Urban Planning Guide

Revised Edition

Prepared by the
Task Committee to Prepare a Planning Guide
of the
Urban Planning and Development Division
of the
American Society of Civil Engineers

Published by the
American Society of Civil Engineers
345 East 47th Street
New York, New York 10017-2398

ABSTRACT

More than any other profession, civil engineers are concerned with infrastructure, the fabric of urban life. Planning for maintenance and expansion of the nation's infrastructure is the subject of this book. The focus of this manual is the practical use of planning tools to solve real life problems. It provides the reader with a broad overview of the planning process and what factors or issues are of particular concern. The first three chapters deal with planning and the planning process in general, describing the process that any planning study must follow from data collection to implementation. The rest of the book covers urban planning in specific areas including land use, housing, urban transportation, intercity highways, airports, railroads, ports, community services facilities, water resources, parks, wastewater management, solid wastes management, energy, environment, and capital improvement programs.

Library of Congress Cataloging-in-Publication Data

Urban planning guide.

(ASCE manuals and reports on engineering practice; no. 49)
Bibliography: p.
Includes index.
1. City planning. 2. City planning—United States. I. American Society of Civil Engineers. Urban Planning and Development Division. Land Use Committee. Task Committee to Prepare a Planning Guide. II. Series.
HT166.U742   1986   307.1′2   86-17335
ISBN 0-87262-546-X

Copyright © 1986 by the American Society of Civil Engineers,
All Rights Reserved.
Library of Congress Catalog Card No.: 86-17335
ISBN 0-87262-546-X
Manufactured in the United States of America.

MANUALS AND REPORTS ON ENGINEERING PRACTICE

(As developed by the ASCE Technical Procedures Committee,
July 1930, and revised March 1935, February 1962, April 1982)

A manual or report in this series consists of an orderly presentation of facts on a particular subject, supplemented by an analysis of limitations and applications of these facts. It contains information useful to the average engineer in his everyday work, rather than the findings that may be useful only occasionally or rarely. It is not in any sense a "standard," however; nor is it so elementary or so conclusive as to provide a "rule of thumb" for nonengineers.

Furthermore, material in this series, in distinction from a paper (which expresses only one person's observations or opinions), is the work of a committee or group selected to assemble and express information on a specific topic. As often as practicable the committee is under the general direction of one or more of the Technical Divisions and Councils, and the product evolved has been subjected to review by the Executive Committee of that Division or Council. As a step in the process of this review, proposed manuscripts are often brought before the members of the Technical Divisions and Councils for comment, which may serve as the basis for improvement. When published, each work shows the names of the committees by which it was compiled and indicates clearly the several processes through which it has passed in review, in order that its merit may be definitely understood.

In February 1962 (and revised in April, 1982) the Board of Direction voted to establish:

A series entitled 'Manuals and Reports on Engineering Practice,'
to include the Manuals published and authorized to date, future Manuals of Professional Practice, and Reports on Engineering Practice. All such Manual or Report material of the Society would have been refereed in a manner approved by the Board Committee on Publications and would be bound, with applicable discussion, in books similar to past Manuals. Numbering would be consecutive and would be a continuation of present Manual numbers. In some cases of reports of joint committees, bypassing of Journal publications may be authorized.

AVAILABLE* MANUALS AND REPORTS OF ENGINEERING PRACTICE

---

*Numbers 1,2, 3, 4, 5, 6, 7, 8, 9, 11, 12, 15, 16, 17, 18, 19, 20, 21, 22, 23, 24, 25, 26, 27, 28, 29, 30, 32, 38, 43, and 48 are out of print.

Dedication

This Manual of Practice is dedicated to Roland J. Frappier (December 13, 1947–December 7, 1984), a committed member of ASCE's Urban Planning and Development Division, who contributed significantly to the preparation of this publication, both as an author and as an ex-officio member of the Peer Committee. As Assistant Chief of the Rhode Island Statewide Planning Program, Roland exemplified dedication to the planning profession and will be missed by all who knew and worked with him.

Acknowledgments

In an undertaking of this nature and scale, there are such a large number of contributors that they cannot possibly all be named here. The work could never have been completed without unselfish and dedicated efforts by many, from authors to reviewers to typists. However, special recognition is deserved by a number of groups and individuals for their long-term commitment to this important effort.

First, to the authors, who each put a great deal of effort into the development of high quality chapters, which collectively add significantly to the base of ASCE publications. Special thanks are due to the authors for their dedication in faithfully incorporating the revisions suggested by the Peer Committee.

Second, to the Peer Committee, who reviewed the Planning Guide and without which this project would never have been completed. For a whole year, the Committee read, reread and "re-reread" a massive amount of material. Throughout, the Peer Committee maintained high standards, commenting on each chapter in detail. Their comments were consistently thoughtful, insightful, detailed and specific, making it easy for authors to respond. The members of the Peer Committee are as follows:

Ruth Fitzgerald—Chairman
Wayne C. Allinson—UPD ExCom Representative
William H. Claire
George D. Barnes
Daniel W. Varin
Roland J. Frappier

We were indeed fortunate for the purposes of continuity that Bill Claire was able to serve on the Peer Committee for this effort, as he served as editor of the original *ASCE Planning Guide*.

Third, to the members of the Task Committee to Prepare a Planning Guide, listed below, who worked so hard to formulate the *Planning Guide* approach and to bring it to fruition. Many from this Task Committee also served as authors of various chapters.

Jarir Dajani	Thomas Koch	Marshall Reed, Jr.
Thomas Debo	John Mackie	Paolo Ricci
Ruth Fitzgerald**	Robert McMahon	John Schoon
Sigurd Grava	James Meek	Gene Willeke
Richard Howe*	Michael Meyer	
James Hudson	John Morrison	

*First Chairman
**Second Chairman

Fourth, to the Executive Committee of the Urban Planning and Development Division, who did not hesitate to provide support to the *Planning Guide* effort despite many delays and changes during the process. Special acknowledgement is given to Richard S. Howe and Wayne C. Allinson, who provided wholehearted support for this effort during their terms as Chairmen of the Executive Committee. Dick Howe originally conceived the idea of this new *Planning Guide*, and first chaired the Task Committee charged with its development.

Final thanks belong to my employer and to the employers of all other major participants who supported our efforts for the duration of this project.

A. Ruth Fitzgerald
CE Maguire, Inc.
New Britain, Connecticut
January, 1986

Preface

In 1969, the *Urban Planning Guide* was published by ASCE as Manual of Practice No. 49. This timely publication attempted to set forth the planning precepts of the time and was a popular and widely read document. After more than a decade of use, ASCE's Urban Planning and Development Division decided to either update the 1969 *Urban Planning Guide* or replace it with a new Planning Guide expanded to cover more of the current complexities of the planning field. The decision was made at that time to pursue the latter route, and a Task Committee was appointed to formulate and carry out the process.

The current *Planning Guide* contains a total of eighteen chapters. The first three chapters deal with planning and the planning process in a generic way, describing the process that any planning study must follow, from data collection to development of implementation measures. The last fifteen chapters are devoted to various specific technical subareas of planning, such as urban transportation planning, solid waste planning, and the environmental assessment process.

Although the *Planning Guide* contains eighteen different chapters, fifteen of them covering technical "subareas" of planning which may be of interest to planners and civil engineers, it makes no claim to full comprehensiveness.

The strong focus of this *Planning Guide* is the practical use of planning tools to solve real life problems. It is intended to be a handbook for practitioners rather than an investigation of planning theory. As such, the information provided in each chapter is not intended to add a new dimension to the field or to provide a step-by-step "cookbook" for carrying out planning studies, but rather to provide the reader with a broad understanding or overview of how the planning process applies to that field and what factors or issues are of particular concern. It is hoped that this *Planning Guide* will not only be useful to practitioners, but that it will serve as a text for use in engineering and planning curricula.

More than any other profession, civil engineers are concerned with infrastructure, the fabric of urban life. Planning for the maintenance and expansion of the nation's infrastructure is the subject of this guide.

TABLE OF CONTENTS

CHAPTER 1

PLANNING CONTEXTS[a]

1.1 ENGINEERS IN THE PLANNING PROCESS

Although this book occasionally refers to "planning" and "engineering" as though they were unrelated professions or disciplines, it does so only to differentiate between two parts of a large process. Planning and engineering are very closely bound to each other, as, indeed, planning is bound to many other disciplines. Planning is essentially the first phase of the development process and, as such, is also the first step in the engineering process.

Traditionally, engineering has been subdivided into five phases: planning, design (preliminary and final), construction, operation and maintenance, and monitoring or evaluation. In some respects, planning has become identified as a separate function, and design, construction, operation, and maintenance are commonly referred to as the engineering elements. It must be emphasized that this is by no means a clear distinction. However, the division of labor that has characterized technology since the Industrial Revolution, combined with the reality of an increasingly complex society, have resulted in the separation of planning, which is the broad view, from design and construction, which are more specifically directed. This division may also be characterized by the statement that design and construction efforts are directed toward meeting a need while planning efforts, in addition to meeting needs, are also concerned with identifying the need and determining the implications of meeting that need in a variety of different ways.

Occasionally, the planning phase of a project results in a recommendation that no further engineering is necessary. Rather, benefits can be most appropriately achieved by a management or operational course of action. For example, the decision to expand bus service rather than construct a rail line, or the decision to implement an aggressive ride-sharing program rather than widen a congested highway corridor, are

[a]Prepared by: Thomas Debo, M.ASCE, Georgia Institute of Technology, Atlanta, GA: A. Ruth Fitzgerald (Affiliate), Vice President, CE Maguire, Inc., New Britain, CT; Sigurd Grava, M.ASCE, Parsons, Brinckerhoff, Quade & Douglas, and Columbia Univ., New York, NY; Richard S. Howe, F.ASCE, Univ. of Texas, San Antonio, TX; C. Thomas Koch, Consulting Engineer, C. Thomas Koch, Inc., Blanco, TX; James Meek, M.ASCE, U.S. Environmental Protection Agency, Washington, DC; John G. Morris, M.ASCE, Morris Environmental Engineering, Inc., Wheaton, IL; Paolo F. Ricci, A.M.ASCE, Electric Power Research Institute, Palo Alto, CA; and Gene E. Willeke, M.ASCE, Institute of Environmental Studies, Miami Univ., Oxford, OH.

examples of nonengineering solutions to problems which originally may have been perceived to need design or construction solutions. Indeed, there is evidence that the high cost of public works projects in recent times, combined with a growing awareness of resource limitations and environmental factors, have increased the incidence of nonengineering solutions to problems. Similarly, and largely for the same reasons, "renovation and reuse" solutions are replacing new construction in many situations.

The increasing emphasis on planning during the last few decades requires that the proposed project must also be viewed in terms of its impacts on society and the environment. The engineer has increasingly become part of a complex system of linkages between project construction and the social, political, economic, environmental, and esthetic implications of the project. Real problem solving in the engineering profession generally requires consideration of both construction and implications, and any successful problem-solving effort requires integration of the several engineering functions. Integration results from an understanding of the various roles an engineer must assume and a working methodology for incorporating all the necessary skills and information.

1.2 TYPES OF PLANNING

Planning can be almost infinitely subdivided into various disciplines and contexts. Each planning situation is different, and each type of planning occurs within its own set of guidelines and methodologies. There is great overlap among the subdisciplines. This should be expected, because urban and regional systems are interrelated.

The field generally referred to as urban and regional planning is comprised of numerous planning elements. Some of these include:

- Transportation planning
- Air quality planning
- Solid waste planning
- Site planning
- Project planning
- Master planning
- Comprehensive planning
- Health services planning
- Water quality planning
- Recreation facilities planning

This is by no means an exhaustive list, nor are these types of planning independent of one another.

Some of the subareas listed, such as site planning, are quite specific while others, such as transportation planning, can be broken down again into several components. These might include:

- Land transportation planning
- Aviation systems planning
- Water systems or port planning

Within these major components exist numerous other possible areas of emphasis. For example, land transportation planning includes the following:

- Urban transportation planning
- Rural transportation planning
- Short-range transit studies
- Long-range facility feasibility studies
- Elderly and handicapped transportation studies
- Paratransit systems planning

Again, this is by no means an exhaustive list. Professional specialization occurs in all these subfields and in many even more specialized areas of study.

The purpose of later chapters of this book is to give some insight into the planning process as it relates to some of these technical areas of specialization.

1.3 GEOGRAPHICAL AND TEMPORAL CONTEXTS

In addition to identification of the various technical contexts in which planning occurs, it is important to consider the application of the planning process to different sized geographical areas and over different time spans.

Planning is appropriate in all geographical contexts, from site planning or project planning, through town planning, regional planning, and state-wide planning, to planning on the national level for considerations such as energy use or air quality. Although the planning process to be described in Chapter 2 can be applied at all of these levels, the outcomes vary depending on the context involved. For example, air quality planning on the federal level may result in national policies for achievement of National Ambient Air Quality Standards, while planning on the local level may result in the development of a new system of signalization to reduce queuing and, therefore, engine idling and excess pollutant emissions.

Planning also occurs on various temporal levels. Various planning processes result in detailed one-year and five-year implementation programs and budgeting. This is typically considered short-range planning and is most appropriate in situations where the recommended actions do not require long lead time for implementation. Long-range planning with a 20-yr to 25-yr (or longer) focus occurs when a significant infrastructure is anticipated requiring a long lead time for design and construction. Again, the outcomes of the two extremes differ considerably.

A short-range plan provides many specifics for development, while a long-range plan is more concerned with general directions and policies. Much mid-range planning also takes place using a 10-yr to 15-yr time frame.

1.4 COORDINATION IN THE PLANNING PROCESS

One important element of the planning process is the provision of a mechanism for coordination with other projects and communication among the various involved parties.

Awareness of and coordination with other projects or plans is critical to the success of any planning effort. If a plan does not reflect these elements and their significance to the project under study, it can present an unrealistic description of the issues involved and a misdirected recommendation for improvement. When a planning effort fails to allow for interface with other planning efforts, the possibility exists that the recommendations will be unimplementable and the process will have to be repeated, as a plan which cannot be implemented is a worthless document. An unworkable plan typically results from lack of comprehensiveness in dealing with significant issues and implications posed by a proposed project or situation. The planning process must never take place in a vacuum.

As a principal area of project interface, planners working on the subject project should investigate both previous planning efforts and concurrent planning efforts for other projects or situations which may affect theirs. This is not as easy as it may appear. In any given area a great many agencies, jurisdictions, and private companies are involved in a great many planning projects. The importance of this interface cannot be overemphasized. It is necessary for project planning to be consistent with other planning in the area. For example, planning a large industrial enterprise in an area zoned for low-density residential development is not consistent with the previous planning efforts which have resulted in the zoning designation. It is also possible that in some cases of conflicting proposals a compromise can be reached—a reflection of changing goals, conditions, and priorities on the part of the affected constituency. Planning for a proposed project in a particular town must, as a minimum, be coordinated with various appropriate town-level agencies, the regional planning agency, various state agencies, other towns in proximity, local and area industry, groups which have expressed interest, and the general public.

Coordination must also be maintained between the planning effort and the legal regulations and requirements of the various involved federal, state, and local agencies. Construction of a highway or rail line, for example, could potentially require a Section 404 Permit from the Army Corps of Engineers, a Section 4(f) Statement for the taking of a recreation area, a Section 6(f) Statement for the taking of land acquired by funding under the Land and Water Conservation Act, an Inland

Wetlands Permit from the local community, a State Traffic Permit, and an Indirect Source Permit from the state. This partial list of possible permits that might be required and regulations that must be complied with is included only to give the reader some concept of the magnitude of the legally mandated coordination effort. Some of these requirements are discussed in subsequent chapters. This is just a small cross section of considerations the planner must be aware of and agencies which must be consulted during the planning process.

Public participation is one of the most important aspects of the entire planning process. Public involvement is an integral part of the planning process, not only because of legal mandate, but also to assure that any planning effort can be implemented. The planner should not lose sight of the fact that planning, whether for general development or for a specific project, is done for a constituency, and the planner's efforts must be directed toward incorporating the needs and desires of those who live and work in the project area.

Interpretation of the way in which the public should be involved has changed considerably over the past few decades. Oversimplification of the issue of public participation should be avoided. There is more involved than just holding a public meeting and hoping people attend. The planner has a responsibility to help the public become involved in a useful way.

The public in a given area faces numerous projects, plans, hearings, referenda, and political issues. The planner's responsibilities include helping them understand the implications and context of the proposed project. Because the tradeoffs and the direct and indirect implications are frequently ill-defined, the public may remain confused about the ramifications of each alternative. It is important that they understand that each alternative, including the "do-nothing" option, of almost any project has positive and negative impacts on some part of the population. Part of effective planning is foreseeing this dilemma and taking appropriate steps toward helping citizens understand the issues. It is important that the planner avoid adopting a position which could be construed as adversarial.

Public participation is not just a matter of keeping the general public intelligently informed, however. "Participation," by definition, means involvement; there are very few situations where the planner can be fully aware of all issues without public input. Localized problems can be dealt with openly and adequately if interface occurs early in project planning; they cannot if the public is expected to give approval to a "selected" alternative near the end of the planning process.

It should be stressed that public participation does not mean just the general public. Provision should also be made for interface and coordination with special interest and advocacy groups. For cases where the project is private or of regional or state-wide scope, the local governmental jurisdictions must also be provided with a mechanism to deal with their concerns and input.

The linkage among the various disciplines and participants within a given project is another critical part of the planning process. The effectiveness of planning and management lies in careful coordination of these various functions. Because it is necessary in planning to coordinate various disciplines, there must be effective communication among project study participants. Planners, architects, engineers, soils scientists, ecologists, historical preservationists, geologists, economists, and others must learn to work toward the same goals which require the input of each. Modification and adjustment of the project may occur as part of this coordination effort.

In summary, planning must serve as the mechanism for two important functions in the development process:

1. The planner must coordinate with other proposed projects, existing plans, various government agencies, special interest groups, public bodies and the general public.

2. The planning process must act as a communications system for the various disciplines involved in a project—for environmentalists, designers, managers, and others involved in some way in the project or planning situation.

1.5 INSTITUTIONAL FRAMEWORK

One of the most important contexts within which any planning effort takes place is the institutional framework governing that particular type of study or functional discipline. Although later chapters of this book consider in more detail the institutional framework for each specific major area of planning, it is appropriate to address the topic here in this discussion of planning contexts.

Over the course of years, governmental institutions at different levels have increasingly mandated planning studies to assure that the projects and developments they are participating in (through funding) at the local level are appropriate to the situation. For example, within the transportation planning field, the federal government has a requirement that all urbanized areas with populations over 50,000 must undertake a long-range transportation planning effort which is "comprehensive, cooperative and continuing." This is just one of a number of federally required planning efforts in the transportation field. In addition, the federal government instituted the National Environmental Policy Act (NEPA) in 1969, mandating review of every major federal action in relation to its impact on the human environment.

Other levels of government have instituted their own planning requirements in the interests of either orderly development or efficient allocation of capital spending. State governments mandate planning studies in a number of fields. In addition, many states have environmental impact analysis requirements on a state level similar in intent to NEPA on the national level.

Local governments become involved in the planning process for several reasons and in several manners. Municipalities often undertake planning efforts associated with a potential federal or state grant application to meet expressed needs. A city desiring a new bus maintenance garage, for example, must demonstrate need for such a facility in a planning study. At other times, local governments undertake planning efforts strictly for their own use in promoting orderly development. Such studies may not be directed specifically toward a particular agency, funding source, or proposed action.

It is important to understand that requirements for planning and participation in the planning process occur at all levels of government. In addition, many private organizations undertake planning efforts based on public agency requirements. Two types of governmental agency interactions are necessary in order to assure a comprehensive planning effort and an implementation program with maximum opportunity for success.

The first consists of horizontal communication across: (1) The various planning subareas which might in any way be involved; and (2) the subject agency's "sister agencies" at the same level. For example, an airport noise control and land use compatibility (ANCLUC) study being undertaken by a city for operations at a municipal airport must be coordinated with existing land use planning in the area, local airfield and aviation planning, utility system expansion, zoning ordinance and building code revisions, and a myriad of economic factors. Many different agencies at the municipal level must be consulted. Generally, the approval and cooperation of a number of agencies will be necessary to ensure successful implementation of the recommended course of action.

The second type of interaction consists of vertical communication among the different levels of government involved. In the ANCLUC study cited above, for example, the airport commission and the municipality itself (as owner and operator of the airport) will have to coordinate and cooperate closely with the county of which it is a part, with the regional planning agency, with the state aviation authority and, perhaps most visibly, with the Federal Aviation Administration. Each of these levels has input to the study and is impacted by the study findings and recommendations.

In summary, the planner must be fully aware of the institutional framework within which the project under study must operate. The planner also has a responsibility to involve all of these agencies or levels to assure comprehensive coverage of all factors, including legislation or regulations, which might affect the outcome of the study. This communication also helps prevent any duplication of effort which may have occurred in a previous planning study, and further assures consistency among various ongoing planning efforts or elements.

THE PLANNING PROCESS[a]

2.1 STEPS IN THE PLANNING PROCESS

Simply stated, planning is a means for preparing for action, and it occurs through a process in which: (1) Information is collected and analyzed; (2) logical alternative courses of action are developed consistent with the goals of a constituency; and (3) a course of action is recommended. Every project has its own set of parameters and dynamics and its own sequence of events.

Because each planning situation is unique, planners necessarily rely heavily on the process of planning. With an adequate process, the difficulties of planning can be surmounted over a period of time. The process of planning is comprised of a number of stages or phases. The phases are not necessarily followed in sequence in all cases, and recycling to an earlier phase is frequently necessary. The general nature of the process is presented in the following subsections.

The steps in the planning process may be described as follows:

- Identification of problem or need
- Data collection and analysis
- Development of goals and objectives
- Clarification and diagnosis of the problem or issues
- Identification of alternative solutions
- Analysis of alternatives
- Evaluation and recommendation of actions
- Development of implementation program
- Surveillance and monitoring

The planning process is shown graphically in Fig. 2-1.

2.1.1 Awareness of Need

The planning process usually begins with the consideration of some problem or need. The need can be stated specifically, such as the need for additional capacity on a highway bridge across a river, as indicated by traffic congestion; or it can be very broadly addressed, such

---

[a]Prepared by: Thomas Debo, M.ASCE; A. Ruth Fitzgerald, Affiliate; Sigurd Grava, M.ASCE; Richard S. Howe, F.ASCE; C. Thomas Koch; James Meek, M.ASCE; John G. Morris, M.ASCE; Paolo F. Ricci, A.M.ASCE; and Gene E. Willeke, M.ASCE. The professional affiliations of the authors are given on p. 1.

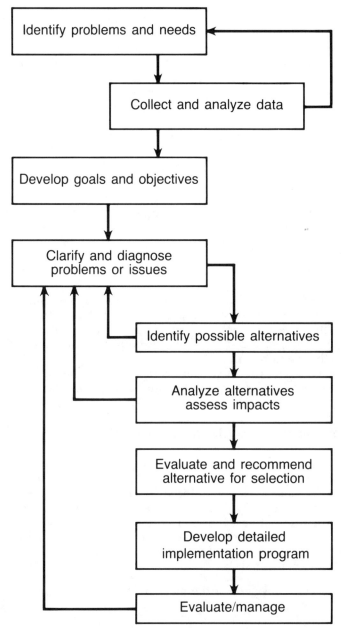

Fig. 2-1. The planning process.

as a town's need for orderly development to protect the quality of life for its residents and assure adequate budgeting for municipal improvements. The problem expression may be entirely based on a description of symptoms (the planner should be careful not to confuse the problem with the symptom), or it may be the outgrowth of earlier studies that have carefully delineated a particular problem needing further study. At this preliminary stage, sufficient information may be available to identify the interested parties and the important issues. Public involvement should begin at this early stage, as should initial coordination with various agencies or groups which must be involved.

2.1.2 Data Collection and Analysis

Based on the awareness that a need or problem exists, the second step in the planning process is to collect and synthesize data so as to know more about the causes of the problem and better understand how it might be solved. Large amounts of data are often available from existing sources, such as census data, economic indicators, and a variety of existing planning documents. Additional empirical data, such as transit boarding counts, origin and destination surveys, or housing surveys, are often also collected as part of the planning process.

Part of the information collected during this phase should be the forecasted variables which aid in ascertaining what the future conditions will be with respect to the situation under study. Whether a 5-yr forecast is necessary, or a 20-yr forecast, or both, is a function of the time frame of the planning effort.

The result of this phase of work will be a better understanding of the needs that presently exist and those which will exist in the future.

2.1.3 Development of Goals and Objectives

The statement of what is hoped to be accomplished in a particular planning effort is the statement of goals and objectives. The terms "goals" and "objectives" are typically used together, sometimes (mistakenly) interchangeably and synonymously. There are distinct differences in their definitions, however.

Goals are general in nature. They are "broad brush" definitions of conditions which are to be striven for but may not be fully attainable. Examples of goals might be:

- Access to all parts of the metropolitan area by public transit
- Clean water and air
- Energy self-sufficiency
- Accurate, up-to-date mapping throughout the country
- Safe water supplies
- Elimination of unsafe, substandard housing

Objectives are more specific, and appear to be attainable. They have been carefully examined, and the plans will be developed to achieve them. In fact, the alternative courses of action proposed to meet the needs of the area will be measured or evaluated in terms of their success in achieving these objectives. Examples of objectives which correspond to the goals stated might be:

- Addition of five crosstown bus routes
- Reduction of phosphorus in municipal effluent by 80%
- Development and application of a public education program for energy conservation
- Conversion of all survey records to the state plane coordinate system within five years
- Determination of procedures for coping with accidental spills into the water supply source
- Better code enforcement and municipal support services in low-income areas

Establishing goals and objectives is a process of discussion and analysis. Public officials and citizens may come to an agreement that the first goal cited is important because: (1) People shouldn't have to own automobiles to live and work in the metropolis; (2) traffic congestion is undesirable; and (3) increased public transit use would reduce energy consumption. The comparable objective of adding five crosstown bus routes will not achieve the stated goal but may be an attainable solution to the most critical transit need in the metropolitan area.

As the list shows, statements of objectives may be either quantitative or qualitative. For example, devising procedures for coping with accidental spills is a legitimate objective, but one that can only be a qualitative one. Qualitative statements are not necessarily less rigorous than quantitative statements; indeed, they are often more so. The principal concern in stating an objective is to apply the terms most appropriate to the issue. Objectives should be worded so as to identify a measure of achievement.

Until recently, the setting of goals and objectives was regarded as the sole prerogative of elected officials, planners, or local planning commissions or boards. In recent years, a significant departure from that practice has been advocated—namely, the participation of citizens and interest groups in goal and objective setting. Much of the sizable literature on citizen involvement or participation in the planning field is devoted to the setting of goals and objectives.

The precise wording of objectives, and their conversion into quantitative terms when appropriate, is usually done by the professional planning team. The planning team's expertise is called upon because of its experience in similar situations and its collective knowledge of what the planning process is intended to achieve. However, the planning team must have the participation and agreement of the elected officials and major interest groups who will ultimately be responsible for implementation of the results.

2.1.4 Clarification and Diagnosis of the Problem

After goals and objectives have been stated, the problem and the environment within which it is found need to be clarified and understood, and a diagnosis of the situation must be developed. With this better understanding of the problem and its environment, the alternatives developed in the ensuing phase can be more responsive to the goals and objectives.

A classic demonstration of the need for clear understanding and diagnosis of a problem and its environment occurs when some increased system capacity (in transportation, water supply, solid waste, energy, etc.) seems to be required. A common misconception is that only an increase in supply will solve the problem, when in some cases alteration of demand may also be a feasible solution. For example, if airport expansion "appears to be needed," whereas rerouting flights would both eliminate the capacity problems and improve service to passengers, then a better understanding of the problem will lead to alternatives not only completely different but also better. Similarly, if there is substantial consumptive waste, as has been the case in water and energy usage, then it may be possible to eliminate the need for increased supply by reducing demand through pricing, controls, or public education methods.

This example is not the only situation in which problem identification and diagnosis can lead to better options. For all projects, the problem and the needs must be clearly understood and articulated if the solution is to be appropriate. Again, the involvement of citizens is essential to understanding and defining the breadth of the problem.

2.1.5 Identification of Alternative Solutions

A number of alternatives can usually be devised to meet the planning objectives, and any one or a combination of several may be appropriate under the given set of circumstances. It is important to have a comprehensive listing of feasible alternatives. The practice of presenting only one course of action for consideration and analysis is both dangerous and inefficient; it is poor planning practice and is contrary to the basic tenets of planning.

All interested parties should be given the opportunity to propose options for evaluation. The experience of agencies such as the U.S. Army Corps of Engineers, state transportation departments, and many local governments has been that occasionally an alternative solution proposed by an interested group or individual is the most appropriate. Maintaining an open mind is a very important part of a successful approach to the planning process.

The method of formulating alternatives bears further discussion. Generally, several objectives will be considered. One approach that has been used is to formulate a course of action that maximizes the benefit of each objective. In the extreme case of such planning, a "multi-objective" alternative is formulated only after evaluation of the single-purpose alternatives. Thus alternatives are formulated to maximize the objectives separately, which is basically contrary to the concept of multi-objective planning. Another undesirable consequence of single-objective alternatives is that much of the study budget and staff resources may be used to evaluate unrealistic courses of action, leaving little time and money to evaluate more reasonable alternatives. Ideally, alternatives should be developed that consider the various objectives simultaneously, inasmuch as the best multi-objective alternative does not simply lie somewhere between the extremes of the single-objective alternatives.

The theory of mathematical programming provides a good model of how to think about the development of alternatives, though it is not often possible to actually employ mathematical programming in this portion of the planning process. The linear programming model, for example, includes two critical elements: (1) An objective function; and (2) constraints.

The objective function states that each objective has a certain weight or contribution to make to the over-all utility of a solution. These weights are multiplied by the degree to which the objective can be achieved. The over-all appropriateness is then the summation of those weights multiplied by the extent to which each objective can be achieved. An optimal solution is one that maximizes or minimizes the objective function, yet it is often one which does not maximize any single objective in the objective function. Rather, it is one in which something is given up for one objective in order to gain something toward another which may make a greater contribution to over-all utility.

The second critical element in linear programming is the set of constraints. This is a list of conditions imposed on the objective function that brings the problem into agreement with the realities of the situation. For example, although some objectives may direct the solution of a water-supply problem toward the construction of a very large reservoir, there may be constraints on the maximum reservoir size that is possible. The reservoir size may be constrained by the physical setting, available budget, legal restrictions on the amount of flow, or limits on the lower pool level for the maintenance of fish life. Such constraints set parameters within which the optimal solution may be found.

In formulating alternatives, the two elements—objective function and constraints—should be utilized at least informally, if not quantitatively. At the very least, a set of constraints should be defined and alternatives should not be proposed that violate them, unless provisions are also made for their alteration.

Public participation must again be encouraged at this critical stage of the planning process. Some means of presenting and explaining the alternatives and the procedures for assessing their impacts must be employed. One way of doing this is through the use of a planning brochure. In successive drafts of a widely distributed brochure, alternatives are described and, as analysis proceeds, the impacts and implications of each alternative are presented. Alternatives can be added, deleted, or modified in successive drafts.

Workshops can also be used. Workshops are held to explain to affected and interested parties the progress of the study since goals and objectives were formulated, and to present the alternatives that have been developed. The participants discuss the issues and the ramifications of identified alternatives. New or modified alternatives may emerge as part of this exercise.

Research on communication to large audiences shows that the methods for explaining alternatives should include both written documents, such as planning brochures and reports, and oral communications, which occur in workshops, briefings, and other public meetings or discussions. In both written and oral communications, graphics should be used as much as possible to help assure accurate transmission of information.

2.1.6 Analysis of Alternatives

The analysis of alternatives is basically the process of determining the effects or impacts of each. This step in the planning process begins with more detailed forecasting of variables to determine the context or environment within which each alternative would perform. The impacts of the various alternatives are subsequently assessed in terms of their physical, social, economic, fiscal, environmental, or esthetic implications on the study area and its environs.

There is a great deal of literature on the analysis phase of planning and on the evaluation and selection phase described in the next section. Cost-benefit and cost-effectiveness literature applies to this phase, and much mathematical programming literature is similarly oriented. Simple approaches, such as goals-achievement matrices and performance profiles, can also be employed.

In recent years, particularly since 1970, the term "impact assessment" has been used with reference to planning analysis. Ordinarily, this term is used as part of a more specific descriptive term, such as environmental impact, social impact, or economic impact. Impact assessment is not only a part of good planning practice, it is also required by legislation by the federal government and many state governments. The catalyst for most of this legislation was the National Environmental Policy Act (NEPA) of 1969, as well as the promulgation of various pieces of legislation within specific technical areas. These laws generally call for consideration of social, economic, and environmental consequences. Other requirements call for consideration of the efficiency, equity, effectiveness, and responsiveness of a proposed alternative. The over-all purpose is to assure that decisions are made in a rational manner, considering the range of data available, and that they are directed toward addressing the problem or need identified.

Impact assessment is done with a large measure of input by affected and interested groups. An element of advocacy is injected into the impact assessment process, as each group evaluates a proposed alternative by scrutinizing it in light of its own specific objectives and concerns.

A key part of impact assessment is the documentation of impacts. It is also appropriate in this context to identify to whom or what the specific benefits or detriments will accrue. Results of the analysis must in some way be displayed so that the parties involved can compare the alternatives. As in the formulation of alternatives, effective communication generally calls on a combination of written, graphic, and oral methods.

It is not uncommon to revise the statement of objectives at this stage, inasmuch as the implications of the objectives often become more apparent than they were earlier in the process. New objectives may be added and those previously formulated may be modified.

2.1.7 Evaluation and Recommendation of Actions

The choice of criteria for evaluation is perhaps one of the most important aspects of the planning process because these criteria provide the basis for selecting a course of action from among the options available.

After the effects of the alternatives have been assessed, a selection must be made of the one or ones that comprise a "best" or at least a "good" solution. Typically, the first step in this selection process is the elimination of those alternatives clearly inferior to others. Once the field has been narrowed by this screening process, a rigorous comparison of the remaining alternatives is possible using evaluative criteria. Evaluative criteria are implicit in the setting of objectives. By the time the selection stage is reached, they should be made sufficiently explicit to allow evaluation of the alternatives.

The various approaches referred to in the preceding subsection culminate in outputs used in the evaluation and recommendation process. Decision makers can be presented with a display of comparisons. Benefit-cost analysis and cost-effectiveness analysis, for example, yield quantitative measures of worth for each alternative analyzed. Benefit-cost ratios, internal rates of return, net benefits, present worth, and annual charges of benefits and costs are all possible outputs of a benefit-cost analysis. In a cost-effectiveness analysis, the alternative offering the highest ratio of effectiveness to cost is preferred. In goals-achievement matrix analysis, the comparison of desired outputs with actual outputs is not aggregated to the extent common in benefit-cost or cost-effectiveness analysis. In profile analysis, a display of comparisons is also presented, though it is somewhat easier to use the profile than the matrix.

One danger in the evaluation process is that of overaggregating the effects. For example, a benefit-cost ratio conceals too much information to provide a complete basis for decision. At the other extreme, of course, if the information about alternatives is so disaggregated as to present dozens of separate impacts without some mechanism to guide the evaluation, it may be impossible to make meaningful comparisons.

2.1.8 Development of Implementation Program

Implementation is the actual carrying out of the selected plan or recommendations. It may proceed in one or two stages. Typically, the plan is adopted and carried into design and construction, or simply into operation, depending on the outcome of the planning process. Occasionally, however, a pilot or demonstration project may be carried out. This allows the implementing agency and its clients to acquire experience with the project and also allows further development and refinement. In some instances the scientific base for the design is inadequate to predict completely the effects of implementation. In this situation, a pilot project allows testing and collection of more useful field data to enable more accurate design. Water quality management, solid waste handling, and new zoning regulations are all fields in which pilot projects or small-scale implementation can precede full-scale implementation.

Implementation is generally the hardest part of the planning process to accomplish. However, the difficulties can be reduced if planning for implementation has been incorporated as part of the process from the beginning. Indeed, consideration of this step is one of the primary safeguards against idealistic, unrealistic plans. By involving the affected and interested parties (public participation) in the setting of goals and objectives, defining alternatives, assessing their impacts, and selecting the one for implementation, support for the selected action is generated among those who will be affected and responsible for the project, thus increasing the assurance of the project's success.

The implementation stage requires assembling the necessary legal documents, securing financing, contracting, hiring or assigning persons to do the work, scheduling milestones, and a myriad of other tasks. All of these needs should be adequately addressed during the preparation of an implementation program so that a minimum number of obstacles is encountered. On occasion, new problems encountered during the implementation phase may require repeating one or more earlier phases of the planning process to attain the objective.

2.1.9 Surveillance and Monitoring

In the surveillance stage the results of the planning process are monitored. Surveillance techniques determine what has occurred as a result of plan implementation, and how well such results conform to the goals and objectives that were identified during the process. The data gathered from monitoring the project during and after its implementation provide feedback to elected and appointed officials as to whether or not the selected course of action is having the anticipated effects. This feedback is used to assess the performance of the planning process and the achievement of the objectives. Midcourse corrections can (and should) be made if needed, and additional problems can be addressed.

It is possible that even if the planning process was carefully and responsibly executed, changing factors in society or the environment can alter the pattern of needs sufficiently to require an update of the development and analysis of alternatives (or even adoption of new priorities or goals). For example, in the transportation planning process, the effects of energy availability and cost can make such changes necessary.

The surveillance and monitoring phase of the planning process is generally the final "closing of the loop" on a project, but it can also be the beginning of the next planning project to meet the dynamic needs of a changing society.

2.2 OTHER CONSIDERATIONS

In this description of the context in which planning takes place and articulation of the planning process, it is appropriate to emphasize several fundamental concepts which have been touched on earlier. These are elements of the planning field which must be recognized if the planner is to operate effectively and if the result of the planning process is to be a useful tool in guiding development.

1. Planning is an ongoing process and, as such, must not be considered rigid or inflexible. It should set the framework for guiding development rather than try to impose rigid development patterns. The process is usually iterative, with data analysis outputs being fed back into the analysis. Objectives decided upon early in the study can change, as can the range of possible options, based on the outcome of other parts of the process.

2. One of the outputs of the planning process must be a detailed program for implementation. Without this, it is doubtful that any plan would be carried out. The implementation process should clearly identify, in detail, what is to be done; who is to do it; when it is to be done; how it should be done; how it can be monitored; and how it will be paid for. In addition, the plan and implementation program should spell out all anticipated capital and operating costs, possible revenues, and sources of funding.

3. Planning is, above all else, an overview in which the "big picture" is of utmost importance. There are two basic types: planning for orderly, efficient, and cost-effective development; and planning for a specific project. Even when one is planning for a specific project, care must be taken to examine that project in light of its surroundings, and to evaluate not only its effectiveness in meeting the need but also its implications for various other aspects of the community or environment.

4. One of the planner's principal responsibilities is to communicate and coordinate with all the agencies, individuals, and regulatory

processes which affect or are affected by the project or area under study. Planners must be aware of all these forces as well as all existing plans which have a bearing on the project or area.

5. Planning is done for a particular area and for the people who reside, work, relax, travel, or have an interest in that area. As such, the planning effort must take into account the needs and desires of these people and must provide a mechanism for them to communicate the issues they feel are important. Each alternative course of action under consideration has implications for some segment of that population, and the planner must consider the interested and affected constituency during all parts of the process. Impacts are perceived differently by various groups of individuals—what is a benefit to one group may be perceived as a detriment by others. It is the planner's responsibility to communicate to the best extent possible the quantitative and qualitative implications of each alternative and the reasons for recommending a particular alternative. Planning is typically not a decision-making function, but it does provide information that will aid in the decision-making process.

CHAPTER 3

PLANNING TOOLS[a]

3.1 INTRODUCTION

Planning is in many respects a quantitative field, particularly in those aspects that touch upon physical systems and services. Perhaps it is not possible to define precisely how families pick residential locations, but once they are there, their trip-making behavior can be predicted quite accurately. An estimate of the number of youth workers needed in a neighborhood is uncertain and transitory, but not the calculation of gallons of water required by the same area. The visual impact of an oil refinery can only be debated, but its olfactory effusions can be measured and their consequences predicted.

As these examples show, planning is somewhere between a soft science and a hard art, and the situation is quite different among the various subareas of planning activity—ranging from the quantitative structuring of a solid waste disposal system to the strictly qualitative esthetic design of a cityscape. But there has been and continues to be a definite trend away from impressionistic, individual judgment toward documented collective rationality as the basis for making decisions about the environment; and there is an accompanying and growing kit of tools. This is a significant factor in the historical perspective of how the urban planning discipline has evolved.

Tracing the ancestral roots of planning approaches, with corresponding states-of-art in methods, may be an interesting exercise. However, examination of current and foreseeable future use of planning tools has a more practical relevance. Basic contemporary trends appear to have two distinct orientations, quantitative and qualitative, both of which fit into a broad definition of systems analysis or systemic planning.

The quantitative orientation has emerged from quantitatively oriented fields such as operations research, engineering, and economics. The resulting tools for planners have been simulation models of various urban aspects, exact budgeting of all resources, and evaluation procedures that try to account for as many variables and interests as possible. The thrust has been toward precision, comprehensiveness, and ratio-

---

[a]Prepared by: Thomas Debo, M.ASCE; A. Ruth Fitzgerald, Affiliate: Sigurd Grava, M.ASCE; Richard S. Howe. F.ASCE; C. Thomas Koch; James Meek, M.ASCE; John G. Morris, M.ASCE; Paolo F. Ricci, A.M.ASCE; and Gene E. Willeke, M.ASCE. The professional affiliations of the authors are given on p. 1.

nality. The quantitative approach has the greatest affinity to the physical and operational systems of a city or region.

Despite a measure of success with simulation modeling, quantitative methods have definite limitations. Most urban systems are extremely complex, involving multiple participants (providers and users) with multiple goals (divergent and sometimes conflicting). Nothing can be completely precise or truly comprehensive unless the constraints of the problem are defined very narrowly. For example, a water distribution network can certainly be designed and built to provide a specified volume at an adequate pressure to a given district, but a planner must also be expected to ask and deal with additional questions, such as:

- What demand conditions are caused by the socioeconomic status of the local population?
- Are there any past or present inequities in supply to be corrected?
- Are domestic use rates going to change (should they)?
- Will fire-fighting demands be modified?
- What about possible conservation practices?
- Does this district have a higher priority than others?
- Is water service among the urgent needs? Are tradeoffs possible?
- What are likely to be the changes in density and building type within the area? With what probabilities?
- How strong are development regulations?
- What are citizen attitudes?

A reorientation of attitudes has taken place over the past several decades, which has found expression in urban policies and regulations. Some of these assumptions may be expressed as follows: preservation and reuse may be more advisable than new building in many instances; access by everybody to a satisfactory level of housing, mobility, and social services is necessary; the environment has to be protected even if the immediate costs are sometimes considerable.

These types of assumptions have led to the qualitative orientation in the development of methods and procedures. This approach embodies the recognition that solutions can only rarely be unequivocal, compromises are usually necessary, many legitimate interests have to be respected, the study process is seldom linear, values and needs change, and that a form of democracy and participatory decision making should be brought into planning at all levels.

Thus, planning tools have been created that stem originally from the social and behavioral sciences, psychology, public administration, business, and even advertising. Techniques such as planning balance sheets, Delphic procedures, alternative analyses, design workshops, client needs assessment and many others have been used successfully and, indeed, have often become indispensable with active public participation programs. Inasmuch as these qualitative study procedures respond to evolving concepts in analysis and decision making, not to mention new statutory requirements, they are now indisputably a part of the inventory of planning tools.

It is interesting to note parenthetically that during the 1970s, unlike the 1960s, relatively little new development can be identified in the quantitative methods. There were elaborations and more involved applications during this time, but certainly no breakthroughs. Conversely, the qualitative but systematic procedures saw vigorous growth and development during the same period.

It is convenient and appropriate from this point to discuss planning tools in the sequence in which they might be applied to a regular planning assignment. While every project is unquestionably different, there are conceptually standardized procedures which allow a chronological review.

3.2 DATA COLLECTION

Data, information, and intelligence are the stock in trade of the engineer and planner. Data are the factual relationships that link observations and reality and are the first of three elements that comprise a concept of knowledge. Figure 3-1 shows the linkages among these elements.

The first concrete tool in the planning process is data availability, scope, and format. There is some evidence that the planning field has started to move away from the traditional approach of collecting large amounts of data. Since better methods are now available, the assembly of needed information can be more purposeful. Nevertheless, data gaps

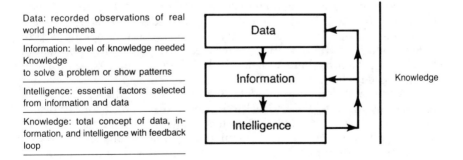

Data: recorded observations of real world phenomena

Information: level of knowledge needed Knowledge to solve a problem or show patterns

Intelligence: essential factors selected from information and data

Knowledge: total concept of data, information, and intelligence with feedback loop

Fig. 3-1. Hierarchy of data, information, intelligence (Source: F.S. So, I. Stallman, F. Beal and D.S. Arnold, eds., *The Practice of Local Government Planning*, ICMA, Washington, DC, 1979)

often exist and may be filled only at great expense to any given project. Consequently, the thrust must be to advance study methods that can use less data or surrogate data, or to develop information collection procedures that are largely automated, utilize material routinely collected for other purposes, or can satisfy several purposes with a single effort.

There are two types of data. Primary data are obtained from the original source. The direct counting of people, observation of natural phenomena, or measurement of distance are examples of primary data. Secondary data are obtained by others and made available for use, such as the data collected by the United States Bureau of the Census. There are many types of data and data collection procedures which respond to the various sectors within planning; however, a few significant sources can be described that illustrate the difficulties and potentials in this area.

3.2.1 Demographic Data

The United States decennial census is the most fundamental source of demographic, social and economic data in this country. Improvements over the years have made the information available quickly and flexibly through the use of computers. In addition, the census data are available broken down into the smallest possible geographic areas (such as blocks) for use in many situations.

Yet from a planning point of view, the census still has two major deficiencies: (1) It is too infrequent (making the data toward the end of any decade somewhat obsolete); and (2) it does not include many of the data items that would be useful for municipal and regional planning purposes, most notably land use and more detailed travel information.

The U.S. government collects demographic data in two broad categories: enumeration and characteristics. The basic data are obtained through a full count, while most of the secondary characteristics are identified through controlled sample surveys. The enumerations provided include births, deaths, marriages, divorces, and population trends. Population characteristics include age, race, sex, education, income, occupation, and mobility.

Additional demographic data may be found in the vital statistics reported by the U.S. Public Health Service and state and county health departments. Municipalities, counties, states or regional planning agencies often develop annual population estimates for their particular jurisdictions. Some private sources of demographic data are also available in some areas. Insurance companies and banks frequently have useful data, and R. L. Polk and Company produces annual city block canvasses that serve to supplement the census. Utility and telephone connections and disconnections as well as postal and tax records can also be useful. Parenthetically, the most difficult demographic data to obtain, validate, and analyze are migration data, as the movement of families and individuals is not recorded in any systematic way.

For some years in most U.S. metropolitan areas, the best data inventory has been assembled under the comprehensive transportation studies sponsored and funded by the Federal Highway Administration. These studies have generated a full set of aerial photographs and maps, economic and demographic updates and analyses, and information generated by home interviews relating to family characteristics and origins and destinations of daily trips of various types. The high expense of home surveys, even if information is gathered for several purposes, has precluded many further large-scale efforts of this sort. The latest trend in transportation studies and updates is toward a minimization of original data needs.

The search for possible substitutes of data sources leads to consideration of remote sensing. The rapid advances in this technology, utilizing high-altitude airplanes and satellites equipped with sophisticated scanning devices, may hold a solution to several urban data needs in the not-so-distant future. The ability to differentiate the character of surface for an area as small as an acre, to identify change over time, to pick out moving elements, to distinguish thermal conditions, and to identify many other sophisticated distinctions may provide the key for planners to maintain adequate data bases in the future, at least for the physical land use aspects of a city or region. This tool is not yet widely available and will have to undergo further refinement before it can be universally used.

It is possible that environmental management programs will be at the cutting edge of new data assembly techniques during the 1980s, just as transportation programs served this role during the 1960s. Environmental analysis requires great volume and depth of data and is also largely sponsored by federal funds. In addition, many aspects of environmental analysis could benefit significantly from the capabilities of remote sensing.

3.2.2 Economic Data

Government reports are a principal source of economic data such as employment and unemployment, labor markets, banking, personal income, investment, consumption, production, sales, and international trade. The principal federal sources are the United States Bureau of the Census, Department of Commerce, Department of Health and Welfare, Department of Education, and Department of Labor. Many state, county and local governments publish similar data. Several privately collected data sources are also available, usually at a cost.

3.2.3 Environmental Data

Reports prepared by or for governmental agencies are a source of much environmental data, such as air quality, water quality, flood plains, wetlands, and flora and fauna lists. The U.S. Environmental Protection Agency, along with its counterparts at the state and local level, is one source of this type of data. Related data sources dealing with land use, soils, and geology are available from the Soil Conservation Service and the U.S. Geological Survey. Meteorological and oceanic data are available from the National Oceanic and Atmospheric Administration. Additional information may be obtained from the U.S. Department of Interior and the U.S. Department of Agriculture as well as from the corresponding state agencies.

3.2.4 Social Data

Social data are available from numerous sources. The Bureau of the Census provides extensive information on housing demand, costs, structural characteristics and condition. Most enumerations and supply data are available in the reports issued by state and local governments and housing authorities as well as by the U.S. Department of Housing and Urban Development. Private sources, such as Dodge, Dow, Dun, and McGraw-Hill, offer housing data on a regular basis. Federal and state banking and savings and loan associations, along with realtors and appraiser groups, are also a source of data.

The principal source of health and welfare data is the U.S. Department of Health and Welfare and its counterparts at the state and local level. Data on education are available from the U.S. Department of Education and its counterparts at the state and local level.

3.2.5 Other Data Sources

Depending on the type of planning study being undertaken, there are generally many other sources of secondary data. Existing planning studies, such as a comprehensive plan of development, metropolitan area transportation study, traffic studies, market studies and environmental impact studies for other projects, all provide a background of information vital to the planner. Many planning efforts, particularly those on a smaller scale, rely heavily on secondary data of this type. The local planning department, public works department, traffic department, redevelopment agency or regional planning agency should be contacted to put the planner in touch with all appropriate existing sources of data. Each individual planning study or project will have varying data needs, dictated by the scope and geographical context of the project.

3.3 FORECASTS

Common to practically every planning assignment is the forecasting of variables in order to estimate future needs in a particular area. The most basic of these are population projections, which provide a direct measure of service needs in many sectors. Usually, forecasts are needed of future population levels, as well as of such characteristics as geographical distribution, income distribution, and age distribution.

Considerable progress has been made in forecasting during the last decade or so, serving to upgrade the tools available for urban planning. These improvements have not been characterized by any breakthroughs in methods, but rather in a more widespread understanding of forecasting tools and their application. Simplistic techniques such as straight-line extrapolation should be applied with constraint and with an understanding of their limitations, while reference to the experience in "comparable" communities should be considered only if no other options exist.

Even the traditional scientific methodology for population projections, cohort-survival calculations, cannot alone be recommended for most urban tasks because of the great uncertainties associated with our changing birthrates and with the migration factor that is so critical due to the high mobility of our national population. It is now generally recognized that only a thorough demographic-economic investigation for at least a full region, which carefully projects forward the basic economic, developmental and social factors, can be regarded practically and theoretically with any favor. Even in such instances, forecasts are presented in ranges rather than simple numbers, reflecting a greater maturity in the understanding of complex urban issues. In any case, the utilization of several methods in parallel for an internal cross-check is most advisable.

It should be noted here that the preparation of formal and highly scientific population forecasts is typically outside the jurisdiction of most planners. Population projections for areas and subareas are generally available from state agencies or regional planning agencies which have prepared forecasts using the most sophisticated means available. It should still be borne in mind, however, that often different estimates are produced by different agencies, and care must be taken to compare the available forecasts and select a "most likely" projection or range of projections based on the latest available trends in the area under study.

Many studies and projects, especially those for service systems that can be implemented or expanded gradually, do not necessitate precise projections for specific dates. Under this approach, after the lead time for implementation of any component is determined and a general growth projection plotted, it is sufficient and, indeed, realistic to monitor existing population size and composition and to start implementation of facilities on an "as needed" basis. This approach conserves resources and runs minimal risks of excess or deficient service. The only obvious refinement that can be added to this procedure, particularly in light of the fact that not all American communities are continuing to grow, is to design also for the removal, conversion, and replacement of facilities as they become obsolete.

In a practical sense, however, the greatest strides in the field of forecasting have been made in applications and continuity of effort. It would be difficult to find today a sizable urban area in the United States for which a comprehensive economic or population forecast, or both, is not available, nor one that is not backed by previous efforts, public discussion, and respectable background studies. There is also frequently a recognized agency that is looked upon as the keeper of this responsibility, under the control of professionals in the forecasting disciplines. In many cases, these units have been established under federal and state requirements for regional monitoring of various programs.

This means, then, that the planners and designers of facilities and services in any given community can fall back on established future scenarios. Indeed, they are usually expected to do so. Nevertheless, adjustments to forecasts are sometimes necessary and can be accomplished by: (1) Scaling down global figures, usually through apportioning techniques; (2) interpreting specific trends from a set of detailed characteristics; and (3) modifying the over-all forecasting results in light of specialized knowledge or studies.

Data forecasting is one of the inputs to the planning process and is generally based on some assumptions. If the planning process outcome affects those assumptions, then the input may also be affected, as planning is an iterative process. For example, a state or regional planning agency which is forecasting population for a metropolitan area may allocate a "top down" forecast among the various towns of the region. One suburban community may be allocated a large amount of growth because of a proposed beltway facility through the community which will greatly improve access and stimulate development. If, during a separate transportation study, however, the beltway is eliminated, the growth allocated to that community may no longer be expected to occur and must be reallocated, thus changing the areawide population distribution which was originally input to the transportation study. For this reason, planners must be vigilant about communication with other planning entities and about documenting assumptions. In an ideal situation, communication and involvement of all concerned parties will be rigorously maintained.

In addition to demographic types of data, it is often necessary to forecast the future levels of economic activity in the area studied. Economic base studies are done to: (1) Assess strengths and weaknesses of available resource and support systems; (2) determine potential for development; and (3) identify constraints to development.

3.4 ANALYTICAL METHODS

Only a limited amount of general comment is possible regarding tools of analysis, because every planning sector, whether it is housing, transportation or health services, has developed its own set of techniques that allow the respective specialists to arrive at their own plans and recommendations. Such an analytical framework for many planning sectors is the focus of many subsequent chapters of this book. There are some study procedures, however, that are common to all planners.

Undoubtedly, the most basic of these methods is standard statistical procedure. It is difficult to envision effective planning without at least some familiarity with such statistical techniques as correlation and regression analysis, basic probability, and similar descriptive procedures. Estimation, testing of hypotheses, and, above all, sample surveys and the preparation of their results are major subactivities underlying much contemporary planning work. For efforts ranging from the United States census, to demand analysis for specific services, to the identification of community preferences, only a limited portion of the total affected or involved population can be surveyed. Such partial data are sufficient when used in advanced analysis techniques.

A variety of methods is used to convert data into information and intelligence. The quantitative methods are usually borrowed from other fields such as statistics, operations research and systems analysis. The more commonly used analytical methods are described in the following subsections. Although many of these tools are highly quantitative, it should be stressed that planning analysis is often qualitative.

3.4.1 Statistics

The basic tools of statistics used in planning are:

1. Frequency and distribution of data as variables.
2. Dispersal of data about the central tendencies.
3. Variance and standard deviation, as the most common measures of the average dispersal about the mean.
4. Tests or procedures that identify relationships among variables such as the chi square test, correlation coefficients, and analysis of variance.

Statistics are used in cross tabulations, scatter grams, and bar charts. Figure 3-2 shows these types of data displays.

3.4.2 Graphics

In addition to numerical techniques, many graphic analysis techniques are also available to the urban planner. Graphic analysis is useful because it allows visual display of a complex situation or trend. A significant analytical tool of urban patterns has been the definition of a descriptive vocabulary and the accompanying graphic techniques regarding the imageability of districts, their components and linkages.

One widely applied graphic method consists of the carefully controlled use of overlay sketches that can provide a meaningful composite—an interpretive and analytical description of conditions, needs, and

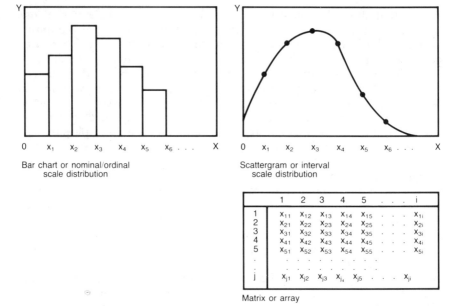

Fig. 3-2. Typical displays of planning data (Source: F.S. So, I. Stallman, F. Beal and D.S. Arnold, eds., *The Practice of Local Government Planning*, ICMA, Washington, DC, 1979)

possibilities. By placing each variable on a separate transparent sheet and expressing its variations by the intensity of patterns, the cumulative effect of any combination of items can be readily discerned visually, and can even be digitized by expressing shades of gray numerically. This technique has been used most widely in landscape and ecological investigations, but other applications are certainly possible.

3.4.3 Models

Models have been defined as symbolic representations of real world phenomena by

$$v = f(x_i \, y_i)$$

in which v = measure of performance;
                       x_i = set of variables the decision maker can control;
                       y_i = set of variables representing conditions, decisions, and environmental factors that decision maker cannot control; and
                       f = functional relationship that can be determined or produced.

Models that use data to simulate real situations can provide a set of scenarios for those variables controlled by decision makers. Models are also useful in predicting the effects of those variables which the decision maker cannot control.

Research in some areas has pointed out that models that work well provide information which may serve as guidelines for coping with the portion of the real world which can be represented by the model. This definition of models is broad enough to include mathematical formulas, computer programs, games, maps, budgets, scenarios, and architectural models.

Models used most frequently in planning involve mathematical or logical symbols (or both) based on beginning algebra and calculus. The models most frequently used by planners are described in the following paragraphs.

Predictive and estimating models.   These are designed to explain real world phenomena and the patterns that may be expected over time. Predicting and estimating models used in planning are usually standard curves fitted to the appropriate data. For example, they are frequently used to predict or explain future trends over time for variables such as population, traffic, housing, income, water use, and sewage flow.

Linear models.   Simple and complex linear models are useful tools in planning analysis, but should be employed with care as they have several limitations which should be noted. First, they assume that the future is an extension of the past. Second, linear models based on a correlation of variables do not show cause-and-effect relationships. Finally, an averaging out occurs in order to make the linearity assumption work. This can distort the results. Figure 3-3 shows a simple linear model. This type of model is a straight-line approximation of historical data.

Nonlinear models.   These are used when linearity does not adequately explain the relationships between variables. Figure 3-3 shows three nonlinear models: (1) Second-order polynomial model; (2) Gompertz model; and (3) logistic model.

Optimizing models.   Given a set of constraints, optimizing models are a group of methods useful in estimating the "best" solution. Among the most commonly used optimizing models are classical calculus, linear programming, nonlinear programming, and dynamic programming.

Stochastic models.   These are optimizing methods used when the terms of the problem are probabilistic (i.e., expressed in terms of uncertainty).

3.4.4 Simulation

Simulations are imitations of real-life situations. There are three types of simulation models: analog, iconic, and symbolic. Analog simulations imitate the real world by use of physical characteristics, such as water in pipes. Iconic simulation relies on scale models. Perhaps the best known example is an airplane model in a wind tunnel. Symbolic simulation uses numerical models and is probably the type most widely used

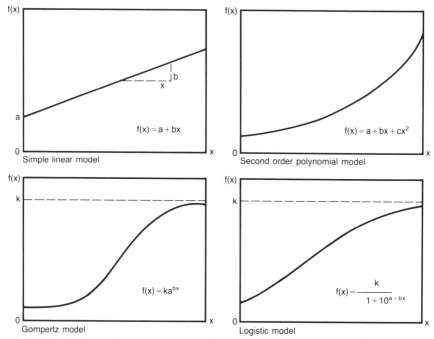

Fig. 3-3. Simple linear model and three nonlinear models (Source: F.S. So, I. Stallman, F. Beal and D.S. Arnold, eds., *The Practice of Local Government Planning*, ICMA, Washington, DC, 1979)

in planning (see subsection 3.4.3 on models). The general mathematical formulation for a symbolic simulation is

$$w = f(U_i, U_j)$$

in which w = a set of numerical characteristics of the problem;
U_i = controllable or uncontrollable variables that generate numerical values;
U_j = independent variables and constraints; and
f = a numerical function.

3.4.5 Gaming

Games are a form of simulation that focus on learning through role playing. There are several operational games available. Among the most widely familiar to planners are Community Land Use Game (CLUG), APEX and Metropolis, and the City and Region Games. These games are primarily useful in a classroom situation.

3.4.6 System Analysis

A system is defined as anything, physical or conceptual, that is composed of interrelated elements. These elements are called subsystems. Subsystems, in turn, are composed of interrelated elements. Systems theory states that a complex system must be dissected so that it can be analyzed and decisions can be made about its over-all optimal performance. The objective is to avoid suboptimization (or the optimal performance of a subsystem) at the expense of over-all system performance.

3.4.7 Summary

Since it is an assumption in the planning profession that many urban operations and facilities can be systematically analyzed, that their internal relationships can be understood, and that logical upgrading actions can be identified in the diagnostic process, simulation model concepts with computer use evolved as an important tool in planning analysis.

Early efforts at application of these techniques were too ambitious, attempting to model all aspects of the urban system. Results of these efforts illustrated the inadequacy of such an undertaking in light of inadequate knowledge, incomplete theory, and the exigencies of real-life situations. As a result, most of the practical work with models can be found within the several distinct sectors of urban services, particularly those that are quantifiable and where cause-and-effect relationships are definable.

There can be little question that the furthest advances in the completeness and reliability of models and in their application have been achieved in the urban transportation field. The old origin and destination survey approaches have been expanded and refined into a chain of procedures that can project future travel needs, distribute them over urban space, and assign trips to existing or proposed channels, thus testing the adequacy of networks and services. From this information, many other dimensions, such as economic and environmental impacts, can be readily analyzed. Ongoing use and review continue to develop greater accuracy and maintain the vitality of the analytical tools.

In the air and water quality environmental field, modeling started later than in the transportation field but has progressed considerably. Techniques are now available that simulate emissions, their distribution and dispersal according to local factors, and the eventual impacts that are estimated to be received at specified locations. From the output of these tools, control and corrective actions can be identified which would bring the pollutant loads within acceptable levels, by either restriction of emissions or treatment of effluents.

These are some of the fields in which the scientific aspects of planning procedures have received their major boost. The federal programs under which these projects are usually executed require a metropolitan approach, insist on a strong demographic, economic, and social base, demand the definition of a future land use or activity pattern or patterns, call for the analysis of alternatives and their consequences in terms of many parameters, and require the preparation of implementation measures. In short, they are a representation of the planning process.

Serious efforts have been made in other sectorial areas to develop usable models. Such areas include housing, retail activity, and the location of institutions. Even if operational models have not always resulted which could be readily and routinely used in practical applications, the work has contributed to the definition of problems in the field and the exploration of frontiers of available knowledge.

Another type of model is represented by programmed land use and development forecasting techniques, which deserve consideration here because they deal with a fundamental planning task from which other service and facility needs are usually determined. The underlying assumption regarding this work is that individual developers, as well as home buyers, manufacturers, and other consumers of urban space, follow a rational thought pattern in seeking advantageous locations for their activities within the available land area. The determinants of locational choice may be various attractive site characteristics (e.g., access), or they may be a series of constraints, not only physical and economic (water availability, soil characteristics) but also social and institutional (availability of various activities).

Most of these simulation models are based on the concept of accessibility as the dominant factor (i.e., that activities favor locations from which other points can be reached most expeditiously), while others emphasize the premise that mobility constraints are less important and that intrinsic site characteristics govern locational choices. The planning tools are hampered greatly by an inadequate understanding of exactly how land development takes place. Some simple theories and descriptive investigations appear insufficient to define precisely this complex process. Recent developments in the issue of energy availability may result in subtle changes in land development patterns and the methods of locational decision making, thus adding to the difficulty in simulating land development.

In summary, great progress has been made in the area of urban activity modeling and some accepted models are operational, but there is room for major improvement. The thrust is now toward sectorial procedures instead of comprehensive models which try to deal with several service areas at once. While there are still uncertainties about the substance and technical methodologies of planning in individual sectors, there is increasing agreement about the form that planning work should take: consensus on objectives, evaluation of alternatives, respect for the needs of various interest groups, and examination of all possible consequences. This approach has brought with it its own set of tools which have received wide application in practically all large-scale projects today.

3.5 INTELLIGENCE INDICATORS

Tools that have been developed to provide intelligence to decision makers include indicator series, scheduling, and information systems.

3.5.1 Indicator Series

Indicator series are based on the idea that a regular, consistent and accurate set of measures of key indicators of economic, environmental, and social conditions will provide decision makers with intelligence that is useful and timely. Indicator series are helpful in fulfilling three needs of decision makers: (1) As "pulse takers" for a region or a state; (2) in monitoring changes; and (3) in the evaluation of operating programs.

3.5.2 Scheduling

Critical path scheduling, with accompanying graphic documentation, has become a standard tool in planning assignments too. More specifically, it is used in the field of planning for planning, that is, the disaggregation of an entire project into defined tasks and their arrangement in a logical relationship to one another. While it is hard to identify an actual planning project that ever followed exactly the sequence and timing originally plotted in the work organization phase, the method is still a very valuable device for scheduling studies rationally, anticipating cross-dependencies among efforts, and monitoring progress. For any large-scale project, particularly if it is sponsored by a public agency, the use of some form of this control tool is mandatory for all practical purposes.

The techniques of Critical Path Method (CPM) employed in planning projects are no different from those used in other fields, and here, as in a number of other instances, planners have freely borrowed or adopted methods from elsewhere. Computer programs are often used to assist in the scheduling process.

3.5.3 Information Systems

An information system is comprised of people, equipment, and software interacting to provide information and intelligence to help in decision making. Figure 3-4 is a schematic diagram of an interactive information system.

Comprehensive data banks result from a coordinated effort to assemble and handle most statistical and factual information under a single umbrella. This concept, although theoretically desirable, has not succeeded in practical terms. There has, however, been considerable success in setting up data systems on a sectorial or special project basis. It is not clear whether these efforts will or should lead to larger,

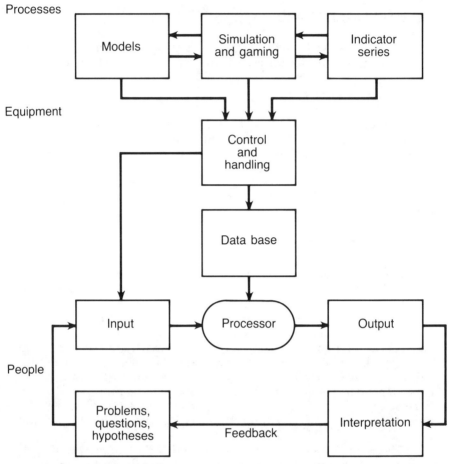

Fig. 3-4. Interactive information system (Source: F.S. So, I. Stallman, F. Beal and D.S. Arnold, eds., *The Practice of Local Government Planning*, ICMA, Washington, DC, 1979)

more integrated ventures. Clearly, a single central data bank at the metropolitan (city or county) level with detailed and recent information would expedite much of the technical work and give a stronger foundation for analysis and, eventually, decision making. But the administrative, political, institutional, jurisdictional, and philosophical—not to mention financial—constraints have so far kept this type of information system from becoming a reality.

Whether data banks are available or not, efforts to secure an adequate information base have increasingly turned to procedures that tap and make available in a workable way factual data that are generated every day by every operational agency of a jurisdiction, ranging from the local police precinct to the state historian.

3.6 PUBLIC PARTICIPATION

Public involvement in planning decisions has not only become a frequently mandated requirement but it generally is (or should be) an integral and constructive part of any planning endeavor. Frequently, a serious attempt is made to create an evaluation process separate and independent from the regular administrative structure.

Besides the standard use of newsletters, public meetings, and review or advisory committees, interesting progress in the field of public involvement has been made with the specific tools utilized in the effort, not only to involve all relevant groups and individuals, but also to streamline the process leading to a consensus on planning proposals. Contributions to such progress include a better understanding of the implications regarding the selection of active participants and their organizations, and recognition of the need to maintain their representation. For example, in any given instance or for any given project, which of the following might provide the most appropriate review: a highly experienced professional task force; a "blue-ribbon" group of leading citizens; a self-selected but small and representative committee; or a large and fluid forum of citizens?

There is also a choice in specific procedures and techniques to be used in public deliberations. No one review group or procedure is superior; each individual project and situation has its own needs for public information and evaluation. Frequently, a combination of review groups or techniques is used. It should be ascertained, however, that the method selected is easily understood by the audience and is presented clearly and comprehensively.

Public involvement is intended not only to keep the public informed of the study status, purpose and findings. An equally important element of public participation is the acquisition by those involved in the planning effort of information or intelligence which will aid in the evaluation and selection of alternatives. Several techniques, described in the following paragraphs, help the planner to gain information.

3.6.1 Survey Research

Survey research based on sound techniques of sampling enables planners to assess people's attitudes in order to determine the levels of public awareness, understanding, and feeling toward complex and sometimes emotional issues. These data can provide information about the qualitative aspects of a situation that would otherwise not be considered. It is essential that care be used in choosing the sample and evaluating results.

3.6.2 Group Techniques

Group techniques are useful tools for providing intelligence to decision makers. This method is a repetitive process based on sequential questionnaires that provide summaries of judgments and opinions from previous rounds.

3.7 EVALUATION

Planning is playing an ever-increasing role in decision making, implementation, and evaluation of possible alternative activities. Although planning is not a decision-making device, its results nevertheless provide decision-making tools that can influence those people who have decision and implementation responsibilities. The purpose of this section is to focus on the evaluation process, its elements, and how the process both affects and is affected by project planners.

There are usually many different ways to arrive at a certain end, whether it be a planning activity or an alternative means to accomplish some task. It is part of the planning process to identify all reasonable alternatives in order not to exclude what might be the most favorable alternative before a systematic analysis can be performed. Thus, all reasonable alternatives should be considered during the initial phases of the evaluation process. The evaluation process is used to select courses of action from the myriad of proposed alternatives.

Planners are often confronted with extremely complex problems involving the interrelationships among many separate elements. These problems must be dissected into elements or processes and the subactivities evaluated as accurately as possible. The information derived from studying the subactivities must then be integrated into a comprehensive analysis of the total problem. The planning process forms a framework within which such detailed analyses can be performed. Many methods can be used to evaluate planning alternatives.

3.7.1 Alternative Selection

The evaluation techniques used in this procedure are usually comparative and are applied to each alternative so as to highlight the differences between alternatives.

Tangible effects. Each planning output will have certain values and consequences which can be measured in physical or monetary units, or both. These units or tangible effects will form the basis for the evaluation process. By measuring or calculating the tangible effects of all outputs, the marginal differences between two or more can be estimated, and the tangible effects of selecting one over another can be determined. It must be remembered that the tangible values and consequences of all outputs must be measured in commensurable units with respect to kind and time, in order to allow direct comparisons.

Intangible effects. Many of the values and consequences of proposed actions cannot be measured in physical or monetary units and are classified as intangibles (for example, loss of life, effects on psychological wellbeing, esthetic degradation, etc.). Even though intangible effects cannot be accurately measured, they must be integrated into the decision-making process if the evaluation and selection process is to have any credibility. The criteria used to evaluate planning outputs should incorporate all positive and negative effects.

The great majority of civil engineering projects generates an array of costs and benefits, some of which are not accounted for through financial analysis, engineering cost estimates, cost and benefit analysis, or other traditional forms of project appraisal and evaluation. Many of the unaccounted impacts are extremely difficult to quantify and require the use of a variety of techniques not normally considered in traditional engineering economics.

Nevertheless it is necessary to enumerate, qualify and, whenever possible, quantify such impacts, since accurate and complete evaluation of a project's alternatives is not only sound planning practice but is frequently required by law. For example, the National Environmental Policy Act (NEPA), Public Law 91-190, 852 (1970), as amended by P.L. 94-83, 89 Stat. 424 (1975), enacted in 1969, requires that the

> . . . Federal Government use all practicable means . . . (to) . . . assure for all Americans safe, healthful, productive, and aesthetically and culturally pleasing surroundings . . . (and to) . . . preserve important historic, cultural, and natural aspects . . . (NEPA, sec. 101!bl)

> . . . All agencies . . . shall . . . identify and develop methods and procedures, in consultation with the Council of Environmental Quality . . . , which will insure that presently unquantified environmental amenities and values may be given appropriate consideration.

The systematic quantification of the "unquantified environmental amenities" (the intangible impacts associated with engineering projects) is crucial if informed choices are to be made among the possible alternatives.

Techniques of project appraisal are employed by the public and private sectors to attempt to assure, in a systematic way, that investment projects actually achieve the desired objectives. For the private sector, objectives may be quite narrowly defined (for example, maximization of the net worth of the firm), while for public sector projects objectives are likely to be broadly defined to accommodate a variety of economic, social, and political goals. Project evaluation techniques are used to assess whether or not: (1) Scarce resources are used in such a way as to contribute to economic efficiency (e.g., cost-benefit analysis); and (2) projects contribute to the achievement of specific objectives (e.g., regional development, airport noise control, equality of opportunity, maximization of employment). In some cases, objectives may be identified to be the avoidance of certain effects, such as overloading government services (e.g., health, recreation, transport), significantly affecting the environment, or depleting the resource base.

Frequently, government bodies are called upon to engage in activities or provide services which cannot be valued in their entirety by market mechanisms and are thus extremely difficult to measure in dollars. These activities may include national defense, education, police and fire protection, roadways, airports, irrigation, health services, recreation, and environmental protection. The problem of valuing marketed outputs of public projects is a central issue in cost-benefit analysis. Nonetheless, nonmarketed outputs may also affect the net benefits generated by the chosen alternatives.

In the past, the difficulties of identifying and measuring intangible costs and benefits often resulted in their omission from analysis in assessing the desirability of a particular project. Benefits and costs which are more easily measured have traditionally been treated as more important considerations in project appraisal. More recently, however, there has been a growing awareness that intangible costs and benefits may be of great significance and thus must be recognized and accounted for. For example, esthetic considerations and improved recreational opportunities may be major considerations behind many river basin development projects. Esthetic enhancement of the United States capital area has been cited as a major justification for the Potomac Basin clean-up, while loss of wilderness areas has been a major concern in making decisions regarding the construction of pipelines in the northern United States and Canada.

The government is increasingly called upon to invest in projects and programs designed exclusively to maintain or improve environmental quality. Few, if any, of these programs can be justified on the basis of their contribution to the gross national product; instead, their value can be determined only by their direct (but difficult to measure) contributions to individuals in society.

There has been a great deal of interest expressed in the intangible environmental costs and benefits associated with various projects and the measurement of these impacts in such a way that they can be taken into account in making decisions among different project alternatives. Along with increased interest, some confusion has arisen surrounding: (1) The nature of environmental intangibles; (2) the terminology used to describe them; (3) the techniques appropriate to measure and evaluate them; and (4) the relationship between these techniques and techniques of project evaluation based on inputs and outputs which are more readily quantifiable and which have dollar values attached to them in the marketplace. Table 3-1 summarizes for quick reference the terms and definitions which are useful in the evaluation of intangibles. Table 3-2 summarizes the possible impacts associated with a typical civil engineering project.

TABLE 3-1 Key Concepts Utilized in the Evaluation of Intangibles

Concept (1)	Description (2)
Opportunity cost	the net present value of the most economical alternative use which is precluded when resources are allocated to a specific project
Equity	the distribution or incidence of real income on selected social groups, e.g., the poor and the rich, and classifications, e.g., spatial, temporal, and racial
Welfare economics	the area of economics that relates individual and collective social utility to monetary values (though noneconomic factors are assumed to be constant, social, political, and institutional aspects enter into the analysis)
Benefit-cost analysis	the net discounted value of net benefits from providing goods and services from a developmental alternative obtained from subtracting from the value of the goods and services, provided the value of those goods and services that could have been produced had the developmental alternative not been constructed; the criterion is to maximize the net discounted value of benefits, given that compensation is made to those who are made worse off by the developmental alternative, to ensure that no one is made worse off, at least someone is better off
National economic development account	the monetary value of the change in goods and services provided, inclusive of the willingness-to-pay aggregated values and the costs incurred by reducing the utilization of existing projects
Regional development account	changes that occur at the regional level, e.g., employment, economic base, population distribution, and environmental quality; direct and indirect changes occurring from a developmental alternative on the region
Environmental quality	physical, biological, and ecological changes imputable to a project, characterized by indicators, e.g., historical, geological, recreational, and environmental
Social well-being account	changes in the distribution of real income, the opportunity to partake in recreational activities, and other social changes affecting individuals
Willingness to pay	the market expenditure made by the individual consumer, plus any additional amount which the consumer can be induced to pay, to assure that he is not excluded from enjoying the output of the

TABLE 3-1 continued

Concept (1)	Description (2)
	developmental alternative; the net willingness to pay is the monetary value of the additional enjoyment gained by utilizing the project, relative to the next best alternative. Willingness-to-pay and demand curve are intimately related
Demand curve	the quantities of a good or service the individual consumer is willing and able to buy at given prices are related through the demand curve; the determinants of demand are quantity demanded, price of the good or service, the price of available substitutes and complementary goods and services; the individual's income, taste, and preference characterize the demand curve
Consumer surplus	the amount of money that an individual actually pays for a given quantity of a good or service resulting from subtracting the amount actually paid from the maximum amount he would be willing to pay; the definite integral of the area under the demand curve, up to the quantity demanded, measures the consumer's surplus and the actual expenditures made to enjoy the output from the project; the utility that the consumer derives, a nonproprietary right, diminishes as more of the quantity is provided to the consumer, diminishing marginal returns
Willingness to sell	the measures of benefits lost by foreclosing options, e.g., flooding a habitat with consequent loss of a species, as the minimum compensation that the sellers would accept to relinquish their rights; such compensation is of such amount that would make the sellers neither better nor worse off than they would have been without the project
Social rate of interest	the rate of discount used to determine the present worth of future value expressing the preference of a society as a whole. Generally considered to be less than the opportunity cost of capital

3.8 IMPLEMENTATION

Plans become reality only when specific actions are taken; implementation is the action step of the planning process. The planning process does not usually participate in choosing a specific action, but it

TABLE 3-2 Economic and Environmental Impacts Associated with a Civil Engineering Project

Type of impact (1)	Costs (2)	Benefits (3)
(a) Primary		
Tangible	materials, labor, concrete, steel	commodity outputs valued at market prices, e.g., electricity production
Intangible	loss of wilderness areas, destruction of wildlife, air and water pollution	water for recreation, irrigation, reduced risk of loss of life due to flooding
(b) Secondary		
Tangible	increased stress on government services, decreased incomes for factors in other areas of the country; generally, costs were determined to equal benefits	local employment, increases in value of local land, returns to local factors and business incomes, tax base, and expansion of ancillary industries
Intangible	environmental impacts of induced activities, including air, water, land, and community	reduction, to a certain extent, of environmental impacts in other parts of the country

does play a key role in the decision-making process by providing information and intelligence about the tools available to implement each alternative course of action. Implementation tools may be categorized as economic, regulatory, administrative, or informational.

3.8.1 Economic Aspect

The principal thrust of the economic aspect of an implementation program is the identification of sources of funds for project implementation, and examination as to whether project operations will be able to recover all or part of the expenditures. These techniques constitute a well-defined subset of knowledge and represent the tools of some other disciplines, namely finance and public administration. However, the planner must be sufficiently familiar with the economic field, because the availability of certain funding programs may encourage or preclude specific alternatives.

The basic economic management tool for many types of public and privately sponsored projects is the capital improvement program, a multiyear schedule of anticipated actions and estimated expenditures for different purposes year by year. In most cases this program is updated annually for a five-year period with the next year's capital improvement budget worked out in great detail. These documents are of the utmost importance in structuring the entire development effort of a municipality (or county or state).

The documentation of a capital improvement program lists projects or items and identifies the sources of funds for each. Several types of financing arrangements can often be considered, and in any given instance a specific choice has to be made regarding the practical suitability and further consequences of each option. For example, the most direct means of financing might be transfers from the current annual revenues. However, because public works improvements are sporadic, such a practice would create intolerable dislocations in the annual budget. Consequently, borrowing is required, which calls for the issuance of bonds, their sale, and repayment over an extended period. This adds interest expenses, but also places the financial burden on the actual beneficiaries of the project, often extending over several decades.

There are two basic types of bonds: general obligation bonds and revenue bonds. The former are backed by the total income generation powers of the community (generally taxes), and tend to be used for projects that benefit the entire population but do not result in specific income, such as schools, roads, and fire stations.

Revenue bonds, on the other hand, are secured by the expected income stream from the specific project and have the additional advantages that they are exempt from municipal debt ceilings and do not require approval through a referendum. They are used for such projects as water supply systems, transportation terminals, bridges and tunnels. Revenue bonds, in effect, depend on user fees; this method can sometimes also be employed directly on small projects or those that rely on private financing.

Another means of financing which is used less frequently today than in the past is special assessments levied on the residents receiving direct benefits. For example, assessments might be placed on all properties within a given distance of a new sewer line or park.

The entire field of public financing mechanisms has changed and continues to change with the introduction and continuing availability of a wide variety of public assistance programs by state and federal governments that encourage and support desirable projects. Such programs exist in education, transportation, health, housing, public safety, water and sewer systems, and almost all other areas of concern to the planner. Federal agencies may pay up to 90% of the capital costs, depending on the particular program. (In some areas, such as public transit, federal funds may also be available for operating assistance if operating subsidy is required.) A "local share" is almost invariably required, although in some cases states may assume responsibility for that portion of funding. Needless to say, the availability of grants and subsidies from higher levels of government frequently becomes the dominant consideration in examining the financial feasibility of a project at the local level.

Federal and state policies have greatly expanded opportunity for local jurisdictions, but there is some feeling that they can also dampen the initiative of municipalities and metropolitan authorities. There is a growing segment of the population and the federal hierarchy which feels that grant assistance programs discourage good financial and operational management on the municipal and metropolitan level.

The available programs are, of course, different in each sector and are constantly changing; their funds become replenished and exhausted at varying rates. Consequently, they must be carefully monitored and evaluated on an individual basis by the sectorial planners in each case. A transportation planner, for example, must be aware of the various grant programs for highways, transit and traffic systems, and should keep updated on the status of the availability and awardability of funds under each.

It should be noted that the economic analysis of a project is not limited to financing aspects alone. There are also nonrecoverable benefits which can improve the economic situation of the larger community. Increases in jobs and efficiency of production, ease of communications, a better business climate, cleaner environment, and even improved local self-image may provide ample justification for project implementation, even though the municipal treasury may not experience any benefits in the short range.

3.8.2 Regulatory Aspect

The possibility exists that some planning recommendations could be unimplementable because they are illegal or in conflict with established institutional or labor practices, or because they are politically unfeasible under the prevailing administration or set of circumstances. These factors enter into the total evaluation matrix and usually represent relative considerations with different levels of severity of constraint. There are also, however, absolute constraints represented by a battery of ordinances and regulations that are in effect in any community. This subsection is concerned primarily with local ordinances.

Local ordinances are enacted by the local legislative body and usually conform to state enabling legislation. This means that a municipality may implement such regulations but is not compelled to do so. Consequently, communities can still be found without some or all of these development controls.

Undoubtedly, the most comprehensive of local regulations is the zoning ordinance. While its antecedents can be traced to various scattered municipal rules, the pioneering document was the 1916 New York City ordinance. The policies and techniques of zoning have changed considerably over the years, but the basic purpose and format remain about the same—to specify for all parts of a locality which land uses and activities are permitted (or barred) and at what densities. In addition, there usually are auxiliary clauses dealing with parking and loading requirements, signs, access by light and air, etc. It is particularly important to note that the zoning ordinance should evolve from and be the principal tool for implementing a community's over-all plan of development or growth. In practice this is not always the case, and the ordinance loses some of its potential effectiveness.

Zoning ordinances, as well as most other local regulations, are not binding on higher levels of government. Since the municipality itself is obviously free to operate as it sees fit within its own legal framework, the zoning ordinance is above all a tool to control individual private development. The over-all objectives are to: (1) Avoid any incompatible combination of uses; (2) protect the livability of residential areas and the productive efficiency of work districts; (3) prevent unsanitary and unsafe conditions; and (4) preclude excessive burdens on public service systems.

Zoning ordinances have been criticized for their rigidity and inability to accommodate superior but unusual developments. In reaction to this criticism, some features of flexibility have recently been introduced, such as clustering of building with compensating open spaces, and adding more square feet for the provision of elements of public benefit. Special districts with a unique set of regulations respecting historical, esthetic, or unusual activity elements can be created as well.

Zoning ordinances have been tested repeatedly in courts as to the extent of their legal authority and adequacy of procedures. The principal current controversies relate to the questions of whether they are used as exclusionary devices to keep low-income families out of suburban communities, and whether they can be used as tools to manage or limit growth.

Another local ordinance that has a direct linkage to project implementation is the official map. It is an ordinance in graphic form and delineates all lands, whether publicly owned or not, that are impressed with a public interest. This includes all rights-of-way, parks, drainage channels, facility sites, etc. It can also include parcels to be acquired in a reasonable time period for planned public improvements. As such, it becomes a powerful implementation tool in the inventory of devices to control and upgrade the urban environment.

Subdivision regulations outline procedures and standards that have to be followed by developers of residential groupings. Such regulations contain specific requirements regarding infrastructure systems (roads, utilities); thus, any planning project operating within this sphere deals with these regulations in detail.

A municipality will usually have a number of other codes and regulations in force in addition to the ones mentioned. However, in descending order, they become less directly concerned with planning issues and address specific technical concerns. For example, municipalities will almost invariably include a building code which deals with structural aspects of construction and is vital to basic safety and livability. There also may be sanitary and housing codes, special parking and sign ordinances, regulations directed at historical and esthetic aspects, and other similar types of regulatory provisions.

The concluding point is that no two communities are ever likely to have an identical of regulations. It is the planners' responsibility working in any area to determine exactly what is allowed, under what circumstances, and what opportunities and constraints exist toward the implementation of any kind of plan or project. Frequently, a basic need to reform the ordinances may be indicated. In many other cases, planners need simply to conform to the intent and letter of the regulations expressing the developmental policies of a locality under its cherished legal powers.

3.9 CONCLUSIONS

It is appropriate to conclude this chapter on planning tools with the observation that the planning process has been reasonably successful in developing procedures and techniques which keep pace with work needs and societal mandate. Many of these techniques have been borrowed and adopted from other disciplines. This is appropriate, since the entire field of planning and analysis relies on the integration of knowledge from many specialties. It is also clear that there are still many areas where further methodological development can take place, because either better procedures are needed, or untapped resources exist that can be utilized.

CHAPTER 4

LAND USE PLANNING[a]

4.1 INTRODUCTION

In a democratic society such as the United States, land has historically been used by its owner for whatever purposes the owner saw fit. As society evolved, limitations came into being that prevented uses of one's land if those uses would detrimentally affect neighboring property. These limitations, in effect, maintained other people's rights pertaining to the uses of their own land.

As awareness grew of the need for decent housing, environmental protection, and other goals, governmental bodies and private concerns saw the need for planning and regulating the use of land. This awareness has become evident at all levels of government. It can be seen at the national level in terms of federal regulations and directives, down to the local county or municipality level, where zoning and subdivision regulations have become the rule rather than the exception, at least in urban communities.

This chapter will provide insight into the current processes, theories, and techniques in land use planning. It will attempt to summarize these processes, theories, and techniques in sufficient detail to enable the practitioner who is unfamiliar with them to perform simple studies without further research.

The term "land use planning" can actually be thought of in two separate contexts. On one hand it can be thought to include all forms of planning. For instance, transportation planning can be considered a form of land use planning since it actually consists of planning for the use of land for transportation purposes. The same is true for housing, recreation, water resource, or any other form of physical planning. Urban, regional, and city planning also can be thought of as subsets of land use planning. The land use planner must therefore have a knowledge of all the various types of physical planning in order to perform in a competent manner. On the other hand, land use planning is its own specific discipline. In its strictest sense it is a very precise art having its own set of theories and techniques that establish specific procedures and processes, all of which form the "tools of the trade."

It should also be noted that land use planning for a developed area is different than for vacant land for a new town (or even a new subdivision), because existing development in an already developed

---

[a]Prepared by the late Roland J. Frappier, M.ASCE, Rhode Island Statewide Planning Program.

area controls plans for that area much more than vacant land does. The overriding factor in both cases is planning for the optimum use of the land, given the physiography, demand, and other planning factors.

The historical material presented next will look at land use planning in the broader sense. Material presented in the remainder of this chapter will look at land use planning in the stricter sense—that is, it will investigate those theories and techniques that are used in that subset of planning known as land use planning, or stated differently, planning for the use of the land.

4.1.1 History

The use of land has been planned to one extent or another for almost as long as the land has been used. The placement and form of the villages established by our prehistoric ancestors had the first rudiments of planning. Most were located on or near bodies of water and were formed so as to aid in the protection of the inhabitants. The ancient cities of Egypt, Greece, and Italy definitely were preconceived in terms of their location and structure. There were many reasons which brought about these early attempts at planning, including such fundamentals as protection, availability of resources such as water, trade economics, cultural and religious activities, or even the dictates and desires of rulers. These rudiments of city planning developed throughout the centuries and were reflected in various European cities.

In America, three early colonial examples of good city planning should be noted. The first is Philadelphia, Pennsylvania (1682), which featured a gridiron street system having open spaces. The gridiron system continues to this day to dominate the American city plan. The second is Williamsburg, Virginia (1699), which has been noted by many historians as one of the first successful attempts to create a town culture in America. Probably the most successful attempt at city planning in colonial America is the third example. It is James Oglethorpe's gridiron with open space plan for Savannah, Georgia (1733). As colonial America developed so did the techniques and plans for colonial cities. L'Enfant's plan for Washington, D.C. (1791) and Frederick Law Olmsted's plan for Central Park in New York City (1857) are highlights of the period from colonial times to modern city planning.

The 1893 World's Fair (known as the World's Columbian Exposition) in Chicago marked the start of modern-day city planning. Even though plans for the development of many cities in the United States predated 1893, the effect of the Columbian Exposition was to last for many years. It was the catalyst that led to the "city beautiful movement." Planning and design of the Columbian Exposition actually began in 1890 by the appointment of a design team headed by Chicago architect Daniel H. Burnham and including Frederick Law Olmsted, landscape architect, Charles Follen McKim of the architectural firm of McKim, Mead and White, and Augustus St. Gaudens, a sculptor. Their design is said to be the first successful attempt to combine esthetics and social consciousness into urban life. From this beginning, the city beautiful movement was formed. Professionals in the field began to realize that there should be a relationship between urban form and architectural scale.

While America was modifying its thinking of urban relationships, Britain was also experiencing a rethinking of its own urban forms. This rethinking was a reaction against the effects of overcrowded, ugly, and disease-prone English factory areas. One of its pioneers was Ebenezer Howard, who proposed to solve the industrial slum problems of England by the creation of small, self-sufficient "garden cities" surrounded by "greenbelts" of privately held lands, which were permanently dedicated to agricultural purposes. This new type of planning was called "garden city" planning and was characterized not only by greenbelts but also by an interest in meeting minimum housing needs. The concept was realized for the first time at Letchworth, England, which was started in 1903. Today it is a city of some 35,000 people surrounded by an extensive greenbelt. The garden city idea, like the city beautiful movement in the United States, caught on and has been influencing planning ever since. There are currently in excess of two dozen such garden cities in the English countryside. They have not evolved as originally conceived of by Howard, as self-contained entities, but have, in fact, evolved into suburbs for some of England's major cities.

At that time, in the United States, another concept which would have far reaching effects on modern city planning was being formulated. A book written by Clarence A. Perry entitled *The Neighborhood Unit, A Scheme of Arrangement for the Family-Life Community* was published in 1929 and documented his premise that the neighborhood should be the basic unit for residential land use planning. Perry's neighborhood unit was envisioned to be of a size that would require and support an elementary school with an enrollment of between 1,000 and 1,200 students. This translated to a total population of between 5,000 and 6,000. Its actual physical size was dependent upon population density. The neighborhood unit was to be bounded on all sides by arterial (or higher classification) streets of sufficient width to facilitate the passage of all through traffic around the unit. The internal street system within the neighborhood would consist of local and collector streets sized to carry local traffic loads. This local street network should be designed to facilitate circulation within the neighborhood but to discourage its use by through traffic. Small parks and open space areas would be planned within each neighborhood and would meet the needs of the neighborhood. Public service facilities should be grouped about a central park or common. Shopping areas of adequate size to service the population should be laid out on the circumference of the neighborhood, preferably at the intersection of various arterials and adjacent to similar uses in adjoining neighborhoods. Figure 4-1 is a schematic portrayal of Perry's neighborhood concept.

One of the most basic assumptions of Perry's concept was that the age distribution within a neighborhood would not change appreciably

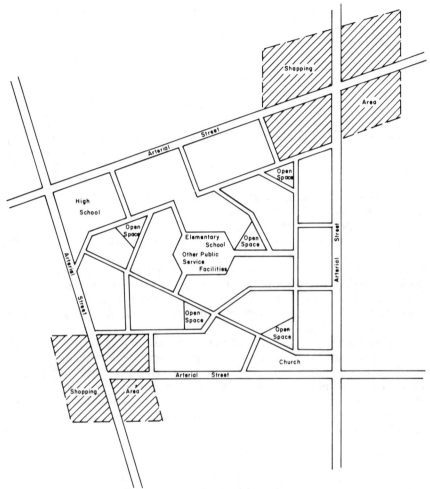

Fig. 4-1. Perry's neighborhood concept

from generation to generation. This assumption is critical since the continued viability of the elementary school within a neighborhood depends upon its correctness, but it is disputed and has been proved incorrect in numerous instances. The result is underutilization of the neighborhood elementary school and public facilities as the age mix of the neighborhood changes. Regardless of this fact, Perry's neighborhood concept may be second only to Howard's garden cities in influencing modern-day city planning.

Frank Lloyd Wright, noted 20th century American architect, adopted and adjusted some of the city beautiful and garden city concepts in one of his expeditions into the realm of city planning. His Broadacre

City, first exhibited in 1935, spread the suburb across the countryside and then dispersed throughout it a mixture of manufacturing areas and large farms. Large houses sat on the highest ground and overlooked the farms and other areas of small residential units.

Another noted 20th century architect, Le Corbusier, took a contrary direction to the garden city and greenbelt concepts in his Ville Radieuse. Here one sees an invasion of the center city by the greenbelt and the incorporation of garden cities within the center of the metropolitan areas. This was done in an effort to open the cities, increase the propensity for movement through the area, and increase the parks and open spaces close to the center. The plan is simple to implement on a new site: simply build radial transportation facilities which lead to large office buildings, then surround the new open center with large residential complexes to house the population. It is usually not considered in terms of renovating existing sites.

A completely different approach from Le Corbusier's was presented by McHarg (24)*. McHarg is an outspoken critic of the traditional notion that urban development must be imposed upon the landscape without regard to its environmental and ecological consequences. In his book, he proves that manmade structures can be accommodated within the natural landscape. His basic premise is to plan, design and develop with the natural landscape, rather than reform the landscape to conform to the plan.

This brief historical survey has touched upon a very small number of concepts that have influenced city planning and its evolution. One needs to have some understanding of the evolution of city planning in order to apply the various procedures and techniques currently in use. Anyone wishing a more detailed historical chronology should refer to Chapter 2 of Reference 36, entitled "Historical Development of American City Planning."

4.1.2 Some Basic Terminology

The following definitions are not meant to be complete but simply set out some basics which will be built upon in following sections.

Comprehensive plan   The basic over-all plan in all planning above the project level is usually the comprehensive plan, also called the master plan or general plan. The comprehensive plan, at a minimum, is an official statement of a geographic unit's policies and intentions pertaining to physical development. In and of itself a comprehensive plan does not have any regulatory effect. It is a necessary and very important item in planning because it establishes a frame to build from. It should include a clear discussion of what, where, when, and, especially, why with regard to all recommendations set forth within the plan.

---

*Numerals in parentheses refer to bibliographic items listed at the end of this chapter.

The land use plan or element is a basic part of the comprehensive plan because it is the major component of that plan. It usually contains extensive background research of the area. It should also contain documentation of the analyses which took place leading to a determination of the best future physical development within the geographic unit.

The geographic unit for which the planning is being performed may be a state or municipality, both of which have definite political boundaries, or a region, which may or may not be defined in terms of political boundaries. One dictionary defines a region as "any large part of the earth's surface especially as distinguished by certain natural or climatic conditions or even more generally as an area, space, or place of more or less definite extent or character."

Citizen participation No matter what geographic unit is being planned, one critical aspect that must not be neglected is citizen participation. In its simplest form citizen participation can be defined as public involvement. The techniques and timing of this public involvement vary organizationally and functionally depending on the geographic scope of the study. These techniques will be specifically described in later sections of this chapter. Definitions of the respective roles of the citizenry, planners, and public officials are critical. The lack of definitions of proper roles for the various parties in the process often causes unnecessary conflicts in situations where adversarial roles have already been established. It is equally critical that the process of public involvement be clearly defined as to when and at what step the involvement takes place.

Implementation   In order for a plan to have an effect once it is adopted, its recommendations must be implemented. Techniques used to implement recommendations from a plan vary with the geographic scope of the plan. The techniques vary from guidelines and legislation at the state or regional level to zoning or subdivision regulations at the municipality and project-specific level.

4.1.3 Interaction With Other Planning Studies

A knowledge of some generalized interactions between land use and other planning studies may prove very helpful. Not only can these other studies assist in filling gaps in data needed to perform the land use studies, but they can serve as a quick cross-check for analyses performed as part of the land use studies.

Transportation studies Transportation studies are a major source of socioeconomic and demographic characteristics for rather small geographic units known as "analysis zones" or "traffic zones." Transportation studies also yield travel or transportation system characteristics. Table 4-1 lists some possible data elements that may be obtained from typical transportation studies. Additionally, transportation studies establish relationships between these various data items that may prove

TABLE 4-1 Data Elements That May Be Obtained From Typical Transportation Studies

Dwelling units
Population, by age group
Employment, by type
Labor force
Income
Autos available
School enrollment
Trips, by purpose
Trips per person
Trips per dwelling unit
Trips per employee
Parking characteristics
Spatial relationships, residential to industrial to commercial areas

helpful when attempting to predict the effects of a specific land use decision or development project.

Economic studies   Economic studies can provide an independent estimate of labor force and total employment, and provide data that relate employment by type (such as commercial or manufacturing) to such things as floor area by use. These relationships can then be used to estimate the requirements of a certain area in terms of the amount of a specific type of commercial or industrial space—for instance, what amount of space will be needed in order to employ some percentage of the available labor force. Table 4-2 lists the data elements that may be obtained from typical economic studies.

Other studies   Although transportation and economic studies have the greatest potential to provide data for land use studies, other studies may also provide helpful material. Previous land use studies can provide material relating to how the area developed and where outmoded or obsolete land uses could be upgraded to higher and better uses through

TABLE 4-2 Data Elements That May Be Obtained From Typical Economic Studies

Employment, by type
Labor force
Floor space, by type
Land uses, by area
Income

private or publicly funded renewal projects. Recreation and open space studies can provide relationships between spatial separation of sites from residential areas and demand for those areas. Inventories of public facilities such as water supply lines, utility lines, and sewer service areas can yield density characteristics that may prove very helpful. Housing studies can be a basis for residential land use planning.

Vast amounts of data are available from other types of studies to aid in land use planning. Such data can be readily adopted for application to land use studies. Research into these other sources can be beneficial to the land use planner. Caution must be taken in researching and analyzing these other sources of data prior to their use. Since all studies "borrow" data, one may end up using data that are outdated or incorrect if sources are not carefully checked.

4.1.4 Land Use Classification Systems

A basic decision in land use planning is which land use classification system to use. A land use classification system is a systematic and consistent way to interpret and document the actual use of specific parcels or cells of land within a specific area. Since land use patterns change from area to area, the system used in a specific area should correspond to the existing and emerging land uses within the area. This can be done by investigating different systems and choosing the one which best suits the needs of a specific area.

Many different types of land use classification systems have been developed. Some systems are new; others are simply variations of an existing system developed to meet the specific needs of an area. Land use classification systems now in use include:

1. Detroit system. The land use classification manual (21) developed by the Detroit Metropolitan Area Regional Planning Commission is designed to easily identify all of the land uses in an entire region and to analyze in detail the land use in a small area. The Detroit system starts with a basic one-digit system (0 through 9) resulting in ten categories (which can be seen on Table 4-3) and builds upon the basic system in order to arrive at its most detailed system of four-digit coding (0000 through 9999) resulting in 10,000 categories (an example of which can be seen in Table 4-4). The key element to this system is that the level of detail can be varied depending on the land use or size of the area. Any detailed four-digit coding may be aggregated simply and quickly with the use of a simple coding convention adopted by the system. In the coding convention all subcategories of category 1 at whatever level have code numbers starting with 1; all subcategories of category 2 have code numbers starting with 2; and so on.

2. "Standard" system. Another generally accepted system is described in the federal government's *Standard Land Use Coding Manual* (42). The system has many of the characteristics of the Detroit system

TABLE 4-3 Basic (One-Digit) Categories in the Detroit System (21)

Identifying digit	Category
0	Residential
1	Extractive and industrial nonmanufacturing
2	Manufacturing
3	Manufacturing
4	Transportation, communication and utilities
5	Commercial
6	Personal, business and professional services
7	Public and quasi-public services
8	Recreational
9	Unused space

TABLE 4-4 Example of Four-Digit Land Coding in Detroit System (21)

1   Extractive and industrial nonmanufacturing

  10   Agricultural

      101   Field crop farms
            1013   Cash grain farms
            1019   Other field crop farms

      102   Fruit, tree nut, and vegetable farms
            1022   Fruit and tree nut farms
            1023   Vegetable farms

      103   Livestock farms
            1032   Dairy farms
            1033   Poultry farms
            1039   Livestock farms not elsewhere classified

      104   General farms
            1042   General farms primarily crop
            1043   General farms primarily livestock
            1044   General crop and livestock farms

      108   Noncommercial farms
            1082   Part-time farms
            1083   Residential farms
            1084   Institutional farms

  11   Agricultural services and hunting and trapping

such as variability of coding level and easy aggregatability. It also has some embellishment which makes it more suitable for use.

    3. Other systems. Both the Detroit and standard systems work very well in urban areas, enabling one to code to great detail within

those areas. Both have one major drawback also; that is, they do not work very well when attempting to classify land in rural areas. Another more recently developed system, called the land use classification system for use with remote sensor data, is more suited for use in rural areas. Its orientation is more towards natural resources. It uses land cover as a surrogate for activity or land use. Because of this it is geared to different data collection techniques than the urban oriented systems. An ideal land use classification system for a mixed rural and urban area would be a combined system, using one of the urban oriented systems for the urban areas and the land use classification system for land use with remote sensor data, or a similar system, for the rural areas.

The following steps should be taken in selecting a land use classification system. First, determine if a land use classification system is in existence for the area. If one is, every attempt should be made to retain it. An analysis of its advantages and disadvantages should be made in order to ascertain whether it is still satisfactory. If it is not satisfactory, the reasons should be analyzed and the existing classification system corrected. Unless the area has changed drastically or the initial decision was incorrect, then that system may still be the best one for the area. Several other reasons for keeping the existing system are: (1) People are familiar with it; (2) much needed information has already been collected and is being used; and (3) there is a possibility that only relatively minor updating may be needed (a much less time-consuming process than starting over).

If, however, the area in question has never been classified, or the decision is made that the existing system is not salvageable, the following should be done:

1. Research areas of similar makeup and size to see if they have a readily adaptable system. Surrounding areas should also be investigated, but caution should be taken in ascertaining whether they are similar in makeup and size. If a prospective system is found, it should be analyzed in order to ascertain what types and levels of detail of data will be needed. If at all possible, the same system should be used not only on the land use study, but also in transportation and other studies which need such a system.

2. Once system requirements have been established, data availability must be determined. Utility companies, colleges or universities, and sometimes local officials can provide much useful data. Available data must be analyzed and techniques to supplement the available data must be established. These could include actual field surveys, or other data collection techniques, or both.

3. Select the unit for which the data will be collected and summarized. A decision must be made on how the system will be established: a grid cell basis, an analysis zone, a census tract, or a parcel basis. The answer depends on the size of the area and the level of detail needed. The more detailed the system, the more specific the data it can

TABLE 4-5 Color Code in Land Use Classification System

Land use category	Color
Residential	orange
Retail businesses	red
Transportation, utilities, communications	ultramarine
Industry and related uses	indigo blue
Wholesale and related uses	purple
Public buildings and open space	green
Institutional buildings and areas	gray
Vacant and nonurban uses	uncolored

provide, but also the more costly and time consuming it can be to establish and maintain. If coding is done at too coarse a level, homogeneity of land uses will be overemphasized and the system will be misleading in that it will not always show differences in land uses even when they are present.

4. Establish the level of detail to which the actual coding will conform. There is no prescribed level of coding suited for all areas. A generally acceptable system for classifying land at its most basic use level has evolved. Table 4-5 illustrates this system. The colors shown on the table have evolved corresponding to the various classifications. This basic level of coding (sometimes with minor variations) is usually used in map presentations. For analytical purposes, much more detailed systems have been developed.

Once the initial decisions have been made, the actual coding of data must be done. At this point, the decision whether to use computers to store and analyze data must be made. This decision will vary from area to area, depending on whether a computer system is readily available, whether knowledgeable personnel are available, what the cost of computerization will be, and other factors. Computerization has many long-term benefits in terms of aggregation and tabulation of data and ease of updating.

4.2 FEDERAL INVOLVEMENT IN LAND USE PLANNING

The federal government's role in land use planning since the 1930s has been to act as a catalyst supplying policy direction and funding to states. The policy direction as well as the funding have at times been fragmented and even inconsistent. Federal funding through grants, loans, or direct federal projects have by their very existence provided policy direction and have usually been successful in this respect. More direct policy setting at the federal level has also been attempted, generally without as much success.

Perhaps the first realization of the need for national planning came in 1937 when the United States Natural Resource Committee, Urbanism Committee, called for "a system of urban research and reporting to be organized at the national level." This call met with little success, in that no funds were ever appropriated for the stated purpose.

4.2.1 Federal Grant Programs

The Catalog of Federal Domestic Assistance (CFDA) is the definitive source for individuals and agencies seeking federal funding through federally sponsored grant and loan programs. During the early to mid 1970s the CFDA contained no less than 110 separate programs that had the potential to impact state and local land use planning. Some of these programs were small and had no real effect; others resulted in significant attention to the planning process used at the state and local levels.

Housing Act of 1954   Section 701 of the Housing Act of 1954 was initially intended to provide funds to generally smaller communities that did not have adequate planning resources. Through a series of legislative amendments and other administrative action, the "701 Program" became the comprehensive planning assistance program for most planning agencies. Section 701 funds were used by state, regional and local planning agencies to perform a variety of planning studies. These ranged from inventories of land use and other existing conditions to population and other socioeconomic analyses; to plans for recreation, conservation, housing and land use; and to preparation of zoning ordinances and subdivision regulations. The program went out of existence in 1981.

National Flood Insurance Act of 1968   The National Flood Insurance Act of 1968 and subsequent amendments thereto established a grant program for land management in flood-prone areas. Originally administered by the federal Department of Housing and Urban Development, in 1978 its administration was moved to the Federal Emergency Management Agency. It supplies funds to states to perform various planning studies of flood-prone areas. It also sets out regulations restricting various uses in certain flood-prone areas if a community joins the program.

Clean Air Act of 1970   The Clean Air Act of 1970 and subsequent amendments thereto (particularly in 1977) made funds available to certain areas designated as nonattainment areas in terms of air quality standards. These funds were made available to the areas so that plans could be formulated and projects implemented which would enable them to reach attainment by specific dates. The plans, entitled State Implementation Plans (SIP), addressed both mobile and stationary sources of air pollution. They evaluate various strategies to reduce carbon monoxide (CO), sulphur dioxide (SO_2) and hydrocarbons (HC), and set forth a recommended action plan.

Rural Development Act of 1972   The Rural Development Act of 1972 established mechanisms for facilitating the development of rural communities through grants, loans and technical assistance. The program includes a number of components dealing with housing, industrial development, water supply, and sewerage development to meet the needs of states and regions. Only very limited planning funds are available through these programs. Section 701 funds were used by many agencies for planning purposes.

Coastal Zone Management Act of 1972   The Coastal Zone Management Act of 1972 and subsequent amendments established a voluntary program in which states could receive financial and technical assistance to formulate a plan for the efficient use of its coastal zone areas within its boundaries. Once the state plan is accepted by the federal government, additional financial assistance, used for plan implementation, becomes available. One additional stipulation of this grant program is that federal agencies will coordinate their own direct federal action to be consistent with the state plan.

Federal Water Pollution Control Act of 1972   The Federal Water Pollution Control Act of 1972 replaced the Water Quality Act of 1965. It established a new approach to water pollution based on enforcing effluent limits rather than ambient quantity. A major section of the act (Section 208) involved planning activities. The planning activities undertaken under the section include programming sanitary and stormwater collection and treatment facilities for a 20-yr period. One key link to land use planning was that planning agencies develop and implement a regular program to control location and construction of any facility that may discharge wastes.

4.2.2 National Land Use Legislation

During the early to mid 1970s a significant groundswell at the national level pushed the federal government to pass some form of national land use legislation. Many different bills were submitted in both the House and the Senate of the United States. Proponents of the legislation presented it as a means to provide resources and incentives to states to establish a program to inventory, designate and manage critical environmental areas and land uses of more than local significance. Opponents of the legislation labeled it as federal intervention of states' rights and unconstitutional. Proposed legislation of this type repeatedly passed the Senate and failed the House.

No matter what version of the national legislation on land use policy is analyzed, there are commonalities. They all incorporate a grant-in-aid program for providing funds to the states. All had review and approval components of the state developed plans. This was one of the factors which resulted in the final demise of the idea. They all had a procedure for the development of guidelines for the states to follow. This was another component the opponents were against. All provided for coordination of federal activities with approved state plans. If states chose not to develop a plan, then a separate coordination mechanism was proposed.

The final attempts at national land use legislation were made in 1975. These attempts met with increased opposition. The future may hold other attempts but this is not likely. Therefore the federal role in land use planning in the foreseeable future will be through individual grants and assistance programs as described earlier in this section.

4.3 STATE, REGIONAL, AND MUNICIPAL LAND USE PLANNING

4.3.1 Geographic Scope

State A state can be easily defined in terms of geographic area. It is a political subdivision having easily definable boundaries within which a single over-all governmental unit has sovereign power. This sovereign power is reserved to the states by the U. S. Constitution, and includes the inherent powers of eminent domain, taxation, and police power. The Tenth Amendment to the Constitution has been interpreted to reserve to the states the authority to regulate all state and private lands and land uses within their territorial boundaries.

Regional A region is more complicated to define than a state, both in terms of what it is from a planning standpoint and how it is defined geographically. A region may be made up of political entities. If it is defined, establishing its geographic area becomes a much simpler task. Regions form where adjacent areas find they have similar problems and concerns. They visualize that they can realize economies of scale by pooling resources to study common problems. Funding may be more easily obtained by aggregate groups rather than individual areas. These are just a few factors which may lead to the formulation of a regional study area.

Regions may be subdivisions of states following municipal boundaries. They may at times split municipalities. Regions may encompass large metropolitan complexes that traverse state lines. An example was the Tri-State Region, which actually included parts of three states: New York, New Jersey, and Connecticut. There are instances where a region consists of an already defined jurisdictional unit such as a state. The State of Rhode Island is unique in that the only regional planning agency within the state is a state agency that performs statewide and regional planning activities. In this case the region has the state boundary as its boundary. Figure 4-2 shows various types of regions.

A major problem with the region as a planning unit exists whether the region is substate or interstate in geographic scope. It is that participation in most regional planning agencies is voluntary; that is, most regional agencies do not have any power to dictate to their local member agencies. Regional agencies are usually funded in part from assessments or contributions from the local member governments that lie within their

Intrastate Regional Planning Area

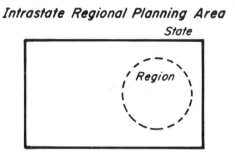

Interstate Regional Planning Area

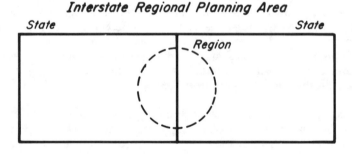

Coterminus State/Regional Planning Area

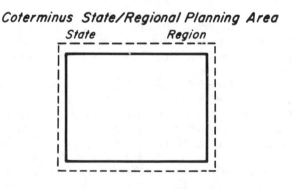

Fig. 4-2. Examples of various types of regions

boundaries. Therefore, regional agencies must tread softly in attempting to implement controversial strategies. This differs from state-level agencies, which have constitutional powers that may be used for implementation. There are instances, many at the interstate level, where states are committed to fund regional agencies through actual contractual arrangements. Most of these agreements have not reached the point where the various participants have committed themselves to follow recommendations resulting from regional agency studies.

Municipal   A municipal planning study is a study at the city or town level. In some respects, this level is the easiest to work with since the political arrangements are generally less complicated, may be defined more easily, and usually consist of only one level. The broadest discretion or greatest power to affect land use is now placed at the local level of government.

4.3.2 Scale of Studies

Scale is the key factor in determining the geographic scope of a municipality, a region, or a state. Scale also helps determine the size of these relative to a project specific planning area. As a general rule state, regional, and local planning encompasses a much greater geographic area than project specific planning. Even though the planning area for a city or town is smaller than for a region or state, the same techniques are generally used for all three. The relative differences in size necessitate different levels of detail in specific studies, but not usually different techniques.

Due to the variability in size of the various state, regional and local planning areas, no single rule of thumb can be established that will fit the needs of all. As an example, consider that Rhode Island collects, codes, and tabulates numerous data elements for use in its environmental and land use studies. These data are coded on a 10-acre grid basis for the entire state. This results in some 87,000 data cells for each element that is coded. If the same basis were used for New York state, some 3,060,000 data cells would be coded; California would have 10,000,000 data cells; Texas, 17,000,000 cells; and Alaska over 36,000,000 cells. This illustration points out that a scale of study that works well in one area could be completely unworkable in some other area. Although the larger states would find data coded to this level of detail very helpful, the cost and time it would take would be prohibitive.

A similar analogy could be made for regional or local studies. The relative size of regions, cities and towns, and the spacing between regions or cities and towns, are the controlling factors. Smaller regions can usually use data at a finer scale than bigger regions. Small local studies may be able to use data at an even finer scale.

Studies performed at the state and regional level are usually accomplished at a greater scale than those performed at the local level. Project level studies are usually performed at smaller scales than local level studies. The smaller the state or region, the more detailed the studies can be. A balance must be struck between the availability of detailed data and the capability or capacity one has to gather, code, analyze, and update data. If the level of study chosen is too detailed, a disproportionate amount of time and money may be spent manipulating data. Then there is a risk of never completing the original study, or having to modify the scope of the study significantly. The finer the detail of the study (within the limitations due to time and budgets) the more uses the data will have. Data may never be detailed enough for all conceivable purposes. A planner should always balance the scale of the various studies to be performed with the goals of the study.

4.3.3 Goals

Planning studies are performed to fulfill a variety of goals. Two separate sets will be considered here: the goals formulated as a result of the land use planning process, and goals of the land use planning process.

Goals formulated as part of the plan are not universal. No single rule of thumb or textbook listing can be given that will suffice for every state or region. Table 4-6 shows the goals listed in the Rhode Island *State Land Use Policies and Plan*. Some goals shown could be found in most plans, while others are unique to Rhode Island. Goals 2 through 5 and goal 9 on Table 4-6 could be found in any state, regional or municipal land use plan. They are generally aimed at making the interface between land use and other planning stronger. Goals 1, 6 through 8, and 10 are more area specific. Goal 1 shows the state's position toward over-all population growth. Goal 6 demonstrates Rhode Island's concern for its remaining open space and agricultural lands. Goal 7 makes a statement about its age and stage of development. Goal 8 is a statement relating to the state's geographic location on the Atlantic coast and also its position on the value of its vast coastal area. Finally, goal 10 reflects its geographic location in the northeast, a high energy cost area. A common characteristic of land use goals is that they must express the attitude of the area toward future growth: favorable, selective, unfavorable, or neutral.

Goals of the land use planning process itself are the more critical, because they actually guide the implementation of the process. This segment on goals will deal with the goals of the process. In order for the goals set out in the plan to be of any use, the process must relate to and address the concerns and needs of the population within the planning area. This is the basis for the first and most critical goal of any land use planning process.

Goal 1: Identify and, in the process, reflect the concerns of the citizenry affected by the plan. Identification of these concerns is not an easy task. Various techniques that can be used in an attempt to ascertain public views will be presented in a subsequent section on public opinion surveys. This primary goal must be met or the process may result in development of a land use plan which may not be adopted. The method

TABLE 4-6 Goals Listed in the Rhode Island Land Use Policies and Plan (31)

1. Relate state land use policies to a population ceiling of 1,500,000

2. Make efficient use of available land and water, producing a visually pleasing, coherent and workable environment

3. Sustain economic growth at a rate adequate to support the state's population, in a manner consistent with the state's characteristics, capabilities or environmental objectives

4. Continuously improve the structure and operation of governments and their responsiveness to their citizens in the area of land use planning and management

5. Control urban sprawl and dispersion

6. Preserve and protect open space, including recreation and conservation areas, vacant and open land, and selected agricultural and forest areas, so as to enhance the total quality of the environment

7. Revitalize older central cities, setting target population levels which reflect stability

8. Preserve, develop and, where possible, restore the resources of the coastal region in order to benefit from its variety of assets

9. Develop a balanced transportation system which provides safe, efficient and economical movement between the component parts of the state; improve interstate transportation

10. Consider energy requirements in plans for land use

Note: Numbers added for discussion purposes only.

by which the concerns of the population are reflected within the process usually takes the form of goals statements within the plan. In that context, the next goal of the process is:

Goal 2: Clearly define the intent of the goals within the plan. The planner should be precise in wording these goals so they can be interpreted correctly. Conflicting opinions of goals tend to indicate generalization. General statements can be interpreted in many ways, while specific statements usually leave little doubt in their interpretation. During the planning process conflicting points of view will necessitate that some goals will have to be written generally. Therefore, the original goals statements should be written as specifically and precisely as possible. It is also quite possible that some goals will be dropped and new goals added. This is part of the process and reflects the dedication to the overriding goal of the process itself. Whenever a new goal is added, it should be set out as specifically as possible so that its intent is clear.

Goal 3: Identify alternatives in as much detail as is necessary to clearly describe and quantify the impacts of each.   The land use planning process should identify alternative courses of action and attempt to define clearly advantages and disadvantages of each alternative. The description of the various alternatives to be considered should be clear, with as much detail on each alternative as possible. Identification of alternatives should take place early in the process. The alternatives to be analyzed should range from the no-action alternative to those alternatives which would yield the most varied results. In this way, the range of alternatives to be tested would include virtually all possibilities. The enumeration of the advantages or disadvantages of each alternative must be clearly presented. The impacts of each should be quantified in terms as precise as possible. General statements should be avoided.

Sometimes during the land use planning process it is inevitable that conflicts will arise. These conflicts may be between goals in the plan itself or even with goals in other comprehensive plan elements. Often conflicts arise between interest groups within the citizenry of the planning area. Therefore, the next goal of the land use planning process is:

Goal 4: Attempt to resolve conflicts whenever possible.   Not all conflicts are resolvable. For instance, a stretch of shoreline along a body of water will frequently bring conflicting points of view from the development interests and the conservation interests. The most that the process can do in a situation such as this is to clearly define the alternatives and quantify the advantages and disadvantages of each conflicting point of view. If this can be thoroughly handled by the planner, the decision makers will have at their disposal the best possible data. Many conflicts are resolvable through discussion and mediation, and every effort should be made to do so before the decision is made to simply quantify both sides of the issue and make no recommendation. Every effort should be made by the planner to resolve conflicts through discussion and mediation so that decisions are not arbitrarily reached.

Goal 5: Explicitly state and precisely define the recommended alternatives, stating their impacts.   Some planning processes and the resulting plans stop short of this goal. They end with the discussion and quantification of alternatives. The planner's judgment should be an influencing factor on the decision makers. If no recommended alternative is set forth the decision makers could interpret this as a sign that none of the alternatives is better than any other. This goal may be the most difficult to fulfill within the entire process. The planner must draw on professional judgment. The judgments should be supported by the results of the various studies and analyses performed earlier in the process. If after performing these analyses no alternative or combination of alternatives is considered best, this may be a sign that more alternatives should be formulated and studied.

Goal 6: Explicitly set forth implementation responsibilities for all recommended alternatives.   This is the single most neglected step in the land use planning process. Failing to fulfill this goal is probably the most important reason why some adopted plans never get implemented. The steps in the implementation process must be clearly set out. Responsibilities for each step in the implementation process should be assigned and documented. If this is done, the chances of having the plan recommendations implemented increase significantly.

If one has fulfilled the previous six goals, the final goal should fall into place without too much additional effort.

Goal 7: Make the plan adoptable. If the plan goals are truly the goals of the citizenry, the various alternatives have been set out and their ramifications quantified, all conflicts resolved and a recommended plan established, there should be no reason why that plan is not adopted. There is one very large unmentioned "given" to this list. That is, that the citizenry within the area has been involved throughout the process through a successful public participation effort.

4.3.4 Studies and Data Requirements

The object of land use studies is to provide basic data on the characteristics of the land within the study area in terms of physical features and infrastructure. The land use planner must have reliable population and other demographic estimates and forecasts. A thorough understanding of the interrelationships of land uses to these forecasts is also essential.

Public opinion surveys Many land use planning studies have used public opinion surveys to attempt to ascertain the goals of the population within an area. Depending on how the questions are structured, additional useful information can be obtained. The formulation of alternatives to be studied can also be strengthened through the public opinion survey process. If public opinion surveys are used, two critical points must be considered: (1) The selection of the survey sample; and (2) the structure of the survey itself.

On the first point, in all but the smallest areas, a representative sample should be used rather than attempting a survey of the entire population. Many texts have been written on random sample selection. A random sample is one in which every person or household within the population of an area has an equal probability or chance of being selected. The selection process for a random sample should not favor any particular group intentionally or unintentionally. A much more efficient and usually less costly approach to obtaining a random sample of the population is to contact various marketing and advertising firms working in the area. It is their business to select random samples for various surveys that they are performing themselves. They will usually assist in determining the proper size sample for your area and questionnaire. Samples obtained in this way should be carefully checked in order to determine whether any bias is inherent in the sample. The coverage should be as complete as possible. If it is not, supplementary samples may have to be obtained from other sources. Supplementing the main sample with other subsamples is also frequently done. Surveys of state, regional, and local officials and legislative bodies may also prove helpful in ascertaining whether the general population and the legislators within an area have the same concerns and ideas. One may discover, for example, that the legislative body in an area is promoting economic development, while the general population is concerned with keeping the area rural.

The structure of the survey itself is the second critical step in the process. Spending a little more time here may save considerable time when analyzing the survey and using its results. A balance must be achieved between ease of analyses and tabulation, and leaving the survey open enough so as not to lead the respondents to answers. Some questionnaires use the direct approach in establishing goals by either asking the respondent to list goals or by providing a list of goals and asking the respondent to put them in order of importance. Other questionnaires never directly ask what the respondents' goals are but ask other questions, the responses to which should lead to a perception of the respondents' goals. It is important to keep the questionnaire as short as possible but not omit a question or series of questions critical to the study. It is also important to strike a balance between open-ended questions (which may result in extremely useful information but may also provide no real response), and "yes" or "no" and multiple choice or rating questions, which will provide real information but will probably not result in any new ideas. A little more time spent in the survey planning stage may make the results received more usable.

Soil and topographic surveys   Soil surveys provide information useful to the land use planning process. The land use planner should have an understanding of soils and their interrelationships with land use. Soils also affect waste disposal systems and water supply. Soil permeability is at times the controlling factor in sizing residential lots in nonsewered areas having no public water supply. The United States Soil Conservation Service has done numerous studies throughout the country. These studies are a valuable source of soils data (if available) for an area. Figure 4-3 shows a sample soils map compiled by the Soil Conservation Service and the corresponding description of one of the soils found on the map. These are valuable since they not only give an indication of the type of soil present in a given area but also describe the characteristics of the soil in terms of its capacity to bear weight, its capability to hold and cleanse wastewater, and its slope. An associated but separate type of survey is the topographic survey, which looks at slopes but also relates adjoining slopes to one another, thereby giving a better picture of the entire area. The characteristics described provide an indication of the acceptable land uses for any given area or, stated differently, the capability of the land to handle stress in any one of many different forms.

Geological studies   Geological studies furnish the planner with data essential to land use determinations regarding earth slides, fault and fracture zones, subsidence and other earth instability characteristics, as well as characteristics of the ground-water potential within an area. Such

SOURCE: *Soil Survey of Rhode Island by the United States Department of Agriculture Soil Conservation Service in Cooperation with the Rhode Island Agricultural Experiment Station (July 1981)*

Fig. 4-3. Sample of soil map (40)

studies may also provide information relating to valuable minerals which may be extracted at a later date.

Water-related studies   Water-related studies provide useful information pertaining to the quality and quantity of the water within an area. Freshwater bodies and streams are usually divided into segments that may be classified to reflect the impacts of point-source discharges of pollution. Point-source discharges are those that can be identified as emanating from a single locatable source. During the 1970s many areas completed Water Quality Management Plans, usually known as "208 Plans" because they became a requirement as a result of section 208 of the Clean Water Act of 1972. These plans concentrated on nonpoint sources or areawide sources of pollution. An example of a nonpoint source of pollution could be the road salting operation after a winter storm. Saltwater bodies are classified by area delineation based on the amount of pollution discharged and the distance needed to dilute the pollution level to each succeeding higher (lower pollution) classification. These classification studies are usually done by the agency responsible for regulation of water in an area. It may be the state or local health department or the department of environmental quality or management. Data on ground-water aquifers or primary recharge areas, if available, can also provide useful information relating to nonsurface waters. These data provide information not only on quality but also on quantity of water.

Drainage studies   Drainage studies may provide other water-related data elements that can prove to be of great help. Flood hazard areas are delineated by the Federal Emergency Management Agency (FEMA). Most municipalities that have entered the regular phase of the National Flood Insurance Program have had flood insurance studies performed. These studies establish areas within a community that are prone to flooding for various rainfall possibilities. Flooding potential is usually measured for frequency and magnitude. For purposes of delineation and management, the 100-yr flood is generally used. The 100-yr flood is the flood resulting from a storm having a likelihood of happening once every 100 years on the average (i.e., having a 1% chance of occurring in any year). However unpredictable the chance of flooding may be, wise land use planning should attempt to minimize future hazards through prevention of development where appropriate, and strict development regulations when development is unavoidable. These data, if available, can usually be obtained from FEMA or the local National Flood Insurance Program coordinator.

Infrastructure   Infrastructure consists of all those basic elements which make an area function: transportation facilities, sewer and water facilities, etc. Knowledge of the infrastructure within an area provides much useful information. Studies of the physical infrastructure will provide information pertaining to existing and planned public facilities, such as schools, hospitals, public water and sewer lines, and transportation facilities. Knowing existing and planned service areas for public water and sewers can provide a good indication of where pressures for development will be the greatest. Major transportation, water and sewer facilities sometimes promote development also.

Organization Studying the actual organizational structure present in an area enables the formulation of intelligent decisions pertaining to where implementation responsibilities should lie for various recommendations. In order to answer these types of questions it is useful to know how the area works organizationally. Is there a governor, mayor or regional commission which acts in conjunction with a legislature or town council? Are there planning boards or commissions? Are there zoning boards? Is the legislature bicameral? Are there other special districts, such as school districts or water and sewer districts? What are the powers of the agencies? How has land use planning or control been handled historically? Similarly, information on existing laws and programs for controlling land use is important in developing recommendations for a land use study. Knowledge of organization is critical.

Other studies Other data that may be available for the land use study include the following. Recreation, conservation and open space areas may have been compiled as part of the State Comprehensive Outdoor Recreation Plan (SCORP). Vegetation cover may have been compiled by the forestry service or the natural resources division of a college or university within the area. Information on historical and archaeological places may be available from the National Register of Historic Places, historical surveys, or the local historical preservation commission. Information on unique natural areas may be obtained from the local department of natural resources or an environmental management agency, or from the natural resources division of a college or university. The more data that can be gathered from these studies, the easier it will be to perform the various analyses that must be completed in order to make intelligent decisions and recommendations.

4.3.5 Data Analysis

Once all available data have been collected and any supplementary studies performed, the actual analysis process begins. Analysis can be done either by computer or manually. The decision as to which method to use depends upon the study area itself. In either the computer or manual techniques, the following six steps can be used. This simplistic procedure is presented only as a general guide. Specific areas may require that new steps be added, or suggested steps skipped.

1. Map existing land uses. This step is important because it sets the current conditions. It should be done using the land use categories decided upon earlier in the process when a land use classification system was chosen. Judgments relating to the stability of land use within a specific area should also be made at this time. For instance, if a specific area is undergoing redevelopment, or is simply changing in character

due to other factors, the fact should be noted because maintaining existing land uses in these areas may not be necessary or even advisable. On the other hand, if existing areas are found to be stable and interacting well with adjoining areas, it is probably advisable not to consider changing their land use patterns.

2. Identify critical areas. Any critical areas identified in the goal setting and data collection phases of the process should be clearly mapped. These could be wetlands, archaeological sites, or historic sites and districts. Special care should be taken when considering alternative adjoining land uses to these areas. Buffers may be required in order to separate them from adjoining land use which may conflict with or detrimentally affect the critical areas.

3. Identify other areas not suitable for development. Other areas not classified as critical may be unsuitable for development, or should at least be restricted to specific types of development. These areas could be prone to flooding, may have poor soils, or may even be on geological fault zones. Such areas should be identified and care should be taken so that compatible land uses can be assigned to them. Ideally these areas should be left to open space or recreation, but some low-density uses may also be acceptable.

4. Estimate amounts of each land use needed for the future. Socioeconomic projections and demographic trends must be analyzed in order to ascertain the population and employment levels expected in the area in future years. Once these projections are made and related to the goals of an area, estimates of the amount of each land use, such as acres of residential land or acres of manufacturing or commercial land, can be made. These are made by applying density factors to the socioeconomic projections. Many sources periodically update these density factors for a variety of different land uses. Current literature should be surveyed to ascertain density factors. References 1 and 20 may be used to arrive at some of these factors.

5. Assign land uses to areas. Once steps 1 through 4 have been accomplished, actual assignment of land use to specific areas can take place. In assigning land use areas, the cautions set out in steps 1 through 4 should be observed. Several different assignments of land uses can and should be made; then each can be analyzed to determine which is the best use of all land within the area.

6. Document analysis. Any assumptions used in steps 1 through 5 should be clearly documented. The advantages and disadvantages of each alternate assignment performed in step 5 should be clearly stated.

4.3.6 Public Participation

The art of obtaining public participation has made great strides in the recent past. During the 1950s and 1960s public participation was the exception rather than the rule. Planners performed their studies and released the results to the public in the form of a glossy, polished final report that was considered, by the planners, to be the end of the study.

This technique worked for most of those two decades. Towards the end of the 1960s, groundswells of opposition to these techniques arose from the general population, and a process of evolution began that is still going on today. The experience of the 1970s pointed out several things to planners. First, the citizenry has a right to be involved in decisions that will affect them in the future. Second, they were demanding to have that right fulfilled. Third, and probably the most important, they can contribute productively to the process if all concerned enter the process with an open mind. In order for the process to be successful there are three critical points relating to public participation that should be addressed prior to its commencement: (1) What techniques should be used; (2) how it should be timed; and (3) what will be done with the results.

Techniques The following account of techniques is not meant to be all-inclusive but is presented to address some of the more widely used approaches. Numerous variations to the basic approaches are in existence and may be adopted for particular situations. One major technique for soliciting ideas from the public has already been discussed in a prior section—the public opinion survey, which has been used successfully for many years. Planners in some areas have taken the opportunity to mail other information of an introductory nature out with the survey itself. This is an excellent technique and should be used whenever possible. Such introductory material could be in the form of a brochure and may even be mailed to each household in the study area. It could include a brief description of the planning process itself, as well as a description of the current situation. The material should be brief and to the point. The material should not be continuous text but should incorporate graphs and charts, as well as actual photographs or illustrations to make points.

Another survey technique, which is actually a variation of the public opinion survey, is the citizen survey. Citizen surveys are simply public opinion surveys performed not by the planning professional but by members of public interest groups. The technique adds credibility to the public opinion survey process and also involves public interest groups in the very early stages of a planning study.

Newsletters are a good medium for disseminating information to large numbers of people. A mailing list of interested individuals should be maintained and periodic mailings made to all parties on the list. Material included in the newsletter can range from summaries of various aspects that have been completed of the over-all study to listings of coming events such as committee meetings or workshops. Newsletters do not have to be as elaborate as brochures, and may address more technical matters.

Various committees can be established to guide the planning process in general, or to work on specific tasks within the planning process. The general committee, sometimes called a project or study advisory committee, should consist of representatives of the key interests involved, such as citizens, various interest groups (environmental groups, builders' or developers' associations or both, interested citizens' organizations) and officials of all affected levels of government and political jurisdictions. Such an advisory committee should be exposed to, and be a part of, the various policy decisions that must be made throughout the study. It should, for instance, be involved in establishing the goals of the area. One or several individual task committees can also be formed to work on the more technical aspects of the study. For instance, one task committee could be formed to establish alternatives, and a second set up to establish criteria and evaluate the various alternatives. It is important to include all of the important interests on a committee, to have a selection process that is perceived as legitimate, and to make clear to a committee what its role is (i.e., advisory). Committees have the advantage of bringing together many interests but the disadvantage of requiring a great deal of time and work for both members and staff.

Public informational meetings and workshops also prove to be very helpful. They may take many different forms. Workshops should be held in both the daytime and evening in order to give as many people as possible ample opportunity to participate and discuss concerns in an informal atmosphere and on a one-to-one basis. Public informational meetings should also be held in both the daytime and evening. They are usually slightly more structured than workshops in that the planning agency may start the program with a brief presentation prior to opening the meeting for general discussion. Such meetings usually do not afford the opportunity for one-on-one interaction. Workshops and informational meetings may be held concurrently or in sequence. Some studies have adopted the technique of holding workshops in the afternoon and holding a public information meeting the same evening. Other studies have held simultaneous workshops and public information meetings by using separate rooms in the same building. This affords people the opportunity to hear a presentation and general group discussion or to have individual questions answered on a one-to-one basis, while attending only one session.

Public hearings, although still held, are now usually more of a formality than of any real help in the process. They are usually held towards the end of the process as part of formal adoption. If the other techniques used in the public participation process have been effective, the formal public hearing should not bring out any new ideas or comments. Other techniques have proved to be much more successful in developing constructive interaction between the planners and the population.

Timing No specific timetable can be set for public participation. The timing of various committee meetings, public informational meetings and workshops are dependent on when sufficient material has been completed and is ready for committee or public review. The public infomation surveys should be done as early in the process as possible since their results may add focus to the study.

Brochures can be done at any time, and maybe more than once.

The only limiting factor is the cost of the brochures. One brochure could be published very early, explaining the process and presenting other general information. Another brochure could be published after alternatives have been developed and analyzed. The timing of the brochures is flexible. Newsletters should be sent out on a more or less regular schedule, monthly or quarterly. The frequency of the newsletter should be in relationship to the anticipated duration of the study; that is, if the study is anticipated to last four months, bimonthly or monthly newsletters would be more appropriate than quarterly newsletters. A 1-yr or 18-month duration study could use either monthly or quarterly newsletters.

The various committee meetings should be scheduled on an as-needed basis. Once a committee is formed, it may meet rather frequently for a short period of time at the beginning in order to become familiar with the process; then less frequently for a longer period as the actual deliberations are made. This really depends on its purpose. Public information meetings and workshops should only be held when sufficient material is available. Holding a workshop at the beginning of a study may not be advantageous since the one-on-one discussions could have no substance. It is advisable to hold a committee meeting, public information meeting, or workshop only when there is sufficient information to present and discuss. The public hearing is usually held at the end of the process when all other forms of public participation have been or are about to be completed.

Use of results It is imperative that the planning process interact with the public participation process. Attempting to go through the motions of public participation without making use of the results often can do more harm than good. The public will quickly realize that interaction is not taking place, and the planning process will lose all credibility. Whenever and wherever possible, questions and comments arising from the public participation process should be addressed and answered. If a good idea comes out of the process, by all means use it and make the public aware that it is being used. This will not only improve the planning process but will add to its credibility and eventually strengthen the chances that the final plan will be adopted.

4.3.7 Implementation Techniques

To this point the only difference in the processes for state, regional, and municipal planning has been scale of study. In this section, various techniques that can be used successfully in land use studies in order to implement specific recommendations will be described with clear indication of where certain techniques are applicable and where they are not.

Comprehensive plan The comprehensive plan is an official public document once it has been adopted by the appropriate government. It indicates in a general way how an area is to develop in the next 20 to 30 years. Because it is general, it is subject to interpretation and is not by itself a sufficient implementation technique. It does form a good base to build upon. It is critical to incorporate a land use element in the comprehensive plan. This is a good implementation technique to use at the state, regional, or local level.

Guidelines   Guidelines for development are sometimes set out as a recommended alternative in a land use plan. If they are adopted as part of the comprehensive plan they become official policy guidelines and have the same impact as anything else in the comprehensive plan. This implementation technique, like the comprehensive plan, is good for use at any level, state, regional, or local. Guidelines can be given more importance as an implementation technique by putting them into legislation.

Legislation   Legislation is an excellent implementation technique. Some recommendations from the land use plan may be transformed into bills that can subsequently be submitted to the legislative body for possible enactment into law. This technique is more appropriate for use at the state level. Several states have attempted to enact legislation pertaining to comprehensive land use management. In instituting such legislation, states typically exercise their sovereign power to plan and regulate. The 1961 Hawaii State Land Use Law is the most noteworthy example of this technique. Hawaii's Land Use Law created a State Land Use Commission which had the responsibility of classifying all land into one of four districts. Regulations were established for the use of the land in each district. The principal groups having regulatory powers are the State Land Use Commission, the Department of Land and Natural Resources, and the county governments. Other states have also enacted some form of legislation for use in managing some or all of their lands.

Special districts   The creation of special districts or the establishment of critical areas or historic districts, usually done through legislation, are also excellent implementation techniques. The approaches usually entail establishing regulations for the use of land in specific areas. They are similar in concept to comprehensive land use management, but the geographic area is more limited. They can be used at any of the three levels, but state legislation is usually needed for enactment.

Official map   The official map is a less used, but useful, technique authorized in the planning enabling legislation of many states. It is a document adopted by the legislative body of a municipality that locates future streets, other public facilities such as schools and municipal offices, and open spaces (parks). Designation of a site on the official map protects it from further development for a limited time, thus giving the municipality an opportunity to acquire the land. Originally, the official map was used to establish building setback lines in order to minimize the impact of future street widenings. The expanded use of the official map to include reservations for a large number of different public facilities provides a municipality with the authority to delay any proposed development for long enough to purchase the property before construction makes it too expensive. Note however, that designation of an area on an official map cannot delay private construction indefinitely. The official map is usually used at the local level.

Codes Housing and building codes are important implementation techniques for land use management. Like subdivision regulations (to be discussed later) these codes can be used to assure the quality of community growth. Building codes establish certain standards for the construction of homes, commercial and industrial facilities. A housing code designates the minimum structural and utility standards for habitable dwellings. When used as part of a growth management system, both techniques can reinforce and complement the various land use approaches adopted by a municipality. Codes are most prominent at the local level but may also exist at the state and regional level.

Zoning Zoning is the oldest and most commonly used legal device available for implementing local land use plans. It is a means of assuring that the land uses of a community are properly situated in relation to one another, while providing adequate space for each type of development. It allows for control of the densities in each area so that property can be adequately served by such governmental facilities as streets, schools, or utility systems. Figure 4-4 is an excerpt from Reference 37 which gives an excellent summary of what zoning can and cannot do.

Historically, zoning ordinances have been described in terms of setbacks, minimum lot size and height restrictions. In the more recent past, zoning ordinances have become flexible so as to allow innovative types of development. These new techniques are used to preserve and protect environmentally sensitive areas or to eliminate from development unsatisfactory portions of a site. One innovative type of development control is cluster development. This is the grouping of dwelling units in closer proximity to each other than would normally be accepted on a site. A prescribed density must be maintained on the entire site. Since the development is constructed on one part of the site, the remainder of the site becomes available for possible uses such as open space, recreation, conservation, or other facilities designed to serve the residential development or the community. Because a prescribed gross density is maintained on the entire development parcel this is sometimes called density zoning. Figure 4-5 is an illustration of the concept.

Another development alternative is planned unit development. This can be defined as the development of a parcel of land that is preplanned in its

> . . . entirety and permits variations in the rigid zoning and subdivision regulations. Typically, the residential development includes a variety of housing types (single family, duplexes, town-

Zoning can:
- Help guide community growth by encouraging the most appropriate use of land throughout the community.
- Protect critical areas, such as prime agricultural land, floodplains, marshes, and heavily wooded areas, from being destroyed through unplanned development.
- Specify permitted land uses within districts which reflect the comprehensive plan for the community.
- Regulate the density of population and intensity of land use.
- Provide regulations designed to reduce traffic congestion.
- Work with what exists today, avoid the repetition of past mistakes, and correct abuses to provide for future improvement.
- Contribute to the solution of problems which are regional or state-wide in scope.
- Give people a voice in land use decision-making.

Zoning cannot:
- Prohibit certain economic and racial groups from locating within certain districts of a community (known as exclusionary zoning).
- Be arbitrary or capricious, favoring some people over others.
- Force existing land uses to be either eliminated or changed after the effective date of the ordinance without due process.
- Guide how a subdivision will be developed or regulate how a building will be built.
- Solve all local development problems overnight.
- Be enforced by anyone outside the given locality, including the state and federal government, except where the courts are involved in individual cases.
- Be used to exclude undesirable but necessary uses of land from a community.

Fig. 4-4. Summary of what zoning can and cannot do (37)

houses, and garden apartments) which are designed to fit together and complement one another. Infrequently, the PUD also includes a mixture of land uses (such as shopping centers, industrial and office parks) which may be in any combination, depending on the local ordinance. A unique feature of the PUD involves the planning and zoning commission, which has considerable involvement in determining the nature of the development. Through negotiations, variations may be permitted in lot size, front and side yard setbacks, street right-of-way, sidewalk location, and height restrictions. (37, p. 57)

Figure 4-6 illustrates the PUD concept. Other innovative zoning techniques, such as performance zoning, incentive zoning, and impact zoning, may also be useful. New approaches are being developed con-

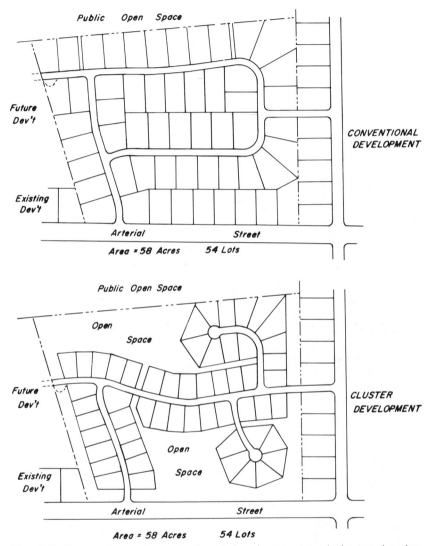

Fig. 4-5. Comparison of conventional development and cluster development (30)

stantly. Zoning as an implementation technique is used almost exclusively at the local level.

Subdivision regulations An associated implementation technique is the subdivision regulation. Such regulations may be adopted to complement the local zoning ordinance; they cannot supersede it. The best way to perceive the relationship between zoning and subdivision regulations is to view the zoning ordinance as a framework in which subdivision regulations fit. Subdivision regulations control the development and change occurring within a community and encourage efficient and desirable local services. When zoning is used to manage density and locations, subdivision regulations assure that the details of the new development are designed to function properly. This implementation technique, like zoning, is used almost exclusively at the local level.

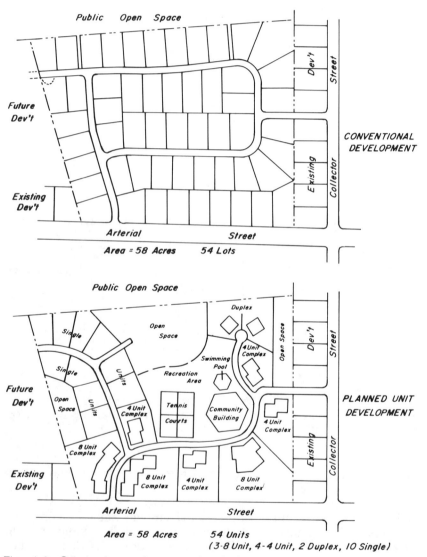

Fig. 4-6. Comparison of conventional development and planned unit development (30)

Capital improvement programs   This plan implementation technique provides funds for proposals which need them. It is used to implement recommendations in all types of planning studies, and is covered in more detail in Chapter 18 of this manual.

Tax structure   The final implementation technique considered here is taxation or tax structure. Changes in tax structure can significantly affect how land is used in various situations. A basic but common instance of the use of tax structures will illustrate this point. If a taxing authority structures its property taxes to assess land for its value in an economic sense (i.e., its prospects for development), the location of that parcel of land will be a critical factor in determining its value. For example, a parcel of land in downtown Manhattan would be taxed much more heavily than a parcel of land on the tip of Long Island. On the other hand, if the assessment is established on the actual use of the land, the parcel of land in Manhattan that is being used as a parking lot may be valued at less than the parcel of land at the tip of Long Island that has an office complex built upon it. The critical distinction here is assessment due to potential versus actual development. This implementation technique is usually used at the local level. Often it is used to protect farmland.

4.3.8 Contents of the Completed Plan

Generally speaking, a land use study and the resultant plan should address three basic aims. First, it should describe the status of various land-use-related activities within the study area. Second, it should present alternative types of actions that will either reinforce or attempt to correct the current ongoing activities. Finally, it should recommend action to promote the stated goals of the area. Techniques vary when a planner is deciding how to present the material that will accomplish the three stated aims. Figure 4-7 shows a generalized outline of the minimum requirements for the plan. This outline is put here simply as a guide and should not be considered to be the only or best way to document a land use study.

There are differences of opinion pertaining to the physical appearance of the plan document. In the past, the general approach was to make the plan a massive document having appendix upon appendix of very detailed and technical material that at times had only superficial relationship to the actual deliberations in the land use planning study. Currently there is a trend to streamline the plan document so that it is much more readable. This does not mean that critical information is left out but that it is presented in a clear and concise form.

Some studies have taken a two-level approach using separate documents. The first is the over-all plan document, which should set out a reasonably concise summary of the plan and the process of its formulation. Included in the document should be all those items set forth in Fig. 4-7. It should include a clear discussion of what, why, where, and

I Introduction
   Historical perspective
   Description of study area
   Objectives of study
   Study procedures

II Goals
   Techniques used to obtain input
   Detailed description of goals
   Reasons for choosing each goal

III Background and Research on Land Use
   Existing land use
   Growth projections
   Capability of land for future development (assets and constraints)

IV Evaluation of Alternatives
   Identification and description of alternatives
   Criteria used for evaluation
   Discussion of each alternative in terms of how it met or did not meet
   criteria

V Recommended Actions
   Discussion of why actions were recommended
   Set up implementation responsibilities

Fig. 4-7. Outline of minimum land use plan content

when with regard to everything advocated for implementation. The second document could be much more streamlined and polished, and it would have a much more general distribution. This document could take the form of a brochure like the ones previously described, having various graphs, charts, and illustrations to make points. No matter which approach is taken, it is critical to have sufficient copies for distribution. There is nothing more self-defeating than to arouse interest in a study through a public participation process, and then to have to deny requests for the final document because insufficient copies were printed.

4.4 PROJECT-SPECIFIC LAND USE PLANNING

The basic philosophy of most planning at the project level is oriented toward development. Whether it be the development of a recreational, commercial, industrial, or residential area, at project level the land use planning process is structured to answer the overriding question: Is it feasible?

4.4.1 Geographic Scope

Physical area The geographic scope of a project specific plan can be defined in one of two ways. The first is the physical area of the project, sometimes known as the site. Project specific geographic areas can range from a lower limit of 1/2 to 1 acre (0.2 to 0.4 ha) for small projects to 5000 acres (2025 ha) or more for projects at the upper limit. A prime example of a very large scale land use planning project is Sea Pines Plantation on Hilton Head Island, South Carolina. This development started in 1957 and is currently the largest development of its type anywhere in the continental United States, if not the world. It comprises nearly 3000 acres of planned resort area having some 75 tennis courts, three golf courses, five miles of beach, as well as numerous swimming pools, bicycle trails, and a 600-plus-acre forest preserve. This development has won numerous awards for its excellent composition and design.

Influence area   The second way to define the geographic scope of a project is to look at its area of influence. This definition becomes critical, especially in the market analysis studies (to be described later) that must be performed. In terms of the smaller (1/2 to 1 acre) projects, the influence area may be only the size of a municipality or even smaller, while the influence area of a large project may actually encompass two or three states or even a larger area.

The physical area of a project can usually be defined quite readily and definitively, whereas its influence area is much more difficult to define. The influence area, also called a market area, although not easily definable, can usually be approximated by analyzing such secondary variables as commuting patterns, transportation networks, location of employment and population centers, migration patterns, and even topography. In project specific studies, the relative difference in the size of various projects usually does not correlate well to the level of detail of specific studies.

4.4.2 Scale of Studies

Small projects are generally planned in detail because they are small. Larger projects are generally also done in considerable detail, because large capital outlays will have to be committed, and developers need considerable assurances pertaining to the feasibility of a large project before they will commit large amounts of funding. It is safe to say that project specific land use planning is always done at a greater level of detail than state, regional, or local level planning.

Varying levels of detail can usually be found at different stages of the same project. For instance, the first cut at a preliminary feasibility study can usually be done at a rather gross scale (mesoscale). Data input into this phase of a planning study may consist of municipal or even state level demographic data and generalized concepts pertaining to the project and associated infrastructure. If the first cut indicates the probability of a successful project, a more refined second-level analysis (macroscale) would be performed, using perhaps the same data elements but at a finer level of detail, such as the census tract or analysis zone level. Other data elements could also be used to expand the analysis. Perhaps some preliminary site planning would also take place in this phase. Again, if this second-level analysis indicates that the probability is still good for having a successful project, a third-level analysis could be performed which might necessitate very detailed demographic data, actual soils samples, and other detailed information (microscale). The results of the microscale analysis could be an actual detailed plan including the specifics of the project. Some project specific studies may need a one- or two-phase analysis, while others may need five or six phases to complete. This again depends upon the scale of the study.

4.4.3 Goals

There are actually two sets of goals to consider. The first set is the goals of the project initiator, which can usually be stated as the goals of the project. If the project was initiated by a profit-making entity, the major project goal may be to make as big a profit as possible. On the other hand, if the project was initiated by a governmental body, the major goal may be to establish a new recreation area to serve the population of the area, or to build a new elderly housing project. The first set of goals is usually established prior to the start of the project specific land use planning process.

The second set is that of the goals of the land use planning process itself. They are the critical goals in terms of bringing a project to its culmination, so the rest of this subsection will center upon the goals of the process. There are two primary goals inherent in the process.

Goal 1: Make the project as good as possible while working within the established constraints. The phrase "as good as possible" can cause some difficulties. It can be interpreted in different ways by different people. A profit-making entity may take this to mean "as good as possible with no increase in costs," while concerned citizens in the area may interpret it to mean "as good as possible regardless of the cost." This is one place where the practitioner must use professional judgment and attempt to balance conflicting interpretations. The "established constraints" could encompass a variety of issues and concerns, from stipulations put on the project by permitting agencies, to a problem with the physical size or topography of the parcel, to a maximum cost established by federal, state, local, and private funding limitations.

The second primary goal is equally important.

Goal 2: If justified, make the project implementable. In order to do this, the following goals should be closely adhered to. Adherence does not guarantee an implementable project, but nonadherence will more often than not guarantee that the result of the process will be an unimplementable project. The phrase "if justified" is there to make one aware that at times a project may be good in terms of some criteria but cannot be justified when looking at the entire analysis. If this is the case, the project should probably not be built. This is another situation where the practitioner must use some professional judgment.

The following five goals are secondary to the two primary goals just stated. These five are important because accomplishing them will usually lead to the accomplishment of the two primary goals.

Goal 3: Explain the project and set out the process to be used in the analysis. It is critical that the project be explained as early as possible and in as much detail as possible. Describing the process should include not only establishing and documenting the planning process, at least to the point where the number of phases to be used is documented, but also including a description of what analysis will be done in each phase. A description of the public participation process to be used in the study should also be set out at this point. Accomplishing this goal should lessen the impact of unsubstantiated claims and rumors by opposition groups. These rumors can take hold rapidly if a project has not been clearly explained. Once this goal has been accomplished the planner may proceed to the next goal.

Goal 4: Determine whether the project is feasible. This may entail performing market analyses or doing some preliminary design work to see if the proposed project can reside on the available site. If the project as presented in goal 3 is not found to be feasible, one of two things can take place: the project can be stopped, or it can be modified. If the decision is made to modify the project, the material formulated in order to fulfill goal 3 should be modified. This modified material should be clearly defined as superseding a prior release, and rereleased. This step is critical since there is nothing more harmful to a planner's credibility than having different versions of the same project being discussed at the same time.

If the project is found to be feasible, work on the next goal should be initiated.

Goal 5: Establish and present preliminary designs. The designs presented at this point should be detailed enough to illustrate the various design elements perceived to be part of the project. Artist's or architectural renderings are very helpful in doing this. Presentation of preliminary designs will usually cause conflicts between opposing groups to surface. The next goal follows logically.

Goal 6: Resolve conflicts. If the conflicts are minor, small design changes may be sufficient. Major conflicts may necessitate iterating back to goal 3 and modifying the project. If this is necessary, be sure to rerelease the modified project description, clearly stating that this release supersedes all others. If it is not possible to resolve all the conflicts, the process may have to proceed regardless. If this is the case, reasons for not resolving specific conflicts should be clearly stated.

Goal 7: Describe the project as it will be implemented and explicitly set out the implementation process. Fulfilling this last goal will usually result in bringing the project to a point at which objecting views have been resolved to the extent possible and implementation may begin.

4.4.4 Studies and Data Requirements

The object of project specific land use studies is to gather data needed to make some basic decisions, first on the feasibility of a specific project, later on the actual design, and finally on implementation of the project. These studies can be divided into four major subdivisions: demographics (economics), physical attributes, infrastructure, and organization. Studies pertaining to demographics are sometimes expanded to look not only at the physical project area but at the entire influence area of a project, and to look at marketability or effectiveness of the project. The studies of physical attributes are usually limited to the physical area of the parcel, and look at soils, water-related studies, vegetation, slopes, and other physical data about the site. The infrastructure studies, on the other hand, may expand the study area in order to investigate the needed interactions with existing infrastructural elements such as water, sewer, or transportation system connections. The studies of the organization of an area may also necessitate the expansion of the study area to surrounding areas. Much of the basic data needed may have already been collected by ongoing state, regional, and local planning studies. A thorough survey of these studies should take place early in the process.

Demographic studies   Demographic studies should attempt to ascertain the characteristics of the population within the influence area. Such stratifications as age, income characteristics, family size, housing information, and other census-related information are critical to the feasibility analysis portion of the study. Economic studies for the influence area are also critical. Indicators such as construction activity, denoted by housing starts or total construction permits issued, can give needed information pertaining to economic trends within the area. Analyses of sales or other economic activity indicators such as employment trends, both total and by Standard Industrial Classification (SIC) code, can provide needed information. Trends in vacant commercial and industrial floor space and rental housing may also provide data needed for the over-all market analysis.

Physical attributes   Physical attributes of the proposed site should also be studied. Soils and geological survey data, such as those mentioned in the section on state, regional, and local planning, can provide invaluable information in the preliminary phase of the study. More detailed soils data may be needed in the final stages. Actual core samples may and probably should be taken in order to cross-check the soils data obtained from such sources as the Soil Conservation Service, especially if construction will take place as part of the project. Water-related studies pertaining to both quantity and quality of water on the site should be obtained. Ground-water table tests should be performed and cross-checked with other tests performed within the surrounding areas. Any wetlands on the site should be noted and analyzed. Research into the various water-related permits that must be obtained should also be undertaken. Flood hazard areas as delineated by FEMA should be researched. Geological analyses are important to identify unstable areas, good foundation bearing soil areas, and mud and mudslide areas. These are very important since building in such areas usually necessitates using different construction techniques or, at a minimum, purchasing additional insurance. Most municipalities are in the National Flood Insurance Program and have flood insurance studies available for inspection. Any other physical data, such as historic places, vegetative cover, or unique natural areas information should also be compiled and analyzed. The sooner problems are uncovered, the easier it is to plan for their solution.

Infrastructure   Studying the infrastructure in the physical area and in the areas surrounding the project is also critical. One of the most important infrastructural elements to be studied is the existing and planned transportation system. They will have a critical impact on the success of any project. New routes may significantly increase accessibility to, and therefore demand for, a project in a location next to them, or they may decrease accessibility and therefore demand if the new route results in a shifting of travel patterns away from the project. These infrastructural studies should also ascertain existing and planned public facilities such as schools and recreational areas, as well as location and size of existing and planned water and sewer lines, and water supply or treatment capacities.

Organization   Organizational studies of an area should include surveying the subdivision regulations and zoning ordinances in order to ascertain any special conditions or regulations that may be placed on the project. One should attempt to ascertain how the various regulatory organizations in the area interact. For instance, how long should a permitting process take, or which organization has permitting power in a coastal zone area? It may be the local department of natural resources, or environmental quality or management, or it may be some other agency. It can even be both agencies. These types of organizational questions must be answered as early in the process as possible so that sufficient lead time is given to obtain the various required permits. Here again, the more data that can be gathered from these various studies, the easier it will be to perform the various analyses that must be completed in order to make the correct decisions on a project.

4.4.5 Data Analysis

After all available data have been collected and supplementary studies have been performed, analysis of the data may begin. The following six-step procedure is presented here only as a general guide.

1. Map existing site. The current surface and subsurface conditions at the proposed site should be carefully identified and clearly mapped. Particular attention should be given to assure clear and accurate mapping areas of severe slopes, wetlands, streams, ponds, ledge and rock outcrops, flood hazard areas, and other surface conditions which could affect development. Subsurface conditions which should be noted include poor subsurface soils (both in bearing capacity and ability to clean sewage effluent), underground utilities, archaeological areas, and ground-water aquifers. It is critical that these are precisely identified in order that the remaining steps are performed accurately.

2. Identify critical areas. Any area of critical concern mapped in step 1 should be clearly identified as a critical area. These could be wetlands, archaeological sites or historical sites or both, and districts not only on the site but adjoining it. Special care should be taken when attempting to allocate land uses on adjoining areas. Buffers may be required to separate the critical area from adjoining areas.

3. Identify other areas not suitable for development. Other areas not classified as critical may be unsuitable, or at least should be restricted in their development. These areas could have severe slopes, be prone to flooding, or have poor soils, or may have some other surface or subsurface feature which makes them less than optimum for development. Such areas must be identified. Care should be taken when developing adjacent to these areas also. Ideally, they should be left to recreation or other open space uses, but at times some low-density uses may be acceptable, depending upon their characteristics.

4. Estimate the development potential of the site. A site-specific study usually begins with a specific development concept for a parcel of land. Once the available data have been collected, supplementary studies performed, and steps 1 through 3 completed, a good estimate of the developable area of the parcel can be made. Kendig (20) or other books that may be available can provide much useful information relating to the density factors and other criteria which may be used to make an estimate of a parcel's adjusted development potential after all critical areas and other unsuitable areas have been removed. Once this estimate is made, it can be compared to the original development concept and costed to determine whether the project is still feasible.

5. Allocate land use districts to site. If step 4 results in the determination that a project is feasible, then the actual allocation of land uses can be performed. Several alternative designs should be established. Each alternative can be costed to determine which has the best cost to benefit ratio. When performing this allocation of land use and design of alternatives, care should be taken to adhere to criteria established throughout the process.

6. Document analysis. Any assumptions used in steps 1 through 5 should be clearly documented. The advantages and disadvantages of each alternative design established in step 5 should be clearly stated.

4.4.6 Public Participation

Public participation at the project level may be thought of as public relations, which is defined as creating a favorable public image with the community. In order to do this, the same three questions raised in subsection 4.3.6 are still asked. They are: (1) What techniques should be used? (2) How should public participation be timed? (3) What will be done with the results?

Techniques　Most of the techniques described in the corresponding subsection under state, regional, and local land use planning are appropriate to use at the project level also. Public opinion surveys may be used to ascertain the views of the citizens in close proximity to the project area. Brochures are a very good technique to inform the public about the project. Newsletters may be used to keep interested citizens up to date on the progress of the project. Committees may be formed to advise the study team on various approaches to use in critical areas or situations. Public informational meetings and workshops should be scheduled at critical points. Public hearings may or may not be necessary. If they are not required, one might give thought to eliminating them completely.

All of the previously mentioned public participation techniques were considered in greater depth in subsection 4.3.6 on state, regional, and local land use planning, and are therefore not discussed in detail here. One more innovative approach to public participation actually more correctly specified as public awareness is to hold contests that publicize the project. For instance, publicity for a new industrial or commercial development project could be incorporated into a contest held to obtain a name for the development, or a new housing development could run a contest to obtain a design for its logo. Contests have two positive aspects. First, they make people in the community aware of the project; and second, they involve the public, making them feel that the project is theirs. The contest approach works only if the public participation efforts up to that point have been performed successfully.

Timing　Timing of public participation, as with state, regional and local land use planning, is variable. Let it suffice to say that the earlier in the process the public is made aware of the project and their comments on the project are solicited, the more time the planner will have to perform corrections or conciliatory actions. The only caution that should be made here is that a definite project must be in existence prior to the commencement of this effort. If a definite project is not established at the outset, then the public may feel that there is deliberate vagueness about the specifics of the project. A more detailed discussion of timing can be found in subsection 4.3.6 under state, regional, and local land use planning.

Use of results　Going through the motions of a public participation process without really contemplating changing the project plan, even if worthwhile suggestions are obtained, is self defeating. Funds will have been wasted on the public participation efforts and credibility will eventually suffer due to a nonresponsive approach. Good suggestions should be used. At least an attempt should be made to use them. If their use is not possible, then the reasons for not using them should be clearly stated.

4.4.7 Contents of Completed Study

Generally speaking, a completed project specific land use study should answer these questions: first, is the project feasible? In answering this question, various items of background material can be incorporated or referred to including the various studies on the demographics, physical attributes, infrastructure, and organization. Second, the final plan to be implemented should be set out in detail. Any changes resulting from the public participation process should be described. Finally, an implementation process that will bring the project to fruition should be clearly and explicitly set out. Staging of various aspects of the implementation process should be documented. Any necessary permits and variances to be obtained should be described, and specific responsibilities for accomplishing those tasks should be defined.

4.5 MODELS

Initial attempts at producing computer oriented land use models (also known as urban simulation models) during the early to mid 1960s proved disappointing. They were generally insensitive to changes in their independent variables, not able to duplicate existing uses, and sometimes contained illegal relationships. A second round of attempts to simulate land use activity and urban growth began during the middle to late 1970s and continued into the 1980s. Most of these second-generation models can be classified into two major categories.

The Lowry derivative models are based on a set of relationships between place of work, place of residence, and, in some cases, shopping place. Several existing models may be grouped into this category. Two of the most noteworthy and well known are the Projected Land Use Model (PLUM) and the Disaggregate Residential Allocation Model (DRAM). A large proportion of these models deals with both residential location and nonbasic or population-serving types of employment. One consistent characteristic of these models is that they all need an externally provided set of basic location-specific employment estimates.

Those in the second category, the EMPIRIC models, usually consist of a set of linear simultaneous equations having no explicit theoretical structure. There are fewer models within this category than in the Lowry category. The primary analytical process inherent in the establishment of other types of models entails statistical analysis of various data in order to determine which specific variables are most appropriate for use in any one application. Urban modelers consider the models nonbehavioral since there is no theoretical structure whatever in this development. These models usually deal with both residential location and the location of all employment types.

In a 1976 study, Putman tested and compared the accuracy, ease of use, and sensitivity of a Lowry derivative and an EMPIRIC model. The results were published in a report (29). Putman's initial plan was to use the PLUM version of the Lowry derivative model for his work, but during his initial analysis of its application in the United States he found that in all but one case, the model parameters had not been properly estimated. The decision was made to use DRAM (the British counterpart to PLUM) for comparison purposes. An EMPIRIC model was chosen and calibrated for several test cities.

The principal conclusions of Putman's research as set out in his report (29) are as follows:

1. Both models require substantial data preparation prior to use.

2. The parameters of either model can be adjusted to yield rather close statistical fits to observed data.

3. Based on these fits, both models appear to be capable of making forecasts of urban form in the absence of attempted policy manipulations. EMPIRIC may have a slight advantage over DRAM in this respect.

4. DRAM is clearly superior with respect to its response to changes in input. This suggests a clear advantage over EMPIRIC whenever policy tests are completed.

Since the time of Putman's work in the mid 1970s, work on urban simulation models has continued with a trend to making them more sensitive to change, less data intense, and generally more sensitive to policy decisions. Before the decision is made as to whether or not to attempt to use an urban simulation model with a specific study, the following should be considered:

1. Is the information needed readily available and in the correct form? If not, how much effort will be needed to collect it in the appropriate form?

2. Are there sufficient resources (time, money, personnel) available to perform the modeling effort, or will this take resources from the more critical aspects of the study?

3. Will the study have more credibility with the incorporation of such a model, or will this one aspect of the study tend to be its focal point while other even more critical points do not get sufficient exposure?

In summary, caution should be used when deciding whether to use a strict modeling process such as that discussed in this section. If, after consideration of the previous material, it is found that application of an urban simulation model would be useful in the study context, then by all means pursue modeling. If the value of performing such an effort is not clear, then a decision to postpone such effort is probably more prudent. The United States Department of Transportation, Federal Highway Administration and Urban Mass Transportation Administration are excellent sources of current modeling techniques and results of model applications. This would be an excellent starting point if the planner decides to attempt urban simulation modeling within an over-all land use study.

4.6 COURT DECISIONS

The following summary of court decisions pertaining to planning was extracted from a publication (27) prepared by the Office of State Planning in New Hampshire in 1979. It is an excellent summary of the various landmark cases that have affected the land use planning process and profession.

There are many other court decisions affecting planning that could be referenced here, and new ones are issued at every court level on a daily basis. Keeping aware of new decisions can greatly increase one's effectiveness in the profession. Many newsletters issued weekly or monthly by various planning organizations have sections on recent court decisions. It may be helpful to the professional to subscribe to one or more of them.

Village of Euclid v. Ambler Realty Co., United States Supreme Court, 1926, 272 U.S. 365 This case established zoning as a legal growth management technique in 1926.

In 1925, Euclid, Ohio, a suburb of Cleveland, was faced with the prospect of uncontrolled growth as industry and housing increasingly sought to build within its city limits. In an effort to provide order to its growth, Euclid passed zoning regulations for the height, area, and density of new development. The regulations were challenged as violating the due process and equal protection clauses of the 14th Amendment.

The United States Supreme Court upheld the city's regulations as being a legitimate exercise of the state's police power, asserted for the public welfare. This case resulted in the establishment of the concept of "public welfare" in that a community should be beautiful as well as healthful, spacious as well as clean, well balanced as well as carefully patrolled. The Supreme Court's decision established local zoning as a legally defensible regulation and formed the basis for local court decisions on land use controls for many years. It was also recognized at this time in history by Mr. Justice Sutherland that the broader public interest may at some time be more important than purely local interests: "It is not meant by this, however, to exclude the possibility of cases where the general public interest would so outweigh the interest of the municipality that the municipality would not be allowed to stand in the way." (272 U.S. 390.)

National Land and Investment Co. v. Kohn, 215 A.2d 597, Pennsylvania Supreme Court, 1965. The court invalidated a local ordinance because it was exclusionary.

A township in Pennsylvania amended its zoning regulation to require a minimum of 4 acres (1.6 ha) in an area a developer wished to subdivide into 1-acre (0.4-ha) lots. The developer sought a variance and challenged the legality of the ordinance before the Board of Adjustment, which ruled against him. The Pennsylvania Supreme Court, on appeal, ruled the zoning law unconstitutional, because it was not based on legitimate concerns for the "health, safety, morals, or general welfare of the community." Zoning laws that are "exclusionary and exclusive" or that seek to "avoid the increased responsibilities and economic burdens which time and natural growth invariably bring" are unconstitutional. A desire to keep the area "the way it was is not a legitimate basis for zoning" nor may zoning be based "solely on aesthetic considerations." But "zoning for density" is legitimate.

The court also ruled that zoning may not impose "unnecessary hardship" on a landowner. However, the mere fact that a developer would suffer economic loss is not sufficient reason to overturn the zoning law.

The court noted that it is "neither a super board of adjustment nor a planning commission of last resort," but rather a "judicial overseer drawing the limits beyond which local regulations may not go, but loathing to interfere..."

Golden v. Planning Board of Ramapo, 30 N.Y. 2d 35 285 N.E. 2d 291, appeal dismissed, 409 U.S. 1003, 1972 This case established a legal defense for timed developed ordinances based on adequate public facilities, capital improvement programming, and a development permit sliding scale.

During the mid-1960s Ramapo residents tried to control the rapid suburban expansion caused by the influx of New York city workers. Population increased approximately 120% between 1960 and 1970. School taxes rose rapidly and residential sprawl became noticeable. The community developed a comprehensive plan and amended its zoning ordinance to create a new residential development use permit. Approval of these special permits was conditioned on the presence of municipal facilities and services, for which Ramapo proposed an 18-yr capital improvement funding plan. This plan scheduled sewage, drainage, road, recreation, and park facilities in stages throughout the municipality. Residential development permits were granted if the site scored a certain number of points on a development scale established by the ordinance, covering the above services and the availability of school and fire-protection facilities. Developers whose sites did not meet the minimum development points were allowed to install the necessary facilities at the landowner's expense in order to obtain the needed building permits. The community had also made provisions in its comprehensive planning for large amounts of low- and moderate-income housing.

The plaintiffs (landowners, builder's association, and development corporation) argued that the plan was beyond the scope of the state enabling legislation, that it resulted in a taking under the Fifth Amendment, and that it was exclusionary. The New York Court of Appeals upheld the town's program, approving their attempt to pace growth and development so as to maximize orderly population expansion.

The court declared:

> The answer Ramapo has posed . . . is, however, a first practical step toward controlled growth achieved without forsaking broader social purposes . . . from being exclusionary, the present amendments merely seek, by the implementation of sequential development and timed growth, to provide a balanced cohesive community dedicated to the efficient utilization of land.

In rejecting the taking argument, the court observed that it was relying "upon the presently permissible inference that within a reasonable time the subject property will be put to the desired use at an appreciated value."

Construction Industry Association of Sonoma County v. City of Petaluma, 375.F.supp 574, U.S. District Court, California, 1974 This was one of the first cases to test and uphold the legality of annual building permit limitations based on the availability of public facilities.

Petaluma, located a short distance north of San Francisco, went from being a quaint agricultural center of 14,000 in 1960 to a commuter suburb of 24,870 by 1970. Due to the community's desire to preserve quality of life, a local citizens' committee, guided by professional planning consultants, established an official development policy called the Petaluma Plan. In 1971, moratoria in rezoning and annexation of land were imposed to determine community sentiment, give the city council and planners a chance to study the housing and zoning situation, and develop their plans. After nine months of study, an advisory measure was placed on the June, 1973 ballot to elicit citizen reaction to a proposed limitation of 500 residential units per year on all projects involving five or more units, and exempting all projects of four units or less. No evidence was presented as to the number of exempt units expected to be built. About 80% of the responding voters approved the plan (the market demand during the 1970-71 period had been substantially in excess of that number). The plan stated the city's desire to

> . . . 1) preserve the city's small town character and surrounding open space by controlling the city's future rate and distribution of growth; 2) tie the rate of development to school and utility capacity;

3) encourage a balance of development between eastern and western sections of Petaluma; 4) provide a permanent greenbelt for definition of urban form and utilize city powers of utility extension and annexation to support the greenbelt policy . . .

Also established was an "urban extension line," a hypothetical boundary intended to mark the outer limits of the city's expansion for the next 15 years. The city contracted for municipal services on the basis of its limited development plan. Any proposed construction in excess of four units was to be evaluated on a sliding point scale, which took into consideration both proximity to public facilities and the quality of design and contribution to community welfare. A citizens' board was established to administer the 500-unit quota and to allocate between 8% and 12% to low- and moderate-income housing distributed within the allowable limit to various districts of the city. The plan also attempted to alleviate existing problems such as rehabilitation of old homes and a deficiency in multifamily units.

The plaintiffs claimed that the Petaluma Plan was unconstitutional. The city argued that while it was necessary for the city to provide adequate sewage treatment facilities, present facilities were inadequate to serve an uncontrolled population. The city also alleged an inadequate water supply. The court rejected these defenses because it saw no connection between the alleged inadequacies and the exclusionary measures taken. The city also contended that by its zoning power it had an inherent right to control its rate of growth and to protect its "small town character." Judge Burke of the district court ruled that certain aspects of the plan unconstitutionally denied the "right to travel" guaranteed by the U.S. Constitution. "A zoning regulation which has as its purpose the exclusion of additional residents in any degree is not a compelling governmental interest, nor is it one within the public welfare."

Ninth Circuit Court of Appeals reversed the decision based on the lack of standing of the association and appellee landowners to assert the claims of third parties allegedly excluded by the plan. It ruled that the economic interests of the appellees that were affected were outside the zone of interest to be protected by the right to travel, and therefore they did not have the requisite standing to raise the issue. (Plaintiffs had standing to sue, not standing to raise the right-to-travel argument for unknown third parties allegedly excluded.)

The court also conceded that the plan had an exclusionary effort but that the regulation was justified by an aspect of the community's police power being asserted for the public welfare and that the exclusion did bear a "rational relation" to a "legitimate state interest." The Ninth Circuit Court did not find that the plan posed an unreasonable burden on interstate commerce nor disrupted its uniformity by Petaluma's reduction of residential growth as contended by the plaintiffs.

Southern Burlington County NAACP v. Township of Mount Laurel,

336 A.2d 713 Supreme Court of New Jersey, March 24, 1975   This case establishes the legal basis for overturning a municipal ordinance that excludes diversified housing opportunities. It is argued that to protect the general welfare, communities must accept their fair share of housing.

Over the years, the Township of Mount Laurel had zoned almost 30% of its land for industrial and related uses, allowing only one permissible residential use: the single-family detached unit. Some multifamily units had been allowed by agreement under a planned unit development ordinance, limited to the affluent, and in an elderly apartment zone. Over a long period of time only a small percentage of the town had any industrial growth.

In 1972, the trial court found the ordinance to be unconstitutional and ordered the township to prepare a plan that would meet the needs of low- and middle-income families. The court, concerning itself with the economic effects, decided that an appropriate variety and choice of housing should be available and that the amount of land set aside for commercial and industrial use should be related to the present and future potential growth of the community. The court also questioned the large percentage of land area that had been zoned half-acre lots on ecological grounds.

The New Jersey Supreme Court, on appeal and based on provisions of the New Jersey Constitution, found Mount Laurel's zoning ordinance to be contrary to the general welfare and outside the intended scope of zoning power.

"General welfare" was defined as extending beyond the boundaries of individual communities; it should not have been limited to the interests of small segments of a particular community. The court concluded that every community must accept its fair share of the region's housing needs and that Mount Laurel should reform its land use regulations to not exclude the plaintiffs or potential residents. The Supreme Court did not hold the entire zoning ordinance invalid and gave the township 90 days to correct specific parts of the ordinance. As noted in Vol. 26 No. 6 (1975) ASPO *Mount Laurel: An Advanced View of Zoning,* "When there is an outstanding need for housing on a regional level, a community should not be allowed to avoid its 'fair share' of growth."

In 1983 the New Jersey superior court issued a second opinion (Mount Laurel II, 456 A.2d 390, January 20, 1983) which reinforced its earlier decision requiring local governments in New Jersey to adopt regulations that permit fair housing opportunities for low- and moderate-income households based on regional housing needs. Mount Laurel II is said to be the most serious limitation to the presumption of validity mutually accorded local zoning by the court since the first validation of police power in the 1920s by the U.S. Supreme Court.

Associated Home Builders of Greater Greatbay, Inc. v. City of Livermore, 18 Cal. 3d 582, 557 p. 2d 473, 135 Cal. Rptr. 41, California Supreme Court, 1976   This court decision reaffirmed the constitutionality of local ordinances that restrict growth based on the availability of municipal services and are reasonably related to the welfare of the region affected.

The City of Livermore enacted an ordinance that prohibited the issuance of further residential building permits until local educational, sewage disposal, and water supply facilities complied with specified standards. The ordinance was challenged by a local home builders' association. On appeal, the California Supreme Court upheld the local ordinance. The court recognized the conflict between the efforts of suburban communities to check disorderly development, with its concomitant problems of inadequate public facilities and pollution problems, and the increasing public need for adequate housing opportunities. However, the court reaffirmed and clarified

> . . . the principles which govern the validity of land use ordinances which substantially limit immigration within a community; we hold that such ordinances need not be sustained by a compelling state interest, but are constitutional if they are reasonably related to the welfare of the region affected by the ordinance.

In determining whether the ordinance was reasonably related to the regional welfare, the court established a three-step test: " . . . forecast probable effect and duration of restriction; identify competing interests affected by restriction; and determine whether ordinance . . . represents reasonable accommodation of competing interests."

Pandover v. Township of Farmington, 374 Mich. 622, 132 NW2d 687 (1965) This court decision pertains to the relationship between planning and zoning. It was not extracted from the previously mentioned New Hampshire publication (27) but seems critical to mention in terms of significant court decisions relating to the planning profession. This case, depicting perhaps the most clear-cut case of zoning based on advance planning, is found in the decision that turned the tide in Michigan, at least for the time being, in a reversal of the position previously adopted by the courts of that state.

An outer suburb of Detroit adopted a basic plan for the development of residential areas. Under this plan, the square-mile areas bounded by section line highways were to be developed at a density of approximately 1/2 acre (0.2 ha) per house. That equates to 1300 houses per square-mile section, less the amount of land that would be needed for streets, community facilities, and other public and semi-public facilities. Under certain assumptions as to the long-term child-family ratio, this was presumed to provide enough children to fill a school of an assumed convenient size, as part of an over-all neighborhood-unit plan. The legal challenge rose in a section where it was difficult to carry out the plan. A district court (writing four opinions) upheld the entire scheme and also its application in this difficult situation.

4.7 REFERENCES AND BIBLIOGRAPHY

1. American Public Health Association, *Planning the Neighborhood*, Public Administration Service, APHA, Washington, D.C., 1948.
2. American Society of Civil Engineers, *Urban Planning Guide*, Report No. 49, ASCE, New York, 1969.
3. Bosselman, F., et al., *The Taking Issue*, U.S. Government Printing Office, Washington, D.C., 1973.
4. Council of State Governments, *A Legislator's Guide to Land Management*, CSG, Lexington, KY, December 1974.
5. Council of State Governments, *Land State Alternatives for Planning and Management*, CSG, Lexington, KY, April 1975.
6. Council of State Governments, *Land Use Management*, CSG, Lexington, KY, November 1974.
7. Council of State Governments, *The Land Use Puzzle*, CSG, Lexington, KY, May 1974.
8. Council of State Governments, *The States' Role in Land Resource Management*, CSG, Lexington, KY, January 1972.
9. Cresti, C., *Le Corbusier—Twentieth Century Master*, The Hamlyn Publishing Group Ltd., London, England, 1970.
10. Eldridge, H.W., ed., *Taming Megalopolis*, 2 vols., Anchor Books/Doubleday, Garden City, NY, 1967.
11. Frieden, B.J., and Morris, R., eds., *Urban Planning and Social Policy*, Basic Books, New York, 1968.
12. Gallion, A.B., and Eisner, S., *The Urban Pattern*, D. Van Nostrand Co., New York, 1975.
13. Goodman, P., and Goodman, P., *Communities—Means of Livelihood and Ways of Life*, Vintage Books/Random House, New York, 1960.
14. Goodman, W.I., ed., *Principles and Practice of Urban Planning*, Municipal Management Series, International City Managers' Association, Washington, D.C., 1968.
15. Hamburger, W.S., ed., *Transportation and Traffic Engineering Handbook*, 2nd ed., Prentice-Hall, Inc., Englewood Cliffs, NJ, 1982.
16. Harriss, C.L., ed., *The Good Earth of America, Planning Our Land Use*, Prentice-Hall, Inc., Englewood Cliffs, NJ, 1974.
17. Hitchcock, H.R., Fein, A., Weisman, W., and Scully, V., *The Rise of an American Architect*, Praeger Publishers, New York, 1970.
18. Hough, B.K., *Basic Soils Engineering*, The Ronald Press Co., New York, 1957.
19. Howard, E., *Garden Cities of Tomorrow*, MIT Press, Cambridge, MA, 1965.
20. Kendig, L., *Performance Zoning*, American Planning Association, Planners Press, Chicago, 1980.
21. Land Classification Advisory Committee of the Detroit Metropolitan Area, *Land Use Classification Manual*, Public Administrative Service, Lincoln Printing Co., Chicago, 1962.
22. Land Use Analysis Library, *A Land Classification Method for Land Use Planning*, Iowa State Univ., Ames, IA, 1973.
23. League of Women Voters, *Land Use*, Philadelphia, 1976.
24. McHarg, I.L., *Design With Nature*, The Falcon Press, Philadelphia, 1971.
25. Merritt, F.S., ed., *Standard Handbook for Civil Engineers*, McGraw-Hill Book Co., New York, 1968.
26. Nelson, R.H., *Zoning and Property Rights*, MIT Press, Cambridge, MA, 1980.
27. Office of State Planning of New Hampshire, *Planning and Development*

Techniques—Options for Managing Community Growth in New Hampshire, Concord, NH, 1979.

28. O'Mara, W.P., et al., *Residential Development Handbook*, The Urban Land Institute, Washington, D.C., 1978.

29. Putman, S.H., *Laboratory Testing of Predictive Land-Use Models, Some Comparisons*, Office of Transportation System Analysis and Information, U.S. Dept. of Transportation, Washington, D.C., October 1976.

30. Rhode Island Department of Community Affairs, *Cluster Development Handbook*, Planning Paper #10, July 1979.

31. Rhode Island Statewide Planning Program, *A Land Capability Analysis for Rhode Island*, Working Paper, January 1982.

32. Rhode Island Statewide Planning Program, *State Land Use Policies and Plan*, Report No. 22, January 1975.

33. Scully, Jr., V., *Frank Lloyd Wright—Master of World Architecture*, George Braziller, Inc., New York, 1960.

34. Smith, H.H., *The Citizens' Guide to Planning*, American Planning Association, Planners Press, Chicago, 1979.

35. Smith, M., ed., *Land Use: Tough Choices in Today's World*, Soil Conservation Society of America, Ankeny, IA, 1977.

36. So, F.S., Stallman, I., Beal, F., and Arnold, D.S., eds., *The Practice of Local Government Planning*, Municipal Management Series, International City Managers' Association, Washington, D.C., 1979.

37. State of Iowa Office of Planning and Programming, *Planning and Zoning Handbook*, Division of Municipal Affairs, Des Moines, IA, 1978.

38. Strom, F.A., ed., *1981 Zoning and Planning Law Handbook*, Clark Boardman Co. Ltd., New York, 1981.

39. Tunnard, C., *The Modern American City*, D. Van Nostrand Co., New York, 1968.

40. U.S. Department of Agriculture in cooperation with the Rhode Island Agricultural Experiment Station, *Soil Survey of Rhode Island*, Washington, D.C., July 1981.

41. U.S. Department of Housing and Urban Development, *Innovative Zoning, A Local Official's Guidebook*, Washington, D.C., November 1977.

42. U.S. Urban Renewal Administration and Bureau of Public Roads, *Standard Land Use Coding Manual*, Washington, D.C., 1965.

CHAPTER 5

HOUSING[a]

5.1 INTRODUCTION

5.1.1 Goal

The goal of providing every family in the United States with a decent home in a suitable living environment has been an integral part of federal housing policy since 1949 (13). It has been in our minds for even longer, given the fact that we had then—and have now in 1985—the best housing for the average family of any country. Yet the field of residential planning is undergoing rapid change toward higher levels of achievement.

For example, constant re-evaluation, on economic and social grounds, of the single-family detached house and its site is leading to improved design. Dwelling units are more concentrated for effective use of land and efficient servicing. Increasing market, financing, and constructing capacities are leading to an enlargement in average project size. Residential developments incorporating servicing and other land uses in substantial amounts are becoming more common (18, 26).

Furthermore, the legal aspects of residential planning have expanded greatly in the last few decades. The number of local nongovernmental community associations managing land for related developments has increased dramatically. Even more spectacular has been the rise in importance of the conceptually similar condominium association. There has been a substantial increase in the number of local government design review boards, as esthetic controls have become popular as a means to achieve continuing development quality.

Zoning in general is evolving from a primitive state, merely categorizing such land uses as residential, commercial, industrial, and agricultural, into a much more performance-oriented concept in which developments are viewed with respect to detailed, scientifically based criteria (32). Beyond local zoning, regional and state development regulations often apply to large projects—Hawaii has a system of statewide zoning—and federal laws and rules often play an important role as well. Increasingly, zoning and other land development regulations are not surviving court tests unless founded on a comprehensive plan.

Planning is for people, not for units, and people differ significantly. They may be predominantly young or old, rich or poor, descendants of

---

[a]Prepared by Ralph Warburton, F.ASCE, College of Engineering, Univ. of Miami, Coral Gables, FL.

original colonists or first-generation immigrants. They may live in large extended-family units or in bachelor's quarters. They may dwell as "mingles," unrelated adults who choose to rent or purchase a unit together, or as single-parent households with many children. There has been a national decline in average persons per unit for several decades, dropping from 3.20 in 1970 to 2.76 in 1980. One-person households were over 22% of the total in 1980. Some people may have increasing leisure time, while others work more than one job. And there are those who live in institutional or military housing. It is clear that people have a variety of backgrounds which influence their behavior; and plans based on some sound theoretical principles may fail if the customs, needs, and desires, as well as the educability, of the subject population is not fully understood (10).

The housing cycle approach to development programs recognizes four distinct periods of typical housing need, which are:

1. A couple forms a family, thus needing a modest rental or ownership unit. The need is usually for a rental unit.

2. The couple has children and their housing needs increase in size and include child-oriented space and location parameters.

3. The children mature and leave the couple as "empty nesters." So housing needs change again.

4. The remaining couple (and survivor) attains retirement and requires a smaller dwelling, perhaps in a new location.

Given the fact that the average American moves fairly often—10% or more per year in recent years—which subject population should a residential development be designed to consider? The answer to this query relates to the estimated characteristics of the population over the physical life expectancy of the housing and development types. The supply of housing best meets the demand if the various dwelling requirements are fully considered and provided for in a range of types, sizes, and costs. Planning in this way avoids substantial inefficiencies in use of human and physical resources, to the end that the improvement of society is facilitated through its residential environment.

5.1.2 Role of Engineers

A residential planner should have the broad capability of properly understanding and synthesizing the many specialty disciplines relating to a residential project, while possessing in-depth expertise in one of them. The better residential planners may well be those who have attained fully registered or certified dual professional status as engineer-planners, architect-planners, landscape architect-planners, economist-planners, etc. One such person should lead the planning team for a project with other specialties playing supporting roles, but the ideal team might consist entirely of generalists with a full range of specialties represented in their backgrounds. More team competence in breadth and depth is required for significant projects, that is, those that have large-scale or complex siting, or both.

The traditional basis of the engineer's competence has been the development and layout of efficient and safe circulation systems, site layout and storm drainage, and utility systems. Large developments and those in sensitive areas will increasingly require additional levels of professional engineering competence. For example, sophisticated seismic risk techniques have recently been used in California involving ground-motion, land-slide and soil-liquefaction factors. Aircraft noise near airports is another quantifiable item (which has health consequences), and there are many conservation issues which demand engineering analyses (6, 22). As the scientific base continues to develop rapidly in these areas, together with computer capacity to handle increasing objective detail, the engineer is in an unusually fine position to contribute to the effort by applying the expanding scientific parameters to residential projects.

From architecture must be drawn an understanding of the various types of residential structure and their relationship over time to user wants and needs, including siting, relationships between units, and requirements for supporting facilities. It must be remembered that beauty can be good business.

Landscape architecture provides a sensitivity for the ecological carrying capacity of the land, and for existing and potential land forms and plant materials, as well as a concern for recreational facilities.

The real estate economist offers evaluations of project budgets and cash flows over time, considering market conditions.

Every substantial project should have a consulting sociologist on its design team, but rare indeed are those who are both able and willing to function in such a creative role. However, to the extent that sociologists can guide other team members to relevant research, their presence can be very valuable. Of concern are the real needs of various population groups as expressed in facilities and service requirements.

Other specialists whose expertise may be required include geologists, atmospheric scientists, biologists, anthropologists, archaeologists, historians, and artists.

5.2 HOUSING IN AN URBAN SETTING

5.2.1 Historical Review

Villages composed of man-made structures date from neolithic times. In Mohenjo-Daro, Pakistan (2500-1500 B.C.), the heights of buildings were proportioned in relation to street width, and there is evidence that disposal lines from dwellings were connected to the underground sewer system. Later, c. 1750 B.C., the codes of Hammurabi heralded the dawn of building regulations. He decreed, in Babylon, that if a building should fall and kill the son of the occupant, the builder's son would be put to death. Babylon consisted largely of three- to four-story dwellings in the 6th and 5th centuries B.C.

In the latter part of the 5th century B.C., the Greek architect Hippodamus advanced the gridiron street system to new levels of sophistication. In Olynthus, for example, streets were oriented and blocks proportioned so that maximum advantage was taken of winter solar heating potentials. Later, towns included underground storm drainage. Greek building regulations typically restricted projections of upper floors of buildings over the street, and windows were not permitted to open onto the street. Also, house water drains were not allowed to empty into the street. During the 5th and 4th centuries B.C., few Greek towns exceeded 10,000 persons. Athens had a population of under 150,000, including slaves and foreigners.

The Romans' development of technology is well known. Their achievements in the design of roads, water supply and distribution systems, drainage and heating systems need no detail here. Not so familiar is the fact that Rome was largely composed of tall residential apartments. Caesar had to restrict building heights to 70 ft (21.3 m) to control land speculators. By the 4th century A.D. there were over 46,000 blocks of apartments, compared to fewer than 2000 private houses in Rome.

In the Middle Ages, housing conditions in European cities were worse than in Rome a thousand years earlier. Half the urban population was decimated by the Black Death plague in the 14th century. It was not until the 17th century that water supply was connected to dwellings in London. This innovation was no doubt also stimulated by the fire hazards caused by several aspects of housing construction, though neither water nor some fire prevention regulations were enough to put out the Great Fire of London in 1666.

During the Renaissance, urban residential areas were opened up a little with avenues and plazas, but behind these open spaces many cities continued to lack water distribution and sewer systems for their high-density populations.

The industrial revolution in the 19th century occasioned further development of water and sewer systems, and initiated significant advances in transportation, communication, lighting and power. It also spawned neighborhoods of factory tenements. In 1867, with a population density of over 300 persons per acre, New York adopted its first law to regulate tenement housing. Later, in 1916, the city adopted the first comprehensive zoning ordinance, which related building height to street width.

Meanwhile, pressures such as population growth and high land costs were forcing the urban dweller farther and farther from the city center. The eventual result was develoment of suburban facilities having the character of satellite communities. An early large-scale residential subdivision was the 1600-acre (645-ha) Riverside, near Chicago, which was carefully planned by landscape architect Frederick Law Olmsted with a curvilinear street pattern related to the land contours. The construction of this subdivision, in 1869, advanced replacement of the easily surveyed gridiron system with one offering more benefits as a living environment.

The last 100 years have been a time of substantial consideration, from three points of view, of the role of nature in the residential environment. First, to what extent should natural open space be immediately and privately associated with each dwelling unit? Second, to what extent should the centers of communities have open space as their focal point, as is the case with many older U.S. towns? And third, should self-contained garden cities of 1000 acres (400 ha), as defined by the British planner Ebenezer Howard in 1898, be surrounded by 5000-acre (2000-ha) agricultural greenbelts to promote harmonious and socially cohesive living? Improved data and analytical capacity are enabling increasingly refined approaches to site-specific answers.

The 20th century has introduced many other influences, actual and perceived, which must be considered by today's residential planner. These include mitigation of crime (4) and the requirements of civil defense, public and private educational facilities and programs, civil rights, religious facilities, and other matters to be considered subsequently.

The planner is left with the inputs concerning housing fairly well identified, although additional ones are always possible given the march of science. However, the values to be applied to each input in determining the design approach in a given situation remain substantially the planner's contribution to society.

5.2.2 The Housing Industry

The housing industry, defined here to include all firms which share in the receipts of expenditures for housing, is one of the most complex industries in the United States' economy (28). It is composed of literally millions of business enterprises. Most are small and specialized. Competition throughout the industry, though imperfect and not ideally beneficial to the consumer, is characteristically fierce.

The housing process can be divided into four phases:

1. Preparation. Potentially developable land is identified and plans are made.
2. Production. Financing is arranged, the site is prepared, and the housing is constructed.
3. Distribution. The house or apartment is marketed. This phase repeats throughout the useful life of the development.
4. Servicing. The housing is repaired and maintained. This phase continues until the end of the housing's economic or physical life.

The participants, the process, and the external influences which affect them are considered in this section.

The evolving housing industry has been generally characterized as localized, fragmented, small-scale, and dependent on outsiders. It is localized because it is largely tied to land and is locally regulated. Only a few home builders, home manufacturers, or consultants look for nationwide markets. The variety of the housing product has led to fragmentation of the industry into an elaborate complex of interlocking production units, resulting in generally inadequate research and development efforts. Most firms are relatively small, due primarily to fluctuations in production caused by seasonality and cyclic variations in the supply of credit. The firms which make up the heart of the industry, mostly home builders and contractors, are dependent on larger enterprises not primarily engaged in housing. Financial institutions constitute the single most important locus of power in the industry.

5.2.3 Outline of Federal Programs

The earliest major federal housing legislation was adopted in 1892, when Congress provided for the investigation of slums in the four cities then having 200,000 or more inhabitants (24). Later, several laws during World War I supported thousands of units of housing for war workers. Of more importance was the law creating a Division of Building and Housing in the National Bureau of Standards (NBS)(23). Since 1921 that organization has evolved into the current Center for Building Technology of NBS, in the Department of Commerce.

In 1931, the President's Conference on Home Building and Home Ownership among other important initiatives gave its recommendation to President Hoover's proposal for a system of home loan discount banks. The resulting 1932 Act established the familiar system of savings and loan associations.

Following another recommendation of the President's Conference, Congress created the Federal Housing Administration (FHA) in 1934, with authority to insure long-term mortgage loans made by private lending institutions (19). Originally for single-family homes, FHA programs have expanded substantially in breadth and depth over its half-century of existence.

Housing programs for farmers were initiated under the Bankhead-Jones Farm Tenant Act of 1937. As these programs expanded, the Farmers Home Administration (FmHA) was created in the Department of Agriculture in 1946.

A more fundamental event was the U.S. Housing Act of 1937, which created the public housing program. Under this Act, loans, annual contributions, and other support are provided to over 3000 local public housing agencies for low-rent housing (12). The Federal National Mortgage Association (FNMA) was chartered in 1938 to establish a secondary market for home mortgages (11).

In 1942 President Roosevelt placed the home loan bank administration, the FHA, and the public housing program under one administrative head in his National Housing Agency, renamed as the Housing and Home Finance Agency in 1947.

The Housing Act of 1949 established the Urban Renewal Program to assist community slum clearance, redevelopment, and development programs (13). In the Housing Act of 1954, participation in the urban renewal program was made contingent upon, among other "workable program" items, presence of a comprehensive community plan, a neighborhood planning analysis, and a housing code (14). In addition the 1954 Act established, in Section 701, a program of planning grants for small communities and for metropolitan areas. Although these programs are no longer funded by the federal government, they have exerted a strong influence on generations of planners and managers in both the public and private sectors, and on succeeding legislation and practice.

By 1961 FHA programs had expanded to include rental apartments, and later included "below-market interest rate" housing for low- and moderate-income families (15). In 1965 a new FHA mortgage insurance program for land development was initiated. The Cabinet-level Department of Housing and Urban Development (HUD), including FHA, FNMA, urban renewal and public housing, was formed in 1965. In 1966 the short-lived Model Cities program was enacted to focus a full range of programs on critical inner-city areas.

The omnibus HUD Act of 1968 established a 10-year national housing goal of 26,000,000 units, 23% of which were to be for low- and moderate-income families. New deep subsidy FHA programs were introduced, and new communities, new technology, flood insurance, riot insurance and interstate land sales regulations were supported. FNMA was spun off as a private corporation, and the Government National Mortgage Association (GNMA) was created to operate special financial assistance functions for subsidized programs (17).

The National Environmental Policy Act of 1969 mandated the now familiar environmental impact statements. Implementation of the resulting kinds of quality increases at federal, state, and local levels has generally raised the cost of housing (22). The HUD Act of 1970 initiated crime insurance, and significantly expanded the new communities program which was phased out in the early 1980s.

In 1974 the urban renewal and model cities programs were terminated, and were generally replaced by the community development block grant (CDBG) program. This shift from "categorial" programs to block grants was undertaken to permit local communities to have much greater discretion in the use of federal assistance (16). Applications to receive CDBG funds must normally consist of: (1) A summary of a 3-yr plan which identifies needs; (2) formulation of a plan-responsive program; (3) identification of efforts to eliminate or prevent slums, blight, and deterioration and to improve community facilities; and (4) a housing assistance plan (HAP).

The housing assistance plan is to survey the condition of the community's housing stock and assess the housing assistance needs of lower-income persons residing in or expected to reside in the community. It also is to specify a reasonable goal for the annual needs of lower-income persons, including the mix of unit types and sizes, project sizes, and types of financial assistance. Furthermore, the HAP indicates the general locations of proposed lower-income housing with a view to furthering revitalization, promoting greater housing choice, avoiding undue concentration of low-income persons, and assuring availability of adequate public facilities and services for such housing.

In addition, the HUD Act of 1974 provided a new "Section 8" housing assistance program. Under this, assistance by HUD in the form of "assistance payments contracts" was authorized on behalf of eligible lower-income families occupying new, substantially rehabilitated or existing rental units. The 1974 Act also required HUD to establish appropriate federal mobile-home construction and safety standards.

The Housing and Urban-Rural Recovery Act of 1983 repealed the Section 8 new construction program, replacing it with a housing development grant program. It authorized a one-time, up-front grant to units of government to spur rental housing construction for lower-income families. Such one-time grants are in contrast to the traditional long-term commitments of federal assistance in the continuing mortgage insurance and low-rent public housing programs.

This has been a brief summary of major federal legislation for housing, which has significantly expanded the governmental role in breadth and depth. Unless there are major new influences, this level of involvement is likely at least to be maintained in the future.

5.2.4 Social Factors

Perhaps one of the most pressing social concerns in housing planning is civil rights. The federal government's involvement began with the 14th Amendment to the Constitution and the Civil Rights Act of 1866, which banned discrimination in some types of housing. Under President Kennedy's Executive Order 11063, issued in November 1962, the intent was stated to prevent discrimination because of race, color, creed, or national origin in all federally assisted housing. It had only a minor impact, but the Civil Rights Act of 1964 prohibited discrimination under any program receiving federal financial assistance. And the more important Civil Rights Act of 1968, which covers about 80% of all housing, became fully effective in 1970.

In 1971, President Nixon stated the federal policies relative to equal housing opportunity thus:

. . . . By equal housing opportunity, I mean the achievement of a condition in which individuals of similar income levels in the same housing market area have a like range of housing choices available to them regardless of their race, color, religion or national origin. . . . We will not seek to impose economic integration upon an existing local jurisdiction; at the same time we will not countenance any use of economic measures as a subterfuge for racial discrimination (20).

This has a great deal to do with housing planning. For example, it can often be shown that housing of high economic value generates a "profit," in that tax receipts exceed local government expenditures for services to that housing. Thus there is an economic incentive to communities to plan for increasing the average value of their housing. When carried to excess, responding to this incentive may result in *de facto* discrimination. In many situations it has done so.

In the famous case of Southern Burlington County NAACP v. Township of Mount Laurel (27), the devices of requiring large minimum house size, large minimum lot size, and large minimum frontage, prohibiting multifamily housing and mobile homes, and overzoning for nonresidential uses resulted in segregated housing. In this example, none of the economic excesses mentioned could be legally justified by any scientifically based planning criteria related to public health, safety or welfare. The New Jersey Supreme Court therefore adopted the doctrine of requiring that municipalities' land use regulations provide a realistic opportunity for low- and moderate-income housing.

Revisiting the situation in 1983, 10 years after the original trial court action, the New Jersey Supreme Court found that the township still determined to exclude the poor, and it strongly reaffirmed its earlier actions. It further suggested that municipalities provide incentives for, or require, private developers to set aside a portion of their developments for lower-income housing (9).

It now seems clear that following the court's direction is mandatory if real attainment of the cellular "neighborhood unit" planning advocated by Clarence Perry in 1929, and often used by planners, is desired. Perry felt that an elementary school should be the focus of a residential neighborhood where no child would have to walk more than 1/4 mile (0.475 km) to school. Following the 1955 U.S. Supreme Court decision in Brown v. Board of Education, which mandated school integration, nonrecognition of civil rights in residential planning where children are concerned has led to extensive school busing in many communities. This removes land planning opportunities to provide social cohesion, conserve energy, efficiently use property tax revenues, and save children's time for educational and other productive pursuits. Of course, neighborhoods which are not planned to have a concentration of school-age children can be organized around a more appropriate activity center.

An additional concern related to children is the adequacy of recreational facilities in moderate- to high-density developments. Are there enough playgrounds, basketball and tennis courts, baseball diamonds and football fields accessible to the children's residences?

Accessibility is also an issue with regard to the elderly. Too many developments for senior citizens are located far away from, for example, major food markets, so busing is also required here. The elderly, and the handicapped, need access to a wide variety of commercial, social, medical, religious and other facilities and services. Busing is only partly successful in relieving access problems, because transit equipment itself may not be fully accessible or available on a convenient basis.

Furthermore, site planning for the elderly and the handicapped needs to consider recreational needs, and not only shuffleboard courts and gardening areas. Careful walk design with easy grades instead of steps, snow melting in cold climates and shade in hot areas, and wheelchair bypasses, etc., will do much to make the land usable by the elderly or handicapped or both.

It should be clear from the foregoing paragraphs that organization of the residential community, project, or site cannot be called "planned" if it merely imposes or conforms to some abstract geometry without social rationale. In fact, one infamous project housing thousands of people (St. Louis' Pruitt-Igoe) was razed after less than 20 years of service because, among other things, it did not follow some of the simple social principles stated and, therefore, became less desirable to the residents than the surrounding slums.

5.2.5 Technological Factors

The evolutionary industrialization of housing can be seen in several areas. Manufactured building parts have become larger and more complex, often incorporating products that were originally developed for a different use. Another indicator is the on-site division of labor; and there is the ever-increasing share of the national housing market captured by the mobile home and manufactured housing industry.

However, the housing industry has lagged behind other sectors of the economy in incorporating new technology. A principal problem has been that the cost savings and quality increases associated with industrialization cannot be realized most effectively unless the mass market is being served. Due to the fragmentation of the industry, the market for housing does not exist as it does for automobiles, for example. Housing producers are not usually in a position to shape their market through extensive advertising so that it can be receptive to new approaches. Thus they cater to more traditional views of consumers, and those shaped by other producers, in order to sell the product. The uncertainty introduced is reflected in a proliferation of housing product models which would be uneconomic to mass produce and are not necessarily tuned to real consumer housing needs.

Furthermore, in contrast to regulation for most consumer products, government regulation of housing—such as building codes, subdivision regulations, development review ordinances, transportation rules, and health laws—is substantially a matter of state and local control. A producer of housing would find it nearly impossible to market a competitive national (or even regionally modified) model home approved by all government authorities. Even gaining nationwide acceptance of significant new materials, products, or methods requires a substantial investment in money and time. Though there have been improvements in recent decades, the period required for introduction and acceptance of new housing concepts appears to be about 10 years.

The major federal attempt to address these issues and stimulate technological development of the housing industry was called "Operation Breakthrough." Launched in 1969 by then HUD Secretary (and former auto industry executive) George Romney, it involved receipt of over 600 proposals from industry (33). A selection of systems was made for design and development work, and construction began of prototype models on prototype sites throughout the country. Criteria for testing the prototype models were carefully developed by NBS on a performance-oriented basis, so that the tested products would find optimum levels of code acceptance (21).

It was recognized early in the program that creative site planning was even more essential for standardized industrial products than for conventional units, so significant efforts were made to retain excellent design teams for the prototype sites and carefully monitor their work. Site plans were required to accommodate new types of building erection processes, as well as to provide functional environments with enough variety to please consumers and encourage land developers to try the new approach. High-quality site plans were produced.

Key to the success of mass producing any industrialized housing is aggregation of a large enough market to justify necessary front-end investments. While market aggregation was part of the Operation Breakthrough plan, it depended substantially on the availability of unit allocations under HUD's subsidized housing programs. When the relevant programs were suspended or reduced in the early 1970s as the result of fraud and other matters unrelated to industrialization, market aggregation was fatally weakened. Thus the major advances under Operation Breakthrough were in the support of forward-looking technical ideas, including mitigation of some of the constraints previously identified. The development of those ideas was greatly accelerated.

5.2.6 Legal Factors

Some aspects of the law relating to residential planning have already been mentioned, but one deserves treatment here in more detail: zoning.

Zoning is the regulation of the use of land on behalf of the public health, safety, and welfare through utilization of the police power. In general, if the public wishes to prohibit an owner from making any use whatsoever of his land, this would constitute a "taking" and is not zoning. The owner would receive just compensation under eminent domain. In the 1970s, zoning entered its third major stage of development.

Nineteenth-century zoning laws dealt with nuisance issues, such as the proximity of slaughterhouses to residences and the establishment of fire districts. Later, courts required evidence dealing with the "character of the community" before ruling on the validity of an ordinance.

Beginning in the 1970s, significant technical documentation has often been a necessary base for zoning matters.

Two U.S. Supreme Court decisions are of immense importance. In 1926, Justice Sutherland pointed out that each community had the right and responsibility to regulate land use within its own boundaries in determining its own character, so long as that did not disturb the orderly growth of the region or nation (31). In 1954, Justice Douglas wrote:

> The concept of the public welfare is broad and inclusive. The values it represents are spiritual as well as physical, aesthetic as well as monetary. It is within the power of the legislature to determine that the community should be beautiful as well as healthy, spacious as well as clean, well-balanced as well as carefully patrolled (1).

Thus zoning, and other land use and development controls such as subdivision regulations, are becoming extensive in breadth and intensive and performance-oriented in depth. The planner must be aware of the intermix between public controls and private covenants which can be creatively used to help assure appropriate continuity of development quality over time.

Private controls through carefully drafted restrictive covenants are particularly important in upper-income, lot-sale, single-family merchant builder's and condominium projects, since local governments may not be able to offer the desired level of protection over time. There must be controls of land and space use, site, architecture, and other details of what goes on the site or buildings, or both. Without controls, misguided persons may develop or remodel sites or structures, or add elements to multifamily buildings, that will adversely affect a whole neighborhood. Fencing, landscaping, lighting, noise, signage and color are elements usually needing attention so that a thoughtless or indifferent owner cannot ruin the adjoining properties.

A design review board is often specified in the covenant to help administer these matters, with respect to criteria established by the planning team. Clearly, such a board should include members with professional expertise in the subject matter of the regulations. Many of the board's concerns may be of a higly technical nature requiring the expertise of a civil engineer with the necessary experience. Examples of such issues include subsidence, drainage, ground-water considerations, and utilities.

Virtually all of the newer concepts of residential planning for all economic levels include land areas of joint use. Unless these are deeded to a local government, arrangements for their ownership and maintenance can also be handled through appropriate covenant provisions, which often establish homes associations or condominium associations to administer the joint property, as well as the project design review board, if there is one. Appropriate approvals at the project level should be obtained before processing plans, etc., through community review procedures, including any community design review board.

5.2.7 Economic Factors

Market and cost analyses are vital early steps in the planning of any residential development. A market analysis for a small project may be made by an experienced developer, but for larger projects there is no substitute for a thorough and objective professional study by a real estate economist, land economist, or market analyst. Such a study can define particular market potentials and provide valuable inputs into the planner's site selection and evaluation processes. It can also discipline the normal tendency to upgrade projects without regard to affordability, or to maximize land profits by building multifamily units where there are few supporting consumers.

Cost analysis includes consideration of cost of land, improvements, and financing. While the true cost of land may be substantially influenced by the method used for its purchase—and this may be important in some analyses—major planning factors include:

1. Suitability for development, e.g., elevation, topography, soil, vegetation.

2. Accessibility, e.g., by road, mass transit, air, water.

3. Utilities, e.g., water, sewer, power, communications.

4. Zoning. In some cases, reliance on existing zoning is not recommended as the community may have a history of "down-zoning" critical property to a less intensive use. Conversely, rezoning to a more intensive use may be possible in other circumstances. A careful review of the applicable community plan is required, together with an appraisal of local views of citizens and elected officials. However, it is wise in critical situations to consider no zoning final until issuance of the building permit.

5. Neighborhood. It has been truly said that the three things that most determine the value of a parcel of land are location, location and location! The existence or potential of noxious impacts, such as those affecting land, water, air, and noise pollution, is relevant. The quality of existing development of the surrounding area and the probable type of development of vacant land are value factors, as are such nearby facilities as shopping, recreation facilities, and schools.

The value of any parcel of land is determined by a consideration of all these factors in relation to future astute development. Value may or may not have any relationship to the selling price to the developer. A wise developer will often take an option on a promising parcel and then obtain a planning feasibility study to evaluate the factors on the list, often in relation to the other economic factors, before completing a land purchase.

Improvement costs are difficult for a nonbidder to estimate reliably even with final engineering plans in hand. Estimating undertaken during the planning phase is an even greater task. It is wise to consider improvement costs as "budget" figures, rather than "construction costs," to avoid confusion with terminology in standard owner-engineer contracts for construction documents. A reasonable contingency must always be included. Furthermore, the budget estimate and other financial data should be indexed to the currency value at the time of planning and cover a specific time period for implementation. Unanticipated delays due to governmental processing, right-of-way purchasing, labor or material shortages, etc., can hold up a development for months. Meanwhile inflation or recession can invalidate the original improvement budget.

Financial budgets are as hard to predict as improvement budgets. In addition to interest charges on any unpaid balance of the land purchase price, there is interest on improvement loans, construction loans, and funds needed for promotion and for carrying charges. (High interest rates beginning in the late 1970s have priced many potential single-family home buyers out of the market.) Significant detailed budgeting, regularly updated, is needed to predict these figures in a fluctuating money market. Furthermore, rates are not always what they seem, given discounting and other financial industry practices. Of particular importance is correctly predicting how fast the project will sell, because the timing of the cash flow return is crucial. Successful projects are usually timed to open during peak periods of real estate activity, and this input from the market analysis facilitates generation of a month-to-month financial plan.

Other costs include professional fees for planning, engineering, market analysis, architecture, landscape architecture, legal services, accounting, etc., marketing and sales costs, and overhead.

Large-scale projects involve greater risks, but often return significant qualitative benefits. The former federal new communities program attempted to put into effect long-term financial guarantees that would permit a large new community to carry the early land and development costs for the very long time required for revenues to offset those expenditures. Such a patient approach is necessary to realize full appreciation of large-scale residential investments.

5.3 HOUSING AND DEVELOPMENT TYPES

5.3.1 Housing Types

The principal housing types are mobile home, single-family detached, duplex-fourplex, town house, low-rise multiple-unit buildings, high-rise multiple-unit buildings, and multitype and multiuse structures. Most of these are so familiar as to need no further consideration here, though definitions may vary by locality. Mobile homes and multiuse structures, however, are treated in some detail in the following paragraphs.

Mobile homes and manufactured homes have become a significant factor in American housing. Growing from an annual production rate of 1300 in 1930, top fabrication reached over 575,000 units in 1972, which represented about 24% of all dwelling units produced in the peak year of U.S. housing production. Although fewer units were produced in 1980, 29% of all detached single-family homes in that year were mobile or manufactured homes. Of those selling for less than $40,000 in 1980, 82% were mobile or manufactured housing units. There are several hundred firms producing these homes from factory sites, and units include plumbing, heating, ventilation and air conditioning, and electrical systems (25).

The Manufactured Housing Institute defines a unit thus:

> . . . a structure, transportable in one or more sections, which, in the traveling mode, is 8 body feet or more in width or 40 body feet or more in length, or, when erected on site, is 320 or more square feet . . .

in floor area. Built on a permanent chassis and designed to be used as a dwelling with or without a permanent foundation when connected to the required utilities, most units made since 1976 have conformed to the HUD standards issued to cover dwelling purposes (29).

About half of the homes are placed on individually owned sites, generally in rural or small-town locations. The others are in mobile or manufactured home communities normally with an average of 150 to 175 sites. Citizen planning and zoning attitudes are generally not favorable to this type of housing, though the need for more affordable housing, and improved unit and site design, may challenge these views (25).

A principal physical problem is esthetics. A much smaller percentage of new manufactured units can stand on their own as objects of beauty than of comparable site-built residences. Landscaping must normally be relied upon to develop a satisfactory community appearance. Many such communities have landscaping in a degree and quality seldom found in subdivisions of site-built homes (2).

Quality communities, or "parks," first developed in Florida, California, and other areas attracting many retired people and second-home owners. Extensive recreational features are essential in parks having a clientele with leisure time. Families who have lived in good-quality residential areas want attractive mobile home surroundings, but somewhat higher densities of 6 to 8 units per acre are normally acceptable (2). The best designed projects are comparable to high-quality subdivisions in pleasing street layout, siting of units, and provision of open space; not just in profuse landscaping around units.

Careful site planning is also an especially important ingredient in successful multitype and multiuse developments. Of particular concern is the ability of the site plan to satisfy the timely needs of all of the users. This requires a significant identification of the various user groups and preparation of site development programs relating to their separate requirements. The value given to each discrete program in preparing the site plan might well relate to the numbers of person-hours a particular population group will be likely to use the residential site.

5.3.2 Development Types

Principal development types include the middle-income single-family subdivision, adult and retirement communities, military and institutional complexes (college housing, correctional facilities, etc.), developments related to golf courses, marinas, or a private airport, housing for low- and moderate-income people, and housing for very high-income families.

Demographic trends indicate a rising demand for adult and retirement housing. For example, life expectancy at birth has recently been increasing at the rate of 0.3 yr per yr. Attention to the needs of this population group is essential for good residential planning, and there will be a need for planners to update their education continually in this area as more facts become available.

Planning for the low- and moderate-income population provides a special challenge to provide facilities that will be of such high quality as to: (1) Further residents' development so that they may make an optimum contribution to society, and (2) have very low maintenance costs, since government subsidies are often involved and the served population may not be able to undertake high levels of maintenance. Thus it is likely that a good site development for this population will have a higher construction cost than an equally appropriate proposal for a middle-income project.

5.4 CRITERIA AND OBJECTIVES

5.4.1 Criteria

Principal criteria for residential planning include those related to climate, geology, topography, open space, utility systems, communications systems, civil defense, mitigation of crime, air, water, and land pollution, noise, energy conservation, and landscaping. Volumes have been and will be written about each of these criteria as the march of science and public interest progresses. It is no longer sufficient to consider only a few of the objective criteria in preparing residential plans.

All of the criteria listed are susceptible to engineering definition, evaluation, and application, including the resolution of some of the conflicts that may arise when applying criteria to a project. In some cases, it may be necessary to overdesign with respect to one criterion in order to meet the minimum value of another.

5.4.2 Objectives

The criteria are, of course, applied at several scales in the planning hierarchy. The scale ranges from an individual unit to a discrete project, a neighborhood, a community, a metropolis.

The traditional theoretical approach involves "cluster planning" principles, wherein living units are somewhat concentrated and grouped around central areas to focus their social life, optimize circulation and minimize land development costs. However, the scales at which these principles are applied need increasingly to be coordinated with scientific findings related to the nature of man's optimum development. For example, if it is desirable to foster the development of small social groups in a project through the use of cul-de-sac streets and cluster planning, that objective is not necessarily fostered by, say, politically based public safety or ground circulation influences on cul-de-sac length.

At larger scales, housing planners should ask whether a neighborhood or community will actually function as intended by the design, given leaps in technology. How can our "civil" planning make us feel as close to our nearby neighbor as we may feel to a friend hundreds of miles away, thanks to telecommunications? Do we, or should we, actually behave in a cellular fashion even if we live in a community of such a design—having all our routine residential contacts within a confined area?

These are important questions which are being addressed in some way by every residential project. The sum total of the answers provided by their planners can well have a substantial impact on the future of our society. The challenge is to plan for millions of additional housing units, each in the right place, having the right attributes, and provided at the right time. In concert with others, society requires civil engineers to apply their traditional breadth of technological acumen to help plan optimum environments for the future.

5.5 REFERENCES AND BIBLIOGRAPHY

1. Berman v. Parker, 348 U.S. 26, 75 Sup. Ct. 98, 99 L. Ed. 27, 1954.
2. Bestor, G.C., "Residential Land Planning," *Urban Planning Guide*, ASCE, New York, 1969.
3. Bolt, Beranek and Newman, Inc., *Noise Assessment Guidelines*, U.S. Government Printing Office, Washington, D.C., 1984.
4. Center for Residential Security Design, *Improving Residential Security*, U.S. Government Printing Office, Washington, D.C., 1973.
5. Claire, W.H., ed., *Handbook on Urban Planning*, Van Nostrand Reinhold Co., New York, 1973.
6. Cohen, S., Krantz, D.S., Evans, G.W., and Stokols, D., "Cardiovascular and Behavioral Effects of Community Noise," *American Scientist*, Vol. 69, Sept.-Oct. 1981, pp. 528–535.

7. *Community Builders Handbook Series—Residential Development Handbook,* Urban Land Institute, Washington, D.C., 1980.

8. DeChiara, J., ed., *Time-Saver Standards for Residential Development,* McGraw-Hill Book Co., New York, 1984.

9. "Excerpts from Decision on Housing," *New York Times,* January 21, 1983.

10. Gans, H.J., *People and Plans,* Basic Books, New York, 1968.

11. House Committee on Banking, Currency, and Housing, Subcommittee on Housing and Community Development, "Evolution of the Role of the Federal Government in Housing and Community Development," 94th Congress, 1st Session, October 1975, p. 6.

12. Housing Act of 1937, Public Law 412, 75th Congress, September 1, 1937.

13. Housing Act of 1949, Public Law 171, 81st Congress, July 15, 1949.

14. Housing Act of 1954, Public Law 560, 83rd Congress, August 2, 1954.

15. Housing Act of 1961, Public Law 70, 87th Congress, June 30, 1961.

16. Housing and Community Development Act of 1974, Public Law 383, 93rd Congress, August 22, 1974.

17. Housing and Urban Development Act of 1968, Public Law 448, 90th Congress, August 1, 1968.

18. Lansing, J.B., Marans, R.W., and Fehner, R.B., *Planned Residential Development,* Braun-Brumfield, Inc., Ann Arbor, MI, 1970.

19. National Housing Act, Public Law 479, 73rd Congress, June 27, 1934.

20. Nixon, R.M., "Statement by the President on Federal Policies Relative to Equal Housing Opportunity," June 11, 1971.

21. Pfrang, E.O., *Guide Criteria for the Evaluation of Operation Breakthrough Housing Systems,* National Technical Information Service, Arlington, VA, 1970.

22. Planning Environment International, *Interim Guide for Environmental Assessment,* U.S. Government Printing Office, Washington, D.C., 1975.

23. Public Law 18, 67th Congress, June 16, 1921.

24. Public Res. 22, 52nd Congress, July 20, 1892.

25. *Quick Facts About the Manufactured Housing Industry,* Manufactured Housing Institute, Arlington, VA, July 1982.

26. Real Estate Research Corporation, *The Costs of Sprawl,* U.S. Government Printing Office, Washington, D.C., 1974.

27. Southern Burlington Township NAACP v. Township of Mount Laurel, 336 Atl. 2d, 736.

28. Sumichrast, M., and Frankel, S.A., *Profile of the Builder and His Industry,* National Association of Home Builders, Washington, D.C., 1970.

29. U.S. Department of Housing and Urban Dedvelopment, "Mobile Home Construction and Safety Standards," *Federal Register,* 40, No. 244, December 18, 1975.

30. Urban Research and Development Corporation, *Guidelines for Improving the Mobile Home Living Environment,* U.S. Government Printing Office, Washington, D.C., 1978.

31. Village of Euclid, Ohio, v. Ambler Realty Company, 272 U.S. 363, November 22, 1926.

32. Warburton, R., "A Progressive Approach to Zoning and Building Codes," *Systems Building News,* July 1971.

33. Warburton, R., ed., *Housing Systems Proposals for Operation Breakthrough,* U.S. Government Printing Office, Washington, D.C., 1970.

CHAPTER 6

URBAN TRANSPORTATION PLANNING[a]

The environment in which transportation professionals operate has changed dramatically during the past 10 years. Throughout the 1960s, the urban transportation "problem" was perceived almost exclusively as one of highway congestion. In response, most transportation planners and engineers considered as their first priority the accommodation of this rising traffic demand by planning new or expanded expressways. This problem definition has changed, however, and so too have the types of solution strategies that transportation planners and designers must consider. The "new" urban transportation problems include at the very least the relationship between transportation and: (1) Energy consumption; (2) air quality; (3) equity; (4) safety; (5) congestion; (6) land-use impact; (7) noise; and (8) more efficient utilization of fiscal resources (1). The different planning methodologies used to address each of these areas, the need to interact with professionals in other disciplines, the requirement to include public input throughout the planning process, and the desire to put transportation planning in the context of the over-all planning process for a metropolitan area make transportation planning an extremely complex process.

The planning process has been made even more complex by a recent shift in the focus of such planning from large-scale, capital-intensive projects to smaller scale, operational improvements which seek the more efficient use of the existing transportation network. The traditional analysis methodologies and the institutional environment for urban transportation planning have thus changed significantly. Now, more than ever, there is a need to have those who do the planning interact with those who design and implement, so that each understands the contraints under which the other operates.

This chapter is organized to address many of the new characteristics of transportation planning. The introductory section will examine the role of transportation in an urban setting, some of the important characteristics of transportation that affect planning efforts, and the types of issues that transportation planners and designers can expect to face during an analysis. The second section will review the major components of a short-range planning process and the types of projects that are typically the product of such a process. Specific attention will be given to the role of the planner, designer, and policy maker in this type of planning activity. The third section will address issues similar to those

---

[a]Prepared by Michael D. Meyer, Massachussetts Dept. of Public Works, Boston, MA.

in Section 6.2 except that the focus will be on long-range planning, i.e., what types of transportation actions should we be considering now that will have an impact in 20-25 years? Section 6.5 will look at how projects are programmed for implementation, some of the schemes that are used for prioritizing, and the relationship between programming and the political environment. The typical process for project development, i.e., how projects are identified, the procedures that must be followed for furthering the project, project design considerations, and project planning implementation procedures will be described in Section 6.6. The purpose of this section is to integrate much of the material presented in the preceding sections within the context of a single project.

6.1 TRANSPORTATION IN AN URBAN SETTING

Basic to an understanding of transportation are the characteristics of urban travel that in many ways define the scope of urban transportation problems. Five such characteristics that will be considered in this section include:

1. Temporal distribution of urban travel.
2. Type of trips made.
3. Modal distribution of urban trips.
4. Environmental impact of transportation facilities.
5. Relationship between land use and transportation.

Where appropriate, examples will be given of the types of transportation strategies that are now being considered to address some of the problems associated with each characteristic.

6.1.1 Temporal Distribution

Congestion has often been identified as the major transportation problem in today's cities. Put simply, congestion denotes a condition of any transportation facility in which service demand exceeds capacity, resulting in increased delays for the users of that facility. This problem becomes apparent if one looks at the hourly variation of urban person trips by mode during the day (see Fig. 6-1). The demand for transportation service during the morning and afternoon peak periods in many cases causes the transportation system to reach high levels of congestion. The solution to this problem during the early 1960s was to expand the capacity of the highway network so that the increased vehicular demand could be accommodated. In most areas, however, such solutions are no longer feasible because of the disruption such expansion would cause neighboring areas, the large cost associated with construction, and the increasing demands on transportation funds for other types of projects.

Other strategies that are currently being considered to handle the

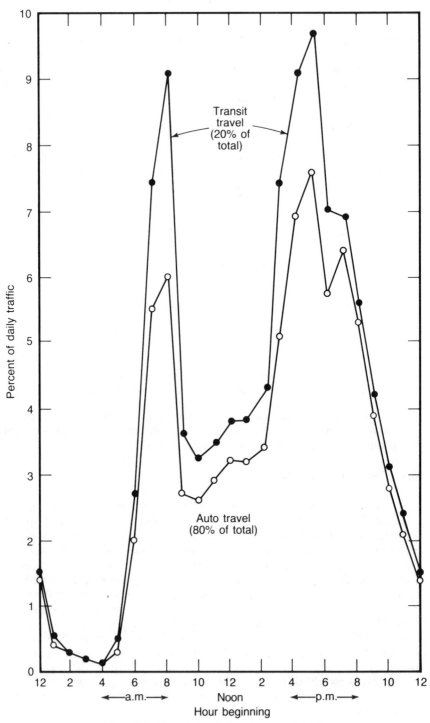

Fig. 6-1. Hourly variation in travel (16)

peaking problem include: (1) To "spread" the peak by arranging work hours such that large groups of employees arrive at different times (variable work hours and flexi-time), and (2) to increase the average occupancy level of vehicles entering a downtown area (ridesharing programs, preferential treatment for buses and carpools, and auto disincentive projects). These types of solutions may be more cost effective than permanent capacity expansion.

6.1.2 Trip Purpose

Trip purpose is also an important characteristic of urban travel behavior. The largest percentage of trip purposes to the Central Business District (CBD) is the home-to-work trips which because of their time of travel usually contribute most to transportation congestion. The second largest category of trips are those taken for social and recreational purposes, which taken in conjunction with shopping trips, account for as many home-based trips as the work trip. The home or dwelling unit is the primary origin of most trips, with more than three-fourths of all urban trips originating from or destined for the home (3). Unique travel patterns are also associated with special purpose activities such as hospitals, universities, and high density business districts (13).

6.1.3 Modal Distribution

One of the most visible characteristics of the transportation system in this country is the dominance of the automobile. From 1950 to 1975, the proportion of American households owning at least one car rose from 52% to 83% (16). Meanwhile, vehicle miles of transit service nationally declined by 37% (25). However, in some cities the percentage of trips to downtown areas served by transit is quite large. Further, given the existing policy trend toward discouraging auto use in metropolitan areas, and the likelihood of fuel shortages in the future, the role of transit and other high occupancy vehicles is likely to become more important.

In the transit field, there has been increased public pressure on providing service distribution according to need, focusing specifically on the mobility deficits of the physically handicapped, the elderly, and the poor. In general, the elderly and poor rely more heavily on transit and taxi travel than the general population does (see Tables 6-1 and 6-2). Effective methods for enhancing the mobility of these groups include: (1) Direct payment of subsidies in the form of vouchers or transit fare discounts; (2) increased demand responsive transportation services; (3) redesign of fixed route service to serve the needs of low-income travelers; and (4) a restructure of transit fares (1).

6.1.4 Environmental Impact

The characteristic of transportation that has gained the most public attention during recent years has been the impact of transportation

TABLE 6-1 Trips Per Capita and by Mode, 1970 (1)

Mode (1)	Percentage of All Trips		Trips Per Capita	
	Persons 65 and over (2)	All persons 16 and over (3)	Persons 65 and over (4)	All persons 16 and over (5)
Auto driver	53.4	62.6	201	531
Auto passenger	35.9	25.7	135	218
Motorcycle		0.2		2
Truck (driver or passenger)	4.2	6.0	16	51
Subtotal: private vehicle	93.5	94.5	352	802
Transit bus	4.3	2.8	16	24
Rapid transit	0.5	0.9	2	8
Commuter rail	0.1	0.2		2
School bus	0.6	1.2	2	10
Taxi	0.6	0.3	2	2
Subtotal: public transportation	6.1	5.4	22	46
Other (airplanes, etc.)	0.4	0.1	1	1
Total	100.0	100.0	375	849

TABLE 6-2 Transit Accessibility by Income, 1970 (1)

Annual household income group (1)	Distance to Nearest Public Transportation (in Blocks)				
	Less than 1, in percentage (2)	1–2, in percentage (3)	3–6, in percentage (4)	Over 6, in percentage (5)	None available, in percentage (6)
Under $5,000	30.3	34.5	17.4	9.2	8.4
$5,000–9,999	20.9	33.2	18.3	15.5	11.7
$10,000–14,999	15.5	29.3	18.3	20.6	16.3
Over $15,000	13.3	23.7	20.6	25.5	15.9
All households	21.3	30.8	18.6	16.6	12.4

facilities and travel on the natural environment. The transportation impact on air quality, for example, emerged during the late 1960s as a significant political issue and has resulted in several federal regulations that guide transportation and air quality planning at the local level. Automobiles account for at least 80% of carbon monoxide (CO) and lead emissions in most metropolitan areas; about 70% of hydrocarbon emissions (HC); and about 50% of the nitrous oxide emissions (NO_x). Many of the severe problems with these primary pollutants result when they chemically combine under favorable meteorological conditions to form secondary pollutants. For example, nitrous oxide emissions react with hydrocarbons in sunlight to form photochemical oxidants (smog) that are not only dangerous to health but seriously affect visibility and the esthetics of a metropolitan area. The automobile is the primary source for both pollutants necessary for this reaction. The types of transportation actions that can be implemented in a metropolitan area, however, can have varied effects on pollutant emissions. As shown in Fig. 6-2, for example, as average speed increases, HC and CO emissions decrease while NO_x emissions increase.

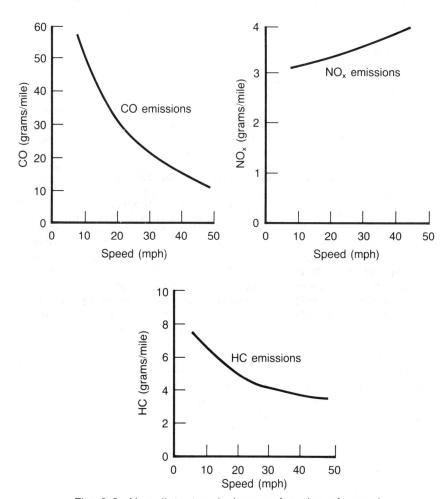

Fig. 6-2. Air pollutant emissions as function of speed

Transportation's impact on energy consumption has also received close scrutiny during the past several years. Gasoline accounts for nearly 40% of all oil used in the United States, and as the availability of oil becomes increasingly scarce, the style of personal transportation could change significantly. Studies have shown that public transit and vanpools are the most energy efficient when compared to all other modes (30). However, most analysts believe that transit alone cannot contribute substantially to a national reduction of petroleum imports because of the low base from which it currently operates, which is at less then 3% of urban passenger travel (7). To truly have an impact, a transportation and energy plan would have to combine automobile disincentives with incentives to use transit service. The planner must therefore view effective transportation strategies as the integration of several transport actions, each affecting one component of the system, but which in total achieve the desired objective (6,14).

6.1.5 Land Use and Urban Development

Transportation and urban development are closely related in a multitude of ways. First, transportation is a critical factor in making parcels of land available for development. A central characteristic of most urban networks is that they serve major activity centers which are a focus for transportation services and are junctions or terminal points for the congested high traffic volume corridors. This relationship produces the high densities of land use in metropolitan areas, and, in turn, the high values of land observed in these centers. Although transportation was clearly a dominant factor in the rapid suburbanization that has occurred during the past 25 years, the highway network in most urban areas is now so ubiquitous that it is doubtful if transportation measures alone can significantly impact metropolitan patterns of land development. Only through such measures as managing the access to the highway network or using local zoning controls related to transportation actions could a significant impact on regional land use be made. Where considerable potential for high-density development exists, however, and other governmental levers such as zoning and tax incentives are utilized, transit and traffic investment could play an important supporting role.

A second factor in the transportation and land use relationship is that transportation facilities occupy land. Between 25% and 45% of the land in central cities (approximately 3% nationwide) is devoted to highways, streets, and parking lots. It was indeed this requirement for large areas of land in densely populated areas and the necessity of displacing large numbers of people that caused some of the reaction against large-scale highway construction during the late 1960s.

The land use and transportation relationship thus becomes an important component in the transportation planning process. This process must include at the least an inventory of land usage and an evaluation of its effect on the performance of the transportation system.

Indeed, most transportation studies use data on land development by traffic analysis zones to predict the number of trips moving between the zones. More will be said about this in the following two subsections.

6.1.6 Institutional Framework for Transportation Planning

Ever since the urban transportation problem first emerged as a public issue in the 1950s, the number of organizations that have been established at all levels of government to deal with it has greatly increased. The proliferation of these organizations, along with a growing awareness that "the" problem was in fact a complex set of problems, created the need for an institutional structure at the regional and local level conducive to coordinated transportation planning. The focus of transportation planning on an integrated transportation system, i.e., where all modes for all trip purposes are coordinated on a geographic basis to improve the movement of goods and passengers, created the need for dialogue between the many agencies responsible for transportation in an urban area. The fragmentation of jurisdictional responsibility and the fact that those agencies responsible for project implementation are often not those undertaking the planning activities has created a complex institutional structure to which every planner and designer should be sensitive (11).

There are many organizations with transportation interests in a metropolitan area, each having its own mandate, constituency, and solution to the transportation problem as defined by its own staff. The metropolitan planning organization (MPO), for example, is an agency in each metropolitan area of over 50,000 population responsible for coordinating the regional transportation planning process. The MPO must deal with transit and highway agencies, parking authorities, planning departments, and local elected officials. The ability of the MPO to carry out this function, however, is hampered by its inability to implement transportation and land use development plans, and its lack of influence in requiring the cooperation of the different actors important to transportation planning.

Because federal agencies such as the Federal Highway Administration (FHWA), the Urban Mass Transportation Administration (UMTA), and the Environmental Protection Agency (EPA) provide a substantial amount of the financial support for planning and project implementation, they also have some say over how the planning process should be structured. For example, the U.S. Department of Transportation has regularly issued planning regulations that require each metropolitan area to have a transportation plan that guides investment decision-making in that area. According to these regulations, the plan shall consist of a long-range element which explores alternative system configurations and policies, and a short-range element which provides for the near-term (1-5 years) transportation needs of persons and goods in the urbanized area (31). Transportation projects are also subject to the National Environmental Policy Act (NEPA), which requires compliance with environmental regulations and preparation of environmental documents for major federal actions.

In general, then, transportation planners or designers often find themselves undertaking activities that have been specified by other agencies, such as UMTA and FHWA, or the state department of transportation. The activities often include using specific techniques in the planning process, complying with the required level of participation of selected groups, and developing documentation necessary to satisfy guidelines. A transportation planner, to be effective, must understand the institutional context of the work. In transportation, this means understanding the roles, responsibilities, and relationships among the federal agencies involved with transportation, the state departments of transportation, the regional planning and implementing agencies, and the local transit operator and traffic engineer.

6.1.7 Urban Transportation Planning Process

A metropolitan transportation planning process should integrate the many different planning activities that occur in a region which affect the transportation system. Within different transportation agencies, for example, the following types of analyses occur (3):

1. Studies of individual traffic generators: industrial plants, shopping centers, universities, and hospitals.

2. Major land use projects: subdivisions, planned unit developments, multiple-use transportation development, urban revitalization projects and transportation centers.

3. Subarea studies: small community planning studies, urban goods movement, and terminal areas.

4. Corridor studies: performance of transit, rail, and highway systems in specific corridors.

5. Transportation plan: metropolitan-wide, multimodal plan for transportation service.

6. Special studies: elderly and handicapped, fare structures, marketing studies, and parking.

7. Programming documents: management plan, unified planning work program, and program for project implementation.

Clearly, the most appropriate and effective planning approach will vary in different cities in both methodology and time frame, depending on the nature of local problems, issues, and characteristics of the area. For this reason, the programming documents mentioned previously are extremely important for managing the planning process and determining the appropriate technical level of effort. Factors such as anticipated population and economic growth rate, existing and anticipated transportation problems and system performance, consideration of environmental and energy concerns, available financial and technical resources, prevailing political and public attitudes, and current status of planning and plans, must be considered for determining the amount of effort that is needed (8). At a minimum, federal regulations require that the following technical activities be included in the transportation planning process in accordance with the size of an area and the complexity of its transportation problems (28):

1. Analysis of existing conditions of travel, transportation facilities, and systems management.
2. Evaluation of alternative short-range transportation improvements.
3. Projection of economic, demographic, and land use activities, and transportation demands based on these activities.
4. Examination of the distribution of costs and impacts of transportation plans and programs.
5. Analysis of area wide new transportation investment alternatives.
6. Refinement of the transportation plan by corridor.
7. Monitoring of urban development and transportation indicators, and regularly reappraising the plan.
8. Development of a Transportation Improvement Program (TIP), a document which lists those projects that are to be implemented in a metropolitan area.
9. Analysis of goods and services movement problem areas.

This list of requirements implies that the planning process should integrate long-range and short-range planning activities into one comprehensive approach. One of the ways integration of these two approaches can be accomplished is by making the long-range plan more sensitive to the actions that are being implemented in the short term. An intergral part of this long-range and short-range balance is the use of corridor or subarea studies which can be used to analyze impacts and tradeoffs among proposed solutions, while specifically taking into account their short-term versus long-term consequences. The corridor study thus becomes a major methodological approach for short-range planning.

6.1.8 Summary

The transportation system is an integral part of any metropolitan area. It provides the major means of movement for persons and goods while also providing the necessary framework for expansion of the city. Urban transportation planning is a comprehensive and continuing process which relates transportation investment decisions to community goals and objectives. Because of the rapid change in problem definition, the role of the transportation planner has changed dramatically during the past 10 years. The planner must interact with those who design the facilities and implement the operational strategies so that technically feasible plans result from the planning process. Given the controversial nature of many transportation projects (especially those which constrain the use of the automobile), the planner and designer must also be sensitive to the political impact of the project. Who is likely to be adversely affected by the project? Who is likely to gain? What are the likely reactions of key elected officials? The integration of project-level concerns with a systemic perspective should also provide a forum for input from citizens. In general then, urban transportation planning has evolved into a complex technical and political process, but one which responds to the needs and desires of a metropolitan area.

6.2 SHORT-RANGE TRANSPORTATION PLANNING

One of the most significant changes in the field of transportation has been the pronounced shift toward planning that is service oriented (rather than facility oriented), that involves relatively inexpensive actions, and that seeks the most efficient use of existing facilities. In essence, the focus of many transportation planning efforts is now on managing and maintaining the existing system. One consequence of this type of planning is that it requires the participation of transportation agencies that never previously thought of themselves as being related to transportation planning because of the previous long-range focus of such efforts. This group especially includes operations-oriented agencies such as local traffic and public works departments, transit operators, port authorities, and so forth (9). Thus, not only does the emphasis on short-range planning and the resulting new types of solutions cause problems of methodology, but it also creates a need for greater coordination and cooperation among the many agencies that now have a significant role to play in the transportation planning process.

6.2.1 Short-Range Transportation Planning Process

One of the interesting characteristics of the short-range planning process as it has been evolving is the introduction of technical simplification and institutional flexibility. Each agency has its own planning approach and preferred solutions, which many times hinders attempts to develop a short-range plan that truly reflects the potential tradeoffs between highway and transit projects. Because the range of problems that short-range actions are supposed to solve is so broad, tradeoffs will be implicit in any strategy. There will be tradeoffs among different types of impacts, between users and nonusers, and among geographic areas or groups of persons affected. A regional approach to short-range planning based on local agency programs is an important component of the regional planning process because it is only through coordinated efforts that effective transportation strategies (those having a significant impact on regional travel) can be developed. In general, a short-range planning process consists of the following elements: (1) The collection of performance data (system monitoring); (2) identification of system deficiencies; (3) formulation of process goals and objectives; (4) identification of potential strategies; (5) development of performance criteria; (6) evaluation of strategies; and (7) ranking of strategies using a cost effectiveness approach. The end product of this process is a list of recommended projects or programs.

In 1975, the United States Department of Transportation (DOT) issued planning regulations which elevated short-range planning to equal partnership with the long-range planning process (26). The transportation plan for each metropolitan area had to include a transportation system management element which was to "provide for the short-range transportation needs of the urbanized area by making efficient use of existing transportation resources and providing for the movement of people and goods in an efficient manner. . . . " Specifically, the TSM elements were to identify traffic engineering, public transportation, regulatory, pricing, management, and operational-type improvements to the transportation system. Subsequent federal regulations removed the term "TSM" from the short-range element of the plan, but reaffirmed the policy goals that it represented. The concept of TSM was now to be incorporated into both the long-range and short-range elements of the transportation plan.

The types of transportation actions that are included under the TSM rubric are shown in Table 6-3. Several characteristics of these actions merit special attention. First, any action by itself is not likely to solve a major transportation problem in a metropolitan area. The planner should thus seriously consider what actions in combination could have a significant impact on the performance of the transportation system (see Fig. 6-3). Second, in some cases, this "packaging" of TSM actions requires the participation of planners from different agencies. For example, the implementation of an exclusive bus lane on a radial freeway with preferential access given at the on- and off-ramps would require coordinated planning efforts between the transit operations manager and the highway engineer, although in all likelihood, many more people would also be involved. Third, TSM actions span a wide range of administrative complexity, including (10):

1. *Routine Internal Administrative or Operational Actions.* These are actions falling within the scope of authority of the traffic engineer or the transit operator, with known consequences, which can be implemented immediately at little or no cost.

2. *Management or Jurisdictional-Level Actions.* These actions are within the area of responsibility of the traffic engineer or the transit operator, but require management or jurisdictional- level budget approval and some degree of project analysis and justification.

3. *Local Multi-Modal Actions.* Included are actions within a single jurisdiction, but which must be coordinated among the traffic engineer, transit operator, and others; require budget approval, and project analysis and justification.

TABLE 6-3 Examples of TSM Actions

Improved Vehicular Flow
   Improvements in signalized intersections
   Freeway ramp metering
   One-way streets
   Removal of on-street parking
   Reversible lanes
   Traffic channelization
   Off-street loading
   Transit stop relocation
Preferential Treatment of High-Occupancy Vehicles
   Freeway bus and carpool lanes and access ramps
   Bus and carpool lanes on city streets and urban arterials
   Bus preemption of traffic signals
   Toll policies
Reduced Peak-Period Travel
   Work rescheduling
   Congestion pricing
   Peak-period truck restrictions
Parking Management
   Parking regulations
   Park-and-ride facilities
Promotion of High-Occupancy and Nonvehicular Travel Modes
   Ridesharing
   Human-powered travel modes
   Auto-restricted zones
Transit and Paratransit Service Improvements
   Transit marketing
   Security measures
   Transit shelters
   Transit terminals
   Transit fare policies and fare collection techniques
   Extension of transit with paratransit services
   Integration of transportation services
Transit Management Efficiency Measures
   Route evaluation
   Vehicle communication and monitoring techniques
   Maintenance policies
   Evaluation of system performance

4. *Interjurisdictional Actions.* Actions affecting one mode but are regional or interjurisdictional in nature, require coordinated budgeting, and require areawide analysis and justification.

5. *Regional Multi-Modal Actions.* These require regional coordination among jurisdictions and modes, areawide project analysis and justification, and coordinated budgeting.

Basic package	Supplementary package							
	Work-hour changes	Pricing techniques	Restricting access	Changing land uses	Prearranged ride sharing	Communications substitutes	Traffic engineering	Transit treatments
Work-hour changes	╳	+	0	0	−	+	−	+
Pricing techniques	+	╳	0	+	−	0	−	+
Restricting access	0	0	╳	+	−	0	+	+
Changing land uses	0	+	+	╳	0	+	−	−
Prearranged ride sharing	−	0	0	0	╳	0	−	−
Communications substitutes	0	+	0	+	−	╳	−	−
Traffic engineering	+	0	−	+	−	0	╳	−
Transit treatments	+	+	+	0	−	0	−	╳

+ Supportive   0 Neutral   − Conflicting

Fig. 6-3. Compatibility of TSM actions (22)

The types of transportation projects that are considered in short-range planning thus range from those that can be handled independently by a traffic engineer or transit operator to those which require higher levels of coordination.

A regional TSM process, as can be seen, requires a great deal of institutional flexibility and cooperation. One way of avoiding many of the problems that are found in the regional approach is to bring the scale of analysis down to the subregional level. In this way, different agency personnel can work together in solving problems that are better defined and are limited in scope. In addition, citizen involvement is often easier to obtain, and more meaningful at this stage. One such approach is based on the major corridors of travel in a metropolitan area.

6.2.2 Corridor Studies

Traditional techniques in urban transportation planning based on large-scale modeling are expensive and require large amounts of time to get final results. Typically, their data requirements are so large, they often severely limit the number of alternative proposals that can be considered. To overcome these problems, planners have adopted a planning approach called sketch planning which reduces the scale of analysis, and permits the use of simpler analysis tools. This analysis, which is usually conducted at the corridor level, includes the following steps: (1) Identify corridors; (2) establish priorities for selecting corridors to be examined; (3) establish the over-all policy direction for the corridor study; (4) use socioeconomic and travel trend information to identify existing or potential problem areas; (5) analyze potential strategies; and (6) recommend actions that can be programmed for implementation. Each of these steps is outlined below.

Corridor identification   The first step in a regional corridor planning program is to divide the region into travel corridors according to the uniformity of land use and dominant travel desires. Although most corridors would most likely be oriented to the center city, there could be cases where routes of major transportation systems, either existing or proposed, lie between outlying activity centers. In general, the following factors are used for identifying corridors in a metropolitan area (24):

1. Existence of perceived problem(s).
2. Barriers, e.g., rivers, rail lines, and airports.
3. Existing transportation facilities.
4. Concentration of economic activities.
5. Concentration of population.
6. Jurisdictional boundaries.
7. Availability of data.

Because some estimate of travel demand in the corridor is usually needed for the analysis, some scheme must be developed for dividing the corridor into uniform analysis units. For most urban areas, a set of analysis units called traffic analysis zones will have already been developed in previous studies and can thus be used (see Fig. 6-4).

Establish corridor selection criteria   Several factors should be considered in selecting the initial corridor to be analyzed, including congestion, safety, the ratio of traffic volume to roadway capacity (V/C), transit service, handicapped and elderly needs, and social, environmental, and economic impacts. Usually though, one or two factors such as congestion, cost, or environmental impact are used to select the corridor, with

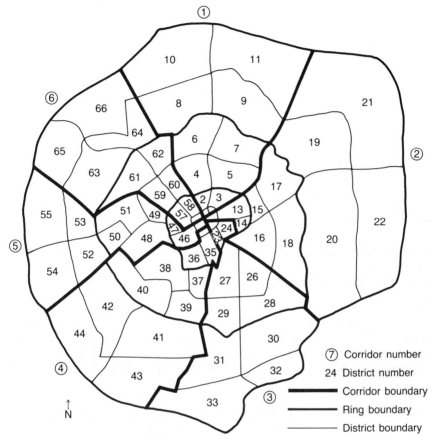

Fig. 6-4. Analysis zones in urban area (30)

the other factors being considered in greater detail during the analysis itself. It is important that a corridor public hearing be held to determine those issues perceived as most important by the public.

Policy direction   Each corridor study should articulate the policies that are directing the planning tasks. These policies should be compatible with and expand upon those in the regional transportation plan and other regional planning documents. In the context of short-range planning, these policies should concentrate on the consideration of low-cost strategies to increase the efficiency and person-carrying capacity of the existing corridor transportation system. Examples of such policy statements include (19):

> Stage short-range transportation improvements to facilitate transition to longer range improvements.

Improve the overall operation of the system within the corridor by increasing the accessibility to the system, by reducing the travel time differential between auto and transit trips, and by providing more frequent and reliable service.

Maximize the person-carrying capacity of the roadway system through the development of high occupancy vehicle projects. These HOV projects should be initially designed to include carpools, vanpools, and buses.

These policies should be formulated through a process in which agencies and other interested parties such as elected officials and representatives of the public participate. Every effort should be made to assure that the set of policies are internally consistent, i.e., that the likely actions resulting from one policy are compatible with the actions resulting from another.

Problem identification   Socioeconomic and travel trend information is used to point out the basic relationships and conditions within the corridor that must be considered in the analysis. The socioeconomic data, which include population, employment, and housing unit trends and forecasts, as well as a variety of population and land use characteristics, are collected based on traffic analysis zones or census tracts. The travel trend information describes past trends and future projections for travel demand, travel patterns, and trip types. The major types of information from both categories include those listed in Table 6-4.

TABLE 6-4 Types of Data Collected for Problem Identification

| Socioeconomic Data (1) | Travel Data | |
	Auto (2)	Transit (3)
Population	volumes	passengers
Employment	accidents	pass/mile
Housing units	V/C	pass/hour
Mean income	speed and travel time	% transfers
Auto availability	energy consumption	average fare
Minority and elderly	air pollutant emissions	revenue/mile
concentrations	noise levels	revenue/hour
Major activity centers		net cost/pass
Residential densities		% ridership growth
Land use types		speed and travel time
Special land/water areas		energy consumption
		air pollutant emissions
		route location

There are several schemes that can be used to identify problem areas in the corridor. For example, specific segments of the highway could be ranked by number of accidents, V/C ratios, air pollutant emissions, and speed. Transit routes could be evaluated by comparing their performance along several service dimensions, i.e., those routes which fall below or above a certain level of performance (a standard) are candidates for analysis (see Fig. 6-5). Even though data would be

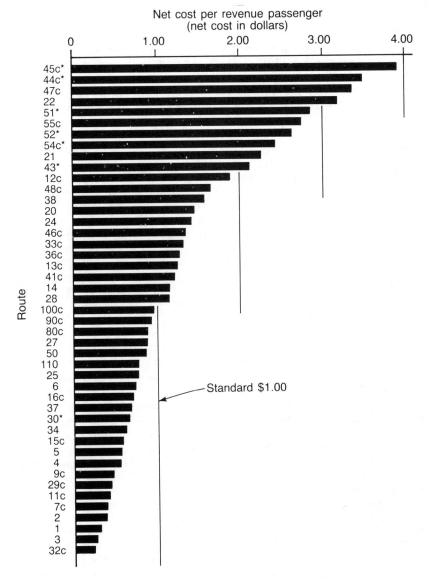

Fig. 6-5. Performance evaluation of transit routes

collected by many different agencies, every effort should be made to include all interested groups in the problem identification task and subsequent analysis activities.

Analyze strategies   The techniques chosen to analyze the different TSM strategies depend on where in the planning process the analysis is occurring. Early in the process, sketch planning models are used to analyze general transportation strategies and to help in identifying which corridors would receive further attention. More complex simulation along with demand and network assignment models can be used in the detailed evaluation procedures. Some of these models, however, require large amounts of input data and are applicable only for a specific range of network size.

The basis for evaluating any transportation action is the set of criteria or performance measures which are used to determine if the action has indeed been successful. The performance measures must (10):

- Be defined as to target.
- Be responsive to the incidence and magnitude of impact.
- Be characterized by geographic area of application and influence—which may differ.
- Be oriented to specific time periods.
- Be formulated at a proper level of detail for type of analysis being formed.
- Be directly or indirectly related to TSM objectives and priorities.

Examples of such performance measures include: (1) Passenger per vehicle-mile; (2) passengers per vehicle-hour; (3) volume to capacity ratios; and (4) accidents per million vehicle miles.

Even though most measures are focused on the direct impacts of service improvements, careful attention must also be given to secondary impacts such as changes in land use and the impact on economic activity. The relationship of project impact to long-term goals and objectives should also be explicitly evaluated.

The number of performance measures used in the analysis depends on the level of sophistication of the analysis and the characteristics of service being analyzed. Evaluation of system performance on a regional basis would most likely use a small number of criteria, e.g., vehicle-miles or vehicle-hours of travel. Assessing the performance of a transit system, however, would require a relatively large number of performance measures.

TSM action recommendation   Once all of the TSM actions under consideration have been evaluated, the planner must attempt to identify the relative merits of each action or package of actions. The evaluation of most candidate actions usually results in the same output, e.g., volume, vehicle- and passenger-miles of travel, speed, etc.; therefore comparison among several alternatives can be made along similar dimensions. However, ranking the alternatives in terms of preference is a difficult task. One alternative does not usually "dominate" all others, i.e., trade-offs between important impacts must be made; the preference for selected alternatives varies dramatically between different agencies, among elected officials, and through all levels of government; and there are also many nonquantifiable factors such as political commitments, project interdependence, project readiness, and political feasibility that heavily influence the scheduling of project implementation. This topic will be covered in more detail in the sections of this chapter titled Programming and Project Development.

6.3 LONG-RANGE TRANSPORTATION PLANNING

Long-range planning has long been the cornerstone of transportation planning in metropolitan areas. The long lead time necessary to plan and construct major transportation facilities requires planners to look ahead and anticipate future problems so that the transportation infrastructure is in place to alleviate these problems when they occur. Furthermore, the planner must also make sure that projects proposed by different planning agencies are compatible with each other, with other components in the existing transportation system, and with community goals and objectives. A long-range transportation plan, which is essentially a statement of future intent, is designed to serve this purpose. Due to changes in policy direction, technology, financial constraints, land use patterns and other factors affecting transportation, long-range plans should be continually monitored and updated so that they can effectively serve as a guide to near-term investments.

Many of the transportation policy trends that have significantly influenced short-range planning have also had a major impact on long-range planning. In any corridor, for example, where major urban transportation investments are contemplated, an analysis of alternatives must be made in which costs and benefits of each alternative are considered. Short-range actions, such as bus and carpool lanes, ramp metering, and transit route modifications, should be included in this analysis. The implementation of fixed guideway systems should also be done incrementally, i.e., corridors which cannot justify major investment in the near term should be provided with levels and types of service appropriate to their needs, with the level of service being progressively upgraded as demand develops. Because major transportation projects usually have a significant impact on the surrounding area, there should also be full opportunity for the involvement in the process of public officials, agency representatives, and citizen groups.

Although the problem-solving approaches for both the long- and short-range planning processes, i.e., problem identification, generation and evaluation of alternatives, and alternatives selection, are similar, the long-range planning process depends on forecasting future transport demand and thus tends to be more complex. This demand forecast is based on an analysis and extrapolation of current travel, and an investigation of its relationship to the patterns of population, employment, and socioeconomic activity (21). The accuracy of these forecasts, however, depends to a large extent on the models and methodologies used to analyze travel demand behavior. There are six major steps in this analysis: (1) Inventory; (2) land-use forecast; (3) trip generation; (4) trip distribution; (5) modal split; and (6) traffic assignment. These six steps constitute what is conventionally known as the transportation planning process (5). Each of these will be briefly examined.

6.3.1 Inventory

The inventory comprises the development of a data base for evaluating existing travel demand and future system requirements. This task is often the most time consuming, expensive, and difficult element of the long-range planning process. In some urban transportation planning studies, for example, up to one-half of the budget is spent on data collection and the development of parameters for various models (15).

There are three major types of data that must be included in a good data base: (1) Inventories of travel; (2) inventories of land use; and (3) data on the transportation system. Because the amount of information gathered in these tasks is so large, conventional transportation studies utilize some sort of spatial aggregation over the metropolitan area. This aggregation usually takes the form of geographical units, i.e., sectors, zones, blocks, in which boundaries are chosen to maintain as much zonal homogeneity as possible in the population's socioeconomic characteristics (see Fig. 6-4). This is necessary for those modeling cases where zonal means are employed as representative of the entire zonal population. (Note: A new approach to demand modeling—individual choice models—does not utilize zonal averages, although the type of information needed is similar to the aggregate approach. Individual choice models will be reviewed in a following section.)

In addition to a zonal system for the analysis area, the transportation network must be coded as a series of links, each of which begins and ends at nodes. Separate networks are coded for highway, bus, rapid rail transit, and commuter rail. Because the coded network is supposed to be a realistic simulation of the real network, the network links are given spatial and locational properties such as length, direction, and capacity. The network coding also includes "load nodes" which are the origins and termini of all trips in the network (see Fig. 6-6). These nodes are usually located in the centroid of population for a specific zone.

There are many types of techniques for obtaining the information needed to complete an inventory. A land use survey based on local zoning maps and field inspections is used to identify types and intensities of land uses in the study area and relating them to trip-generating or trip-attracting characteristics. Surveys are also used to obtain information on the types of trips made in an urban area and the socioeco-

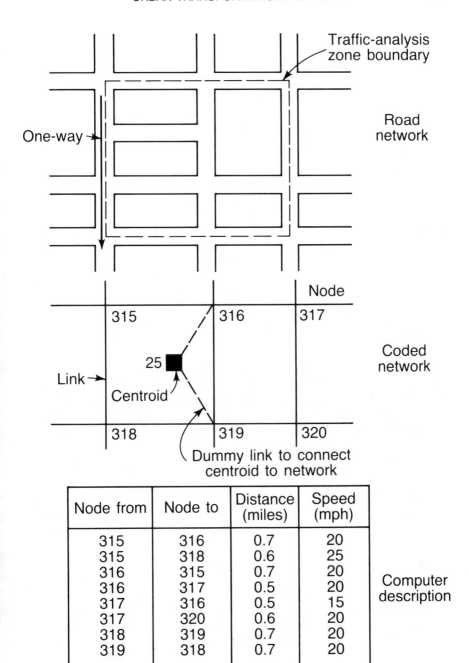

Fig. 6-6. Network coding

nomic characteristics of the travelers. Alternative methods for collecting this information include:

    1. Home interview survey. Teams of trained interviewers interview household members using predesigned survey forms and questioning procedures. Information is collected on the number and type of trips made by each member as well as the socioeconomic characteristics of the household. Households should be selected in such a manner as to be representative of the characteristics of the area.

    2. Roadside and transit ridership survey. Motorists are stopped at interview stations (which are located at strategic points on the survey boundary line) and questioned as to their origin, destination, and trip purpose. Similarly survey teams ride bus routes or question commuters at transit stations to obtain the same type of information.

    3. Mail surveys. Questionnaires are mailed to auto drivers randomly identified through the vehicle registry listings or, if a specific corridor is the subject of analysis, license plates are noted by data collectors and forms are sent to the drivers, again after they have been identified through the vehicle registry information.

    4. Telephone survey. This is similar to the home interview method in terms of information received, only it is done through telephone contact.

    Because the amount of effort needed to survey every traveler and household in a metropolitan area is prohibitively large, only a fraction of the total number is used. For example, the sample size for home interviews is typically 1% in larger cities and can range as high as 10% in smaller urban areas. The value, of course, of the information collected in this fashion depends upon the procedures used for selecting the sample (29).

    The 1980 census has provided the Urban Transportation Planning Package (UTPP), which provides detailed information on origin, destination, and mode for work trips. This is a significant improvement over scanty previous census travel information, and is being used successfully to validate travel data and so to eliminate the need for the costly survey process.

6.3.2 Land Use Forecast

    The effectiveness of the transportation system is significantly influenced by the land use patterns in a metropolitan area. Thus, land use forecasts are important inputs to the transportation modeling process. Indeed, the accuracy of travel forecasting is only as great as the accuracy of the input data from the land use forecast.

    Specific outputs of land use forecasting include items such as population or households, stratified by income or other measures, and employment stratified by an industrial class. Forecasts are made for analysis zones which range in size from that of a traffic analysis zone to that somewhat larger than a census tract (12). This information is then used to estimate by land-use type the number of trips generated throughout the urban area (see Fig. 6-7). These forecasts should then be subjected to validity checks to assure that they realistically reflect the characteristics of the areas.

6.3.3 Trip Generation

Trip generation provides the linkage between land use and travel patterns. Land use is described in terms of intensity (e.g., square feet of retail space), character of the land use activities, and location within an urban area. Existing land use and travel are linked utilizing techniques such as cross classification, trip rates, or regression analysis (27). These relationships are then applied to estimate future travel based on the forecasted change in land use (this assumes that the relationship between land use and travel is constant over time).

While there are several methods for specifying trip generation models, cross-classification analysis has become most widely accepted

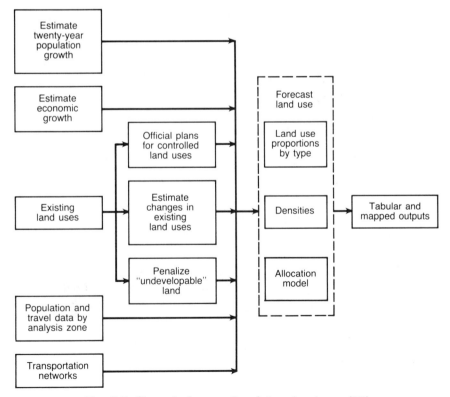

Fig. 6-7. Steps in forecasting future land use (19)

and will be the only one considered in this section. The forecasting of trips produced by zone is based on relating trip-making to various household characteristics such as income, auto availability, or household size. Additionally, total trip productions are categorized by trip purpose. For this task, three categories of trip purpose are usually used: home-based work (HBW), home-based other (HBO), and nonhome-based (NHB). Based on this information, curves which relate expected split of trips to socioeconomic characteristics can be formulated by trip purpose [see Fig. 6-8 (a and b)]. In order to estimate the

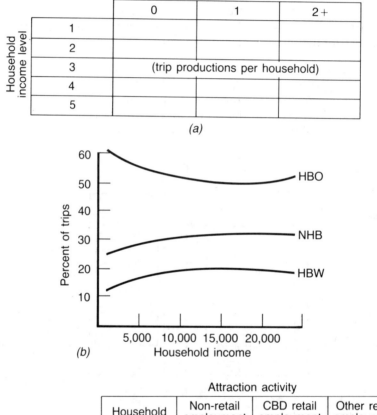

Fig. 6-8. Cross-classification analysis for trip distribution

number of trips attracted to certain activities, a similar analysis procedure is undertaken which relates trip ends by purpose to the amount and character of the activities [see Fig. 8 (c)]. After calculating the total number of trips produced and attracted in an area, the planner must check to see that both totals are the same. In most cases, they will not be in balance; therefore the trip attractions by zone are multiplied by the ratio of total productions to total attractions so that the totals will be equal. The data developed are used in the next phase of travel demand forecasting.

6.3.4 Trip Distribution

Trip distribution is the process of distributing the trips generated in each zone to all the possible destination zones available. As in trip generation, there are several types of models for accomplishing this: (1) Growth factor models; (2) intervening-opportunity models; and (3) gravity models. The most widely used model—the gravity model—will be reviewed in this subsection.

In the gravity model, the number of trips between two zones is directly proportional to the product of the number of trips produced in one zone and attracted in the other, and inversely proportional to the degree of separation between the two zones represented as a function of travel time. Put in mathematical terms, the model formula is

$$T_{ij} = \frac{P_i A_j F(t)_{ij}}{\displaystyle\sum_{j=1}^{n} A_j F(t)_{ij}} \tag{6.1}$$

in which T_{ij} = number of trips produced in zone i and attracted to zone j; P_i = number of trips produced in zone i; A_j = number of trips attracted to zone j; $F(t)_{ij}$ = friction factor (usually travel time raised to some power between zones i and j); and n = number of zones in study area.

Simply stated, this equation says that areas with large amounts of activity, or separated by short distances, or both, will tend to exchange more trips than areas with small amounts of activity, or separated by long distances, or both.

Before a trip distribution model can be used in the planning process, its results must be compared with travel information obtained from surveys to determine model reliability. If this comparison shows statistically significant differences, adjustments must be made to the model.

6.3.5 Modal Split

Modal split analysis is the process of assigning person-trips to available modes of transportation. There are three major factors that need to be considered in this analysis: (1) Characteristics of the traveler; (2) characteristics of the trip; and (3) characteristics of the transportation system. Although there are many characteristics that can be considered in this analysis, those most commonly used are income and auto availability for the tripmaker, trip purpose for trip characteristics, and travel time and cost for characteristics of the transportation system.

The types of techniques that have been used in the development of mode-split models include regression analysis, diversion curves, and cross-classification. Recent research, however, has examined a different modeling approach called individual choice models which is based on the following relationship: "The probability that an individual will choose a particular alternative is a function of the characteristics of the individual and of the over-all desirability of the chosen alternative relative to all other alternatives" (2). These models have certain properties which make them desirable for use in the urban transportation planning process. First, the amount of data needed to calibrate individual choice models is considerably less than that for aggregate models (which need large numbers or observations to obtain a stable value for zonal means). Second, individual choice models are less likely to be biased by correlations among aggregate units and can themselves be used at any level of aggregation. Third, policy sensitive variables are easily included in the modeling framework. Finally, calibrated individual choice models may be transferable to other urban areas.

Individual choice models use

$$P_i = \frac{e^{U_i}}{\sum\limits_{j=1}^{n} e^{U_j}}$$

(6.2)

in which P_i = the probability of choosing alternative i; U_i = the linear utility expression for alternative i; and n = the set of feasible modes.

The utility expressions are assumed to be a linear combination of variables that reflect socioeconomic characteristics (household size, income, and automobile ownership), mode-specific variables (automobile bias and availability of transit), and generalized travel cost (money and time). For example, a typical expression for a utility function would be

$$U_m = C_m + C_1 t_m + C_2 \frac{X_m}{d} + C_3 \frac{C_m}{y}$$

(6.3)

in which C_m = mode-specific parameter; $C_{1,2,3,}$ = mode-independent parameters; t_m = in-vehicle time; X_m = out-of-vehicle time; d = distance; C = out-of-pocket cost; y = income; and m = auto, transit.

Individual choice models such as Eq. 6.2 have become an important transportation planning tool, and will most likely become more important in the future. Not only does the smaller expense associated with these techniques make them more attractive, but their formulation is based on behavioral and economic theory which provides a firm foundation for analysis.

6.3.6 Traffic Assignment

Traffic assignment constitutes assigning the distributed volumes of trips, by mode, to individual network links. The basis for this assignment procedure is that choice of route is basically a decision to minimize total travel time through a transportation network. The several techniques that can be used in the assignment procedure—minimum path, minimum path with capacity restraint, and multiroute probabilistic assignment—all have this basis for their operation. The minimum path algorithm determines a minimum route from any node by considering successive closest nodes and building up a "tree" which represents the minimum path from that node to all other nodes (23). The capacity restraint algorithm considers the relationship between speed and volume in the assignment procedure, i.e., as volume increases, speed decreases. Thus, as links in the network become congested, the time needed to travel that link increases, which could potentially make another route the minimum path, thus diverting traffic. The multiroute probabilistic assignment procedure recognizes that several routes between two nodes might have equal impedances and should therefore receive equal use.

Similar procedures are used to assign passengers to a transit network. The required input data include: (1) Vehicle headways; (2) vehicle capacities; (3) travel speed; and (4) estimates of walk and wait time. The minimum path through the network is approximated by the "minimum weighted time path" where different weights are given to categories of time (walking, waiting, and riding).

6.4 TRANSPORTATION SYSTEMS EVALUATION

The evaluation process for transportation plans is a process for judging the worth of alternative investment, policies, or courses of action in a manner responsive to public needs and welfare (20). Central to this evaluation process is the identification and measurement of impacts due to changes in the transportation system. As has been mentioned previously, however, the measurement of impacts has long created a problem in those cases where the impacts were nonquantifiable. The basis for this problem is the ability or inability of measurement techniques to deal with the concepts of efficiency and effectiveness. Traditional evaluation techniques such as net present worth, benefit and cost ratios, and rate of return are more concerned with measuring the efficiency of alternatives, i.e., obtaining a good monetary return for the investment. Such an analysis methodology requires that the unit of measurement for costs and benefits be the same, in this case monetary units. Effectiveness, on the other hand, relates the performance of each alternative to the goals and objectives of the study, i.e., the alternative which most helps achieve goal attainment is the most effective one. The cost-effectiveness framework for evaluating transportation alternatives thus relies on the structuring of information to articulate the relationships between the alternatives and the trade-offs or compromises that must be made to choose one alternative over the others (22).

The cost-effectiveness evaluation framework includes as much information as is necessary to reach an informed decision. In this regard, careful attention must be given to the selection of factors that will be considered in alternatives selection, because the quality of the final decisions depends on the comprehensiveness and comprehension of this information. Presenting too much information is liable to burden the decision-makers with too many facts and figures, while not enough information runs the risk of missing important factors that could become extremely controversial during project implementation (32). In general, the decision-maker is most interested in the consequences of implementing (or not implementing) a particular alternative, because this is where political considerations are most important (see Table 6-5).

As mentioned previously, one manner of making the evaluation process more meaningful to public officials and citizen representatives is to reduce the scale of analysis. A system-wide evaluation framework can thus consist of prioritizing subareas within a region for investment in transportation improvements. One of the most important aspects of this planning effort is data management, i.e., the structuring of available data so that it can be readily accessed throughout the process. The planner usually finds all too soon that the major stumbling block in most studies is the poor quality or lack of data. In a regional study based on subarea analyses, the effective management of the data resources becomes even more critical.

Costs of alternative plans are also an important consideration in an evaluation framework, although dollar costs associated with alternative plans do not always give a good indication of the true social costs of the resource expenditures. There are several types of cost models that are used to estimate the monetary costs of implementation. For example, one could categorize costs associated with planning, designing, constructing, and operating a facility or system. A more frequently used framework separates costs according to the types of components that are purchased (20):

Centralized Costs	User Costs
1. Right-of-way	1. Vehicle depreciation
2. Traveled-way structural	2. Fuel and oil
3. Terminal facility construction	3. Tires
4. Initial mobile components	4. General maintenance
5. Materials and equipment for operation and maintenance	5. Insurance fees
6. Labor for operations	6. Net accident
7. Management and other	7. Time
	8. Other

TABLE 6-5 Consequences of Transportation Actions

Consequences of Inputs
   Opportunities lost due to resource commitments
   Changes in employment
   Changes in real income
   Scarcities of material resources
   Promotion of previously unused resources
   Social disruption due to purchase of right-of-way
   Modifications of human activity patterns and resource allocations due to the
      taking of land pacels
   Others
Consequences of Performance Outputs
   Changes in community growth patterns
   Changes in market areas and competitive positions of various activities
   Social unification due to increased accessibility
   Expanded social, economic, and cultural realms of people due to increased
      accessibility
   Modifications of human activity patterns and resource allocations due to
      changes in accessibility
   Changes in the prices of public and private goods due to changes in
      accessibility
   Changes in employment patterns due to changes in accessibility
   Lives and resources saved or lost due to changes in transportation
      safety
   Others
Consequences of Concomitant Outputs
   Social and psychological effects of creation or destruction of physical barriers by
      transportation facilities
   Esthetic impacts of facilities
   Changes in crime rate created by transportation structures
   Physiological effects of air pollution due to transportation
   Psychological and physiological impacts of sound and light emitted by transpor-
      tation vehicles and facilities
   Effects of changes in the safety properties of the interface between transporta-
      tion facilities and their environments
   Modifications of human activity patterns and resource allocations because of
      changes in site characteristics due to concomitant outputs
   Others

The costing structure is not only of interest from the point of view of government fiscal policy, but also helps to identify the types of skills necessary to construct a project, and serves to identify the time sequencing of expenditures. The combination of this cost information with a description of the consequences of plan implementation can thus serve as a firm basis for the decision-making process.

6.5 PROGRAMMING

Rather than viewing the product of short- and long-range planning as the choice of a target system, transportation planning should identify the implications of near-term choices in terms of potential long-term impacts, and the future options left open or foreclosed. The best mechanism for shifting the focus of transportation planning toward concern for short-range decisions is the programming process. Programming has been defined as "the matching of available projects with available funds to accomplish the goals of a given period" (17). In the context of Sections 6.2 and 6.3, programming also involves the development of an implementation schedule that accounts for both short-range choices and longer range system options. Thus, while funding is the most important parameter, programming should consider several factors.

Federal planning regulations, which have placed great significance on program and budget review at the metropolitan level, reflect the failure of the comprehensive plans of the 1950s and 1960s to bridge the gap between long-range plans and short-range decisions. Specifically, these regulations require that each metropolitan area develop a programming document—the Transportation Improvement Program (TIP)—which specifies the projects that will be going from the transportation plan into preliminary engineering, design, right-of-way acquisition, and construction. More importantly, however, the projects programmed in the TIP must be drawn from the short-range element of the transportation plan, which is in turn based on the long-range plan, thus making explicit the link between planning and programming.

The programming document is a staged, multiyear program of transportation improvement projects, some of which are proposed for partial funding by federal and state sources, and some projects which are proposed for funding solely from local resources. Those highway, transit, and airport projects which are to receive highest implementation priority should be clearly indicated in the document. However, there are several points to keep in mind in understanding the complexities facing a programmer (17):

- The program is rarely new; it usually contains commitments from previous years and to other agencies or groups.
- The projects are in all stages of development from basic planning studies to final design. At any point and for any number of reasons, a project may be stopped temporarily and thrown off schedule.
- The funds available may be restricted to certain categories of use, although there may be some flexibility with regard to transferring funds between categories or reassigning projects to different categories.
- Priorities may be constantly changing because of changing philosophies, transportation needs, economic conditions, energy availability, political conditions, and other factors affecting individual or collective priorities.

The environment in which the programmer operates is constantly changing, so to produce an acceptable program of transportation improvements means that the programmer must be aware not only of the technical justification for a specific project, but also where that project is placed on the agenda of key officials.

A transportation program usually consists of several elements: (1) A description of the project; (2) delineation of agency responsibility; (3) an estimate of project cost by program year; (4) the identification of the funding source for these costs; and (5) often a sense of what priority is assigned to the project. Each of these elements is susceptible to the turbulent environment just described.

Project prioritization Assigning project priorities based on quantifiable variables can have an important influence on project selection. Such a scheme reduces the complexity inherent in selecting those projects to be implemented among the many projects that need to be considered. However, as mentioned previously, there are other nonquantifiable elements that influence a project's selection, including multiple and conflicting objectives, geographical constraints, special-purpose allocations, network and project interrelationships, and, perhaps most importantly, budget constraints. Thus, the role of project prioritization is unclear, although it could certainly contribute to decision-making if some of these elements are held constant, e.g., if projects within one funding program were compared separately from those in other programs. It is important to realize, however, that technical priorities can be outweighed by other factors in the process of project selection (see Table 6-6).

Early attempts at technical prioritizing focused on those variables that could be easily quantified, e.g., volume and capacity, vehicle miles traveled, accident reduction. Recent efforts, however, have attempted to identify and assess transportation improvement impacts affecting both transportation users and the community at large. One method, based on a linear programming analysis, provides an estimate of the staging of projects given yearly budget constraints (4). The three major areas of inputs in this method include:

1. Benefits and disbenefits. An estimate of the project impact on regional development, users, operators, social structure, environment, and right-of-way is the major element in this category. Typical variables include travel-time savings, operating cost reductions, noise reduction, and improved air quality.

2. Costs. Costs include expenditures for capital construction and maintenance.

3. Budget. The programmer must estimate available budgets for each planning year. More will be said about this process in Section 6.6.

Although most planners do not use the methods described previously, the general approach they represent does occur in all transpor-

TABLE 6-6 Factors Involved in Priority Ratings (26)

Quantifiable Factors
  Physical condition (deterioration): road surface, pavement structure, foundation, shoulders, drainage
  Geometrics: pavement width, shoulder width
  Alignment: horizontal, vertical
  Bridges: condition rating, operating rating
  Safety rating: accident totals or rates, or both
  Capacity rating: volume/capacity
  Benefit/cost rating
  Cost-effectiveness index
  Recreational use
  Social: families displaced
  Economic: businesses displaced, direct routings, jobs during construction, use of air rights
  Environmental: air, noise, and water pollution
Nonquantifiable Factors
  Social: neighborhood cohesion, minority-elderly-handicapped impacts, disruption, proximity
  Economic: build vs. no-build, economic base, mobility, accessibility, employment after construction
  Environmental: effect on natural resources, esthetics, water pollution, vibration, noise
  Land use impacts: future development, community standards
  Transportation need
  Uncertainty: public support, court cases
Interrelationships
  Impacts on connecting facilities
  Impacts on competing facilities
  Stage construction
  System continuity
  Agreements and commitments (other agency plans)

tation agencies. This approach, however, suffers from the same problem that previous efforts have often ignored, i.e., whereas quantifying variables such as travel time and cost savings is conceptually straightforward, the same is not true for social and economic impacts. In most cases, an index of some sort is put into the equation so that the outputs are at least minimally sensitive to such impacts. The budgeting process is often recognized as the key parameter, and other considerations are either ignored or minimally addressed. At the very least, a sensitivity analysis should be conducted to determine the degree of sensitivity of the output to different magnitudes of input parameters.

Another approach for ranking projects assigns points to projects along certain service dimensions. For example, a rating system could assign points to highway projects based on the current condition of road service, improvement to safety, socioenvironmental factors and energy savings. The problem with this approach is that the subjective assignment of points to projects is highly dependent upon the person responsible for the task. Because each individual is sensitive to different factors in the project selection, it is doubtful that a listing of projects using this method would yield consistent results if different evaluators were used. A standard system for evaluation must be defined.

One of the most important uncertainties in programming transportation improvements is the weight that political considerations have in the process. Because each metropolitan area has its own institutional structure and groups of political actors, it is difficult to generalize about the role that such considerations have in programming. Political considerations are not the only important concerns in this regard. Items such as commitments to other agencies, project interdependencies, and the position of a project in the implementation schedule become critical constraints in the programming process as well. This last factor, position in the schedule, becomes especially important when one considers that projects take several years to advance through planning, design, and construction. Given this time frame, it is difficult to alter programs when changes in officials and policies require their alteration.

Financial planning   One of the most important tasks of the programmer is estimating the level of funding that can be expected for transportation improvements during future years. This is not a particularly easy task because it requires a sense of the trends in priorities and funding on the part of Congress, state legislatures, city councils, and agency officials. In most cases transportation improvements can be funded from three general sources: (1) Federal aid; (2) state and local taxes; and (3) property owners. By far the most important source of funds is the federal government which, through allocated and discretionary funds, provides significant support for all modes of transportation. Planners, however, must estimate not only federal sources of revenue, but also local sources and user revenues. For example, transit officials must estimate not only the federal contribution to transit operations, but also revenues from fares and local subsidies.

6.6 PROJECT DEVELOPMENT

As the preceding sections have shown, urban transportation planning and programming are extremely complex processes. Not only are the analysis procedures different for various types of projects, but the amount of intergovernmental participation in the development of a project makes the planner both a liaison with other agencies as well as a technical analyst. One way of demonstrating the complexities of project planning is to follow the development of a transportation project from project initiation to construction.

Projects are identified from a variety of sources. Technical sources include such things as planning studies, special studies, information obtained from periodic review of facility performance, or observations made from maintenance or safety inspection staff. Projects identified through these means usually end up in a normal administrative procedure for handling them. Nontechnical sources of project initiation are relatively few in number—local public officials, citizen groups, and individual citizens—but they often demand immediate and serious response.

Once the project has been identified it is placed on the agenda of a transportation agency. The priority of the project depends upon several factors, including the backlog of projects in the agency, the need for fast turnaround to qualify for specific funding programs, the degree to which the project complements existing agency programs, and the individual or group of individuals who initiated the project. Assuming that the project warrants further investigation, preliminary planning procedures are begun.

6.6.1 Preliminary Planning

Preliminary planning consists of such items as determining end points of the route, approximate locations of critical intersections or terminals, the alternative types of projects that could solve the problem, and the level of effort that would be necessary for a detailed analysis. Information such as traffic and passenger counts, accident records, level of service, and approximate cost figures are collected and used in a brief description of the project. This initial planning effort amounts to nothing more than a feasibility study, i.e., does the project make sense? Can it be implemented? Several actions can then be taken depending on the standard operating procedures of the agency and the size of the project. If the project is large in a sense that it will require significant resources, or that it will have a major impact on the surrounding area, a public meeting might be held. In another case, a preliminary planning project report would be sent to a policy committee or any other overseeing body which would recommend further action. In most cases, however, the project is reviewed within the sponsoring agency and the decision is made there on whether further design efforts are desired.

6.6.2 Project Programming

The programming decision, i.e., when the project should be listed in the Transportation Improvement Program (TIP) occurs at different times in the project development process in different metropolitan areas. Programming a project in the TIP is dependent on the type of funding to be used on the project. Federally funded projects should be included in the TIP at all stages of the project for which program action is proposed. In some areas, if a project has been assigned a preliminary cost estimate and a tentative construction date, it is included in the TIP at this stage of development. The TIP may also reflect locally funded projects at the discretion of the agency which approves the TIP at the local level.

Engineering design is most often thought of as a routine process, consisting primarily of using standard methods to meet the needs of the specific problem. Although some design problems do fit into this category, most do not. Almost all design problems are subject to regulations and standards such as the allowable level of noise and air pollution, minimum design speeds and lane widths, and warrants for traffic control devices. A planner must therefore be conscious of the trade-offs involved in satisfying design objectives within the constraints imposed by available resources and regulations.

From initiation to construction, project development is a complex and demanding process. Not only are there a large number of agencies which can influence the way in which a project evolves, there are also several planning and design considerations which must be addressed as well.

6.7 CONCLUSIONS

The transportation planning process is currently in a period of transition. Fiscal constraints, a possible reorientation of federal transportation policies, and an increasing reliance on local commitment and decision-making are all likely to influence the future of transportation in urban areas. Even with these pressures, however, local governments will still need to examine options that will maintain or improve the existing operation of the transportation system. This need is based on the fact that the efficient operation of the transportation system is a necessary prerequisite for healthy economic development in the metropolitan area and for attaining social objectives related to the mobility of different groups.

The transportation planning process described in this chapter is particularly well suited to the demands of the 1980s. This process not only provides different scales of analysis, but also relates planning to the programming process. In the latter case, it seems likely that, with limited resources available for improvements to the transportation network, much of the interest of decision-makers will be focused on the programming and budgeting process. The type of planning process described here is also one sensitive to alternative viewpoints on problem definitions and solutions, and one which recognizes that valuable information can be obtained from individuals or groups not directly involved with the process.

6.8 REFERENCES

1. Altshuler, A., *The Urban Transportation System: Politics and Policy Innovation*, 1st ed., The Massachusetts Institute of Technology Press, Cambridge, Mass., 1979.

2. *Applications of New Travel Demand Forecasting Techniques to Transportation Planning*, Urban Planning Division, Washington, D.C., Mar., 1977.
3. Baerwald, J., ed., *Transportation and Traffic Engineering Handbook*, Institute of Transportation Engineers, 4th ed., Prentice-Hall, Inc., Englewood Cliffs, N.J., 1976.
4. Bellomo, S., Mehra, J., Stowers, J., Cohen, H., Petersilia, M., and Reno, A., "Evaluating Options in Statewide Transportation Planning/Programming," *National Cooperative Highway Research Program Report 179*, Transportation Research Board, Washington, D.C., 1977.
5. Creighton, R., *Urban Transportation Planning*, 1st ed., Univ. of Illinois Press, Urbana, Ill., 1970.
6. Davis, C.F., "A Framework for the Assessment of Progress in Achieving Air-Quality Goals," *Traffic Quarterly*, Vol. 33, No. 2, Apr., 1979, pp. 263–274.
7. "Energy Conservation Potential of Urban Mass Transit," *Conservation Paper 34*, Federal Energy Administration, Washington, D.C., 1976.
8. Fleet, C., Kane, A., and Schoener, G., "Achieving A Long-Range/Short-Range Planning Balance with an Appropriate Level of Effort," U.S. Department of Transportation, Washington, D.C., June, 1978.
9. Gakenheimer, R., and Meyer, M., "Urban Transportation Planning in Transition: The Sources and Prospects of Transportation System Management,: *Journal of the American Planning Association*, Vol. 45, No. 1, Jan., 1979, pp. 28–35.
10. "Handbook for Transportation System Management Planning," *Vol. 1*, North Central Texas Council of Governments, Dallas, Tex., March, 1978.
11. "Institutional Framework for Integrated Transportation Planning," Public Technology, Inc., Washington, D.C., 1978.
12. *An Introduction to Urban Development Models and Guidelines for Their Use in Urban Transportation Planning*, Office of Planning, Urban Planning Division, Washington, D.C., Oct., 1975.
13. Keefer, L., and Witheford, D., "Urban Travel Patterns for Hospitals, Universities, Office Buildings, and Capitols," *National Cooperative Highway Research Program Report 62*, Highway Research Board, Washington, D.C., 1969.
14. Manheim, M. L., Suhrbier, J., Bennett, E., Neumann, L., Colcord, F., and Reno, A., "Transportation Decision-Making: A Guide to Social and Environmental Considerations," *National Cooperative Highway Research Program Report 156*, Transportation Research Board, Washington, D.C., 1975.
15. Morlok, E., *Introduction to Transportation Engineering and Planning*, 1st ed., McGraw-Hill Publishing Co, Inc., New York, N.Y., 1978.
16. "Motor Vehicle Facts and Figures, 1978," Vehicle Manufacturer's Association, Detroit, Mich., 1978.
17. "Priority Programming and Project Selection," *National Cooperative Highway Research Program Synthesis of Highway Practice #48*, Transportation Research Board, Washington, D.C., 1978.
18. Remak, R., and Rosenbloom, S., "Implementing Packages of Congestion-Reducing Techniques," *National Cooperative Highway Research Program Report 205*, Transportation Research Board, Washington, D.C., June, 1979.
19. *Route 8 Transportation System Management Corridor Study*, Comprehensive Planning Organization, San Diego, Calif., 1978.
20. Stopher, P., and Meyburg, A., *Transportation Systems Evaluation*, 1st ed., D.C. Heath and Co., Lexington, Mass., 1976.
21. Stopher, P., and Meyburg, A., *Urban Transportation Modeling and Planning*, 1st ed., D.C. Heath and Co., Lexington, Mass., 1975.

22. Thomas, E., and Schofer, J., "Strategies for the Evaluation of Alternative Transportation Plans," *National Cooperative Highway Research Program Report No. 96*, Highway Research Board, Washington, D.C., 1970.
23. *Traffic Assignment*, Urban Planning Division, Office of Highway Planning, Washington, D.C., Aug., 1973.
24. *Transit Corridor Analysis, A Manual Sketch Planning Technique*, Urban Mass Transportation Administration, U.S. Department of Transportation, Washington, D.C., May, 1976.
25. *Transit Fact Book*, 1976–77 ed., American Public Transit Assoc., Washington, D.C., 1977.
26. "Transportation Improvement Program," *Federal Register*, U.S. Department of Transportation, Washington, D.C., Sept. 17, 1975, pp. 42976–42984.
27. *Trip Generation Analysis*, Urban Planning Division, Washington, D.C., Aug., 1975.
28. United States Code, Title 23: Highways, U.S. Congress, by the Committee on Public Works and Transportation, U.S. House of Representatives, *Print 95-2*, March, 1977.
29. "Urban Origin-Destination Surveys," Highway Planning Program Manual, *Transmittal 143*, Federal Highway Administration, Vol. 20, Appendix 34, U.S. Department of Transportation, Washington, D.C., 1973.
30. "Urban Transportation and Energy," by the Congressional Budget Office, Committee on Environment and Public Works, U.S. Senate, 95th Congress, 1st session, *Serial No. 95-8*, Sept., 1977.
31. U.S. Department of Transportation, "Urban Transportation Planning," *Federal Register*, Aug. 6, 1981, pp. 40170–40179.
32. Wilson, D., and Schofer, J., "Decision-Maker-Defined Cost-Effectiveness Framework for Highway Programming," *Transportation Research Record 677*, Transportation Research Board, Washington, D.C., 1978.

CHAPTER 7

INTERCITY HIGHWAY PLANNING[a]

7.1 INTRODUCTION

Intercity highway planning may be defined as the development of a highway system capable of moving people and goods between cities safely, efficiently, and economically. Since highways are but one of several modes available for the movement of people and goods, it follows that intercity highway planning should be one element of the intercity transportation planning process. Intercity transportation includes the highway, air, rail, waterway and pipeline modes.

A recent report by the National Cooperative Highway Research Program (NCHRP) indicates that multimodal, intercity transportation planning is not, however, the general method of approach. The report indicates that most states develop plans one mode at a time, and combine the single-mode plans in a statewide transportation plan. Irrespective of the procedures used to develop the statewide transportation plan, the interrelationship and impact of one mode on other modes is of significant importance. A well-defined, systematic approach is required to identify and properly consider these intermodal relationships and impacts.

The first step in developing a systematic approach should be to identify significant issues, and to articulate the goals and objectives of the planning effort. Analytical work should then be structured to focus on these issues and to develop the information required to make informed decisions. All work should be coordinated with involved agencies at the state, regional and local levels, including public utility or service commissions and private operators.

Issues confronting intercity highway planners are both broad in scope and complex. For example, intercity bus transportation poses difficult problems: revenues that are just keeping pace with rising operating costs, inadequate service to smaller communities, and threatened termination of service on low-patronage lines. There is also the issue of energy availability and cost which will influence the nation's intercity passenger system. Increases in modal operating efficiencies will have an impact on the market share captured by the individual modes. In addition, the United States freight system has been dominated by economic regulations for more than 50 years. The process is complicated and has resulted in trucks and waterways eroding rail's market base. Further erosion of the rail system will place a greater stress on the

---

[a]Prepared by Martin J. Fertal, M.ASCE, COMSIS Corporation, Pittsburgh, PA.

intercity highway network—a network that in some areas is already severely strained.

The foregoing paragraphs provide some insight into the complexity of planning transportation facilities at the intercity level. The process is demanding in terms both of professional expertise and informational requirements.

Civil engineers not formally trained in transportation planning often assume a major role as members of intercity highway planning project teams. The effectiveness of the civil engineer in this role can be increased with a basic understanding of the methods and procedures employed by the transportation planner.

The following sections of this chapter review some of the more common datasets and methods required to perform comprehensive, intercity highway analyses, and to evaluate the results obtained through this process. The steps to be followed in using this output to develop the transportation plan are then outlined.

7.2 INTERCITY DATA REQUIREMENTS

The planning of intercity highway facilities can be accomplished in a manner similar to that employed in the urban transportation planning process, by means of data collection, data analysis and model development, travel forecasting, and systems analysis and evaluation. This planning process requires a variety of information to simulate base year conditions and develop forecasts of future travel demand and facility needs. The types of data required can be grouped into three general categories: (1) Socioeconomic; (2) facility; and (3) travel. The same general categories have often been referred to as characteristics of the trip, the trip-maker, and the transportation system. The terminology used is unimportant. Information describing all components of travel is, however, of utmost importance.

7.2.1 Socioeconomic Data

Socioeconomic data refer to the characteristics of study areas and people that affect the demand for travel facilities. Examples of these data include population, employment, vehicle ownership, average family income, land use patterns, and employment by type. The importance of this information is that it describes an area and its inhabitants and provides the facts required to develop relationships with existing trip-making characteristics for use in forecasting models.

The most readily available source of social and economic statistics is provided by the U.S. Bureau of the Census. Many state and regional planning agencies have additional data available as a result of local surveys and sources. Also, a great deal of data is typically available directly from private carriers and other organizations.

7.2.2 Facility Data

Facility data provide information on the existing condition and performance of the system. This information is required to develop traffic assignment computer models, measure system performance, structure traffic engineering improvements, and undertake the many additional analyses requiring facility input.

Highway facilities   Highway facility information required by link (see Fig. 7-1) or section, or both, includes pavement type, administrative and functional classification, capacity, volume, average operating speed, vehicle miles of travel by type, and number and percentage of trucks by type. Other data, including surface condition and geometrics, are desirable for safety planning purposes. Information relative to total cost and total revenue is necessary to perform the economic analysis portion of any comprehensive planning effort. The prime source of this information is a state department of transportation (DOT). If the DOT does not have it and does not know where to obtain it, it is highly probable that the facts are unknown and must be collected.

Other facility data   Intercity highway facilities serve autos, buses, and trucks engaged in the movement of persons and goods. The intercity transportation system also includes the air, rail, water and pipeline modes. It is a complex system requiring a broad planning perspective.

Required intercity bus and truck information includes: passenger and freight schedules; equipment available (type, age, capacity, etc.); annual revenues and cost; number of persons carried; tons of freight moved; size, location, and other attributes of terminal facilities. In most instances, this data-collection work will require direct contact with the private carriers (e.g., Greyhound Bus Company) and most probably the state public utility or public service organization.

7.2.3 Travel Data

Travel data are required to establish existing travel patterns. Information on the origin and destination of existing passenger trips and

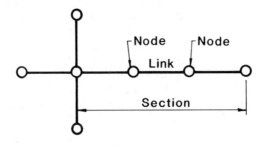

Fig. 7-1. Node, Link, Section Example

freight movements must be obtained before any understanding of existing travel can begin to develop. In addition, other attributes of these trips, such as purpose, income level of trip-maker, mode utilized, time of day and day of week trip was made, and cost of trip should be obtained. With information of this type, models to simulate existing conditions and to forecast future conditions can be developed and calibrated.

The collection of existing travel data is difficult, time consuming and expensive. For these reasons, every effort should be made to locate and utilize existing sources. These existing sources should be carefully reviewed to assure their usefulness. The alternative is the collection of new travel data for intercity highway planning purposes. This could be accomplished, depending on the goals and objectives of the planning study, with cordon counts, roadside interviews, home interviews, mail, telephone, on-board transit, special truck, or combinations of the survey methods. Irrespective of the method used, the objective of the data-collection phase is to assemble socioeconomic, facility, and travel data to the level of comprehensiveness required to address and satisfy the established goals and objectives.

Upon completion of the data-collection work, the next phase is the analysis of available data and the development of computerized planning models for use in the travel forecasting phase.

7.3 DATA ANALYSIS AND MODEL DEVELOPMENT

The data-collection phase of any planning effort can produce a great deal of interrelated yet uncoordinated information. Summary and analysis of this information is required to establish the validity and reasonableness of the base dataset, and to assist in its orderly, efficient use.

It used to be that simply to summarize various sources of information was not an easy task. Computer resources were not always available to analysts. Where computer resources were available, expertise and software, or both, were often unavailable. As a result, a substantial amount of data reduction and analysis work was done manually. The introduction of the low-cost microcomputer and user-oriented software is dramatically changing data reduction and analysis efforts. In the past, many pages in many manuals were filled with instructions on how to use a certain program to obtain simple tabulations. Most agencies now have the capability to summarize data quickly and easily.

The summary and analysis of base data are prerequisites to the development of transportation planning models. The following subsections will examine the three basic models in the transportation planning process: (1) Trip generation; (2) distribution; and (3) assignment. These models can be employed, irrespective of area, in any highway or transportation planning effort. They can be employed at any scale, e.g., on a main-frame computer, a mini, a micro, or even manually, as explained in Reference 7. A general understanding of the models is important to any civil engineer involved or associated with a planning function.

7.3.1 Trip Generation Modeling

Trip generation is a term used by the transportation planner to describe the relationship between trip characteristics and land-use or socioeconomic characteristics. For example, it is intuitively known that the number of work trips originating in a residential area is related to the labor force residing in that area. Furthermore, it can be generalized that the number of work trips attracted to an area is somehow related to the employment in the area. The quantification of these and other similar relationships produces a set of equations which collectively are termed the trip generation model.

The trip generation model is an integral element in the transportation planning process. However, the model answers only one question: How many trips start or end in a given analysis unit? In the planning process, these analysis units are normally referred to as traffic analysis zones. Other questions about the trip such as mode, direction, length, duration, and routing are answered by other planning models. The trip generation model thus quantifies the relationship between the number of trips beginning or ending in any analysis unit with that unit's land use and socioeconomic characteristics. From this basic understanding of the interaction between travel and the surrounding environment, forecasts of future travel can be made that are both meaningful and responsive to changes continually occurring in study areas.

The primary purpose of this subsection is to provide an overview of the generation model. For this reason, the material does not include information relative to background or theory, which can be found in numerous publications, including two published by the Federal Highway Administration (4, 11).

Analysis techniques   Three basic analysis techniques have been used to develop trip generation relationships: (1) Simple rate; (2) regression; and (3) cross-classification. To illustrate, assume that a data-collection effort was undertaken and produced information by analysis unit of a type shown in Table 7-1.

Analysis of the data in Table 7-1 would show, for example, that the average number of trips per person in the study area is equal to 2.10 (1010/480). More detailed investigation would show a meaningful relationship between median family income and trip-making expressed in terms of trips per person. A plot of the actual data points and a least-squares fit of these data with a linear regression line of the form $Y = A + BX$ would be as shown in Fig. 7-2.

Another way of analyzing these data might be to compute the average number of trips per person by automobile ownership group; e.g., 1.00 or less autos per dwelling unit, greater than 1.00 but less than 2.00 autos per dwelling unit, and greater than 2.00 autos per dwelling

TABLE 7-1 Transportation Planning Data (Hypothetical Five-Zone Study Area)

Zonal Characteristics	Traffic Zone					Total
	1	2	3	4	5	
Total population	100	150	90	70	70	480
Number of dwelling units	33	43	30	29	28	163
Median family income, in dollars	10,000	7000	11,000	13,000	18,000	N/A
Autos per dwelling unit	1.0	0.8	1.1	1.2	2.0	N/A
Total number of trips	200	225	200	175	210	1010
Home-based work trips*	66	100	60	46	50	322
Home-based other trips	67	50	100	100	110	427
Non home-based trips	67	75	40	29	50	261
Trips by auto	160	169	170	157	200	856
Trips by transit	40	56	30	18	10	154

*A home-based trip is defined as a trip having one end at home. A non home-based trip is defined as one having neither end at home.

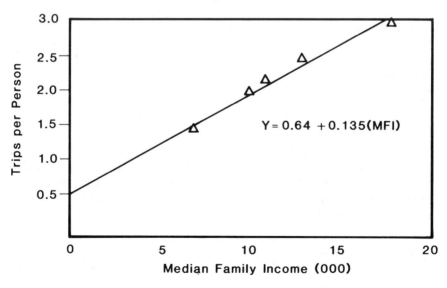

Fig. 7-2. Trips per person versus median family income

TABLE 7-2 Trips per Person as Related to Autos per Dwelling Unit

	Autos per dwelling unit		
	1.00 and less	**1.01–2.00**	**2.00+**
Trips per person	1.70	2.34	3.00

unit. This analysis would result in the type of information shown in Table 7-2.

The preceding has demonstrated three methods of developing relationships between a dependent travel variable (number of trips, trips per person) and independent socioeconomic variables (persons, median family income, autos per dwelling unit). The first method falls into the category of a simple rate or average. The second demonstrates a data fitting or regression technique. The third fits the category of cross-classification. All three techniques are used in the planning process to define the relationship between travel and socioeconomic factors. The relationships thus defined have come to be known as the trip generation model.

7.3.2 Trip Distribution Modeling

The trip distribution model is a major element in the integrated transportation planning process. The purpose of the model is to convert zonal trip ends into travel movements or, in other words, to tell where the trips are going. To accomplish this objective, two trip distribution models—the Fratar model and the gravity model—have been used most extensively. Examples of the method of computation for both models follow.

Fratar model   The Fratar model can be classified as an iterative, growth-factor type trip distribution model. The model is structured on the premise that:

1. The future volume of trips out of a zone is related to the present volume of trips out of the zone and the growth estimated for the zone.
2. The future distribution of trips from a zone is proportional to the present distribution of trips from the zone modified by the growth expected in the zones to which the trips are attracted.

To illustrate the working of the model, consider the three-zone example shown in Fig. 7-3. There are now 10 trips between zones A and B ($tab = 10$), 20 trips between zones A and C ($tac = 20$), and 15 trips between zones B and C ($tbc = 15$). Also, the trip production of zone A is expected to double ($Fa = 2$), the trip production of zone B is expected

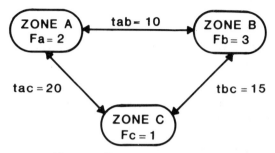

Fig. 7-3. Three-zone example

to triple ($Fb=3$), and the trip production of zone C is expected to remain constant ($Fc=1$). An estimate of the future distribution of trips between zone A and zones B and C is obtained in a seven-step, iterative manner. The calculation underlying the Fratar process can be found in Section 7.7 of this chapter.

The computations are made for each zone in the study area. Modified growth factors are computed and used in a second iteration of the model. The iterative process continues until all factors converge to within acceptable limits of 1.00. Two points should be recognized relative to the Fratar model: (1) The model can only work if given an existing trip matrix to expand, and (2) it does not consider the characteristics of the transportation system.

Gravity model The second trip distribution model to be considered is the gravity model. In essence, the gravity model says that the distribution of a given zone's trip production of P_i is directly proportional to the attraction power of other zones A_j and inversely proportional to some function of the spatial separation between the two zones, d_{i-x}. In equation form

$$T_{i\cdot j} = \frac{P_i \dfrac{A_j}{d_{i\cdot j}^{\,z}}}{\displaystyle\sum_{x=1}^{N} \dfrac{A_x}{(d_{i\cdot x})^z}} \tag{7.1}$$

in which $T_{i\cdot j}$ = trips from zone i to zone j; P_i = trips produced at zone i; A_j = trips attracted at zone j; $d_{i\cdot j}$ = measure of impedance (spatial separation) between zones i and j; Z = empirically derived exponent; N = number of zones; and, A_x = trips attracted at zone x.

The denominator of the gravity model is usually referred to as the accessibility index. It represents the total accessibility of any zone i to all zones in the study area. More relating to accessibility is included in later sections of this chapter.

A slight rearrangement of the gravity model formulation makes it easy to see that the model merely distributes trip productions of zone i to other zones on the basis of another zone's attractiveness relative to total system attractiveness.

In reference to the examples, it should once again be noted that the Fratar model is not responsive to changes in the transportation system. It has no way of accounting for a change in travel patterns that would occur as a result of transportation system changes such as a new bridge or a circumferential highway. On the other hand, the gravity model is responsive to changes in the transportation system. These changes are reflected by the model through the use of zone-to-zone travel imped-ances (e.g., travel time).

Each model has its role in the planning process. The Fratar can be used to develop estimates of revised zone-to-zone trip interchanges resulting from changes that are not changes in the highway system. An example would be expected, unequal growth in various cities in the state. The gravity model can be used to develop similar estimates reflecting, for example, improved accessibility between a given city pair.

7.3.3 Traffic Assignment Modeling

Traffic assignment is a process used to develop loadings on a network of transportation facilities. The result of the assignment process is an estimate of user volumes on each segment (link) of the network as well as the turning movements at intersections of the links. Traffic assignment is used to simulate existing traffic volumes on a transporta-tion system and to forecast probable future volumes. This simulation requires the use of trip interchanges (trip table) obtained in the origin-destination (O-D) survey or developed as a result of the distribution process. The volumes used may be number of vehicles, number of total persons, number of transit riders or any other user characteristic that can be described by an origin, a destination, and some quantifiable trip interchange characteristic. Traffic assignment is used for many reasons, including:

1. The development and testing of alternative transportation sys-tems.

2. The establishment of short-range priority programs for trans-portation facility development.

3. The detailed study of traffic generators and their effects on the transportation system.

4. The development of a specific location for facilities and service within a transportation corridor.

5. The development of design hour volumes.

6. The development of necessary input and feedback to other planning tools.

Required inputs Input to the traffic assignment process, regardless of the type of network to be considered (transit, highway, rail, etc.), includes:

1. Network geometry. A description of the links and their interconnections, this may be viewed as a map containing the network to be studied.
2. Network parameters. The assignment process requires network link values in order to determine routes through the network under study. Only one value is required and may be, for example, travel time, distance, cost, or a combination thereof. No other network parameter is required, but other parameters are highly recommended for special analytical purposes.
3. Interchange values. The unit to be loaded onto the transportation network by the assignment process is described by an origin, a destination, and an interchange value. The value may be, for example, vehicles, persons, tons of cargo, etc.

Assignment outputs   The output of the traffic assignment process consists basically of loads on each link of the transportation network. These may be 24-hr vehicular highway traffic volumes, peak hour transit volumes, or yearly volumes of freight flow. In addition to the link volumes, the assignment process produces turning movements at link intersections, minimum routings through the transportation network, and the minimum summation of impedances between origins and destinations.

Assignment techniques rely on the determination of routes through a network of facilities based upon link impedances such as time, distance, or cost of travel. Interchange values described by an origin and destination are then accumulated on the network links comprising the path or paths calculated between the origin and destination. The accumulation of all O-D interchange values on the network links is the load on the transportation network.

The traffic assignment process is but one procedure in the transportation planning process. The results are, however, widely used because they are readily understood by administrators, the public, and general planners. In addition, intermediate results (e.g., zone-to-zone impedances) are used for other analytical procedures such as modal split, trip generation, and land use distribution. Since the final link loads probably receive more exposure, analysis, and evaluation than any one other output of the process, it is recommended that considerable care be used to assure their reasonableness.

Uses of traffic assignment   The assignment technique is first utilized in the planning process to assess the adequacy of the trip data obtained in the O-D survey. The coded and factored survey trips are assigned to the network for survey validation purposes. The assignment technique provides an inexpensive and efficient means of accumulating O-D trips across screenlines as well as through corridors for comparison with ground counts. In addition, the selection of traffic analysis zones and network coding should be evaluated by traffic assignment to assure reasonable link volumes.

Traffic assignment is also used to obtain zone-to-zone impedances for input to other planning tools. These impedance values are initially based upon travel time surveys; however, network calibration and capacity restraint will modify these initial values. The effect of these modifications should be well understood by the analyst, since the zone-to-zone impedances will be used as a basic input to subsequent trip distribution and modal split modeling. Also, these impedance measures are used by several land use distribution models currently in use.

The trip distribution and modal split model calibration process also relies on traffic assignment; i.e., model trips are loaded on the base network and compared to O-D travel. Comparisons are normally made by screenline, portions of screenlines, functional classification, and individual links. The basic types of traffic assignments made in a comprehensive study include:

- Existing trips to the existing network.
- Future trips to the existing plus committed network.
- Future trips to the existing plus committed plus proposed networks.

These types of assignments are made to aid in formulating and evaluating alternative transportation systems for serving future demand. Additionally, traffic assignment is used for:

- Priority planning through the assignment of travel for intermediate years to their corresponding systems.
- Detailing of route locations through established corridors and studying in more detail features such as alternative interchange location.
- Evaluating the effects of new and large generators such as airports, housing developments, and commercial complexes on the surrounding transportation system.
- Development of design hour volumes and other factors necessary for the detailed design of facilities.

7.4 TRAVEL FORECASTING

Projections of population and economic activity have long been the basic inputs underlying forecast of travel demand. Since there is a great deal of uncertainty in any forecast of population or economic activity, it follows that there is a great deal of uncertainty in any forecast of travel demand. The degree of uncertainty has become even greater with major adjustments in the economic and energy sectors. These adjustments and uncertainties dictate that single point forecasts are probably inadequate for all but the least important and least comprehensive planning efforts. Efforts of significance should attempt to measure the impacts of various scenarios designed to bound the probable range of outcomes.

Once basic input variables are available, the travel models that utilize these variables can be solved to produce travel demand estimates. These input variables include future estimates of all independent variables used in the base-year travel models. Examples of typical independent variables include population, employment, highway speed, highway capacity, and transit operating cost.

It should be noted that forecast data are not always readily available; furthermore, that forecast data are subject to error. Judgment is required in the development of the base-year models to assure that necessary future-year inputs are both obtainable and reliable.

The specifics of the travel forecasting process will vary from state to state, and possibly from project to project. A generalized approach is presented by Fig. 7-4, which illustrates the major work elements in the travel forecasting process and the interrelationship between the elements.

7.5 SYSTEMS ANALYSIS

At the conclusion of the travel forecasting phase, a large amount of information will be available. This information will include projected traffic volumes, minimum time and distance paths, travel patterns,

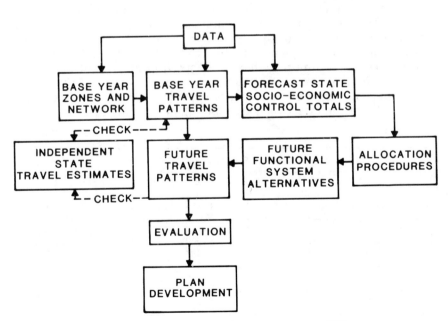

Fig. 7-4. Statewide forecasting steps (10)

vehicle-miles of travel, insight into the economic and social impacts of various alternatives, and other associated data.

The next phase of the transportation planning process is systems analysis. It can be concisely summarized as a three-step process: (1) What is the problem? (2) What are the alternatives? (3) What is the best alternative? For example, if the problem is to reduce transportation energy consumption, the alternative that minimizes vehicle-miles of travel is a logical, best alternative.

In practice, the selection of the best alternative is rarely as straightforward as the example. There are typically many system performance measures of varying importance to be considered. Many analysts handle this problem by completing a table similar to Fig. 7-5. The weight attached to each measure is normally obtained by soliciting input from involved participants.

To illustrate the systems analysis process, assume the problem is to evaluate the quality of existing intercity bus service and the effect of proposed intercity bus improvements. The structuring of the systems analysis effort could be accomplished in many different ways. The extent of the analysis effort is largely dependent on the availability of resources. In any event, performance measures to be used in evaluating alternative improvement plans must be developed. As in almost all analyses, the cost of the proposed improvements is an important performance measure. In addition, the problem indicates that the quality of existing intercity bus service and the effect of proposed improvements is to be quantified.

In this example, the use of a relative service index—the ratio of intercity bus travel time (including access, egress, and transfer time) to intercity auto time—is an appropriate performance measure. This index provides a method of quantifying the relative level of existing intercity bus service and testing the effect of proposed improvements.

The development of the relative service indices for all city-to-city pairs can be rather easily accomplished using the Urban Mass Transportation Administration's Urban Transportation Planning System (UTPS).

	Performance Measure					
	1	2	3	n	Weighted	
Alternative	WT1 =	WT2 =	WT3 =	WTn =	Total (WT)	Rank
1						
2						
3						
n						

Fig. 7-5. Table of alternatives

The work involved to establish base year conditions includes the coding of the intercity networks and a series of computer runs. The work involved to reflect proposed service improvements involves revisions to the coded networks and additional computer runs.

The information presented in this section briefly illustrates the systems analysis phase of the urban transportation planning process. The scope of this phase is dependent on the complexity of the problem and available resources. The structure of this phase should, however, be relatively constant. Articulation of the problem, identification of the available alternatives, and selection of the best available alternative on the basis of well defined performance measures are the keys to professional systems analysis.

7.6 CONCLUSION

Intercity highway planning is a complex area requiring a broad perspective, a reasonable level of staff expertise, and adequate resources. The perspective required is a function of the goals and objectives of the planning effort. It is important that the goals and objectives be well defined at the beginning of the project and that technical work be structured to focus on these areas.

Adequate methodology and computerized procedures are available to address most intercity highway planning projects. These methods and procedures form a planning process. The major steps in the planning process are the articulation of goals and objectives, data collection, data analysis and model development, travel forecasting, and systems analysis and evaluation. Each step has been described in a previous section of this chapter.

The use of these methods and procedures provides a structured approach to analyze the capability of existing highway systems to meet current and future needs. They also provide a capability to analyze future alternative systems and their ability to meet future needs. It should be recognized, however, that the networks used to represent systems in the planning process must be translated into plans and then into projects. This involves additional work not described in this chapter. This additional work can include engineering feasibility analyses, cost estimation, environmental appraisal, and other similar analyses.

The structured planning process described in this chapter is a good foundation on which to build an intercity planning effort. It does, however, have its limitations. It is highly demanding of data, computer resources, expertise and time. A decision is therefore required early in the process relative to the methods and procedures to be employed. The decision as to the appropriate analytical approach will be largely influenced by time and budget constraints. Proper systems analysis at this point in the process may dictate that the best approach is an approach other than that described, that is, the manual NCHRP 187 methodology (7).

It is not possible to provide a recommended approach for a subject as complex as intercity highway planning that will be valid for each individual effort. It is, however, possible to provide a general structure for developing a recommended approach for each intercity planning effort. Briefly, the steps are:

1. Articulate the goals and objectives of the planning effort.
2. Define study constraints, e.g., time, cost, available resources, etc.
3. Employ basic systems analysis procedures to select the most appropriate method of approach; What is the problem? What are the alternatives? What is the best alternative?
4. Use the selected approach to produce probable impacts of alternative systems.
5. Evaluate the various alternatives again, using the basic systems analysis approach in conjunction with previously agreed upon performance measures to select the best available alternative.
6. Translate the best alternative into an implementation plan including individual project statements.

The use of a systematic approach similar to the one described above will provide structure to the planning process and produce results consistent with the stated goals, objectives and available resources.

7.7 APPENDIX A—FRATAR DISTRIBUTION MODEL

Use of the Fratar model follows a seven-step iterative calculation procedure. The first step is to estimate trips between zone A and zone B considering the growth of zone A, by means of

$$Tab\ (a) = \frac{tab\ (Fb)\ [\Sigma(tax)]\ (Fa)}{\Sigma(tax)\ (Fx)}$$

$$Tab\ (a) = \frac{10(3)\ (30 \times 2)}{(10 \times 3) + (20 \times 1)}$$

$$Tab\ (a) = 36.0$$

Next, estimate trips between zone A and zone B considering growth of zone B, using

$$Tab\ (b) = \frac{(10 \times 2)\ (25 \times 3)}{(10 \times 2) + (15 \times 1)}$$

$$Tab\ (b) = 42.8$$

Arrive at the best estimate of trips between zone A and zone B by means of

$$Tab \quad = \frac{(tab\ (a)\ +\ tab\ (b))}{2}$$

$$Tab \quad = \frac{36.0 + 42.8}{2}$$

$$Tab \quad = 39.4$$

Estimate trips bewteen zone A and zone C considering growth of zone A, using

$$Tac\ (a) = \frac{(20 \times 1)\ (30 \times 2)}{(20 \times 1) + (10 \times 3)}$$

$$Tac\ (c) = 24.0$$

Estimate trips between zone A and zone C considering growth of zone C, using

$$Tac\ (c) = \frac{(20 \times 2) + (35 \times 1)}{(20 \times 2) + (15 \times 3)}$$

$$Tac\ (c) = 14.7$$

Arrive at the best estimate of trips between zone A and zone C by means of

$$Tac \quad = \frac{tac\ (a)\ +\ tab\ (c)}{2}$$

$$Tac \quad = \frac{24.0 + 14.7}{2}$$

$$Tac \quad = 19.3$$

Compute modified growth factor to be used in next iteration of model by means of

$$F'a \quad = \frac{\Sigma\ tax\ (Fa)}{Tab + Tac}$$

$$F'a \quad = \frac{(30 \times 2)}{(39.4 + 19.3)}$$

$$F'a \quad = 1.18$$

7.8 REFERENCES

In the preparation of this chapter, reference was made to Chaps. 1, 2, 3, and 6 of this Urban Planning Guide. Other useful references are:

1. COMSIS Corporation, *Estimating Long Range Highway Improvements and Costs*, prepared for the U.S. Department of Transportation, Washington, DC, August 1977.
2. COMSIS Corporation, *Nebraska Public Transit Study*, Nebraska Office of Planning and Programming, Lincoln, NE, 1973.
3. "Evaluating Options in Statewide Transportation Planning/Programming," *Report No. 179*, Transportation Research Board, Washington, DC, 1977.
4. *Guidelines for Trip Generation*, Federal Highway Administration, Washington, DC.
5. Klink, W.D., and Yu, J.C., "Propensity of Statewide Multimodal Transportation," *Journal of the Transportation Engineering Division*, ASCE, Vol. 101, No. TE4, November 1975, pp. 639–655.
6. Levinson, H.S., "Highways, Transport, and Energy: A Look Ahead," *Journal of the Transportation Engineering Division*, ASCE, Vol. 108, No. TE5, September 1982, pp. 447–456.
7. "Quick Response Urban Travel Estimation Techniques and Transferable Parameters," *Report 187*, National Cooperative Highway Research Program.
8. "State Transportation Issues and Actions," *Special Report 189*, Transportation Research Board, Washington, DC, 1980.
9. "Statewide Transportation Planning," *Report No. 95*, Transportation Research Board, Washington, DC, November 1982.
10. "Statewide Travel Demand Forecasting," *Transmittal 147*, Vol. 20, App. 59, U.S. Department of Transportation, Washington, DC, November 1973.
11. *Trip Generation Analysis*, Federal Highway Administration, Washington, DC.

CHAPTER 8

AIRPORT PLANNING[a]

8.1 INTRODUCTION

Powered flight had its historic beginnings with the Wright brothers on December 17, 1903, at Kitty Hawk, North Carolina. Propelled by a single four-cylinder engine, the Flyer carried Orville Wright a distance of 120 ft (36.5 m) for 12 sec, at a speed of just over 7.5 miles per hr (12 km per hr). Modern aircraft are now capable of carrying over 600 passengers on a single flight at speeds in excess of 500 miles (805 km) per hr. In 1946, commercial air travel in the United States represented by revenue passenger miles stood at 6 billion a year, increased to 224 billion in fiscal year 1983, and are projected to increase to 400 billion by 1995 (see Table 8-1 and Fig. 8-1). Similar growth trends are seen for air cargo and U.S. mail.

General aviation activity, i.e., aviation other than commercial airlines, also increased significantly since 1953. The growth of this element

TABLE 8-1 U.S. Domestic Air Carrier Passenger Enplanements and Aircraft Instrument Operations, 1980–1996

Fiscal year (1)	Enplanements, in thousands (2)	Instrument operations (3)
(a) Historical		
1980	278.2	10.6
1981	264.3	10.2
1982	272.8	9.5
1983	290.3	10.1
1984	313.2	11.3
(b) Forecast		
1985	336.4	11.6
1986	348.1	11.8
1987	366.7	12.0
1992	456.0	13.3
1996	530.8	14.2

[a]Prepared by Gordon Y. Watada, F.ASCE, Howard Needles Tammen & Bergendoff, Los Angeles, CA.

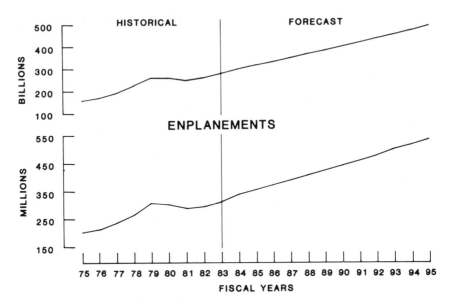

U.S. CERTIFIED ROUTE AIR CARRIER
SCHEDULED PASSENGER TRAFFIC RPM'S

SOURCE : 1975–83 CIVIL AERONAUTICS BOARD
1984–95 FAA FORECASTS

Fig. 8-1. Commercial air travel passenger miles

of civil aviation is projected to continue and require additional airport facilities. The active general aviation fleet increased from about 70,000 aircraft to about 210,000 between 1960 and 1983. The Federal Aviation Administration forecasts the net annual increase to the general aviation fleet between 1984 and 1995 to average about 7300 units per year (see Fig. 8-2).

Air transportation has affected all segments of American society. It has increased personal mobility; provided access into remote communities; allowed overnight delivery of freight and cargo; and established airports as major transportation terminals, commercial facilities and industrial centers. The economic well-being of many communities and regions is often dependent on the benefits derived from the air transport industry.

Civil engineers have traditionally been on the leading edge of the airport planning profession. In recent years, airport congestion has been recognized as a major constraint to the ability of the air transport system to handle future demand. Therefore, it is expected that the civil engineer's role in planning airport facilities will become crucial if the capacity of the airport system is increased to meet forecasted growth.

This chapter will attempt to review the major attributes of the

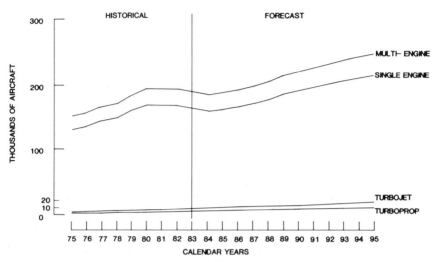

TOTAL ACTIVE GENERAL AVIATION AIRCRAFT*

SOURCE : 1975-83 FAA STATISTICAL HANDBOOK OF AVIATION
1984-85 FAA FORECASTS
*INDIVIDUAL AIRCRAFT TOTALS ARE ADDITIVE

Fig. 8-2. General aviation fleet

present U.S. air transportation system; describe the airport planning process; provide information on the sources and availability of airport planning and design standards; and give the history of the federal airport grant program.

8.2 CHARACTERISTICS OF THE AIR TRANSPORTATION SYSTEM

Civil aviation comprises two principal classes of activity: scheduled air transport and general aviation. Scheduled air transport refers to air carriers which hold certificates of public convenience and necessity under Section 401 of the Federal Aviation Act of 1958 (49 USC 1371), as issued by the Civil Aeronautics Board to conduct scheduled services over specified routes and a limited amount of nonscheduled operations.

Scheduled air transport also refers to commuter airlines which operate small aircraft up to a maximum size of 60 seats and which schedule at least five round trips per week between two points or carry mail. Commuters operate principally under Part 298 of the Civil Aeronautics Board Regulations or Part 135 of the Federal Aviation Regulations. The air transport category can also refer to a number of charter airlines which operate exclusively on a nonscheduled basis.

General aviation embraces all other civil aviation activity not classified as air carrier, including air taxi, business and pleasure flying, and military operations.

The operations, maintenance and safety of the United States air transportation system are affected by federal statutes and regulations promulgated principally by the Federal Aviation Administration. The principal role of states, counties and municipalities is to plan, design, develop, operate, and maintain airport terminal facilities in accordance with federal guidelines and standards. Under certain conditions, states are permitted to promulgate standards for general aviation airports.

8.2.1 Federal Role in Air Transportation

Federal regulation of the United States civil air transportation system is vested principally in two agencies, the Federal Aviation Administration (FAA), and the Civil Aeronautics Board (CAB).

The FAA (a part of the U.S. Department of Transportation) is responsible for the safe and efficient operation of the airport and airway systems, operation and maintenance of the air traffic control system, and administration of an airport capital grant program. The FAA discharges its responsibilities through the publication of guidance material contained in advisory circulars or through administrative rules in the form of federal aviation regulations (FARs).

The federal role in airport development increased substantially as a result of the Airport and Airway Development Act of 1970 (Public Law 91-258). This Act, and its subsequent amendments, set forth the amounts of annual funding for grants to public agencies for airport planning and development. After a modest beginning of $280,000,000 in 1971, the Airport and Airway Improvement Act of 1982 extended the federal grant program for airports for an additional 10 years. It provides for $800,000,000 in fiscal 1984, increasing to over $1 billion by fiscal 1986.

The CAB, established in 1938 as the Civil Aeronautics Authority, is responsible for the federal government's economic control over commercial air transportation. Between 1938 and 1978, the CAB exercised regulatory powers over route awards, fares, mergers and flight schedules. The Airline Deregulation Act of 1978 (Public Law 95-504) substantially reduced the CAB's regulatory authority and contained a "sunset" provision declaring that the Board shall cease to exist after January 1, 1985, unless Congress deems an extension to be appropriate. The U.S. Department of Transportation will assume much of the CAB's authority after "sunset."

8.2.2 Airline Deregulation

Airline deregulation has seen a proliferation of "new entrant" airlines into many markets. The ease with which airlines may enter or withdraw from service in a particular market or from service to a community creates major fluctuations in demand for facilities at many airports. This has affected the planning, development, and financing of many airport improvement programs.

The characteristics of the scheduled air carrier industry have undergone many changes since deregulation. The major trunk airlines took it as an opportunity to restructure route systems to serve the more profitable markets and eliminate marginal routes. The local service airlines generally adopted the same operational pattern and also expanded service beyond old regional boundaries. This often put them in head-to-head competition with the major trunk carriers. Former intrastate carriers also expanded their routes to include interstate and international points. Deregulation also created a new factor for established airlines to contend with: competition from low cost airlines operating in the high-density markets.

The Airline Deregulation Act has also been a significant cause of the recent growth of the commuter airline industry. As the established trunk and local service carriers restructured their route systems and withdrew service from smaller communities, commuter airlines began to fill the void. In many cases, commuter service has meant greater frequency and, thereby, has generated greater passenger demand. Financial encouragement for seeking replacement service was made available through the CAB's Small Communities Program under Section 419 (49 USC 1389) of the Federal Aviation Act. Beginning in 1972, commuter revenue passenger miles have increased on the average over 16% a year.

During 1983, seven airlines were added to the list of scheduled certificated carriers bringing the total increase since deregulation to 53. At the end of 1983, there were 84 airlines in scheduled service.

8.2.3 Airports

The airport serves many functions. Its principal role is providing facilities for arriving and departing aircraft. It is an intramodal and intermodal transfer center. The large air traffic hub airports are major commercial and industrial centers, and thus, major ground traffic generators. In 1983, the United States had recorded 12,562 airports, 2697 heliports, and 454 seaplane bases. Of these, approximately 600 are airports with scheduled airline service.

Air traffic hubs are not airports, but cities and Standard Metropolitan Statistical Areas (SMSAs) requiring aviation services. Individual communities fall into four hub classifications as determined by each community's percentage of total enplaned revenue passengers in all services, and all operations of U.S. certificated route air carriers within the 50 states, the District of Columbia, and other areas designated by the Federal Aviation Administration (see Table 8-2). Geographic locations of large air traffic hubs are shown on Fig. 8-3.

Airports serving commercial traffic are publicly owned by city, county or state agencies. Airports are also owned by quasi-governmental commissions, such as the Port Authority of New York and New Jersey (LaGuardia, Newark International and John F. Kennedy Interna-

TABLE 8-2 Enplaned Passengers in the Hub Classifications for 12 Months Ending December 31, 1982

Hub classification (1)	Percentage of total enplaned passengers (2)	Number of enplaned passengers (3)
Large (L)	1.00 or more	2,777,510 or more
Medium (M)	0.25 to 0.99	694,378 to 2,777,509
Small (S)	0.05 to 0.24	138,876 to 694,377
Nonhub (N)	less than 0.05	less than 138,875

tional Airports) and The Massachusetts Port Authority (Logan International Airport). Washington National Airport and Dulles International Airport, both serving the nation's capital, are the only commercial service airports owned and operated by the federal government.

Airports principally serving general aviation traffic are both publicly and privately owned. The number of privately owned airports for public use has declined from 2900 in 1969 to 1490 in 1983. This decline has created a large demand for services by general aviation aircraft at publicly owned airports, including those with large volumes of commercial traffic. The integration of commercial and general aviation operations has resulted in congestion at many large hub terminal facilities. The FAA has instituted a major program of reliever airport development to

Fig. 8-3. Location of air traffic hubs

attract general aviation away from the larger congested airports in order to secure additional capacity for commercial operations.

Joint use of military airfields can offer an attractive alternative to the relatively high investment costs, construction lead times and environmental limitations associated with new airport development. In 1983, there were 15 joint use airports in the United States.

A limited number of public use heliports exist in the United States. Most helicopter operations are conducted from airports designed for use by fixed wing aircraft, private heliports, or military facilities. Helicopters have had limited use in scheduled air carrier service. This has been attributed to their relatively high operating costs, rotor noise generation at environmentally sensitive airports and city center landing sites, and incompatibility with approach and departure operating characteristics of fixed wing aircraft. However, recent advances in helicopter technology have reduced noise and operating and maintenance costs, as well as increased their reliability and safety. Helicopters are widely used by business corporations and by government agencies such as police departments, forest and park organizations, and emergency units.

8.2.4 Environmental Impact

The impact of aircraft noise on a surrounding community is reflected in recent increases in court actions, operating restrictions, curfews, and sanctions against airport development. Aircraft noise restrictions can be a significant factor in negating aviation's primary role as a prime mover of people and goods. In order to reduce the impact of aircraft noise, the FAA encourages land use compatibility planning (ANCLUC studies) through enforcement of Part 150 of the Federal Aviation Regulations and the institution of aircraft noise abatement procedures in flight under FAR Part 91. FAR Part 36 sets forth maximum noise levels to be achieved by all aircraft in commercial service by January 1985. This will, in effect, remove most older jets, such as 707s and DC-8s, and some BAC-111s, 727s and 737s from active service, although there are exemptions for service to small communities until 1988.

Atmospheric pollution caused by jet aircraft operations is evident from the distinctive kerosene-like smell from engine exhaust emissions. The Environmental Protection Agency is the appointed lead federal office in control of engine emission requirements and has published standards that must be considered in the design of new power plants for aircraft.

No single piece of recent federal legislation has had a more profound effect on airport development than the national Environmental Policy Act of 1969 (Public Law 91-190). The Act established a broad national policy for the preservation of the environment and was designed to assure that environmental concerns are given careful consideration in all actions taken by the federal government. The requirements of the Act cover all federal grants, loans, contracts, leases, construction, research, rule-making and regulatory actions, certifications and permits, and plans submitted by state and local agencies which require FAA approval. The environmental process generally consists of an impact assessment study, public hearings by the initiator of the proposal requiring a federal action, and a finding by the FAA that the proposal is consistent with the national policy on the environment. The absence of such a finding usually means that a proposal cannot proceed or requires further study.

8.2.5 Future

"Change" is probably what best characterizes the aviation industry from its formative years after the turn of the century, through the high growth period of the 1960s and early 1970s, and during the recent era of declining profits, rising operating costs, and a new competitive environment.

Control of operating costs and capital formation should continue to be major challenges to the commercial segment of the aviation industry for the remainder of the 1980s. Many commercial aircraft need to be replaced because they do not meet federal noise regulations or have high operating costs. Certain airlines will have to follow the recent trend of seeking wage concessions from employees as a means of reducing costs. Airlines that do not generate sufficient earnings or borrowing power must continue to fly less efficient airplanes and face the possibility of sanctions because aircraft do not comply with noise regulations. In terms of passenger enplanements, U.S. domestic carriers are forecast to approach 41,500,000 by 1994, up from 19,500,000 in 1984.

Major changes are also occurring in the general aviation element of the industry. It represents a very important means of travel for American business, as evidenced by the growing percentage of business jet aircraft comprising the general aviation fleet. About 90% of general aviation jet aircraft sales are for business use. Approximately 80% to 85% of turboprop aircraft and about 60% to 70% of multiengine piston aircraft enter the business aircraft fleet each year. The general aviation fleet is expected to sustain its present annual growth rate of just under 4% through 1994.

Ultralight aircraft represent a growing element of the general aviation fleet. This is attributable to their lower price, cheaper operating costs, and less restrictive regulation. The growth of ultralight activity could make it a significant factor in regional aviation systems planning because of requirements for terminal airspace and landing facilities. Some type of regulation, either at the federal or state level, can be expected if ultralight activity continues to grow at its present rate.

Helicopters show a potential for considerable growth in the next decade. Their unique operating characteristics have made them most adaptable to emergency and rescue operations, offshore oil exploration, and other missions that are not suited for fixed wing aircraft. The helicopter fleet is forecasted to increase at a rate of about 5% a year through 1994.

8.3 AIRPORT PLANNING PROCESS

Airport planning refers to the process of formulating sound and efficient plans to direct the initiation and staging of airport improvements. Such planning takes place at the national, state, regional and local levels. The National Airport System Plan (NASP), prepared by the FAA, is a compilation of the nation's civil airport development needs for all classes and categories of public use airports. Indicative of recent federal emphasis on the systems aspect of transportation planning at the federal level, the next version of the NASP will be redesignated the National Plan of Integrated Airport Systems.[1]

In order for the NASP to reflect local goals and objectives, federal planning grants are available to public agencies for state and regional airport system plans and for local airport master plans. The statutory objectives of the federal planning grant program are to promote the appropriate location and development of individual airports, provide for the proper allocation of resources, and develop and maintain an effective national system of airports.

8.3.1 State and Regional Airport Systems Plans

State system plans provide an over-all frame of reference for the development of individual airports within one state. The plans recommend the general location and characteristics of new airports and the nature of improvements needed at existing ones. These plans are also sensitive to linkage with other modes of transportation and are often used by state transportation agencies for the allocation of their own resources to maximize benefits to the general population of the state.

Regional airport system planning focuses on the needs of the region and is usually prepared under the same guiding principles as state plans. Elements common to state and regional plans include: (1) Forecasts of passengers and aircraft operations; (2) demand to capacity relationships; (3) airfield facilities and passenger terminal building needs; (4) environmental impacts; (5) financial requirements; and (6) ground access and egress provisions.

Regional airport system plans are usually prepared by regional governments or regional transportation agencies. Additional information on the preparation of state and regional airport system plans is available in FAA Advisory Circulars 150/5050-3A, "Planning the State Airport System," and 150/5070-5, "Planning the Metropolitan Airport System."

---

[1]Information on the national plan is available from: Chief; National Planning Division, APP-40, Federal Aviation Administration, 800 Independence Avenue, S.W., Washington, D.C. 20591.

8.3.2 Airport Master Plans

Airport master plans provide a detailed level of airport planning and serve as the programming instrument for the development of future facilities on the airport. Greater precision or detail is required for master plans than for either regional or state system plans. Elements of an airport master plan include: (1) Forecasts; (2) demand and capacity analysis; (3) terminal area plan; (4) facility requirements; (5) environmental impacts; (6) airport layout plan; (7) airport access plan; and (8) financial plan. Before initiating the preparation of an airport master plan, it is important to consult Advisory Circular 150/5070-6, "Airport Master Plans." This document was revised in 1984 and is an excellent reference.

Forecasts Forecasts are generally established for five, 10 and 20 years into the future and include passengers, aircraft operations, categories of aircraft, cargo, and airport access data. Aviation demand is based on socioeconomic, environmental, and technical factors. The FAA publishes annual statistics on passengers and aircraft operations at airports operating within the U.S. National Airspace System (4). The FAA also publishes 10-year forecasts covering some 900 airports in the country (16). These documents provide an excellent source of reference for preparing aviation forecasts.

Demand and capacity analysis Demand and capacity analysis is the basis for determining the adequacy of current facilities to handle existing and future demand for airport services. The analysis focuses on such facilities as runways, apron and gates, terminal buildings, access roads, and parking. Documentation is available from the FAA which sets forth procedures for determining the capacity of an airport runway system. Procedures for analyzing and sizing passenger terminal facilities are available from the FAA, the International Air Transport Association, and the Air Transport Association of America (2, 7, 9).

The use of computers has proved effective in analyzing the service capabilities of facilities, particularly at major airports. The computer is also a proficient design tool in determining the geometric configuration of airfield facilities and the sizing of passenger processing accommodations.

Terminal area plans The terminal area plan includes such facilities as terminal and cargo buildings, aprons, gates, hangars, shops, and parking lots. The terminal area plan is developed to achieve the most efficient use of land for servicing vehicular traffic, passengers, and aircraft. Such plans are conceived through conceptual studies and drawings to establish the general locations of facilities and order-of-magnitude size. More detailed studies are conducted during the design phase to fix exact location and size.

Facility requirements This element of an airport master plan project establishes the specific list of airport facility needs to accommodate future aviation demand. The list of items could include: (1) Length, strength (weight-bearing capacity) and number of runways; (2) number of aircraft gates; (3) passenger processing facilities in the terminal building; (4) vehicular parking spaces; and (5) type and alignment of ground access roads, and transit needs.

Consideration of the interaction between general aviation and commercial aircraft operations is an important aspect of establishing total facility requirements. Major airports such as Phoenix Sky Harbor, Salt Lake City, and Oakland experience general aviation traffic in excess of air carrier operations. Provisions for dedicated runways or segregated approach paths for general aviation may improve operating efficiency. Future facility needs for general aviation, such as hangars, tie down areas, maintenance facilities, etc., are best obtained from fixed based operators.

Airport layout plan   The airport master plan is the basis for preparing a new or updated airport layout plan (ALP). An ALP is a graphic presentation, to scale, of existing and proposed airport facilities, their location on the airport, and the pertinent clearance and dimensional information required to show conformance with applicable standards. It represents the ultimate development of the airport, as established by the latest master plan. The most important aspect of an ALP is that one must be approved by the FAA as a prerequisite to receipt of a federal grant for an airport.

Environmental assessment   Environmental factors must be considered carefully in the development of an airport master plan. Environmental studies consider the impact of construction and operation of a new airport or an airport expansion upon accepted standards of air and water quality, noise levels, and the ecology. All airport development projects financed under a federal grant program must be reviewed for environmental impact in accordance with NEPA before funds are released.

Airport access plan   This element of the master plan indicates proposed routing of ground access to central business districts and other major commercial and industrial centers. It should consider facilities for all interconnecting modes of transportation, including ground vehicles (truck terminals, bus stations), rail, and short-haul aircraft.

The airport access study element of an airport master plan should be general in nature and done in conjunction with the programs of local highway departments, transit authorities, and regional planning bodies. Airport-bound travelers are affected by the relative efficiency of the urban highway network. Passengers headed for a number of major U.S. airports are exposed to severe congestion problems during peak traffic periods. The airport master plan process is not the panacea to ground access constraints. Ground access problems are properly addressed by urban transportation planners as part of local, regional, and state planning projects.

Financial analysis   Schedules and cost estimates of improvements proposed in the master plan should be developed on the basis of five, 10, and 20 years. These cost estimates include capital needs and maintenance and operating expenses.

Financial feasibility is determined by a revenue-expense study. Expenses usually include the annual cost to retire debt service plus maintenance and operation expenses. Revenues include lease rents, landing fees, concession and parking income, and federal grants.

8.3.3 Airport Planning Guidelines

A principal source of airport planning material is the Federal Aviation Administration, which prepares and publishes advisory circulars to communicate guidance and general information in designated subject areas. Advisory circulars are issued in a numbered-subject system. Airport planning information is provided under the 150 series in the numbered-subject system.[2] Advisory circulars are not considered standards unless used in compliance with a Federal Aviation Regulation. For example, FAR Part 152 specifies the 150 series advisory circulars that become a standard in connection with a project under a federal grant program, unless exemptions are granted by the administrator.

An important international body concerned with the establishment of airport planning and design guidance material is the International Civil Aviation Organization (ICAO). ICAO is an agency of the United Nations and discharges its responsibilities through resolutions and International Standards and Practices that are published as Annexes to the Convention on International Civil Aviation held in Chicago in 1944.

The airport planner should be familiar with the ICAO document "Aerodromes, Annex 14 to the Convention on International Civil Aviation" (15), which contains design standards and recommended practices applicable to nearly all airports serving international air commerce. Most U.S. airports are designed to FAA guidelines and standards, although major international airports are in general compliance with Annex 14. Most FAA standards equal or exceed those of ICAO.

Texts on airport planning and design, and handbooks published by aviation trade organizations such as the International Air Transport Association (IATA) and Air Transport Association of America (ATA) provide information and guidance from the private sector.

The aircraft manufacturers publish useful information in the form of flight manuals and aircraft characteristics documents. Flight manuals

[2]Information on obtaining advisory circulars is available at any Government Printing Office bookstore, or by writing to: U.S. Department of Transportation, Distribution Requirements Section, M-481.1, Washington, D.C. 20590.

provide information on runway length, and the aircraft characteristic documents describe the physical dimensions and ground maneuvering procedures for each type of aircraft. Advisory Circular 150/5335-4 sets forth FAA standards for determining runway length. Aircraft gross weight, maximum stage length (nonstop distance), and airport meteorological conditions are primary factors an airport planner must consider in determining runway length.

Airport planners must also recognize the need to protect the integrity of terminal airspace from intrusion of high structures and other obstructions that would constitute a hazard to air navigation. Two principal documents govern the determination of hazards to air navigation. They are:

    1. United States Standard for Terminal Instrument Procedures (TERPS).
    2. FAR Part 77—Objects Affecting Navigable Airspace.

As is often the case, there is no single text, advisory circular or handbook that can be directly applied throughout a project. It is up to the planner to understand the principles outlined in the documentation and tailor them to the specific situation.

8.4 FEDERAL GRANT PROGRAMS

The first major federal airport grant-in-aid program was authorized under the Federal Airport Act of 1946. Under this program, funds were made available out of the U.S. Treasury General Fund to support airport development projects. Allocation of annual authorizations to each airport was left to the discretion of the FAA Administrator. Between 1946 and 1969 an average of $52.5 million was allocated annually for this program.

In the mid 1960s, capacity shortfalls became evident at many of the high density traffic airports. Lengthy queues were appearing at the ends of runways, formed by aircraft waiting for takeoff clearance. Additional runways, taxiways and navigational aids were sorely needed to increase airport capacity. The Airport and Airway Development Act of 1970 was enacted into law to provide a major source of development funds to improve airport and airway system capacities.

The principal source of funds would be raised through a series of user taxes (excise taxes on tickets, aviation gas and tires, aircraft registration fees, freight waybills, etc.). Allocation of funds for capital improvements is administered by the FAA and grants are made directly to airports served by air carriers under an entitlement formula (based on passenger enplanements). Additional grants are made from the Secretary of Transportation's discretionary fund. The capital grant program under the 1970 Act was commonly referred to as the Airport Development Aid Program (ADAP) and covered airport improvement projects considered necessary by the FAA for maintaining or upgrading airport safety. Project eligibility under the federal grant program is generally limited to runway and taxiway construction, airfield lighting and marking, approach lighting, apron paving, airport fire and emergency equipment, and land acquisition. Funds are available for public areas in terminal buildings on the condition that all eligible safety-related improvements associated with aircraft landings and takeoffs have been constructed by the airport.

The 1970 Act also established a Planning Grant Program (PGP) administered by the FAA to provide funds to public agencies for airport system planning and airport master planning. Approximately $15,000,000 was made available each year for this program.

In the Airport and Airway Improvement Act of 1982 (Public Law 97-248), Congress extended the airport capital grant program for another 10 years. A major change created by this legislation was combining ADAP and PGP into one program and designating it the Airport Improvement Program (AIP). Program authorizations between fiscal years 1982 and 1987 are indicated in Table 8-3. Any owner or a public use airport may submit to the FAA a project grant application. On receipt of such application, the FAA must review it to determine if:

1. The airport and project are in the "National Plan."

2. Project is consistent with the general land use plan of surrounding jurisdictions.

3. Local project sponsor has sufficient funds to cover project costs above federal grant authorization, and project will be completed without delay.

4. Fair consideration has been given to the interests and land use plans of surrounding jurisdictions.

5. A full and complete review has been given to effects upon the environment.

The federal share is 90% of the total project cost at most airports. However, airports enplaning 0.25% or more of the total number of annual passengers at commercial airports in the United States are limited to a federal share of 75%.

TABLE 8-3 Airport Improvement Program Authorizations

Fiscal year	1982	1983	1984	1985	1986	1987	Total
Airport grants, in millions of dollars	450	600	793.5	912	1017	1017.2	4789.7

More detailed information on the federal grant program is available in the Airport and Airway Improvement Act of 1982 (PL97-248, September 3, 1982), (Reference 5), and FAR Part 152, "Airport Aid" (14). Assistance in determining project eligibility and in the grant application process is available from the Airport Division in FAA regional offices or in FAA airport district offices.

8.5 SELECTED REFERENCES

1. *Air Transportation Bibliography*, prepared by the Transportation Research Board for the Federal Aviation Administration, Washington, D.C., December 1978.
2. "Airline Aircraft Gates and Passenger Terminal Space Approximations" *AD/SC Report No. 4*, Air Transport Association of America, Washington, D.C., June 1977.
3. *Airplane Characteristics for Airport Planning*, published by aircraft manufacturers to present information on aircraft characteristics needed by airport planners. Documents may be obtained from:

   • Boeing Commercial Airplane Company
   P.O. Box 3707
   Seattle, Washington 98124
   Attention: Manager, Airport Development
           Mail Stop 6E-29

   • Lockheed-California Company
   P.O. Box 551
   Burbank, California 91520
   Attention: Department Manager, Airport Compatibility

   • McDonnell-Douglas Corporation
   Douglas Aircraft Company
   3855 Lakewood Boulevard
   Long Beach, California 90846
   Attention: Chief Airport Aircraft Compatibility Engineer
           Mail Stop 35-97

4. *Airport Activity Statistics of Certificated Route Air Carriers*, joint publication of Federal Aviation Administration and Civil Aeronautics Board (annual), Washington, D.C.
5. Airport and Airway Improvement Act of 1982, Public Law 97-248, 97th Congress.
6. *Airport Planning Manual*, Part 1—Master Planning; Part 2— Land Use and Environmental Control, 1st ed., International Civil Aviation Organization, Montreal, Canada, 1977.
7. *Airport Terminals Reference Manual*, International Air Transport Association, Montreal, Canada, December 1976.
8. *Airport User Traffic Characteristics for Ground Transportation Planning*, Institute of Transportation Engineers, Washington, D.C., 1976.
9. *The Apron and Terminal Building Planning Report*, prepared by the Ralph M. Parsons Company, Pasadena, Calif., for the Federal Aviation Administration, March 1976.
10. *CTOL Transport Aircraft Characteristics, Trends, and Growth Projections*, Aerospace Industries Association of America, Inc., Washington, D.C., January 1979.

11. *Environmental Assessment of Airport Development Actions,* prepared by Greiner Environmental Sciences, Inc., Baltimore, Md., for the Federal Aviation Administration, March 1977.
12. *FAA Air Traffic Activity,* Federal Aviation Administration, Washington, D.C., (annual).
13. *FAA Statistical Handbook of Aviation,* Federal Aviation Administration, Washington D.C., (annual).
14. Federal Aviation Regulations, Part 152, "Airport Aid," Federal Aviation Administration, Washington, D.C.
15. *International Standards and Recommended Practices— Aerodromes,* Annex 14 to the Convention on International Civil Aviation, 7th ed., International Civil Aviation Organization, Montreal, Canada, June 1976.
16. *Terminal Area Forecasts,* Federal Aviation Administration, Washington, D.C. (annual).

CHAPTER 9

RAILROAD PLANNING[a]

9.1 INTRODUCTION

In 1970 two events occurred that would dramatically affect planning for the future of United States railroads. First, the bankruptcy of the Penn Central, followed quickly by the bankruptcy of several other railroads in the northeast and midwest, shocked state and federal governments into direct involvement in planning that had been largely the domain of the carriers themselves. Second, the enactment of the National Environmental Policy Act (NEPA) introduced expanded public involvement in planning for the abandonment of lines and the construction of new lines and facilities.

Problems for the railroads were compounded through the 1970s. The energy shortage and high inflation and interest rates, coupled with recession conditions, placed unprecedented management dilemmas before all railroad officials. Freedom to meet these challenges was enhanced through passage of federal deregulation bills such as the Staggers Rail Act of 1980.

As we enter the middle of the 1980s, we see the rail carriers meeting these financial challenges through merger, consolidation of operations, and modernization of facilities. We also see the federal government divesting itself of the apparently now viable Conrail (the federally created railroad that took over operations of the Penn Central and other bankrupt railroads of the northeast and midwest in 1976) and reducing its financial commitment to a more stable and efficient National Railroad Passenger Corporation (Amtrak).

Planners at all levels of government and industry have had a hand in shaping the events of the 1970s and 1980s that have in many ways reorganized the railroad industry to better deal with the challenges of the future. They will continue to face some of the same challenges and many new ones in the years to come. Economists, management strategists, and public policy planners will be most interested in issues related to providing a competitive and financially efficient service in today's marketplace. Operating practices, labor contracts, rate making, government regulation, mergers, market trends and capital formation are examples of these kinds of issues.

Transportation engineers and planners, on the other hand, will be most interested in issues related to creating a rational operating envi-

---

[a]Prepared by Thomas E. Barron, M.ASCE and Winn B. Frank, De Leuw, Cather & Company, Denver, CO.

ronment and developing the physical plant necessary to provide a competitive and financially efficient service. This chapter emphasizes those planning problems most frequently faced by the transportation engineer and planner. In this context, planning for railroads involves:

1. Systems planning for main lines, which involves analyzing the demand, capacity, and operating practices of the major line-haul elements of the railroad system from the broadest perspective.

2. Planning for improvements to the existing system, including providing new and improved intermodal transfer facilities, improving terminal and yard operations and access, rationalizing rail system configurations in urban areas (from land use and operating efficiency perspectives), and eliminating at-grade crossings of roadways.

3. Planning for light-density lines, by evaluating proposed abandonments, developing cost-sharing agreements, and preserving and using abandoned rights-of-way.

4. Planning for intercity rail passenger service, using conventional, high-speed and super-speed systems.

9.2 CONDITION OF UNITED STATES RAILROADS

The transportation engineer and planner must have some understanding of those factors that contribute to the present condition of U.S. railroads and may affect future conditions. This section reviews briefly some of the more important events and trends that define the environment in which the railroads operate. The impact of the energy crisis, investment trends, railroad mergers, railroad labor practices, and major legislative actions are reviewed with an aim of providing a context for the planning process. Finally, the State Rail Planning Process is introduced as a framework for much of the public sector involvement in railroad planning.

9.2.1 Energy Crisis Impact on Railroads

Shortages and the high cost of petroleum-derived fuels have caused railroads to be more prominent in transportation planning activities. Two impacts are immediately apparent: (1) Railroad utilization as a partial substitute for highway transport, and (2) railroad transport of substitute energy material, particularly coal.

Coal transportation has had the most significant impact on the railroad industry. The impetus has come from both domestic and export markets. On the domestic scene, for example, construction of new coal-fired generating plants and the slowdown in construction of nuclear plants have caused a proliferation of new unit coal train movements (a unit train is an integral train having a given set of cars and locomotives dedicated to shuttle service between one origin and one destination, normally for a single commodity). For example, the

Burlington Northern Railroad first started its unit coal train operations in 1969. As of 1980, the railroad had 152 unit train sets operating in coal service. Approximately 100,000,000 tons (90,700,000 metric tons) of coal were hauled, requiring an average of 30 coal trains a day to be originated throughout the system. Coal exports have shown similar expansion. The Chessie System handled 35,000,000 tons (31,750,000 metric tons) in 1980, a 70% increase over 1979. For the first time, export coal began moving through west coast ports (Los Angeles, Long Beach, Stockton) to Pacific rim countries such as Japan and Malaysia.

9.2.2 Investment Trends

Financial statistics for the railroad industry have been improving, as Table 9-1 shows. These data indicate a continued investment by the railroads in their physical plant and rolling stock. Particularly important is the uptrend exhibited by the return on net investment. Although the rate seems less significant when compared to that of other major industries, the new legislative freedoms, augmented by management action, are expected to promote a continued upward pattern.

The 1981 Economic Recovery Tax Act replaces the traditional retirement-replacement-betterment (RRB) methods of depreciation with the new Accelerated Cost Recovery System (ACRS). ACRS will provide for complete cost recovery on most plant and equipment expenditures based on a 5-yr depreciation schedule. Under RRB, only the salvage value was recoverable. Therefore, significant financial advantages are apparent in utilizing ACRS. In addition, equipment leasing and research activity have been granted favorable tax provisions.

9.2.3 Railroad Mergers

Railroad mergers are having profound effects on the rail industry and shipping public. From the national standpoint, railroad corporate identities are practically unrecognizable from those of 1970. A partial listing of merged railroads and their antecedents is provided in Table 9-2. For brevity, some "intermediate" mergers (e.g., Penn Central) have not been listed. Considerable speculation has been made regarding the

TABLE 9-1 Railroad Industry Financial Statistics for 1975 and 1980

Financial indicator (1)	1975 (2)	1980 (3)
Net railway operating income, in millions of dollars	350.6	1337.0
Rate of return on net investment, as a percentage	1.20	4.25
Capital expenditures on roadway and structures, in millions of dollars	486.4	1275.0
Total capital expenditures, in millions of dollars	1724.7	3621.2

TABLE 9-2 Some Merged Railroads and Their Antecedents

Merged railroad (1)	Antecedent railroads (2)
Conrail	New York Central
	Pennsylvania
	New York, New Haven & Hartford
	Erie
	Lackawanna
CSX Corporation	
Seaboard System R.R.	Atlantic Coast Line
	Seaboard Airline
	Louisville & Nashville
	Clinchfield
	Georgia
Chessie System	Baltimore & Ohio
	Chesapeake & Ohio
	Western Maryland
Norfolk Southern Corp.	Norfolk & Western
	Southern
Union Pacific System	Union Pacific
	Missouri Pacific
	Western Pacific
Burlington Northern R.R.	Chicago, Burlington & Quincy
	Great Northern
	Northern Pacific
Santa Fe Southern Pacific	Santa Fe
	Southern Pacific

reasons for the "merger movement." Although no readily identifiable single reason presents itself, factors such as shifting world trade patterns, economies of scale, competitive advantage and self protection are frequently cited.

From the shippers' perspective, changes may be expected in routing of freight as lines and facilities are consolidated to achieve economies of scale. Also, short-line railroads are proliferating as the large railroads divest themselves of the unprofitable lines and sell them to others who can make profits.

9.2.4 Railroad Labor

One of the most significant factors affecting the railroad industry is labor. In 1981 and 1982, approximately 39% of railway operating revenues were paid out in the form of wages. Competing modes (e.g., waterway, slurry pipeline) have argued that because of the high labor component in railroad expenses, rail rates will continue to rise at inflationary rates, whereas their rates will remain more stable because they are less labor intensive. The heart of the question, then, becomes whether railroads will be able to negotiate real productivity gains in future labor contracts.

During the recession years of 1981-83, important labor concession events took place in reaction to economic conditions and to gain new traffic from competing modes. For example, Amtrak was able to negotiate significant train crew reductions on its Auto Train service between Virginia and Florida. Numerous reduced-crew trains handling trailer-on-flatcar traffic and bulk commodities have been instituted by a number of railroads to compete for truck traffic. Railroad labor agreed to changes which helped Conrail and the Milwaukee Road, another bankrupt railroad, to keep operating. These concessions by railroad labor represent a realistic assessment of the economic and competitive climate faced by the railroad industry.

Another aspect of the labor picture concerns human relations and employee morale. As in U.S. industry in general, the railroad companies are becoming increasingly aware of the importance of people in their organizations. Most railroads now utilize management development and training programs. The Southern Pacific Railroad, for example, instituted a Transportation Problem Solving program that enables contract employees and management to openly explore ideas which may improve the railroad's competitive position.

The trends exemplified by the concessions made during the recession period, and the increasing awareness of employee importance, indicate that there is flexibility in labor negotiations and that railroads are more attuned to the total impact of labor relations than they were in the past. However, the most important component in productivity negotiations will continue to be the elasticity between increased wages (reflected in higher rates) and traffic lost due to the higher rates.

The interests of the railroad labor unions are an important consideration in developing solutions to planning problems. Changes in operating practices or modifications to other physical features that may have a detrimental effect on safety will be of prime concern to the unions. Their requirements should be considered early in the planning process in order to develop solutions that can be implemented.

9.2.5 Railroad Legislation

Since the early 1970s, major legislation has been passed by Congress that directly affects railroads. This legislation includes the Regional

Rail Reorganization Act of 1973 (3R Act), the Railroad Revitalization and Regulatory Reform Act of 1976 (4R Act), the Rail Services Act of 1975, and the Staggers Rail Act of 1980. With respect to planning, several provisions are noteworthy:

1. Local rail service continuation provisions of the 3R act provide a timely procedure for line abandonments and the opportunity for states to continue certain rail line operations with assistance of federal funds.

2. Railroad rehabilitation and improvement financing (Title 5 of the 4R Act) permitted railroads to apply for federal guarantee of financial obligations, resulting in the establishment of the Rail Trust Fund. In 1980, for example, the Southern Pacific utilized the sale of $48,500,000 in redeemable preference shares to the Federal Railroad Administration to help finance a $97,000,000 track rehabilitation program between Santa Rosa, New Mexico, and Topeka, Kansas.

3. Regarding contract rates, regulatory easing actions taken by the Interstate Commerce Commission (ICC) and reinforced by the Staggers Act of 1980 now enable railroads to negotiate transportation contracts. Contracts may cover any or all aspects of the relationship between service and product, railroad and customer. Contracts have the propensity to encourage increased utilization of railroad services, thus promoting transportation stability from which lower unit costs may result. The potential for traffic diversion from highways is increased.

4. With regard to selective rate deregulation, in 1979, the ICC deregulated the haulage of most fruits and vegetables. Further deregulation of bulk food commodities occurred in 1980, and in 1981 all piggyback traffic was deregulated. These actions had significant impact on Conrail, for example, as 19,431 trailer loads of perishables from the west moved to east coast markets in 1981, compared to 6915 loads in 1980.

The trend in federal legislation, then, has been toward encouraging the railroads to streamline and reorganize, providing some of the financing needed to do it, and allowing them the management freedom needed to compete in today's marketplace.

9.2.6 State Rail Planning Process

The collapse of the Penn Central and other railroads in the northeast and midwest led directly to passage of the 3R Act. The 3R Act, in turn, led to the creation of the Rail Services Planning Office (RSPO) and the United States Railway Association (USRA) as the planning and funding agencies for the Consolidated Rail Corporation (Conrail). Conrail began operations in April 1976. The 3R Act also provided funds for rail service continuation on lines that were not to be continued under USRA's Final System Plan, and, in Section 402(c) (1), directed that each state, as a prerequisite for eligibility to receive rail service continuation subsidies, establish "a State plan for rail transportation and local rail services which is administered or coordinated by a designated State agency . . . '' The program was limited to most of the midwest, the entire northeast, and adjacent parts of Wisconsin, Missouri and Kentucky.

Section 803 of the 4R Act extended both the local rail service continuation program and the rail transportation planning process to all states in the nation. Section 203(j) further refined eligibility requirements by requiring each state to establish "an adequate plan for rail services in such State as part of an overall planning process for all transportation services in such State, including a suitable process for updating, revising and amending such plan."

The Federal Railroad Administration's *Rail Planning Manual* (11, 12) is the most definitive accounting of the state rail planning process. The reader is encouraged to consult that document for detailed information on the planning processes and analysis techniques that are reviewed in the sections that follow.

9.3 SYSTEMS PLANNING FOR MAIN LINES

System level planning for railroads focuses on the consolidation or selective improvement of railroad main lines and is primarily the domain of the railroad companies themselves. In fact, prior to the 3R Act in 1973 little, if any, systems planning was done outside the railroad companies themselves. As a result, comprehensive planning techniques are still in their infancy by comparison to highway, transit, and airway system planning. This results in part from the somewhat unique data and analysis requirements associated with the ownership, rate structures, operating practices and routing decisions of the railroads. For example, Section 15 of the Interstate Commerce Act allows the originating carrier, unless otherwise dictated by the shipper, to specify the routing for a particular shipment. The carrier will normally attempt to maximize the line-haul mileage on its own property or select a routing based on an agreement with a connecting carrier. This can result in less than optimum routing and makes freight-flow simulation and the development of forecasting models difficult. Nonetheless, railroad systems planning techniques are fundamentally the same as those used for urban transportation planning or any other network simulation and forecasting system.

The *Rail Planning Manual* suggests three stages of planning for mainline railroads. These are illustrated in Fig. 9-1 and described as follows:

- Stage I Planning. Initial stage. Involvement largely limited to obtaining an initial familiarity with main lines and other components of the rail system. Planning largely an individual response to particular problems or issues. Some broad policy planning.
- Stage II Planning. Intermediate stage. Limited development of a

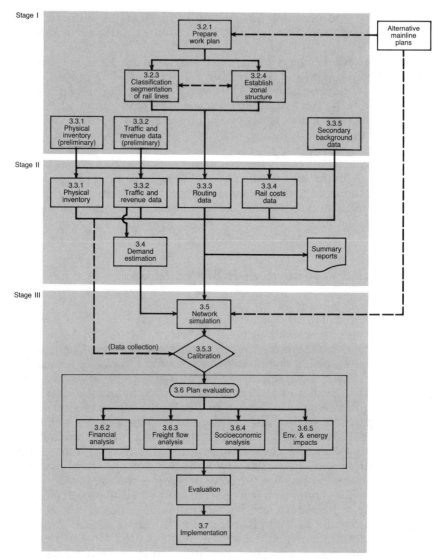

Fig. 9-1. Steps in executing mainline studies (12)

systems planning capability for main lines and other rail system components. Initial use of analytical techniques for forecasting demand, network simulation, and assessing impacts. More sophisticated, quantitative response to particular problems or issues. Deeper understanding of factors influencing demand and mode choice.

• Stage III Planning. Advanced stage. Full development of a comprehensive freight transportation systems planning process of which rail planning is one portion. Full-scale application of the more sophisticated techniques for demand estimation, mode split, network analysis, economic evaluation, and impact estimation (12, p. 3-6).

Initial steps in the process involve the classification and segmentation of lines and the designation of analysis zones. For the purposes of mainline planning, the best source for an initial functional classification of lines is that developed under Section 503 of the 4R Act and published under the title *Final Standards, Classification and Designation of Lines of Class I Railroads in the United States* (2). For a particular regional study, classification of lines can take any form that provides a logical and useful division and recognizes the specific planning, implementation, administrative or regulatory purpose of the study.

Segmentation of rail lines is merely a division of the lines into links for the purpose of recording and manipulating data by computer. The link will have generally uniform characteristics (physically and functionally), and will be defined by two nodes which correspond to points of change in those characteristics (such as a yard, intersection, major traffic generator, or political boundary).

As the basis for forecasting traffic generation and origin-destination movements, the geographic study area should be delineated and divided into zones. The study area boundary should be sufficiently large to permit identification of all tributary market areas and all flows to, from, through, or within the study area. Zone size and definition will vary depending on the purpose and level of refinement required.

9.3.1 Data Collection

The data needed to conduct mainline studies include a physical system inventory, freight flow and revenue data, routing data, and cost data. Figure 9-2 lists the kinds of physical inventory data normally required and suggests possible sources for them. The inventory should be collected and coded in a form which corresponds to the links as previously defined. This form permits efficient storage and manipulation, particularly if computer analysis is envisioned.

Freight-flow and revenue data are more difficult to obtain than physical data. The ICC maintains confidentiality of the shipment data collected and compiled by the railroads. What is available, however, is an ICC/FRA one-percent sample of revenue waybills for carloads terminated by line haul railroads, which can be expanded to provide a basis for large-scale mainline analysis. The one-percent sample files contain detailed information on origin, destination, commodity type, and rate.

Routing data are fundamental to the accurate assessment of the impact of proposed actions that divert traffic from established patterns. Because most long-distance shipments involve several carriers, routings are not always on the minimum time or distance path. For this reason,

Data item	Possible source(s)
1. System name	employee timetables
2. Division name	track charts, employee timetables
3. Line name	system maps, official railway guide, track charts
4. Link length	employee timetables, USGS maps, track charts
5. Link type (passenger or freight)	system maps, transportation zone maps
6. Link use status (active, petitioned for abandonment, etc.)	index of abandoned lines
7. FRA track class	track charts, FRA records
8. Number of tracks	system maps, transportation zone maps, track charts, employee timetables
9. Weight of rail	track charts
10. Signal type	signal charts, transportation zone maps, employee timetables
11. Maximum speed	employee timetables, track charts
12. Speed restrictions	employee timetables, record of speed restrictions
13. Maximum weight on rail	track charts, employee timetables, clearance guide
14. Horizontal clearance	clearance guide
15. Vertical clearance	clearance guide
16. Maximum horizontal curve	track charts
17. Maximum grade	track charts
18. Passing siding capacity	employee timetables, track charts
Optional:	
19. Functional class	—
20. Mode type (station interchange yard, etc.)	system maps, transportation zone maps, equipment register, employee timetables
21. Mode location (coordinates)	USGS maps, transportation zone maps
22. Location name	transportation zone maps, track charts, employee timetables
23. Standard location code	freight station accounting code directory, SPLC directory
24. SMSA	statistical abstract of U.S.
25. Production area	U.S. census of transportation
26. Region	—

Fig. 9-2. Sources of rail inventory data (12)

a variety of sources must be consulted to construct an accurate simulation of flows. The waybill sample previously mentioned gives some information, but railway guides, through freight schedules, shippers and railroad personnel should also be consulted.

It is extremely difficult to measure the cost of moving each carload of freight from origin to destination, so cost data must be derived using elaborate accounting procedures. System-wide data are available from each railroad's annual report to the ICC. The ICC also develops variable and fixed unit costs by car type, as well as information on the cost of interchange and switching services, trailer-on-flatcar (TOFC) or container-on-flatcar (COFC) shipments, loss and damage claims, etc., which it publishes under the title *Rail Carload Cost Scales by Territory and Commodity* (10).

9.3.2 Demand Forecasting

Demand forecasts are essential for economic impact analysis and the simulation of freight flows. The available approaches are shown in Fig. 9-3 and described as follows (note that, in this section only, numbers in parentheses refer to numbers in Fig. 9-3):

- An economic forecast (1) that estimates sales by industry type is required for all approaches, although the level of detail of industrial classification and geographic zoning may vary substantially.
- For Stage II planning, the economic forecast (1) is used to expand present rail shipments and receipts in carloads (2) to a horizon year in terms of numbers of carloads shipped and received. This

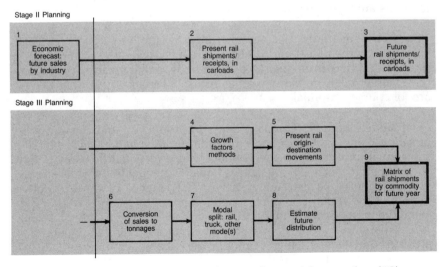

Fig. 9-3. Alternative approaches to demand forecasting (12)

output can then be used to expand shipments from light-density lines and main lines, so that general orders-of-magnitude of freight traffic increases will be known.

- For Stage III planning, the simplest approach is to apply the economic forecast (1) to a table of present origin-destination movements (4) using growth factors methods (5). This will produce a matrix of rail shipments by commodity type for the horizon year (9).
- For more sophisticated Stage III planning, the economic forecast (1) can be converted to tonnages (6). Then a mode split model can be applied (7) to estimate tonnage movements by all freight modes, including rail, truck, water, and possibly pipeline or air. The rail proportions can be used to modify a present origin-destination table (4), or a new distribution pattern can be estimated (8) to produce the horizon year matrix of rail shipments (9). Since there have been no applications of this technique to state or even multistate regional planning, this method must be considered as under development (12, p. 3–46).

The starting point for railroad demand forecasting is an economic forecast of producer and market factors. Quantitative methods, time series methods, or qualitative methods may be used.

Quantitative methods   There are four types of quantitative methods: (1) Regression analysis; (2) simultaneous equation systems; (3) input-output models; and (4) economic base studies. In complexity, the economic base studies are the simplest; the input-output models and simultaneous equation systems are much more complex. All methods depend upon time series data for the region (and any subregions) for which economic forecasts are being made.

Time series methods   Time series analysis and projection, or trend extension, is the oldest and probably the most widely used forecasting method. It differs from quantitative methods in that no attempt is made to explain or relate demand to other "causal" variables. Time series data are, of course, essential.

Qualitative methods   Dramatic shifts in production and consumption of various commodities can be expected from time to time and will have substantial impacts upon the volumes and directional flows of freight shipments. In such circumstances, qualitative methods of economic forecasting may be extremely useful. The essence of the qualitative method is the application of reasoned judgment by persons who understand the industries producing, consuming, or moving freight and who, from experience, may be able to estimate changes in freight demand that are caused by factors which cannot be described adequately with available statistical methods or data.

A combination of qualitative and quantitative methods may be useful. Qualitative methods include the Delphi method, market research, panel consensus and anticipation surveys.

The economic forecasts are converted to freight demand forecasts by applying the results to known shipments and receipts of freight carloads (Stage II forecast) or known origin-destination movements (Stage III forecast).

9.3.3 Network Simulation

Simulation of freight flows involves a procedure that is very much like the traffic assignment procedure used in passenger transportation modeling. Each requires schematic networks, routing procedures or algorithms, and either trip interchange tables or trip interchange models. Freight shipments, however, are considerably more complex in that they involve more modes of transportation, more types of vehicles, more complicated physical distribution facilities, more complicated routing decisions, and literally thousands of discrete commodity groups.

The Federal Railroad Administration (FRA) has developed a computer simulation model for analysis of the national railroad network. The model is a modified version of the Federal Highway Administration's traffic assignment package. It consists of an extensive railroad network (approximately 20,000 links and 16,000 nodes representing over 200,000 route miles and 332 different railroad carriers), several traffic interchange data bases, and a series of 45 computer programs to process the data. The procedure is shown in Fig. 9-4.

The major weakness of the FRA network model has been its dependence on a minimum impedance (time, distance, cost) algorithm that does not necessarily replicate actual routing decisions. Nonetheless, it provides a useful starting point for development of a project specific network simulation for mainline studies. Several states have also developed network simulation procedures for use in state rail planning. These should also be consulted prior to making decisions on which procedure is most useful and efficient for a particular purpose.

9.3.4 Plan Evaluation

Mainline consolidation and improvement alternatives will have financial, operational, environmental, social, and economic implications. Financial analysis procedures, such as FRA's Revenue, Expense and Equipment Forecast (REEF) model or the unit variable cost procedure can be used to evaluate operational or system configuration changes from the capital and net operating cost perspective.

Freight volumes should also be compared with rail line and interchange capacity to identify potential bottlenecks and measure delay. Rail line capacity is not a quantity that can be precisely determined, since intolerable delays and increased operating costs occur long before capacity conditions are realized. Rail line capacity is best determined using a performance simulator, but a fixed capacity, dependent on a limited

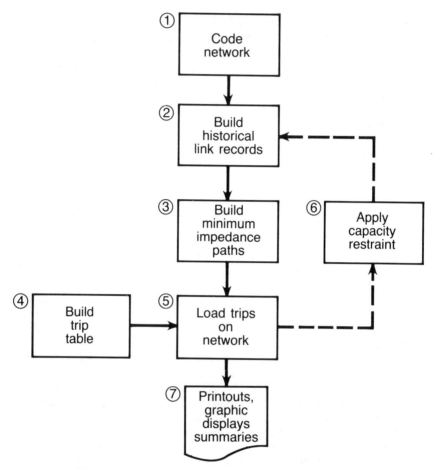

Fig. 9-4. Macro-diagram: FRA network model (12)

number of simple variables, is often used for an initial indication. Table 9-3 gives one estimate of capacity developed by the U.S. Department of Transportation.

Other operational parameters should also be considered in evaluating mainline modifications. A circuity analysis, for example, can be performed by calculating the ratio between actual mileage traversed and short rail path mileage. Train performance, blocking and classification, labor, schedule and reliability studies may also be appropriate.

Economic and social impacts resulting from mainline modifications will be derived largely from changes in shipping cost. Possible effects include corporate bankruptcy or relocation, employment changes, social dislocation, tax base changes and changes in railroad employment or viability.

Finally, the evaluation of mainline modifications should take into

TABLE 9-3 Rail Segment Capacity (13)

Number of Tracks (1)	Automatic Block Signal System		Centralized Traffic Control System	
	Trains per day[a] (2)	Gross tons per year,[b] in millions (3)	Trains per day[a] (4)	Gross tons per year[b] in millions (5)
Single	40	62	60	93
Double	120	186	160	250

[a]Total both directions.

[b]Gross ton miles per route mile; total both directions.

Note: This table represents the engineering capacity of the respective lines. Practical capacity will be affected by terrain, train size, tonnage, operating procedures, and other factors.

consideration the environmental effects of alternatives under consideration. Aggregate measures of fuel consumption and pollutant emissions can be calculated if projected diversions from truck to rail or vice versa can be derived from the forecasting technique. New lines or significantly increased traffic on existing lines may also result in adverse noise impacts, changes in land value, effects on the natural environment, or an increase in safety or automobile delay problems associated with at-grade crossings (see Sec. 9.4.4).

9.4 PLANNING FOR IMPROVEMENTS TO EXISTING SYSTEM

From the railroad and shipper perspective, much can be done to improve the efficiency, reduce the transit time and reduce the cost of rail transportation. From the community perspective much can be done to make railroads a better neighbor, particularly in urban areas where rapid growth has placed a heavy strain on the interface between railroads and their environment. Issues like improved intermodal terminals, modernization and expansion of yards, urban rail bypasses and grade separations are at the forefront of present-day railroad planning. Planning for these improvements is fairly straightforward, but lack of funding, institutional problems and environmental considerations have constrained their implementation.

9.4.1 Intermodal Operations

Since the 1950s, intermodal transport of freight has captured an increasing share of intercity traffic. Trailer-on-flatcar (TOFC) and container-on-flatcar (COFC) services are particularly competitive for transport distances of over 500 miles (800 km) and can be cost competitive for distances as low as 200 miles (320 km). Intermodal service of this nature is distinguished from conventional rail service, not only by specialized hardware, but by unique truck-rail cooperative arrangements in rate-making, billing and operations. Continued growth in intermodal transport is hampered, however, by the difficulties involved in coordinating with the trucking industry and unions and the lack of funding for construction of efficient intermodal terminals.

Estimating the demand potential for intermodal transport requires extensive data on the costs, rates and travel time of the truck and rail modes. This would normally be undertaken as part of a larger systems planning effort as described in the previous section. One technique for use in forecasting diversion to intermodal transport is the modal preference matrix (see examples in Fig. 9-5). It shows the expected percent-

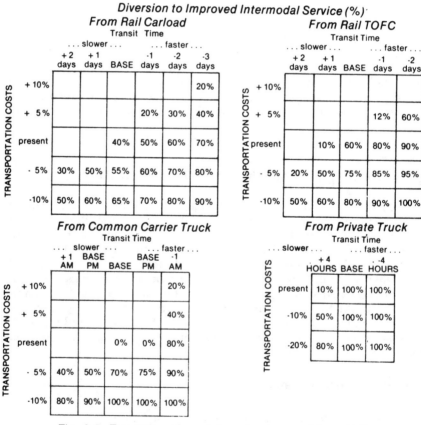

Fig. 9-5. Examples of modal preference matrices (14)

age of diverted traffic as a function of changes in cost and transit time. These matrices are generally constructed from the results of a shipper survey of modal preference.

The facilities for intermodal transfer have more often than not consisted of a simple ramp used to back trailers onto a string of flat cars connected by bridge plates. This method is very inefficient, but requires the least capital investment. More modern facilities for large-scale intermodal transfer utilize gantry cranes or sidelift (large forklift) trucks. In locating and designing these facilities, particular attention must be given to rail operations, highway (truck) access, and environmental considerations.

Intermodal transfer facilities are also of interest at ports (ship-to-rail) and mines (conveyor or truck-to-rail). The proliferation of unit train movements for coal and grain and of bridge trains for international cargo has demanded efficient, high-capacity transfer facilities at these terminals. In this case, bridge trains refer to trains operating from one port region to another port region carrying traffic for transshipment to or from ships.

9.4.2 Improved Terminal and Yard Operations

A 1974 U.S. Department of Transportation study found that the typical freight car had a 25.6-day cycle, of which 7.3 days (29%) was spent in terminal yards, 8.5 days (33%) in intermediate yards, 6.0 days (23%) with the consignor or consignee, 1.8 days (7%) in empty backhaul, and only 2.0 days (8%) actually hauling freight in revenue producing operation (12). With over 62% of the cycle involving yard switching operations, it is clear that productivity improvements should be focused on these facilities.

There are four basic types of yards in the rail system: (1) Classification yards that break down, sort and assemble road trains; (2) industrial yards which serve as collection points for classifying freight cars into local trains serving industrial sidings; (3) interchange yards where cars are exchanged by connecting railroads; and (4) intermodal yards described in Sec. 9.4.1. Some yards also provide support services such as car inspection, repair, weighting, and cleaning. Often more than one type of yard function is provided at a single location.

As the FRA *Rail Planning Manual* points out, there are three major categories of problems which are encountered in planning for more efficient yard operations:

Primary among these is that of railroad operational problems, such as locomotive shortages, yard configuration, and equipment failures. These problems are frequently aggravated by institutional arrangements, such as trackage rights and labor rules, which can restrict the flexibility of train movements. Finally, the yards create neighborhood and community problems of noise, safety and land use which must be studied. (12, p. 4-115)

Any comprehensive planning effort aimed at solving rail terminal problems must consider a broad spectrum of interested parties. The railroad companies, the unions representing railroad employees, the affected shippers, local government planners and officials, neighborhood associations and potential funding institutions should all be consulted through some structured involvement process. The steps suggested by the *Rail Planning Manual* present one approach:

1. Determine who is interested in the problem and why.
2. Determine the physical layout and typical work load of the yard.
3. Set up system to measure terminal operations.
4. Meet with the railroad officials, labor union officials, and shippers to find out what operational problems they perceive, what are their needs or requirements, what are possible solutions not requiring capital investment, and what are potential long-term alternatives.
5. Distribute a draft of the study plan to interested parties.
6. Using a rail advisory committee, hold meetings on the draft report to solicit comments and identify further needs.
7. Identify and evaluate alternative operational procedures.
8. Monitor progress toward making yards more efficient.

The most comprehensive effort to date to rationalize terminal operations at a major gateway is the St. Louis Gateway Terminal Restructuring Project. This project represents a good source of information and a starting point for structuring similar terminal area improvement programs in other areas.

9.4.3 Rationalizing Rail System Configurations in Urban Areas

The quality of life in our urban areas is often significantly affected by the presence of railroad lines and terminal operations. These facilities may no longer be optimally located or may be vastly underutilized, even from the railroads' perspective, because of the suburbanization of industry and their adverse impacts on high-density abutting development. The problems include train delay due to speed or operational restrictions at grade crossings; auto traffic delay at grade crossings; safety problems related to grade crossing accidents, trespassing or movement of hazardous materials; the rail barrier effect on neighborhood cohesiveness; and the intrusion of rail noise, vibration, air pollution and visual blight.

As with terminal area planning, the planning process for urban rail rationalization includes a wide range of interested parties and the potential solutions to these problems are numerous. Aside from a handful of federal demonstration projects, there is no single, dedicated source of funding to alleviate these problems. The initiative for their resolution must come from energetic local leaders working to bring a variety of resources to bear.

Options for alleviating urban rail problems include changes in train operations, rerouting of through traffic movements, relocation of yard operations, closing of streets to eliminate grade crossings, constructing grade separations, elevating or depressing rail lines, and providing noise or esthetic shielding. The reader is referred to Moon et al. (7) as one source of techniques to evaluate alternative solutions to these problems, which suggests a neighborhood oriented approach to evaluating the impacts of five types of railroad system changes: (1) Removing a railroad from a neighborhood; (2) adding a railroad to a neighborhood; (3) reducing the level of traffic on an existing railroad; (4) increasing the level of traffic on an existing railroad; and (5) adding a grade separation structure. The general procedure is to identify how each alternative introduces one of these five changes into each uniquely affected neighborhood, to analyze the impact of the changes on the neighborhood, and then to summarize the neighborhood impact of each alternative.

Perhaps two examples would best serve to illustrate some of the options used to solve urban rail problems. Project Lifesaver in Elko, Nevada, was dedicated in November 1983, becoming the first of 18 demonstration projects funded under the Federal Aid Highway Act of 1973 to be completed. Prior to that time as many as 60 slow-moving freight trains a day blocked 13 grade crossings in downtown Elko for extensive periods. Now the Western Pacific and Southern Pacific Railroads have a fully grade-separated, 2.8-mile (4.5-km) corridor around the downtown area, as well as new yard facilities with practically unlimited expansion potential. The $43,000,000 project also included rechannelization of the Humboldt River along the new corridor to solve flood control problems for the city. The old rights-of-way running a block apart through the downtown area are now available for development, landscaping, and other enhancements.

The coordination aspects of the Elko project were extensive. Early phases involved development of alternative track alignments, cost and benefit analyses, a comprehensive environmental impact statement, hydraulic analyses, a downtown and riverfront joint development plan, and extensive traffic planning. In addition to local agencies and the residents of Elko, extensive negotiations were carried on with the two railroads to establish financial participation and operating, maintenance and construction agreements.

In Providence, Rhode Island, expansion of the central business district into vacant land between it and the state capitol has been hampered for years by the elevated embankment of the Northeast Corridor mainline tracks. With extensive local impetus and partial funding from the federally-sponsored Northeast Corridor Improvement Project (see Sec. 9.6), the alignment is being shifted and depressed to allow for the comprehensive development of commercial, residential, and open space, and highway and transit improvements. The project satisfied the objectives of the railroad while at the same time satisfying the broader urban planning objectives of the community. Extensive coordination, local impetus and a broadly based funding package were the keys to planning that is solving an urban railroad problem.

The options are almost limitless, but unless they solve a particular problem for the railroad in a cost-effective way, they are seldom initiated by the railroad planner. Rather, they are part of a comprehensive improvement in the broader urban planning context that will utilize techniques described throughout this planning guide.

9.4.4 Grade Crossings

With an average of one crossing per mile of track throughout the nation and accidents at crossings injuring or killing over 4000 people in 1981, much attention has been focused on the protection or elimination of rail-highway grade crossings. The Highway Safety Acts of 1973 and 1976, and the Surface Transportation Assistance Act of 1978, provided funding authorizations to individual states for safety improvements at public crossings.

From the planning perspective, efforts have been focused on ranking grade crossings using some form of hazard index to identify priorities for elimination of the crossing or upgrading of crossing protection. Several indices have been developed at the state and federal level. The variables considered in calculating these indices include accident history, number of trains, train speed, gradients, angle of approach, protection device, sight distance, daylight versus nighttime trains, traffic volumes, number of tracks, and number of traffic lanes. Data sources for these analyses include the joint DOT-AAR *National Rail-Highway Crossing Inventory* and the *Railroad Accident/Incident Reporting System* (RAIRS), both available through the Federal Railroad Administration.

Eliminating crossings through construction of grade separation is clearly the most desirable action from a safety and traffic delay perspective. Analysis of the benefits of grade separation should recognize the accidents avoided, the reduced delay to road users, the reduced fuel consumption and air pollution associated with queued vehicles, the reduced train noise associated with horn blowing at crossings, and the improved reliability of emergency services. Balanced against these are the high costs, changes in land value, visual intrusions and other potentially adverse environmental effects associated with grade separation structures. Short of actual elimination of the crossing, some upgrading of protection has been shown to be effective (8). Upgrading may include a change from passive protection (signs or crossbucks) to flashers, or from flashers to flashers with gates.

9.5 LIGHT-DENSITY RAIL LINES

Light-density rail lines are normally defined as lines that carry less than 1,000,000 gross tons per mile per year. This is equivalent to Class B Branchlines as defined by the U.S. Secretary of Transportation (2, p. iv). Such lines typically provide originating and terminating freight service to feedmills, lumber yards, mines, factories, grain elevators, and other establishments that are of economic importance to local communities and states.

Planning for the proposed termination of service on light-density lines has been and continues to be the primary focus of state rail planning agency efforts. The prospects for abandonment of light-density lines increased with the reorganization of the bankrupt railroads in the northeast and midwest, and with the easing of ICC regulations and procedures for abandonment petitions nationwide mentioned in Sec. 9.2. The choice for states was reduced to: (1) Permitting abandonment to take place, thus accepting any social costs that result, or (2) continuing rail service through government or shipper subsidy.

The proposals for service abandonment occurred in two ways. First, the USRA's Final System Plan excluded certain uneconomical lines that were not to be made part of the Conrail system. As previously stated, the 3R Act provided funds to the states for planning assistance and for rail service continuation on these lines. Second, any railroad can petition the ICC for a certificate of public convenience and necessity allowing a line to be abandoned. The relationship between the ICC abandonment process and planning for light-density lines as promulgated by the 3R Act is shown in Fig. 9-6.

Often the planning undertaken by states in reaction to the Final System Plan or an ICC abandonment petition was too late to provide meaningful input. More recently, states have caught up, in the sense that state rail planning has incorporated studies of all light-density lines so that early input to an ICC petition is possible. However, these studies are complex, time consuming and data intensive. Eligibility for local rail service assistance requires each state to adopt a state rail plan and a program of projects that addresses the following administrative and product requirements:

(i) Freight traffic and characteristics of shippers on the line of railroad; (ii) revenues derived from rail freight services on each line and the cost of providing those services; (iii) a discussion of the condition of the rail plant, equipment, and facilities; (iv) an economic and operational analysis of present and future freight service needs; (v) an analysis of the effects of abandonment with respect to the transportation needs of the state; (vi) the relative economic, social, environmental, and energy costs and benefits involved in the use of alternate rail services or alternate modes, including costs resulting from lost jobs, energy shortages, and the degradation of the environment; (vii) an evaluation of methods of achieving economies in the cost of rail service operations on lines on which service will be continued including consolidation, pooling, and joint use of operation of lines, facilities and operating equipment; (viii) the competitive or other effects on or by profitable railroads; (ix) for lines or projects which the state may consider for rail banking, a description of future economic potential, such as development of fossil fuel reserves or agricultural production; (x) a statement of the state's projected future

INTERSTATE COMMERCE COMMISSION   PLANNING FOR LIGHT DENSITY LINES

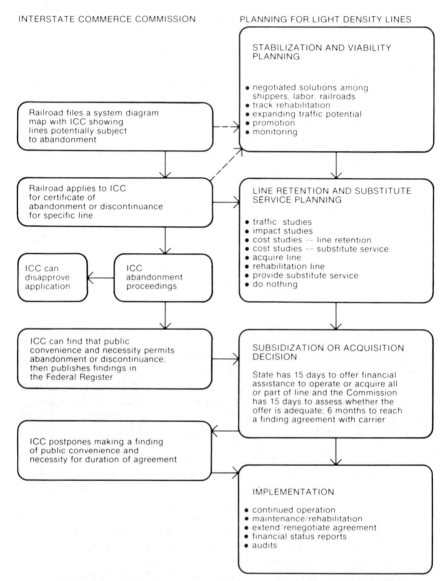

STABILIZATION AND VIABILITY
PLANNING

- negotiated solutions among
  shippers, labor, railroads
- track rehabilitation
- expanding traffic potential
- promotion
- monitoring

Railroad files a system diagram
map with ICC showing
lines potentially subject
to abandonment

Railroad applies to ICC
for certificate of
abandonment or discontinuance
for specific line

LINE RETENTION AND SUBSTITUTE
SERVICE PLANNING

- traffic studies
- impact studies
- cost studies -- line retention
- cost studies -- substitute service
- acquire line
- rehabilitation line
- provide substitute service
- do nothing

ICC can
disapprove
application

ICC
abandonment
proceedings

ICC can find that public
convenience and necessity permits
abandonment or discontinuance;
then publishes findings in
the Federal Register

SUBSIDIZATION OR ACQUISITION
DECISION

State has 15 days to offer financial
assistance to operate or acquire all
or part of line and the Commission
has 15 days to assess whether the
offer is adequate; 6 months to reach
a finding agreement with carrier

ICC postpones making a finding
of public convenience and
necessity for duration of agreement

IMPLEMENTATION

- continued operation
- maintenance/rehabilitation
- extend/renegotiate agreement
- financial status reports
- audits

Fig. 9-6. Planning for light-density lines as it relates to ICC abandonment
process (12)

for the line or project upon the expiration of Federal assistance under
Section 5 of the Act (including such considerations as: profitability,
state or shipper subsidy; state, shipper or carrier acquisition; termination of rail service; and the substitution of other transportation);
(xi) a detailed description of alternatives evaluated, including sub-

sidy or discontinuance, and abandonment of service and potential
for moving freight by alternate rail service or alternate modes, an
explanation of the analysis of each alternative, including the criteria
considered in selecting or rejecting the proposed line or project for
assistance and identification of the relative costs and benefits of each
alternative; (xii) the conclusion of the state as to whether or not the
line or project should be selected for Federal or state assistance and
(xiii) a discussion of how each line or project selected for assistance
is related to the criteria established as a part of the overall state rail
planning process. (3)

The six major components of light-density line studies may be
defined as: (1) Study design; (2) data collection; (3) financial analysis; (4)
community impact analysis; (5) implementation planning; and (6) monitoring. The study design is a management plan that designates lines to
be studied, selects analytical methods, determines data requirements,
develops a work schedule, and estimates staffing and budget requirements. The other five elements of light-density line studies are briefly
described in the following subsections. Once again the reader is referred
to Reference 12 for a more detailed review of procedures and techniques.

9.5.1 Data Collection

The data requirements for light-density line studies include physical and operating data about the line, traffic flow data, shipper characteristics, carrier data, direct and indirect impact estimates and alternative
mode characteristics. Table 9-4 gives a detailed listing of data requirements and potential sources.

A primary technique for data collection is a shipper survey, which
may be conducted by personal interview, telephone or mail-back questionnaire. Each technique has different advantages and disadvantages
with regard to response rate, completeness, quality of data and manpower requirements. Other sources of data for carrier records include
the Association of American Railroads Data Package, which contains
detailed physical and operating data for light-density lines, and the
Branch Line Accounts of the individual railroads, which under 49 C.F.R.
Part 1121.20 and Part 1201, Section 920 (a), are required to be kept by the
railroads for lines in some danger of abandonment or operated under
subsidy agreement.

9.5.2 Financial Analysis

Financial viability of a light-density line is measured by subtracting
the costs which the operator will save if it discontinues service on the
line (avoidable costs) from the revenues which accrue to the carrier from
operation of the line (attributable revenue). Although railroads are
required to provide these data, the states will want to have an independent verification for use in subsidy decisions.

TABLE 9-4 Data requirements of light-density lines (12)

Data Item	Study Design	Data Collection	Financial Analysis	Community Impact Analysis	Implementation Planning	Monitoring	Shipper Survey	Carrier Records	Secondary Sources	Field Inspection
Physical and operating										
1. Length of rail line	●	●	●	●	●	●		●	●	
2. Annual one-way locomotive trips			●			●		●		
3. Average grade per mile segment				×				×		
4. Average curve per mile segment				×				×		
5. Average running speed				×				×		
6. Number of defective crossties				×				●		●
7. Number of defective rails								●		●
8. Quantity of ballast required			●					●		●
9. Terrain type			●		●					
10. Traffic density on adjoining trunk lines			●	×	●			×	×	
11. Capital cost and salvage values			●	×	●				●	
a. ties										
b. rail										
c. ballast										

Shipper/consignee characteristics
(For each shipper/consignee)

1. Identification
   a. name
   b. address
   c. phone no.
2. Private siding/team track
3. Distance to nearest alternate team track facility at which service will be continued
4. Estimated job losses due to:
   a. plant closing
   b. transfer of operations
   c. reduced production
5. Nature of business (SIC type)
6. Annual sales volume ($)
7. Total present employment of firm
8. Estimated annual sales loss (if aband.)
9. Estimated annual wage loss (if aband.)
10. Annual property tax; tax jurisdictions
11. Anticipated capital investment due to abandonment
12. Radius of firms market (selling area)
13. Mode to be used in the event of abandonment

Traffic flow data

1. For each shipper/consignee currently using rail service by commodity (STCC):
   a. annual no. of carloads
   b. annual tonnage
   c. shipment origin
   d. shipment destination

TABLE 9-4 continued

Data Item	Phase of Study						Potential Source(s)			
	Study Design	Data Collection	Financial Analysis	Community Impact Analysis	Implementation Planning	Monitoring	Shipper Survey	Carrier Records	Secondary Sources	Field Inspection
2. Average weight per carload by commodity	●			●			●		×	
3. Revenue/car-mile by commodity			●	×				●	×	
4. Overhead traffic density			●	×				●		
Carrier data										
1. System and branch operating expenses	×		●					●		
a. maintenance of way and structures										
b. maintenance of equipment										
c. traffic										
d. transportation rail line										
e. miscellaneous operations										
f. general										
g. taxes										
2. System and branch revenue	×		●			×		●	×	
3. System and branch operating statistics			●			×		●		
a. train-miles										
b. locomotive-miles										
c. car-miles										
d. gross ton-miles										
e. train-hours										

4. Freight car costs:
   a. per diem rates
   b. capital cost
5. Railroad crew size
6. Railroad wage rates
7. Transshipment (loading & unloading) cost by region

Direct and indirect impacts
1. Number of employees by industry type for each impact area
2. Average wage by county
3. Average wage of secondary sector employees
4. Per capita income from sources other than wages, salaries and proprietor's income
5. Population by MCD
6. Average household size
7. Weekly unemployment payments by wage class; total payments
8. Average period of unemployment
9. Public assistance payments by household size
10. Political boundary locations
11. Total new unemployment claimants-previous year
12. Federal and state income tax rates by salary level
13. Exhaust emission factors for locomotives and trucks
14. Identification of critical air basins within the state
15. Ambient pollutant levels
16. Environmentally sensitive areas
17. Historic sites

TABLE 9-4 continued

Data Item	Study Design	Data Collection	Financial Analysis	Community Impact Analysis	Implementation Planning	Monitoring	Shipper Survey	Carrier Records	Secondary Sources	Field Inspection
Alternate mode characteristics										
1. Local highway condition ratings				x						x
2. Pavement serviceability index by highway segment				x						x
3. Construction cost per mile by highway type				x						x
4. Maintenance cost per mile by highway type				x						x
5. Design term by highway segment				x						x
6. Highway license, fuel and use taxes				x						x
7. Highway bridge conditions and weight restrictions				x					x	x
8. Trucking costs per ton by region				●					●	
9. Trucking wage rates				●				●		

Note: SIC = Standard Industrial Classification; STCC = Standard Transportation Commodity Code; MCD = Minor Civil Division.

● = data items needed to compute impacts of moderate to high potential importance.

x = data items needed to compute impacts of low potential importance.

Three methods have been developed for calculating the avoidable costs and attributable revenues for light-density lines. (12, p. 2–102):

1. The RSPO method calls for detailed accounting data and many individual calculations. It is the only method given official status in 4R Act subsidy funding applications.

2. The USRA method requires less specific data, and although complex, has been programmed for computer use.

3. The abbreviated method is a simplified version of the USRA method which can be used when time or data are insufficient.

The RSPO method will ultimately supersede all methods so it may be wise to invest in its application from the start. The ICC and RSPO have jointly issued "Standards for Determining Costs, Revenues, and Return on Value" which provide more detail on the RSPO financial analysis method (4). The USRA method is described in detail in Reference 15.

9.5.3 Community Impact Analysis

Balanced against the net avoidable cost associated with the abandonment of a light-density line is the social and economic impact on the community derived from plant closures, employment declines or use of alternative modes of transport. Table 9-5 summarizes the kinds of impacts that can be expected. Many of the techniques used to quantify these impacts have been developed and applied by the individual states and in environmental impact assessments for a variety of transportation modes. The reader is referred to References 1, 6, and 9, and the *Rail Planning Manual*, for procedures and analysis techniques.

9.5.4 Implementation Planning and Monitoring

Implementation planning is aimed at examining the alternatives to outright abandonment by: (1) Identifying measures that might improve the profitability of the line to break even and thus avoid abandonment altogether; or (2) planning for substitute service or line subsidy to minimize or avoid intolerable impacts. Improving the viability of the line can be done through some combination of increasing revenues and decreasing costs. Revenues can be increased through:

- Increased traffic
- Better marketing
- Industrial relocation and expansion
- Increased rates
- New facilities.

Operating costs can be reduced through:

- Rehabilitated track
- New facilities

TABLE 9-5 Summary of Potential Community Impacts (12)

Potential impacts (1)	Person or group feeling impact (2)	Impact area (3)
Economic:		
Losses in personal income	individual	labor market
Increased unemployment compensation, public assistance payments	government	local, state
Retraining and other miscellaneous costs	government	local, state
Loss of income tax revenue	government	state
Loss of property taxes	government	local
Higher transport costs	plants	functional[a]
Increased trucking employment and income	trucking firms	local
Absorbed transport cost increases	plants	functional[a]
Increased highway construction and maintenance costs	government	local, state
Social:		
Jobs lost	individual	labor market
Persons forced to relocate	individual	labor market
Changes in accident levels	individual	functional[b,c]
Environment and Energy:		
Changes in energy consumption	national economy	state, nation
Changes in air pollutant production	individual	functional[b]
Changes in noise levels	individual	functional[b]

[a]Plants presently served by the light-density line.
[b]Highways receiving increased truck volumes.
[c]Light-density line grade crossings.

- Improved operating practices
- Changed labor rules.

Retention of service through subsidy may involve direct operating subsidy to the existing carrier, or planning for acquisition of the line and an operating agreement with the same or another carrier. Subsidy of rehabilitation costs may also be sufficient to assure a break-even condition without a long-term operating commitment.

Substitute services to be considered in the event that abandonment is inevitable include: (1) Construction of new connections, team tracks, new storage facilities; (2) change of railroad; (3) change to TOFC or

COFC operation; or (4) industrial relocation. If substitute rail service is not possible, planning efforts may be concentrated on plant modifications to permit trucking operations and planning for the acquisition and alternative use of the rail line right-of-way.

The monitoring of substitute or subsidized service is important to the periodic reevaluation of financial commitments. This monitoring process should be structured to be consistent with rail planning efforts for all light-density lines in the state, so that changes in priority for the commitment of limited funding can be identified.

Finally, the difficulty in assembling a linear right-of-way in an urban area suggests careful evaluation if a railroad plans to sell off an abandoned right-of-way for piecemeal development. Public use of abandoned railroad rights-of-way can include transitways, roadways, landscaped buffers or recreational paths for walking, bicycling, snowmobiling or horeseback riding. All light-density lines should be evaluated in the context of urban transportation and open-space planning and, if necessary, purchased and land-banked for longer-term public use. Evaluation should take into account the possibility of reestablishing rail service.

9.6 PLANNING FOR INTERCITY RAIL PASSENGER SERVICE

9.6.1 Amtrak

The National Railroad Passenger Corporation (Amtrak) was created by the Rail Passenger Service Act of 1970 and began operations on May 1, 1971. Amtrak now operates all intercity rail passenger service in the United States, having taken over the Rio Grande Zephyr, previously operated by the Denver and Rio Grande Western Railroad between Denver, Colorado and Salt Lake City, Utah, in 1983.

With a few segments excepted, the Northeast Corridor main line between Washington, D.C., and Boston, Massachusetts, and branch lines between New Haven, Connecticut, and Springfield, Massachusetts, and between Philadelphia and Harrisburg, Pennsylvania, are owned and operated by Amtrak. All service outside the Northeast Corridor is provided over track owned by the various freight railroads. A service agreement provides that the owning railroad supply train crews and other support services while utilizing equipment mainly owned by Amtrak.

The Amtrak of the mid-1980s is vastly improved over its first decade of operation. Cars and locomotives are now modern and reliable. On-time performance is hovering around 80%. Revenues are covering 56% of operating costs, ahead of the 50% target set by the Amtrak Improvement Act of 1981 for fiscal year 1984. In fact, 80% of short-term avoidable costs are covered by revenue, and management has a goal of no short-term avoidable loss. As a result, Amtrak is chipping away at its

$700,000,000-plus federal subsidy. Finally, direction from Congress is more clearly defined than it has ever been, and relations with the railroads over which Amtrak operates are better than they have ever been.

With this orientation toward stability, quality of service, and an improved revenue-to-cost ratio, significant growth in the Amtrak system is unlikely in the immediate future. Despite this, intercity rail passenger service improvements continue to be planned and implemented. Amtrak itself has cautiously implemented new services on experimental routes, and some have become permanent parts of the system. Some states have taken advantage of the provisions of Section 403(b) of the Rail Passenger Service Act which permits Amtrak to enter into a joint agreement to provide new services. States or localities must provide 50% and eventually 100% of the operating subsidy.

In 1976, the federal government committed over $2 billion to the Northeast Corridor Improvement Project to upgrade the mainline railroad between Washington, D.C., and Boston, Massachusetts, for passenger service at speeds up to 120 miles (194 km) per hr. The renovation, repair or replacement of trackwork, bridges, traction power systems, stations, grade crossings, maintenance facilities and other elements are virtually complete as of the mid-1980s. The major remaining work is in the train control and communications systems. Significantly improved reliability and travel time reductions are already evident.

Several private groups and government agencies are studying the feasibility of high-speed passenger service in corridors across the country. The success of French, Japanese and British high-speed and superspeed services has sparked new interest in their possible application in the U.S. In 1981, for example, the American High Speed Rail Corporation was incorporated, with Amtrak help, to seek private capital for high-speed service in corridors such as Los Angeles-San Diego. Similar efforts are under way in Nevada, Pennsylvania, Texas, Ohio, Florida and other areas.

9.6.2 Market Analysis

The depth of market analysis required to evaluate new or expanded rail passenger service must be closely related to the investment and risks involved. Typically, rail service will be expensive to provide and not always economically or operationally feasible. Cooperative agreements for joint Amtrak-state and local services under Section 403 of the Rail Passenger Service Act, for example, must be based on a market feasibility study which will:

> take into account the current and estimated future population and economic conditions of the points served, the adequacy of alternative modes of transportation to those points, and the cost of adding such service. (Section 403(a))

Figure 9-7 illustrates one method for carrying out such a study. A feasibility study for high-speed or super-speed ground transportation would go beyond this to include assessment of available technology, costs, rights-of-way, track alignment, ridership, population, economic trends and alternative modes.

9.6.3 Demand Estimation

Central to the market feasibility studies for rail passenger service is the forecast of demand. Ridership levels will influence revenue, equipment requirements, frequency of service and, as a result, operating cost.

Several models have been developed for predicting intercity travel demand. The *Rail Planning Manual* describes six models which are summarized in Table 9-6. The data required for these models generally include:

1. Modal service characteristics: frequency, travel time (line haul and door-to-door), speed, cost (private out-of-pocket and public), comfort, reliability and energy consumption.
2. Modal network characteristics—location and vehicle capacity.
3. Value of time.
4. Demographic characteristics.
5. Population size and growth trends.
6. Land use.
7. Work travel patterns.
8. Proportions of work and recreational travel.

As can be seen in Table 9-6, the data requirements and complexity of the models vary widely. Each should be evaluated in terms of desired results and available resources for a specific application.

9.6.4 Operational Issues

Of particular concern in proposing new rail passenger service are the operational problems associated with the joint use of track. Passenger trains are much lighter and faster than freight trains. As a result, passenger trains require a larger "window" in the schedule to avoid overtaking freight trains in sections of limited track capacity. The result can be a significant deterioration in freight schedules since intercity passenger trains, by ICC regulation, are given track priority.

Implementation of joint use passenger service should therefore be based on a detailed operational study using train graphs or computer simulation techniques. The results may dictate the need for capital investment in additional track capacity, such as passing sidings, or the need to provide upgraded signal and communications systems.

In general, the freight railroads are much less strongly opposed to accommodating passenger service than they may have been when Amtrak first took over the system. Reliable equipment and financial

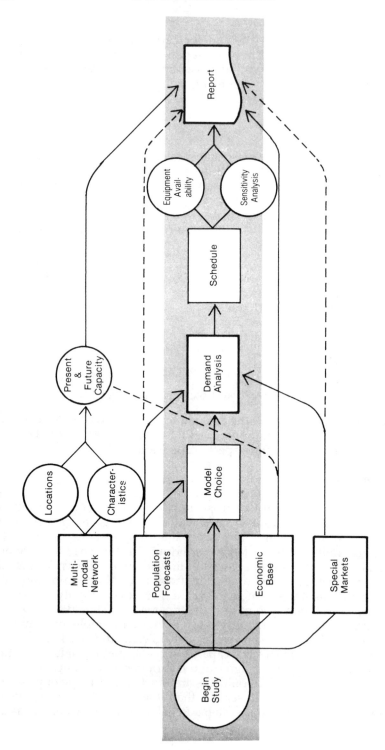

Fig. 9-7. Market analysis study process (12)

TABLE 9-6 Comparison of Selected Models (12)

Models (1)	Type of distribution (2)	Time needed (3)	Data needed (4)	Complexity (5)	Amtrak compliance (6)	Computer required (7)
	Characteristics					
Relative shares	post	medium	medium	medium	high	computer
Amtrak	direct (before)	medium	medium	medium	high	hand
STAR	post	high	high	high	medium	computer
Cross elasticity	post	high	high	high	high	computer
Aerospace	post	high	high	high	high	computer
HSPT diversion (NYSDOT)	before	low	low	low	medium	hand

incentives have been the key. Amtrak is expanding its use of incentive clauses in agreements with the operating railroads. These clauses provide a financial incentive for on-time performance, and most of the railroads are taking full advantage of them. Even maintenance officers of the railroads are supporting Amtrak service since they find it easier to justify high track standards because of the provisions of the operating agreement.

9.7 CONCLUSION

Railroad planning presents some unique opportunities and problems to the transportation engineer and planner. Despite the fact that the railroad predates the automobile, truck and airplane, comprehensive planning techniques for railroads are not well developed by comparison. Some of the unique operating practices of the railroads themselves have contributed to the difficulty in developing sophisticated planning techniques.

On the other hand, federal intervention in railroad financial problems through the 1970s, and public scrutiny of them, have reaffirmed the importance of railroad transportation in the United States. Work to be done includes optimizing mainline operations, improving terminal facilities, restructuring underutilized or poorly located facilities in urban areas, eliminating at-grade crossings of roadways, evaluating the proposed abandonment of light-density lines, and evaluating the feasibility of new conventional, high-speed or super-speed rail passenger services.

9.8 REFERENCES

1. *Analysis of Community Impacts Resulting from the Loss of Rail Service*, United States Railway Association, Washington, D.C., October 1974.

2. *Final Standards, Classification and Designation of Lines of Class I Railroads in the United States*, Secretary of Transportation, Washington, D.C., January 1977.
3. 49 CFR (Code of Federal Regulations) Part 266.15(c)(4). Office of the Federal Register, U.S. General Services Administration, Washington, D.C.
4. 49 CFR (Code of Federal Regulations) Part 1121. Office of the Federal Register, U.S. General Services Administration, Washington, D.C.
5. International Business Machines Corp., *FRA Network Model, Users Manual*, Vol. 1, Gaithersburg, Md., May 1975.
6. Massachusetts Institute of Technology, *Framework for Predicting the External Impacts of Railroad Abandonment*, prepared for the USDOT, M.I.T., Cambridge, Mass., March 1975.
7. Moon, A.E., et al., *Guidebook for Planning to Alleviate Urban Railroad Problems*, Stanford Research Inst., for the FRA and FHWA, Washington, D.C. August 1974.
8. Morrissey, J., *The Effectiveness of Flashing Lights and Flashing Lights with Gates in Reducing Accident Frequency at Public Rail-Highway Crossings, 1975–1978*, Input-Output Computer Services. Inc., for the FRA, Waltham, Mass., April 1980.
9. *Rail Abandonments and Alternatives: A Report on Effects Outside the Northeastern Region*, U.S. Dept. of Transportation, Washington, D.C., October 1974.
10. *Rail Carload Cost Scales by Territory and Commodity*, U.S. Government Printing Office, Washington, D.C.
11. *Rail Planning Manual, Vol. I: Guide to Decision-Makers*, Federal Railroad Administration, Washington, D.C., 1976.
12. *Rail Planning Manual, Vol. II: Guide for Planners*, Federal Railroad Administration, Washington, D.C., 1976.
13. *Rail Service in the Midwest and Northeast Region*, Secretary of Transportation, Washington, D.C. February 1974.
14. Reabis Associates, Inc., *An Improved Truck/Rail Operation: Evaluation of a Selected Corridor*, prepared for the USDOT, Federal Highway Administration, Washington, D.C., 1975.
15. *Viability of Light-Density Rail Lines—the USRA's Analytic Policies and Procedures*, United States Railway Association, Washington, D.C., March 1976.

CHAPTER 10

PORT PLANNING[a]

10.1 WHAT IS PORT PLANNING?

Port planning is the process of identifying optimal patterns of future development and recommending projects and strategies to accomplish that development. It is typically done by or for a municipal or state port authority, since port planning is primarily a function of the public sector. A particular terminal operator or port user might perform or commission a market or feasibility study, but the growth of port authorities during and after World War II created an opportunity, as well as a need, for port planning. The use of planning in port development has occurred, in part, as a result of centralization of control in these port authorities.

In the United States, port planning on the national level mainly involves studies or technical assistance by the Maritime Administration (MarAd) or the Army Corps of Engineers, but control over development remains with port authorities or local and state governments. Some regional coordination of port development has occurred, particularly in the northwestern United States. The New York-New Jersey Port Authority is an example of an interstate port authority.

The National Environmental Policy Act (NEPA) of 1969 and the Federal Coastal Zone Management Act (CZM) of 1972 formalized and institutionalized the need for planning in the port development process, in order to assure the protection of environmental quality and the compatibility of port development with adjacent uses. As a result of these laws, federal, state and local agencies were given a role in the port planning and development processes. Inflation, the rise in energy prices, the economic impacts of technological changes, and increasing recognition of the importance of transportation systems have presented economic and political incentives for planning in the capital-intensive port development process.

10.1.1 Historical Overview of U.S. Port Development

Prior to World War I, ports consisted of privately owned terminals and federally managed harbors and waterways. Terminals were typically owned and operated either by railroads, terminal companies orga-

---

[a]Prepared by Victor V. Calabretta, M.ASCE, Vice President, Robert H. Wardwell, Project Manager, and David A. Veshosky, Port Consultant, CE Maguire, Inc., Providence, RI.

nized for that purpose, or industries that generated port cargo, and were run as businesses. There was little, if any, coordination among these port users and, in fact, they were often involved in direct competition.

During and after World War II, U.S. international waterborne commerce increased dramatically and several port authorities were established, frequently buying privately or municipally owned terminals and operating them or contracting for their operation. This trend centralized the control over facilities, although not over harbors and waterways.

The rapid trend toward containerization since about 1960 has revolutionized cargo handling, storage and control, and on-land transportation requirements. Prior to containerization, general cargoes were handled in breakbulk form, as pallets, crates, drums, etc. Typical terminal configurations involved finger piers perpendicular to the shoreline with transit sheds located on the piers, in order to maximize the land-water interface and minimize the distance between vessel and terminal covered storage.

Figure 10-1 illustrates a typical breakbulk cargo marine terminal operation. Such facilities were not suitable for container traffic, however, as containers do not require covered storage, except for stripping (unpacking) and stuffing (consolidation) of partial container loads. Containers do require large open areas adjacent to the berth, which could not be

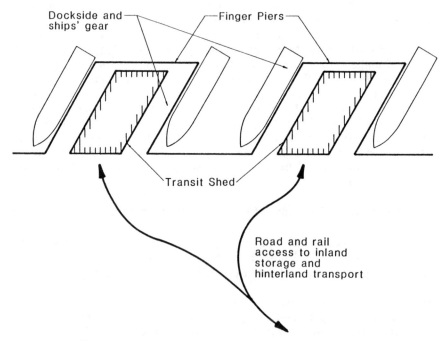

Fig. 10-1.Typical breakbulk cargo marine terminal

provided on finger piers. Facilities for stripping and stuffing partial container loads are also necessary, but can be provided by using transit sheds. Figure 10-2 illustrates a typical container terminal.Since containerization allows improved productivity and control in cargo handling, shippers and shipping lines have enthusiastically containerized all possible cargoes. In some U.S. ports, 80% or more of all exports are containerized; imports are generally containerized to a lesser but increasing degree. Containerization has not been as pervasive in developing countries because it is capital intensive and requires less labor than breakbulk cargo. Increased use of containers by shippers led to construction of vessels designed specifically to carry containers and development of specialized terminals, with portal cranes, marginal wharves, and large backup areas. This has caused the underutilization and early obsolescence of breakbulk terminals, and created a rapid demand for container facilities.

The capital intensiveness of containers, container ships, and container handling equipment has also increased the need for improved efficiency and productivity in port operations. The greater degree of cargo control available due to containerization has made such improvements possible. Container ships require quicker turnaround time than breakbulk vessels in order to be cost effective. Containers themselves represent a capital investment, so, when not in use, they are a liability. On the other hand, containerization allows improved control to reduce loss and theft, is compatible with automated inventory systems, and allows greater efficiency in cargo handling.

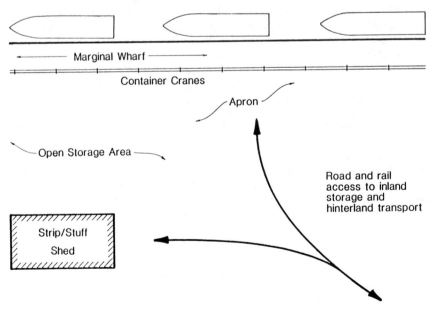

Fig. 10-2. Typical container terminal

Containerization has also affected intermodal transportation systems and terminal yard handling equipment. Containers are carried on rail flatcars (containers-on-flatcars, or COFC) rather than boxcars, which were used to transport breakbulk cargoes. Roll-on/roll-off (RO/RO) cargoes, with containers on chassis driven on and off vessels, are transported inland as semitrailers or on rail flatcars (trailers-on-flatcars, or TOFC). In either case, typical breakbulk facilities were not adequate, so development of COFC and TOFC facilities and specialized container handling systems became necessary.

In addition to containerization, several other developments in shipping technology have affected ports. These include the use of large, specialized vessels for carrying bulk commodities, introduction of unit trains (trains of 100 to 120 cars with a common origin and destination), and the use of "land bridges."

Land bridges involve the movement of cargo via a water-rail, rather than all water, route. An example of a typical land bridge is the use of container ships between the Far East and the U.S. east coast. At U.S. west coast terminals, the cargo is unloaded and moved across the country by rail. The previous method was to deliver the cargo to a U.S. east coast port via the Panama Canal. A "minibridge" is a modification of the land bridge, in which the on-land portion is shorter and may be the link between two water routes. Plans are currently under way to develop a land bridge across Mexico, with container terminals on the Pacific and Gulf coasts, and surface transport across the country.

The development of specialized ships and equipment for transporting and handling bulk materials, both liquid and dry, has also improved the efficiency and productivity of bulk transport and led to new terminal and transportation system requirements. Offshore moorings for vessels can be used instead of piers or wharves for berthing specialized single-commodity carriers. In addition, mechanical, pneumatic, or slurry systems on land can handle bulk materials in a cost-effective manner that requires significant capital investment but reduced labor.

In response to these technological trends, the shipping industry has moved toward fewer port calls, with vessel service occurring between a few selected ports in order to reduce dead time in port. Initially, the large amount of capital required to develop container and specialized bulk terminals limited the number of ports capable of efficiently handling these cargoes, so the choice of port calls was partly determined by capabilities. The use of distance-dependent rates for transporting containers by rail, as opposed to breakbulk cargo rates which are uniform to or from all ports in a coastal range (east, west, or Gulf coasts), also directed cargo to certain ports. Ports with advantages in these factors—equipment and inland transport rates—benefited from the technological and operational trends as they became load centers for containerized cargo. New York-New Jersey, Baltimore, Hampton Roads (Norfolk, Portsmouth, and Newport News, Virginia), Miami, Oakland, and Los Angeles are examples of ports whose roles have intensified as a result of these and other trends. Demographic and economic conditions and trends, obviously, also affect port use.

More recently, most ports have developed container capabilities and begun to compete for markets. A major factor in capturing new markets and expanding existing markets has been the use of comprehensive port master plans to encourage and direct the most cost effective use of port resources. Sound planning tends to minimize the expense and adverse impacts of unnecessary development.

10.1.2 Definition of Terms

Port   For the purposes of this chapter, a port is defined as any geographically identifiable group of facilities directly related to waterborne commerce or industry. A single terminal or group of terminals and facilities may constitute a port. The Port of Hampton Roads, for example, includes port facilities in Chesapeake, Norfolk, Portsmouth, and Newport News, each of which (and particularly the last three) could be considered a separate port. In this chapter, therefore, a port is considered to be self-defining: the Port of Hampton Roads, the Port of New York and New Jersey, the Port of Los Angeles, etc.

Port development   Due to the changing needs of port users, maritime industry trends, and fluctuations in the types and levels of port use, port development is a continual process of maintenance, improvement, modification, replacement, modernization, and expansion of port facilities.

Port planning   Port planning involves identification of port needs, capabilities, opportunities, demands, and courses of action which, when implemented, will most efficiently and effectively direct port development, within the institutional and functional framework in which the port exists. Since port planning is the process of directing future development, it also must be a continual process. Port planning may involve preparation, review, or modification of a port master plan, or the analysis of specific projects or port operational issues, within the framework of optimal port development.

Cargo types and modes   Several defining terms are typically applied to commodities and cargoes: breakbulk, general cargo, containers, RO/RO, bulk, etc. In this chapter, these terms will be used in the following sense:

1. Bulk cargo: liquid and dry commodities (petroleum products, coal and metal ores, grains, chemicals, sand and gravel, molasses, vegetable oils, etc.) handled without packaging. Some commodities may be handled as bulk cargo in large-volume shipments and as general cargo, in drums or sacks, in small-volume shipments.

2. General cargo: all non-bulk shipments, including those handled in breakbulk form (pallets, drums, sacks, slings, etc.), as well as in containers [20-ft and 40-ft (6.1-m and 12.2-m) long standard units], and as

roll-on/roll-off (RO/RO) cargo (trailers, automobiles, mobile equipment, etc.). Some commodities, including wood and paper products, iron and steel, and automobiles (when transported in a dedicated auto carrier) are referred to as neobulk cargo when handled in shipload or large lots.

3. Project cargo: large shipments destined for the same location, typically a major construction or energy development project.

10.2 THE PORT PLANNING PROCESS

Port planning is intended to assure that an adequate supply of port facilities and services is available to satisfy future demand, cost effectively. As with any planning process, it requires the establishment of a set of goals for development and use, analysis of conditions and trends to identify potential alternatives, and evaluation of these alternatives with regard to benefits, costs, impacts, and feasibility. The product of the port planning process must show what should be done when, and why; how it can be done; and who should do it.

Ports must be able to respond to and serve the needs of business, industry, and the general public. Port planning and development involve extensive interaction between the public and private sectors. Private stevedore or terminal companies are predominantly responsible for the day-to-day handling of waterborne commerce in U.S. ports; ports are a link in a transportation network consisting of public roads, highways, waterways, public and private railroads, and private trucking and steamship companies; and ports are often under pressure to operate as businesses, on a profit basis. Since port development is capital intensive in nature, involves significant commitments of public resources, and always affects societal conditions, decision-making primarily is a governmental action. Port planning can be an important tool in assuring that the interaction between the public and private sectors is as smooth as possible, and can provide the link between the operational, marketing, engineering, and financial functions of a port.

10.2.1 Establishment of Purposes, Targets, and Criteria

Institutional framework   Port planning must conform to the policies, plans, strategies, programs, goals, and objectives of a number of public agencies, at the local, state, and national levels. It must also meet the demands of the private sector. Since the enactment of NEPA and CZM regulations, planning for port development is legally mandated and involves a variety of public agencies. The fact that port development must be consistent with the policies and plans of these agencies should be considered in the planning process. The establishment of purposes, targets, and criteria in the port planning process satisfies this need and also provides a set of guidelines for identification and evaluation of alternatives.

Typical institutions involved in port planning and development include:

- Port authority or agency with responsibility or authority for the port
- Local planning agency or conservation commission, or both
- State environmental protection agency
- State natural resource management agency
- State transportation or public works department, or both
- Army Corps of Engineers
- Federal Environmental Protection Agency (EPA)
- Coast Guard.

If national parks are located in or adjacent to a port area, the Department of the Interior is involved; if outer continental shelf support activities are located in the port, the U.S. Geological Survey and Bureau of Land Management may be involved. The U.S. Fish and Wildlife Service also administers laws which affect port development. The most direct responsibility and authority for port development is held by local and state agencies and the Corps of Engineers. Conformance with state environmental quality standards generally satisfies NEPA requirements.

The chartered and traditional roles of a port authority are key factors in the institutional context of port planning. A port authority is generally chartered by a city, town, or state, and the first level of oversight occurs there. The role of a port authority in marketing, financing, development, and operations is determined by: (1) Its enabling legislation or charter; (2) requirements for review or approval, or both, by the chartering government; and (3) traditional roles of the port authority, port users and relevant agencies.

Local agencies may include a municipal planning department, conservation commission, or regional planning agency. These agencies assure that plans for port development are consistent with local land use, transportation, and development planning. Residential, commercial, and recreational uses of the waterfront compete with port facilities for space, and port development affects adjacent areas. Planning for major development was mandated initially by NEPA and CZM. An increasing number of port authorities have prepared or commissioned port master plans to complement local planning efforts.

State agencies have the most direct responsibility for protection and management of natural resources and environmental quality. State energy offices also may be involved in coastal energy siting decisions, or may set policy that affects energy-related development.

Roles of state and local governments differ, depending on the organizational structure of public ports in a particular state. In addition to having a semi-autonomous state port authority, state governments may provide funding, coordination, and regulation affecting port development. Similarly, local governments complement port development within their jurisdictions. Common responsibilities of local governments include the planning and provision of access roads, compatible zoning of port and port-related areas, and assisting with port promotions. Coordination remains a common requirement for public and private port planning and related state or local government activities.

The two primary federal agencies involved are the Corps of Engineers and EPA. The Corps is responsible for channel maintenance and improvements and has been involved with the problem of lack of dredge spoil disposal options and frustration with the permitting process. The Corps must also approve construction in navigable waters. EPA is responsible for discharge permits for air and water emissions and for on-land dredge spoil disposal. It is jointly responsible, with the Corps, for ocean disposal of dredge spoil.

The Corps of Engineers has traditionally been closely involved with port authorities at the state and local levels. Corps funding for navigational improvement begins with the congressional appropriations process, which in turn emanates from local or state sponsors. The conventional cost-benefit analyses used by the Corps to test the validity of projects emphasize individual channel evaluations, further strengthening state or port ties to the local district offices of the Corps.

Continued federal funding of navigational channels is the subject of extensive debate within the federal government. Legislation to impose the costs of channel improvements and maintenance on local sponsors, rather than the federal government, has been introduced. This potential reduction of the federal role in port development could drastically alter the port planning process. Local port planning would extend beyond shoreside, and development decisions would depend upon cost recovery of channel expenditures as well as those for facility improvement.

In recent years, federal funding to assist in port planning has been available. While there have never been any specific, categorical grants for ports, funds from the Economic Development Administration (EDA) and the Maritime Administration (MarAd) have been used in preparing long-range port plans. EDA funds have been allocated to assist preparation of individual port master plans, while MarAd has funded a series of regional plans which included several port authorities or states within a common coastal or riverine area. The Community Development Block Grant (CDBG) program has also been used for financing specific development studies. Recent federal budget reductions have severely limited these funds.

Shoreside port facilities have traditionally been provided by government at other than the federal levels and by private industry. Although some public port authorities operate their own common user facilities, the predominant role of public authorities is that of landlord, with private terminal companies responsible for the operation of common user or proprietary facilities. Private companies also construct port facilities on navigational channels or waterways. Most private facilities operate for single purposes, normally for the exclusive use of an integrated business. There are, however, private marine terminal operations providing public transfer and storage capacities for a variety of shippers and consignees.

The provision of port facilities is, therefore, a completely decentralized activity. While nearly every state with navigable waters has an organization involved in the development of its ports, the actual planning and development involve a variety of public and private entities. The Maritime Administration has classified types of port ownership into three categories: (1) State governments or agencies; (2) local governments, municipal or county agencies, and special districts; and (3) private profit-making or nonprofit organizations or cooperatives. The results of a MarAd inventory are presented in Table 10-1.

As Table 10-1 shows, it is difficult to generalize about the type of local organization involved in port planning. Regional customs, state policies, and the nature of trade seem to be common denominators. For example, private ownership is common on the mid-America inland waterways; state port authorities are prevalent in parts of the South Atlantic and eastern Gulf coast; and local port authorities are common on the west coast. Commonalities due to the nature of trade include these: liquid and dry bulk commodities are normally handled through proprietary terminals, whereas general cargoes are handled through facilities normally provided by public port authorities. Even with these rules of thumb, however, there are exceptions and, even within a single harbor, there may be several varieties of marine terminal ownership.

Cost effective planning The cost of port development more than doubled between 1960 and 1970, and rapidly escalating energy costs increased the need for cost effectiveness in terminal design, construction, and operation. As a result of these two factors, many ports have replaced aggressive, growth-oriented development policies with policies aimed at improving the productivity and efficiency of existing facilities and reuse or rehabiltation of deteriorating or obsolescent facilities. Recent trends toward reductions in government spending and increased reliance on the private sector make it likely that capital development will continue to be difficult and costly to arrange.

TABLE 10-1 Type of Port Ownership by Region (3)

Region (1)	State (2)	Local (3)	Private (4)
North Atlantic	28	24	48
South Atlantic	34	32	34
Gulf	48	8	44
South Pacific	10	61	29
North Pacific	0	48	52
Great Lakes	4	19	77
National average	12	37	51

Port efficiency and productivity can be restrained by several elements in the port system, including lack of adequate equipment or facilities and inefficient facility layout. In the port planning process, constraints to throughput capacity, efficiency, or productivity should be identified and the most cost effective improvements recommended. The process should first consider management or operational changes, or changes involving relatively minor construction or development, before more capital-intensive, major improvements are considered. For example, a port that is experiencing delays in entry and exit of containers should consider management or operational measures, such as increasing the hours of gate complex operation or providing more response in gate direction, before additional gate facilities are constructed.

In particular, improvements in layout, equipment, management, and operations should be attempted before costly construction is begun. At the same time, relatively inexpensive development items, such as open storage areas and terminal equipment, should not be allowed to constrain the efficiency or productivity of major port items, such as berths and cranes.

Port planning, therefore, should give maximum consideration to the most efficient use of existing facilities and minor development that allows more productive use of major port elements. Berths and other major elements should be provided, if necessary, and should certainly never be allowed to impair the ability of a port to satisfy the demands of port users or respond to new opportunities. The planning process should assure that the least capital-intensive improvements are considered first, and that productivity and efficiency of the port are maximized before major improvements are implemented.

Productivity improvements may require the replacement of labor-intensive activities with capital-intensive equipment, e.g., breakbulk loading procedures which handle fewer tons per unit of time than do container operations. Although capital-intensive, modern port facilities are relatively productive compared with other U.S. industry. The need for capital investment in growth areas such as container terminal facilities in certain ports in the South and West has been identified, and investment should enhance productivity.

In places where land is very scarce (such as in urban ports) improvements in productivity may be the only means of increasing throughput or reducing costs. It may require new equipment or modifications to port layout or operations. In large container ports, such as Seattle, Oakland, and Baltimore, the combination of growing container flows and scarcity of waterfront lands emphasizes the need for productivity improvements in order to enhance or maintain competitive position.

Many sources are available for information on trends in port development and operation. Port and shipping industry periodicals, such as *Cargo Systems International, Bulk Systems International, World Wide Shipping/World Ports, Seatrade, American Shipper,* and *Container News* provide information on equipment and facility development. Equipment manufacturers offer product literature, and many ports publish magazines which contain articles on industry trends.

10.2.2 Analysis of Port Capabilities

The ability of a port to meet present and future needs is determined by a number of factors, including transportation access, terminal capacities, and suitable land available for port and port-related use.

Analysis of these factors to identify potential opportunities, advantages or constraints can be done in a range of levels of detail and used in connection with marketing efforts as well as in the port planning process. On a macro-planning level, national, regional, or portwide capacity can be estimated, with major transportation networks considered. Recommendations may be broad statements of policy, or more specific facility or infrastructure improvements. On a micro-planning level, with a single project or terminal as the focus of analysis, the process becomes more refined and quantified. The level of detail necessary is determined by the purpose for which planning is being done.

Terminal capacity analysis   The ability of a cargo terminal to transfer cargo may be quantified, to some extent, by analysis of the facilities and operating systems available. The number of berths, equipment, storage space, entry and exit points, and operational procedures affect the amount of cargo handled efficiently at a terminal. The capacity of a port to handle various types of cargo is related to the capacities of the individual terminals.

Quantification of these factors is a difficult and sometimes futile process. On the macro-planning level, capacity of a terminal can be estimated based on study of the terminal and the experience of terminal operators, or through one of several methodologies developed for the purpose. On a micro-planning level, analysis of terminal capacity becomes a time and motion study or a response to a specific problem.

The two most commonly used methodologies for estimating terminal capacity were developed for the Maritime Administration. Both methodologies require the input of information regarding physical terminal facilities and equipment, as well as information on terminal operations. Information on most U.S. ports is available from the Army Corps of Engineers Port Handbook Series and the Maritime Administration Port Inventory. Samples of Corps and MarAd data are shown in Figs. 10-3 and 10-4, respectively. Physical data are available from many ports in their facilities handbooks and, of course, from port authority records. Most port authorities collect and develop information on terminal operations to some degree.

The MarAd methodology (1) separates terminals into nine classifications:

1. Breakbulk general.
2. Neobulk general.

PIERS, WHARVES, AND DOCKS

Easterly shore of New Haven Harbor

Corps of Engineers Port Code No. 01646

REFERENCE NUMBER ON MAP	16 Dock Code No. 114			17 Dock Code No. 112			18 Dock Code No. 111		
NAME	Getty Refining and Marketing Co., New Haven Terminal Wharf.			Gulf Refining and Marketing Co., New Haven Terminal Wharf.			Gulf Refining and Marketing Co., New Haven Terminal Pier.		
LOCATION ON WATERFRONT	Below Tomlinson Bridge. 85 Forbes Avenue			Approximately 600 feet below Tomlinson Bridge. 500 Waterfront Street			Approximately 1,100 feet below Tomlinson Bridge. 500 Waterfront Street		
OWNED BY	Getty Refining and Marketing Co.			Gulf Refining and Marketing Co.			Gulf Refining and Marketing Co.		
OPERATED BY	do.			do.			do.		
PURPOSE FOR WHICH USED	Receipt of petroleum products by tanker and barge.			Receipt and shipment of petroleum products by tanker and barge.			Receipt and shipment of petroleum products by barge.		
TYPE OF CONSTRUCTION	Timber pile, timber-decked, offshore platform, with 240- by 9-foot approach supporting walkway and pipelines; 2 timber breasting dolphins in line with face at each side.			Steel and timber pile, timber-decked, offshore wharf with 160- by 18-foot, timber walkway and pipeline trestle approach; angular catwalks extend from sides of wharf to 4 steel bresting dolphins in line with face and to other mooring dolphins in rear.			Timber pile, timber-decked pier; additional 215 feet of berthing space available on lower side at inner end along a timberpile, timber-decked wharf and in line with row of timber mooring piles with 14- to 16-foot water depths.		
DESCRIPTION	Face	North side	South side	Face	Upper side	Lower side	Face	Upper side	Lower side
Dimensions (Feet)	25	10	10	60	39	39	43	400	380
Depth Alongside at MLW Do.	15–20	–	–	35	–	–	25	25	25
Breasting Distance Do.	260w/dolphs.	–	–	520w/dolphs.	–	–	–	400	380
Total Berthing Space Do.	260	–	–	735	–	–	–	400	380
Width of Apron Do.	Open.			Open.			Open.		
Height of Deck Above MLW Do.	10			13			10		
Load Capacity (Lbs. per Sq.Ft.)	250			450			250		
Lighted or Unlighted	Lighted.			Lighted.			Lighted.		
TRANSIT SHEDS Number and Description	None.			None.			None.		
Length and Width (Feet)									
Height Inside Do.									
Floor Area for Cargo (Sq.Ft.)									
Load Capacity per Sq.Ft. (Lbs.)									
Cargo Doors									
MECHANICAL HANDLING FACILITIES	One overhead chain hoist on steel tower for handling hose.			One steel tower on wharf equipped with pneumatic hoists for handling hose.			None.		
RAILWAY CONNECTIONS	None.			None.			None.		
HIGHWAY CONNECTIONS	Via driveway, asphalt, 15 feet wide, from Forbes Avenue, asphalt, 35 feet wide.			Via driveway, asphalt, 15 feet wide, from Waterfront Street, asphalt, 30 feet wide.			Same as Ref. No. 17.		
WATER SUPPLY (Available to Vessels)	None.			None.			None.		
ELECTRIC CURRENT (Available to Vessels)	A.C., 220 volts.			None.			A.C., 110 volts.		
FIRE PROTECTION (Other than City)	Foam hydrants, hand extinguishers, and security patrol.			Hand extinguishers and foam monitors.			Hydrants, hose, hand extinguishers, and foam monitors.		
REMARKS	One 14- and one 6-inch pipelines extend from platform to 4 steel storage tanks, total capacity 91,000 barrels.			One 20-, four 16-, and one 10-, and one 6-inch pipelines extend from wharf to 19 steel storage tanks at rear, total capacity 1,026,050 barrels. Facilities connected to Jet Lines, Inc., 12-inch inland pipeline.			One 10-inch pipeline extends from south side of pier to storage tanks described under Ref. No. 17.		

Fig. 10-3. Sample of Army Corps of Engineers data

3. Containerized general.
4. Dry bulk, silo storage.
5. Dry bulk, open storage—low density.

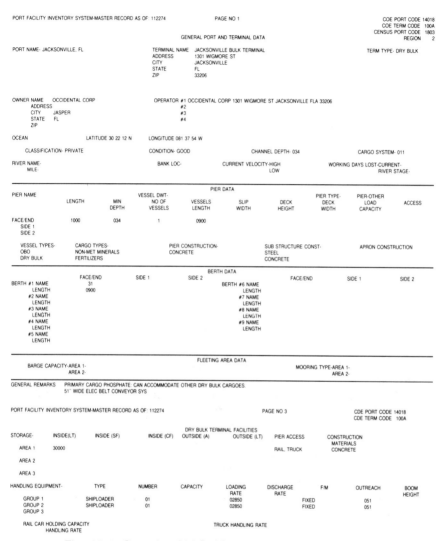

Fig. 10-4. Sample of U.S. Maritime Administration data

6. Dry bulk, open storage—high density.
7. Liquid bulk, other than petroleum.
8. Petroleum, bulk, up to 50,000 DWT ships.
9. Petroleum, bulk, 30,000 DWT to 200,000 DWT ships.

The methodology allows analysis at three levels of detail and presents typical, broad-based values for a first-level analysis, shown in Table 10-2. Second-level estimates can be made if data are incomplete. Typical values can be used, and the methodology presents some examples. For

TABLE 10-2 Typical Annual Cargo Throughput by Module[a] (1)

Single berth terminal, by cargo class (1)	Cargo throughput, in tons per year (2)
Breakbulk general	66,000
Neobulk general cargo	130,000
Containerized general cargo	360,000
Dry bulk, silo storage	1,000,000
Dry bulk, open storage, low density	500,000
Dry bulk, open storage, high density	1,000,000
Liquid bulk, other than petroleum	80,000
Petroleum bulk, up to 50,000 DWT ships	1,500,000
Petroleum bulk, 30,000 to 200,000 DWT ships	6,000,000

[a]Based on the minimum cost-effective level of utilization. If a higher level of utilization can be expected, throughput could be double or triple the values shown.

a third-level estimate, detailed knowledge of the terminal's physical plant and operations is necessary.

For second and third-level analyses, the MarAd methodology presents modules for a variety of terminal uses and arrangements, with components in each module to determine such factors as ship to apron transfer capability; apron to storage capability; storage capability; and storage to inland transport transfer capability.

The other methodology, developed by the Northern California Ports and Terminals Bureau (2), estimates capacity by analyzing eight elements of the terminal which could limit throughput capacity or efficiency. They are:

1. Ship to apron transfer.
2. Apron storage transport.
3. Storage to truck transfer.
4. Shed truck spots.
5. Customs truck spots.
6. Gates.
7. Covered storage area.
8. Outside storage area.

A series of modifiers, such as allowable waiting time, peaking component, and efficiency are applied to physical plant and operational characteristics to develop a capacity.

As can be seen, the two methodologies, and other systems, are very similar. They examine real or potential constraints to the efficient flow of cargo through a terminal. From this pipeline-type analysis, a graphical representation of cargo flow and constraining port elements can be developed, showing the necessary timing of improvements and the relative importance of alternate improvements on terminal capacity.

Use of either methodology for a detailed analysis requires a great deal of information or typical data based on assumptions. The methodologies can be modified, and data requirements reduced, based on analysis of terminal operations and discussions with terminal operators and users. Practical constraints to throughput or existing problem areas can be identified and analyzed in more detail, with less attention paid to other less critical areas.

Several factors are important to consider in assessing terminal capacity, whichever method is used. The first is an understanding of the concepts of capacity. Capacity refers to the physical and operational ability of a terminal to handle cargo efficiently. Full utilization of physical plant is generally not desirable or achievable, because of the need for capacity in excess of average use to accommodate peak loads cost effectively. Terminal facilities should be provided to the extent necessary to keep waiting times within acceptable limits. Frequent delays in excess of those limits may lead to dissatisfaction and loss of customers, but the high cost of development prohibits the building of facilities to meet peak demands. Determination of acceptable delay times (for vessels, cargo, etc.), degree of utilization acceptable and desired, and a definition of capacity are important steps, therefore, in estimating terminal capacity. Quantification of these variables involves comparison of development costs and benefits. Several analyses of demand, using queuing theory and network analysis, have been performed. Analysis of alternative levels (and directions) of terminal development versus increases in capacity can be done in a cost- benefit framework. Since facility demand necessarily involves projections and assumptions regarding future use, however, quantification of terminal capacity should consider the level of detail necessary.

Transportation access analysis Transportation access, including road and rail systems, waterways, and pipelines, affects the ability of a port to handle cargo efficiently, defines a port's hinterland, and determines, in part, types and levels of port use. Local road and rail connections to national systems can be constraints on port operations or growth potential. Analyses of road and rail capacities should utilize the tools and methodologies of a transportation planner. The mix of cargo transported inland by road and rail systems is a critical factor in identifying potential constraints of surface transportation on port use. Since construction of new road and rail systems represents a major investment, removal of surface transportation constraints is generally a long-range project beyond the direct control of the port authority or terminal operator. Minor improvements, such as route identification, signalization, and switching are more likely to be accomplished in the short term than is new construction.

Water access has increasingly become an issue in port planning. The use of large bulk vessels and longer container vessels, in order to reduce shipping costs, has created a need for deeper channels and berths, longer berths, and improved navigation and traffic control. A typical breakbulk cargo ship is approximately 700 ft (214 m) in length, with a beam of 75 to 80 ft (22.8 to 24 m); a container ship may be 1000 ft (305 m) long with a beam of up to 110 ft (34 m), the maximum for passage through the Panama Canal. Bulk carriers may have drafts of up to 60 ft (18.3 m), as opposed to 30 to 35 ft (9.2 to 10.7 m) for general cargo vessels. As the traditional role of the federal government in funding channel improvements and maintenance has come into question, it appears that ports may be required to provide funding for dredging and dredge spoil disposal in the future. The details and arrangements are not defined, but several alternatives now under discussion could affect the economic competitiveness among ports.

While it is necessary to consider transportation access in port planning, and useful to assess potential advantages as part of port use projections, the inability of a port authority to improve access limits the freedom of action available. Transportation access, therefore, is typically an external factor in the port planning process.

Potential for expansion   A final factor in determining port capability is the potential for expansion. Adequate area available and suitable for port and port-related development is necessary to sustain port growth. Zoning, existing and planned land use, transportation and utility systems, and physical or environmental constraints define the areas available for port and port-related use.

Since port facilities have historically tended to be located in urban areas and have helped to stimulate growth in adjacent areas, many ports find expansion constrained and surface transportation systems congested. Development of port facilities in isolated, undeveloped areas frequently involves substantial infrastructure costs, often generates opposition based on potential environmental or social impacts, may create transportation problems for the labor force, and may cause abandonment of existing port facilities, with resultant decay of inner port areas.

In port and local planning efforts, attempts should be made to distinguish between water-dependent or water-enhanced activities, and activities that do not need location on a waterfront. The latter should be encouraged to locate inland, to the extent possible. Priority in the use of waterfront sites should be given to water-related activities. Use of waterfront areas for water-enhanced activities (such as residential and commercial facilities) as opposed to water-dependent activities (such as terminals, marinas, and ship repair facilities) is an issue in the port and local planning processes that requires policy decisions.

Reuse, renewal, and rehabilitation of obsolete or underutilized port facilities has gained impetus from the increasing costs of new construction and the reduction in availabilty of public funds. The choice of rehabilitation or new construction should be based on social as well as economic and financial factors. In some cities, notably Boston and Baltimore, commercial and residential use of inner harbor areas has been accomplished as part of urban renewal efforts, with port and industrial development occurring in the outer harbor area. This allows the rehabilitation of the urban waterfront, but does limit the potential for future use of those areas by port-related activities. Demographic and economic trends must be considered to assure that rehabilitation of port areas for nonport activities does not constrain the future ability of the port to satisfy demands placed on it and respond to new opportunities.

The potential for expansion is important not only for growth of port facilities, but also for port-related industry that may consider development. Such industry may not require direct water access and can be accommodated in an area with good access to the port.

10.2.3 Projecting Maritime Commerce

The demand side of the planning equation consists of examining historical trends, identifying the impacts of significant causal factors, and forecasting future cargo flows. This subsection presents: (1) What the important demand information is; (2) why this information is relevant; and (3) where some basic data can be obtained.

Regional economic information   The business of ports is cargo, and the volume and character of that cargo reflects the economy of the region served. Pertinent statistics and analysis of certain key economic indicators within a region can help determine existing and potential trends. Important indicators include industrial growth, population growth, income, and investment.

In most cases, the area surrounding a port contributes the majority of cargo volume and is the most important. Surveys on the origin and destination of cargo are most valuable in defining the parameters of the extended cargo hinterland. For each case, statistics on population distribution, growth, and density are relevant for the purposes of consumption and availability of labor. The U.S. Bureau of the Census is the principal source of data. Demographic information by states and Standard Metropolitan Statistical Areas (SMSA) is available from the Bureau of the Census.

Data on employment and income further define the potential business of a local port. Employment by sector defines the manufacturing base of the regional economy, while per capita income is an important variable in forecasting foreign trade. The U.S. Bureau of Labor Statistics provides data on employment by sector. Comparative analyses between the relevant region, competitive regions, specific SMSAs and the entire U.S. are valuable. Information on per capita income, available from the U.S. Bureau of Economic Analysis, can similarly be compared as background to defining a port's business.

The manufacturing sector of a regional economy normally generates substantial cargo flows for a port. Similarly, the agricultural and mining sectors provide raw materials for export that stimulate adjacent port development. However, while a regional economy may have strong service, government, and retail trade sectors, the area's ports may experience minimal cargo activity. Hence, the nature of a region's industrial activity is an important element in defining waterborne trade.

Even a strong manufacturing sector may not create waterborne commerce. For example, the production of goods of high value, such as jewelry or electrical equipment, normally utilizes air transportation and will not substantially affect waterborne commerce. Analysis of these industrial data provides a useful background to further investigation. The Annual Survey of Manufacturers by the Bureau of the Census provides basic data. Additional sources include the U.S. Department of Agriculture for agricultural output and the U.S. Department of Interior for mining materials.

Data on capital spending within a region are also relevant as economic background information. These initial investments in both the private and public sectors will stimulate additional economic activity as well as serve as measures of the economic well-being in a region. Sources of data on capital spending by industry and region are available from the Bureau of Economic Analysis, U.S. Department of Commerce.

Historical waterborne trade   Much of the trade enjoyed by individual ports has historically utilized the same transportation routing. Forest products through Pacific Northwest gateways, coal through Chesapeake Bay ports, petroleum through Texas terminals, and imported energy materials through New England ports are a few examples. Although significant routing shifts occur, particularly with high value intermodal traffic, the tracking of historical cargo flows through a port is still the best barometer of future trading prospects.

Trend Analysis.   A trend analysis of historical waterborne trade will depict commodity types, volumes, and growth rates. A 10-yr time frame is normally sufficient, although longer time frames may illustrate certain specific trends. The prospective domestic coal movements to New England ports, for example, can benefit from analyzing past records of similar routings of the 1930s and earlier. Historical data should be gathered for exports, imports, and domestic receipts and shipments.

Various sources of commodity data are available from government and private organizations. The origin of trade statistics is the Bureau of Customs through collection of shipper export and import documentation. The Bureau of the Census is the primary disseminator of historical foreign trade data. Available on computer tapes for waterborne foreign trade (305/705 Series), Census data provide monthly and annual information on individual and groups of commodities. The data are available on commodity tonnage and value. Other federal agencies provide trade data, but unfortunately the lack of statistical standardization inhibits compatibility of data from different sources.

Another traditional source of port tonnage is the Corps of Engineers' *Waterborne Commerce of the United States*, published annually in a five-part series and also available on computer tapes. It is the principal source for domestic waterborne commerce, with statistics also available for exports and imports. The Corps data document waterborne commerce through each federally approved channel, while the Census data are by district. Handbooks, brochures, reports and periodicals from port authorities, shippers, and shipping lines can also be helpful.

Principal Commodities and Cargo Handling Modes.   Examination of historical cargo flows for individual ports or groups of ports can identify important commodities and the range of competition among them. Further investigation into specific commodities, relevant industries, and foreign trading partners can identify important demand and supply factors affecting principal commodities. Interviews with major export-import companies will often clarify certain causes of fluctuations in waterborne commerce volume. Additional sources of information on specific commodities include trade associations, university research, and international agencies.

For matching cargo demand with the available supply of port facilities, individual commodity tonnages must be translated into actual cargo handling modes. Published government sources have traditionally been deficient in these vital conversions. While dry and liquid bulk commodities can be readily identified for individual port areas, the analysis of other cargoes by handling modes such as breakbulk general cargo, container cargo, and RO/RO cargo is more complex. Often, information on cargo handling mode is collected by port authorities and terminal operators. Innovative use of trade and vessel computer files has also produced data on cargo at ports carried in certain vessel types. Thus, container cargo, for example, can be estimated based on tonnages carried on container vessels plying certain trade routes. The Maritime Administration has published reports on these trade and vessel data.

The common denominator for depicting cargo throughput is tonnage. While there are several variations of measurement, such as short tons, metric tons, long tons, and revenue tons, the important point is consistency. Port planning efforts often distinguish between container-izable and noncontainerizable general cargoes. Container cargo is typically depicted in 20-ft (6.5-m) equivalent units (TEUs), as the number of boxes is an important determinant in estimating total container terminal capacity, and particularly the capacity of storage areas. The growth of containerization, which now handles 60% to 70% of general cargo in U.S. trades, the capital-intensive requirements of container terminals, and the problems with published statistics make the reasonable approximation of cargo handling mode a critical step in the port planning process.

Cargo Origin and Destination.   Information on the origin and destination of waterborne commerce illustrates the geographic sphere of influence or hinterland of a port. It is vital data for marketing port services as well as for planning new facilities. Although the Customs Bureau collects data on the names and locations of shippers, the tabulation of origin and destination data has been limited to periodic surveys by the Bureau of the Census.

Another source of origin and destination data is *The Journal of Commerce*. This daily trade journal sells timely information through publications and on-line computer systems. Many port authorities, terminal operators, and steamship lines subscribe to these services, and many port planning efforts rely on them for determining the competitive hinterland. Original data can also be collected through mail surveys and questionnaires, although shippers are often reluctant to release any data for fear they might be of use to competitors. In virtually every case, collection of origin and destination data is expensive and difficult because of the requirement to maintain the confidentiality of shippers.

While origin and destination data identify domestic shippers, information on principal trading partners will further define the port's sphere of influence. Sources of data on trading partners include *The Journal of Commerce* and Bureau of the Census reports. More generic information may be obtained by analyzing the trade routes and vessel services calling at a port. The identification of primary trading partners and principally employed trade routes will illustrate U.S. port competition as well as emerging shifts in trading trends. Macro-economic analysis of various trading countries should illuminate strengths and weaknesses which, in turn, should depict reasons for fluctuations in trade volumes and identify emerging trading opportunities.

Factors affecting cargo flows   Many factors define the business of a port. To understand the reasons for specific cargo routing and prospects for future trade, the port planning exercise should examine these important causal factors. Some may be amenable to change, while others are not. An evaluation of these elements is a critical precursor to forecasting maritime commerce. They include:

- Geography
- Frequency of vessel service
- Available port facilities and services
- Competitive pressures
- Labor and management
- Maritime technology and trends
- Government regulations and actions.

Geography.   Ports are, foremost, elements of geography. Virtually all major metropolitan areas have developed near access to waterborne transportation. In turn, a critical mass of cargo emanates from large metropolitan areas and passes through adjacent port facilities. Distances to deep water, inland manufacturing centers, and foreign trading partners are important determinants and are fixed in a port's geographical location. The resulting advantages and disadvantages are important concepts in both port planning and marketing.

Frequency of Vessel Service.   The frequency of vessel service on foreign trade routes is a primary factor in the attraction of cargo to a port. Scheduled ocean liner services are often a port's primary selling item.

General cargo of value is particularly attracted by liner service rather than by inland transportation cost savings. The absence of certain services will eliminate cargo for many ports, while the availability of frequent sailings may draw cargoes from a neighboring port. For planning purposes, it is important to document vessel services which illustrate strengths to certain markets and vulnerabilities to competitive routings. Frequency of services, critical to general cargo trade, is far less important for bulk commodities. For those commodities, vessel service is typically nonscheduled and depends on the accumulation of cargoes or decisions of large shippers.

Available Port Facilities and Services. While economic and geographic elements are more significant determinants, availability of port facilities to accommodate the needs of shippers and vessel operators is basic to cargo attraction. Port facilities should match the requirements of hinterland cargoes, and services should be flexible enough to satisfy customers for compensatory fees. In port planning, it should be determined if the lack of appropriate port facilities is a constraint to port growth. Additionally, port services should be examined to determine responsiveness to market conditions. While an overcapacity of expensive port facilities will not necessarily attract commerce, some excess capacity is required to bring in new business.

Competitive Pressures. With over 150 U.S. ports handling waterborne trade, competition for available commerce is constant. A regional assessment of neighboring ports' capabilities and services is required to determine an individual port's competitive position. Cargo growth, capital improvements, vessel services, and market shares should be evaluated for a range of competitive ports. An individual port's plan should identify competitive strengths based on this assessment, and recommended actions should follow these advantages to capture natural cargoes. At the same time, competitive weaknesses should be documented and investments in facilities that duplicate those of neighboring ports with stronger positions should be avoided.

Labor and Management. Port planning routinely deals with physical development and strategic planning, but differences between ports in labor and management can also affect cargo flows. Problems with continued labor slowdowns or inept management decisions can divert local cargoes to competitive ports. It is more difficult to document than other factors, but the labor-management relationship is an important determinant. Sources for this information should include interviews with shippers, freight forwarders, and steamship lines. Cooperation between labor and management can identify deficiencies and competitive imbalances. Follow-up actions can attempt to remedy cost factors or clarify issues to minimize or exploit competitive differences affecting cargo flows.

Maritime Technology and Trends. Port development, as a long-term investment, must anticipate changes in maritime technology over time by providing appropriate shoreside facilities to remain competitive. Certainly, the advent of containerization required vast changes to conventional breakbulk general cargo terminals. While technological advances in the future may not rival those of the container revolution, the adaptation of port equipment and infrastructure for appropriate cargoes and vessels is a continual process. An assessment of maritime technology with particular emphasis on relevant trade routes and opportunities for the individual port is an ingredient in the planning process.

Nontechnological trends in maritime trade can also affect commerce and must be anticipated in port planning. Examples include container feeder services from secondary ports to load center ports, land-bridge movements extending the hinterland of certain ports, and numerous international trade policies and events. The impacts of these trends can shift traditional cargo routings and should be assessed in individual port plans.

Government Regulations and Actions. Numerous government regulations affect cargo flows, transportation, and port development. The impact of bureaucratic rules on competitive ports is not always uniform. The recent deregulation of railroad and trucking rates, for example, has eliminated some rate equalizations and shifted advantages to strategically located ports. Additionally, proposed government actions to impose user fees on ports for navigational improvements may affect the competitive posture of ports. For planning purposes, the impact of government regulations and proposed actions should be assessed with attention paid to cargo routings and competitive imbalances. State and local government actions, as well as federal actions, should be evaluated under this category.

Cargo forecasting Forecasting waterborne trade prospects, like all economic projections, is, at best, an inexact science. As depicted earlier in this section, trade expectations are based on trends in historical cargo flows and assumptions regarding the future impact of important causal factors. Trade projections should be attempted for various time intervals through a 20-yr time horizon. Intervals of three, five, 10, 15, and 20 years should be sufficient for planning future demand expectations.

Several statistical techniques exist to extend historical trends into the future and to correlate commodity growth with important variables. Additionally, there are generic trade projections available from several federal agencies. Projections can be compared and judgmental factors added through interviews and supplementary reports on specific cargoes, industries, or trading partners. It is common to develop low, medium, and high level trade scenarios through the 20-yr forecasting horizon.

The most basic forecast extends annual commodity growth rates into future years. A regression analysis produces another level of sophistication by projecting commodity growth as a function of important variables such as, for exports:

1. Output levels of relevant producing industries.
2. Population of foreign trading area.

3. Gross domestic product of foreign area.
4. Per capita income of foreign trading area.

Significant variables for imports include:

1. Level of production of consuming industries in hinterland.
2. Per capita income and population of hinterland.
3. Gross regional product of hinterland.
4. Level of exports from trading area.

Different commodities can be dependent upon changes in different variables. Additionally, this forecasting exercise will depict the relative importance of certain variables as key indicators of prospects for future port traffic.

Cargo forecasts are more difficult to make for individual ports and terminals than for broader geographic areas. One technique includes using available national forecasts as a base and, through market share analysis, projecting regional, subregional, and local port growth into the future. The Maritime Administration publishes a long-term forecast for United States trade routes and regional port areas. Many port planning efforts use these MarAd data as baseline information. Local judgment often adds optimism to federal government forecasts, while, on the other hand, local estimates normally reflect more timely events than do the commonly delayed federal agency forecasts. Particular attention must be paid to the conversion of groups of commodities into cargo handling mode. This is significant for containers and other commodities requiring special port handling. A common practice is to group commodities as containerizable, marginally containerizable, and noncontainerizable. Results can be depicted in TEUs and tonnages for comparison to facility throughput capacity.

Several statistical and econometric computer models exist to assist in forecasting port traffic. Nevertheless, judgmental factors are most important, while short-term projections are inherently more reliable than are the longer range forecasts. A recent innovation in port planning involves the utilization of economic impact estimates in the planning process. The results of port economic impact exercises portray the number of jobs, revenues, and taxes that are provided to an area because of port activities. Prior to recent improvements, port economic impact data were considered more promotional than objective. Research advances by the Maritime Administration, however, have improved the creditability of port economic impact techniques. A regional model uses an input-output computer model to depict the importance of port activities to other industries and the surrounding economy. The model provides flexibility and contains the capability to address contingency questions regarding future possible scenarios affecting the port. Planning tools, such as this regional economic impact model, should be employed as pressures for rationalized investment continue to affect port improvements.

Port development strategies   By comparing existing port capacity estimates with projected cargo flows over a 20-yr period, required facilty improvements and expansions can be identified and scheduled. Depending upon the level of detail in both the marine terminal capacity estimates and cargo forecasts, facility requirements can be stated in cargo terminal equivalents or actual incremental improvements, handling equipment and land requirements. Comprehensive development strategies can also include detailed implementation plans and action steps depicting alternate approaches to accommodate anticipated directions and levels of port use.

Cargo Handling Facility Requirements. This section of the plan matches the supply of port facilities with cargo demand by handling mode. Supply factors are derived from an inventory of marine terminals and estimates of throughput capacity. Cargo forecasts should depict the demand for facilities by handling mode through the planning time horizon. Typical matching cargo–facility categories include containers, breakbulk general cargo, special-purpose neobulk or bulk cargo, general liquid bulk cargo, and general dry bulk cargo.

Assumptions should be made regarding the planning impact of multipurpose terminals and obsolete or damaged facilities. Subsequent implementation strategies can determine a development policy concerning new construction as opposed to rehabilitation. Because of the high cost of capital and potential constraints due to environmental considerations of new development, modernization of a port facility is a viable option for increasing port capacity in many harbors.

A common matching procedure will depict existing capacity for each cargo type, actual waterborne trade for current year, and forecasted trade for planning intervals through the next 20 years. Capacity shortfalls will be identified where trade forecasts exceed existing capacity estimated (see Fig. 10-5), and can then be converted to incremental facility requirements. Individual terminal equivalents will result from this matching procedure, with project phasing estimated from the timing of anticipated cargo growth. Facility requirements can be presented by phased additions in marine terminals for each cargo type as well as estimated capital expenditures for itemized port development.

Additional Factors Affecting Future Port Development. Prior to implementation, realistic factors affecting a port's ability to accommodate the identified growth should be analyzed. An obvious potential constraint could be the availability of suitable port-owned and undeveloped waterfront land. An important consideration in analyzing the availability of land and harbor area is the ratio of acres to water frontage on a parcel-by-parcel basis. Several cargo handling modes, such as containers, RO/RO, and certain bulk commodities require waterfront property with large surrounding acreage for storage and distribution. Land use should be evaluated and criteria of suitability for port use should yield a list of priority properties for terminal location. Constraints to property acquisition or engineering suitability should be identified and subsequent

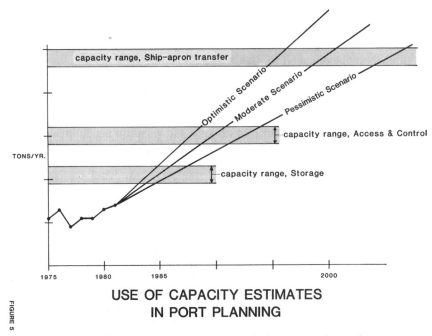

USE OF CAPACITY ESTIMATES
IN PORT PLANNING

FIGURE 5

Fig. 10-5. Trade forecasts versus existing capacity estimates

implementation strategies should weigh the costs and benefits of alternate actions to provide required additional port capacity.

Environmental regulations as well as protected wetlands should be identified and evaluated in connection with land use and port development requirements. Existing government documents contain regulations affecting port development. The dredge and fill rules of the Corps of Engineers and coordination responsibilities of the Environmental Protection Agency, National Marine Fisheries Service, and Fish and Wildlife Service should be understood and reflected in the suitability appraisal of potential port use sites. Similarly, local zoning ordinances, adopted land use comprehensive plans, and adopted shoreline master programs should be applied to the port plan. Other environmental problems including visual impacts, noise-related impacts, and recreational interests should be anticipated. Shortage of land in urban ports and protected wetland issues in rural ports are typical constraints, while dredging and spoil disposal concerns are normal environmental constraints limiting development in virtually all U.S. ports.

The quality and nature of inland transportation access are critical to port growth. Although inland transportation comes under separate authorities, deficiencies in rail and road access need to be identified, and action steps recommended to address constraints to port growth. Earlier data gathering should have identified the principal transportation modes serving the port. Additional data on cargo growth will depict the anticipated growth pressures on rail or road services. More detailed research on existing systems which are considered to be constraints should be undertaken, with alternate development actions recommended to relieve constraining elements. Similar analysis should be done for navigational channels and locks and dam, if applicable.

Alternate Development Scenarios. Accommodating future port growth can be accomplished by different means. Old facilities can be modernized, incremental improvements, such as storage, can be made to terminal elements, and completely new facilities can be constructed in alternate waterfront locations. A logical planning approach is to propose several alternate development scenarios for economic, engineering, environmental, and public evaluation. Advantages and disadvantages of each development scenario should be depicted and rated for the costs and benefits to the port community. At this point, policies should be made regarding the public and private sector responsibilities to provide port growth. As port development is traditionally a mixed responsibility, with trends differing in various regions and for different types of cargoes or port services, the alternate development scenarios should contain clear options. The roles of public port authorities and private companies will filter down to specific action steps in financing, marketing and operations in the recommended implementation program. The analysis of alternate development scenarios should conclude with a recommended development plan. Flexibility should be programmed into the plan through established contingencies to anticipate uncertainties inherent in financing and constructing major waterfront developments.

Implementation Plan. A typical implementation plan should consist of a physical development plan and required action steps to accommodate desired port growth. As an over-all master plan, this typical end product should include the following elements:

1. Land use and location of facilities.
2. Specific site plans and proposed terminal layouts.
3. Scheduling and costs of improvements.
4. Investment plan.
5. Marketing and other required action steps.
6. Monitoring.

A series of harbor or riverine maps should characterize existing and proposed locations of port facilities. Transportation access and services, as well as proximity to navigational channels, should be illustrated for existing and proposed waterfront developments. Locations of anchorages, barge fleeting areas, and dredge spoil disposal areas could also be depicted on the plans. Oversize harbor use maps should be included in the final planning report, displayed at public meetings, and provided for reference in the comprehensive land use plan of the local jurisdiction.

For terminals requiring modernization or for new areas, specific site plans depicting proposed terminal layouts should be included as part of the implementation plan. Since planning, in this context, is essentially a public process, specific site illustrations are basically appropriate only for public terminals. Private decisions regarding additional land use or connections with public facilities are relevant, but site-specific layouts for proprietary terminals are normally outside the port planning process. The portrayals of public terminal layouts should be considered graphic descriptions of required physical changes to accommodate cargo growth, not terminal designs.

Order-of-magnitude cost requirements and phasing of capital expenditures should be outlined in the implementation plan. Estimated costs for new terminals, buildings, and major equipment purchases should be given. Scheduling of investments can be annual or projected for a range of years. This capital expenditure schedule should be compatible with the budget scheduling of the port authority.

An investment plan should consist of strategies to finance the identified improvements. Mixtures of retained port earnings, bonds, and government appropriations should be recommended. Emphasis on long-term financial planning should emanate from this implementation plan. Trends in port financing should be examined to identify feasible avenues for cost effective financial sources. Major bond issues should utilize the supply and demand factors identified in the port planning exercise.

To obtain desired levels of cargo growth, improvements in marketing port services may be needed. The analysis of competitive factors and the advantages and disadvantages of the subject port may uncover marketing opportunities that have not previously been recognized. In addition to changes in marketing strategies, the long-range nature of the port planning process may initiate adaptations to operations, promotion, community relations, and other relevant activities affecting successful port development.

10.3 THE CONTEXT OF PORT PLANNING

Port planning is a relatively new field, linked to the growth of port authorities and regulatory requirements. Recognition of the importance of ports and port development to economic and social conditions, the capital intensive nature of port development, and extension of public control over terminal facilities and operations has highlighted the need for effective planning for port development.

In many large ports, planning is done on a continuing basis by port authority staff. Consultants are often used by larger ports, however, when port authority staff do not have the resources available, particularly in specialized areas, are not in working contact with national or regional trends and activities, or may want a second or more neutral opinion. Some very large U.S. port authorities, such as New York-New Jersey and Oakland, have developed staff expertise that gives them the ability to provide consulting services to other ports, as some private European port agencies have done (Felixstowe in England, for example). In small ports, planning may be done by staff or consultants, or both.

Short-term planning and continual analysis of relevant conditions and trends are generally done by staff or terminal personnel out of necessity or ability.

The role of a consultant in a planning study for a port authority involves effective communication with and encouragement of communication among terminal operators and users, as well as functions in port marketing, finance, and engineering. Definition of the goals and objectives of port development and operation must be undertaken in conjunction with responsible policy-makers, since commitment of funds necessarily involves the political process.

As a final note, it must be kept in mind that flexibility and responsiveness in port development are necessities, due to the interaction of the public and private sectors in port development. The need to serve business and industry, and pressure to operate as a business, require an ability to respond to opportunities and market trends, while public control over and responsibility for port development necessitates planned and formalized use of public funds. The planning process should, of course, attempt to predict and identify opportunities and relevant trends, but no planning process foresees every situation. It is important, therefore, that a plan be continually or periodically monitored, reviewed, and updated, and that the plan allow flexibility and responsiveness.

Major terminal improvements, such as berths and capital equipment, must be planned and funded in advance. Less major improvements (to storage facilities, for example) or repairs may require rapid decision-making and action. Planning must consider the horizon of decision-making, and long-term master planning that does not allow for flexibility and responsiveness constrains the ability of port operators and users to respond to new situations; short-term planning, for a specific issue or decision as the focus of investigation, can address specific projects in more detail. Continual or periodic analysis of current and projected port use allows timely responses to changing conditions in the port operating environment.

10.4 REFERENCES

1. Hockney, L.A., *Port Handbook for Estimating Marine Terminal Cargo Handling Capacity*, for Moffatt & Nichols under contract nos. DO A0178-003093 and MA-Port-970-80013 for the U.S. Maritime Administration, Long Beach, CA, September 1979.
2. Northern California Ports and Terminals Bureau, report developed for the U.S. Maritime Administration, National Technical Information Service, Springfield, VA, August, 1976.
3. U.S. Maritime Administration, *National Port Assessment, 1980/1990*, Washington, D.C.

CHAPTER 11

COMMUNITY SERVICE FACILITIES PLANNING[a]

11.1 INTRODUCTION

Community service facilities deliver goods and services to the community through a system of facility networks. The traditional models of planning for community service facilities relied mainly on analyses of optimum location and capacity based on the concept of minimum travel distance for the delivery of services to the target population. The environment for planning in general, and community service facilities in particular, has substantially changed over the last few decades. Accessibility is no longer the single most important criterion in planning community service facilities. There have been many changes which necessitate a careful analysis of new quantitative and qualitative aspects of facilities planning.

First, a significant number of communities in the post-industrial era have been transformed into heterogeneous entities, economically, politically, racially, and socially. This change has resulted in an increase in the level of conflicts and controversy over community decision making, and drastic alteration of the concept of community needs. Second, the planning process has become more complicated than ever due to the increased level of public participation and regulatory procedures mandated by the government. For example, many planning projects are now subject to legal requirements for citizen participation and impact assessments. Third, the qualitative characteristics of many community service facilities have become more complex. For example, many facilities once considered as having neutral impacts are now perceived by community residents as undesirable. Fourth, scarcity of funds and increasingly higher costs of labor and capital have made it difficult for communities to provide an adequate level of services.

These circumstances call for a thorough evaluation of traditional models of planning for community service facilities, and for the development of a more relevant framework of plan-making for community based service facilities. Recent developments in community service facilities planning clearly note the changing environment of decision making (31) and argue for a reorganization of facilities location theories (4). This chapter is intended to provide a framework of planning for

---

[a]Prepared by Gill C. Lim, M.ASCE, Department of Urban and Regional Planning, University of Illinois at Urbana-Champaign, Urbana, IL., and David Bernstein, Atlantic Commodities.

community service facilities with special reference to new characteristics which have not been adequately addressed by current professional practice and conventional studies. Attention will be given to needs analyses, examination of location analysis models, plan evaluation, and development of planning models under conflicts of interest and public controversy.

11.2 NATURE OF PLANNING FOR COMMUNITY SERVICE FACILITIES

11.2.1 Definitions

The term "community" is frequently used to refer to a territorial unit having certain common characteristics. But these common characteristics can be diverse. They can be political, administrative, social or economic. The difficulty of defining a community arises from the complexity and heterogeneity of the contemporary social fabric. Therefore, the most immediate task in defining a community is a search for the most crucial common characteristics.

Janowitz and Street (14) focused on the concept of sustenance needs as the most crucial common feature of a community. They define a community as "a geographically based form of social organization that directly supplies its members with the major portion of their sustenance needs." Most of an individual's sustenance needs involve transactions of goods and services on a daily basis. Therefore, the daily commuting pattern is an important criterion in determining a metropolitan region. In this sense, a metropolitan region can be defined as the largest community which is organized around the sustenance needs of individuals. On the other hand, some of the daily sustenance needs such as recreation or food shopping can be satisfied within a range of a block or a neighborhood. In this chapter, a community is defined as a contiguous geographical unit—ranging from a small block to a large metropolitan region—whose members share the major portion of daily transactions of sustenance needs.

The central function of service facilities is to provide services to their users. Therefore, community service facilities can be defined as those facilities which provide services to members of a community who live in a geographically contiguous area and share the major portion of daily transactions of sustenance needs. These facilities can be either in the private sector, the public sector, or part of a joint public-private organization. Whether a particular type of service is furnished by the public or private sector depends on economic, political, and historical factors. Although certain types of services are most efficiently supplied by the market, some services cannot be efficiently supplied by the free market system.

TABLE 11-1 A Matrix to Classify Service Facilities

Community unit (1)	Sector Providing Services		
	Private (2)	Joint public–private (3)	Public (4)
Block	corner grocery		mailbox
Neighborhood	movie theater grocery	neighborhood social center	post office school fire station
Municipality	department store	municipal day care center run by private agency and funded by the public sector	hospital municipal park
Metropolitan region	regional shopping center	metropolitan emergency shelter run jointly by the public and private sectors	regional hospital water system power plant regional park

11.2.2 Classification

Using the definition of community presented above and the different sources of community services, we may create a matrix for classifying community service facilities. Table 11-1 shows various facilities classified by this system. Alternatively, community service facilities can be classified by their method of delivery. Massam classifies service facilities into two major groups: punctiform and linear facilities (16). Table 11-2 shows examples of punctiform facilities, such as a fire station, school, and park, and linear facilities, such as subways, highways, and power lines.

11.2.3 Planning Process

A typical planning process involves the following steps:

1. Problem definition.
2. Formulation of goals and objectives.
3. Development of alternatives.
4. Evaluation of alternatives.
5. Selection of one alternative that can best meet the objectives.
6. Implementation.

TABLE 11-2 Basic Classification of Facilities (16)

Type of facility (1)	Example (2)
Punctiform: emergency services	fire station police station ambulance depot
social services	hospital, clinic social center school
industrial	factory, processing plant warehouse extraction site, mine industrial park
utilities	waterworks power plant sewage plant
leisure and recreation	park, playground
Linear: below ground	subway utility lines (gas, water, electricity) pipeline
surface	highways railways utility corridor
elevated	power lines

In a traditional analysis of service facility planning, problems are usually defined in terms of service needs and the single objective of efficiently providing services. Efficiency is defined as either minimizing costs or the number of facilities, or maximizing the use of facilities or user access. However, where multiple objectives exist, trade-offs between different objectives complicate the planning process. McAllister noted the efficiency-equity trade-off in facility planning (18). It is now widely recognized that there are no universally accepted criteria to evaluate the trade-off between two conflicting objectives. This difficulty suggests the need for evaluation of facility planning from the viewpoint of multiple objectives. Later in this chapter, plan evaluation methods that deal explicitly with the issue of multiple objectives will be presented.

Two additional important characteristics of community service facilities should be carefully considered in the planning process. First, the service recipients of most community facilities are selective; many community service facilities are not used by the entire community. Second, geographical differentiation exists in the external effect of community service facilities on individuals. For example, the effect of undesirable facilities on property values may be represented by a distance-decay function—the adverse effects decline with distance. These features of community service facilities, i.e., (1) selectivity of service beneficiaries and (2) variation in their external effects, often lead to conflicts and controversy among different groups of the community. For example, conflicts are often found in the siting of facilities such as mental health centers. The existence of conflict may add to the cost of planning and construction by causing delays in project implementation and additional expenditures for mediation, legal counsel, and additional studies.

Further complications in planning community service facilities arise from the various regulations existing in local communities. The primary source of local regulations is zoning and land use control. The most desirable location for a particular service facility may be zoned for residential use and therefore unavailable. Local regulations such as zoning serve the purpose of reducing impacts of certain types of land use on the community but could complicate the planning and implementation processes.

Complications of traditional planning procedures suggest that successful planning for community service facilities requires a more judicious and sophisticated combination of analysis and strategy for negotiation and implementation. Figure 11-1 describes a revised version of a typical planning process presented at the beginning of this section. The new model is intended to make the planning process more relevant and useful in addressing the special characteristics of the community facilities previously described. Key elements of the model presented in Fig. 11-1 are explained next.

11.3 NEED ASSESSMENTS AND DEMAND ANALYSIS IN PROBLEM DEFINITION

If a community's current needs for services are adequately met by the current level of service provision, the community may claim that it is free from problems regarding community services. However, changes in population structure and service provision may indicate a significant gap between needs and services in the future. In that case, the community will face a problem of community services. Therefore, the most important element of defining the problem of community service facilities relates to an assessment of community needs for various services. Broadly, there are two approaches to determining a desirable quantity of such facilities: (1) The per capita requirement approach, and (2) the demand approach.

11.3.1 Per Capita Requirement Approach

This approach uses a predetermined value as an amount of community services required "per capita," or for each person in the popu-

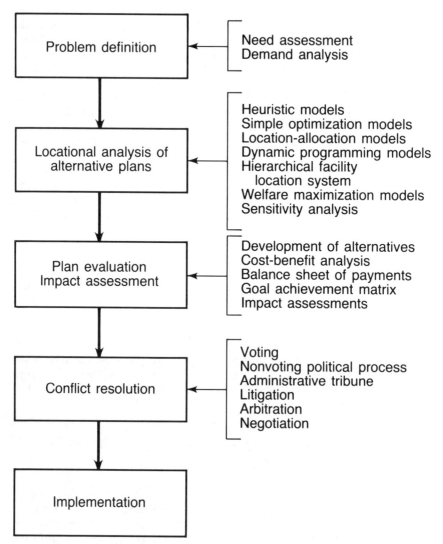

Fig. 11-1. Planning process for community service facilities

lation. To calculate the over-all size of a community facility, it relies on a projection of the community's population. It usually involves the following steps: (1) Projection or estimation of population to be served for a target year; (2) selection of a per capita requirement for service facilities in question; (3) calculation of over-all size of facilities by multiplication of target population and per capita requirement; (4) comparison of existing service facilities and needs; and (5) consideration of available resources and other constraints.

To illustrate the procedures described, it would be useful to consider a case of recreational facilities. Suppose a suburban town which expects a fast growth in the next decade is planning for a system of playgrounds, neighborhood parks, playfields, and community parks. As a first step, planners need to estimate the population change in the next decade. Second, they must decide upon the per capita requirements for various recreational areas. Table 11-3 shows standards for various recreational areas per 1000 population, size of site, and service radius. Third, knowing population estimates and per capita requirements, planners can calculate the over-all needs for recreational facilities. Fourth, by comparing the needed amount of recreational areas and existing recreational areas, they estimate the gap between needs and services. The fifth step is to look at the resource constraints. The town may not have enough land to satisfy all the needs estimated by this approach. In that instance, the town must consider other alternatives, such as adjusting the per capita requirements, buying land from neighboring jurisdictions, or controlling the growth of population itself.

Various cities, counties and regions have established per capita requirements for different community service facilities. Organizations such as the National Recreation and Parks Association have also suggested standards for service provision. Since there is no absolute standard norm in selecting per capita requirements, community service facility planners are advised to consult the information provided by these agencies, and to determine per capita requirements by examining the economic, demographic, social and other characteristics of their community.

11.3.2 Demand Approach

While the per capita requirement approach applies a simple rule of thumb to calculate the needed quantity of community service facilities,

TABLE 11-3 Standards for Recreational Areas (21)

| Type of Area (1) | Acres per 1000 Population (2) | Size of Site, acres[a] | | Radius of Area Served, in miles[b] (5) |
		Ideal (3)	Minimum (4)	
Playgrounds	1.5	4	2	0.5
Neighborhood parks	2.0	10	5	0.5
Playfields	1.5	15	10	1.5
Community parks	3.5	100	40	2.0
District parks	2.0	200	100	3.0
Regional parks and reservations	15.0	500–1000	varies	10.0

[a]1 acre = 0.405 hectare.
[b]1 mile = 1.61 kilometers.

the demand approach is based on the concept of how much people want to consume in association with the cost of services. Given the scarcity of land and the fact that community members must pay for certain facilities through taxes or user fees, the demand approach is a more realistic way of determining the desirable quantity of community service facilities.

If there is reliable price information for the provision of community service facilities, the demand for service equation can be estimated by employing regression analysis. Typically, demand functions are estimated by using output as the dependent variable and income, price, and other variables as independent variables. These functions can be used to project the desirable level of services in the future.

In the absence of reliable price signals, a proxy for price is used. For example, the demand for a regional health facility can be estimated by using the travel distance from home to hospital as a proxy for price.

Economists have produced a number of studies on demand for community services such as police, fire, recreation, and cultural services (13). These studies do not provide a simple rule of thumb to estimate a community's demand for services, but they do provide a useful guideline to examine whether typical need assessments using per capita requirements are realistic from the viewpoint of willingness to pay and affordability.

11.3.3 Locational Considerations

Typical needs assessments and demand analyses deal with the aggregate quantity of community service facilities. Community needs for services, however, vary over space, and the location of facilities also affects the level of satisfaction of service recipients. Therefore, locational analysis is another important element of planning for community service facilities. The next section is devoted to this subject.

11.4 MODELS OF LOCATIONAL ANALYSIS FOR COMMUNITY SERVICE FACILITIES

Several models of location decisions for community facilities have been developed over the years. They can be broadly classified as heuristic models, simple allocation models, location-allocation models, dynamic programming models, hierarchical facility location models, and welfare maximization models. A great deal of thought has been given to their theoretical construct and efficiency. However, relatively less attention has been given to the analysis of their pragmatic aspects. The purpose of this section is to: (1) Briefly review the various types of public facility location analysis models, and (2) evaluate their relevance to the planning of community facilities.

11.4.1 Heuristic Models

Heuristic models were developed to locate public community facilities at a general level. Such models impose several restrictive assumptions, and they lead to a good, if not optimal, solution, if properly employed. They are basically analytic attempts to use a given theory. One of the more commonly used theories is the central place concept.

Morrill and Kelley (19) developed a model of this type which includes such variables as the number, size, and location of public facilities. Their model minimizes the distance betwen services and users subject to the constraints: (1) That minimum thresholds of population must be nearer to a possible activity location than to any other such location, and (2) that since larger communities have a better chance to support an activity than smaller ones, the priority of possible areas to be the location of an activity is a function of community size.

Using this model, facilities of the proper size can be allocated to zones in a community according to their priority. Unserviced areas can then be combined with adjacent areas until the minimum population level is met, and a facility can be allocated. The minimum population level thus obtained is called the threshold population level. If no further combinations can be made, the remaining areas should be allocated to the nearest facility after appropriately adjusting the size of that facility.

Since heuristic models are based on limited assumptions, they can be applied only to a small number of cases. The models can be used when planners have a limited amount of time, resources, and information. The following problems, however, must be clearly understood.

The first problem associated with heuristic models is the lack of a test of efficiency. Although it is true that they will allocate a sufficient service level, there are many other possible distributions which can satisfy an area's needs. Heuristic models lack the ability to compare different alternatives in order to determine the optimal (or even comparatively better) solution.

Closely linked with this problem is the issue of threshold population levels. Even within a well-defined region, threshold population levels should be allowed to change from site to site. It is unrealistic to apply the same criterion to both the central city and its suburban ring. Heuristic models make no allowances for this problem. A third problem of heuristic models is their treatment of the area as an isotropic plane. By using distance instead of time, they implicitly assume equal access in all directions. This assumption clearly ignores many aspects of locating service facilities which are essential to the proper formulation of problem solving.

Another problem is the arbitrary assignment of communities. Heuristic models fail to recognize the possibility of splitting a community between two facilities.

Finally, heuristic models include only demand (obtained from population levels) and distance. Other factors such as rent, competitive uses, heterogeneity of services, adjacent uses, and physical constraints (including the size of the facility) must also be included in order to serve a useful purpose in planning community facilities.

11.4.2 Simple Optimization Models

Simple optimization models are a more useful group than heuristic models. They incorporate various measures of accessibility, including distance, time, and travel cost. The basis of these models is the problem of minimizing (or maximizing) the objective function subject to various constraints. In the most basic example this can be seen as a problem of assigning a given number of facilities to the same number of sites while minimizing the cost of assignment.

In terms of the linear programming problem, a simple optimization model can be represented as

$$\text{Min} \qquad \sum_{i=1}^{n} \sum_{j=1}^{n} d_{ij} x_{ij} \qquad (11.1)$$

Subject to

$$\sum_i x_{ij} = 1 \qquad (11.2)$$

$$\sum_j x_{ij} = 1 \qquad (11.3)$$

$$x_{ij} \geq 0 \qquad (11.4)$$

in which i = the ith of n facilities, j = the jth of n locations, d_{ij} = cost of assigning facility i to site j, and x_{ij} = magnitude of flow from i to j.

One of the more specific problems is the optimization of the pattern of flows between sites where each site has a given supply and demand. The objective of this type of model is to minimize the cost of the flow. The model can be further extended to include minimizing initial (setup) costs as well as transportation costs. In addition, it can be modified so that the optimal solution will include a facility at each site where any demand exists. This model need not be restricted by threshold population levels.

It should also be noted that simple optimization models can overcome the heuristic models' assumptions of equal access. By including a matrix of either time or cost between facilities and sites, they can be made much more realistic than the heuristic models. However, in doing so they are restricted to a predetermined number of facilities. Simple optimization models merely allocate a given number of facilities among several locations without considering whether the number of facilities is optimal.

11.4.3 Location–Allocation Models

Location-allocation models attempt to both locate community service facilities and allocate demand to those facilities. They are considered discrete space models if there is a given set of potential locations to choose from, and continuous space models if there are no known possible locations.

In discrete space these models can be characterized by several features. First, there are n known destinations located in Cartesian space (as in a two-dimensional graph) at the coordinates x_j , y_j (for $j = 1, \ldots , n$), and each location has a cost β_i related to the amount of services delivered. Second, there are m facilities to be located, and the cost of distance between sites and facilities α_{ij} is a matrix from which a subset is chosen. Finally, the subject specifies assignments of facilities to sites. The problem is to find values for both (x_j , y_j) and α_{ij} .

In the case of continuous space, the location-allocation model can be made even more general by assuming that: (1) Demand is unique to each destination j; (2) destinations can be assigned to more than one source; and (3) facilities have a given capacity c_i . When demand is included in the objective function and a zero one choice variable is defined, this model is known as the optimal partitioning problem.

Location-allocation models still do not account for economic rents or existing surrounding uses. In addition, they ignore the problems of a time horizon, of whether accessibility is an accurate measure of welfare, and of how to allocate services that are hierarchical in nature. Nevertheless, they provide a convenient scheme to determine the location and allocation of demand at the same time.

11.4.4 Dynamic Programming Models

Dynamic programming models introduce time-dependence into the modeling procedure, so taking into account the fact that facilities cannot be located simultaneously. In this process facility construction is established in a time frame so as to minimize long-run costs. In general such processes are very complicated, because with m facilities there are $m!$ possible development schemes. For instance, with 10 facilities there are $10 \times 9 \times 8 \ldots 2 \times 1 = 3,628,800$ possible development schemes. Dynamic programming handles this problem through a recursive technique, which specifies that at any period t the optimal solution consists of the costs of choosing a particular state i, having selected state j previously, plus the cost of the optimal time-path leading to state i at period t–1.

Suppose the problem is to locate five service facilities given that facilities may be constructed only one at a time. There are, then, 120 possible schedules for development. The objective is to account for the fact that service will be provided at different levels during construction, and that the optimal schedule will service the largest number of people at the lowest cost during the construction period. Dynamic programming models solve this problem by assuming that for a given number of completed facilities, e.g., two completed facilities at stage i, the optimal solution to the entire problem can be found by optimally completing the remaining facilities, e.g., the three facilities still to be constructed by stage j, if the completed facilities were already constructed optimally.

Dynamic programming models solve the problem by working backwards in time and resolving the problem at each stage. In this way, the number of development schedules considered is substantially reduced.

11.4.5 Hierarchical Facility Location Systems

Banerji and Fisher studied the location of service hierarchies in areas where infrastructural relationships exist (3). Their objective was to find both an efficient and equitable spatial organization, in which efficiency is defined as minimizing travel distance between sites and facilities, and equity is defined in terms of a maximum allowable travel distance. Levels in the hierarchy are defined by the relative allowable travel distances associated with a group of services, starting with those services which occur most infrequently. Optimal location patterns are determined in the model in two separate steps. In the first step an algorithm is used to determine the optimal number of facilities. The second step involves locating these facilities in such a way as to minimize user cost.

The Banerji and Fisher model works from the highest level of the hierarchy downward and treats the location of facilities already determined as constraints at subsequent levels. When the number of facilities is too few to meet demand satisfactorily, an additional facility is added.

Dokmeci developed a similar type of model to find the optimal number, size, and location of hierarchically coordinated facilities in an area so that the total cost of the system is minimized, and the demand in the area is fully met (5). The model is solved using a step-by-step heuristic approach beginning at the lowest level of the hierarchy.

These models are extremely useful for practical purposes, because they deal with the determination of the number, size and location of community service facilities within a single framework.

11.4.6 Welfare Maximization Models

Welfare maximization models can be employed to find a better measure of social welfare than the commonly used variable of accessibility such as a distance-cost relationship. The two models described here were developed by Wagner and Falkson (30). They operate in discrete space and attempt to choose socially optimal levels of service for each of n communities, and to locate these service facilities by maximizing consumer and producer surplus. The first model, known as a public fiat model, assumes that consumers can be assigned arbitrarily to facilities and can be denied services.

The second model is a modification of the first. It assumes that consumers cannot be denied service and are free to choose any facility. This is called a "serve-all-comers" model. In order to transform the model, two sets of constraints must be added. The first set is added to assure that consumers are assigned to the closest facility in terms of travel cost. A second set of constraints must be added to guarantee that all consumers who present themselves for service are served.

It is important to point out that welfare maximization models require a few basic assumptions. First, a production function must be available for a given facility. Second, there must be an estimable willingness-to-pay function for all consumers. Finally, all assumptions for consumer and producer surplus theory must hold.

11.4.7 Sensitivity Analysis and Other Issues

Before concluding the section on models of locational analysis, it is important to mention two additional issues: sensitivity analysis and mental maps.

Sensitivity analysis is a technique used to determine the stability of location models. It should be applied first to determine if small changes in the weighting schemes result in large changes in the outcome. If this is the case, it is important to be careful in estimating weights and to understand that these weights might change over time and so affect the results significantly.

Another use of sensitivity analysis is to test the relationshp between the number of supply points and the average distance. It is important to look at the marginal gain or loss which can be obtained by adding and subtracting sites. This factor is especially relevant in models where these numbers are exogenously determined; the number of sites is determined prior to the analysis.

The other issue to be considered is the difference between absolute and relative locations (8). People's perception of the physical environment— their mental map—often diverges from the actual environment. This divergence questions the nature of the objective function: what should these models minimize?

For example, many factors, including stress, risk, environmental concerns, and social biases, might lead an individual to perceive incorrectly the distance between sites and facilities. If so, using cost functions based on map distances will not correctly state the costs involved.

Several studies addressing the issue of perception in planning have significantly improved our understanding about the relationship between spatial perception and behavior (1, 7). It is advisable to include in the background analysis a survey of people's perceptions of their environment, and to use the results of this survey in conjunction with distance-cost information in locational analyses.

11.5 PLAN EVALUATION

Techniques of locational analysis described in the previous section are mainly concerned with finding an optimal solution for a location and a level of community services. Depending on the type of analysis employed and assumptions about constraints, a number of different alternatives can be proposed. This section reviews evaluation and impact assessment processes.

11.5.1 Development of Alternatives

There are many alternatives to attain a set of given objectives. Simply by changing a few assumptions or by employing slightly different techniques, numerous alternatives can be generated as possible solutions to a problem. These alternatives must be evaluated in order to determine their relative advantages and drawbacks. Several methods are available for this type of comparative analysis, and some of them are considered next.

11.5.2 Methods of Plan Evaluation

Cost-benefit analysis   Cost-benefit analysis is a procedure formulated to evaluate whether the benefits of a program outweigh its costs (9, 28). Both benefits and costs are recorded in monetary terms and are then discounted back to their present value so that they can be compared. In this way, different plans can be compared, and the plan with the greatest net benefits can be identified.

The technique may seem quite simple, but the difficulty lies in assigning monetary values to nonmonetary items. For instance, what is the value of a park? To deal with the problems associated with nonmonetary items, concepts such as consumer surplus, shadow prices, and required compensation have been developed. In addition, it should be noted that for the purpose of evaluating alternative plans, exact identification of a monetary value is not always necessary. If the same standards are used, it is often possible to rank alternative plans, even though it may not be possible to determine exact monetary values.

Balance sheet of payments   The balance sheet of payments technique is very similar to cost-benefit analysis (15). The difference is that, in the balance sheet of payments technique, all individuals are divided into two distinct groups: producers and consumers. As a result of various transactions, each group can incur costs and benefits. These costs and benefits are not listed simply in monetary terms. They are divided into: (1) Monetary items; (2) nonmonetary items; and (3) nonquantitative, nonmonetary items.

Once these items are grouped, the nonmonetary categories can be ranked. This ranking can be accomplished by surveying a sample of individuals and by using aggregation techniques, such as comparative matrices and average ranking, in order to determine a final scale. Alternative plans can then be compared by examining both the monetary and nonmonetary items.

Although this technique is often used because it does not attempt to define everything in monetary terms, it does suffer from some drawbacks. One is that the ranking system can be as arbitrary as the monetary values assigned in cost-benefit analysis. In addition, this ranking can only be compared if all items appear on the lists of benefits or costs for all alternative solutions.

Goal-achievement matrix   In an attempt to combine the better points of the cost-benefit analysis and the balance sheet of payments method, the concept of goal achievement was developed to evaluate alternative plans (12). Underlying this method is the belief that both costs and benefits can be defined only in terms of their relationship to the intended goal.

In this process, a matrix is developed which shows the various groups affected by a plan, the relative weights assigned to each group, and the costs and benefits associated with each group and each particular goal. The matrices for the various plans can then be compared and the best alternative recommended.

The process is not quite as straightforward as it seems. The question to be considered is, how can the matrices be compared? It is difficult to make fine distinctions. However, if the matrix points out the relevant relationship and the groups that will be affected, it is useful in evaluating plans even though weights cannot be determined.

Impact assessment   Leopold's environmental impact assessment matrix is one of the most widely used techniques of impact assessment (16, 17). The purpose of the technique is twofold: (1) To provide a weighting scheme for various impacts, and (2) to provide information for the preparation of an environmental impact assessment. These objectives are important in the evaluation of alternative plans for community service facilities.

Leopold's matrix consists of the rows, representing the existing condition of the environment, and the columns, describing actions which may cause environmental impacts. All actions included in the plan are identified in the matrix. Usually, the magnitude of impact is expressed on a scale of 1 to 10. Each cell can then be assigned two values representing the magnitude and the importance of the impact. Alternative plans can be more easily compared once a matrix is prepared for all alternatives. This process is proposed as a technique for ordering the numerous possible impacts. There is no good numerical technique available to summarize over-all impacts. The main advantage of using the impact assessment matrix is to bring to the attention of planners various possible impacts of community facilities which are not clearly addressed in typical project evaluation methods such as cost-benefit analysis.

11.6 CONFLICT RESOLUTION IN COMMUNITY SERVICE FACILITIES PLANNING

In some situations, planners may be requested to conduct an analysis of benefit distribution and external effects on different groups and individuals in a community. A scheme may be prepared which details compensation, charges, and concessions to equalize the net effect of community service facilities among all members of a community. Two problems are inherent in this process. First, planners may not have sufficient information to conduct an objective calculation of the net effects of a facility on all members of the community. Second, planners usually do not have full authority over the implementation process. Unless there exists cohesive, centralized political power and a high level of consensus in the community, a rational planning process faces serious difficulties.

11.6.1 Conflict in Community Facilities Planning

Conflicts over facilities planning arise mainly because of the selectivity of service beneficiaries and the geographical variations in the external effects. Even in a homogeneous community where all residents receive the benefits of certain facilities, the differential external effects on individuals can lead to conflicts over facility siting decisions. Conflicts would be more intense in a case involving a selective-user facility which generates a high level of external effects. A classification of community facilities may be developed according to the varying levels of conflicts (Table 11-4).

It is important that planners have information about the factors affecting the level of conflicts and consider their implications at the initial stage of the planning process. When the necessary technical analyses and the specific plans for the community facilities are completed, planners should be prepared to deal with the inevitable conflicts.

11.6.2 Modes of Conflict Resolution

There are several approaches to resolving conflict in planning community service facilities. They include:

TABLE 11-4 Degree of Conflict

External effects (1)	Beneficiaries of Service Facilities	
	Entire community (2)	Part of community (3)
Minimal	I lowest level of conflict	II higher level of conflict
Substantial	III higher level of conflict	IV highest level of conflict

1. Voting.
2. Nonvoting political process.
3. Administrative tribunal.
4. Litigation.
5. Arbitration.
6. Negotiation.
7. Mediation.

Voting is based on the concept of majority rule. A referendum on a particular community facility may result in a decision. Usually a referendum will show only a positive or negative decision about the establishment of a specific facility. Such subtle issues as compensation and concessions within the context of multiple facilities are easily ignored. It is possible to influence the outcome of the voting by disseminating relevant information through public hearings or other channels.

Nonvoting political processes are often more influential than referenda. The result of political processes depends on political strategies which deal with the demands of interest groups either opposing or supporting specific aspects of a community service facility. The conventional political strategies, which distinguish between the groups to be placated and those which can be ignored, become explicit in the political process (26). This process may lead to a failure to compensate those groups which are severely affected by the negative aspects of a siting decision but which are politically ineffective (25). Planners may understand benefit distribution and the effects of a facility upon different subgroups in a community, but the final outcome may be considerably different from what was initially envisaged as optimal.

In some cases, an administrative tribunal system can be set up to resolve conflicts. In some countries, tribunal systems play a key role: in Britain, for example, a dispute over land development may be brought to an administrative tribunal (11). Tribunal systems work well in areas characterized by central control but are not popular in communities where power is diffuse and decentralized. In a decentralized political environment, the settlement of dispute is frequently referred to the courts.

Community facility planners often have to deal with litigation. Certain groups in a community which oppose the idea of having a service facility on a particular site may bring the issue to court. Planners may also resort to litigation for settlement of disputes. Litigation adds substantially to the over-all costs of planning and implementation, which include legal fees and the costs associated with project delay. The cost of litigation often serves as an incentive for the parties involved in a controversy to reach a settlement outside the court. Arbitration is a process by which a dispute is submitted for settlement to an impartial party selected by mutual consent or by statutory provision.

Negotiation, in a broad sense, is a means of getting something accomplished when the parties involved must deal with each other in order to reach an objective (27). Community facility planners should understand the various methods of negotiating because they typically face various community groups and must deal frequently with bargaining, compensation, and concessions. The negotiation process does not necessarily involve a third party. Mediation refers to a particular type of negotiation in which a third party, a mediator, plays a key role in resolving the conflict. Mediation is playing an increasingly important role in resolving the conflicts that arise as attempts are made to reach equitable decisions about community facilities.

11.7 SUMMARY

This chapter has dealt with the process of planning for community service facilities. Community service facilities are defined as a system of service delivery for contiguous geographical units whose members share a major portion of daily transactions of sustenance need. Particular attention was given to: (1) Describing the nature of community service facilities; (2) need assessments; (3) evaluating the models available to planners for locating facilities; (4) a discussion of plan evaluation; and (5) examining alternative methods of resolving conflicts.

It was noted that even the most sophisticated mathematical models of locational analysis do not provide planners with an optimal solution for all members of a community. The most difficult problems arise from the very nature of community service facilities—selectivity of service beneficiaries and geographical variations in external effects.

Two additional planning concepts should be included in the conventional analytical models of location decisions. One is a rigorous plan evaluation procedure which scrutinizes the goals, impacts, and costs of community service facilities on various members of the community. The other step is conflict resolution. To successfully plan and implement a project, planners should have a clear understanding early in the planning process of the nature of the conflicts over facility planning that may arise between different groups of the community. Planners should be familiar with various methods of dealing with the inevitable disagreements. The planning process is a tool to provide decision makers with adequate analyses and up-to-date information. As such, planners must remain aware of the limitations of the technical aspects of planning and of potential conflicts which might arise.

Essential for facility planners is an understanding of the political power structure in their community, a familiarity with litigation procedures, and a knowledge of the techniques of arbitration and negotiation. The importance of conflict resolution in the successful planning of community facilities suggests a need to supplement the technical and analytical training of planners and engineers with study in these fields.

11.8 REFERENCES

1. Abelson, R.P., and Tukey, J.W., "Efficient Conversion of Non-Metric Information into Metric Information," *Proceedings of the Social Statistics Section*, American Statistical Assoc., 1959.
2. Bacharach, S.B., and Lawler, E.J., *Bargaining: Power, Tactics and Outcomes*, Jossey-Bass Publishers, San Francisco, 1981.
3. Banerji, S., and Fisher, H., "Hierarchical Location Analysis for Integrated Area Planning in Rural India," *Papers of the Regional Science Assoc.*, Vol. 33, 1974, pp. 177–194.
4. Dear, M., "Planning for Mental Health Care: A Reconsideration of Public Facility Location Theory," *International Regional Science Review*, Vol. 3, No. 2, 1978, pp. 93–111.
5. Dokmeci, V., "An Optimization Model for a Hierarchical Spatial System," *Journal of Regional Science*, Vol. 13, No. 3, 1973, pp. 439–451.
6. Goodkind, D.R., "How to Reduce Construction Claims Through Mediation," *Civil Engineering*, Vol. 53, No. 3, March ,1982, pp. 52–53.
7. Gould, P., *On Mental Maps*, Michigan Inter-University Community of Mathematical Geographies, Ann Arbor, 1965.
8. Gould, P., and White, R., *Mental Maps*, Penguin Books, Inc., New York, 1974.
9. Gramlich, E., *Benefit-Cost Analysis of Government Programs*, Prentice-Hall, Inc., Englewood Cliffs, N.J., 1981.
10. Hakimi, S.L., "Optimum Locations of Switching Centers and the Absolute Centers and Medians of a Graph," *Operations Research*, Vol. 12, 1964, pp. 450–459.
11. Hall, P., "Urban and Regional Planning in Britain and America: Ends and Means," *International Review*, Vol. 1, No. 1, U.S. Department of Housing and Urban Development, Washington, D.C., November, 1978, pp. 85–95.
12. Hill, M., "A Goals Achievement Matrix for Evaluating Alternative Plans," *Journal of the American Institute of Planners*, Vol. 32, 1968, pp. 19–29.
13. Hirsch, W., *Urban Economic Analysis*, McGraw-Hill, Inc., New York, 1973, Chapters 11 and 12.
14. Janowitz, M., and Street, D., "Changing Social Order of the Metropolitan Area," *Handbook of Contemporary Urban Life*, by D. Street, et al., Jossey-Bass Publishers, San Francisco, 1978, pp. 90–97.
15. Litchfield, N., Kettle, P., and Whitbread, M., *Evaluation in the Planning Process*, Pergamon Press, Oxford, England, 1975.
16. Massam, B.H., *Spatial Search*, Pergamon Press, New York, 1980.
17. McAllister, D.M., "Efficiency and Equity in Public Facility Location," *Geographical Analysis*, Vol. 8, 1976, pp. 47–63.
18. McAllister, D.M., *Evaluation in Environmental Planning*, MIT Press, Cambridge, Mass., 1980.
19. Morrill, R., and Kelley, P., "Optimum Allocation of Service: A Hospital Example," *Annals of Regional Science*, Vol. 3, No. 1, 1969, pp. 55–66.
20. Mumphrey, A.J., Seley, J.E., and Wolpert, J., "A Decision Model for Locating Controversial Facilities," *AIP Journal*, Nov., 1971, pp. 397–402.
21. Inter-County Regional Planning Agency, *Standards for New Urban Development*, Denver, Colo., 1960.
22. ReVelle, C., Marks, D., and Liebman, J., "An Analysis of Private and Public Sector Location Models," *Management Science*, Vol. 16, No. 11, 1970, p. 692–707.

23. ReVelle, C.S., and Swain, R.W., "Central Facilities Location," *Geographical Analysis*, Vol. 11, 1970, pp. 30–42.
24. Scott, A., "Location-Allocation Systems: A Review," *Geographical Analysis*, Vol. 2, 1970, pp. 95–119.
25. Seley, J.E., "Participation in Urban Renewal: The Germantown Case," Discussion Paper II, *Research on Conflict in Locational Decisions*, University of Pennsylvania, Philadelphia, 1970.
26. Seley, J.E., and Wolpert, J., "A Strategy of Ambiguity in Locational Conflicts," *Locational Approaches to Power and Conflict*, K. Cox, D. Reynolds, and S. Rokkan, eds., Sage Publications, Beverly Hills, 1971.
27. Strauss, A., *Negotiation: Varieties, Contexts, Processes and Social Order*, Jossey-Bass Publishers, San Francisco, 1978.
28. Squire, L., and VanderTak, H.G., *Economic Analysis of Projects*, Johns Hopkins University Press, Baltimore, Md., 1975.
29. Teitz, M.B., "Toward a Theory of Urban Public Facility Location," *Papers of the Regional Science Association*, Vol. 21, 1968, pp. 35–52.
30. Wagner, J., and Falkson, L., "The Optimal Nodal Location of Public Facilities with Price-Sensitive Demand," *Geographical Analysis*, Vol. 7, No. 1, 1975, pp. 69–83.
31. Wolpert, J., "Opening Closed Spaces," Working Paper 16, School of Architecture and Urban Planning, Princeton University, Princeton, N.J., 1975.

CHAPTER 12

WATER RESOURCES PLANNING[a]

12.1 INTRODUCTION

12.1.1 Uses and Issues

Water is essential for human life, for agricultural and industrial production, and for water-based recreation and transportation. It is central to many national concerns, including energy, food production, environmental quality, and regional economic development. Water is often taken for granted, even though it is unequally distributed in time and space, thereby causing problems of "too much" or "not enough."

Although water is a vital resource and a basic need for individuals and society, it can also be a deadly enemy. Major floods regularly bring death and destruction throughout the world, and polluted waters can have serious health ramifications and render water unfit for most uses. In view of the many demands for water, its uneven distribution, and the potential hazards from pollution and flooding, water resources planning is an important activity in modern society. Water can no longer be treated as a free good, but as a limited resource whose use must be carefully planned, and whose impacts must be anticipated. Planning is the first step in dealing with water related issues, whether for immediate needs or for those anticipated at some future time. We must emphasize long-range comprehensive planning rather than the project planning that has been so much a part of our water resources management.

Consideration must be given in comprehensive water resources planning to a variety of concerns, such as economic development, environmental quality, flood protection, and political acceptability. Conflict frequently arises between developmental interests, environmental organizations, and other parties regarding which objectives should be pursued. Which of the infinite possible variations of water resource systems and policies should be implemented? The planning process is important in attempting to achieve appropriate uses of water in the face of competing and often conflicting demands, and with due consideration of many alternative schemes.

Water resources planning covers the broad spectrum of concerns just indicated, but not always simultaneously. One can deal with specific aspects of water resources, such as water supply or pollution control, or can be concerned with a comprehensive treatment of water resources

---

[a]Prepared by Andrew A. Dzurik, M.ASCE, Associate Professor, Department of Civil Engineering, FAMU/FSU College of Engineering, and Department of Urban and Regional Planning, Florida State University, Tallahassee, FL.

over a broad area. We have gradually come to the point of considering socioeconomic and environmental impacts, and the interrelations among the many facets of water resources, even when dealing with one specific aspect. The emphasis changes over time and differs by location depending on needs. For example, water supply has been a crucial issue in southern California for years, but it is becoming an increasing concern in many parts of the United States as supplies are stressed by extensive agricultural irrigation and urban growth. Since the early 1970s, water quality has been the object of great concern nationally as increasing pollution of the nation's rivers and lakes became evident. In the early years of the nation and continuing to the present, navigation has been viewed as essential to national economic development. In all of these cases, planning helped to clarify needs, identify alternatives, assess impacts, and select appropriate courses of action.

This chapter focuses on three major categories of water resources planning: water supply, water quality, and floodplain management. It also covers other minor categories in much less detail, and provides an overview of relevant legislation, planning procedures, and quantitative models.

12.1.2 Basics of Water Resources

Water is clearly one of the world's most important natural resources. A region that is blessed with abundant surface and ground water must deal primarily with protecting the quality of those resources, whereas water-short regions must first contend with the problem of obtaining adequate supplies.

An important step in understanding a region's water resources is to examine the freshwater budget or balance. A water budget is an important analytical tool for measuring the flow of water through the hydrologic cycle.

The hydrologic cycle (Fig. 12-1) is no more than a summary of flows in the water system. Precipitation (rain, snow, hail) falls to the earth and may follow several paths. Some will evaporate before reaching the ground, a large portion will infiltrate into the earth, and the remainder will enter into surface or depression storage. As excess precipitation accumulates, water will overflow and move across the surface. This runoff ultimately reaches streams, lakes and other surface water bodies, and much of it returns to the atmosphere via evaporation. The water that infiltrates into the ground enters the soil zone, where it may be taken up by the soil and plants, and part of it is given up by evapotranspiration. A portion may evaporate from the soil surface or pass into the saturation zone and into aquifers. Aquifers are composed of sediments and rocks that store and transmit significant amounts of water. An unconfined aquifer has water in direct vertical contact with the atmosphere, whereas a confined aquifer is bounded on top and bottom

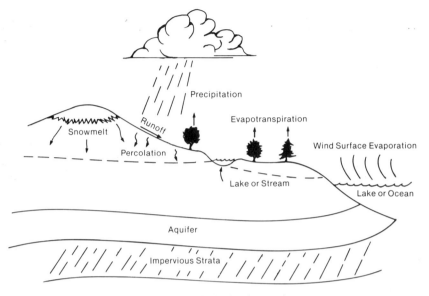

Fig. 12-1. Hydrologic cycle

by relatively impermeable layers and its work is usually under pressure (artesian).

Figure 12-2 shows a hypothetical water budget with the inflows and outflows expressed as a simple balance sheet. These numbers are typically very approximate in practice, but they should be reliable enough to give a general indication of flows in the system. The difference between inflows and outflows is the change in storage from year to year. Some years will have gains, while others remain the same or show a loss. Some regions of the country show a continual decline, particularly in areas where the ground water is being tapped heavily. A review of a series of annual water budgets in such places will indicate there are trends giving cause for concern. Essentially the water budget serves a similar purpose to a bank book; it gives a record of deposits, withdrawals, and net balance.

Several observations can be made regarding the hydrologic cycle and the water budget. Rainfall not only exhibits an uneven distribution during the year, but also shows variations from year to year. Use of "average" rainfall data can be misleading from a water management perspective, because of an upward skew of averages from relatively infrequent but particularly heavy events. Thus, average annual rainfall will have different implications in the State of Washington and in Florida.

Evapotranspiration typically accounts for a major share of the water budget. This combined measure of evaporation and transpiration indicates the extent to which precipitation is needed merely to break

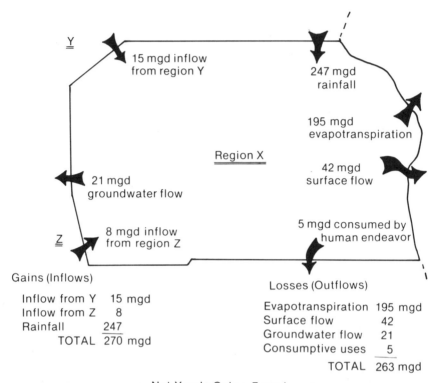

Gains (Inflows)

Inflow from Y	15 mgd
Inflow from Z	8
Rainfall	247
TOTAL	270 mgd

Losses (Outflows)

Evapotranspiration	195 mgd
Surface flow	42
Groundwater flow	21
Consumptive uses	5
TOTAL	263 mgd

Net Yearly Gain = 7 mgd

Fig. 12-2. Hypothetical water budget

even. Certainly a tropical climate will have a much greater evapotranspiration rate than a temperate area.

Ground water is extremely important in many areas as the major source of water. The volume of water beneath the ground is often many times that on the surface. It is important to have a reliable measure of ground-water supply in a region with high rates of use, and to determine whether the potentiometric surface has been declining over time. The potentiometric surface is the level to which water would rise in a cased well into an aquifer. Surface water is similarly important in many regions. The volume of water stored over time should be measured, as well as capacity of surface waters and channels to carry and to store water under excessive runoff conditions.

Depending upon climatic conditions and various elements of the hydrologic cycle, storage of water may be extremely significant to a region. Storage—surface and subsurface, natural and man-made—is the buffering system which absorbs excess inflows during wet seasons and gradually releases water during dry seasons. Surface storage may occur naturally in lakes, rivers, and wetlands, whereas subsurface storage occurs in soil moisture, shallow water table aquifers, and various deep aquifers. This storage can be augmented by man-made reservoirs, river impoundments, diking of lakes on the surface, and through artificial aquifer recharge and injection wells for ground water.

12.2 LEGAL FRAMEWORK

State property rights form the basis for the two general categories of water law in the United States: the riparian rights doctrine and the appropriation rights system. The riparian doctrine, which is most common in eastern states, provides that landowners whose property is bounded by a watercourse have the right to the reasonable use of the water as long as their use does not interfere with the use of the water by downstream residents. "Reasonable use" is often subject to a balancing test by most courts in cases of conflict between riparian landholders.

In the arid western portion of the country, water use is based upon an appropriations system, whereby the consumptive use of water is the right of the individual who puts the water to beneficial use first. Because of the complexity often involved in appropriations rights conflicts, most appropriations states have opted for some type of permit system for regulating water withdrawal and use. Certain traditionally riparian states, such as Florida and Mississippi, have also developed water use permitting systems. Several other doctrines, such as absolute ownership and correlative rights, have also been formulated (mainly in western states) for the allocation of ground-water supplies.

The following subsections present an overview of water resources planning legislation. Note that the term "legislation" as it is used here pertains to the administrative rules that have been instituted to protect water quality and water supplies, rather than to the strictly judicial water law system described above. The administration of water management regulation is divided among federal, state, and local government agencies. The federal government administers national water policies and legislation through various councils, commissions, and cabinet level departments, and states interpret and apply these policies and laws to water within their boundaries. Local governments, in turn, enact their own community water supply regulations in accordance with federal and state standards. Because of the variations encountered in this three-tiered system, each level will be examined separately.

12.2.1 Federal

Water resources legislation on a national scale has been extensive since the 1950s and has strongly influenced the direction of water resources planning. The more recent legislative acts include the Water Resources Planning Act (1965), the Federal Water Pollution Control Act

Amendments (1972), the Safe Drinking Water Act (1974), the Resources Conservation and Recovery Act (1976), and the Clean Water Act (1977).

The Water Resources Planning Act established the policies of Congress toward developing "the conservation, development, and utilization of water and related land resources on a comprehensive and coordinated basis by the Federal Government, states, localities, and private enterprise" (11). The Act created the former Water Resources Council (WRC), whose main functions were to study and catalog the nation's water resources and needs and to oversee the implementation of federal water management plans by the various national river basin commissions (which could be established by the WRC or by appropriate states).

The Federal Water Pollution Control Act Amendments of 1972 are not concerned as much with water quantity as with water quality. The main directive of the Amendments is the elimination of pollutants into navigable waters by 1985, with interim goals of "fishable, swimmable" waters by 1983. Reduction and elimination of discharges are to be accomplished by way of federal financial assistance for the construction of wastewater treatment works and wastewater treatment management planning.

The Safe Drinking Water Act was a response to studies starting in 1970 that dealt with the deterioration of water supply. The Act provides for the setting of national drinking water quality standards by the Environmental Protection Agency (EPA), with the states responsible for enforcing those standards. Primary standards require public water systems to maintain a level of quality for the protection of public health, whereas secondary standards are for maintaining satisfactory taste, odor, and appearance. The Act also provides for protection of underground sources of drinking water through a program of state regulation and enforcement.

The Resources Conservation and Recovery Act is also more concerned with water quality than with water quantity. The Act's main application is in the regulation and prevention of the introduction of hazardous industrial wastes into the environment. However, the Act does touch on water supply and wastewater treatment in that sludge from treatment plants can be included under a hazardous solid waste category. Waste materials from treatment plants other than sludge can also be regulated under the RCRA as hazardous wastes. Current penalties for noncompliance are quite strict and could have a definite impact on the future handling of wastes by water supply treatment facilities.

The Clean Water Act of 1977 consists of further amendments to the Federal Water Pollution Control Act. In the aggregate, the Clean Water Act can be viewed as the cumulative Federal Water Pollution Control Act because of its focus on federal assistance for the construction of public wastewater treatment plants and on the coordination between federal, state, and local water agencies. The Act directs state and local authorities to develop areawide wastewater management plans and to establish management agencies to implement the plans (specified in Section 208 of the Act).

Two other pieces of federal legislation, though not expressly concerned with water quality or water supply, deserve mention. The first is the National Flood Insurance Act of 1968. Floodplains and, indirectly, water quality are protected by provisions in the Act that contribute to land use management in flood-prone areas. The second legislative act is the Coastal Zone Management Act of 1972. The CZMA encourages the development of state coastal zone management plans which could influence the quantity and quality of water supplies and fresh and saline wetlands in coastal areas.

Numerous other federal laws affect water resources planning. Among them are:

- River and Harbor Acts (1899, 1909, 1915, 1962, 1965, 1968, 1970)
- Flood Control Acts (1938, 1944, 1960, 1962, 1968, 1970)
- Water Supply Act of 1958
- Land and Water Conservation Fund Act of 1965
- Water Project Recreation Act of 1965
- Wild and Scenic Rivers Act of 1968
- National Environmental Policy Act of 1969
- Marine Sanctuaries Act of 1972
- Flood Disaster Protection Act of 1973
- Water Resources Development Act of 1974.

12.2.2 State

States have enacted many of their water resources policies and regulations in coordination with and as a result of federal water policies. State water resources legislation has long been influenced by federal statutes such as the federal reserved right to water use. Western states, especially, because of the predominance of the prior appropriations doctrine of water use in western water law, have had to consider the reserved rights doctrine because of the possibility that an existing state water right may become subordinate to a federal reserved right (36). Nevertheless, states have developed statutes concerning the use and regulation of water within their boundaries in accordance with the laws of prior appropriation, riparian rights, or a water use permit system (2).

Aside from statutory regulation of water use and supply, state water management is usually accomplished by agencies which administer water rights by permit authorization or which administer and oversee water pollution regulations. Also, there are a number of federal-state commissions, committees, or councils which coordinate water resources planning and management. Examples would include Federal-State Compact Commissions, which carry executive powers, and the Basin Inter-Agency Committees, composed of representatives from various state and federal water resources agencies (35). Regional river basin commissions, such as the New England River Basin Commission, were established to plan and coordinate (but not authorize) water resources activities and to integrate all three governmental levels of water management.

Four types of state legislation relate primarily to water supply distribution: (1) Public utility acts, which are usually administered by public utility commissions and which set water service standards concerning quality, quantity, etc.; (2) state water supply statutes, which are basically health and safety standards similar to federal enactments; (3) environmental statutes, usually relating to federal regulations or environmental impact assessments; and (4) water supply agreements, which are implemented mainly through local water authorities and are usually applied in western states. The amount and degree of enforcement of these regulations will vary from state to state in a way similar to water rights statutes.

Legislative authority for state water resource planning is similarly diverse. Two states, Delaware and Florida, require statewide comprehensive water resources planning and management under the direction of a single state agency. Other states require either continuous comprehensive water planning (14 states), static comprehensive planning (7 states), or continuous comprehensive planning with a static water plan (4 states) (49).

12.2.3 Local

Local water resources legislation is usually implemented through municipal and county water authorities or districts and deals primarily with drainage, water supply, or wastewater treatment. Much local water management is a result of federal and state delegation of powers. For example, the Intra-State Special Districts are water management bodies that are "local units of government established by state law for planning, constructing, and ensuring the maintenance of local works" (11). Most municipalities also have their own water treatment or management authorities, and most areas implement some type of water supply agreement to assure provision of sufficient quantities of water.

12.2.4 Summary

In summary, U.S. water resources legislation is represented by:

- application of common law and jurisprudence in regulating private use of water at the state level, based on the riparian rights doctrine in eastern states and on the prior appropriation doctrine in the western states;
- comprehensive water resources development programs defined and executed by various federal, federal-state, interstate, state, and local agencies, coordinated and otherwise;
- recent creation of legal instruments for water resources planning and management, on a national scale; and

- recent legislation aimed at developing a comprehensive program for elimination of water pollution, on a national scale (11).

12.3 ORGANIZATIONAL STRUCTURE

All of the various pieces of legislation mentioned in the foregoing section require some form of implementor. In the United States, water supply and water quality legislation is administered by government agencies at federal, state, and local levels. In addition, certain regional organizations, composed of various agencies from the three levels, have been formed to aid in coordination of water resources planning efforts. What follows is a descriptive breakdown of the water resources management organizational structure found in the United States.

12.3.1 Federal

Water resources planning and the administration of water resources programs in the U.S. are performed within a diverse organizational structure. On the federal level, water resources management and program preparation have been historically the responsibility of cabinet level departments, principally the Departments of the Interior, Agriculture, and Defense.

The Department of the Interior is the main cabinet level body in charge of the nation's water resources. Within the Department of the Interior (DOI), the U.S. Geological Survey (USGS) is responsible for financing water resources research at universities and various institutes. USGS also prepares technical reports on new and existing water management practices and techniques, and is responsible for the monitoring and collection of data for the nation's ground and surface water supplies. The Bureau of Reclamation, also part of the DOI, is responsible for the monitoring and development of appropriate irrigation and agricultural land reclamation projects in the western states.

The Department of Agriculture deals with water resources planning and development through the Soil Conservation Service, Forest Service, Agricultural Research Service, and Economic Research Service. The Soil Conservation Service is the most notable of these, particularly with regard to irrigation and flood control.

The Army Corps of Engineers, under the Department of Defense, is the nation's oldest water resource agency. It deals mainly with water resources through the construction and maintenance of navigable streams and harbors and the physical structures found on them. Its planning activity is closely tied to its construction activities. One of the Corps' main responsibilities is for flood control, and it has gained many friends and foes through its construction of numerous dams. In recent years, greater consideration has been given to nonstructural techniques.

The Environmental Protection Agency (EPA) is the foremost federal agency with respect to water quality. It administers the Clean Water Act, and has had major responsibilities in pollution control enforcement, funding of municipal sewage treatment plants, and managing the Section 208 program for areawide planning.

Other cabinet and executive level agencies and departments have some input into the nation's water resource development. The Federal Emergency Management Administration (FEMA) promotes floodplain management through the National Flood Insurance Program. The Department of Commerce (through the National Oceanic and Atmospheric Administration), the Department of Transportation (through the U.S. Coast Guard), and the Council on Environmental Quality have played significant roles in the development of water resources programs in selected areas.

One of the most important and influential federal water resources agencies in recent years was the former Water Resources Council. The Council, established by the Water Resources Planning Act of 1965, was composed of the secretaries and directors of various federal departments and agencies, including the Departments of Interior, Agriculture, Defense, and Transportation; the Council on Environmental Quality; the Office of Management and Budget; and the Attorney General. The WRC was established to oversee water resources planning and development from a federal level, and to establish the basic structure and legislative framework for the solution of water resources problems. The WRC was to design the planning structure for the identification of such problems, and to coordinate and guide federal, state, and local water resources planning programs and policies.

12.3.2 State and Local

State water resources management is usually administered by agencies dealing with permit authorization or water pollution control. Various state departments with responsibility for natural resources management are usually the main administrative bodies, much like the Department of the Interior at the federal level. State public service or public utility commissions frequently have some authority concerning water supply and wastewater treatment.

Local water resources management organizations usually include municipal or county water authorities and local wastewater management departments. Other local water planning organizations may be found in areas where unique water resources characteristics require special management policies and programs.

Regional independent agencies also exist for the coordination of federal, state, and local water management policies. These agencies include Interstate Compact Commissions, Federal-State Compact Commissions, Interagency Committees, Federal-State Regional Councils, and Intra-State Special Districts (11). All are composed of federal and state or a number of state departments, and all have varying degrees of planning, executive, and coordinative powers concerning water resources management.

12.3.3 Recent Trends

The change in the federal administration in 1980 brought major changes in the water resources organizational structure, as well as some proposed changes in water resource legislation itself. These changes, in turn, are having significant effects on water resources planning at the state and local levels.

Perhaps the biggest change came when the Water Resources Council effectively closed its doors in September of 1982. Funding for the Council was eliminated in President Reagan's budget proposal for Fiscal Year 1982–83, though limited funding was approved for the nation's River Basin Commissions. Funding for existing Council programs would continue through FY 1985, and through FY 1984 for the River Basin Commissions (5). The Council itself, however, was eliminated, with its coordinative and planning functions assumed by the new Cabinet Council on Natural Resources and the Environment, and its review of water projects transferred to the Office of Management and Budget. The River Basin Commissions, though minimally funded through FY 1984, lost six commissions by the end of 1981 because of a lack of sufficient operating funds (6).

The Office of Water Research and Technology (OWRT) survived initial budget cutbacks and elimination proposals but was finally abolished in August 1982. Its programs were divided among three branches of the Department of the Interior: the Bureau of Reclamation, the Geological Survey (USGS), and the Office of Water Policy in the Secretary of Interior's office. By October 1983, the Office of Water Policy was transferred to USGS as directed by Congress, and a year later Congress directed that the remaining programs under the Bureau of Reclamation also be transferred to USGS. Responsibility for programs that were once in OWRT now lie fully in the Water Resources Division of USGS.

Differences continue to arise between the administration and Congress as to the exact orgnizational structure to be created to manage the nation's water resources. Legislators have proposed their own national board of water policy and state water advisory committee, to be similar in function to the administration's Cabinet Council on Natural Resources and the Environment yet more responsive to Congress (7).

Changes in the administrative framework for national water resources legislation and policies have also been proposed. Guidelines for planning and management are to be formulated in relation to national economic development. In line with the administration's "New Federalism" proposals, state and local water planning agencies are to assume a greater role and responsibility in the development of water management policies and programs. Private organizations are also expected to become more involved in the provision of water service projects. Also, proposals have been made to amend certain sections of the Clean Water

Act, specifically the funding of wastewater treatment construction grant programs and construction of reserved capacity facilities, and the lowering of industrial water emissions standards.

State water resources planning and management is also undergoing a shift in direction. Many states and regional commissions are moving the focus of their studies from advisory and program-planning functions to hydrological studies and ground-water investigations. Also, legislative authority for water management is shifting toward some type of permit authorization system, particularly in the southeast and mid-Atlantic regions. Such a system emulates the western appropriation system of water law, with prior state authorization often required before water use can begin (49).

All of the aforementioned changes in the nation's water resources management structure and legislation are in flux. Recent water shortages and water quality problems point to the urgent need for proper management of the nation's water resources.

12.4 WATER SUPPLY

Of all the major categories of water resources planning, none is more crucial than water supply, for a dependable water supply is essential to human activity. Whether drawing water in the home for drinking, cleaning and bathing, or from the fire hydrant for extinguishing fires, or from wells and canals for irrigation, a day without water would cause severe hardships. The many users of water in modern society expect to have it readily available. Planning for water supply involves knowledge of present consumption and future needs compared with available supplies. The task then is to prepare alternatives for meeting future needs. In some cases water supply can expand greatly, whereas others may require reuse and conservation strategies.

Of the 4,250 bgd (billion gallons per day)[1] of water that falls on the United States annually in the form of rainfall, approximately 1,450 bgd can be found in ground or surface storage and in rivers and streams. Of this 1,450 bgd, "only 675 is considered available 95 out of 100 years" (47). Withdrawals of water in 1980 amounted to 450 bgd with 361 bgd coming from surface water and 89 bgd from ground-water sources (38).

Offstream use of this total withdrawal can be categorized into: (1) Those uses which return the water withdrawn to a ground or surface water source; and (2) those that consume or do not return water directly to a source. An example of the former would be an industry that withdraws water for cooling purposes and then returns the water unchanged except for an increase in temperature to a ground-water or a surface water source. An example of the latter would be the transpiration

---

[1]Use the SI conversion factor 1 gallon = 3.8 liters, so that, for example, 361 bgd = 1372 bL/day.

of water from irrigated vegetation into the atmosphere. Of the 450 bgd withdrawn in the U.S. in 1980, approximately 100 bgd was for consumptive use. Irrigation alone was responsible for the consumption of 83 bgd in 1980 (38).

In examining the demand, supply, and conservation aspects of water resources planning, it is useful to break down the use of water into three major categories of use: agricultural, industrial, and municipal. These categories are not all-inclusive, yet they represent over 90% of all water consumed in the U.S. Steam electric generation, the other major category of water use, is not a very great consumer of water (less than 5% of total consumption). Because the water in steam electric generation is returned almost entirely to a ground or surface water source, and because reuse and recirculation of the small amount of water consumed is so prevalent, it was not included in this examination of planning for water use.

Most of the available water withdrawn for the three uses named is obtained from traditional sources and by traditional practices. In other words, water is obtained from ground-water deposits, reservoirs and storage areas, or streams and rivers. Traditional practices mean that water is obtained by mining of ground-water deposits, upstream watershed management, or transfer of water from one region to another (e.g., the California Aqueduct). As the supply of water begins to diminish, however, it becomes necessary to examine closely the methods and sources of supply and the projected demand for each type of use. Such investigation will give insights into those areas where conservation, reuse, and supply augmentation can provide the most appropriate solution to a region's water needs.

12.4.1 Agricultural Use

Agriculture is the largest user of water nationally. Of the 155.6 bgd used for agriculture in 1980, irrigation accounted for 150 bgd (97%) with the remainder going to rural domestic use and livestock production. A vast portion of the water used in irrigation was utilized in the arid western states, particularly California, Colorado, and Idaho.

Ground-water withdrawals for irrigation account for approximately 40% of all water used for irrigation. This heavy dependence on ground water has led to serious depletion of regional aquifers. The huge Ogallala Aquifer, extending from northern Texas to southern South Dakota, was once thought to be inexhaustible. The aquifer, however, has dropped from an average saturated water thickness of 58 ft (17.7 m) in 1930 to a thickness of about 8 ft (2.4 m) in 1985 as a result of increased withdrawal for irrigation. Serious aquifer depletion is also occurring in the Texas-Gulf and Rio Grande Water Resources Regions.

Surface water depletion from irrigation is also a major concern in the western states. The Colorado River has been reduced to a mere trickle as it enters the Gulf of California, as a result of appropriation of its waters by the states through which it flows. Much of this appropriated water is used for irrigation purposes in central Arizona and Southern California, though a substantial portion is used for municipal supplies. Another example is Pyramid Lake in Nevada, which has dropped by as much as 70 ft (21.4 m) from its level in 1906, primarily a result of decreased inflow because of the diversion of water from the Truckee River for irrigation.

Demand for water for agricultural purposes is not expected to decline despite the depletion of major sources of supply. Agriculture will remain the leading consumptive user of the nation's water supply, with consumptive use of water for irrigation projected to increase from 83 bgd to 93 bgd in the year 2000. Competition for the use of the available ground and surface water supply is expected to be heavy, however, as population and industry continue to expand in arid regions such as the Southwest.

Because of its high withdrawal and consumption needs, the potential for water conservation in agriculture is very high. Supply augmentation is not very feasible in many places because of the economic and environmental constraints involved in creating new reservoirs or diverting water from distant sources (though recharge of ground-water deposits with waste agricultural water may be practical in specific areas). Conservation and reuse of irrigation waters appear more appropriate and would include: (1) Development of more productive or salt-tolerant crop species, or both; (2) increased use of chemical fertilizers, pesticides, and herbicides; (3) lining of irrigation canals or the use of pipelines to prevent seepage loss; (4) "trickle" or "drip" irrigation practices to reduce the quantity of water necessary for continued crop yield; and (5) the reuse of municipal and agricultural wastewater for direct irrigation or for recharge of ground-water deposits. All of these practices involve conscientious management of irrigation water, and most require either significant economic expenditures or changes in traditional methods of crop management. The savings in the long run, in terms of water supply and capital expenditures, may be worth the effort.

12.4.2 Industrial Use

Self-supplied industrial uses of water, excluding thermoelectric power plants, accounted for 45.3 bgd of the total water withdrawn in 1980. Of this total, 29 bgd was withdrawn from freshwater surface sources, 10 bgd from fresh ground water, and 6.3 bgd from saline water sources. Some industrial supplies are obtained from public water systems referred to in the following subsection.

The figures given do not provide the total picture of manufacturing use of water. Total gross water utilized by industries amounts to 2.2 times the amount withdrawn. This difference is accounted for by the fact that water withdrawn for industrial uses is recirculated extensively in the manufacturing process (47).

Demand projections for the industrial sector do not indicate an increase in the need for water. The WRC Second Assessment (47) states that "combined fresh- and saline-water withdrawals are . . . projected to decrease from the present 60.9 bgd to about 29.1 in the year 2000." However, consumption in manufacturing processes in all water resources regions is expected to increase by the year 2000, the result of the perfection and widespread use of recycling and recirculation practices, as well as a projected increase in manufacturing production.

According to the American Society of Civil Engineers' Task Committee on Water Conservation, federal water quality regulations regarding wastewater discharges have been the primary impetus for reduction of industrial demand (40). This reduction in demand for water withdrawals has been brought about mainly through water reuse, recycling of internal wastewater, and water use reduction measures. Total industrial intake of water was reduced by 36% over the 1954 to 1968 period, much as a result of the implementation of these conservation practices.

The reuse and recirculation of wastewater is restricted by the economic feasibility of reuse (i.e., whether it is cheaper to recycle or to purchase from a public supply) and the quality of the recycled water for industrial processes. Over-all, however, the outlook for continued conservation of industrial water supply appears promising.

12.4.3 Municipal Use

In 1980, 34 bgd of water was withdrawn for municipal use, with approximately 7.1 bgd of this amount being consumed. Domestic and public use accounted for 22 bgd, whereas industrial and commercial uses amounted to 12 bgd. Ground-water sources supplied approximately 35% of the total while surface-water sources supplied the remainder.

Demand projections for municipal water use have been relatively consistent with projections for population increase. Though over-all municipal withdrawal is expected to increase by 32% by the year 2000, certain regions, particularly Florida, California, Texas, and Arizona, will experience a higher growth in demand for water than the rest of the nation because of increased population growth in those areas. Expansion of water supply sources in these and other regions, however, will be inhibited by increasing costs of expansion and competition among different users for available local and distant supplies. Municipal water conservation, then, presents itself as a major factor in future municipal water supplies.

Conservation of municipal water supplies can be attempted in a number of ways. First is maintenance and repair of existing facilities. Antiquated and deteriorated water supply systems are great wasters of water, yet with proper repair they can continue to provide sufficient quantities of water for domestic and commercial use. Costs are high, however, for such maintenance and repair, showing the need for other conservation measures.

Residential water conservation methods can contribute significantly to over-all municipal water conservation. Certain economic measures, such as water pricing policies, can be utilized to reduce the demand for water. Related to this is the need for metering water use. Water use restrictions (e.g., fines for illegal water use during times of drought, restrictions on outside water use, etc.) can be effective in reducing water consumption during emergency shortages or peak demand periods. Pressure reductions, improved plumbing equipment, changes in landscaping methods and maintenance, and public conservation education can all contribute to a reduction in water demand.

Possibly the most progressive step toward increased municipal water conservation can be made in the area of municipal water management. All too often, institutional and jurisdictional differences will prevent the formulation of a coordinated water conservation program. Responsibility for assuring a continued supply of municipal water is not always clearly defined in terms of who is in charge of service provision or funding. A more centralized water supply authority may be necessary before savings in municipal water conservation are realized.

12.4.4 Planning for Water Supply

Planning for water supply must start with the identification of uses and estimation of demand for these uses. Estimating water demand relationships is one of the most important steps in water resources planning and management. This subsection provides an overview of the major considerations in dealing with water demand and supply, focusing primarily on municipal and industrial uses.

Demand   Most water supply agencies rely on relatively crude methods for determining the future demands on an area's water supply capabilities. Common approaches for municipal demand focus on population size and households, while industrial demand may be determined by number of employers. Such variables are used in simple mathematical calculations to project future demand, develop water supply management strategies and, occasionally, to determine the need for conservation practices. The realization has grown, however, that other less salient factors need to be examined in water use analysis.

Water use forecasts in most cases are long range, for up to 50 years, and deal with average daily use. This stems from the fact that projections are usually used to plan major facilities, and these facilities are typically large projects such as dams and reservoirs. Shorter range projections may be made for smaller facilities or management strategies, and may deal with variations in water use by season, month, or week.

The available forecasting techniques are varied, even though most agencies use simple approaches. The following paragraphs describe the more important techniques. They are reviewed more fully in a report by the Institute for Water Resources, Corps of Engineers (4).

Time Extrapolation.   This technique considers only past water use records, and extrapolates into the future using graphical or mathematical methods. It assumes a continuation of changes over time, but may use a variety of functional forms. Time and water use are the only variables in this technique, which is not highly reliable, especially for long-term projections.

Single Coefficient Methods. The most commonly used technique estimates future water demand as the product of service area population and per capita water use. The per capita use coefficient may be assumed to be constant, or it may be projected to increase or decrease over time. Population projections may be obtained for the service area through rough original work or from local sources, such as local planning departments, or from higher level agencies such as state projections, or federal level OBERS projections. The OBERS projections (USDC Bureau of Economic Analysis/USDA Economic Research Service) are used as standard practice in water resources planning at the federal level, and are also appropriate at lower levels. The per capita approach is usually applied to municipal water use or to aggregate use. Many studies have shown population to be a reliable indicator of water use. The method may be refined by using separate per capita coefficients for different use categories: residential, commercial, public, and industrial. The coefficients can also be disaggregated by geographic area and by season. A variation of the per capita approach is to use the number of customers of the system within the study area.

Single coefficient methods may also be applied for industrial use. For example, water use per employee may be used with projections of employment in the industrial sector. Commercial forecasts may be done in terms of use per employee, or per square foot. In all cases, the single coefficient method relies entirely on projections of a variable, and assumptions regarding future water use as a function of that variable. The method is reliable for short-range forecasts, but becomes increasingly questionable in long-term projections.

Multiple Coefficient Methods. This approach defines future water use as a function of two or more variables that are associated with water use. Regression analysis is typically used as the statistical technique for estimating the coefficients. This may be done based on historic time series data for the study area, or on cross-section data from a number of similar areas. To forecast water use, the future values of the independent variables must be determined by some other means. As an example, average water use in million gallons per day in a region W may be defined as a function of number of employees in manufacturing E and number of households H as follows:

$$W = a + b_1 E + b_2 H + e \qquad (12.1)$$

in which a, b_1, b_2 = parameters to be estimated statistically, and e = error term to account for the unexplained variation in W. To estimate the equation, historic data would be applied to the regression analysis technique. Future water use would then be determined by using the estimated equation with projected values of E and H for the forecast period.

Demand Models. The term "water demand" is often used loosely in water use projections. In economics, demand is functionally related to price, whereby a price increase is associated with a decrease in demand. Water use projections in the absence of price considerations are more appropriately termed "water requirements" (1). Water demand models are a subcategory of the multiple coefficient methods described above. The key difference is that price of water is included as an explanatory variable, and some measure of personal income is usually included. Perhaps the most significant of the studies of this type was by Lina-weaver, et al. (26). Their model showed that the most important variables in residential water use were climatic factors, economic levels of consumers, irrigable lawn areas, and number of homes. Another important study, by Kindler and Bower (25), showed that water demand relationships can be analyzed at four levels (Fig. 12-3). The primary advantage of demand models is that they usually contain more complete sets of explanatory variables and can reflect important policy considerations with respect to price as a management tool. Substantial price increases may, in fact, reflect actual changes in water supply costs as well as deliberate pricing policy.

Probabilistic Analysis. The models described above use regression analysis to explain variations in water use, but the technique also

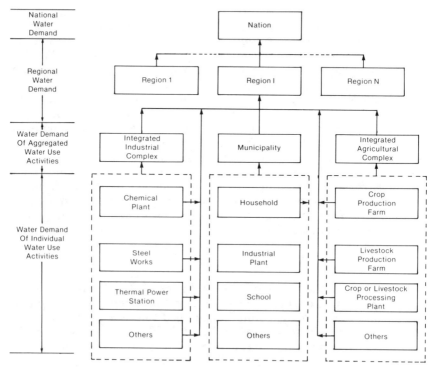

Fig. 12-3. Levels of water demand analysis (25)

includes the error term e to account for unexplained variation. If the remaining variance is random and not explained by other variables, water use then can be identified as a stochastic process (4). Probabilistic analysis includes not only explanatory variables to estimate future use, but also a probability distribution of that estimate. In practice, probabilistic methods have not been highly successful.

Planning for future water use requires reliable projections, regardless of technique. A statement from Reference 46 (18 CFR 713.113) provides a useful summary:

> Future water use shall be projected by sector, in consideration of seasonal variation, and shall be based on an analysis of those factors that may determine variations in levels of water use. Projections shall include the effects of implementing all expected nonstructural and/or conservation measures required by or encouraged by federal, state, and local policies, and by private actions.

Supply The supply side of water supply planning requires knowledge of the sources available to meet the projected demand and the amount that can be provided from these sources, as well as the costs and environmental effects. For all practical purposes, water is available from ground water or surface water. In some places, desalinization plants have been used to provide water, but the comparative costs are usually much higher than for other alternatives.

Ground-water supplies are plentiful in many parts of the country and are frequently used for municipal, industrial, and agricultural purposes. The essential information required is the depth to aquifers, and the amount that can be withdrawn without impairing the quality or quantity of water in the aquifer. In many cases, ground water has been withdrawn to such an extent as to cause a significant lowering of the water level and contamination by salt water intrusion.

Surface water provides naturally abundant supplies where lakes and rivers have sufficient capacity to safely meet demands. In this situation, plans must be developed only for providing the necessary infrastructure for treatment, storage, and distribution of water. In many cases, however, reservoirs are needed to provide regulation of the distribution of surface water flows and volumes (29). Essentially, reservoirs are for temporary storage of surface water flows over relatively long periods of dry weather and low flow. Keep in mind, however, that many reservoirs serve purposes other than water supply, such as flood damage reduction, hydroelectric generation, and water-based recreational activity. Figure 12-4 shows three major components of reservoir storage-capacity requirements: (1) Active storage for firm and secondary yields; (2) dead storage for sediment collection, hydropower production, and recreational purposes; and (3) flood storage for reduction of downstream flood damages (28). Firm or safe yield is defined as the maximum amount of water that can be "guaranteed" from a reservoir based on historical streamflow record, whereas secondary yield is the amount greater than firm yield (28).

Mass Diagram Analysis. A common and simple method for determining reservoir storage requirements is a mass diagram which is based on the assumption that past flows will be repeated in the future. The curve shows total cumulative inflow to a stream at the point of the proposed reservoir plotted against time. Determination of required capacity involves finding the maximum difference between cumulative inflows and cumulative demand. The example in Fig. 12-5(a), based on data in Table 12-1, shows cumulative monthly flow and assumes that average demand or required release R_t is 5.0 units per time period. The difference between total inflow and release is the quantity required to meet demand. The demand is drawn as a sloped line and placed tangent to the cumulative inflow curve. In months when the stream flow is lower than demand, the demand slope is greater than the supply slope, and thus the reservoir must make up the deficit. The maximum demand needed for this particular period of analysis was 10 units. The graphic approach can be done readily if demand in each time period is the same. If demand varies, the cumulative differences between inflow and demand can be plotted as in Fig. 12-5(b). The maximum vertical distance between the highest peak of the cumulative difference curve and the lowest valley to its right represents the required capacity.

In order to determine storage capacity required over time, an estimate of the mean probability of unregulated stream flow makes it possible to define the probability of any particular reservoir yield. Thus, if we had a 20-yr record of stream flow, and the required reservoir capacity for each of those years, a frequency analysis of the record would allow selection based on recurrence intervals. Designing for the lowest flow of record in this case would be a 20-yr recurrence interval, or 5% drought.

Sequent Peak Method. The mass diagram method is still used today, but a more manageable modification is the sequent peak procedure (29). Storage capacity required at the beginning of period t is K_t, and R_t is the required release in period t. Inflow is represented by Q_t. If we set

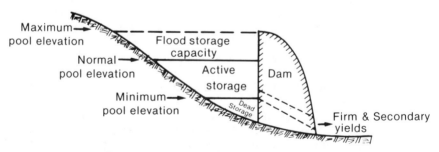

Fig. 12-4. Reservoir storage zones (28)

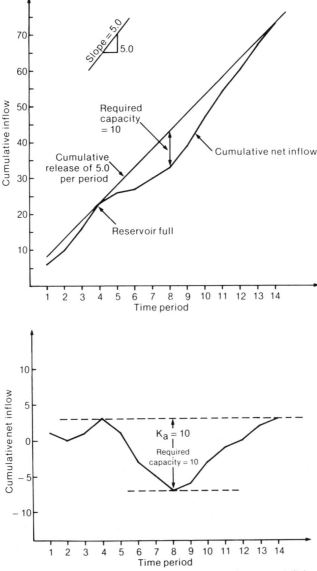

Fig. 12-5. Mass diagram using (a) cumulative inflow, and (b) cumulative net inflow

$K_0 = 0$, the procedure calls for calculating K_t for up to twice the total length of record using

$$K_t = \begin{cases} R_t - Q_t + K_{t-1} & \text{if positive} \\ 0 & \text{otherwise} \end{cases} \qquad (12.2)$$

TABLE 12-1 Calculation of Storage Capacity by the Sequent Peak Procedure

Period, t	Required release, R_t	Inflow, Q_t	Previous required capacity, K_{t-1}	Current required capacity, K_t [a]
1	5.0	6	0	0
2	5.0	4	0	1
3	5.0	6	1	0
4	5.0	7	0	0
5	5.0	3	0	2
6	5.0	1	2	6
7	5.0	3	6	8
8	5.0	3	8	10 [b]
9	5.0	6	10	9
10	5.0	8	9	6
11	5.0	7	6	4
12	5.0	6	4	3
13	5.0	7	3	2
14	5.0	6	2	1

[a]Greater than or equal to zero.
[b]Maximum required storage capacity = 10.

If the critical sequence of flows occurs at the end of the record, this method assumes that the record repeats. The maximum of all K_t is the required storage capacity for required release R_t. The method is demonstrated in Table 12-1 with data for 14 periods.

Optimization Models.   The mass diagram and sequent peak methods account for few variables, and cannot incorporate such considerations as evaporation losses, lake level regulation, or multiple reservoir systems. Mathematical models have been developed for such purposes, based on mass-balance equations which explicitly define inflows, outflows, and net storage. Some of these models are reviewed briefly in Sec. 12.9.

12.5 WATER QUALITY

Water quality is a relative term. Different processes which use water can function satisfactorily with water sources of varying quality. Water that contains a high amount of dissolved solids is often inadequate and low in quality for textile manufacturing. The same water, however, may be of satisfactory quality for industrial cooling, mining processes, and even carbonated beverage manufacturing.

The word "pollution" is often mentioned in the same breath as water quality. Water pollution can be defined about as differently as water quality, though the most basic and frequently used definition is the introduction of concentrations of a particular substance into water for a long enough period of time to cause deleterious effects. Much of the water resources planning legislation in the United States has been aimed at preventing such introduction.

The major focus of water resources planning since the early 1970s has been on surface water quality, especially under the impetus of the Federal Water Pollution Control Act Amendments of 1972 and more recently the Clean Water Act of 1977. Section 208 of the 1972 Amendments provided for regional basin-wide planning in many areas throughout the country, and included provisions for planning the control of nonpoint source pollution of surface water systems (i.e., pollution that does not come from a particular waste outfall). Later, the Resource Conservation and Recovery Act of 1974 was enacted to address pollution of surface and ground water from hazardous wastes.

Water quality planning stems from several important sections of the 1972 Amendments and the Clean Water Act, Sections 201, 208, 209, and 303(e). In addition, Section 305 provides a broad framework for the states' water resources planning activities.

Section 305. Under Section 305(b) of the Act, each state prepares and submits an annual report on the water quality of all waters in the state. This evaluation of water quality problems is the basis of the state strategy which describes the state's long-range plans and programs for water quality management.

Section 303(e) Plans. Basin plans prepared in accordance with Section 303(e) of the Act represent the first phase of a two-phase planning process. Whereas the first phase emphasized surface and non-surface water discharges, Phase II will add an intensive study of nonpoint sources. Section 303(e) basin plans also provide an information base for the development of Section 208 areawide management plans and Section 201 facilities plan.

Section 209 Level B Plans. This section requires preparation of Level B plans for all basins in the United States. These are preliminary or reconnaissance level water and related land plans prepared to resolve complex long-range problems identified in broader framework plans.

Section 208 Areawide Plans. Section 208 is the Act's most comprehensive vehicle for in-depth water quality management on an areawide basis. The objective of Section 208 is to meet the 1983 goal of the Act. The planning requirements of this section are intended to formulate a comprehensive management program for collection and treatment of wastes, and for control of pollution from all point and nonpoint sources in areas with complex pollution control problems.

Section 201 Plans. The overall objective of Section 201 facilities planning is to provide for the development of cost-effective, environmentally sound and implementable treatment works which will meet the requirements of the Act. The purpose of these plans is to insure that investments in treatment works will proceed in an orderly fashion and will achieve maximum protection and enhancement of water quality.

As can be seen, the various sections are extensive in their goals for achieving comprehensive national and regional water quality planning. Unfortunately, the implementation of the sections and the attainment of their goals has not been realized, particularly in the control of nonpoint source runoff. A Conservation Foundation report in late 1981 (34), when debate over the extension of the Clean Water Act was under way in Congress, mentions that, since 1972

over 200 water quality management plans were approved by EPA. All of these plans addressed both nonpoint and point-source problems. Yet observers familiar with the program suspect that most 208 plans are not being implemented.

States, municipalities, and areawide management agencies have had to wrestle continually with budget and grant cutbacks in trying to implement Section 208 plans and Section 201 wastewater treatment works projects. The lack of reliable information and accurate data bases has also helped prevent implementation of Section 208 nonpoint pollution control measures.

Despite these administrative difficulties, water quality remains a primary concern of many environmental engineers and planners, government officials, private agencies, industry, the public, and others. This concern has prompted a complex but necessary scheme of regulations, ordinances, and laws as well as a complicated network of administrative and enforcement mechanisms.

12.5.1 Measurement of Water Quality

In examining the potential impacts of pollutants on water quality, it is important to delineate water quality characteristics. These characteristics can be assigned to three basic categories of parameters: chemical, physical, and biological (bacteriological).

Chemical parameters include both organic and inorganic substances. Major organic compounds that can lead to significant water pollution problems can be found in fertilizer and pesticide residue runoff, improperly treated sewage effluent, vehicular wastes (oils and grease), and industrial wastewater. Inorganic properties that may affect water quality are pH, heavy metals (mercury, zinc, copper, etc.), hardness, salinity, nitrogen compounds, phosphorus, chlorides, and sulfur compounds.

An important problem associated with organic chemical water pollution is the potential impact on the dissolved oxygen (DO) content of a water body. In flowing streams, this characteristic is commonly depicted by an oxygen sag curve, shown in Fig. 12-6. Curve A depicts an oxygen sag without anaerobic conditions, and curve B shows DO levels with anaerobic conditions resulting from a heavy pollution load. A sufficient level of dissolved oxygen in water is necessary for most organisms to survive. Water in unpolluted streams usually has a DO concentration of 10 ppm or less (3 to 5 ppm is the established lower limit in which fish can survive over a long time period) (39).

Chemical decomposition of one or more chemical pollutants can significantly reduce the amount of DO in local aquatic environs. Also of importance is the rate at which the DO is consumed by bacterial action. This rate of oxygen use is measured by the biochemical oxygen demand (BOD), which is defined as "the amount of oxygen required by bacteria in decomposing organic material in a sample under aerobic conditions at 20°C over a 5-day incubation period" (8). Aside from DO and BOD measurements, tests for chemical oxygen demand (COD), total oxygen demand, and total organic carbons can also be performed to determine water pollutant levels.

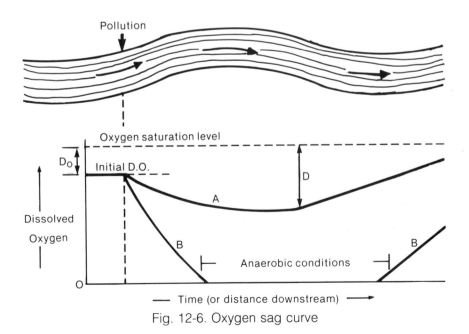

Fig. 12-6. Oxygen sag curve

Physical properties of importance include temperature, turbidity, color, odor, and suspended solids. Turbidity can affect the amount of sunlight available for aquatic microorganisms and plant life—essential components of the aquatic food chain. High temperatures can reduce local dissolved oxygen levels as well as drive off or kill native vegetation and wildlife. Odor and unnatural color can be sources of great nuisance.

Biological parameters are primarily related to those bacterial pathogens (fecal coliforms, viruses, etc.) that pose a health threat to man or wildlife. High coliform counts in water bodies are usually a result of the disposal of untreated or improperly treated human wastes. Also, nonpoint runoff from feedlots and livestock holding areas can contribute to the presence of bacterial pathogens.

12.5.2 Surface Water

Surface water consists of those bodies of water held by impermeable or semipermeable basins such that they are exposed to the atmosphere for relatively long periods of time.

In the past, mankind frequently used surface water as a convenient place to dump untreated wastes, particularly those bodies of water subject to currents or tidal action. The common belief was that wastes would be dissolved and diluted by the turbulent movement of the water. These practices were eventually halted in many countries after the link between disease and contaminated water was established.

There are primarily two different source types for surface water pollutants: point and nonpoint sources. Point sources are those sources that emit pollutants from a clearly indentifiable or discrete source, such as the mouth of a pipe. Nonpoint sources emit pollutants over a relatively wide, dispersed area and are thus frequently more difficult to identify. Some examples of nonpoint sources include spray from crop-dusting planes, fertilizer runoff from fields, and "acid rain."

12.5.3 Ground Water

Whereas polluted surface waters may be restored to safe conditions within a relatively short time span, ground water can take decades or centuries to divest itself of contaminants. This is primarily due to the very slow rate of ground-water flow when compared with surface-water movement. There are several variables which may dictate ground-water flow: precipitation levels, infiltration, water table slope, and soil characteristics to include permeability (37). Additional factors that may affect flow velocity and direction are local water demand and outflow-inflow sources (such as wells). Many aquifer systems are interconnected; thus, when one aquifer becomes polluted, it may affect other contiguous aquifers.

Ground water remains a vital source for relatively pure water. It is still frequently taken for granted by many people that ground water is safe as is, without regard to possible contamination.There are actually many potential types of and sources for aquifer pollution. Discharge of improperly or inadequately treated wastewater onto land (e.g., sprayfields) is an occasional source for pollution. Septic wastewater disposal can have a significant impact on ground-water quality since leachate from septic disposal systems can foul underground water reservoirs. Eight hundred billion gallons of sewage are discharged annually into the ground by residential cesspool and septic tank systems (37). In areas where septic systems are common and of close proximity (such as many subdivisions lying outside city limits), contaminated well water may be an important problem. Landfills may also adversely affect ground-water supplies as leachate filters into them.

Sanitary landfills are not the only waste disposal sites that contribute to ground-water pollution. National attention has recently focused on the problems associated with hazardous and toxic waste disposal. Frequently, the materials placed in hazardous waste landfills are those that will not degrade naturally with any relative celerity and whose toxic effects are somewhat unpredictable at any concentration. If landfills are not properly underlined with impervious materials or entirely contained, hazardous toxic substances can be introduced into ground-water supplies through natural leaching processes. Even with complete landfill containment, some hazardous wastes are so corrosive that, over time, they can still seep into ground-water deposits.

Accidental (and purposeful) pollutant spills may enter ground water, particularly in areas with very porous soils. Leaking pipes, sewer lines, and petroleum storage tanks are also frequent sources of ground-water contamination. Mine tailings and sludge are usually stored in holding ponds. These too may percolate through the soil and enter the aquifer. Fertilizers and pesticides, especially after soaking rains, may also enter the ground water.

Salt-water intrusion has become an occasional problem in coastal areas. This phenomenon is largely the result of local overdemand for ground water. Overpumping allows salt water to move in and replace the normal freshwater aquifer. This is a serious problem now faced by populous coastal municipalities and regions. It also affects several major agricultural areas located near the coasts.

Proper planning and extramunicipal considerations are necessary for assuring safe, adequate ground-water supplies. Ground water is still an abundant resource for most regions in the United States, although it has been frequently misused and abused in the past.

12.5.4 Urban Storm Runoff

The disposal and treatment of urban runoff (primarily storm water runoff) has become an increasingly important problem associated with continued development and large population centers. Multiplying the number and size of artificial nonporous areas, such as paved streets and parking lots, adds substantially to the problem. Storm water runoff can lead to erosion, flooding, and pollution, and can seriously overburden wastewater treatment facilities.

Precipitation tends to help cleanse the atmosphere of many impurities. "Acid rain" is an example of precipitated "dirty water." These impurities often add to a municipality's sewage disposal load where storm sewers and sanitary sewers are combined. Perhaps even more significantly, as precipitation becomes storm water runoff, it also flushes surface areas, picking up dust, litter, fertilizers, oils, grease, etc. These pollutants are also added to the sewage load.

More often than not, runoff impurities originate from nonpoint sources such as litter, vehicular waste, construction activities, and lawn maintenance residues. These nonpoint pollutants are very difficult, if not impossible, to control at their sources. Instead, control efforts have been directed toward retention, filtering, and treatment of storm water runoff. These methods can range from the simple (street cleaning broom) to the more complex and efficient (physical treatment, retention basins, swales). Such techniques are a cornerstone to effective control and disposal of runoff pollutants. Other recent innovations include the use of porous paving materials to enhance percolation of rainfall into subsurface strata.

Considerable work has been done on urban storm runoff (44), but it remains one of the major factors affecting the quality of the nation's rivers and lakes.

12.6 FLOODPLAIN MANAGEMENT

Flooding is a natural phenomenon that occurs regularly. Nonetheless floods inflict major economic loss with annual regularity and genuinely catastrophic damage to large regions of the nation. Since the mid 1960s, a changing philosophy has caused floodplains to be viewed as areas to be carefully managed. Increasing concern with flood hazards and environmental values of floodplains has led to considerable legislation and administrative action to provide new management tools. This section focuses on the various planning and management techniques for dealing with flood hazards.

12.6.1 Flooding

Flooding is primarily associated with two phenomena, hurricanes and excessive stream flow. Accordingly, flooding can be categorized as coastal or riverine.

Coastal or tidal flooding results primarily from hurricanes and other major storms. A hurricane is centered on low atmospheric pressure which causes a storm surge or raised water level. This is compounded by large, high-energy waves. Under the worst possible conditions, a storm surge on top of normal high tides combined with large waves can raise water level to as much as 10 to 15 ft (3 to 5 m) or more above mean sea level. In unusual circumstances (e.g., The Netherlands), structures have been used to minimize flooding. Most coastal areas, however, must rely on various nonstructural techniques.

Riverine and backwater flooding is caused by exceptional rainfalls and spring thawing, and the inability of a stream channel to accommodate the runoff from its watershed. Continued development in floodplains has increased the potential hazard, but the situation is further complicated by the fact that such development typically increases problems to downstream areas originally out of the hazard zone. The solutions to flood hazards are varied, ranging from various structural techniques to numerous nonstructural approaches.

Hydrologic principles about flood magnitude are especially important in floodplain management. Dunne and Leopold provide an excellent introduction to hydrology and flooding for planners (15), and they argue that planners can and should understand basic concepts.

A simplified method for estimating peak runoff rates in small areas is the rational formula

$$Q = CIA \tag{12.3}$$

in which Q = peak rate of runoff, in cubic feet per second; C = coefficient of runoff based on the type of surface area under consideration; I = rainfall intensity, in inches per hour; and A = drainage area, in acres. The method has been used for many years, but its use is generally limited to urban catchment areas of less than 200 acres (81 ha). At best it is an approximation for dealing with drainage problems.

A more important tool to the planner is the hydrograph, which shows discharge over time at a given point in a channel. As an example, Fig. 12-7(a) shows hypothetical inflow and outflow hydrographs for a given channel. The particular pair of hydrographs indicates reservoir action within the valley. In other words, water flows in at a faster rate than it flows out. As water flows in, it is progressively stored and raised, causing the outflow to increase. If the inflow accumulates more than the channel capacity, it will overflow its banks onto the floodplain. The unit hydrograph [Fig. 12-7(b)], derived from actual hydrographs for a given basin, is the hydrograph of 1 in. (25.4 mm) of storm runoff generated by a rainstorm of uniform intensity over a specific time period. The hydrograph and the unit hydrograph are for estimating storm runoff and to predict flooding levels under certain climatic conditions. They are used in the planning and design of flood control structures, and for assessing the influence of flood control structures in reducing peak floods.

The methods used for determining potential flooding, whether coastal or riverine, range from the simple rational formula (Eq. 12.3), to hydrographs, and to complex computerized models. Regardless of the prediction technique, the norm for floodplain management is generally the 100-yr storm or 100-yr floodplain. This implies an area that will be

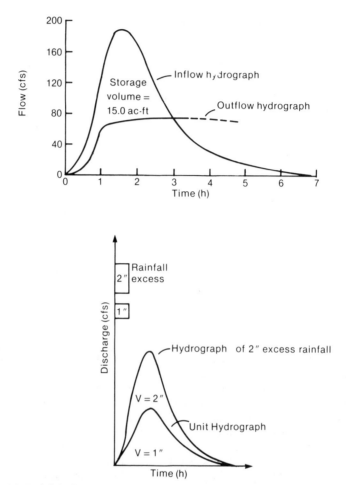

Fig. 12-7. (a) Inflow and outflow hydrographs; (b) unit hydrograph

flooded to a certain level on average once in 100 yr. In other words, the probability of a 100-yr flood in any given year is 1%. This concept may be misleading, for it does not mean that such a flood will occur only once in a given 100-yr interval. It is a probability estimate based on long-term data. Historical information on precipitation and floods is essential for planning associated with rivers, coasts, and floodplains, for land use planning and regulation, engineering design, and other aspects of floodplain management.

Once the potential flooding in a given area has been determined, a variety of methods can be used to minimize flood damage. The following subsections describe different approaches for dealing with potential losses from flooding.

12.6.2 Flood Damage Reduction Measures

Comprehensive floodplain management requires that the various modes of floodplain management be coordinated and systematically implemented, but this is not often done (16). A sound approach to floodplain management may be formulated in conjunction with the WRC report on "A Unified National Program for Flood Plain Management" (48). The program's basic framework provides decision-makers with a management perspective that encourages a comprehensive assessment of alternative floodplain uses. Four general principles from the WRC report were used to establish the background for floodplain management:

1. Although the federal government has a fundamental interest, the basic responsibility for regulating floodplains lies with state and local governments.

2. The floodplain must be considered a definite area of interrelated water and land to be managed within the context of its community, its region, and the nation.

3. Flood loss reduction should be viewed as one of several management considerations which must be addressed in planning for economic efficiency and environmental quality.

4. Sound floodplain management is built upon the following premises: the goals and objectives of floodplain management are defined as wise use, conservation, development, and planning of interrelated land and water resources; decision-making responsibility is shared among various levels of government and private individuals; future needs and the role of the floodplain must be understood in the context of both the physical and the socioeconomic systems of which it is a part; all strategies for flood loss alleviation must be given equal consideration for their individual or combined effectiveness; there must be full accounting for all benefits and costs and for interrelated impacts likely to result from floodplain management actions; all positive and negative incentives must be utilized to motivate individuals who make decisions influencing the floodplain; government programs must be coordinated at and between all levels of government, as well as among the different areas of floodplain management; and there must be ongoing evaluation of management efforts with periodic reporting to the public.

The basic objective of floodplain management is to achieve an acceptable end of direct or indirect impacts of flood losses to the individual and the community. A variety of options, tools, or alternative strategies for producing desired uses or changes in uses of the floodplain may be employed to attain this objective. Flood hazard problems, whether caused by coastal hurricane or interior riverine flooding, should be evaluated in the context of possible alternative strategies. The WRC has categorized alternative strategies as will be described next.

12.6.3 Modifying Susceptibility to Flood Damage

This strategy attempts to avoid unwise use of the floodplain and dangers associated with flooding. It includes land use regulations, development and redevelopment policies, disaster preparedness plans, flood forecasting, floodproofing, and evacuation, as follows:

1. Land use regulations are suited for the management of the floodplain in areas adjacent to streams or coastal areas that are not intensely developed. Measures that can be used to regulate construction and encroachment on the floodplain are zoning ordinances, subdivision regulations, and building code permits.

2. Development and redevelopment policies may be applied at all levels of government through the design and location of utilities and services, open space and easement acquisitions, redevelopment, or permanent evacuation of an area.

3. Disaster or emergency preparedness and response plans are suited to any area in which risk to life exists due to flooding, or in which property damages due to flooding could be mitigated by protective actions.

4. Flood forecasting and warning systems can be designed and installed to give adequate notice of potential dangers.

5. Floodproofing can provide for development in lower risk floodplain areas by reducing or eliminating flood damages through preventing water from entering the structures. Damages can be reduced by relatively simple measures such as waterproofing, elevating, or diking around flood-prone structures.

In many communities, growth pressures cause urban encroachment on flood-prone areas, and development occurs in the floodplain because of recreational and esthetic benefits obtained from being on or near open water. The latter trend is likely to continue; hence, use of flood-prone lands and construction of dwellings on them should be given special consideration by communities in order to reduce potential flood damages. Lowlands which are subject to flooding and are unsuitable for high-density development should be used for open space purposes.

To discourage development in flood hazard areas, local governments should adopt policies that resist the extension of utilities and streets and the construction of schools and other facilities in these hazard areas. Infrastructure development on nonflood-prone lands should be given priority, and land management tools, such as zoning, should be used to supplement infrastructure policies.

Tax adjustments can be effective in preserving floodways. Increased tax valuation of rural lowlands adjacent to developing urban areas and of open lands within urban areas is increasing throughout the nation. Tax increases may reach the point where land productivity is marginal (e.g., for agricultural purposes), or where it no longer can be used profitably for open space, but appropriate tax adjustments could prevent this. The tax adjustment procedure also can be used to encourage property owners to use flood-prone lands in a manner consistent with a proposed land use plan. It may include assessment on the basis of current use rather than potential use, and deferred payment of taxes on land sold for development prior to public purchase. These tax abatements involve agreements by the owners to forfeit certain development rights in return for a reduced tax assessment over a period of time. This procedure is most often known as preferential assessment.

Another floodplain management tool is open space planning and preservation. Open space and recreational plans should always be included in planning over-all development for a community.

Permitting is an appropriate land use control technique where it is not feasible to define usage controls adequately. Insofar as modifications to physical conditions in coastal areas are concerned, the most significant example of the technique is the permit authority of the U.S. Army Corps of Engineers governing the approval of any construction or other actions which affect navigable waters, wetlands, tributaries, and lakes, or effectively all waters which drain into navigable waters.

12.6.4 Modifying Flooding

The strategy of modifying floods involves construction of dams and reservoirs; dikes, levees, and floodwalls; channel alterations; on-site detention measures; bridge and culvert modifications; and tidal barriers. Flood modifications may change the volume of runoff, peak stage of the flood, the time concentration and direction, the extent of areas flooded, and the velocity and depth of flood waters. In most instances, flood modifications acting alone, without other nonstructural strategies, leave a residual flood loss potential and may encourage inappropriate uses of land being protected because of an unwarranted sense of security. Specific flood modification measures are:

1. Dams and reservoirs that help to control the broad range of flood flow velocities, extent of area flooded, timing, etc. Flood reservoirs may function singly or in combination with other purposes (e.g., water supply, recreation). Flood control may also be aided by construction detention structures to delay local runoff for the purpose of reducing downstream flood stages.

2. Dikes, levees, and floodwalls to protect portions of the floodplain from flooding by acting as a barrier to confine flood waters. These structures must include provision for discharging interior drainage from precipitation which falls inside the protected area, and they must be built high enough to contain a high level of flooding.

3. Channel alterations that work to reduce flood stages by improving flow conditions within the channel and thereby increasing the flow capacity of the stream. Methods generally used to obtain improve-

ments of channels include straightening to remove undesirable bends; deepening or widening to increase the size of a waterway; clearing to remove brush, trees, and other obstructions; and lining the channel with concrete to increase the flow efficiency. An important consideration is that channel alterations should not increase flood problems downstream, but this often happens with channel alterations.

4. Land treatment measures that modify flooding by increasing infiltration rates and decreasing the runoff rate and volume. Measures include change in vegetative cover, strip cropping, contour plowing, runoff interceptors and diversions, and small detention and erosion control structures and terrains. They are effective in headwater areas, and function in combination with other measures to ameliorate flood conditions in larger watersheds.

5. On-site detention measures can provide temporary storage of urban runoff waters by retarding flows and thereby extending the period of runoff to reduce flood peaks. This strategy works well in growing communities within small river basins, and could be incorporated into master drainage plans for urban areas.

6. Bridge and culvert modifications can be made to hydraulically inadequate bridges and culverts to provide sufficient capacity for stream flow. Doing this would also reduce damages caused by water backing up behind such structures.

7. Tidal barriers that prevent high tide stages from inundating a developed area. They are generally designed with gate or navigation openings to provide drainage from the protected area and maintain normal uses of the watercourse. These systems are costly and are usually major construction projects for protection of large urban areas.

12.6.5 Modifying Impact of Flooding

This approach is designed to assist the individual and the community in the preparatory, survival, and recovery phases of floods. Tools include information dissemination, arrangements for spreading the costs of the loss over a period of time, and purposeful transfer of some of the individual's loss to the community. Note specifically that:

1. Information and education on flood hazards is essential in an effective floodplain management program.

2. Flood insurance is a mechanism for spreading the cost of losses, both over time and over a relatively large number of similarly exposed risks. While flood insurance does not reduce flood damage, it does provide a means for minimizing flood losses to individual property owners.

3. Flood emergency measures, such as floodproofing and flood fighting plans, can be completed in anticipation of flooding for areas where flood warning time would permit these actions.

5. Postflood recovery requires a plan to assure that public facilities and services are restored and aid is given to individuals suffering flood damages. Recovery plans are also needed where poor natural conditions prevail and assistance is needed to drain flooded subareas when rivers and tidal floods recede.

Flood insurance is available through the National Flood Insurance Program (NFIP). When a community becomes a participant in the program, property owners within a flood hazard area may apply to have structures and their contents insured. Flood insurance does nothing to reduce existing flood hazard or damages; it lessens but does not eliminate the economic burden of flooding on the floodplain occupants. However, over the long term, the land use regulations required for participation in the flood insurance program should reduce floodplain development. This "relocation by attrition" aspect of the flood insurance program has been strengthened by passage of the Flood Disaster Protection Act of 1973, which provides that no federal agencies or federally backed financial institution shall approve any financial assistance for acquisition or construction purposes in flood hazard areas unless the community in which the area is located is participating in the NFIP.

To participate in the NFIP, a community must agree to require building permits for all proposed construction or other improvements in the flood hazard area and to review building permit applications in that area to determine whether the proposed building sites will be reasonably safe from flooding. Building permits are required only in the identified flood-prone portion of the community, i.e., if a map designating these areas has been issued by the Flood Insurance Administration. It is required that structures within the flood hazards be designed and anchored to prevent flotation, collapse, or lateral movement. For residential structures within the area of flood hazard, the community must require new construction and substantial improvements to existing structures to have the lowest floor elevated to or above the level of the base flood. Further regulations state that building in a coastal high hazard area is also not permitted unless the site is landward of the mean high tide level, and the lowest floor is elevated to the level of the base flood plus an allowance for wave action on adequately anchored piles. The space below the lowest floor must be kept open and free of obstruction. The low structural members of the floor system of a new building in this area, or any part of the outside wall, should be above the base flood elevation.

Elevated structures should be serviced by mechanical equipment that is also elevated or floodproofed above the base flood level and by utility systems that are designed to minimize or resist flood damage and infiltration. Owners, builders, developers and communities that have no alternative but to construct in a flood hazard area should anticipate utility disruptions and seek comprehensive engineering data and professional guidance to prevent and minimize them.

12.7 OTHER PLANNING CONCERNS

There are several other areas with which a water resources planner should be familiar. Among them are navigation, recreation, wetlands, fish and wildlife, and the interrelationship between water and land use. This section summarizes them briefly to indicate that the scope of water resources planning goes beyond the categories reviewed previously. Although not considered in this chapter, additional issues that might require contributions from water resources planners are hydroelectric power, beach erosion, hurricane protection, and irrigation.

12.7.1 Navigation

A specialized subarea of water resources planning involves navigation, primarily commercial navigation which uses large vessels. Navigation might be viewed as an aspect of transportation planning, but the requirements for developing and maintaining channels, turning basins, locks and dams, and protective structures such as jetties, are in the domain of water resources planning.

Navigation planning requires knowledge of many aspects of water transport: shipping technology, terminal facilities, minimum depth of water, channel width, climatic influence, seasonal variations, currents, and tidal influences. Three methods for improving river navigation require planning studies. Open channel methods attempt to improve existing channels for navigation, primarily through dredging. Lock-and-dam methods require dams to create a series of water pools through which vessels can move, and locks to lift or lower vessels from one pool to the next. Canalization methods provide a new channel by artificial means to connect two navigable waters (48). For additional information, see Chap. 10 on Port Planning.

12.7.2 Recreation

The importance of water-based recreation has increased greatly in recent years. This phenomenon has largely been the result of a greater population with shorter average work week which has steadily increased the demand for recreational opportunities. Federal, state, and local governments have recognized this rising demand for outdoor recreational outlets by providing and enhancing many acres of public land in the form of parks, beaches, trails, picnic areas, wilderness sanctuaries, and wildlife refuges. Many types of outdoor leisure pursuits are either directly or indirectly related to water: swimming, fishing, boating, sailing, waterskiing, picnicking beside a stream, birdwatching in a marsh, and similar activities.

These activities are important to water resources planning because of the direct relation between many types of water resources projects and recreational benefits. Outdoor recreation is, for the most part, produced and maintained as a public good. Recreation is usually a by-product of a water resources plan, but an important one that must be evaluated as a benefit (or a cost if recreational opportunities are lost). In some cases, recreation may be cited as one of the objectives of a plan.

Many bodies of water have become polluted by urban and agricultural runoff, municipal wastewater, industrial discharges, and thermal release from power plants and other industries. Frequently, these bodies of water are no longer healthy sites for recreational activity. Additionally, the continuing drainage of many existing lakes, ponds, bogs, and swamps has substantially eliminated other potential recreational sites. These are common problems associated with development and an increase in both population and standard of living. It is therefore important for planners at all levels of government and the private sector to consider the impact of proposed development on any existing or potential water-based recreational opportunities (see Chap.13 on Recreation Planning).

12.7.3 Wetlands

Wetlands occur in many forms such as swamps, bogs, marshes, shallow lakes, estuaries, ponds, salt flats, sloughs, and floodplains. In the past, these areas were regarded as wasted space and were frequently drained to create new agricultural or urban land—only relatively recently have they been widely recognized for their inherent values.

Wetlands furnish essential habitat for many species of waterfowl, mammals, fish and other wildlife. They act as important ground-water reservoirs, an important function now being recognized by many farmers. Frequently, wetlands serve as natural barriers to fire, erosion, storm waters, and flooding. They serve as convenient natural laboratories for scientists and students. In addition, they provide excellent opportunities for bird-watching, fishing, hunting, timber production, and production of various cash crops: for example, plant mass from bogs may become an important energy source. Wetlands can also improve local water quality by acting as a natural filtration system for various pollutants.

Wetlands preservation is currently being undertaken at many levels of government and by private individuals as their importance and value becomes more widely recognized. Under the Water Pollution Control Act Amendments of 1972, Section 404 gave the Corps of Engineers the authority to control alteration of wetlands, but the federal government did not start a comprehensive program to protect wetlands until 1977. Prudent planning and development can greatly enhance the survival potential for remaining wetlands.

12.7.4 Fish and Wildlife

The nation's water resources are of paramount importance to many species of fish and other wildlife. No living species can exist without water in some form. Most wildlife species require water that is of a high level of purity. The pollution impacts of massive urban, agricultural and industrial projects have led to the disappearance of substantial natural wet habitat acreage. The loss of critical habitat has, in turn, led to the extinction or near-extinction of many species.

America's heritage has always been richly imbued with an appreciation of its native wildlife. Innovative land and water management practices combined with due consideration of conservation and preservation goals have been major steps toward comprehensive national and local policies designed to protect both the environment and wildlife. Planners should be aware of both positive and negative effects on local wildlife when considering project feasibility and implementation.

12.7.5 Water–Land Use Interrelations

There is a common concern for considering the interrelations of water resources and land use. For years, those administering federal programs have talked of "water and related land resources." In reality, however, the interrelationship has received inadequate consideration, largely because of organizational conflicts. For example, the Corps of Engineers and other federal water resources agencies have maintained that land use regulation is a local responsibility, and so they have not intruded into this area of control. At the same time, however, local land use planning and decision-making must incorporate many aspects of water resources, even though management of the resources may be at a higher level of government. Accordingly, intergovernmental cooperation is essential in dealing with water–land use interrelations.

Perhaps the most significant relationship between land use and water is in the matter of flooding. The nation annually suffers great losses from flood damage, largely because development was allowed to take place in a floodplain. In recent years, many communities have adopted floodplain zoning restrictions as described earlier.

Water supply planning is another aspect of water–land use interrelations. In many growth areas, development has been allowed to take place with little regard for the availability of services, including water supply. In the Charlotte Harbor area of southwest Florida, for example, land was platted for subdivisions which could add 2,000,000 people. The water supply requirements to accommodate such a population would be eight times greater than current consumption, and would have to be met through new storage capacity. Similarly, many rapidly growing areas of Texas, Arizona, and California have allowed land development with little regard for available water resources.

Other ways in which land use may have an impact on water resources stem from design practices. Clustering of residential lots, for example, can reduce water demand merely by reducing the amount of lawn to be watered. The nature of land development may dramatically alter runoff characteristics and the effectiveness of aquifer recharge areas. A few innovative developments have created commercial and residential complexes with reuse of water for irrigation.

The relationship between land use and water is also very strong regarding surface-water quality. Urban storm runoff, which can have serious effects upon receiving waters, is a direct function of urban land use. Similarly, agricultural runoff is a function of rural land use and land management practices. It is important for planners to recognize and incorporate the many interrelations between water resources and land use in their plans.

12.8 PLANNING PROCESS

There is a history of formalized planning procedures in federal water resources planning, but the first major statement was a set of Interagency Policy Guidelines known as the "Green Book" prepared in 1950. The guidelines were updated in 1962 by the President's Water Resources Council. The National Environmental Policy Act led to significant changes that included recognition of environmental values in the WRC's "Principles and Standards" (46) adopted by presidential order in 1973, and revised in 1979. Planning for water quality has been influenced strongly by Section 208 of the Federal Water Pollution Control Act Amendments of 1972. Publications on the 208 planning process were prepared by EPA to guide federal, state, and local planning activities under this program (43, 44, 45). Various other federal guidelines for water resources planning have also had influence at all levels of government.

The planning process as applied to water resources is comparable to other types of planning. It is a logical series of steps, beginning with identification of needs and culminating in recommendations for action. The planning process goes further to include implementation and monitoring. As described in Chap. 2, the planning process has the following components: (1) Awareness of need; (2) data collection and analysis; (3) development of goals and objectives; (4) clarification and diagnosis of the problem or issues; (5) identification of alternative solutions; (6) analysis of alternatives; (7) evaluation and recommendation of actions; (8) development of implementation program; and (9) surveillance and monitoring. This section elaborates on these components as applied to water resources issues.

12.8.1 Awareness of Need

Identification of concerns with respect to the water resources of an area comes under this heading. Competing and conflicting interests are often involved, and they should be clarified. Problem identification should reflect the concerns of different private and public groups, and be in sufficient detail to receive adequate attention in the planning process. Public involvement as well as coordination of various agencies and groups should begin at this stage.

Specific needs usually stem from a problem experienced (such as flooding) or anticipated (such as water supply inadequate to meet future needs). In some instances, water resources planning studies may be more general, and may not deal with any single problem or need. River basin studies and areawide water quality studies typically are of this type.

As part of problem identification, the study area should be defined and existing information about it analyzed for relevance to the problem. Relevant geophysical, biological, social, and economic characteristics of the area should be identified. Problem identification activities may be summarized as follows:

1. Identify public concerns.
2. Analyze water resources problems.
3. Define the study area.
4. Describe base conditions.
5. Project future conditions.

12.8.2 Data Collection and Analysis

Following problem identification, pertinent data should be obtained. Existing information for the study area, including geophysical, biological, social, political and economic characteristics, as well as anticipated future conditions shown by existing planning documents, should be obtained and analyzed for relevance.

There is a large set of data typically available on water resources. The USGS maintains a large volume of information on surface water and ground water; municipal utilities have information on water use for each account; and water quality information is maintained by the EPA and responsible state agencies. Still, it may be necessary to obtain primary data in some instances. Examples are questionnaires on water use, gaging stations to give water flow at specific points in a stream, and samples to determine water quality in a water body.

As part of the data collection process, forecasts should be made of appropriate variables to determine likely future conditions of the problem under investigation. They may include future flooding and flood damage, water requirements to support future growth and development of a region, and water quality in selected areas. In all cases, these projections are based on certain assumptions regarding the future, such as levels of population growth, economic development, and changes in technology.

12.8.3 Goals and Objectives

Specifying relevant planning goals and objectives, and defining their relative importance, are two of the most difficult tasks in water resources planning. There are many divergent interests that often generate competing and conflicting objectives. For example, the conflict between extreme economic and environmental objectives is common-place in water resources planning. There is no single plan that satisfies all economic and environmental objectives, and therefore the plan formulation process must allow for trade-offs among conflicting interests. Until the 1970s, economic objectives dominated water resources planning, with the benefit-cost criterion stated in the Flood Control Act of 1936 as the guiding objective: " . . . the benefits, to whomsoever they may accrue, are in excess of the estimated costs." In other words, the prime objective in federal water resources planning was to maximize the net aggregate monetary benefits to all parties affected by a water resources project.

Statements of goals and objectives will indicate what the planning effort hopes to accomplish. Goals are broad and general, such as the attainment of clean water or provision of adequate water supplies. Although general, goal statements relate human values to natural resources and the environment (9). Objectives are more specific statements toward which plans will be developed. Often several objectives are required to attain a goal. They will provide the basis against which to evaluate alternatives. Examples of objectives are attaining water quality that meets federal standards with regard to specific measures, or providing 50 mgd of municipal water supply.

To illustrate goals and objectives, it is appropriate to consider federal laws and actions. National water resources goals are incorporated in numerous legislative acts, executive orders, and administrative laws. The Federal Water Pollution Control Act Amendments of 1972 summarize and state the national goals with regard to water quality:

> That the discharge of pollutants into the navigable waters be eliminated by 1985.

> That wherever attainable, an interim goal of water quality which provides for the protection and propagation of fish, shellfish, and wildlife and provides for recreation in and on the water be achieved by July 1, 1983.

These goals were not fully achieved, and, in fact, the first one may be unrealistic if taken literally. They did provide, however, a statement of direction for the federal government, and a basis for EPA to set a number of objectives which resulted in programs for implementing the act.

12.8.4 Problem Diagnosis

A thorough analysis and clear understanding of the problem is needed at this point so that the alternative solutions that are developed will respond to the objectives. Clear understanding of a problem may indicate that there are numerous and widely divergent solutions. Thus, a flooding problem may be met by nonstructural as well as structural solutions, or a water supply problem may be solved by a conservation program or different management, rather than by building new reservoirs.

12.8.5 Formulation of Alternatives

The purpose of this task is to address the problems and objectives defined above. Alternative plans must be formulated to help the decision-maker see how they relate to the objectives, and to understand the trade-offs among them.

Formulation of alternatives begins with identification of measures that will satisfy the defined needs. Public and interagency participation is important at this point to assure that a full range of measures is considered. When possible, the alternatives should range from capital intensive structural measures to nonstructural management solutions. Structural measures tend to be relatively expensive and irreversible, whereas nonstructural approaches involve low initial costs and tend to be reversible if changes are needed.

The development of alternatives to meet objectives narrows the range of alternatives by focusing only on those that are directed to the stated objectives. If different objectives are given, alternatives should be developed to meet each one. The WRC Principles and Standards, for example, required objectives for a National Economic Development Plan (NED) and an Environmental Quality Plan (EQ). The NED plan has economic efficiency as its primary objective, while the EQ plan focuses on preservation or restoration of the environment. Accordingly, alternatives would have to be developed for each of these objectives, among others.

There is no standard for the number of alternatives to be developed. Judgment must be exercised to determine which plans are appropriate, and to decide which altenatives to carry forward for more detailed study.

12.8.6 Analysis of Alternatives

This stage has two major aspects, economic evaluation and impact assessment. The purpose is to provide identification and measurement of changes that would result from the alternative plans being considered. In all cases, it is useful to have a "no action" plan to provide a basis for comparing alternatives. Under the "no action" plan, projections are made of future conditions assuming that no plan is implemented.

Economic evaluation of each alternative provides an important basis for plan comparison. Different plans may involve different projects with different economic lives. Cost-benefit analysis has been developed to allow comparisons on a common basis. There is a large body of literature on this subject, especially as applied to water resources, so only a few comments are provided here. In simplest form, cost-benefit analysis compares the present value of all costs with the present value of all benefits. If the benefits exceed the costs, then a plan is economically justified. The present value approach is appropriate if the economic lives of alternatives are the same. If they differ, it is more appropriate to convert each time stream of net benefits to an equivalent average annual net benefit for purposes of comparison. Cost-benefit analysis is more detailed and complex, but a good understanding of this useful technique is essential to water resources planning (14).

Impact assessment includes environmental, social, and economic impacts, but the major concern is environmental impact, stemming from NEPA of 1969. Most water resources projects are undertaken directly or indirectly with at least partial federal funding. NEPA requires that all proposals for major federal actions have an environmental impact statement (EIS) prepared, and thus most water resources planning is tied to requirements for an EIS. Even in the absence of NEPA, environmental assessment of alternatives is just as important and valid as an economic evaluation. The environmental assessment is essentially an analysis of the potential environmental impacts, positive and negative, of a given alternative. Although no single measure of environmental impact can be obtained comparable to the benefit-cost ratio, the environmental assessment of each alternative allows a detailed comparison of potential impacts which allows for more informed decision-making.

12.8.7 Evaluation and Recommendations

Evaluation is the process of analyzing alternative plans to compare their beneficial and adverse contributions for the purpose of recommending a plan. Several determinations must be made to assure that plans are adequate and unique (41):

1. Determine how well an alternative satisfies component needs, including beneficial and adverse effects on all component needs.
2. Compare the performance of each alternative with all others. Alternatives that differ only slightly represent an incremental variation of a unique alternative and should be treated as one alternative.
3. Analyze the trade-offs between economic efficiency and environmental quality.

Specific criteria used by the Corps of Engineers are useful in evaluating plans and reducing the number of alternatives (41):

1. Acceptability. Assess the workability and viability of a plan in terms of its acceptance by affected parties and its accommodation of known institutional constraints.
2. Effectiveness. Appraise a plan's technical performance and contribution to planning objectives.
3. Efficiency. Assess the plan's ability to meet objectives functionally and with least cost.
4. Completeness. Assess whether all necessary investments to fully attain a plan are included.

5. Certainty. Analyze the likelihood of the plan's meeting planning objectives.

6. Geographic scope. Determine if the area is large enough to fully address the problem.

7. Benefit-cost ratio. Determine economic effectiveness of the plan.

8. Reversibility. Measure the capability to restore a complete project to original condition.

9. Stability. Analyze sensitivity of the plan to potential future developments.

The significance of each of the tests listed in comparing plans is a matter of judgment, and will vary with the type of plan being developed.

Plan selection is done by those decision-makers with legal authority, based on comparisons and recommendations set forth by planners. The selection should be based on the best use of resources considering all effects, monetary and nonmonetary. Usually only one plan is selected, although the planning process may be repeated to develop new alternatives or combinations of existing alternatives.

12.8.8 Implementation

Implementation means carrying out a selected plan or set of recommendations. At this stage, the plan is adopted and put forward for design and construction, or for adoption of laws, policies, and management procedures. Although implementation is usually difficult, a thorough approach to the preceding steps and continuous consideration of implementation will make the alternatives realistic and the selected plan more capable of being carried out. Often in water resources planning, considerable effort goes into developing plans that are never adopted. Sometimes a plan is approved and adopted but never carried out, or it is set aside for years. In the latter case, care must be taken not to implement a plan that was adopted years ago unless it has been thoroughly reevaluated. In like fashion, a recently adopted plan that is being implemented should be continuously reviewed to resolve any problems that might arise.

12.8.9 Surveillance and Monitoring

As was stated in Chap. 2, the surveillance step is considered to be "closing of the loop." Although a water resources plan may be fully implemented, the project should be monitored to see how well it satisfies the original goals and objectives. Many water resources projects require long-term investments, so it is likely that modifications will be needed as conditions change, long before the useful life of the investment is ended.

12.9 MODELS IN WATER RESOURCES PLANNING

Chapter 3 gave a brief overview of the use of models in planning and noted that considerable progress has been made in the field of water resources. Since the 1950s, mathematical modeling of water resources phenomena has grown to become an important part of water resources planning and management. One of the first teams to begin the development of water resources systems analysis was part of the Harvard Water Program. A seminal publication in water resources modeling, *The Design of Water Resources Systems* (30), was published in 1962 as a result of that effort. Other early works include those by Ekstein (17), Hufschmidt and Fiering (23), Hall and Dracup (20), and Hamilton, et al. (21).

The body of literature has increased dramatically since the late 1960s because of rapid increases in computer technology combined with substantial federal funding of this relatively new area. The funding came about largely because of growing interest in systems analysis throughout government and industry, and concern for environmental quality and improved resource management. Evidence of the institutional commitment to water resources modeling in the U.S. exists today in the form of three major centers: the Center for Water Quality Modeling of EPA in Athens, Georgia; the Hydrologic Engineering Center of the Corps of Engineers in Davis, California; and the International Ground Water Modeling Center of the Holcomb Research Institute, Indianapolis.

Models are briefly defined as representations of real world phenomena. Water resources planners and engineers have long used analog models of water resource systems, such as a scale model of a hydraulic system. We are concerned here with mathematical models of water resource systems, in which a series of equations depicts real world phenomena. Water resource models are analytic tools that help to forecast the quantity or quality of water in some specific place, or to determine the consequences of some proposed actions. A model uses numbers, symbols, and relationships in mathematical form to represent a system. Even the most complex model is a simplification of the system it represents, for it is not possible to account for every detail in a complex system, nor is it desirable. A model's value is in its ability to represent the important features of a system, reduce the number of factors under consideration to manageable size, and depict the characteristics of interest and how they change under different conditions, so that meaningful results are obtained.

Water resources models can be categorized in any number of ways. The most convenient, and perhaps most common, division is between water quantity and water quality models. Other features are important, however, in understanding the uses and types of models. Descriptive models can aid in analyzing how a system works, whereas predictive models are useful in determining some level of water quantity or quality based on a set of given conditions. Models can also be designed as optimizing tools to determine the best available outcome that satisfies a set of given requirements or constraints. Another differentiation of models is between deterministic and probabilistic. Deterministic models have the relationships among the elements of the system fixed, and give results of an event as a single outcome, i.e., they are completely determined by the model with the given set of data. Probabilistic, or stochastic, models yield results that are given as a range of probable outcomes, taking into account the random nature of many parts of the system. Finally, models can be viewed as static or dynamic. Static models evaluate steady-state conditions in which the values of the variables do not change over time. Dynamic models are used when some parameters vary over time, or when the effects of transient phenomena must be evaluated.

12.9.1 Optimization Models

A number of texts deal with various aspects of water resources modeling (e.g., 3, 18, 29, 32). This subsection provides an overview of the more commonly used techniques, including calculus and LaGrangian multipliers, and mathematical programming techniques which have considerable application in water resources planning.

Most optimization problems focus on maximization of some function (e.g. benefit), although the minimization aspect (e.g. cost) is equally appropriate. The first significant step in formulating optimization models is to select adequate objective criteria, such as maximization of system efficiency or minimization of operational cost. The mathematical formulation of a specific objective is known as the objective function. Together with this function is a set of mathematical relationships among the variables, known as constraints. As an illustrative example we may have a simple water quality problem with wastes generated along a stream at sites 1 and 2. Without some form of treatment at these sites, water quality at site 3 downstream may be below the acceptable standard. The task is to find the level of treatment required at sites 1 and 2 to achieve desired standards at site 3, at minimal cost. The problem may be stated as follows (29):

Objective function:

$$\text{Minimize } Z = C_1 (X_1) + C_2 (X_2) \tag{12.4}$$

Constraints:

$$a_{13} W_1 X_1 + a_{23} W_2 X_2 = Q_3 \tag{12.5}$$

$$X_i \geq 0.30, i = 1, 2 \tag{12.6}$$

$$X_i \leq 0.95, i = 1, 2 \tag{12.7}$$

in which C_i = cost of treatment per unit at site i; X_i = fraction of waste removed at site i; q_3 = actual quality in milligrams per liter at site 3; Q_3

= desired quality in milligrams per liter at site 3; W_i = waste input at site i; and a_{ij} = transfer coefficient (improvement in water quality index at site j per unit of waste removed at site i). The objective function is to minimize the total cost of removal of waste fractions X_1 and X_2. The required constraints are to satisfy water quality standards at site 3, Q_3; to have at least 30% waste removal at each site x_i corresponding to primary treatment standards for municipal waste; and to have a maximum of 95% waste removal at each site, corresponding to best available technology.

The situation is formulated in Eqs. 12.4 through 12.7 as a linear programming problem, wherein the objective function and all constraints are linear mathematical functions. This technique is widely used to obtain optimal allocation of limited resources. Linear programming packages are available at most major computer centers, so the analyst needs only a knowledge of using the program and applying it to the specific water resource problem. Other optimization techniques are less readily available and are not as widely used. The most important of them is the dynamic programming formulation, which solves sequential decision problems where a system can be broken down into many subsystems. Recursive sets of equations are structured for successive solution, with the solution at each stage being optimal.

12.9.2 Simulation

Simulation models are the most common among water resource planners. They are essentially descriptive, computerized formulations in which characteristics of a system, in the form of functional relationships, are used to assess the response of selected outputs to the input variables.

A simulation may be time-sequenced or event-sequenced (29). The time-sequenced form uses a fixed time interval to examine the state of the system (e.g., flows, quality) at successive time intervals. If the time interval selected is small, the simulation will use more computer time; but if it is too large, many of the approximations on which the model is based may not be valid. An event-sequenced model simulates a sequence of events when they happen. The time between events is random, and the model focuses on the events of interest. The structure of water resources data makes the time-sequenced model appropriate for most uses. A simulation model is often run many times with various input and parameter data to generate corresponding outputs. Development of a simulation model requires the following:

1. Components. Design variables or economic decision points at which investment can change the value of the response.
2. Relationships. Rules by which the components are operated; rules that specify the physical features of the prototype; rules that govern the response computation.
3. Variables. Symbolic representations of components of the system; conditions affecting the system, both external and internal.
4. Time interval. A finite characteristic time interval operating over the period of analysis.

Simulation is a multiple-trial technique rather than an analytic process that yields optimal output. Accordingly, it is useful to question how reliable the results are for a given number of trials, and how the analyst proceeds from trial to trial. One of the key problems in simulation modeling is to determine the number of design and operating policies that need to be simulated. The general question of how to take the sample points is central to sampling and search procedures.

The search technique draws on sampling theory for its various approaches. The random sampling approach consists of choosing feasible values of the decision variables randomly. It is a complex process, particularly in the matter of deciding how many samples to take. The nature of the results of each simulation is an important indicator of how many additional trials to take. Fortunately, most responses in water resources simulations are reasonably uniform, allowing the analyst to approach convergence near the optimum.

The uniform grid sampling approach requires analysis of uniformly spaced values of decision variables. Typical water resources simulation models have many decision variables. Therefore, a model evaluation using this approach requires many simulations.

Unlike the random sampling or uniform grid approaches, sequential search procedures use results from previous simulations to calculate subsequent trials. The most common sequential search procedure is trial and error, because it is simple, and because many models are too large to use a formal sequential search procedure (29). The trial-and-error method calls for the analyst to intuitively move in the direction he feels will give the greatest change in performance. Another sequential search method uses partial derivatives of the objective function to indicate the path of steepest ascent in selecting subsequent values for decision variables.

The various search techniques each have their own advantages, and often a combination of methods is used. The essential point is that the analyst must be able to determine when a sufficient search has been made.

12.9.3 Statistical Techniques

A large body of statistical techniques is applicable to water resources models, especially to describe hydrologic processes associated with runoff problems. Multivariate techniques provide efficient methods for describing statistical relationships among system variables, which may then be incorporated into other system models. Multivariate techniques include regression analysis, principal component analysis, factor analysis, and discriminant analysis. These and other statistical techniques are presented in detail in numerous texts on statistics.

In general, multivariate analysis deals with several variables, such as the flow or water quality at different gaging stations. Each contains records of observations at that particular point. Multivariate analysis is used to determine relationships between the variables, and to determine the individual effects of interrelated data.

Regression analysis will generate an equation which shows a dependent variable as some function of a set of independent variables. The coefficients in the equation are determined by the set of empirical obserations on the different variables. Principal component analysis creates a new variable or index which is a combination of a number of observed variables that are related. Thus, rather than having many different measures of water quality, a single variable can be created which is a composite of the original variables. Factor analysis is similar to principal components, but somewhat in reverse fashion. Rather than working from given data to generate a composite measure, a model is assumed and the data are analyzed to estimate pertinent parameters. Discriminant analysis is a procedure for classifying observations as belonging to one of several populations. The preceding methods are by no means an all-inclusive set of statistical techniques, but they are the ones commonly used in water resources modeling.

12.9.4 Some Current Models

Many water resources models have been developed since the late 1960s, and some of them are becoming standard tools of the water resources planner. Several books are important in providing overviews of existing water resources models.

Three publications by the federal government are noteworthy. The Office of Technology Assessment, U.S. Congress, prepared a report on the use of models for water resources management, planning, and policy (42) in 1982. It provides an assessment of the capability to use models more effectively and efficiently in analyzing and solving water resources problems, and the ability of federal and state agencies to apply the models. EPA prepared a critical review of currently available water quality models (27) in 1973, and a report in 1976 on evaluation of water quality models (19). It is intended as a handbook for water resources planners and managers, and gives much information on water quality modeling, including procedures for model evaluation and selection, integration of modeling with planning activities, and use of contractors for modeling services. A massive volume by EPA provides proceedings of a 1976 conference on environmental modeling and simulation (33). Although the book includes numerous environmental concerns, the sections on water resources modeling are substantial. Included are over 60 papers on water resources.

Several books have been prepared outside government on various aspects of modeling (e.g., 12, 13, 22, 31). Basta and Bower (1) bring together information on methods of analyzing natural systems. Their purpose is to guide the use of publications and reports on models in a planning and management context. The chapters on water resources give: (1) An overview of principal approaches to developing models; (2) detailed summaries of many operational models; (3) factors to consider in selecting a model; (4) procedures to select a model; and (5) methods to incorporate information on new models into an existing framework. Included in Reference 1 are Tables 12-2, 12-3, 12-4, and 12-5 which give

TABLE 12-2 Sample of Mathematical Models of Receiving Waters (1)

Model category or model name (1)	Commonly used acronym (2)	Originator (3)
Streeter-Phelps Dissolved Oxygen Equation	—	Indiana State Board of Health, Bloomington, Indiana
Simplified Stream Model	SSM	Hydroscience, Inc., Westwood, New Jersey
Simplified Estuary Model	SEM	Hydroscience, Inc., Westwood, New Jersey
Dissolved Oxygen Sag Model	DOSAG-I	Texas Water Development Board, Austin, Texas
Dissolved Oxygen Sag Model (revised version)	DOSAG-3	Water Resources Engineers, Austin, Texas
SCI DOSAG Modification	DOSCI	Systems Control, Inc., Palo Alto, California
Estuary Model	E3001	U.S. Environmental Protection Agency—Region II, New York, New York
River Quality Model	QUAL-I	Texas Water Development Board, Austin, Texas
Dynamic Estuary Model	DEM	Water Resources Engineers, Walnut Creek, California
Tidal Temperature Model	TTM	U.S. Environmental Protection Agency, Pacific Northwest Laboratory, Corvallis, Oregon
Receiving Water Model Module of SWMM	RECEIV	Water Resources Engineers, Walnut Creek, California
Receiving Water Model (modification)	RIVSCI	Systems Control, Inc., Palo Alto, California
Receiving Water Model (modification)	WRECEV	Water Resources Engineers, Austin, Texas
Deep Reservoir Model	DRM	Water Resources Engineers, Walnut Creek, California
Lake Ecologic Model (modification of Deep Reservoir Model)	LAKSCI	Systems Control, Inc., Palo Alto, California
Reservoir Water Quality Model	EPARES	Water Resources Engineers, Austin, Texas
Hydrocomp Hydrologic Simulation Program	HSP	Hydrocomp, Inc., Palo Alto, California

TABLE 12-2 continued

Model category or model name (1)	Commonly used acronym (2)	Originator (3)
Coastal Circulation and Dispersion Model	CAFE/ DISPER	Ralph M. Parsons Laboratory, Massachusetts Institute of Technology, Cambridge, Mass.
Estuary Water Quality Model	EXPLORE-I	Battelle Pacific Northwest Labs, Richland, Washington
Outfall Plume Model	PLUME	U.S. Environmental Protection Agency, Pacific Northwest Laboratory, Corvallis, Oregon
Estuary Hydrodynamic/ Salinity Model	HYD/SAL	Texas Water Development Board, Austin, Texas
River Quality Model (QUAL-I modification)	QUAL-II	Water Resources Engineers, Walnut Creek, California
Lake Ecologic Model (DEM modification)	LAKECO	Water Resources Engineers, Walnut Creek, California
Estuary Ecologic Model	ECOMOD	U.S. Environmental Protection Agency, Washington, D.C.
Estuarine Aquatic Ecologic Model	ESTECO	Texas Water Development Board, Water Resources Engineers, Austin, Texas
Lake Phytoplankton Model	LAKE-1	Department of Civil Engineering, Manhattan College, New York, New York
Water Quality in River-Reservoir System	WQRRS	U.S. Army Corps of Engineers, Hydrologic Engineering Center, Davis, California
Narragansett Bay Hydrodynamic Model	—	Department of Ocean Engineering, University of Rhode Island, Narragansett, Rhode Island

characteristics of a number of water runoff and water quality models. They are followed in the book by full-page summaries of each model.

Among the major water runoff models, the Stanford Watershed Model (SWM) is perhaps the oldest and most widely used (10, 24). It uses hourly precipitation and potential evapotranspiration as input data.

Table 12-3 Receiving Water Models and Their Relevance to Specific Problems (1)

	Water Body Characteristics		Major Problems	

Water Body Characteristics:

- **Water body type:** Streams, Rivers, Lakes, Estuaries, Offshore waters
- **Flow conditions:** Constant streamflow, Variable streamflow, Tidal action, Steady state lake levels, Variable lake levels

Major Problems:

- **Temperature:** Ambient variation, Waste heat inputs, Thermal stratification
- **Salinity:** Natural belt sources, Irrigation return flows, Saltwater intrusion, Salinity stratification
- **Erosion and sedimentation:** Bedload transport, Suspended solids transport, Absorbed residuals transport
- **Eutrophication:** Carbonaceous oxygen demand nonpoint sources, Carbonaceous oxygen demand point sources, Nitrogenous oxygen demand, Instream oxygen demand
- **Dissolved oxygen:** Nitrogen kinetics, Phosphorous kinetics, Minor nutrients
- **Total substances:** Heavy metals, Pesticides, Refractionary-synthetic organics, Radioactive material
- **Biological effects:** Decomposers inc. coliforms, Primary producers, Zooplankton-invertebrates, Fishes, Ecosystem-level indicators

Model

SSM
SEM
DOSAG-1
DOSAG-3
DOSCI
E3OOI
QUAL-I
DEM
TTM
RECEIV
RIVSCI
WRECEV
DRM
LAKSCI
EPARES
HSP
CAFE/DISPER
EXPLORE-I
PLUME
HYD/SAL
QUAL-II
LAKECO
ECOMOD
ESTECO
LAKE-I
WQRRS
Narragansett Bay Model

• applicable; ○ applicable if treated as discrete particles; ★ applicable if treated as conservative constituent

TABLE 12-4 Runoff Models (1)

Name (1)	Com-monly used acronym (2)	Originator (3)	Applic-able land area (4)
Rational Method	—	—	urban
Hydroscience Simplified Models	—	Hydroscience, Inc., West-wood, New Jersey	urban
Midwest Research Institute Loading Functions	MRI	Midwest Research Institute, Kansas City, Missouri	nonurban urban
Storm Water Management Model. Level I	SWMM—Level I	Dept. of Environmental Engineering Sciences, Univ. of Florida, Gaines-ville, Florida	urban
Environmental Pollution Assessment-Erosion Sedimentation and Ru-ral Runoff Model	EPARRB	National Environmental Re-search Center, Environ-mental Protection Agency, Athens, Georgia	nonurban
Simplified Storm Water Management Model	Simplified SWMM	Metcalf and Eddy, Inc., Palo Alto, California	urban
Agricultural Chemical Transport Model	ACTMO	Agricultural Research Serv-ice, USDA, Beltsville, Maryland	nonurban
Agricultural Runoff Man-agement Model	ARM	Hydrocomp, Inc., Palo Alto, California	nonurban
Hydrocomp Simulation Program	HSP	Hydrocomp, Inc., Palo Alto, California	nonurban urban
Nonpoint Source Model	NPS	Hydrocomp, Inc., Palo Alto, California	nonurban
Quantity-Quality-Simulation Model	QQS	Dorsch Consult., Munich, Germany and Toronto, Ont., Canada	urban
Storage, Treatment, Over-flow and Runoff Model	STORM	Hydrologic Engineering Center, Corps of Engi-neers, Davis, California	urban nonurban
Agricultural Runoff Model	AGRUN	Water Resources Engi-neers, Inc., Walnut Creek, California	nonurban
Calcul des Reseaux d'assainissement (Calculation of Sewage Networks)	CAREDAS	SOGREAH, Grenoble, France (also New York, New York)	urban

TABLE 12-4 continued

Name (1)	Commonly used acronym (2)	Originator (3)	Applicable land area (4)
Storm Water Management Model	SWMM	Metcalf and Eddy, Palo Alto, California; University of Florida, Gainesville, Florida; Water Resources Engineers, Walnut Creek, California	urban nonurban
Simplified Storm Water Management Model	SWM-IV	Department of Civil Engineering, Stanford Univ., California	nonurban
National Weather Service River Forecast System	NWSRFS	Office of Hydrology, National Weather Service, Silver Spring, Maryland	nonurban
Urbsn Hydrology for Small Watersheds	TR-55	Soil Conservation Service, USDA, Washington, D.C.	urban
U.S. Geological Survey Rainfall Runoff Model for Peak Flow Synthesis	USGS	U.S. Geological Survey, Reston, Virginia	nonurban urban
HEC-1 Flood Hydrograph Package	HEC-1	Hydrologic Engineering Center, Corps of Engineers, Davis, California	nonurban

Inflow to channels is determined by simulation of interception, surface retention, infiltration, overland flow, interflow, ground-water flow, and soil-moisture storage. SWM was followed by several refined versions and a variety of other models based on the SWM structure. Other important runoff models are HEC-1 and STORM, used by the Corps of Engineers. HEC-3 and HEC-5 are other Corps models for multipurpose planning and operating of reservoir systems for flood control, hydropower, and water supply.

Several water quality models were introduced in the mid 1960s for defining and evaluating water quality management programs, but the use of water quality models grew rapidly under the impetus of the Federal Water Pollution Control Act Amendments of 1972. One of the largest and most comprehensive models for simulating sewer systems, treatment facilities, and impacts on receiving waters is EPA's Stormwater Management Model (SWMM). It is also one of the most widely used

TABLE 12-5 Applicability of Runoff Models to Various Problem Characteristics (1)

Problem Characteristics

Model name	Applicable land area				Temporal properties			Spatial properties		Hy-drology				Hy-draulics					Quality processes											Residuals								
	Urban	Agriculture	Forests	Wetlands	Single storm events	Continuous simulation	Annual or seasonal average	Single catchment	Multiple catchments	Surface/total hydrograph generation	Subsurface processes	Snowmelt	Dry-weather base flow	Flow routing in channels/pipes	Backwater, surcharging, pressure flow	Flow controls and diversions	Storage/reservoir routing	Surface generation	Routing in channels/pipes	Sediment/erosion	Scour/deposition in channels/pipes	Parameter interaction	Soil/sediment-parameter interaction	Routing through storages	Treatment removal in storages	Treatment processes	Organic/MOD/COD	Nitrogen specter	Phosphorus	Suspended solids	Coliforms	Pesticides	Arbitrary or other conservative	Arbitrary or other nonconservative	Economic analysis

	Hydroscience	MRI	SWMM-Level I	EPARRB	Simpl. SWMM	ACTMO	ARM	HSP	NPS	QOS	STORM	AGRUN	CAREDAS	SWMM
		•										•		•
	•				•	•					•			
	•	•		•		•	•	•	•	•		•	•	•
	•				•	•								
	•	•		•						•	•			•
	•	•	•			•	•			•	•			•
	•	•	•	•	•	•	•	•			•			•
	•	•	•	•	•	•	•	•			•			•
	•	•	•	•			•	•			•			•
	•			•					•	•				•
									•	•				•
	•					•			•	•		•		•
		•			•	•		•						
					•									
				•										•
		•		•		•	•	•		•	•			•
						•		•			•	•	•	•
	•	•	•	•		•		•	•	•				•
				•		•		•	•			•	•	•
						•		•				•	•	•
								•				•	•	•
						•		•			•	•	•	•
		•				•		•	•			•	•	•
				•	•	•	•		•					•
				•	•	•		•						
	•		•		•	•	•	•	•	•	•	•	•	•
				•	•	•	•		•			•	•	•
	•	•	•	•						•				
	•	•	•	•										
				•	•	•	•	•	•					•
		•				•	•		•		•	•	•	•
		•					•							
	•		•			•	•							
	•		•		•	•	•			•				
	•	•	•	•	•		•	•	•	•			•	•

models, because of its reliability and widespread availability. Other important water quality models are QUAL-II, a stream water quality model; SWMM/RECEIV, an urban runoff model; and ARM, an agricultural runoff model.

Perhaps the most noteworthy achievement to date in the application of water resources modeling is in the cooperative agreements reached in 1982 for water supply in the Washington, D.C. metropolitan area. After three decades of uncertainty regarding the area's water supply, water resources modeling and management techniques were adopted to optimize water supplies for years to come with only moderate capital expenditures of $30,000,000. The achievements include (50):

1. Combination of optimization and simulation techniques to provide practical operating rules for the entire system.

2. The first large-scale use of the National Weather Service River Forecast System, which is based on a soil moisture accounting model.

3. The combination of distribution analysis and hydrologic models for developing operating procedures for a major, complex water distribution system.

4. The use of gaming simulation to test and improve operating procedures and to demonstrate their use to decision-makers.

Considering the fact that eight separate agreements were reached among federal, state, and local agencies, that the alternatives studied over many years ranged from $200,000,000 to more than $1 billion, and that the adopted solution is based primarily on low cost, improved operation of existing facilities using systems analysis techniques, the Washington, D.C. metropolitan water supply project has brought water resources modeling a major step forward. It has demonstrated that nonstructural engineering alternatives using the techniques of water resources modeling can solve complex "sociopolitical problems and achieve substantial cost savings" (48). The capabilities of water resource models vary significantly among applications, but many usable techniques exist for both quantity and quality. Their continued development, and the rapidly increasing availability of computer technology, should make models an important element of water resources planning.

12.10 GLOSSARY

Aquiclude.—An impermeable geologic formation that confines water in an adjoining formation.

Aquifer.—An underground bed of porous rock or soil that carries or holds water.

Artesian aquifer or well.—Water held under pressure in porous rock or soil confined by impermeable geologic formations. An artesian well is free flowing.

Biochemical Oxygen Demand.—The amount of oxygen consumed by microorganisms (mainly bacteria) and by chemical reactions in the biodegradation process (BOD).

Brackish.—Mixed fresh and salt waters.

Dissolved Oxygen.—A measure of water quality indicating free oxygen dissolved in water.

Drainage Basin.—The area of land that drains water, sediment, and dissolved materials to a common outlet at some point along a stream channel.

Estuary.—A surface area where fresh and salt waters mix; for example, where a river joins the ocean.

Eutrophication.—Process of aging of lakes and other still water bodies, characterized by excessive aquatic growth.

Evaporation.—The process whereby water from land areas, bodies of water, and all other "moist" surfaces is absorbed into the atmosphere as a vapor.

Evapotranspiration.—The combined processes of evaporation and transpiration. It can be defined as the sum of water used by vegetation and water lost by evaporation.

Floodplain.—Any area that is subject to flooding.

Ground water.—All water beneath the surface of the ground (whether in defined channels or not).

Hydrograph.—A graph of the rate of runoff plotted against time for a point on a channel.

Hydrologic Cycle.—Movement or exchange of water between the atmosphere and the earth.

Hydrology.—The study of the occurrence and distribution of the natural waters of the earth.

Infiltration.—Movement of water into the soil.

Infiltration Rate.—Quantity of water (usually measured in inches) that will enter a particular soil per unit time (usually one hour).

Nonpoint Pollution.—Nonpoint sources are diffuse or unspecific in nature and discharge pollutants into waters by dispersed pathways.

Oxygen Sag.—Drop in dissolved oxygen following pollution of a stream, with subsequent recovery.

Percolation.—The slow seepage of water into and through the ground.

Permeability.—Generally used to refer to the ability of rock or soil to transmit water.

Potentiometric Surface.—The level to which water will rise in cased wells or other cased excavations into aquifers, measured as feet above mean sea level.

Potable Water.—Safe and satisfactory drinking water.

Recharge.—Generally, the inflow to an aquifer or ground water.

Recharge Area.—Generally, an area that is connected with an underground aquifer by a highly porous soil or rock layer. Water entering a recharge area may travel for miles underground.

Recharge Rate.—The quantity of water per unit time that replenishes or refills an aquifer.

Recurrence Interval.—The average interval, in years, between the occurrence of a flood of specified magnitude and an equal or larger flood (sometimes called return period).

Runoff.—Generally defined as water moving over the surface of the ground, consisting of precipitation (rainfall) minus infiltration and evapotranspiration.

Salt Water Intrusion.—Contamination of a freshwater aquifer by movement of saline water into it; usually caused by excess pumping and drawdown of the freshwater aquifer.

Stage.—Elevation of the water surface in river investigations, usually above some arbitrary datum.

Surface Water.—All water on the surface of the ground, including water in natural and man-made boundaries as well as diffused water.

Transmissivity.—The ability of an aquifer to transmit water.

Transpiration.—The process whereby water vapor is emitted or passes through plant leaf surfaces and is diffused into the atmosphere.

Unit Hydrograph.—The hydrograph of one inch of storm runoff generated by a rainstorm of fairly uniform intensity within a specific period of time.

Watershed.—All land and water within the confines of a drainage divide.

Water Table.—The water level or surface above an impermeable layer of soil or rock (through which water cannot move). This level can be very near the surface of the ground or far below it.

Water Well.—An excavation where the intended use is for the location, acquisition, development, or artificial recharge of ground water (excluding sand-point wells).

Wetlands.—Swamps, marshes, bogs, wet meadows, and tidal flats where water stands on the ground surface.

12.11 REFERENCES

1. Basta, D.J., and Bower, B.T., *Analyzing Natural Systems*, Resources for the Future, Washington, D.C., 1982.
2. Bird, J.W., "Origin and Growth of Federal Reserved Water Rights," *Journal of the Irrigation and Drainage Division*, ASCE, Vol. 107, No. IR1, March, 1981, pp. 11–24.
3. Biswas, A.K., "Systems Approach to Water Management," *Systems Approach to Water Management*, A.K. Biswas, ed., McGraw-Hill, Inc., New York, 1976, p. 5.
4. Boland, J.D., Baumann, D.D., and Dziegielewski, B., *An Assessment of Municipal and Industrial Water Use Forecasting Approaches*, U.S. Army Corps of Engineers, Institute for Water Resources, Ft. Belvoir, Va., 1981.
5. Business Publishers, Inc., *Clean Water Report*, Silver Spring, Md., May 19, 1981, p. 95.
6. Business Publishers, Inc., *Clean Water Report*, Silver Spring, Md., September 22, 1981, p. 185.
7. Business Publishers, Inc., *Clean Water Report*, Silver Spring, Md., December 28, 1981, p. 255.
8. Canter, L.W., *Environmental Impact Assessment*, McGraw-Hill, Inc., New York, 1977, p. 89.
9. Costello, L.S., *Establishing Goals and Objectives for Urban Water Resources Management*, CH2M Hill, Inc., Reston, Va., 1973.
10. Crawford, N.H., and Linsley, R.K., *Digital Simulation in Hydrology: the Stanford Watershed Model*, Technical Report No. 39, Dept. of Civil Engineering, Stanford University, 1966.
11. Cunha, L.V., et al., *Management and Law for Water Resources*, Water Resources Publications, Inc., Ft. Collins, Colo., 1977.
12. de Neufville, R., and Marks, D.H., eds., *Systems Planning and Design*, Prentice-Hall, Inc., Englewood Cliffs, N.J., 1974.
13. Dorfman, R., et al., *Models for Managing Regional Water Quality*, Harvard University Press, Cambridge, Mass., 1972.
14. Douglas, J.L., and Lee, R.R., *Economics of Water Resources Planning*, McGraw-Hill, Inc., New York, 1971.

15. Dunne, T., and Leopold, L.B., *Water in Environmental Planning*, W.W. Freeman and Co., San Francisco, Calif., 1978.
16. Dzurik, A.A., *Floodplain Management and Intergovernmental Coordination*, Research Paper No. 6, Board of Engineers for Rivers and Harbors, U.S. Army Corps of Engineers, Ft. Belvoir, Va., 1976.
17. Eckstein, O., *Water Resource Development*, Harvard University Press, Cambridge, Mass., 1958.
18. Haith, D.A., *Environmental Systems Optimization*, John Wiley and Sons, Inc., New York, 1982.
19. Grimsrud, G.P., Finnemore, E.J., and Owen, H.J., *Evaluation of Water Quality Models: A Management Guide for Planners*, Office of Research and Development, U.S. Environmental Protection Agency, Washington, D.C., July, 1976.
20. Hall, W.A., and Dracup, J.A., *Water Resources Systems Analysis*, McGraw-Hill, Inc., New York, 1970.
21. Hamilton, H.R., et al., *Systems Simulation for Regional Analysis: An Application to River Basin Planning*, M.I.T. Press, Cambridge, Mass., 1969.
22. Holcomb Research Institute, *Environmental Modeling and Decision Making*, Praeger, New York, 1976.
23. Hufschmidt, M.M., and Fiering, M.B., *Simulation Techniques for Design of Water Resource Systems*, Harvard University Press, Cambridge, Mass., 1966.
24. Hydrocomp International, Inc., *Hydrocomp Simulation Programming Operations Manual*, Palo Alto, Calif., 1968.
25. Kindler, J., and Bower, B.T., "Modeling and Forecasting of Water Demands," presented at the November 28–29, 1978, Conference on Application of Systems Analysis in Water Management, held at Budapest, Hungary.
26. Linaweaver, F.P., Geyer, J.C., and Wolff, J.B., *A Study of Residential Water Use*, U.S. Dept. of Housing and Urban Development, Washington, D.C., 1967.
27. Lombardo, P.S., *Critical Review of Currently Available Water Quality Models*, for Office of Water Resources Research, Hydrocomp, Inc., Palo Alto, Calif., 1973.
28. Loucks, D.P., "Surface-Water Quality Management Models," *Systems Approach to Water Management*, A.K. Biswas, ed., McGraw-Hill, New York, 1976.
29. Loucks, D.P., Stedinger, J.R., and Haith, D.A., *Water Resource Systems Planning and Analysis*, Prentice-Hall, Inc., Englewood Cliffs, N.J., 1981.
30. Maas, A., et al., *Design of Water Resource Systems*, Harvard University Press, Cambridge, Mass., 1962.
31. Major, D.C., and Lenton, R.L., *Applied Water Resource Systems Planning*, Prentice-Hall, Inc., Englewood Cliffs, N.J., 1979.
32. Meta Systems, Inc., *Systems Analysis in Water Resources Planning*, Water Information Center, Inc., Port Washington, N.Y., 1975.
33. Ott, W.R., ed., *Environmental Modeling and Simulation*, U.S. Environmental Protection Agency, Washington, D.C., 1976.
34. Rastatter, C.L., "Congress Braces for New Fight on Water Quality," *Conservation Foundation Letter*, September, 1981, p. 8.
35. Reinke, C.E., and Allison, R.C., "State Water Laws: Effect on Engineering Solutions," in *Legal, Institutional and Social Aspects of Irrigation and Drainage and Water Resources Planning and Management*, ASCE, New York, 1979, pp. 204–218.
36. Snyder, D.J. III, "Federal Water Law Policy," in *Legal, Institutional and Social*

Aspects of Irrigation and Drainage and Water Resources Planning and Management, ASCE, New York, 1979, pp. 138–142.

37. Salvato, J.A., *Environmental Engineering and Sanitation*, John Wiley and Sons, Inc., New York, 1972.
38. Solley, W.B., Chase, E.B., and Mann, W.B. IV, *Estimated Use of Water in the United States in 1980*, Geological Survey Circular 1001, U.S. Geological Survey, Washington, D.C., 1983.
39. Swenson, H.A., and Baldwin, H.L., *A Primer on Water Quality*, Dept. of the Interior, U.S. Geological Survey, Washington, D.C., 1965.
40. Task Committee on Water Conservation of the Water Resources Planning Committee of the Water Resources Planning and Management Division, ASCE, "Perspectives on Water Conservation," *Journal of the Water Resources Planning and Management Division*, ASCE, Vol. 107, No. WR1, March, 1981, pp. 225–238.
41. U.S. Army, Corps of Engineers, *Manual for Water Resources Planners*, Board of Engineers for Rivers and Harbors, Ft. Belvoir, Va., 1976.
42. U.S. Congress, Office of Technology Assessment, *Use of Models for Water Resources Management, Planning, and Policy*, U.S. Government Printing Office, Washington, D.C., 1982.
43. U.S. Environmental Protection Agency, *Guidelines for Preparation of Water Quality Management Plans*, Washington, D.C., 1974.
44. U.S. Environmental Protection Agency, *Water Quality Management Planning for Urban Runoff*, Washington, D.C., 1974.
45. U.S. Environmental Protection Agency, *Guidelines for Areawide Waste Treatment Management Planning*, Washington, D.C., 1975.
46. U.S. Water Resources Council, *Principles and Standards for Water Resources Planning*, Washington, D.C., 1973.
47. U.S. Water Resources Council, *Second National Assessment of the Nation's Water Resources*, U.S. Water Resources Council, Washington, D.C., 1978.
48. U.S. Water Resources Council, *A Unified National Program for Flood Plain Management*, Washington, D.C., September, 1979.
49. U.S. Water Resources Council, *State of the States: Water Resources Planning and Management*, Washington, D.C., April, 1980.
50. "Water Supply," *Civil Engineering*, Vol. 53, No. 6, June, 1983, pp. 50–53.

CHAPTER 13
RECREATION AND OPEN SPACE PLANNING[a]

13.1 INTRODUCTION

13.1.1 Definition of Terms

Recreation, parks, and open space are interrelated concepts and planning for their provision is generally done in concert. The key terms in this chapter are defined as follows:

- Open space. Any parcel or area of land or water essentially unimproved and set aside, designated or reserved for public or private use or enjoyment, or for the use and enjoyment of owners and occupants of land adjoining or neighboring such open space.
- Park. A tract of land, designated and used by the public for active and passive recreation.
- Recreation, active. Leisure time activities, usually of a more formal nature and performed with others, often requiring equipment and taking place at prescribed places, sites or fields. (Activities such as running, bicycling, hiking and picnicking are not usually considered active recreation.)
- Recreation, passive. Any leisure time activity not considered active.
- Recreation facility. A place designed and equipped for the conduct of sports, leisure time activities and other customary and usual recreational activities (23).

Open space is the broadest term, because it includes all parks as well as other undeveloped or marginally developed land which may be publicly or privately owned. Open space may be accessible to the public or, like the common open space of an apartment complex, cluster subdivision, or planned unit development, only to a limited group. It may be relatively inaccessible or unusable for geographic or public safety reasons, such as land surrounding a water supply reservoir, a traffic island, or a swamp (although permanent bodies of water would not generally be considered open space). Such areas do fulfill the environmental and esthetic functions of open space, which are reviewed in Sec. 13.1.3.

---

[a] Prepared by Curtis R. Bynum, Design Specialist, Rebecca Kemmerer, Senior Planner, and David W. Wright, M. ASCE, Vice President, Presnell Associates, Inc., Louisville, KY.

"Recreation" is really an abbreviation for "recreational facilities, recreational programs, or both," since the planner, engineer or administrator is generally concerned with providing the opportunity for individuals to recreate. Recreation can take place in public parks, other open spaces, and any number of other public and private places, including fully developed and indoor locations. Recreation includes activities such as bowling, video games, and movies (which are almost entirely provided by the private sector), as well as indoor public facilities such as community centers.

To further classify recreation facilities, two additional definitions are provided (23, p. 154):

- Recreation facility, commercial. A recreation facility operated as a business and open to the public for a fee.
- Recreation facility, private. A recreation facility operated by a nonprofit orgnization and open only to bona fide members and guests of such nonprofit organization.

13.1.2 Context for Planning

Recreation, parks and open space planning takes place at several jurisdictional levels, within numerous agencies at the local level, and in the private sector. Agencies responsible for parks and recreation planning include the National Park Service, State parks departments, metropolitan, city, and county parks departments, public and private nonprofit zoos, nature centers, and other facilities. Such planning is also typically done by local, regional, and state planning agencies, often as one element of the comprehensive plan. The private sector provides much of the public and semipublic open space such as golf courses, downtown plazas, subdivision open spaces, swimming and waterfront developments, and commercial recreation facilities. Private and commercial facilities represent an important segment of the recreational opportunities available to the public and must be considered in public recreation and open space plans.

The focus of a planning agency, regardless of jurisdictional level, is on the land use, transportation system, and general development of the area or community. In this context, open space is one of the basic land uses that helps to shape and structure development. It may be part of an over-all environmental protection and enhancement program. It is often one of the functional elements of the comprehensive plan, along with land use, transportation, housing, and other community facilities. When carried out by a parks and recreation agency, the planning focus is somewhat narrowed and correspondingly more detailed as the agency organizes the facilities and programs for which it is responsible.

Recreation facilities and open space are among many possible uses for our resources. The priorities of communities will differ from area to area and over time. Therefore, planning must be flexible enough to adapt to changing conditions and not rely too heavily on historical use patterns and standards.

Many of the factors which affect the planning process may change rapidly. Demographic, economic, and environmental conditions in the planning area, the region, and the country as a whole should be considered. Some of the changes of the late 1970s and early 1980s having a significant impact on open space and recreation planning are:

1. Changing attitudes toward recreation, particularly physical fitness.

2. Changing family patterns, including more single-person and single-parent households, lower birth rates, and a growing elderly population.

3. Economic conditions which have included inflation, recession, and unemployment; regional shifts in economic development.

4. Changing housing patterns, with smaller houses and more multifamily housing due to rising costs of construction, land, energy and financing.

5. Energy shortages; changing attitudes towards energy.

6. Technological changes, such as widespread availability of computers, electronic games, and cable TV.

7. Changing environmental concerns and goals.

13.1.3 Functions of Open Space

The functions of open space can be characterized as follows: (1) To meet human needs for recreation and esthetics; (2) to protect and enhance the environment; and (3) to shape the extent and patterns of development in a community (12, pp. 187–188).

Meet human needs   Open space and parks meet a multitude of human needs from physical to social and psychological. First and most obviously, they provide space and facilities for recreation, both active and passive. Recreation itself has important positive effects on the individual.

Second, open space provides health benefits such as sunlight and fresh air. It can provide a buffer between incompatible land uses that is physically as well as psychologically important, by separating residential areas from a heavily traveled highway, for example. The importance of vegetation, especially trees, in the ecosystem is only recently becoming widely understood. Wooded areas can improve air quality and lower ambient air temperature in urban communities.

Third, open space provides social and psychological benefits. A neighborhood park or apartment complex courtyard may serve as the social focal point of a neighborhood, helping to establish a sense of identity and community which benefits the individual and the community. The esthetic benefits, though difficult to measure, are real and significant. Open spaces have long served ceremonial and symbolic functions, often incorporated with boulevards and monuments. The Mall and Federal Triangle area of Washington, D.C., the Champs-Elysées and Arc de Triomphe of Paris, and Washington Square in New York are examples of such spaces.

Protection and enhancement of environment   Land varies in its capacity for development. Some land can be developed only at great expense; some land can handle only limited development. Land-based resources that may require protection include unique wildlife habitats and areas with delicate ecology or physiography. Wetlands, coastal zones, and steep hillsides are among the environmentally sensitive areas that can be protected as open space. Floodplains can be kept free of development that limits the storage of potential floodwaters by designation as an open space easement, public open space, or semideveloped park. Some of these areas may be suitable for active recreational areas, some only as greenbelt areas or passive parks. A lasting contribution of the environmental movement of the 1970s has been the realization by the public and by government decision-makers that natural resources are not unlimited. Thus, management of land-based resources takes on greater importance than if only recreational opportunities and esthetics are considered.

Shaping development   The size, nature, and location of parks and open spaces can have a major impact on development decisions in a community. In an area endowed with attractive natural resources, well planned open spaces may be the basis of a local tourist-based economy. In a metropolitan area, parks and recreation facilities affect patterns of residential and commercial development. Such spaces can define neighborhood centers and boundaries, as well as affect the relative desirability of different neighborhoods, the downtown, and other commercial areas.

An open space system is often incorporated into the design of a new development as the predominant feature of a clustered subdivision or planned unit development. By reducing individual lot sizes while maintaining over-all density, land is available for common open space that can be used for such purposes as jogging paths, common gardens, or retention of existing trees. Finally, the importance of open space and recreational facilities as a community amenity should not be overlooked. It is one of the "quality of life" factors that helps to make a desirable, livable community and may, in the long run, have an effect on economic development.

13.1.4 Historical Perspective

Parks for public and private use in developed areas have a history going back to ancient times. Sufficient perspective can be obtained in a review of parks since the American Colonial period, recognizing that values and standards had important antecedents in Europe and the Middle East.

One of the first tracts of land to be dedicated to public use in America was the Boston Common, established in 1634. Its original purpose was to provide pasture for transient livestock, but the Common has been put to various uses including military parades and training, public execution, celebrations, public addresses, and sports. Boston was also the site of the first public botanical garden in the United States, in 1852, and the development of the "Emerald Necklace" concept of parks in 1888 as green space around the perimeter of the city, bringing open space closer to every inhabitant (17).

In his plan for Philadelphia of 1682, William Penn set aside 10 acres of open space in the center of the city and eight acres for each area of the town under residential development. James Oglethorpe planned for a system of public squares in his 1733 design for Savannah, Georgia. The original plan for Washington, D.C. designed by Pierre L'Enfant provided for a generous number of open spaces incorporated into the axial network of ceremonial avenues and monumental buildings (12, pp. 9–12).

As industrialization and urbanization occurred in the latter part of the 1800s, many urban open spaces were being replaced with high-density residential development. The resulting congestion and unsanitary living conditions, particularly in large cities such as New York, led to the development of reform movements, including the park planning movement.

Growing public and political support for urban parks led to the establishment of the first large urban park, New York City's Central Park. Acquisition of land began in 1853. Frederick Law Olmsted was named superintendent and, with Calvert Vaux, submitted the winning design for the park. This work had a tremendous impact on the parks movement, as well as on the City Beautiful movement and city planning. It has influenced the design of parks all over the country. The principles set forth by Olmsted have been a major influence on planners to the present day. Some of the most important of Olmsted's park planning principles may be summarized as follows:

Human Objectives.

1. Park planning should be based on well defined objectives.
2. Urban residents need the healthful respite offered by permanent open spaces. Furthermore, all social classes should have access to parks and recreation facilities.
3. Park facilities should meet the needs of different groups, such as children, adults and families.
4. Park planning should be integrated with other service systems in order to provide for a variety of recreational needs.

Park Design.

1. The natural landscape should be preserved and provide the basis for design. Any changes that must be made should appear to be

natural. Plantings should consist of native trees and shrubs. Informality should prevail, with formal design in limited areas.

   2. Locate large open lawns and meadows in central areas, separating different use areas with natural features.

   3. Potentially conflicting areas should be separated and compatible recreation uses grouped together. Traffic circulation should be by means of curvilinear roads, with grade separations for different modes of travel (16).

   Many of these principles are apparent in the design of Olmsted's many parks around the country. Iroquois Park in Louisville, Kentucky (see Fig. 13-1) is a good example of one such park.

National Recreation and Park Association   With the growing parks movement came the establishment of the National Recreation Association in 1906. At its first meeting, the organization adopted a report outlining the need and space requirements for certain recreation facilities (3, p. 7). Since then, this organization, later renamed the National Recreation and Park Association (NRPA), has been responsible for the development and recommendation of community recreation standards nationwide.

13.2 THE RECREATION AND OPEN SPACE PLANNING PROCESS

13.2.1 Institutional Structure

   The institutional structure for recreation planning includes agencies at the federal, state, regional, and local levels, along with private

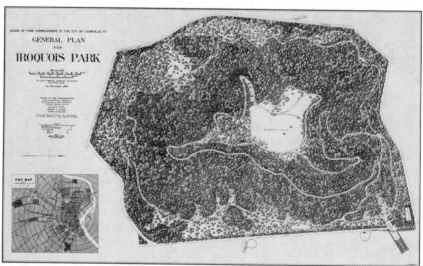

Fig. 13-1. General plan for Iroquois Park (Courtesy: National Park Service, Frederick Law Olmsted National Historic Site)

organizations. Many federal agencies are involved in open space, parks, or recreation planning—among them the Department of the Interior, including the National Park Service and National Fish and Wildlife Service; the Department of Housing and Urban Development; and the Department of Agriculture, including the U.S. Forest Service. The U.S. Army Corps of Engineers does open space and recreation planning in conjunction with its reservoirs. The Tennessee Valley Authority is similarly involved in recreational use of reservoirs along with its regional planning function.

These agencies may produce comprehensive plans for their areas of jurisdiction, such as a plan for the National Parks System. There are three major impacts of federal agencies on open space and recreation.

First, federally-owned lands, both developed and undeveloped, comprise the vast majority of open land in the country and are a major recreational resource. Second, several federal agencies provide funding for the planning, acquisition, and development of open space by state and local governments. Third, the regulations that are concomitant with such funding have influenced and will continue to influence open space and recreation planning. For example, state comprehensive outdoor recreation plans were initially done as prerequisites for federal funding.

Each state may have several departments that concern themselves with different aspects of open space, parks, and recreation planning. These may include state parks departments, state planning agencies, fish and game commissions, community and economic development departments, and environmental protection and natural resources departments.

Most if not all states have an agency charged with preparing and maintaining a state comprehensive outdoor recreation plan (SCORP). While their title implies recreation facilities, the plans often include undeveloped public open space. State plans may be an excellent source of data, and may present a classification system and set of standards for use by local agencies. A state plan is typically a broad policy statement, establishing specific objectives and standards within a midrange (3-yr to 5-yr) planning period.

At the local level, a variety of organizations—planning commissions, parks and recreation agencies, other bodies of local government, and regional agencies—all may be involved with some aspect of recreational and open space planning. Any organization providing recreation facilities may do planning for its own area of concern. However, the responsibility for coordinated, comprehensive recreation and open space planning generally rests with a regional or local parks authority or planning commission. Where more than one agency has some responsibility, it is best for the agencies to coordinate their plans, or for one agency's plan to incorporate the others. In a typical situation, a city-county planning commission is charged with preparing a comprehensive plan. This plan has a recreational facilities element and also includes open space and parks as categories in the land use element. In the same community, the parks and recreation commission owns and operates the parks system and prepares the parks and recreation policy plan. Clearly, conflicting or inconsistent policy plans would not serve the community's interests. Such problems are sometimes ameliorated by memoranda of understanding between federal and state agencies, state and local agencies, or two state agencies.

13.2.2 Functional Hierarchy of Plans

Open space and recreation plans can be organized into three general categories: (1) The policy plan (also known as a comprehensive parks and recreation plan); (2) the site-specific master plan; and (3) program plans or operation and maintenance plans. These form a hierarchy in the sense that there is an order or rank to the various plans. They differ in function, scope, time frame, and level of detail, yet should be consistent with and explicate each other.

Preparation of the policy plan and site master plan will be described in some detail in following sections. The operation and maintenance plan is an action plan which establishes short-term goals for facilities and programming, scheduling, standards, and operational policies. This would be prepared by the individual park agency (18, p. 25). The planner or engineer is seldom involved in its preparation.

13.3 PREPARING THE POLICY PLAN

A schematic diagram of a model for the recreation and open space planning process (see Fig. 13-2) shows the phases and tasks comprising the planning process (18, pp. 26-27). Several major steps lead to the policy plan.

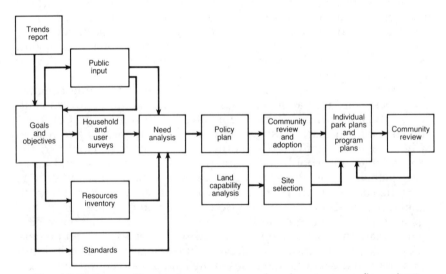

Fig. 13-2. Recreation and open space planning process flow chart

13.3.1 Establish Goals and Objectives

The first major step in policy plan formulation, as in all planning efforts, is the establishment of goals and objectives. Goals may be defined as ideals expressed in abstract terms which provide direction; they are values or ends to be sought after. Objectives provide more specific expression of goals and can also represent intermediate end states. Objectives can be both attained and measured (36). The objectives established at this stage will provide the basis for standards—an even more specific expression of community values—to be developed later. Public input through elected bodies, community representatives, attitude surveys, and direct participation in goal-setting meetings is necessary to assure goals and objectives that truly represent community wishes.

13.3.2 Trends Report

A planning model develped by the Austin (Texas) Parks and Recreation Department in 1980 for its 5-yr master plan has been reported by the NRPA as adaptable for any community (18, p. 8). This model includes the preparation of a trends report, which summarizes the status of planning in the community and the current national and local trends in recreation and leisure. It serves as an interim guide until the recreation plan is completed, and also provides a framework for the planning effort.

Such a report may or may not be appropriate for a given community. An up-to-date comprehensive plan may serve a similar purpose in relating recreation and open space planning to the over-all needs and directions of the community.

13.3.3 Needs Assessment and Analysis

This is the core of the recreational open space planning process. The basic components are the existing supply, the demand, and an analysis of unmet needs based on a set of standards developed for a given community. The needs analysis should result in a summary of what is available and in what measure. It should identify needed facilities that are not available, inadequate quality or quantity of facilities or open space, and geographic areas where facilities or open spaces should be acquired, developed, improved, or preserved.

Open space and recreation demand The task of determining the demand for various types and locations of park facilities includes assessing actual levels of participation in terms of numbers of visits or visitor hours of an activity, leisure behavior patterns and motivations, needs of different groups, and citizen perceptions and preferences. The primary sources of information about open space and recreation demand are surveys of community residents (usually households) and current park users, and direct public participation via neighborhood or community meetings. Referring to the planning process flowchart (Fig. 13-2), these subtasks are represented by the boxes labeled "public input" and "household and user surveys." At this stage, the neighborhood meetings also serve to allow public input into goals and objectives, which may then be revised. One approach is the administration of a questionnaire to a sample of households by mail, telephone, or door-to-door survey. Such a survey conducted in the Austin planning process included questions covering the following areas (18, p. 29):

1. Park maintenance levels desired.
2. Constraints on park use.
3. Alternative recreation delivery methods.
4. Pricing of recreation services.
5. Visitor safety in parks.
6. Factors motivating leisure activities.

To this list might be added:

7. Types of facilities desired, in rank order of importance.

Any questionnaire should be coded geographically to differentiate results by location. It also should include demographic and socioeconomic status questions (such as age, sex, and income) to help identify user groups which have varying needs. The specific questions to be asked will be unique to each community.

Existing park user surveys Another approach is to determine actual use of existing facilities. Combined with household survey data and the results of neighborhood meetings, such information helps assess demand for both existing and new facilities by listing type of activity, location, and frequency. Participation figures are typically derived from surveys of residents and visitors. Surveys can also establish visitor preferences, perceptions and images of parks. A profile of park visitors can be established including their characteristics, composition, recreation interests, and overt behavioral patterns within the park. Such a profile, while not essential to policy planning, may be useful as a basis for proposing and evaluating improvements to an existing park or as a guide to designing a new park.

Reed and Perdue (25) suggest that planners employ multiple research methods to determine user estimates. They recommend the following procedures:

1. Prepare a demographic profile of park users, including socioeconomic characteristics and trends (age, sex, income, education, ethnicity, household size, proximity of residence).

2. Identify the leisure behavioral patterns within the park. Obtain visitation records including available activities, and number of participants peak and average daily. Record users' behavioral patterns and characteristics (this usually requires systematic observation).

3. Conduct direct interview of users to establish visitor preferences and perceptions of the park.

4. Employ participant observation as a means for obtaining personal experiences within the park, taking note of both satisfaction-producing as well as satisfaction-limiting aspects of the park.

5. Obtain, if possible, information on those leisure behavior patterns outside the park that affect use within the park (alternative activities competing with park use).

Behavioral and demand studies are vital in establishing actual trends in participation rates and demand for facilities that are unavailable. Patterns and levels of participation are specific to population groups differing in age, family status, socioeconmic status, ethnic group, and regional location.

The importance of public opinion concerning perceived recreational needs cannot be overemphasized. Public participation and input has become mandatory, regardless of whether the facility is in the public or private sector. Citizen input often is very site-specific and project-specific; the greatest interest is generated for a park or improvement in the immediate neighborhood at the present time. A balance must be struck between short-range action and objectives and long-range planning. Part of the planner's job is to assist the community in visualizing the long-term ramifications of decisions.

A multifaceted public participation program which includes direct input from meetings, household surveys, visitor observation and surveys of park users will maximize the potential for obtaining complete and accurate assessment of demand.

13.3.4 Resource Inventory

The resource inventory is a compilation and evaluation of all open space, parks, and recreation facilities in the community. It should include private and semiprivate facilities, with qualifications noted as to the use limitations on a nonpublic facility. For example, the existence of private swim clubs will reduce the over-all need for public swimming facilities, but cannot be considered as important a resource as a public pool which is open to all. The inventory also should include publicly and privately owned open space such as greenways, stream and river floodplains, cemeteries, forest and nature preserves, and large tracts of undeveloped land. It should include the acreage and evaluation of the facilities, maintenance, site characteristics, accessibility, safety, and other qualitative aspects of each site.

A separate survey of other leisure services in the community is important to put public outdoor leisure facilities in the proper context (18, p. 30). The potential park user makes choices on how to spend leisure time, and the options include movies, video arcades, bowling alleys, and theme parks as well as public parks.

An analysis of each facility will include a description, an over-all evaluation, and a rating in each of several categories (facilities, maintenance, accessibility, etc.). A sample evaluation form is shown in Fig. 13-3. The sample shows a summary of all parks in the Austin, Texas system; however, each park would also receive a separate rating.

An evaluation presumes a set of standards for measurement. Section 13.4 presents the 1983 national standards and an approach to the development of a community's own open space and recreation standards.

Geographic distribution: equity model This phase of the assessment is concerned with the geographic distribution of parks and recreational facilities. The Austin park planning program includes an equity model which is a means of judging the fairness of the geographic distribution of facilities. This model, which could be adapted to any community, has

Park Evaluation Form
Austin Parks and Recreation Department

Park:	All Parks
Zone:	All Zones
Average Score:	6.24

Legend		
O	10	Good
◑	5	Fair
●	1	Poor
⊖	—	Not Applicable

	Score
Design Suitability	6.4

◑ Land Resources
◑ Water Resources

	Score
Quality of Environment	7.3

◑ Soils
◑ Turf
O Underbrush
◑ Shade Trees
◑ Water Bodies
O Air
◑ Noise Level
◑ Aesthetics

	Score
Quality of Development	4.1

◑ Buildings
● Interpretive Exhibits
◑ Play Equipment
O Ballfields
◑ Courts
O Swimming Pool
● Picnic Areas
◑ Trails
◑ Support Facilities
◑ Lighting

	Score
Maintenance	7.7

O Groundskeeping
◑ Litter Pickup
O Vandalism
O Irrigation

	Score
Multiple Use Opportunity	6.2

◑ Range of Ages
◑ Range of Physical Ability
◑ Active/Passive Activities

	Score
Linkages	4.8

◑ Greenbelt
◑ Community Activity Center
◑ Schools

	Score
Accessibility/Circulation/Parking	5.8

◑ Pedestrian/Bicycle
◑ Mass Transportation
◑ Automobile

	Score
Personal Safety	7.6

O Pollution Hazard
O Isolation
O Deviant Behavior
O High Crime Area
O Loose Animals

	Score
Total	49.9

Fig. 13-3. Sample park evaluation form (Reprinted with permission of the National Recreation and Park Association)

both quantitative and qualitative features (18, p. 30). Recreation investment per capita is calculated for zones (defined by neighborhood, census tract or other appropriate subcommunity level) so that areas which are inadequately served can be targeted. The population base for the per capita calculation is adjusted to reflect socioeconomic variables such as age, household size, and income level. This adjustment reflects the belief that low-income areas with larger, younger families have greater needs for public recreation than older and wealthier areas.

The supply of recreational areas in each zone is also adjusted to reflect qualitative differences by means of an on-site suitability study of existing parklands. Park evaluations (see Fig. 13-3) can provide this information. The resulting analysis of per capita investment by zone is a guide for locational decisions about future open space and recreational investment.

The results of the equity analysis, leisure marketing and user surveys, direct public input, and the resource inventory are incorporated into an area profile which sets priorities for each area.

13.3.5 Policy Plan Report: Review and Adoption

The final steps in policy planning include preparation of a report; review by and input from the public, government officials, and technical staff; and adoption by the appropriate body. The report should include collected and analyzed data and all major conclusions of the surveys. It should translate the objectives and assessments into a set of policy alternatives that recommend directions for public investment and decision making. Important issues uncovered in the planning process should be clarified. The implications of alternative policies and programs should be addressed.

The policy plan should represent a statement of community values regarding open space, parks, and recreation. It should also provide a guide for specific capital improvements and program development. Thus, it should be general and flexible, yet specific to the needs and resources of the community and geared toward filling any gaps in the community resource base.

Public participation is important throughout the policy planning process but particularly important at plan report preparation. Public meetings, at both the neighborhood and community levels and supported by information dissemination and media coverage, are most often used to generate input, involvement, and support. There should be an opportunity for public review and comment, and possible revision of the plan, before it is presented to official bodies for adoption.

13.4 PARKS AND RECREATION STANDARDS

13.4.1 Approaches to Developing Standards

Standards are the specific criteria that translate community goals and objectives into programs, facilities, and actions. The standards established in the policy planning process translate such broad goals as "adequate recreational opportunities" to "one neighborhood park for each 3000 persons, with a maximum 1/2 mile (0.8 km) service area." In addition to space standards, there are facility and development standards which provide guidelines for park and recreation facility development (18, p. 40). Such standards would specify the types and quantities of facilities provided in parks, and the amounts and locations of undeveloped public or private open spaces, or both. They would also clarify objectives such as preservation of unique natural areas, designing to take advantage of natural features, quality construction, and safety.

Recreation space standards have been established in the United States since 1906, when the National Recreation Association first published national standards. The standards have been revised by that organization (later known as the NRPA) in 1934, 1962, 1971, and 1983. While many cities have developed their own standards, the NRPA standards remain the most important guidelines within the profession. They have evolved over the years to be much more flexible and community-specific than in the past.

There are four primary approaches to space standards:

1. Population ratio: total park and recreation space expressed in a population ratio, such as acres per 1000 people.

2. Area percentage: the percentage of area dedicated to parks and other recreational uses and open space in the community (for example, 10% of gross area).

3. User orientation: recreation needs determined by user characteristics or demand projections.

4. Carrying capacity: the practical limits to the use of land.

Population ratio The population ratio method is the oldest, most widely used and perhaps the simplest. It provides the basis for NRPA space standards. There has been much criticism of this method in recent years as being too strictly interpreted and oversimplified. According to one critic, this approach " . . . emphasizes these general concepts: 1) quantity over quality, 2) physical over social objectives, 3) form over function, 4) exploitation over conservation of human and natural resources, and 5) the community rather than the individual" (9). The NRPA's ratio-based set of standards is accompanied by a disclaimer: that the standards should be used as a flexible guideline, and adapted to the particular community and situation.

Area percentage The area percentage method defines the percentage of the total land area within a jurisdiction that should be set aside for open space and recreation. This is of limited usefulness in a developed urban area, as it does not take into account population density or local recreational use patterns. It is very useful, however, in assuring adequate open space in new development, and has been used in subdivision and planned development ordinances for this purpose.

User orientation   The shortcomings of the traditional acreage-popul-
ation approach has led to the development of alternative methods that
are oriented specifically around user demand. This analysis identifies
the nature of user demands for existing recreational resources and
projects future demands. It is assumed that recreational needs will vary
not only among various individuals and groups, but also for each
individual due to changing needs over the course of the user's lifetime.
User orientation, or demand, is affected by several factors such as: (1)
Age; (2) disposable income; (3) levels of education; (4) occupation; (5)
family status; (6) regional characteristics; and (7) opportunities for user
participation. Research indicates that diverse groups in various sections
of the country maintain relatively consistent recreational patterns and
interest in particular types of leisure activities. These patterns of interest
and activity may be correlated with geographic, age, and socioeconomic
characteristics of potential users to identify user-oriented groupings.
National, state, and local recreation surveys usually contain some user-
oriented or demand emphasis.

Carrying capacity   Carrying capacity is the level of use a renewable
resource can withstand and still remain productive. It is the highest level
of yield that can be sustained over an extended period. Short-run actions
therefore must be examined in terms of their expected long-range
effects. Carrying capacity is particularly useful in large regional parks or
open space where the natural landscape or the historic or cultural
significance of the site is the main attraction. If a park is to be a nature
preserve, for example, limitations on use may be based on carrying
capacity: how many visitors can be allowed at peak times without
damaging the environment and thus the fundamental purpose of the
park? For a fully developed urban park, carrying capacity is somewhat
less useful.

   The measurement of carrying capacity is not a precise calculation.
In determining it, the planner must estimate optimal total effects from all
foreseeable viewpoints. This may involve personal judgment and
weighting of criteria to reach a highest value. Three variables involved in
the analysis of carrying capacity that are particularly difficult to predict
are:

   1. Seasonal, daily, and hourly variations in use rates and their
impacts.

   2. Seasonal variations in site productivity as affected by climatic
differences.

   3. Social carrying capacity or the issue of crowding and the user's
perception of resource value.

   Implementation of the carrying capacity concept is difficult. The
technique is often so loosely applied that the analyst can determine that
carrying capacity has been exceeded only when the recreation site begins
to show signs of permanent deterioration. By then, it may be too late to
alter designs and user patterns. This should not suggest that the concept

is of no practical use: analysis of carrying capacity is of great value as a guiding principle, even though the quantification is somewhat imprecise.

13.4.2 Space Standards

Each community or planning organization should adopt a set of standards that reflects the needs of that community. The NRPA national standards or standards developed by another city would be a good starting point. The NRPA outlines the following steps in development of a community's own standards (18, p. 43).

1. Review literature and existing data, including existing plans for parks and open space, economic development, and educational facilities; comprehensive plans of the community, region and state; demographic data; and the inventories and user studies described earlier. The recreation plans and standards of other communities, similar or not, might also be reviewed.

2. Collect any data not obtained in the review of existing sources, which may be data collected in the course of policy plan preparation. They should include more specific articulation of goals and objectives and should delineate the scope of the standard. The criteria used for inclusion or exclusion of land from the baseline will have a critical impact on the selection of which features of a site or potential site are to be evaluated.

3. Use the data to develop the standard. This is the analytical step wherein standards are selected. It may begin and end with the adoption of another community's standards, based on a review of standards that have been developed elsewhere. Ideally, however, the community's standards will evolve from its own peculiar circumstances, recreational patterns, and resources, which would be described in the first two steps. The NRPA outlines several methodologies for developing local park space standards and facility standards, and the reader is referred to that organization's 1983 standards publication for a complete discussion.

13.4.3 Classification of Open Space, Parks, and Recreation Areas

The NRPA has recommended a means of classifying the various types of park and recreation areas. This classification system includes a hierarchy of parks and recreation facilities based on an area to population ratio and a theoretically bounded service area, ranging from small neighborhood facilities to the largest regional parks. In addition, there are many special-use parks and recreation facilities and resource-based open spaces which are independent of any user-based demand determination.

Figure 13-4 shows the NRPA's classification system, along with space standards, function, service area and population, and location. As a general minimum, NRPA recommends 6.25 to 10.5 acres (2.5 to 4.25

Component	Use	Service Area	Desirable Size	Acres per 1000 Population	Desirable Site Characteristics
Local or close-to-home space					
Minipark	Specialized facilities that serve a concentrated or limited population or specific group such as tots or senior citizens.	Less than ¼ mile radius.	1 acre or less	0.25 to 0.5	Within neighborhoods and in close proximity to apartment complexes, town-house development or housing for the elderly.
Neighborhood park/ playground	Area for intense recreational activities, such as field games, court games, crafts, playground apparatus area, skating, picnicking, wading pools, etc.	¼ to ½ mile radius to serve a population up to 5000 (a neighborhood).	15+ acres	1.0 to 2.0	Suited for intense development. Easily accessible to neighborhood population. Geographically centered with safe walking and bike access. May be developed as a school-park facility.
Community park	Area of diverse environmental quality. May include areas suited for intense recreational facilities, such as athletic complexes, large swimming pools. May be an area of natural quality for outdoor recreation, such as walking, viewing, sitting, picnicking. May be any combination of the above, depending upon site suitability and community need.	Several neighborhoods. 1 to 2 mile radius.	25+ acres	5.0 to 8.0	May include natural features, such as water bodies, and areas suited for intense development. Easily accessible to neighborhood served.

Total close-to-home space = 6.25 to 10.5 acres per 1000 population

Fig. 13-4 NRPA suggested classification system (reprinted with permission of the National Recreation and Park Association)

Component	Use	Service Area	Desirable Size	Acres per 1000 Population	Desirable Site Characteristics
		Regional space			
Regional/metropolitan park	Area of natural or ornamental quality for outdoor recreation, such as picnicking, boating, fishing, swimming, camping, and trail uses; may include play areas.	Several communities. 1 hour driving time.	200+ acres	5.0 to 10.0	Contiguous to or encompassing natural resources.
Regional park reserve	Area of natural quality for nature oriented outdoor recreation, such as viewing and studying nature, wildlife habitat, conservation, swimming, picnicking, hiking, fishing, boating, camping, and trail uses. May include active play areas. Generally, 80% of the land is reserved for conservation and natural resource management, with less than 20% used for recreation development.	Several communities. 1 hour driving time.	1,000+ acres, sufficient area to encompass the resource to be preserved and managed.	Variable	Diverse or unique natural resources, such as lakes, streams, marshes, flora, fauna, topography.

Total regional space = 15.20 acres per 1000 population

Space that may be local or regional and is unique to each community

| Linear park | Area developed for one or more varying modes of recreational travel, such as hiking, biking, snowmobil- | No applicable standard. | Sufficient width to protect the resources and provide maximum | Variable | Built on natural corridors, such as utility rights-of-way, bluff lines, vegetation patterns, and roads, that |

Component	General description	Standard	Desirable size	Service radius	Location
(Linear park, cont.)	ing, horseback riding, cross-country skiing, canoeing and pleasure driving. May include active play areas. (Note: Any included for any of above components may occur in the linear park.)			use.	link other components of the recreation system or community facilities, such as school, libraries, commercial areas, and other park areas.
Special use	Areas for specialized or single-purpose recreational activities, such as golf courses, nature centers, marinas, zoos, conservatories, aboreta, display gardens, arenas, outdoor theaters, gun ranges, or downhill ski areas, or areas that preserve, maintain, and interpret buildings, sites, and objects of archeological significance. Also plazas or squares in or near commercial centers, boulevards, parkways.	No applicable standard.	Variable depending on desired size.	Variable	Within communities.
Conservancy	Protection and management of the natural or cultural environment with recreation use as a secondary objective.	No applicable standard.	Sufficient to protect the resource.	Variable	Variable, depending on the resource being protected.

Note: 1 acre = 0.405 hectare.

Fig. 13-4 (continued)

ha) of developed open space per 1000 population. The following paragraphs summarize the park and open space classes developed by several different communities, as reported by the NRPA (18, pp. 65–82).

Miniparks   Not all communities include miniparks as a separate clasification, though nearly all maintain small, special function parks or open spaces. The District of Columbia calls this class "Block and Street Space," and differentiates between "Play and Decorative Areas" and "Miniparks." According to the D.C. standards, the play or decorative area is to serve a radius of 2 blocks, with a size of up to 0.6 acres (0.24 ha) and capacity of 60 persons; a minipark is larger, at 0.6 to 3 acres (0.24 to 1.2 ha), has a capacity of 110 persons and serves a ⅜ mile (0.6 km) radius.

Neighborhood parks   Neighborhood parks are the backbone of a metropolitan park system. While there is variation in different communities' standards, they all describe a basically similar type of facility. The neighborhood park should serve a walking population—generally a radius of ⅜ to 1 mile (0.6 to 1.6 km)—with sidewalks and otherwise safe access. The population served will vary with density, but is roughly 1000 to 5000 persons. The neighborhood park serves all age groups, but primarily children and the elderly. Typical facilities include active recreation areas segregated by the age group to be served: playgrounds for preschoolers and older children; playing courts and ball fields; and an adult area with benches, picnic tables, shelter, game tables, and less active sports such as shuffleboard. Trees, open fields and undeveloped natural areas are also an important part of the neighborhood park.

Some community plans recommend locating a neighborhood park near a school to avoid duplicating facilities. Indoor recreation facilities are recommended in the District of Columbia standards, in either the school or a separate recreation center.

Community parks   The community park serves as a supplement to neighborhood parks by providing facilities that are too expensive or require too much space to be provided in each neighborhood. There is, however, some overlap in the function of the two types. The size of a community park can vary widely. The typical area standard for parks of this type is 10 to 75 acres (4 to 30 ha), with 15 to 40 acres (6 to 16 ha) most common. With a service area of 1 to 2 miles (1.6 to 3.2 km) and 1.5 to 3 acres (0.6 to 1.2 ha) per 1000 population, 20,000 to 60,000 persons are served. Desirable facilities include all those listed for the neighborhood park along with swimming facilities, picnicking, lighted ball fields and tennis courts, a community center, and adequate off-street parking. It is important that the community park be located on or near major thoroughfares and also be easily accessible by foot. This type of facility can include indoor recreation and cultural and educational programs in the community center as well as outdoor recreation. Landscaping and natural areas should be included in a community park.

Regional and metropolitan parks   This class includes major metropolitan parks serving a radius of 3 to 15 miles (4.8 to 24 km), as well as more regional facilities serving people of a relatively large geographical area, generally within an hour's travel. The standards for parks of this type include more variation than those for smaller parks. The size of the regional park may vary dramatically, but 100 acres (40.5 ha) would be considered a desirable minimum, with some as large as several thousand acres. The facilities and opportunities afforded by these parks vary just as widely. Some are left mainly as "natural" sites, while others contain extensive man-made developments. Some facilities typically found in such parks include picnic areas, nature centers, day camp areas, trail systems, boating, summer and natural water areas, a golf course, and major sports centers. County governments or other regional authorities, as well as cities, generally hold the responsibility for providing these major parks, which may be in urban, suburban, or rural locations.

Special recreational facilities   There is a wide range of special types of facilities, such as zoos, ice skating rinks, stadiums, beaches, amphitheaters, botanical gardens, arboretums, historic sites and cultural centers. The design, space, and location of special use facilities will be indicated by the specific demands of the activity. For scenic, historic and cultural sites, the park would be developed around an existing natural attraction or historic site. The NRPA's Facility Development Standards, shown in Fig. 13-5, apply to sports facilities including some of the special uses.

Open space: parkways and greenbelts   Open space that is undeveloped or marginally developed into hiking trails, bikeways, riding trails, or public boat camps is essential to an adequate parks system. This includes linear parks such as protected land around natural bodies of water or scenic parkways. Water-based parks include publicly owned land, some of which may be developed in recreational facilities, as well as private land on which little or no development is permitted. The scenic parkway is essentially an elongated park with a roadway extending throughout its length which connects units within the park system and provides a pleasant means of travel within the city. The parkway effect may be created by the acquisition of adequate right-of-way [generally 200 to 300 ft (61 to 92 m) in width] and through appropriate landscape design.

Environmentally sensitive or unique areas are protected by the establishment of preserves or parks. Beaches, wetlands, unique natural habitats, mountains, and forests are among the areas often preserved in this way. Such areas can be made available for study and limited recreational use with careful planning. Special attention must be given to the design and treatment of public use areas, to avoid destruction of fragile soils and other environmentally sensitive natural features. Activity, access, and program design can permit general public interpretation of unusual environments and provide unique opportunities for

Activity	Recommended Space Requirements	Recommended Size and Dimensions	Recommended Orientation	Number of Units per Population	Service Radius	Location Notes
Badminton	1620 sq ft	Singles 17 ft × 44 ft Doubles 20 ft × 44 ft with 5 ft unobstructed area on all sides.	Long axis north-south.	1 per 5000	¼ to ½ mile	Usually in school, recreation center, or church facility. Safe walking or bike access.
Basketball: Youth High School Collegiate	2400–3036 sq ft 5040–7280 sq ft 5600–7980 sq ft	46–50 ft × 84 ft 50 ft × 84 ft 50 ft × 94 ft with 5 ft unobstructed space on all sides	Long axis north-south.	1 per 5000	¼ to ½ mile	Same as badminton. Outdoor courts in neighborhood and community parks, plus active recreation areas in other park settings.
Handball (3–4 wall)	800 sq ft for 4-wall. 1000 sq ft for 3-wall	20 ft × 40 ft. Minimum of 10 ft to rear of 3-wall court. Minimum of 20 ft overhead clearance.	Long axis north-south, front wall at north end.	1 per 20,000	15–30 min travel time	4-wall usually indoor as part of multipurpose facility. 3-wall usually outdoor in park or school setting.
Ice Hockey	22,000 sq ft including support area.	Rink 85 ft × 200 ft (minimum 85 ft × 185 ft). Additional 5000 sq ft support area.	Long axis north-south if outdoor.	Indoor, 1 per 100,000 Outdoor, depends on climate.	½ to 1 hr travel	Climate important consideration affecting number of units. Best as part of multipurpose facility.
Tennis	Minimum of 7200 sq ft single court (2 acres for complex)	36 ft × 78 ft. 12 ft clearance on both sides; 21 ft clearance on both ends.	Long axis north-south.	1 court per 2000.	¼ to ½ mile	Best in batteries of 2 to 4. Located in neighborhood–community park or adjacent to school site.

	Size	Dimensions	Orientation	Number of units per population	Service radius	Location notes
Volleyball	Minimum of 4000 sq ft	30 ft × 60 ft. Minimum 6 ft clearance on all sides.	Long axis north-south.	1 court per 5000.	¼ to ½ mile	Same as other court activities (e.g., badminton, basketball, etc.)
Baseball: Official	3.0–3.85 acres minimum	Baselines 90 ft. Pitching distance 60½ ft. Foul lines-min. 320 ft. Center field 400+ ft.	Locate home plate so pitcher throwing across sun and batter not facing it. Line from home plate through pitcher's mound run east-northeast.	1 per 5000 / Lighted, 1 per 30,000	¼ to ½ mile	Part of neighborhood complex. Lighted fields part of community complex
Little League	1.2 acres minimum	Baselines 60 ft. Pitching distance 46 ft. Foul lines 200 ft. Center field 200–250 ft.				
Field Hockey	Minimum 1.5 acres	180 ft × 300 ft with a minimum of 10 ft clearance on all sides.	Fall season, long axis northwest to southeast. For longer periods, north to south.	1 per 20,000	15–30 min travel time	Usually part of baseball, football, soccer complex in community park or adjacent to high school.
Football	Minimum 1.5 acres	160 ft × 360 ft with a minimum of 6 ft clearance on all sides.	Same as field hockey.	1 per 20,000	15–30 min travel time	Same as field hockey.

Fig. 13-5 NRPA suggested facility development standards (Reprinted with permission of the National Recreation and Park Association)

Activity	Recommended Space Requirements	Recommended Size and Dimensions	Recommended Orientation	Number of Units per Population	Service Radius	Location Notes
Soccer	1.7 to 2.1 acres	195 ft to 225 ft × 300 ft to 360 ft with a 10 ft minimum clearance on all sides.	Same as field hockey.	1 per 10,000	1–2 miles	Number of units depends on popularity. Youth soccer on smaller fields adjacent to schools or neighborhood parks.
Golf driving range	13.5 acres for minimum of 25 tees	900 ft × 690 ft wide. Add 12 ft width for each additional tee.	Long axis south-west-northeast, with golfer driving toward northeast.	1 per 50,000	30 min travel	Part of golf course complex. As a separate unit, may be privately operated.
¼-mile Running track	4.3 acres	Overall width 276 ft; length 600.02 ft. Track width for 8 to 4 lanes is 32 ft.	Long axis in sector from north to south to northwest-southeast with finish line at northerly end.	1 per 20,000	15 to 30 min travel time	Usually part of high school, or in community park complex in combination with football, soccer, etc.
Softball	1.5 to 2.0 acres	Baselines 60 ft. Pitching distance 46 ft (men), 40 ft (women). Fast pitch field radius from plate 225 ft between foul lines. Slow pitch 275 ft (men), 250 ft (women).	Same as baseball.	1 per 5000 (if also used for youth baseball)	¼ to ½ mile	Slight difference in dimensions for 16 ft slow pitch. May also be used for youth baseball.

Multiple recreation court (basketball, volleyball, tennis)	9840 sq ft	120 ft × 80 ft	Long axis of courts with primary use is north-south.	1 per 10,000	1 to 2 miles.	
Trails	not applicable	Well defined head maximum 10 ft width, maximum average grade 5% not to exceed 15%. Capacity, rural trails 40 hikers/day/mile; urban trails 90 hikers/day/mile.	not applicable	1 system per region	not applicable	
Archery	Minimum 0.65 acres	300 ft length × minimum 10 ft wide between targets. Roped clear space on sides of range minimum of 30 ft, clear space behind targets minimum of 90 ft × 45 ft with bunker.	Archer facing north + or − 45°.	1 per 50,000	30 min travel	Part of a regional/metro park complex.

Fig. 13-5 (continued)

Activity	Recommended Space Requirements	Recommended Size and Dimensions	Recommended Orientation	Number of Units per Population	Service Radius	Location Notes
Combination skeet-trap field (8 station)	Minimum 30 acres	All walks and structures occur within an area approximately 130 ft wide by 115 ft deep. Minimum cleared area is contained within two superimposed segments with 10-yd radii (4 acres). Shotfall danger zone is contained within two superimposed segments with 300-yd radii (36 acres.)	Center line of length runs northeast-southwest with shooter facing northeast.	1 per 50,000	30 min travel	Part of a regional/metro park complex.
Golf						
Par 3 (18-hole)	50 to 60 acres	Average length— varies, 600 to 2700 yd	Majority of holes on north-south axis.	—	½ to 1 hr travel	9-hole course can accommodate 350 people per day.
9-hole standard	Minimum 50 acres	Average length, 2250 yd		1 per 25,000		18-hole course can accommodate 500 to 550 people per day.
18-hole standard	Minimum 110 acres	Average length, 6500 yd		1 per 50,000		Course may be located in community or dis-

Swimming pools	Varies on size of pool and amenities. Usually ½ to 2 acres site.	Teaching: minimum of 25 yd × 45 ft even depth of 3 to 4 ft. Competitive: minimum of 25 m × 16 m. Minimum of 27 sq ft of water surface per swimmer. Ratios of 2:1 deck vs. water.	None, although care must be taken in siting of lifeguard stations in relation to afternoon sun.	1 per 20,000 (pools should accommodate 3% to 5% of total population at a time).	15 to 30 min travel	trict park, but should not be over 20 miles from population center. Pools for general community use should be planned for teaching, competitive, and recreational purposes with enough depth (3.4 m) to accommodate 1-m and 3-m diving boards. Located in community park or school site.
Beach areas	not applicable	Beach area should have 50 sq ft of land and 50 sq ft of water per user. Turnover rate is 3. There should be 3 to 4 acres supporting land per acre of beach.	not applicable	not applicable	not applicable	Should have sand bottom with slope a maximum of 5% (flat preferable). Boating areas completely segregated from swimming areas.

Notes: 1 ft = 0.305 m; 1 sq ft = 0.093 sq m; 1 acre = 0.405 hectare.

Fig. 13-5 (continued)

research. The overriding concern in any development of such areas is, however, preservation of irreplaceable natural resources.

Figure 13-6 shows a visitor contact station at the Great Dismal Swamp, which is located in Virginia and North Carolina. A plan prepared for this national wildlife refuge will allow limited public use for recreation and education while avoiding destruction of fragile soils, wetlands, and other environmentally sensitive natural features.

13.5 SELECTION OF SITES

The needs analysis and equity model (or geographic distribution analysis) of the policy plan indicate general locations where parks and recreation facilities are needed and the class or type of facility required. The possible location for resource-oriented parks and recreation areas will be largely dictated by natural features such as rivers, lakes, steep slopes, and existing undeveloped land. An areawide land capability analysis should serve as the basis for this determination. Such an analysis generally would be undertaken as part of a comprehensive land use plan. Rather than duplicate effort, the recreation planner (most likely the parks and recreation agency) should utilize any existing land analyses done by local or regional planning agencies.

13.5.1 Land Capability Analysis

If no existing analysis is available for the planning area, then the park and open space planning effort should include a land capability or suitability analysis. Very little, if any, original data collection should be required; the U.S. Geological Survey, Soil Conservation Service, and various local, regional, state, and federal agencies collect and map the kind of data that will be needed. Maps and descriptions should include the following (12):

    1. Surface water resources: streams, lakes, rivers, ponds, and coastline areas; hydrology and drainage.
    2. Land resources: topography, including steep slopes, flood plains, forests, soils, minerals resources, flora and fauna.
    3. Water-related resources: wetlands, ground-water supplies, water table, aquifers.
    4. Air: air quality, climatic patterns, prevailing winds.

The information can be mapped as a series of overlays or electronically combined using computer graphics techniques, yielding a composite map which indicates areas appropriately conserved as open space or developed into parks.

McHarg (22) has pioneered the use of land suitability analysis as a basis for land use decisions. In his study of Staten Island, New York, the

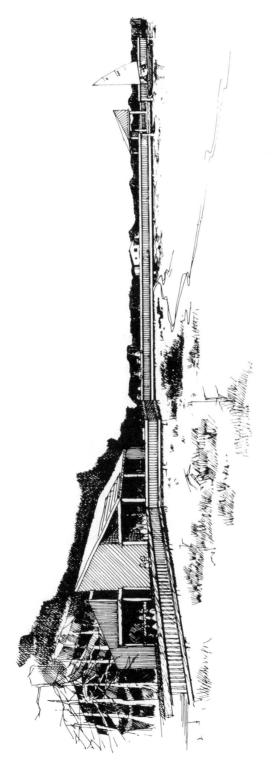

LAKE DRUMMOND VISITOR CONTACT STATION

Fig. 13-6 Lake Drummond visitor contract station and pier, Great Dismal Swamp

factors he selected as most suitable for passive and active recreation were:

Passive. Unique physiographic features; scenic water features, streams; features of historic value; high-quality forests; high-quality marshes; scenic land features; scenic cultural features; unique geologic features; scarce ecological associations; water-associated wildlife habitats; and field and forest wildlife habitats.

Active. Bay beaches; expanse of water for pleasure craft; fresh water areas; riparian land; flat land; and existing and potential recreation areas.

Each region will, of course, have its own unique resources. Furthermore, the same feature will have different perceptual impact in different areas, given different settings, climates, and the rarity or contrast of that feature with the over-all landscape.

Generally, potential sites should be selected according to the needs analysis and land capability or suitability analysis. The next step is preparing the master plan for the individual site.

13.6 PREPARING THE MASTER PLAN

The plan for a given site typically includes several levels of plans: master plan (sometimes called a concept plan), site plan, construction plans, planting plan, the programming plan, and operations and maintenance plans.

13.6.1 Site Analysis

The first step in preparing the master plan is analysis of the site. This can utilize information from the land capability analysis done for the planning area, carried out in greater detail as needed.

The potential of an area to be a recreation facility or park is based on a number of resource characteristics that must be carefully evaluated. Evaluation requires gathering data, obtaining existing information from maps and reports, and site inspections of the proposed recreation area. Such data could include the location of, and information about, particular on-site factors such as the following.

Elements of the built environment

- Legal and physical boundaries, private holdings, and public easements
- Buildings, bridges, and other structures, including those of historical and archeological significance
- Road, paths, and sidewalks, both on and adjacent to the site
- Availability of public transit
- Electric lines, water, sewer, and gas mains
- Land use: residential, commercial, industrial, and others

- Applicable ordinances, such as zoning regulations and health codes.

Natural resources

- Topography, including high and low points, slope gradients, and drainage patterns
- Soil types and characteristics including ground surface permeability, percolation, stability, and fertility
- Water bodies, including permanence, level fluctuations, and other characteristics
- Subsurface geology, including existence of commercially or functionally valuable material (e.g., sand, gravel, water)
- Vegetation types: indigenous and adaptive specimens.

Natural forces These include both macroclimactic and microclimactic characteristics.

- Temperature: day, night, and seasonal norms, extremes and their durations
- Sun angles during various seasons and times of the day
- Wind directions and intensities as they occur seasonally and daily
- Precipitation: rain and snow, seasons and accumulations, as well as storm frequencies and intensities.

Perceptual elements

- Significant views into and out from the site
- Sounds, smells and their sources
- Spatial patterns involving the specific site
- Esthetic value of lines, forms, textures, colors, and scales which give the site its peculiar character
- Over-all image of the site.

The planner should also accumulate information beyond the site boundaries and consider the important off-site elements and relationships which may influence the purpose and function of the park. Analysis of the various perceptual, natural and built environment characteristics of the immediate off-site area should follow the format prescribed for the on-site area, although less detail may be required.

The development concept of the master plan must be fitted to the specific topographic and landscape features of the site, while maintaining the desired positions of the recreation faciles and circulation patterns. Terrain characteristics will often determine the physical constraints of the locations; each type of recreation site will have its own peculiar requirements. Vegetative and physiographic patterns should be examined in matching the plan to the site. Figures 13-7 and 13-8 show

MAP UNITS

$\dfrac{X}{x}$ Capital letter over small letter = canopy over understory

X Capital letter over line = understory undetermined

x Capital letter alone = canopy with sparse or absent understory

$\dfrac{XX}{xx}$ Vegetation in either canopy or understory listed from left to right in order of dominance

Ax Altered vegetation category

SYMBOLS

Needle-leaved or broad-leaved deciduous canopy-ranked by moisture tolerance from wet to dry

C Cypress

G Water tupelo and black tupelo

M Maple-dominated mixed hardwoods: maple, tupelo, and ash

Y Mixed hardwoods: yellow poplar, sweetgum, and maple

B Mesic hardwoods: beech and oak

Needle-leaved Evergreen Canopy

P Pine

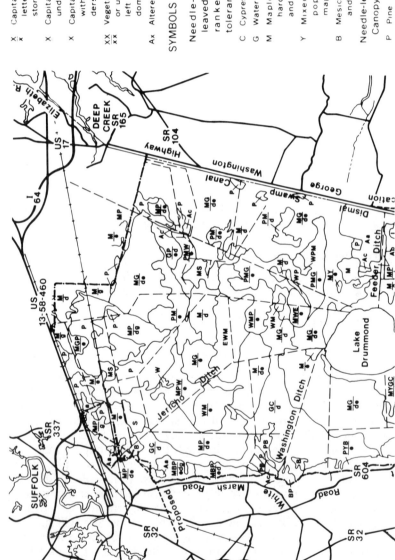

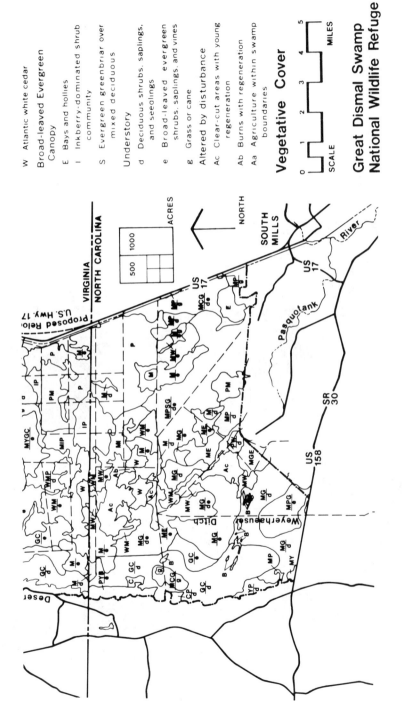

Fig. 13-7. Great Dismal Swamp—vegetative cover

LEGEND

MINERAL SOILS - Soils with Organic Layers less than 16" thick.

ORGANIC SOILS - Includes Terric Medisaprists (Organic Layers more than 16" thick but less than 51") and Typic Medisaprists (Organic Layers more than 51" thick).

SOIL SURVEYS

S   "Soil Survey, Suffolk, Va." Unpublished field survey. Jerry S. Quesenberry, Soil Scientist, U.S. Department of Agriculture, Soil Conservation Service, 1977.

N   "Soil Survey, Norfolk County, Virginia," 1953. U. S. Department of Agriculture, Soil Conservation Service.

NR   "Soil Survey, Norfolk County, Virginia," 1953, with partial revisions, principally to organic soils, from an "in-progress" revision of this Survey by Jerry S.

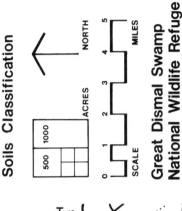

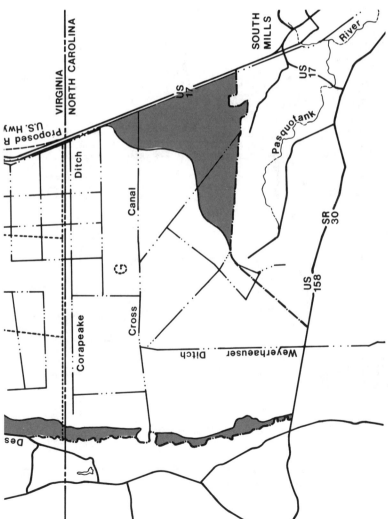

Fig. 13-8. Great Dismal Swamp—soils classification

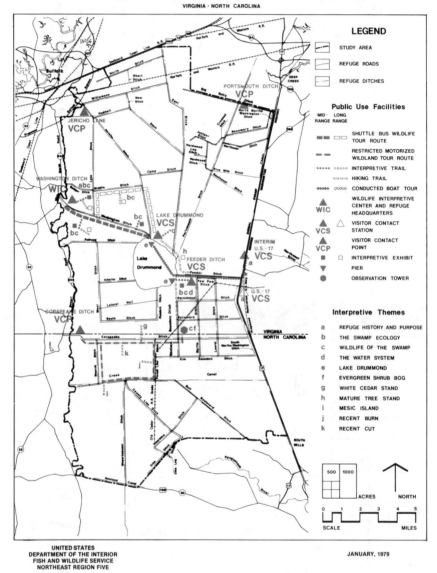

Fig. 13-9. Great Dismal Swamp development plan

two of several overlays prepared for the Great Dismal Swamp plan to characterize the natural features of the site.

13.6.2 Components of the Master Plan

The master plan delineates the essential organization of the park: the types of uses and facilities (if any) to be provided; circulation movements; and major spatial relationships, such as park to surrounding areas, use areas to site, different use areas to each other, and major structures to use area. The master plan will require a narrative description and plans, typically drawn at a fairly small scale (e.g., 1 in. = 100 ft or 1 in. = 200 ft). At such a scale, the entire site can be displayed on one sheet, showing the over-all concept but limiting the detail that can be shown. The master plan is the initial statement of facility intent and should illustrate the interrelationships that affect design decisions. The plan should show how all the individual components of the recreation plan will fit together and complement one another. The master plan may also include a phasing plan if budgetary constraints prohibit the immediate total construction of a project. By showing both the existing and proposed developments at any given stage, the master plan can be continually updated. Changes in recreation demand that occur during the interim period of design and construction can thus be charted and analyzed. The development plan for Great Dismal Swamp is shown in Fig. 13-9. The type and level of detail is typical of master plans.

The more explicit design features are indicated on the site plan. This plan is usually drawn at a larger scale (e.g., 1 in. = 20 ft or 1 in. = 50 ft). This allows the planner or designer to illustrate more precisely the esthetic character, spatial relationships, and location of various minor components of the park. The site plan brings the park designer closer to actual construction through the use of more precise graphics, and pinpoints locations of facilities, equipment, major landscaping features, paths and roads.

The construction plans and specifications spell out exactly what equipment is to be installed, measurements, structural details, and appropriate calculations. This is the guide which assures that the final product will implement the concept plan.

The site plan should also include a planting plan, a type of construction plan that should be produced by a landscape architect as a guide for the selection and location of plant material.

The programming and operation and maintenance plans translate the physical improvements in the master plan into potential recreation experience by users. This may include summer day camp programs for children, adult craft classes at a recreation center, softball leagues, nature study center staffing, and any number of programs necessary to make full use of a site. The operation and maintenance plan is the nuts-and-bolts guide to running the recreation facility or park and related facilities.

Each of these plan types (most notably the master plan) may be supplemented by certain schematic plans that represent primary spatial networks, circulation patterns, maintenance programs, or any other elements that the planner or designer feels would enhance the over-all effectiveness of the project. Schematic plans are often presented as reinforcement for verbal or written reports which provide an explanation of the plan. A brief outline follows of the components of a "complete" set of park (or recreation facility) plans.

Master plan.   The master plan contains:

   1. Over-all design scheme.
   2. Type and placement of all facilities without layout details.
   3. Road location and stationing.
   4. Survey information (horizontal and vertical control, baselines, etc.).
   5. Proximity-location map.
   6. Orientation, scale, legend.
   7. Aerial photo coverage (usually for larger parks).

Site plan.   A surveyed and plotted map, the site plan contains:

   1. Lot lines, easements and property ownership.
   2. Permanently established ground control (survey baselines, etc.).
   3. Contour lines [interval of 1 ft or 2 ft (0.3 or 0.61 m)].
   4. Map scale.
   5. Features, including surface and subsurface hydrology (lakes and streams, as well as flow direction and critical high water marks); existing vegetation and proposed plantings; existing structures (both on-site and off-site) that may influence park design; existing and proposed utilities; and proposed structures or other features to be constructed.

13.7 IMPLEMENTATION STRATEGIES

Many new techniques have been developed in recent years for assuring adequate open space and implementing parks and recreation plans. In addition to traditional public parks acquisition, metropolitan areas have been preserving sensitive and unique natural areas through development restrictions, leaseback and saleback arrangements, easements, and requirements that open space can be set aside in subdivision and commercial development. There are three major categories of techniques: acquisition, regulation, and taxation (12).

13.7.1 Public Acquisition

Ownership of land, either outright or via easements, provides the greatest control over its use and is essential when further expenditures (such as for recreation facilities) are to be made on the site. Land may be acquired for public open space and recreation facilities through donation, condemnation, or purchase. Donation is often used as a way of

obtaining park or future school sites within a new subdivision; a requirement of a certain number of acres per unit or per capita projected
population may be incorporated into subdivision regulations. Donation
is also utilized for park acquisition where the owner is willing to part
with the land for the tax benefits. Condemnation has been upheld in the
courts as legal so long as a public purpose is served. While condemnation is at times unpopular, it may be necessary where a chosen site is
held by several different landowners, or where the site location is
dictated by a natural feature and the owner is unwilling to sell.

Leasebacks and salebacks   Using leaseback and saleback techniques, a
public body acquires the property and leases it or sells it to private
individuals or organizations with use restrictions. In this way, farmland
can be preserved as such and recreational use can be assured with less
investment of public funds.

Easements   An easement is a right or set of rights that is purchased
from the owner, or it may be a set of restrictions on the uses which the
owner is permitted. Easements are effective when full ownership of the
land is unnecessary or too costly an option. Positive easements are
typically used to create bikeways, hiking trails, or public access to bodies
of water for swimming, fishing, and boating. Conservation easements
are negative easements whereby the owner is compensated for limiting
the use of his land to farming, forestry, or other undeveloped use. Scenic
easements have been used in several communities to achieve local goals.
For example, in Prince George's County, Maryland, scenic easements
have been granted to land along the Potomac River in order to assure a
rural view from Mount Vernon (12, p. 200). Scenic easements can also be
used to create scenic parkways along public roads.

13.7.2 Regulation

Regulation is used by local government to achieve open space
goals, along with other land use goals. The primary types of regulation
are zoning, subdivision regulation, site plan review, and the official
map.

Zoning   Zoning ordinances can incorporate provisions to achieve open
space objectives. The primary zoning classifiactions used to obtain open
space are residential cluster zones, planned development zones, and
natural resource zones such as floodplain, agricultural, and forest classifications. The cluster and planned development zones allow a developer to build at higher densities in sections of a project, while providing
public open space which keeps the total development density lower.
Figure 13-10 shows a planned unit development where an open space
system is incorporated throughout the single-family portion of the
development.

Natural resource zoning restricts the development of any land

PLAINVIEW

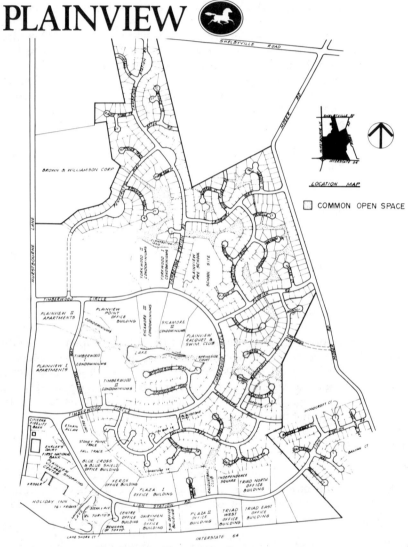

Fig. 13-10. Planned unit development

designated in these zones. Used alone, it is not very effective in preventing urbanization where significant development pressures exist. Floodplain zoning is an exception to this, largely due to federal restrictions on floodplain development.

Subdivision regulation   Subdivision regulations can fulfill similar purposes to cluster and planned development zoning. Typically, a developer is required to contribute land or pay a fee in lieu thereof for parks or open space. Such a contribution is called an exaction. An alternative to the exaction is the impact fee, whereby a per unit charge is made for use of public facilities. Impact fees are most often used to finance water and sewer extensions, but have been applied for the use of public parks and recreational areas.

In order to utilize exactions or impact fees, the municipality must be authorized to do so by state statutes. The state courts have varied considerably in how specific an authorization is required. A municipality would be well advised to rely on its legal department when instituting such requirements.

Exactions. Many exaction requirements were (and continue to be) based on a flat percentage of the subdivision's land, such as 7% or 10% of gross area to be donated for public open space (or the equivalent value in cash). This has been struck down by the courts in some states as an unconstitutional taking of private property, since a flat percentage bears no relationship to the need for facilities created by that development. Elsewhere, notably in California, courts have ruled that exactions can be required even if the need for the land for recreation facilities is not due to the development in question but to the general public need.

The predominant position in the courts in 1985 is that exactions and in lieu fees must bear a relationship to the needs created by the subdivision. A developer should pay for the proportion of a facility for which that subdivision created the need (26).

Impact fees. Impact fees differ from in lieu of land exaction payments in that they are imposed outside the subdivision regulatory process, and so can be applied to condominium, apartment, and commercial facilities or previously platted subdivisions. While there is considerable variation from state to state, generally speaking, a successful (legal) impact fee will bear some reasonble relationship to the burden a new development places on public facilities.

Broward County, Florida, has developed an exaction and impact fee system which includes contributions for both regional and local parks. Figure 13-11 shows a methodology for designing a park impact fee system developed by that county's planning office. Figure 13-12 is a sample system of formulas.

13.7.3 Taxation

Preferential tax assessment or tax deferral can be used to preserve undeveloped land. This would be particularly effective at the fringes of metropolitan areas. Tax rates are kept low, or taxes deferred, as long as the agricultural, recreational, or undeveloped use is maintained. With tax deferral systems, all deferred taxes become due when the land is developed.

13.7.4 Public Programming and Capital Budgeting

It is the purpose of the local community policy plan to establish the parks and recreation needs for both new facilities and improvements or

Analysis and Planning Phase

1. Determine current population and housing characteristics (e.g., 50,000 residents, 20,000 units, avg. residents per unit by type)
2. Project future population and housing characteristics (e.g., 100,000 residents, 40,000 units)
3. Inventory existing park and recreational facilities (e.g., 220 acres)
4. Establish reasonable park and recreational standards (e.g., 5 acres for every 1000 residents)
5. Prepare and adopt a future plan for park and recreational facilities.

Current Needs Phase

1. Determine current park needs based on existing population and standards (e.g., 50,000 residents × 5 acres/1,000 = 250 acres − 220 acres = 30 acres)
2. Determine the estimated current cost to acquire and improve parks (e.g., $30,000 per acre)
3. Determine the estimated total cost to accommodate current needs (e.g., 30 acres × $30,000 per acre = $900,000)
4. Identify revenue sources which do not come from new development to correct any current deficit (e.g., federal/state grants, special taxing districts, current funds).

Future Needs Phase

1. Determine the cost per resident to provide new park facilities (e.g., $30,000 per acre × 5 acres/1,000 = $150 per resident)
2. Determine the cost of new park facilities by type of unit.

Unit type	Residents per unit		Cost per resident, in dollars		Cost per unit, in dollars
Estate	3.3	×	150	=	495
Single family	3.0	×	150	=	450
Townhouse	2.7	×	150	=	405
Duplex	2.5	×	150	=	375
Garden apartment	2.2	×	150	=	330
High rise apartment	1.8	×	150	=	270
Mobile home	2.4	×	150	=	360

3. Draft and adopt an ordinance which requires the payment of an impact fee with the issuance of any residential building permit and provides for: schedule of specific fees based upon actual costs per unit; a Parks Trust Fund into which all collected fees are deposited; expenditure policies which insure reasonable benefits; and provisions for granting waivers when in the public interest.
4. Prepare and adopt a plan-based capital improvements program for parks and recreational facilities which incorporates both current and future needs.

Fig. 13-11. How to design park impact fee system (Courtesy: AICP Workshop on Land Use Law, Broward County Planning Office, March 1984)

1. Land dedication requirement =

$$\frac{3 \text{ acres}}{1{,}000 \text{ residents}} \times \text{ units } \times \text{ density}$$

2. Fees in lieu of dedication =

> Acres required × value per acre (highest of
> assessed or appraised value)

3. Per unit impact fee =

Unit type	Size	Fee
SF, TH, villa	2 BR	$185
	3 BR	238
	4 BR+	280
Apartment	1 BR	110
	2 BR+	171
Mobile home	1 BR	129
	2 BR	169
	3 BR+	243

Fig. 13-12. Park impact fee formulas (Courtesy: AICP Workshop on Land Use Law, Broward County Planning Office, March 1984)

changes in existing facilities. In order to translate these policy directions into recreation facilities, a program for capital improvements is necessary.

A list of projects is derived from analysis of the needs assessment and resource inventory, in light of the community objectives and standards articulated in the policy plan. The projects are further detailed by geographic area, as indicated by results of the equity model, to assure that investment is directed to areas with the greatest need. Preliminary cost estimates are made for any proposed improvements or new acquisitions. The projects are then assigned priorities with respect to urgency and timing. The recreation agency's schedule of capital improvements is incorporated into the over-all capital improvements program of the community.

The recreation agency should also establish a programming plan, delineating recreation programs for different age groups and facilities such as summer recreation programs, swimming leagues, adult classes, and other activities desired by the community. Particularly for new programs, this may be a phased plan indicating in which year funds will be needed for proposed programs.

13.8 REFERENCES AND BIBLIOGRAPHY

1. Banks, H.P., and Mahler, S. "Users of Local Parks," *Journal of the American Institute of Planners*, Vol. 36, No. 5, September 1970.
2. Behnke, W. A. and Associates, *Cleveland Parks and Recreation Study*, 1976.
3. Buechner, R.D., ed., *National Park Recreation and Open Space Standards*, National Recreation and Park Association, Washington, D.C., 1971.
4. Clawson, M. and Knetsch, J. L., *Economics of Outdoor Recreation*, The John Hopkins Press, Baltimore, Md., 1966.
5. Dee, N. and Liebman, J. C. "Optimal Location of Public Facilities," *Naval Research Logistics Quarterly*, Vol. 19, No. 4, 1972.
6. Eathorne, R.H., "Evaluating the Efficiency of Urban Recreation Services: The Investigation of Use Versus Non-use," presented at the annual meeting of the Association of American Geographers, Louisville, Kentucky, 1980.
7. Fogg, G.E., *Park Planning Guidelines Revised*, National Recreation and Park Association, Washington, D.C., 1981.
8. Gold, S.M., *Recreation Planning and Design*, McGraw-Hill Book Co., Inc., New York, 1980.
9. Gold, S.M., *Urban Recreation Planning*, Lea and Febiger, Philadelphia, Pa., 1973.
10. Gold, S.M., "Nonuse of Neighborhood Parks," *Journal of the American Institute of Planners*, Vol. 38, No. 5, November 1972.
11. Goodall, B., *The Economics of Urban Areas*, Pergamon Press, New York, 1972.
12. Goodman, W.I., and Freund, E.C., eds., *Principles and Practice of Urban Planning*, International City Managers' Association, Washington, D.C., 1978.
13. Guggenheimer, E.C., *Planning for Parks and Recreation Needs in Urban Areas*, Twayne Publishers, Inc., New York, 1969.
14. Holman, M.A., "A National Time-Budget for the Year 2000," *Sociology and Social Research*, Vol. 46, No. 1, October 1961.
15. Jensen, C.R., *Outdoor Recreation Planning*, W. B. Saunders Co., Philadelphia, Pa., 1976.
16. Jubenville, A. *Outdoor Recreation Planning*, W. B. Saunders Co., Philadelphia, Pa., 1976.
17. Knudson, D.M., *Outdoor Recreation*, Macmillan Publishing Co., New York, 1980, p. 170.
18. Lancaster, R.A., ed., *Recreation, Park and Open Space Standards and Guidelines*, National Recreation and Park Association, Washington, D.C., 1983.
19. Lavery, P., ed., *Recreational Geography*, John Wiley and Sons, New York, 1974.
20. Louisville and Jefferson County Planning Commission, *Urban Parks and Recreation Recovery Master Action Plan*, Louisville, Ky., 1982.
21. Lovingood, P.E., Jr., and Mitchell, L. S., "The Structure of Public and Private Recreational Systems: Columbia, South Carolina," *Journal of Leisure Research*, Vol. 10, No. 1, 1978.
22. McHarg, I. L., *Design with Nature*, Doubleday/Natural History Press, Garden City, N.Y., 1971.
23. Moskowitz, H.S., and Lindbloom, C.G., *The Illustrated Book of Development Definitions*, Center for Urban Policy Research, Piscataway, N.J., 1981, pp. 137, 139, 153.
24. Mumford, L. *The City in History*, Harcourt, Brace & World, Inc., New York, 1961.

25. Reed, D.J., and Perdue, R.R., *Park Planning and Design: An Evaluation Approach*, National Recreation and Park Association, Washington, D.C., 1979.
26. Richards, S.L., and Merriam, D.H., "Land Dedications, In Lieu of Fees and Impact Fees: When are they Legal," paper prepared for the American Planning Association Workshop on Land Use Law for Planners and Lawyers, Louisville, Ky., March 1984.
27. Rutledge, A.J., *Anatomy of a Park*, McGraw-Hill Book Co., Inc., New York, 1971.
28. Shivers, J.S., and Halper, J.W. *The Crisis in Urban Recreational Services*, Associated University Presses, Inc., East Brunswick, N.J., 1981.
29. Staley, E.J., "Determining Neighborhoood Recreation Priorities: An Instrument," *Journal of Leisure Research*, Vol. 1, No. 1, 1969.
30. Steiss, A.W., *Models for the Analysis and Planning of Urban Systems*, Heath and Co., Lexington, Mass., 1974.
31. Theobald, W.F., "Recreation Resources Planning: An Analysis of Traditional and Contemporary Approaches, and a Conceptual Framework for Use in Urban Planning," dissertation presented to Columbia University, New York, in 1971, in partial fulfillment of the requirements for the degree of Doctor of Philosophy.
32. U.S. Army, *Planning and Design of Outdoor Recreation Facilities*, U.S. Government Printing Office, Washington, D.C., 1975.
33. U.S. Department of the Interior, *Cutback Management: Rational Approaches to Weathering Budget Reductions for the Park and Recreation Administrator*, U.S. Government Printing Office, Washington, D.C., 1982.
34. U.S. Department of the Interior, *Evaluation of Public Willingness to Pay User Charges for Use of Outdoor Recreation Areas and Facilities*, U.S. Government Printing Office, Washington, D.C., 1976.
35. U.S. Department of the Interior, *National Urban Recreation Study—Executive Report*, U.S. Government Printing Office, Washington, D.C., 1978.
36. Young, R. C., "Goals and Goal Setting," *Journal of the American Institute of Planners*, Vol. 32, No. 2, March 1966.

CHAPTER 14

PLANNING FOR WASTEWATER COLLECTION AND TREATMENT[a]

14.1 INTRODUCTION

Until the end of the 19th century, raw sewage discharged from cities and communities in the United States was absorbed into the water environment and eventually purified through natural processes. In highly populated areas, wastewater concentrations were so high that the streams, rivers and estuaries adjacent to municipalities often emitted undesirable odors due to prevalent anaerobic conditions. The natural processes worked well only where the receiving lakes, rivers, seas and oceans had a very large dilution capacity compared to the small volume of effluent discharged. In today's environment, such favorable aquatic conditions are almost impossible to find in any area with significantly large population. Thus, additional, controlled treatment of wastewater is almost invariably required.

During the same period in which urban areas began to employ municipal treatment facilities, rural areas switched for much of their sanitation needs from using commodes and outhouses to disposing of waterborne wastes in cesspools (individual rock-lined seepage pits). The sophistication of these on-site facilities resulted in the septic tank and tile field systems which we use today. Location and effectiveness of early cesspools were erratic, and many areas without knowledgeable sanitarians risked possible contamination of well supplies. The design, siting, and construction of on-site sewage disposal has improved over the years, reducing the health hazard in rural areas due to waterborne disease (14).

Wastewater is most often defined as "spent water." It is a combination of the liquid and water-carried wastes generated by residences, commercial buildings, industrial plants and institutions, together with any ground water, surface water and storm water that may be present. These liquid wastes are collected and transported via sanitary, storm, or combined sewer systems from their origin to wastewater facilities for treatment and ultimate discharge or disposal (1, 2). Various types of treatment processes are described later in this chapter.

Ultimately, wastewater collected from cities and towns must be returned to our land and waters. To minimize the impact of human and industrial wastes on our environment, it is necessary to balance both the

---

[a]Prepared by Paul T. Carver, M. ASCE, Vice President, and A. Ruth Fitzgerald, Affiliate, Vice President, CE Maguire, Inc., New Britain, CT.

loads and load receiving capacity at reasonable levels. Therefore, wastewater characteristics must be identified and quantified.

Planning for wastewater collection and disposal requires consideration of the following (13):

1. Wastewater volumes and strength.
2. Location, type, and sizing of collection system.
3. Location and type of treatment facility.
4. Disposal of liquid effluent and solid wastes.

The ultimate disposal of treated wastewater and resulting sludge (concentrated contaminants removed by treatment) is one of the most difficult and costly problems in the field of wastewater engineering. Ultimate disposal of wastewater effluents can occur by assimilation into receiving waters, discharge onto land, evaporation, or seepage into the ground. Disposal by assimilation (after treatment) into lakes, rivers, estuaries and oceans is, by far, the most common method (8). Treatment of the waste remaining in the effluent continues in these waters by natural biological and physical means until these constituents are reduced to their most basic forms before starting their life cycle again.

The disposal of wastewater contaminants removed or converted by various processes into sludge is more difficult to accomplish now than in years past. This is due partly to more complex industrial base and waste sources in the United States, and partly to the fact that economic pressures have relegated disposal of wastes to a low priority in terms of land use planning.

The purpose of wastewater planning is to balance the varying environmental loads created by man's wastewaters, including treatment, costs, proper disposal, and land use, with the various mitigating factors of our ecosystem.

14.2 LEGISLATIVE FRAMEWORK

As in the various other subareas of planning, the planning for wastewater collection and disposal is guided by a framework of legislation. This legislation is intimately connected with (and was created as a response to) water quality issues. Prior to the development of water quality guidelines, wastewater disposal was often erratically handled, occasionally resulting in severe water pollution and disposal problems. Federal legislation has not only provided guidelines and helped set more balanced standards in the field, but has also provided funding to assist local communities in meeting these requirements.

14.2.1 Federal Legislation

The basic federal law of water pollution control is contained in the Federal Water Pollution Control Act, which was adopted in 1956 (PL 83-660), but assumed its present form through a comprehensive set of amendments passed in 1972 as PL 92-500. Under the 1956 law, the U.S.

Public Health Service was charged with administration of the act. In the early 1960s, this charge was transferred to a new agency, the Federal Water Pollution Control Administration (FWPCA). The FWPCA regulated the discharges of pollutants from "point sources," primarily industrial and municipal sewage treatment plants and agricultural feedlots. Point sources are specifically identified sources such as treatment plants and industries, while nonpoint sources are general sources of pollution, such as agricultural or urban runoff. Nonpoint-source pollution is less easily controlled.

The FWPCA established separate regulatory schemes for two classes of point source discharges: (1) Discharge directly into navigable waters; and (2) discharge into publicly owned treatment works. The FWPCA provided for water quality standards and effluent standards for both existing and new sources. A federal grant program was established, initially funding 30% of the cost of constructing public wastewater facilities, including treatment plants and interceptor sewers. In the late 1960s, the Refuse Disposal Act of 1899 was reactivated, authorizing the federal government (through the U.S. Army Corps of Engineers) to establish a discharge permit program. This permitted the federal government to initiate a system regulating point discharges, which was incorporated into later water pollution control legislation as the National Pollutant Discharge Elimination System (NPDES).

The 1972 amendments to the Federal Water Pollution Control Act also established the U.S. Environmental Protection Agency (EPA) and further defined the national system of permits to control discharges by industry, municipalities and other sources of pollution. NPDES permits are issued by EPA or by states through authority delegated by EPA.

As a result of this legislation, it was possible for the first time to catalog waste discharges across the nation and to fully ascertain the serious nature of water pollution. Each permit must specify which substances may be discharged, the amounts, and a timetable for effluent quality improvements. Administration of the permitting system provides for monitoring, reporting and enforcement of penalties, and corrective action when permit violations occur. Permits are currently (1985) issued for a 5-yr period, although there is some likelihood that the permitting period will be lengthened to 10 years.

The 1972 amendments to the Federal Water Pollution Control Act authorized $5.0 billion dollars per year (for five years) for the program, to include grants and funds for regulatory agencies as well as for research and publication efforts. The most important provision, however, was an increase in federal grants to cover 75% of eligible project costs. This provision gave the needed boost to allow states and localities to earnestly tackle the problem of degradation of the nation's waters from the effects of wastewater disposal.

The stated goal of the 1972 legislation was to eliminate degrading pollutants by 1985 with an interim goal of improving all water bodies to "fishable" and "swimmable" quality by 1983. The Act also promulgated requirements for state and local authorities to develop areawide wastewater management plans and basin plans, and to establish agencies to implement the plans [Sections 201, 208, 303(e), and 305]. Section 209 required that basin plans be prepared and adopted for the entire country. This provision was intended to assure that water quality concerns be addressed within the broader context of water resources, including water supply, recreation, navigation, fish and wildlife habitat, flood hazards, and other matters.

The Clean Water Act of 1977 (PL 95-217) amended the 1972 Federal Water Pollution Control Act. The Clean Water Act continued, for another five years, the program of federal assistance for the construction of public wastewater facilities in conjunction with federal, state, and local water pollution control agencies. The funding authorization remained the same. To encourage use of innovative and alternative technology (I/A), which includes energy conservation, the 1977 law provided an additional 10% in grant funding for wastewater facilities meeting such requirements.

The Resource Conservation and Recovery Act (RCRA) of 1976 (PL 94-580) was concerned with regulating and preventing the introduction of hazardous industrial wastes into the environment. This is particularly significant to ground-water protection. In the area of wastewater treatment and collection, the act regulates contaminated sludge from treatment plants as a hazardous waste. (Certain other waste materials from wastewater treatment plants may also be classified as hazardous wastes.) Where hazardous substances are not present, municipal wastewater systems are essentially exempt from RCRA provisions.

Another important federal law related to pollution control and the provision of wastewater treatment facilities includes the National Environmental Policy Act of 1969 (NEPA). This law directs all federal agencies to develop guidelines to assure that all federal actions undergo a process of environmental evaluation. Major actions require the preparation of an environmental assessment or environmental impact statement to identify potential impacts and provide measures for their mitigation. (See Chap. 18 of this planning guide for more detailed consideration of NEPA and the environmental assessment process.)

The status of the EPA grants program as of August 1985 includes reduction in the federal share of eligible facilities from 75% to 55%, dropping combined sewer overflow (CSO) projects from eligibility (except as carryover of the 1983 and 1984 funds), and increasing grants for I/A technology from an additional 10% to an additional 20%. Lateral sewers are also excluded from eligibility by law. It is still possible to fund CSOs under Marine CSO appropriation under 201(M)2, or by exception under a Governor's discretionary provision up to 20% of a state's allocation. Lateral sewers may also be funded under a Governor's discretionary provision.

14.2.2 State and Local Legislation

States, regions and municipalities play a leading role in environmental protection, as state and local governments are on the front line of essential planning, management and enforcement. In many cases, state and regional water quality implementation plans and areawide waste treatment management plans are as important as federal rules and regulations. All state and local laws and regulations must be consistent with or comply with federal laws. States have enacted many of their water resource policies and regulations in coordination with and as a result of federal water policies. About 50% of the states have accepted delegation of NPDES permitting from EPA.

Aside from statutory regulation of water use and supply, state water pollution control management is usually accomplished by agencies which administer wastewater permits, administer and oversee water pollution regulations and grant programs, and monitor and oversee operation of wastewater facilities. Also, there are a number of federal-state commissions and interstate commissions, committees, or councils which coordinate water resources and wastewater planning and management.

Local water pollution control legislation may be implemented through a municipal department, special district, or a local, regional or county authority. This type of legislation deals primarily with creation, treatment, and disposal of storm drainage or wastewater, or both. Local water pollution control management powers are regulated by the state, requiring local or regional bodies to undertake planning, construction, operation and management of wastewater facilities.

In many ways, the most important part of an effective water pollution control program is the legislative and regulatory effort at the local community or municipal level. Local governments normally have the power to adopt ordinances for control of discharges to sewers and water bodies within their jurisdictions, and to determine the rates for user charges. Local communities also usually have control over the design, location and inspection of individual sewage-disposal systems and septic tanks, tile fields and wells, as well as plumbing and drainage installations in buildings and on private property.

14.3 WASTEWATER TREATMENT PROCESSES

While a significant portion of our population still lives in rural and semirural areas served by individual, on-site wastewater disposal systems, many of our most critical problems are experienced in cities and towns with large wastewater plants which must provide a relatively clean effluent before discharge. To plan for wastewater treatment and disposal, it is necessary to have an understanding of the various types of treatment systems that may be utilized. Treatment processes may be generally categorized as liquid or solid processes. The reader is referred to the glossary (Sec. 14.7) for a definition of the more technical terms in this section.

14.3.1 Liquid Processes

When developing planning criteria for wastewater treatment, it is necessary to consider the various wastewater treatment processes available to meet the degree of treatment required by the receiving waters. A treatment plant can be designed to accomplish as much pollutant removal as may be required, subject, of course, to cost considerations. The three recognized levels of treatment are primary, secondary, and advanced waste treatment (AWT, sometimes referred to as tertiary treatment).

Primary treatment usually results in the removal of 50% to 60% of the suspended solids (SS), and with it 25% to 35% of biochemical oxygen demand (BOD). Primary treatment alone may only be considered where the effluent will be discharged to open ocean waters through a long ocean outfall. Although the EPA has generally required secondary treatment for ocean outfall discharges, under recent legislation primary treatment alone may be permitted in certain ocean disposal projects subject to evaluation on an individual basis.

Secondary treatment, with removal of 85% to 95% of the BOD and suspended solids, is the minimum degree of treatment permitted by EPA for discharge to inland waters and streams. Advanced waste treatment generally provides effluents with greater than 95% removal of BOD and suspended solids, as well as nutrient removal. It is required where secondary treatment cannot provide the degree of treatment adequate to meet receiving water quality needs or standards.

The following process descriptions are brief to provide the planner and engineer with an overview of the various wastewater treatment processes (2, 3, 5, 9, 17).

Primary treatment   Primary treatment is the minimum practical treatment which may be applied to wastewater. It normally serves as a preliminary step for higher degrees of treatment and often consists of the following unit operations:

1. Screening: removal of coarse solids.
2. Comminution: grinding of sewage solids.
3. Grit removal: removal of grit, sand, and gravel.
4. Skimming: removal of floating solids, grease, and oils.
5. Sedimentation: removal of settleable solids.

These processes involve physical removal of wastewater substances, primarily by gravity.

Secondary treatment   Secondary treatment may be accomplished by a variety of different processes, but is generally classified as either a biological treatment process or a physical chemical treatment process.

Biological Treatment.   Biological treatment of sewage consists of bringing the effluent, normally from primary treatment, into contact with a mass of active biological microorganisms. (However, many plants operate without primary sedimentation prior to the biological treatment. One well-known example is the Miami, Florida treatment plant.)

The method of contacting the sewage with the organisms, or biomass, provides for three major types of biological treatment: (1) Activated sludge; (2) biological contactors (i.e., trickling filter, rotating biological disk, etc.); and (3) aerobic stabilization ponds. The activated sludge process is used in both large cities and small communities. Biological contactors are more frequently used in smaller cities and towns, while aerobic stabilization ponds are best utilized in small towns where a large amount of land is available.

Physical Chemical Treatment. The physical chemical process for secondary treatment may consist of primary treatment followed by a chemical coagulation-sedimentation process and mixed media filtration. The sewage might then be introduced into a reactor-clarifier where a coagulating chemical is introduced and mixed with the sewage. The mixture is agitated to form a floc to increase settling efficiency. It then settles in the clarifier area where it is collected as sludge. The effluent may then flow to a series of mixed media filters where further substances are removed from the wastewater prior to discharge of the effluent.

Physical chemical treatment plants often are best utilized where toxic wastes are present which inhibit biological treatment. (Physical chemical treatment is also used as a polishing process in AWT facilities.) In order to be economically competitive with biological processes, the coagulating chemical should be recoverable.

Advanced waste treatment AWT unit processes are considered to be a step advanced from the secondary treatment process. They are needed where removal of 95% or more of BOD and suspended solids, as well as removal of phosphorous or nitrogen nutrients, are required. Several individual processes are available which can be broken down into three major categories: biological, physical chemical, and biochemical.

14.3.2 Solids (Sludge) Processes

The solids removed by the liquid treatment processes include grit, screenings, primary sludge, secondary sludge, and chemical sludge from physical chemical treatment plants. The problems of dealing with sludge are complicated by the fact that it contains those materials that make raw sewage offensive and sometimes toxic. Most of the sludge is water. Therefore, an important facet of sludge disposal operations is the reduction of the water and organic content of the sludge.

The basic operations used in sludge processing may be subdivided into the following categories: concentration, digestion, conditioning, dewatering and drying, incineration, wet oxidation, sludge and ash disposal. Many of these processes may be used alone or in conjunction with other processes.

The solids removed as sludge from wastewater are concentrated, stabilized, and reduced in volume in preparation for final disposal. The method of final disposal determines the type of stabilization and the amount of volume reduction required. Land disposal and ocean disposal are both utilized to varying degrees for the ultimate disposal of wastewater solids.

The most frequently used methods of land disposal are land application and landfill disposal (9, 12, 18). Land application involves spreading the sludge on soil for full utilization as a soil conditioner or fertilizer. In some cases, use as a fertilizer may require further processing and drying before application. A sanitary sludge landfill may also be used for the ultimate disposal of sludge, grease and grit. With daily coverage of newly deposited wastes, nuisance conditions, such as odors and flies, can be minimized.

Ocean disposal of sludge has been utilized over the years by some large coastal cities. Sludge is transported by barge and released at the surface, resulting in widespread distribution prior to ultimate disposition on the ocean floor. This practice is generally not desirable as a long-term solution for sludge disposal due to long-term environmental impacts on the ocean. For such a disposal system, the marine areas should undergo in-depth predisposal environmental inventory and analysis, as well as long-term careful monitoring of all potential environmental impacts.

As an example of problems with ocean disposal, some of the municipalities in the greater New York metropolitan area have barged their sludge (and other waste) in the New York bight area for decades. The method and location of sludge disposal have resulted in significant areas in the inner continental shelf becoming entirely devoid of benthic species, and pelagic species throughout the bight have been greatly reduced. Under certain conditions, the sludge deposits are carried toward the shore and have been observed on both western Long Island and northern New Jersey beaches. Large parts of the bight have become so severely degraded that the entire area is currently the subject of intensive study by a number of environmental agencies and marine laboratories.

14.4 WASTEWATER PLANNING

A comprehensive plan for any wastewater project is requisite for the orderly and efficient development of collection, treatment and disposal facilities to meet the needs of the community at present and in the future. Comprehensive planning takes into account the physical, social, economic, environmental and related characteristics of an area, and evaluates various alternative plans for meeting identified needs (6).

Comprehensive wastewater planning for a particular community should consider past, current and projected community growth; existing sewerage facilities; the projection of sewerage needs; the development and evaluation of alternative ways to meet those needs; the recommendation of alternatives; and development of an implementation program, including costs, scheduling and financing aspects.

In a typical community, the planning process may proceed as follows. Due to growth, outdated facilities, or pollution problems, the community perceives a need and makes a decision to plan for improved or expanded wastewater handling. A facility plan is prepared under EPA guidelines. This plan documents existing conditions, projects future flows (need), and proposes and evaluates alternatives. Following input from the community, an alternative is selected and an implementation program prepared. The selected alternative must undergo the environmental process to evaluate potential impacts and identify ways to lessen them. When the environmental document has been accepted, a grant application can be prepared and local and other nonfederal monies committed. Receipt of the grant will be followed by construction and operation of the new or expanded facilities. This abbreviated example illustrates the general flow of events.

In order to plan properly for a wastewater facilities project, it is important to understand a community's needs, what it wants, what it can afford, and what is technically possible. The planning process is intended to shed light on these questions and generally consists of the following steps:

1. Problem identification.
2. Development of goals and objectives.
3. Data collection and analysis.
4. Forecasting of need.
5. Development and evaluation of alternatives.
6. Plan development.
7. Implementation program.
8. Operation and monitoring (surveillance).

The following subsections review the steps in this planning process.

14.4.1 Problem Identification

Identification of the wastewater problems of an area is often complicated by the presence of competing and conflicting interests. Problem identification should reflect the concerns of different private and public groups and be in sufficient detail to receive adequate attention in the planning process. Public involvement and coordination of various agencies and groups should begin at this early stage.

As part of problem identification, the study area should be defined and existing information for the study area analyzed for its relevance to the problem under consideration. This includes identification of geophysical, biological, social, and economic characteristics of the area. Further, it should be determined whether or not the study area is experiencing problems with its individual sewage disposal systems and whether or not these problems are documented.

Problem identification activities may be summarized as follows: (1) Define the study area; (2) document public concerns; (3) analyze water and wastewater problems; and (4) document wastewater system failures.

14.4.2 Development of Goals and Objectives

The statement of goals and objectives should take into consideration community aspirations and environmental quality. Goals and objectives reflect the community's expectations of what will be achieved through the planning process. While goals can often be expressed as "motherhood-and-apple-pie" statements, objectives are more specific targets toward which plans will be developed. Often, several objectives are required to obtain a desired goal. They also serve as a basis for evaluating alternatives and selecting a recommended program. This aspect of the planning process can best be accomplished on a team basis with representatives of various community agencies and interested groups and citizens.

14.4.3 Data Collection and Analysis

Existing information for the study area is obtained and analyzed for its relevance to the problem during this phase of the project. It may include geophysical, social, political and economic characteristics of the area, as well as anticipated future conditions shown by existing planning documents, particularly as related to wastewater.

Meetings with community staff, wastewater facility operators, and the pertinent regulatory agencies will provide insight into current conditions of the receiving water body, treatment plant, and system operations, and into difficulties being experienced with individual disposal systems. Field surveys will expand the existing data base and will permit assessment of the existing wastewater facilities, including their excess capacity or capacity deficiency. Specific data collection items of major importance are described in the following paragraphs.

Socioeconomic and land use characteristics   The distribution of population in any given community depends on a number of factors, such as income characteristics of the population, the land use and zoning patterns within the community, and the influence of national and regional socioeconomic trends.

In addition to population, it is necessary to collect data on the location and type of commercial and industrial activity in the community. Some types of industries are extremely large users of water and producers of wastewater, while others use and produce less than a single, typical residence. One of the major purposes for collecting socioeconomic information is to gain an understanding of the existing and projected wastewater needs of the community.

Existing wastewater facilities   A survey of existing sewerage facilities should be conducted to establish their condition and utility, because these facilities will form the baseline of the comprehensive facilities plan. The existing systems may include individual disposal systems (see below) or may already include a structured sewer system and wastewater treatment plant.

Individual Disposal Systems.   For study areas where a portion of the community is served by septic tanks and tile fields, a field survey and review of the sanitarian's records will give indications of the failure rates of the systems (14). Where data are not available, it may be necessary to meet with septic tank pumping firms to get septage pumping data from the various sectors of the community. Combining these data with state records, soils data, and current operating conditions, potential problems and future failure rates can be extrapolated. These data become integral to the analysis of alternatives.

Sewer System.   The existing collection system, although it consists primarily of buried pipe, is often the most expensive portion of a wastewater system and, as such, must be carefully maintained and optimally expanded. During the data collection phase a collection system must be analyzed from both capacity and condition perspectives (1).

Capacity actually refers to hydraulic capacity. Knowledge of existing capacity is necessary for the determination of residual capacity or deficiency for future growth. System condition can be evaluated by measuring inflow and infiltration. High inflow/infiltration (I/I) rates not only use up future sewer and sewage treatment capacity, but also affect the efficiency of the treatment plant. In some cases, a detailed I/I study or sewer system evaluation survey (SSES) may be desirable and cost effective to reduce wastewater flows. Separation of combined wastewater and storm water flows, while generally considered desirable, may be so costly that a system of treated or screened overflows may be the most cost effective method of meeting effluent quality requirements.

Treatment Facilities.   The review and analysis of existing sewage treatment plant units and their effectiveness in meeting effluent requirements for both current and future growth patterns may be determined by meeting with the plant operators. A well run facility will have operating records with influent and effluent measurements of flow (daily average, maximum, and minimum), BOD, suspended solids (SS), as well as sludge solids handled, volatile solids (VS), gallons of sludge pumped, and other pertinent data. The state regulatory agency will also have records, both those submitted by the plant operator and those taken by the state regulatory agency staff. Summary and interpretation of these data form a picture of current operations and deficiencies.

Treated Wastewater Discharge and Receiving Waters.   The method used to discharge treated wastewater effluent to receiving waters is important in terms of dispersion both into a moving stream or river and (even more critical) into quiet waters, large freshwater bodies, estuaries, or oceans (8, 10, 15, 19). While stream, river and lake modeling of wastewater effluent loading relates to most of the country, estuary and ocean discharges through outfalls play an important part in design of wastewater facilities for seacoast municipalities. Sewage effluent dispersion models are affected by currents, thermoclines (temperature), wind, and wave action. These are all mechanical effects. Environmental effects on sea and estuary life, both plant and animal, are impacted by the level and concentration of nutrients, microorganisms, and dissolved oxygen (DO) as the effluent is dispersed. Health aspects relate to effluent pathogenic populations which are primarily controlled by disinfection at the wastewater plant, receiving water dilution, and die-off rates.

Waste loading of flowing rivers and streams may be critical from a biological nutrient loading point of view. Modeling techniques have been developed in most waters of the country. However, verification of allowable limits is often necessary. The quality of receiving waters for the wastewater effluent has been established by states in their receiving water and river basin studies. Depending upon the date of these studies, data may have to be updated or supplemental field data collected to dovetail the existing data into a current model of stream and receiving water conditions, requirements, and needs. Meetings with the state or applicable regulatory agency will clarify the status of these standards.

The basic data collection process will, therefore, serve to identify and define favorable and unfavorable natural and man-made environmental conditions as they apply to the wastewater planning and engineering needs of the community. Upon completion of these studies and analyses, the goals and objectives previously developed should be reevaluated as to their applicability, and then revised, if necessary.

14.4.4 Forecasting of Need

The data collection studies and analysis serve as an inventory of existing conditions, establishing current deficiencies (or excess capacities) and identifying problems. They may also provide initial direction for future rehabilitation and improvement programs. This information base may also include nonphysical considerations, such as ordinances controlling individual wastewater disposal systems (home septic tanks and tile fields) and data on their effectiveness or lack thereof when related to community geological and soil constraints.

The future needs, based on demographic and socioeconomic analysis (i.e., population, industry, local economy, etc.), are developed from the data collection and analysis stage. Wastewater flows and biological loading must also be forecast for the study area.

Projections must be made of the waste assimilation characteristics of receiving waters. Meetings with regulatory agencies regarding receiving water limitations are critical at this point. If these agencies have not completed a stream or river basin load allocation planning document or data to date, producing such a document may become a requirement of the planning study.

14.4.5 Development and Evaluation of Alternatives

A thorough analysis and clear understanding of the problem form the basis for developing alternative solutions that respond to goals and objectives. Review meetings with community staff and officials are important at this stage, in order to present deficiencies of the existing wastewater system in terms of both physical plant and operation and maintenance. Meetings with regional and state water pollution control regulatory agency staff should also be held to review findings on existing systems and discuss future considerations. Understanding of a problem may indicate that there are numerous and widely divergent opinions, as well as a number of possible solutions.

After analysis of current conditions and identification of future needs, preliminary system design criteria can be developed to aid in the identification of workable alternatives. One step in preparing the design criteria is setting forth the design period or useful life of the system, which is the number of years from the date of plant startup to the date when the facilities would require replacement or major rehabilitation. This time period will vary with the type of wastewater facilities, community needs and growth patterns, useful life of system components, cost of financing, and historical considerations. Normal accepted useful life of pipelines is 50 to 100 yr, structures 20 to 30 yr, and mechanical equipment 5 to 20 yr. Treatment plant and pumping station design periods are commonly set at 20 yr and sewers at 50 yr (6, 20).

Location of wastewater treatment facilities can be one of the most critical features of wastewater planning. Desired gravity flow of sewerage systems restricts the number of appropriate wastewater treatment facilities locations, and the "don't-put-it-near-me" syndrome further complicates locational decisions for treatment plants, and even for pumping stations. Long-range planning for acquisition of sites with public land buffers around the wastewater facilities can reduce location problems significantly.

In planning to meet future needs, it is necessary to balance project constraints against alternative ways to meet those future needs. Each alternative will have its varying costs, advantages, and disadvantages. With needs established and existing facilities evaluated, alternative plans should be formulated to address the parameters and objectives of the project, utilizing a variety of techniques to achieve them.

Each alternative should include a specific set of plan elements (collection system, treatment plant, disposal technique), as well as a detailing of construction, operation and maintenance, and user costs. Public and interagency participation is important at this point to assure understanding of the full range of measures considered. The alternatives may range from new capital intensive structural measures, such as new treatment plant and interceptor sewers, to nonstructural management solutions, such as operation and maintenance measures. Each alternative should also contain an assessment of potential environmental impact. Structural measures tend to appear relatively expensive and, at first look, irreversible, whereas nonstructural approaches tend to involve low initial costs. However, the latter may ultimately be more expensive and less effective when total costs (including operation, maintenance and costs of other constraints and effects) are included. On the other hand, they tend to be sometimes easier to modify if changes are needed. A financial analysis of alternatives which will add to the decision-making tools available is essential.

The development of alternatives to meet objectives narrows the range of alternatives by focusing on those that can successfully achieve the stated objectives. The economic evaluation of each alternative provides an important basis for plan comparison. Different plans may involve different projects with different economic lives of the facilities. A cost-benefit analysis is made in an attempt to facilitate comparisons on a common basis. For example, the cost-benefit analysis may compare the present value of all costs with the present value of all benefits. Costs and benefits that cannot be quantified must also be identified and considered. Depending upon the scope of the project, the analysis should include alternative methods of waste transport and treatment, as well as handling and disposal of sludge and effluent.

An impact assessment to analyze the environmental effects of alternatives is required by NEPA and by laws of many states. An environmental assessment (EA) is prepared for those projects which are not anticipated to have significant adverse impacts.

Should the potential impacts be significant, EPA will require an environmental impact statement (EIS). An EIS examines in detail the impacts which might occur as a result of implementation of any of the feasible alternatives and presents measures to mitigate those impacts. The EIS is structured to concentrate on those concerns identified as major during a scoping process.

It is sometimes assumed that the EIS requirement significantly lengthens the project planning phase, but EPA provides for a "piggy-back" process wherein the facilities planning and environmental evaluation occur simultaneously. The process thus becomes shorter and provides responsive planning.

The evaluation and analysis of alternative plans is conducted to compare their beneficial and adverse contributions for the purpose of recommending a plan. The alternative of optimizing performance of existing facilities should receive careful consideration. Following initial screening of alternative plans, a limited number of the most feasible options should be evaluated in detail. Each alternative needs to be re-evaluated and compared after refinement and estimation of monetary costs, environmental effects, and other considerations and concerns. Each alternative, including its cost and environmental effects, will again be displayed to inform the public and solicit public opinion to help select a plan.

Recommendations and alternatives may change after public scrutiny, particularly if public involvement has not been made an integral part of the planning process from the beginning. In some cases, it may be necessary to develop a new alternative or a composite of alternatives to serve as an acceptable compromise.

14.4.6 Plan Development

Following evaluation, one alternative is selected for plan development. During this phase, the plan is fully detailed with costs, design criteria, and an implementation program.

14.4.7 Implementation Program

An implementation program must recognize the needs and goals of the community, as well as the social and environmental constraints within which the selected wastewater treatment system must operate.

Construction cost estimates and the timetable of expenditures provide the basic data required to prepare that section of the capital improvement program dealing with wastewater facilities, and to obtain approval of the program. However, when it comes to developing a long-term financing program, operation and maintenance costs must also be included in order to evaluate the total and annual cost of such facilities and the ability of a community to pay for its wastewater improvement program.

Financing also involves working with the financial community in developing bond costs, and assessing tax implications and sewer use charges—sometimes even going to the legislature of the state to implement the program. Development of new or revised sewer use ordinances and user charges are also part of the planning and implementation process.

Implementation involves bringing to fruition the selected plan or recommendations. At this stage, the adopted plan is put forward for design and construction, regulations and ordinances are adopted, any laws needed are passed or policies amended, management procedures are established, and financing arrangements are completed. The procedures and costs should have been generally worked out throughout the planning process, but must be rechecked in detail at this time to be sure that they are current and consistent. Although implementation is often a complex and frustrating process, care taken during the planning steps and continuous awareness of implementation needs will make the alternatives realistic and the selected plan more capable of being carried out.

Because wastewater facilities may often be programmed over a period of years, they should be included in a community's long-range and short-range capital improvement program. Large projects may often be scheduled in phases to lessen the impact of the project or projects on the financing ability of the community and its budget process in any single year or short period.

14.4.8 Operation and Monitoring

Once a project is completed and brought on line, it should be monitored to see how well it satisfies original goals and objectives. Because shakedown and startup operations take time and can run into various snags, an allowance must be made for unforeseen events occurring during this period. As many wastewater projects require long-term investments, conditions and needs change, and new more efficient processes are developed, it is likely that modifications may be needed long before the useful life of the investment is reached. The best insurance for an effective wastewater system is a good operation and maintenance budget, adequate staffing by qualified personnel, and quality management. These will extend the useful life of any system and should be established during the planning process and public participation period to gain proper community and administrative support. Modifications would be anticipated as the project comes on line and moves into its mature stages.

14.4.9 Summary of Planning Tasks

The level of detail in a wastewater plan will vary according to the nature, scale, location, and need for the project (4). An outline of a comprehensive wastewater planning report, showing the elements that are common to many wastewater projects, is presented at the end of this chapter (Sec. 14.8). The EPA Guidelines for Facility Planning have a similar outline which were designed to answer specific portions of the Clean Water Act of 1972 (PL 92-500) as amended. This outline covers most or all areas of concern in wastewater planning for projects that require comprehensive planning.

14.5 FUNDING AND FINANCING PROGRAMS

While the logical order of steps in developing the implementation program leads to consideration of financing at this point, this factor really has its seeds in the development of the alternatives and selection of the recommended plan. It would be pointless to consider an alternative or a recommended plan which is clearly beyond the community's financial capability, or one which has excessive cost to the individual taxpayer and sewer user. Therefore, before finalizing recommendations, it is necessary for the success of the project to contact the community's finance director and bond counsel as well as area bankers that work with the community, to obtain the latest estimates on the cost of borrowed funds, both short term (during construction) and long term. National trends are available from several sources, but local bankers are likely to have a better picture of the community bond rating and interest costs. These costs and project contingencies are to be included in the cost to be borne by the taxpayers and users. (In estimating and funding project costs, it should be kept in mind that the taxpayer and sewer user may or may not be the same—the latter especially in a community with large unsewered areas.)

The cost to the taxpayer is best extrapolated by reviewing trends over the past five or 10 years of total tax valuation, correcting for any tax reevaluation or adjustments during the period or any anticipated in the near future. Projected tax rates are then applied to an average valued house or housing unit. This provides a base to which are added the costs of constructing, financing, operating, and maintaining the wastewater treatment facility contained in the proposed program. Other costs, such as construction of lateral sewers to extend service to new areas and connection fees, must also be considered.

Normally, most annual operating and maintenance (O&M) costs are recovered from the users by a sewer use charge based either upon a fee per housing unit or on water usage. Some communities partially subsidize O&M costs from general tax revenues, while in others the user charge includes recovery of a portion of the annual capital costs as well as O&M costs through user charges. This subject is addressed in a detailed financing manual published by the Water Pollution Control Federation (20).

14.5.1 Bond Issues

Funding of wastewater programs is generally more complex than water system financing. Many states have specific laws related to financing sewer programs which are sometimes included under or along with other public works projects. Superimposed on state bonding requirements are both the state and federal water pollution control laws and regulations. It is important to note that almost all federal regulations related to funding requirements, contracts, sewer user charges, etc., are only applicable to a particular wastewater project if federal grant monies are involved. This generalization is subject to individual state laws and regulations.

Current federal regulations require that at least the annual O&M costs of a wastewater system be financed by sewer user charges. The charges may be based upon housing units or a similar unit for simple sewer systems, or upon water meter flow usage if the sewer system users are served by a metered public water system. Other methods used are based on variations of these. A variation quite common prior to the 1972 Federal Water Pollution Control Act was that of general taxation. This method is no longer permitted by federal statute except under very specific exemptions that had to be applied for prior to 1976.

The remaining project costs or capital improvement costs may, according to federal regulations, be funded by a municipality by general obligation bonds or can, by choice, be included in the user charge.

A sewer authority, district or regional authority may, subject to state laws, fund its capital improvements by general obligation or revenue bonds. Recent changes in the bond market include minimum bond units of not less than $5000.00. This requirement narrows the bond market to major and institutional investors, which affects those smaller communities where issuance of bonds in smaller denominations facilitated their purchase by small investors.

Some states only permit bond retirement schedules by equal principal (serial) retirement each year. This forces a greater financial impact on the user during the first year of issue when the principal and the full interest is paid. The interest payment will decrease in a straight line on serial issues each year to the last year, and so the greatest impact on the user or taxpayer will be during the first year when the least sewer use most likely occurs. To the user, the level payment (initial low principal coupled with full interest), similar to home mortgage payments, is the easiest to handle, but many states do not permit its use by municipalities. Sewer authorities or districts under special legislation are often permitted to use revenue bonds which may have a level payment feature.

14.5.2 Federal and State Grants

Under the Water Pollution Control Grant Program of 1956 and subsequent amendments, a federal grant program has been available for public sewer and treatment plant construction programs, first at 30% and 33%, then 50% and 55%, then increased in 1972 to 75% of eligible portions of the cost of wastewater treatment and collection works. The recent amendment of 1982 has reduced the percentage to 55% for fiscal year 1985 and cut back the 1972 funding authorization level from $5.0 billion annually to $2.4 billion. Additional provisions of the Act provide supplemental grants for I/A technology and energy effective systems, as well as a reserve of funds for small systems and those involved in nonstructural approaches such as septic tanks and tile fields. Congress is considering modification of some of the supplemental funding programs in light of the cutback in over-all funding level authoriziation.

Various states have enacted supplemental state programs of grants and loans to match the federal grant program. These vary all the way from 40% matching grants to just loans. (Several states still match to 95%, e.g., New Hampshire, Maine, and others.) In addition, many states have enacted wastewater grant programs independent of federal programs.

14.5.3 Other Grant and Loan Programs

Other programs for sewers include Community Development Block Grant funds administered by the U.S. Department of Housing and Urban Development. Recently, many states assumed administration of this program for fund distribution and administration for communities under 50,000 population. Another program is administered by the Farmers Home Administration for small communities. The latter funds grants up to 50% and provides loans for the remainder under complex rules and a formula related to community size and income. Interest rates have recently been tied to national rates, and repayment can be level payment or equal principal payments up to 30 or 40 years, subject to state law.

14.5.4 Control of Financing Costs

Funding sewer capital improvement programs and effective operation and maintenance programs is not simple. The full costs to the user must be developed as part of wastewater system planning. In fact, cost disclosures are required by federal regulations and most state laws to be presented by public notice and at public hearings. Therefore, it is important to undertake these tasks as an integral part of the planning process. Detailed methods of financing sewer systems and developing user charges have been set forth in an ASCE, APWA and WPCF publication on finances and charges (20). This is an update of WPCF's 1973 Manual of Practice. It details some of the finer points of financing sewer programs, such as coverage requirements for bond financing. It includes accounting procedures for handling annual budgets and numerous details required for financial operation of sewer or water pollution control systems.

14.6 WASTEWATER MANAGEMENT ISSUES AND TRENDS

14.6.1 Funding Programs

The nation's water pollution control program may be in jeopardy due to the potential wind-down of current Clean Water Act funding construction grants to municipalities. In 1982, the grant program budget was $2.4 billion, which amounted to only 48% of the 1972 authorization. Effectively, it was much less than 48% because of erosion of the 1972 construction dollar. The federal share of the grant program will be reduced from 75% to 55% in 1985 for eligible items. While the most recent National Needs Survey (conducted semiannually by EPA) indicates a need of $128 billion in 1984 costs, Congress is considering only a 5-yr to 8-yr extension from 1985, probably at a $2.4 billion authorization of grants per year, with a federal loan program after 1986 combined with a decreasing level of grants.

There is some concern that the federal program should be extended to the year 2000 so that communities in the middle of the existing programs are not penalized. Of rising concern is the need of communities for federal assistance to help defray the high cost of reversing deterioration of water pollution system infrastructure and meeting special needs, such as correction of older combined sewer systems. Because of budget constraints in most communities, it is fiscally difficult to properly maintain the wastewater infrastructure. In addition, these maintenance costs increase each year, particularly as delayed and deferred maintenance causes the infrastructure to further decline in the same scenario as the country's bridge system.

As federal funding programs are cut back and phased out, states and localities face the issues of how to complete projects already under way and start other necessary projects. Fiscal pressures because of federal cutbacks are falling on state and local shoulders. Enforcement of clean water legislation will also be more difficult with the cutback in federal funding.

14.6.2 Privatization

Although privatization has been a trend in some other aspects of "public works" planning, it has not fully taken hold in wastewater collection and treatment systems. Privatization works on the principle of project syndication maximizing the tax status of municipalities to pass along benefits to investors as tax-free investments. In addition to unique tax status, depreciation writedowns are also part of the enhancement to encourage private investment. A good description of the mechanics and implication of this type of financing appears in the most recent WPCF Manual on Finances and Charges (20).

14.6.3 Handling Growth Areas

A problem to be faced in the future is how better to handle population growth with respect to pollution control, particularly in those largely undeveloped areas adjacent to metropolitan areas. Should such new and developing areas have individual wastewater disposal systems, or should nearby existing sewer systems be extended and increased in capacity to accommodate them? How should planning and engineering provide direction and control? Should needed wastewater programs be initiated on a project-by-project basis, or should an over-all inclusive program be devised?

14.6.4 Land Use Implications

Current developmental and economic policies in many communities call for limiting extension of public sewer systems to rapidly growing areas at the edges of established areas, or to areas with special drainage problems. Any development beyond these areas is now usually supported by individual systems. Individual systems are normally not permitted in areas of compact soil conditions, high ground water, or steep slope areas, and so growth in these areas is restricted. Unfortunately, tilled farmland areas have the best drained soils and low slopes and are, therefore, ripe for development with resulting loss of good farmland. Hilly land and rocky areas, which have less long-range value for crop and food production, are less likely to be developed for residential or other purposes. Land use policies and wastewater planning must be carefully coordinated toward protection of land resources.

14.6.5 Site Selection Implications

For conventional municipal sewage collection systems, the treatment facility normally serves areas defined by a drainage basin or group of drainage basins. It may also include service areas not under the jurisdiction of the community building or operating the system. The selection of a site for any new treatment facilities is of utmost imporance, not only from a cost point of view, but because of acceptance by the populace of the area it serves. Problems can also occur where an existing plant may require expansion.

It is often nearly impossible to find a site that will meet all the conditions desired—either those which authorities recommend as being essential or those of public acceptance, least cost, etc. Therefore, an evaluation of various potential sites is not only desirable but necessary. From an economic point of view, particularly with today's high energy costs, the planner must always consider how to maximize gravity flow and minimize the number of pumping stations. This is not only for economical operation, but for reliability in operations and service. Unfortunately, this preference may lead to selection of sites in floodplains or wetlands, introducing additional problems and costs.

Sites for treatment facilities must be evaluated to minimize adverse environmental and esthetic impact as well as cost of construction. Other selection factors include costs for the collection system and plant outfall, subsurface conditions, proximity to housing to minimize possible odor concerns, zoning or land use, sufficient area to accommodate future expansion, accessibility to utilities (sewage treatment plants are energy intensive), and transportation for the facility's service needs.

14.6.6 Reuse Alternatives

Many citizens feel that the need for water by municipalities, industries, and agriculture is outgrowing the supply of fresh water. They are concerned about careless use of potable water, both in terms of wasting a water resource and its implications in the waste of the chemicals, electrical energy, and fuels consumed in the development, treatment, and distribution of potable water. Finally, when it is discharged by the users, it is sewage, which must be conveyed and treated.

Wastewater renovation and reuse is a possible solution to reducing water demands on water supply and increased sewage flow, particularly in the semi-arid areas of the United States. Sewage effluent can be purified through advanced waste treatment, and thereby made available for municipal or industrial use (21). However, such treatment is extremely expensive and is only feasible where no other alternative is available. The reuse of treated wastewater for industrial purposes can contribute to the conservation of potable water. However, the energy consumed in preparing wastewater for industrial reuse and its subsequent cost may be excessive.

Planners need to recognize that alternative methods are available by which to use renovated wastewater: direct reuse, aquifer recharge, direct piping to high volume users such as industry, and extremes where gray waters are used for flushing and only bottled water is distributed for potable usage.

Wastewater reclamation techniques have been popular in arid or semi-arid regions. In recent years, they have been used in less water-scarce areas. The greatest use for reclaimed wastewater has been for crop or landscape irrigation and ground-water recharge (12, 18, 21).

Treatment of wastewater for reuse is extremely expensive, unless it is applied as irrigation water. In mildly sloping terrain, even spray irrigation is feasible. This use is subject to limitations of climate and nutrients or toxic substances present in the wastewater. Northern areas require up to six months storage during periods when frozen ground makes irrigation impossible, with costs that may be at least two times higher than secondary treatment.

Irrigation in the southern United States is significantly more economical than in the north due to decreased storage requirements. Critical are concerns with aerosols, movement from the spray during windy periods, and odor problems. Also important is potential accidental pollution of ground-water supplies. Studies have been made in Florida of the effectiveness of soil filtering to determine whether significant removals of viruses can be achieved. Use of wastewater for irrigation creates limitations on types of crops that may be grown. Perhaps only forage crops that are not directly used as food for human consumption could be considered fully safe.

14.6.7 Conservation

Many have pressed hard for conservation of water with resulting savings of wastewater and reduced requirements for treatment. The effort by some types of industry, particularly those using large amounts of water, has been notably successful through recycling. There is usually an economic limit, since water savings are often traded for the increased power and chemical costs involved in many industrial recycling processes.

Some of the most effective ways of reducing water use and sewer flows have been taking place unheralded in many industries. Recently in Connecticut, a major manufacturing plant, as part of its pretreatment program, and coupled with the initiation of a new sewer use charge by the city, cut its discharge to sewers by nearly 50%. Part of this decrease was due to recycling, part to removing the plant's cooling waters from the sanitary sewer system, and part just to reduction in flows.

Conservation in the individual home does not offer such dramatic results. Conservation is even more difficult in apartment complexes which offer no incentive to conserve water without individual water meters. Approaches to residential conservation may include low water-use toilets, low-flow showerheads, and similar reduced flow devices. To a fault, water flow can be reduced to such a low level that we could revert to the commode, hand basin, and bucket basin of rural America of the early 1900s. It should not be forgotten that this period was troubled by disease due to such low-flow or no-flow sanitary systems and aggravated, of course, by poor hygiene and sanitation. Those who have used chemical toilets are well aware of their problems. Conservation and reuse are available, but they have many practical limitations.

14.6.8 Toxic Substances

The impact of toxic substances on the nation's smaller municipal systems has become a decreasing problem since the 1972 Clean Water Act. Discharge permit requirements, as well as pretreatment requirements for industry, are starting to have their effect on reducing discharge of such wastes. In larger municipal systems, toxic spills still occur, though less frequently. The problem with large systems is enforcement because it is very difficult to trace offenders who dump wastes into a large system. PL 94-580, the Resource Conservation Recovery Act (RCRA) of October 1976, has also had a major effect in reducing hazardous waste. This law requires that hazardous wastes be tracked with a paper trail of forms from generation of waste to its treatment and disposal. It will further decrease problems caused by industrial spills at operating wastewater treatment plants.

14.6.9 New Treatment Systems

About one or two significant new treatment systems come on line per decade. In the 1970s, oxygen activated sludge treatment systems were developed. This process had tremendous impact on some of the nation's larger systems, such as Miami and Detroit, where high land cost or extra strength sewage were impact factors as related to total treatment system costs. In the 1980s, it is the sludge belt press, an expensive machine that dewaters sludge economically, at consistently greater liquid removal, with less maintenance, and lower power costs. Continued technological development is anticipated, but is unlikely to result in a complete change in basic wastewater treatment processes or facilities in the foreseeable future.

14.6.10 Operation and Maintenance

As construction of needed water pollution control facilities proceeds under the stimulus of the nation's water pollution control program, noticeable improvement of the receiving waters is becoming apparent. Focus on the effectiveness of the programs is beginning to shift emphasis and efforts towards proper operation and maintenance of the facilities. Increased effort in this area now will also help defer or ease massive rehabilitation of wastewater system infrastructure needs in the future.

14.6.11 Planning and the Future

How do all these factors affect future planning of wastewater collection and treatment systems? Money has always been a problem, equipment often breaks down, maintenance is required, and salaries and operating costs will continue to rise. The biggest impact will probably come from a decrease in federal funding, putting greater demands on state and local dollars. Planning on how to minimize the latter and still build needed systems is the real task. Financing is and will remain a key planning problem.

The technical knowledge to maintain a livable and clean environment is available today. Wastewater treatment processes are available to meet such needs subject, of course, to costs. The pollution problem is becoming more crucial with time. In the past, these concerns were often met with apathy. It appears today, however, that there is a general public awareness of pollution and a strong willingness to do something about it.

Planning plays a key part in the success of the nation's water pollution control program. It is concerned not only with the preservation of our aquatic environment, but also with the interplay and demands of our modern civilization, from land use policies and population shifts and growths, to our increasing demands for water, one of our most important resources.

14.7 GLOSSARY OF TERMS

Brackish. Mixed fresh and salt waters.

Biochemical oxygen demand, BOD. This is one of the major biological parameters or indicators of pollution, and is an indirect quantitative measure of organic compounds in water which are capable of oxidation or reduction by biological process, or both. It most commonly refers to carbonaceous or first stage BOD demand.

Drainage basin. The area of land that drains water to a common outlet at some point along a stream channel.

Degradation. That activity that occurs in flowing streams and rivers where man-made or natural pollution loads exceed the natural ability of the stream to maintain aerobic conditions.

Dissolved oxygen. Free oxygen which is in solution with the water or wastewater. It is an important parameter in stream pollution analysis.

Estuary. A coastal bay or surface area where fresh and salt waters mix; for example, where a river joins the ocean.

Eutrophication. Process of aging of water bodies such as lakes and slow moving water bodies, characterized by excessive biological and aquatic growth.

Evaporation. The process whereby water from land areas and bodies of water surfaces is absorbed into the atmosphere as a vapor.

Evapotranspiration. The combined processes of evaporation and transpiration. It can be defined as the sum of water used in assimilation by vegetation and water lost by evaporation.

Ground water. All water beneath the surface of the ground.

Inflow. Surface waters that enter into sanitary waters from surface flows into manholes and other sources. Inflow is direct, infiltration indirect.

Infiltration. Movement of water from soil into sewer from ground water through leaking joints or cracked pipes.

Life cycle costs. Those costs used to construct, operate and, maintain a unit, and replace it in time, all brought to present-day value.

Milligrams per liter. The standard measurement of small quantities of substances in water and sewage (formerly measured as parts per million, ppm).

Nonpoint pollution. Nonpoint sources are diffuse or unspecific, in nature or man-made, and discharge pollutants into waters by dispersed pathways.

Nonstructural wastewater considerations. Generally might include resolving wastewater problems on a legislative basis, ordinances, maximizing use of individual disposal systems, etc.

Oxygen sag. Drop in dissolved oxygen following significant additional pollution to a stream, and its subsequent recovery through biological activity of microorganisms and physical processes such as settling.

Percolation. The slow seepage of water into and through the ground. Important parameter for individual sewage disposal systems.

Potable water. Safe and satisfactory drinking water.

Reach. Reach of a river, stream, or estuary in which the flow characteristics, such as velocity, quality of nutrients, and configuration, are somewhat uniform. A river study and model is split up into working reaches and the significant features and characteristics cataloged for use in model studies.

Runoff. Generally defined as water moving over the surface of the ground, consisting of precipitation (rainfall) minus infiltration and evapotranspiration.

Septage. Those solids and liquid which are pumped out of septic tanks.

Settleable solids. Those solids which are readily removable from raw sewage by plain settling. Usually measured after 1 hr in milliliters per liter.

Sewage. Those liquid wastes originating from residences and commercial and industrial establishments. When carried in sewers, it would also include such ground water, surface water and storm water as may be present. Also commonly referred to as wastewater.

Sewer. A pipe or conduit used to collect and carry away wastewater, sewage, and storm water runoff from the generating source to treatment plants, receiving plants, or receiving streams.

Sewerage. The entire system of sewage or wastewater collection, treatment and disposal.

Structural wastewater systems. Those systems and components such as sewers, pumping stations, force mains, treatment plants.

Surface water. All water on the surface of the ground, including water in natural and man-made boundaries.

Suspended solids, SS. Those solids which can be filtered from sewage (by weight).

Thermocline. Term used in deep lake and ocean outfall designs related to the temperature/density level which effectively traps treated effluent below this level until thorough mixing takes place.

Total solids. The total residue of sewage solids by weight after evaporation.

Transpiration. The process whereby water vapor is emitted or passes through plant leaf surfaces and is diffused into the atmosphere.

Wastewater. Water which has been used for a particular purpose, contains pollutants from that use, and must be disposed of. Also commonly referred to as sewage.

Watershed. All land and water within the confines of a drainage divide.

Water table. The water level above an impermeable layer of soil or rock.

Wetlands. Swamps, marshes, bogs, wet meadows, and tidal flats where water stands on the ground surface.

14.8 TYPICAL OUTLINE FOR COMPREHENSIVE PLANNING REPORT

A. Letter of Transmittal. To the contracting agency.

B. Acknowledgements. List of individuals and agencies submitting information or assistance during the project.

C. Table of Contents.
- Index of text
- List of tables
- List of figures

D. Finding, Conclusions and Recommendations. Many times included in Letter of Transmittal.

E. Need and Scope of Project.

F. Background.
- General and historical
- Geography, hydrology, meteorology, geology, surface and ground water, etc.
- Soil characteristics and subsurface conditions
- Demographics: population density and characteristics (past, present, future)
- Employment: industry, commercial, service, government
- Transportation and mobility; adequacy and effects produced, both present and future
- Residential, industrial, commercial, recreational, agricultural, and institutional development and redevelopment
- Land use: present and future (including land use in detail in the vicinity of existing and proposed wastewater facilities)
- Drainage, water pollution control, and flood control management.

G. Water Pollution Control Conditions.
- Field surveys and investigations (including physical, chemical, biological and hydrological characteristics of receiving waters)

- Existing methods of municipal and industrial wastewater collection, treatment, and disposal
- Characteristics of municipal wastes and wastewater volumes, strengths, flow rates
- Characteristics of industrial wastes, quantities, and amenability to treatment with municipal wastes
- Water pollution control requirements, federal, state, and interstate receiving water classifications
- Wastewater reduction, reclamation, reuse
- Extent of interim and private on-site sewage disposal (adequacy, present and future)
- Suitability of soils for on-site disposal
- Overview

H. *Wastewater Collection.*
- Existing collection systems (condition and adequacy, including infiltration, surface, and storm-water flows)
- Areas needing collection systems (and timetables)
- Soil, rock, ground-water conditions
- Routing and rights-of-way
- Storm-water drainage and collection systems impacts
- Storm-water separation (feasibility holding tanks, special considerations, local ordinances, enforcement) on older systems

I. *Preliminary Analysis for Wastewater Treatment and Disposal*
- Pollution load, degree of treatment required, and outfall considerations
- Facility siting requirements, including buffer zone, foundation conditions
- Areas served, areas not served
- Trunkline and pumping stations
- Property and easement acquisition problems
- Industrial waste flows and pretreatment (if required)
- Effect of storm-water flows (on receiving waters, need for holding tanks or treatment)
- Treatment plant and outfall sewer design considerations
- Grit, screening, and sludge handling and disposal
- Design criteria summary

J. *Alternatives*
- Alternative solutions, total costs, and annual operating cost
- Evaluation and analysis of alternates
- Environmental assessment
- Summary and recommendations

K. *Regional Considerations.*
- Alternative solutions and plans
- Economic, social, and ecologic evaluation of alternatives
- Site development and reuse plans
- Regional planning development
- Recommendations

L. *Administration and Financing.*
- Public information
- Administrative arrangement, management and costs
- Financing methods: general obligation bonds (alternate revenue bonds or special assessment bonds); grants; incentives; federal aid; state aid; or sewer use charge
- Cost distribution
- Legislation, monitoring, enforcement

M. *Summary and Recommendations.*
N. *Appendices.*
- Applicable laws
- Special data
- Charts, tables, illustrations

O. *Glossary.*
P. *References.*

14.9 REFERENCES

1. ASCE, *Design and Construction of Sanitary and Storm Sewers*, Manual of Practice 37, ASCE, New York, 1969.
2. ASCE, *Sewage Treatment Plant Design*, Manual of Practice 36, ASCE, New York, 1977.
3. Benefield, L.D., and Randall, C.W., *Biological Process Design for Wastewater Treatment*, Prentice-Hall, Inc., Englewood Cliffs, N.J., 1980.
4. Berry, J.L.B., and Horton, F.E., *Urban Environmental Management, Planning for Pollution Control*, Prentice-Hall, Inc., Englewood Cliffs, N. J., 1974.
5. Cherrmisinoff, P.N., and Young, R.A., *Pollution Engineering Practice Handbook*, Ann Arbor Science, Ann Arbor, Mich., 1975.
6. Cohn, M.M., *How to Plan, Design, Finance and Build Modern Sewer Systems — Sewers for Growing America*, Certain-teed Products Corp., Ambler, PA 1966.
7. D'Itri, F. M., *Land Treatment of Municipal Wastewater*, Ann Arbor Science, Ann Arbor, Mich., 1982.
8. Grace, R.A., *Marine Outfall Systems Planning, Design and Construction*, Prentice-Hall, Inc., Englewood Cliffs, N.J., 1978.
9. *Guides for the Design of Wastewater Treatment Works*, New England Interstate Water Pollution Control Commission, Boston, Mass., 1980.
10. James, A., *Mathematical Models in Water Pollution Control*, John Wiley & Sons, New York, 1978.

11. Klein, L., *River Pollution 2: Causes and Effects*, Butterworths, London and Boston, 1962.
12. Loehr, R.C., ed., *Land as a Waste Management Alternative*, Ann Arbor Science, Ann Arbor, Mich., 1977.
13. Major, D.C., and Lenton, R.L., *Applied Water Resource Systems Planning*, Prentice-Hall, Inc., Englewood Cliffs, N.J., 1979.
14. McClelland, N. I., ed., *Individual Onsite Wastewater Systems*, Proceedings of the 1st National Conference held in Ann Arbor, 1974, by National Science Foundation, Ann Arbor Science, Ann Arbor, Mich., 1977.
15. Nelson, L. N., "Receiving Water Quality Objectives," *Scientific Stream Pollution Analysis*, McGraw-Hill Book Co., Inc., New York, 1972, pp. 163–231.
16. Odum, H.T., *Environment, Power and Society*, Wiley-Interscience, New York, 1971.
17. Salvato, J. A., Jr., *Environmental Engineering and Sanitation*, John Wiley & Sons, New York, 1982.
18. Toreey, S., ed., *Sludge Disposal by Landspreading Techniques*, Noyes Data Corp., Park Ridge, N.J., 1979.
19. Velz, C. J., *Applied Stream Sanitation*, Wiley-Interscience, New York, 1970.
20. WPCF Task Force on Financing and Charges, *Finances and Charges for Wastewater Systems*, American Public Works Association, American Society of Civil Engineers, and Water Pollution Control Federation, 1984.
21. WPCF, *Water Reuse*, Manual of Practice SM-3, System Management, WPCF, Washington, D.C. 1983.

CHAPTER 15

SOLID WASTE SYSTEMS PLANNING[a]

15.1 INTRODUCTION

The solid waste collection and disposal system is one of the essential elements of the community facilities plan for an urban area comprehensive plan.

To provide the best possible service to society, solid waste systems must be efficiently integrated within the urban environment in which they function. This chapter reviews some of the basic planning methodologies currently used in the solid waste disposal and resource recovery fields and indicates how these methods may be used to develop efficient, integrated systems. Much of it focuses on the direction in which planners and decision-makers are moving, rather than describing the planning techniques in common use.

A solid waste disposal and resource recovery system is composed of three basic functions:

1. Collection and transportation, covering such items as containers, trucks, collection crews, and district routing and scheduling strategies.

2. Processing and disposal, covering transfer stations, incinerators, resource recovery facilities, and landfills.

3. Auxiliary services, such as management, planning, administration, marketing, and the enactment and enforcement of ordinances and legislation.

It has been estimated that about 80% of the cost of municipal solid waste management is spent on the collection and transportation function (7). While it can be expected that this proportion might drop as capital-intensive resource and energy recovery facilities are built, it will remain a significant part of the total cost. Thus, the planning and design of collection systems lie at the core of municipal solid waste management planning and, indeed, are often the actual determinants of the number, size, location, and type of processing and ultimate disposal facilities developed.

For industrial wastes, and particularly those defined as hazardous, the reverse is true. The major issue is locating and implementing a suitable disposal site, and high collection and transportation costs will

---

[a]Prepared by James F. Hudson, A.M.ASCE, Urban Systems Research & Engineering, Inc., Cambridge, MA., and Jarir S. Dajani, M. ASCE, Abu Dhabi Fund for Economic Development, Abu Dhabi, UAE

generally be accepted for transport to an acceptable site. Hauls of up to 1500 miles (2400 km) are common for some types of waste. This trend will continue as regulations under the federal Resource Conservation and Recovery Act proceed through implementation, and similar programs are enacted by the states.

Over-all cost figures clearly show that collection is the most significant component of the municipal solid waste management effort. For example, a community of 500,000 people which spends about $10,000,000 annually for solid waste collection and about $2,000,000 for disposal is paying about $20.00 per capita per year for collection alone. Furthermore, there is typically one collector or driver for every 600 persons, and one truck for every 2000 persons. While only about 60% of the population receives collection service, the national total is over 200,000 employees and 70,000 trucks.

The costs of municipal solid waste collection can be reduced in a number of ways. The most effective is an improvement in collection efficiency through the adoption of better methods of asset utilization and operation, including both equipment choice and the uses of that equipment. Two other possibilities are: (1) Reduction of residential waste volumes at the source, through household technologies, regulations, or source separation programs; and (2) improvements in disposal technology or facility siting. These topics are covered in the sections that follow.

15.2 PLANNING METHODOLOGY

15.2.1 Questions and Decisions

In planning solid waste collection processing and disposal systems, a number of basic decisions must be made concerning:

1. What materials to collect, in what type of containers, how often, and from where.

2. Who will collect the materials with what equipment, using what routes, what crew size, and what schedules for the crews.

3. What type of processing and disposal facilities (including material recovery and energy conversion) should be included in the system plan.

4. How many transfer stations (intermediate facilities) are needed, what their capacity should be, and where they should be located.

5. How many incinerators, landfills, or other types of processing and final disposal facilities are needed, at what capacity, and where they should be located.

6. To which set of intermediate and final facilities the waste generated in a given location should be sent.

7. How special wastes, and particularly hazardous waste, will be managed as part of the whole system.

Figure 15-1 shows a flowchart outlining the variety of decisions facing the systems planner in addressing the problems involved in the collection, transport, processing, and ultimate disposal of residential solid wastes. Similar decisions must be made for other types of waste.

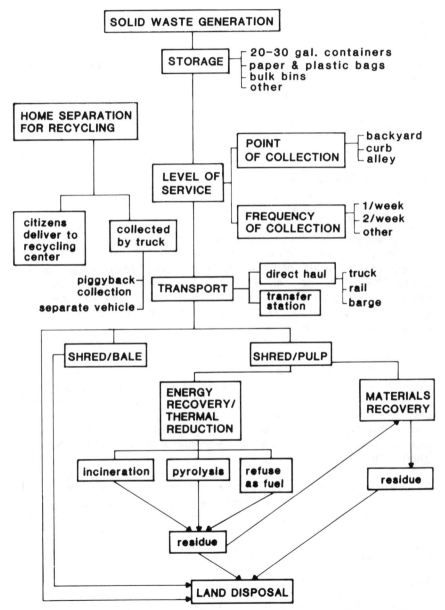

Fig. 15-1. Decision options in solid waste systems planning (7)

The first and foremost question is, what geographic area to plan for? It is usually determined on the basis of existing political and taxing jurisdictions. There may be considerable merit in combining a number of these jurisdictions into a single solid waste district, particularly by making it possible to implement economies in large processing and disposal facilities. However, these larger facilities sometimes involve larger unit cost for collection and transportation. Trade-offs do exist between large and small systems, and it is often possible to determine a minimal cost system. Intergovernmental cooperation should be considered whenever the savings resulting from large-scale transfer, intermediate handling, and final disposal facilities outweigh the additional costs incurred as a result of collecting the waste generated from a larger geographic area.

Solid waste systems planning is a complex process involving considerations of technology, economics, finance, management, and public policy. There is no single technique which incorporates all of these issues into a rigorous analytical pattern. Therefore, comprehensive planning remains very much an art. At present, effective planning of solid waste systems may be more dependent upon logic and an intuitive balance of planning inputs than upon the ability to command sophisticated analytical techniques. Use of these techniques, as presented below, may add to the knowledge of the planner. However, the techniques are limited, and the primary skill required in comprehensive planning is the ability to discriminate among the broad universe of possible planning activities in order to choose those elements essential to the success of the plan. Once the critical elements of a given plan have been identified, the specific tools and techniques of analysis can be utilized in developing an acceptable plan solution.

In this section, the general planning process in the area of solid waste systems is described. Sections 15.4 and 15.5 describe specific techniques for obtaining answers to the basic questions raised earlier in this chapter. The long-range planning of processing and disposal can be expected to consume an increasingly larger proportion of the total bill, and an even larger portion of the total planning effort. Therefore, it is considered first. The key long-range questions address the siting of facilities, choice of processing and disposal technology, and some of the organizational arrangements.

This is followed by Sec. 15.5 on short-range planning, which focuses on residential collection. Here, the decisions range from day-to-day operations through intermediate-range concerns such as the selection of collection equipment. It should be noted that short and long-range planning are not mutually exclusive activities, especially since long-run decisions can be expected to have a significant bearing on the cost and efficiency of the daily collection activity.

15.2.2 Planning Process

According to the U.S. Environmental Protection Agency, planning "is the conscious process for achieving proposed objectives which rationally and fully considers any likely contingencies and alternatives'' (42). In effect, this process should be viewed as a controlled, flexible activity subject to continual revision. It has a formal structure which can be described as a systematic method for recognizing a problem, establishing objectives, collecting relevant data, generating alternative solutions, choosing a recommended solution, and, finally, evaluating the ultimate success of the solution.

In the most basic sense, planning is an aid in the decision-making process (33). However, planning is not a necessary prerequisite to decision-making, for decisions will be made by public officials, political leaders, and businessmen even in the absence of planning. Thus, the burden borne by the planner includes not only the job of determining a solution to perceived problems but also the task of presenting this solution in a manner which is both understandable and acceptable to the decision-makers. This double burden is particularly evident in the field of solid waste systems planning.

The term ''planning'' has been used to denote a wide variety of activities, ranging from a simple physical design to a complex social arrangement. A spectrum of planning activities, consisting of part design at one end and regional plan at the other, can be ranked according to an increasing degree of inherent complexity, as shown in Fig. 15-2. A planning study can be directly concerned with changes in any of these items.

In general, the greater the geographic area encompassed within a plan, the more general and less specific are its objectives. Objectives are the guiding lights towards which a plan is directed. They may be narrowly technical in scope, as in performance criteria for collection vehicles, or broadly policy oriented, as in statewide goals for solid waste regionalization. In the entire planning process, the formulation of objectives is probably the most critical and yet least understood aspect (see Chap. 1).

Fig. 15-2. Spectrum of planning activities

A comprehensive solid waste management plan should serve the following five general functions:

1. Act as an internal policy guideline to the implementing organization.

2. Provide the public with a framework of standards for assessing the implementation.

3. Provide for integrated management of various solid waste activities.

4. Establish procedures for achieving actual design and operation.

5. Promote any desirable legislative or regulatory improvements.

Serving these functions requires consideration of a broad range of planning inputs, which include technical, financial, institutional, and restrictive issues.

Technical   Technical issues involve the engineering analysis and design of physical facilities and system operations associated with collection, transportation, processing, and disposal. For the solid waste engineer, these activities traditionally are treated as deterministic problems contained with a fixed set of assumptions regarding costs, organizations, and policies. More often than not, however, little or no consideration is given to the dynamic aspects, such as legislative changes and institutional constraints. Since effective comprehensive planning deals more with the interrelationships between these various subject areas than with the specific details of any one area, the planner must become sensitive to the issues affecting systems development to contribute significantly to plan success.

Financial   Financial issues include both the over-all expenditure of resources to achieve certain system objectives and financial flows occurring within the system. In solid waste systems, as in most public services, the resources include labor, management, equipment, physical facilities, and money. An efficient utilization of system resources implies either minimum resource use for a given set of system outputs or maximum system outputs for a given level of resource inputs. The techniques of economic analysis, such as cost-benefit analysis and cost-effectiveness analysis, are often used in the evaluation of alternative system plans (9).

The financial aspects deal less with intrinsic system worth and more with the ability of a system to generate sufficient monetary flows to remain solvent. Among the various ways of financing solid waste systems are tax revenues, user charges, general obligation bonds, revenue bonds, corporate bonds, and private leasing arrangements (14, 51). Bond issues can require sophisticated financial advice, and consequently most communities prefer to finance ordinary solid waste collection and disposal out of general tax revenues.

This financing method is appropriate for continuing operations. In contrast, the development of capital-intensive resource recovery facilities has been dominated by private investment, often with some government assistance (particularly commitments to use the facility). Thus, greater attention now is paid to financing modes involving corporate bonds, lease arrangements, and tax treatments. In all cases, capital and recurring costs usually involve different sources of financing. Capital costs are lump-sum investments for new equipment and facilities, while recurrent costs are continuous expenditures necessary to meet the ongoing operation and maintenance expenses of the system.

Institutional   Institutional issues include the types of organizational structures within which solid waste operations are conducted, the role of management, and the establishment of administrative guidelines. Solid waste systems may be managed by public institutions such as cities, counties, councils of government, or state agencies. They also may be managed within the private sector as privately owned, publicly regulated utilities or as pure private enterprises. Sometimes an over-all solid waste system may be divided between the public and private sectors, either vertically (such as collection services operated privately and disposal facilities operated publicly) or horizontally, with some customers or classes of customers served by public collection and others by private collection. A critical issue of concern is the extent to which small systems should be integrated into larger regional systems in order to obtain greater efficiencies of operation and improved levels of service. Manpower planning and industrial relations also are growing in importance as the tendency for municipal employees to unionize and strike for improved conditions of employment grows in all parts of the country. Under such circumstances, solid waste systems engineers and planners in the public sector must learn to take into account problems of management and administration that formerly were of concern only in the private sector (7).

Restrictive   Restrictive issues refer to the constraining effects of institutions, policies, and legislation on solid waste systems. Institutional constraints include limitations on the authority of system managers to change their methods of operation or to expand their areas of service. The limitations will vary considerably among systems.

Policies also can have indirect effects, as in the case of industrial attitudes towards the appearance, convenience, and cost of packaging materials. Private industry traditionally has placed great emphasis on the marketing aspects of packaging and little on the disposal aspects. As a result, there has been a great increase in the generation of solid wastes. Because of the importance of such indirect effects, comprehensive solid waste systems planning must attempt to take into account both organizational policies and prevailing community values.

Legislative constraints include the laws and regulations that control and guide the planning and management of solid waste systems. The federal Resource Conservation and Recovery Act of 1976, and its predecessors, have established the basic federal policies for solid waste management (37). Most of the states have followed the lead of the federal government. During the early 1970s, many states enacted new solid waste management statutes, some of them for the first time. Typical provisions in these state acts were general adherence to improved environmental quality, strong injunctions against open refuse fires and open dumps, moderate encouragement of regional solid waste management efforts, and relatively ineffectual support for resource recovery and conservation. The state responses, however, varied greatly. Some states did nothing, while others not only enacted new legislation, but also established major funding programs to support implementation of the acts (38, 48). This process has continued in numerous additional laws and regulations in hazardous waste management.

Despite these trends, legislative controls upon solid waste systems are not always benign. Local restrictions on siting of facilities can severely hamper an otherwise useful solid waste plan. Similarly, resource recovery has been discouraged by many legislative acts and administrative rulings which provide preferential freight rates, tax depletion allowances, and packaging requirements for virgin materials over recovered materials (44). None of these restrictive issues is immutable; all are dynamic and subject to change. Nevertheless, the actual presence of such constraints, as well as the possibility of their changing for better or worse in the future, calls attention to their importance in solid waste systems planning.

Developing a plan   Incorporating the full range of these issues is no easy task, and it is unreasonable to expect the individual planner or engineer to have a firm grasp of them all. Moreover, no planner has the luxury of unlimited time and resources to study in detail all aspects of the plan. Resources available for planning purposes always are limited and frequently are considered, by the planners at least, to be insufficient. The development of an appropriate solid waste systems plan, therefore, involves an initial identification of the critical planning inputs essential to plan success. Out of the almost endless array of possible plan activities, the planner must choose those key inputs allowed by available resources of time, staff, and funds. Figure 15-3 presents a model of the major activities included in the development of a solid waste systems plan. The model links plan formulation with subsequent plan implementation, which in turn is followed by systems monitoring and evaluation. These latter activities provide information and insights which should be included as inputs in new planning activities.

Although the planning, implementation, and evaluation activities are correctly viewed as a closed, continuous process, as shown in Fig. 15-3, a useful starting point for descriptive purposes is the recognition of a solid waste problem. The next step is to formulate basic goals for the solution of the problem. The goals lead to an iterative process involving data collection and the generation of alternatives. Within each alternative, the basic technical, financial, institutional, and restrictive issues

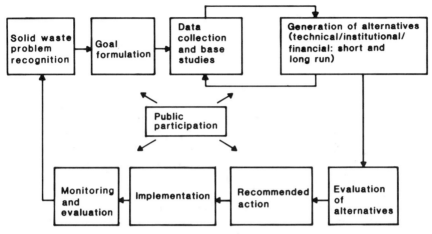

Fig. 15-3. Solid waste systems planning model

referred to earlier should be considered. Once an appropriate range of alternative solutions has been formulated, various analytical techniques are available to evaluate the alternatives and to select one or more recommended courses of action. Comprehensive planning must go beyond data collection and analysis to include specific recommendations whenever appropriate.

Continuing with the model, the next general step in systems planning is plan implementation. This is followed by monitoring of system performance and over-all evaluation of plan success. The results of the monitoring and evaluation steps logically feed directly back into the planning process again by calling attention to new problems requiring solution. Contained within the entire planning-implementation-evaluation process should be a steady input of public participation in the form of public hearings, citizens' committees, open meetings, and wide publicity. Public participation should be encouraged, not only because of increasing legal requirements for such inputs, but also because of the important benefits to be obtained from the open discussion of proposed solid waste systems affecting the general public.

15.2.3 Waste Generation and Composition

Before entering into detailed systems planning, it is important to look at the quantities and composition of the waste to be handled. The question to be answered first, however, is what information should be gathered about quantities and composition. The answer depends on the type of planning being done.

For analyzing large-scale processing systems for municipal and commercial waste, good knowledge is needed of the amounts of waste available in various areas, and the composition of that waste (particularly with respect to issues such as BTU values and quantities of aluminum or other high value components). In the analysis of collection, simple measures of total volume and weight (to get density) may be sufficient, though it may be important to see how this varies across income groups or types of housing, particularly for route balancing.

If the problem is one of hazardous waste disposal, however, the analysis must be detailed enough to allow proper consideration of waste characteristics in designing and operating disposal sites. Capacity must be available for handling each type of waste, without mixing incompatible components. While long-term planning requires less information than site operations, it is still necessary to get some detail on industrial waste characteristics, so that it can be included in planning.

Several sources exist for information on typical waste generation rates (7, 30). Others provide details on the performance of various tests (3, 46, 50) or composition measurements (11, 31). Still others have modeled the waste generation functions for households, including explicit consideration of yard waste, income, housing type, household size, and collection and pricing policies, which may affect the quantities and types of waste (20).

In addition, as part of their water pollution control efforts, most major cities have implemented industrial waste questionnaires. Similar questionnaires can be used for analyzing solid wastes. As a precursor to this step, which is likely to be part of a regulatory program, local input-output tables have been used to estimate total solid waste production for an area, by converting projected firm outputs to waste generation using standard multipliers (39, 40).

All of these methods are covered in the literature, and can be used for planning, with the choice depending on the characteristics of the particular problem being analyzed. Any one of them, and particularly any use of actual data, would be preferable to the common practice of assuming some national value [5 lb (1.9 kg) per day, or 3 lb (1.1 kg), or 2 lb (0.75 kg), for example] and applying it in a local situation.

15.3 EVALUATION METHODOLOGY

15.3.1 Purposes and Objectives

The ability to evaluate the productivity of solid waste systems is a necessary prerequisite to the proper planning of actions pertaining to those systems. In order for management to take appropriate actions pertaining to long or short-range planning and resource allocation, it must have an adequate data base and an adequate mechanism for providing the necessary inputs for decision-making on a continuous basis. Such mechanisms are not currently available. The problem lies mainly in the fact that the output of a public service function is a multidimensional array of both quantitative and qualitative factors affecting different clusters of people at different points in time. The definition of these outputs is not an easy matter—nor is their assessment.

It is common to find two communities of equal size, only a few miles apart, allocating inordinately different amounts of resources per capita to the solid waste effort. It has become a standard argument that private collection may be a more efficient and less costly solution to the solid waste collection problem than public collection or vice versa. In either of these cases, it is not clear whether the more expensive undertaking provides an over-all service which is better or worse than its "more efficient" counterpart. Neither is there a conceptual framework, a data base, or an adequate mechanism for providing the answer to such complex problems. Typically, the kind of data available for decision-making has been operational data, such as the cost per ton collected or disposed. Such data, however, do not provide any insight into the extent to which a service is achieving its proposed goals. Only during the last few years have such questions been addressed. The concept of productivity is meaningless unless it is measured in terms of both the efficiency and effectiveness of the system in question.

Evaluation implies measurement and the ability to compare. The results of the evaluation process become, in turn, inputs into the planning process, so that a plan generates a condition warranting evaluation which then provides feedback to guide future planning. In this manner, planning and evaluation can be seen as two poles of an iterative field of action, with each taking outputs from, and providing inputs to, the other. The task facing the solid waste planner is to develop a systems plan which provides for relevant, yet practical, measurement of plan objectives. This interaction of planning, evaluation, objectives, and measurement is basic to comprehensive solid waste systems management.

15.3.2 Evaluation Process

Much of the difficulty in the evaluation of solid waste systems stems from a lack of a conceptual framework and from confusion in the use of terminology and definitions, which vary from place to place. The evaluation process must therefore be based upon models which clearly differentiate between the types of system consequences and indicate the interrelationships between inputs and outputs. Such models should incorporate consideration of the efficiency, effectiveness, and ultimate social impacts of solid waste systems.

The initial measurements of system performance involve the direct outputs of the production process, such as number of tons collected, number of housing units served, and vehicle-miles driven. The efficiency of the process can be defined as a ratio of outputs to inputs which results in measurements such as tons per vehicle-mile or tons per worker-day. These direct measurements, however, do not measure the real goal of the system, which is the quality of service. It is difficult to compare efficiency measures across geographic boundaries because of variations in local conditions affecting the utilization of resources. The key to the measurement of performance of a solid waste system, therefore, is the effectiveness of the system.

Effectiveness is a compound over-all measure of the different components that make up the quality of service. Since effectiveness is influenced by both expectations and subsequent satisfaction, the degree of effectiveness of a solid waste plan will vary from community to community and from neighborhood to neighborhood. Since there are no universal measurements, it is necessary to define the process for developing effectiveness measurements in a given community.

The effects of a solid waste plan do not stop with the operation of a system: they may have far-reaching effects on other aspects of society. These impacts are the secondary and indirect consequences of the system upon the community and region. It is convenient to classify these impacts into the categories of social wellbeing, economic development, and environmental quality. In the broadest sense, however, these impacts encompass the ultimate purposes of all public works planning: the improvement of the general welfare of society as a whole.

15.3.3 Public Systems Evaluation Model

Definition Figure 15-4 shows a generalized form of the three-level model of system outputs just described. This public systems evaluation model has been found to be applicable for the assessment of a wide variety of public services, including water supply and wastewater disposal (47), urban mass transit (16), statewide resource recovery efforts,

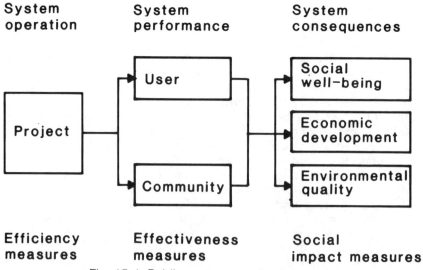

Fig. 15-4. Public systems evaluation model

and solid waste collection (8). Since the model distinguishes different levels of outputs, it also can be used for the assessment of productivity.The efficiency level contains only physical inputs and outputs under the direct control of the system manager. These primary responses can be viewed as the basic "costs" of the system, and an efficient system will minimize these costs. The effectiveness measures also are primarily physical in nature, but they require interaction, or usage, by the public for the responses to occur. These secondary responses can be viewed as basic "benefits" of the system. It is the responsibility of the system manager to maximize these benefits. Since both the efficiency and effectiveness measures are defined in physical terms, they can be readily quantified and evaluated. This is true both for solid waste systems and for most other public services. Thus, the model allows a straightforward definition of efficiency and effectiveness that clearly separates these immediate and quantifiable aspects from the indirect and often unquantifiable impacts that occur in the areas of social wellbeing, economic development, and environmental quality.

Within the specific field of solid waste systems, the public systems evaluation model can be utilized in the following manner. The efficiency level comprises the operation of a solid wastes system and is determined by technical production functions under the control of the system manager. As indicated earlier, measurements of system operation are scaled in terms of physical units of weight, volume, distance, time, energy, etc. This level reflects the capabilities, or the technical potential, of the system and is not dependent upon specific project usage by the community. Project operation and technical outputs at the efficiency level are the primary concern of the planner.

At the effectiveness level, the efficiency outputs interact with the users and the general community. System performance is based on the usage of system outputs by the public. For solid waste systems, typical areas of concern include street cleanliness, public cooperation, worker productivity, and policy implementation. The latter includes legal power to perform the action and to obtain funding, institutional capability, and political feasibility. Policy concerns should be interpreted broadly, to include issues such as public health and morbidity.

Effectiveness measures often are stated in per capita terms, such as collection costs per capita, waste generation per capita, system complaints per capita. In all cases, the measurement must reflect some degree of interaction between the solid waste system and the public. If a system is poorly utilized by the public, measurements should show a low degree of effectiveness.

This interaction between system outputs and the users of the outputs is independent of the theoretical efficiency of the system. It is conceivable that a system with a high efficiency rating could have a low effectiveness rating and vice versa. The outputs which occur at the effectiveness level usually are the primary concern of physical planners and of engineers interested in over-all system performance.

The social impact level includes the ultimate consequences of solid waste systems. Outputs at this level may involve changes in social wellbeing (public health, social opportunities, community attitudes), economic development (employment opportunities, new business formation), and environmental quality (green space, public recreation, community esthetics). There may be no discernible link between the initial solid waste system input and the ultimate social impacts. It would usually be erroneous, for example, to claim direct causality between an improved solid waste system and a subsequent increase in industrial employment. Furthermore, it could be difficult, if not impossible, to show even indirect linkages between system input and employment output. Too many intervening factors can and do occur to allow a definite tracing of even indirect causality. Nevertheless, it is not unreasonable to contend that an improved solid waste system is one of several inputs contributing to the ultimate impact of increased employment. Over-all, the project related consequences that occur at the social impact level are primarily the concern of policy-makers.

Each of the three levels in the public systems evaluation model can be rated in terms of general dimensions relevant to solid waste systems and the needs of the systems planner. These dimensions include the time necessary for a given system output to occur, the degree of causality linking the system input to output of interest, the present state of knowledge concerning the input-output relationships, and the ease of measuring the output in the field. Over the three levels, the effects of these evaluation dimensions can be characterized as shown in Table 15-1.

At present, the state of the art in the evaluation of public systems in general, and solid waste systems in particular, suffers from a lack of consensus as to evaluation concepts, measurement techniques, and over-all methodology. Until such time as evaluation is seen as an integral part of the planning process, the development of solid waste systems will be hampered by an inability to take full advantage of past experiences and actions.

Example applications   Figure 15-5 demonstrates the application of the public systems evaluation model to solid waste collection efforts. The measurement and assessment of the effectiveness of such effort is based

TABLE 15-1 Characteristics of Evaluation Dimensions (47)

Characteristic (2)	Efficiency (2)	Effectiveness (3)	Impact (4)
Delays between action and effect	immediate	short	long
Degree of causality	direct	direct	indirect
State of knowledge	good	moderate	limited
Ease of measurement	easy	variable	difficult

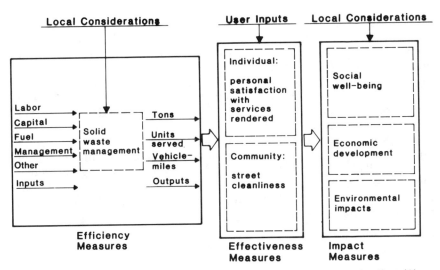

Fig. 15-5. Logical framework for solid waste systems evaluation (8)

on a three-dimensional analysis involving: (1) Users' satisfaction; (2) the effects of the service on the community; and (3) societal values and preferences.

The users' perceptions of and level of satisfaction with the quality of service are measured by direct questioning of a representative sample of the user population. Questions measuring the satisfaction of the citizens are analyzed by giving the various responses point values. A user satisfaction index (U.S.I.) is thus defined as

$$\text{U.S.I.} = \sum_i^q R_i \qquad (15.1)$$

in which R_i = value of question i, and q = total number of questions.

The user satisfaction index assumes maximum value (100 in this case) when all of the responses are given maximum values, indicating complete satisfaction with all the components that constitute the over-all quality of the service. The weights given to different items can be varied to reflect community preferences. An example of a questionnaire designed to measure citizen satisfaction with municipal services is given in Reference 8. The immediate objectives of an effective solid waste collection system are to provide a clean environment which is free from health hazards and esthetically pleasing. Attention thus should be focused on defining, measuring, and weighting the different variables that make up the community effects component of the effectiveness mode.

Over-all street cleanliness can be measured through the institution of a continuous program of visual inspection of block faces conducted by trained inspectors. The visual inspection scheme described here is similar to the one used in Washington, D.C., and other cities. It is based on training an inspector to rate block faces on a scale of 1 to 4, with the lower end of the scale representing a clean street and the higher end a heavily littered street. As the inspector traverses a street, he or she records the visual cleanliness verbally on a cassette tape. The recorded data are later transcribed and analyzed. It has been found that a trained inspector can cover as many as 250 block faces in an 8-hr working day. Several methods have been developed for such ratings (4, 8). A community effects index (C.E.I.) can be calculated by combining the aggregate effects of all block faces in the neighborhood and normalizing the values obtained so that an impeccably clean neighborhood would have a rating of 100 (this condition is all but impossible to obtain). To calculate the community effects index, use

$$\text{C.E.I.} = 100 - \frac{100}{3} \frac{\left(\sum_{1}^{b} S_i - 1\right)}{b} \qquad (15.2)$$

in which S_i = cleanliness rating of the ith block face, and b = number of block faces in the neighborhood.

Societal values are the most difficult to evaluate quantitatively. Their use is suggested in the proposed model in order to provide guidelines for the development of thresholds of societal acceptability and the formation of different combinations of the user satisfaction and community effect indexes. Societal values will reflect such factors as a community's resource allocation decisions, its budgetary appropriations, its priorities, and its citizen participation activities. This area has not yet been fully explored, and further research will be needed to translate conceptual suggestions into workable processes. It should be emphasized, however, that the approach described attempts to independently evaluate the performance of a system, as perceived by the users themselves, within a general framework of accepted societal values.

The model determines the effectiveness of a public service relative to three independent variables and combines these factors into a new measure of "level of service," which is intended to describe the relative performance of alternative proposals, solutions, and management strategies. Figure 15-6 is a graphic representation of the level of service concept. Each of the numbered circles on the graph represents the combination of user satisfaction and community effects indexes prevailing in a given neighborhood. Neighborhoods ① and ③ are thus characterized as having a combination yielding a level of service which is perceived to be excellent, while neighborhood ⑤ has a combination of indexes warranting a fair level of service. The partitioning of the two-dimensional user-community space is dictated by the priorities,

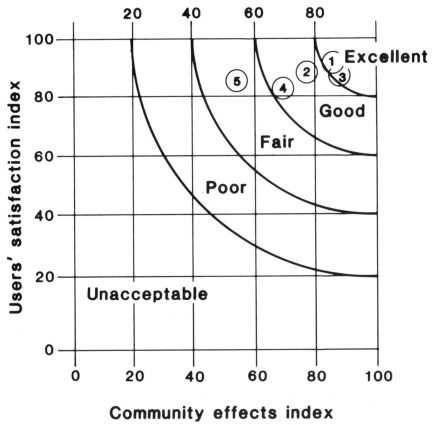

Community effects index

Fig. 15-6. "Level of service" concept (8)

values, and perceptions of a given community. It also reflects the level of physical improvement and public investment needed in each subdivision of the city. When properly applied, the level of service concept can be used by city management to help determine community development priorities.

The National Commission on Productivity, in a recent study of the productivity of solid waste collection, has described the level of service as:

> . . . a matter of community choice, with citizens of any jurisdiction having the option of deciding what they want and how much they are willing to pay for it. Sometimes citizens are adamant in their preference for one level of service over another, . . . In other cases, citizens have simply grown accustomed to a given level of service; never stopping to question whether it could be changed, how much a change would cost, or how much would be saved by making the change. (29)

In order to use the model, data must be obtained for calculating the levels of both user satisfaction and community effects. These two levels then are plotted two-dimensionally and an appropriate level of service for the area at a given time is identified. Once this is accomplished for one town or area, the same procedure can be used for establishing the level of service in other areas of the city and in other cities, or for evaluating the change in the level of service which might result from community or governmental actions. The main value of the model lies in its capability to provide comparative, quantitative evaluations of the effectiveness of community services, which, in turn, provide useful inputs into the decision-making processes within the community.

15.4 LONG-RANGE PLANNING

The long-range solid waste planning options which should be considered can be classified into three basic categories:

1. Technological options, including the number, location, size, and type of processing and disposal facilities.
2. Scale and sizing options, including the consideration of the viability and extent of interjurisdictional cooperation among adjacent units of government.
3. Temporal options, concerning the timing of implementation of the technological and scale options.

Decision-makers should be told what the cost and efficiency implications of different actions might be at various future points in time. They also should be told whether regionalization will contribute to a more efficient provision of service and, if so, what information should be obtained to assist them in setting up future interjurisdictional cooperation. Decision-makers must be able to determine whether (or under what conditions) the introduction of processing, incineration, or resource recovery plants will contribute to cost reduction and over-all system efficiency. Ultimately, new landfills of all types must be opened and old landfills eventually must be closed. It is essential, in an economic sense, to be able to forecast when such actions will be necessary. For siting of new facilities to be successful, the community needs an understanding of the actual costs and risks of environmental protection. Note that cross-media issues such as sludge handling may, in certain cases, be of critical importance to long-range planning.

Decisions relating to issues usually found within the long-range planning function can be made in a variety of ways. At one extreme is intuitive judgment based on personal experience and opinions about the status quo. A more analytical approach would attempt to enumerate a range of possible future courses of action and assess the costs and benefits associated with each in order to develop a plan most suitable for the jurisdiction in question. The most rigorous of the rational planning methods utilizes the power inherent in mathematical programming and optimization theory to select the most efficient combination of technological, scale, and temporal options open to the community. Many such models have been developed within the last 15 years, examples of which are given in References 17, 18, 21, 25, 26, 41, and 43. All are basically concerned with balancing the economies of scale expected to result from larger processing and disposal facilities against the additional costs of transportation needed to supply these facilities with the waste generated in the region.

15.4.1 Mathematical Programming Approaches

The U.S. Environmental Protection Agency developed a computerized model which has the capacity of performing this long-range planning function (45). Termed WRAP for waste resources allocation program, this model produces outputs which provide a dynamic profile of regional solid waste management solutions in terms of the location, size, and type of facilities needed and the specific waste-generating areas supplying each facility at various points in time. It is not the intention here to delve into the mathematical details of problem formulations and algorithmic solutions, but it is instructive to present a formulation of a typical long-range planning problem. The formulation presented provides the basic form of most of the optimization models. This simplified example is of the static variety; it presents the optimal solution at one specific future time. A dynamic model would include different time periods as additional variables in the optimization problem.

Consider the area shown in Fig. 15-7, which has been divided into a number of waste generation zones, each representing an area with relatively homogeneous population, land use, and waste generation characteristics. Each zone is assigned a centroid, which is assumed to be the point at which all wastes are generated within the zone. The tons of waste generated in each zone are estimated for each year X_i. Potential intermediate processing and final disposal sites available in the general area are selected for use. Intermediate processing sites include transfer stations and resource recovery facilities. Final disposal sites denote landfill locations. Whenever one processing location has the potential for a number of alternative processes, each combination of mutually exclusive processes is given a different number, although they may be contenders for the same site. Material flows, thus, are denoted by W_{ij} for flows between sources i and disposal sites j, and by W_{ik} for flows between sources and processing facilities k. Flows between processing and disposal facilities are denoted by W_{kj}. Transportation costs in dollars per ton between these three sets of facilities are designated by C_{ij}, C_{ik} and C_{kj}, respectively. Similarly, the capacities of disposal and processing facilities are denoted by Q_j and Q_k, respectively. Since processing facilities will result in some reduction of the total amount of waste, it is necessary to define an indicator of the magnitude of reduction for each process being contemplated. This indicator is defined as the ratio of the

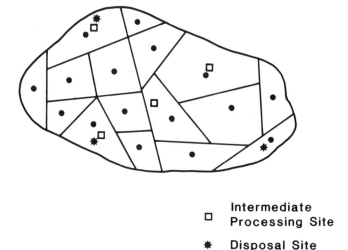

□   **Intermediate**
    Processing Site

＊   **Disposal Site**

●   **Zone Centroids**

Fig. 15-7. Hypothetical solid waste planning problem

weight of the outputs of the process to the weight of the inputs and is denoted by a_k.

The final item required for the development of the model is that of facility cost data. Such costs usually are given in terms of two components: fixed and variable. The simplest (though not very realistic) assumption is that of a linear cost function, as shown in Fig. 15-8(a). Most processing and disposal facilities, however, have a cost function similar to that shown in Fig. 15-8(b), which represents declining incremental costs with increasing capacity. This indicates the existence of economies of scale, which is another way of saying that the cost per unit of capacity decreases as the size of the facility increases. Such functions usually are approximated by a number of straight-line segments. For the purposes of this example (and most models), a linear relationship similar to the one shown in Fig. 15-8(a) will be assumed. Each processing or disposal facility will have a fixed charge needed to set up the facility, F_j or F_k, and a variable cost which is dependent on the actual size of the facility, V_j or V_k.

The above inputs provide all the necessary variables to formulate and solve an optimization problem. A solution algorithm selects that combination of size, location, and waste assignment which will handle the wastes of the region at the lowest possible cost. In a simple case involving two zones, one disposal site, and two possible intermediate transfer process options, all waste routing options would be as shown in Fig. 15-9. Each arrow represents a possible flow of raw or processed waste, and the optimization algorithm selects that combination of waste

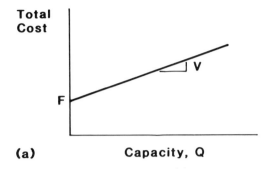

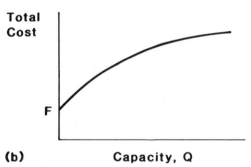

Fig. 15-8. Cost functions for disposal and processing facilities: (a) Linear; (b) with economies of scale

flows which results in the lowest total system cost. The objective function is to minimize (transportation costs + fixed charges + variable costs). This objective function must be minimized subject to the following constraints:

1. All wastes generated in a given zone are processed and disposed of.

2. Flows leaving an intermediate processing facility are equal to a processing efficiency parameter times flows entering it.

3. Inputs to each intermediate facility do not exceed the capacity of that particular facility.

4. Flows to a given disposal site over time do not exceed the ultimate capacity of that site.

5. The usual mathematical restrictions for linear programming formulations apply: all variables greater than or equal to zero, for example.

It should be stressed that the example given represents a static linear

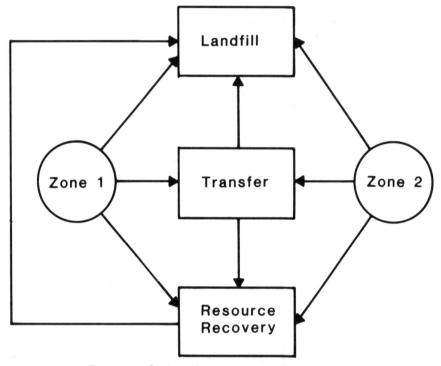

Fig. 15-9. Options in simple hypothetical case

formulation of the problem, with all the constraining effects that it implies. There are at least three ways in which it may be useful to extend the model:

- By including multiple objectives, rather than just cost minimization
- By allowing shifts over time, as new facilities are developed, quantities of waste change, or existing landfills become full
- By adding an associated simulation mode, which will test the results of the optimization model for their realism.

Any model of this type should be used primarily for "screening"; that is, to limit the set of possibilities to those which appear to be both fairly efficient and relatively acceptable to the decision-makers and public. Most models to date have been like the simple example presented above: they have been based purely on finding the least-cost alternative for the system without looking at possibilities for implementation or ways to get from the present situation to that "least-cost" system. They have also been used for detailed planning, even where the model assumptions make this unreasonable.

Optimization models of the type described can be used to analyze multiple objectives. For example, they can look directly at the cost savings which could occur under regionalization. Such models can do this dynamically as well. The structure is fairly similar, though the solution costs may rise as the problems become more complex. In one case study, for example, an analysis was done of the Boston area (15) which developed the curve shown in Fig. 15-10. In essence, this curve (and others like it) show how cost is related to waste shipment. In one ideal situation, each community would manage its own wastes, and cost would be minimized. This example shows directly how costs depend on the amount of waste shipped between communities for processing and disposal, and gives the trade-off between the objectives. There is no single best option for all parties, but instead a range of efficient options which can be used for negotiation.

Once the optimization model has helped the local decision-makers to narrow the range of solutions, it may be useful to develop a simulation to test the solutions or the options in more detail. Optimization approaches are good for looking at a large number of options, but they gain this ability through simplification. Simulations, on the other hand, can

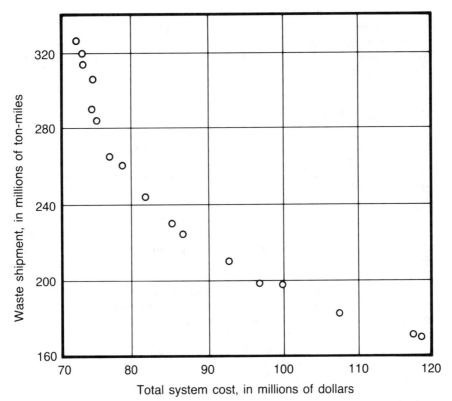

Fig. 15-10. Trade-off curve: system cost versus system equity (15)

include significantly more detail, but only look at one option at a time. For planning of large-scale facilities, the two approaches work well in conjunction, as has been shown in a number of studies (23, 24).

15.4.2 Resource Recovery: Sources and Markets

Models such as those described are useful in planning processing and disposal systems, and may provide information on what options appear to have the least total costs over the planning period. However, these models generally assume that all the waste in an area is sent to the desired processing facilities, and that markets are available for the materials or energy produced by those facilities. Engineers or planners who have actually been involved in resource recovery facility implementation agree that the key constraints for the facilities are not the technologies. The main concerns are whether the waste will be supplied with the right quantities and characteristics (and dumping fees), and whether the products can be sold at a reasonable price over the long term.

EPA has published introductory materials about these problems, and studied the effects of waste markets on the economic feasibility of existing plants (44). However, there is very little completed research in this area, and experiences differ considerably. For the purposes of this guide, therefore, it is only possible to state that the vast majority of the planning effort in implementing a resource recovery facility is likely to be spent in analyzing the economic feasibility of the plant, based on input waste quantities and final product markets, rather than analyzing its technical feasibility.

15.4.3 Siting of New Facilities

Models are useful in helping to guide the planner on what type of transfer, processing, and disposal system would be efficient, effective, or meet other systemwide objectives. However, the real long-range planning problem is likely to be qualifying and gaining approval on individual sites. The technical feasibility of particular sites for given technologies, types of waste, and climates is well beyond the scope of this chapter. Technical concerns are the subject of engineering design manuals, not planning documents. The planner must be aware that these concerns typically include soils, hydrology, climate, traffic, and other factors.

The political issues in local support or opposition to sites are of concern, but are also an area where relatively little can be said beyond the traditional advice to planners. However, there are a few developing trends which should be watched and considered.

Public participation programs are probably critical to obtaining a site. The times are gone when the solid waste system planners could select an area and implement a site without local opposition. Impacts on traffic, ground water, property values, and other neighborhood or travel route characteristics will be of concern, and need to be dealt with directly. Reference 10 provides some case studies of successful and unsuccessful programs.

It is often necessary to go beyond simple public involvement in the process, and consider mitigation, compensation, or incentives (2, 28, 32). Mitigation involves changes to the facility's design or operating procedures to reduce impacts (for example, changing access routes, providing for independent monitoring of impacts).

Compensation programs admit that there will be adverse impacts on the area receiving the facility, and provide the host community or area with some offsetting benefit. This might be a direct monetary payment, or an implicit payment (such as reduced dumping fees). It might be tied to a particular impact—for example, fear of fire in a compaction plant might be compensated by providing the community with an extra fire station or truck. Alternatively, fear of lowering property values might be offset by land value guarantees to nearby property owners. Compensation funds can be set up to include performance bonds, post-closure funds for recovery of the area, or the like.

Incentives are not directly related to the impacts of the project. Examples include building roads in the host community, or the provision by the facility developer of open space or parkland. Incentives essentially show good faith without requiring direct ties between the project and the type of community assistance.

All three approaches have been successful, though they are not appropriate for every case. It is clear that there are perceived impacts from facilities, and these approaches may be useful in reducing the fears of nearby residents or host communities. The result can be an easier siting process.

However, the best way to reduce fears is to have good evidence that the facility is needed, and that the fears are groundless. This requires an effective planning process and, even more important, effective operation of the existing system so that the concerned parties can see that the current operations have minimal impact. Nothing is more effective in siting than a good track record for the existing sites.

15.5 SHORT-RANGE PLANNING—COLLECTION

Short-range planning deals with decisions which do not involve capital-intensive undertakings and which cover actions that can be implemented within a short period of time. The area of solid waste collection frequently involves issues of short-range planning. An extensive review, *Solid Waste Collection Practice*, published by the American Public Works Association, should be read by any engineer or planner concerned with the planning problems in this field (1). This section will not repeat APWA's review of current practice but will explore ways to improve planning of solid waste collection.

15.5.1 Source Separation

For residential wastes, there was always a question of whether to have separate collection of rubbish and garbage. The concern now is whether to segregate and collect materials for recycling, such as newspapers, cans, and bottles. Mandatory separation ordinances and separate collection systems do reduce the quantities of waste consigned to landfills, and increase the amount recycled. Separate collection, though, is expensive, and the markets for recycled consumer waste are volatile. A large number of recycling centers and similar programs are started each time the price of newsprint rises; many fail when the price drops.

From the perspective of a solid waste system planner, source separation looks attractive, as does any other strategy which reduces the amount of landfill capacity used each year. However, there are two major concerns facing any sort of resource recovery at this point, and source separation is no exception: system costs, and availability of markets for the reclaimed materials. Both of these factors deserve careful analysis before implementing a separate collection system.

15.5.2 Frequency

The frequency of collection is another important factor which varies significantly from one location to another. In general, there has been a nationwide shift in the 1970s and 1980s from a twice-weekly collection schedule to one which calls for a single weekly collection, and this is because of collection cost savings on the order of 30% (7, 25, 43). In warmer areas, such as the south, twice-weekly collection was considered necessary to interrupt the 5-day fly breeding cycle (12, 13). Widespread use of plastic bags with closed seals and standardized high-quality containers has reduced this problem, and weekly collection may be acceptable for sanitation.

15.5.3 Transportation

Several methods are in common use for transporting the waste from premises to collection vehicles. At one extreme, residents may be required by city ordinances to place their waste containers at the curb or alley for pickup by collection vehicles. This is the most economical method from the standpoint of the city, though it may not be the most desirable from the resident's point of view. The alternative, that of the city or contracting firm collecting the containers from the back door, can be about 50% more expensive. Use of standardized automatic loading wheeled containers can significantly reduce costs.

15.5.4 Vehicles

The choice of the collection vehicle may have some significant effects on the over-all efficiency of the collection effort. The most common types of vehicles are compactor trucks with capacities of between 16 cu yd and 40 cu yd (12 cu m and 31 cu m), with mechanical loading for large containers at apartments, commercial buildings, and industrial wastes. Until recently, the trend has been strongly towards larger equipment, higher levels of mechanization, and smaller crews, based on savings in system costs. Table 15-2 shows estimates of the costs of solid waste collection under various service arrangements based on a major survey (34). The table shows that the least-cost systems are those with the smallest crews and the lowest level of service: weekly collection from curbside. Requiring use of plastic bags or containers which can be loaded mechanically reduces these system costs even further. However, it may increase the costs to residents, if they have to purchase the special bags or containers.

Vehicle choice is important, and methods of evaluating the vehicles should be carefully considered. Analytic approaches have been used for choosing vehicles in the past (5, 6, 22) which involve scoring each contender on a number of factors (expected maintenance requirements, fuel efficiency, etc.) and weighting the scores. Even if a less formal method is used, it is apparent that these are major decisions, and the data for choice are finally being made available in a useful form through organizations like the Waste Equipment Manufacturers Association.

15.5.5 Route Allocation

Solid waste collection agencies must allocate routes to their collection crews. One approach is to allocate a definite daily task to each crew by segmenting the community into areas of a size equivalent to about one day of work for a crew. In this manner, a crew will be assigned three to six collection routes per week, depending on the frequency of collection. Such an approach allows residents to know the collection days (a requirement for curbside collection) and provides the crew with an incentive to finish early. Labor problems may arise, however, if the schedule cannot be maintained. The rigidity of the approach makes it susceptible to breakdowns and interruptions. An alternative way of allocating definite tasks to crews includes assignments on a weekly basis, in which a crew continues each morning at the ending point of the previous day until the assignment is completed. It sometimes is desirable to have a standby crew available to assist the regular crews when unusually high load volumes occur in a single area. It may also be useful to provide a central overflow route which is collected by whichever set of the crews serving surrounding routes finishes early. Both of these techniques are designed to add flexibility to the collection effort.

15.5.6 Economics

The economics of over-all solid waste collection, processing, and disposal are a function of all of the preceding considerations. There are other factors which depend on the nature of the community and the

TABLE 15-2 Collection Costs and Cost Determinants (34)

Cost Determinant (1)	Cost[a] and Service Level					
	Cost per ton			Cost per household per year		
	Once-per-week curbside (2)	Twice-per-week curbside (3)	Once-per-week backyard (4)	Once-per-week curbside (5)	Twice-per-week curbside (6)	Once-per-week backyard (7)
Crew size						
1 worker	11.79 (10)[b]	14.69 (2)	28.97 (1)	29.38 (14)	44.06 (5)	26.53 (3)
2 workers	26.53 (21)	31.63 (12)	24.48 (5)	31.40 (43)	35.80 (20)	37.61 (10)
3 workers	19.46 (24)	25.03 (31)	39.40 (4)	28.33 (30)	33.77 (34)	46.78 (10)
Incentive system						
yes	21.01 (47)	25.69 (41)	22.10 (11)	30.60 (73)	36.12 (58)	35.63 (22)
no	18.12 (13)	27.41 (7)	48.09 (3)	28.48 (23)	31.63 (10)	49.52 (6)
Absentee rate						
>7.9%	20.32 (24)	27.87 (25)	31.95 (3)	26.08 (27)	33.65 (30)	40.83 (8)
<7.9%	19.02 (27)	23.95 (19)	23.06 (9)	30.79 (46)	38.36 (31)	33.19 (15)
Truck capacity						
<20 cubic yards	21.62 (35)	27.68 (34)	31.51 (8)	33.94 (59)	37.00 (42)	38.21 (18)
>20 cubic yards	18.65 (25)	21.71 (14)	22.56 (6)	23.96 (37)	32.97 (26)	37.32 (10)
Percentage rear-loading trucks						
<90%	12.63 (22)	25.95 (17)	17.49 (6)	25.57 (28)	36.15 (24)	33.21 (11)
>90%	24.87 (38)	25.94 (31)	35.31 (8)	31.96 (68)	35.08 (44)	42.10 (17)
Truck capacity per crew member						
<9.1 cubic yards	20.31 (26)	27.22 (32)	31.87 (7)	29.74 (36)	35.20 (37)	40.65 (15)
>9.1 cubic yards	20.33 (34)	23.39 (16)	23.47 (7)	30.31 (60)	35.76 (31)	36.25 (13)
Over-all	20.38 (60)	25.94 (48)	27.67 (14)	30.10 (96)	35.46 (68)	38.61 (28)

[a]All costs adjusted by the ratio of the national average wage to wages in a particular city.
[b]Number of observations in parentheses.

selected methods of disposal. Population density is a significant determinant of costs. A community having a density of less than 10 dwelling
units per acre can expect to pay up to 50% more in collection costs per
ton than a community which is developed at twice that density. Land
use and zoning regulations have a definite effect on the distribution of
activities in the community and, consequently, the distribution of waste
generation and the distances to be traveled by collection vehicles.

15.5.7 Selection of Collection Routes

One output of the long-range planning process is the assignment of
waste generation areas to processing and disposal facilities of given
characteristics. In order to translate this information into a short-range
working plan for collection, processing, and disposal, the planner needs
to take two further steps. It is necessary to divide each waste generation
area into specific collection routes, and to determine the actual path to be
followed by each collection vehicle. The first of these steps is referred to
as districting and route balancing, while the second is called microrouting. Methods for both of these steps have been described by several
writers, and some approaches are presented in the following paragraphs
(19).

Districting and route balancing   This is the process of determining the
optimum number of services that constitutes a fair day's work and of
dividing the collection task among the crews to give them equal workloads. It can be used for a variety of purposes, such as estimating the
number of trucks and workers needed for a system, evaluating crew
performance or system changes, and assessing the costs of changes in
the levels of collection services. It is best accomplished by simulating the
total effort required for performing the collection effort on a vehicle-by-
vehicle basis. Reference 36 provides useful approaches.

The simulation starts by determining the number of waste generating units to be serviced per vehicle load N, using

$$N = \frac{x_1 x_2}{x_3} \tag{15.3}$$

in which x_1 = vehicle capacity in cubic yards; x_2 = vehicle load density
in pounds per cubic yard; and x_3 = generation unit service load in
pounds per unit.

The next step is to determine the number of loads that can be
completed in a working day through an analysis of the time budget of a
vehicle and its crew. The time spent by each collection vehicle and crew
during a given day can be separated into the following components:

A = travel time from garage to beginning of route;
B = collection time on route;
C_1 = travel time from route to disposal or processing site;

C_2 = travel time from disposal or processing site back to route;
D = waiting time spent at site;
E = travel time from disposal site back to garage at end of day;
F = time spent on official breaks;
G = time lost to breakdowns and unforeseen events; and
K = number of loads per day for a given vehicle.

For a vehicle which carries K loads per day, the total hours Y in a working day are

$$Y = A + B + K (C_1 + C_2 + D) - C_2 + E + F + G \qquad (15.4)$$

By subtracting the over-all nonproductive time spent traveling to and from work and on rest periods and breakdowns $(A + E + F + G - C_2)$ from the total time available Y, the available time remaining for actual collection and disposal $[B + K (C_1 + C_2 + D)]$ can be determined.

All of the time values in Eq. 15.4 can be estimated from actual operating experience. The collection time B is equal to $T \times S$, in which T = estimated collection time per service unit, and S = total number of units to be serviced per day. The value of S is equal to the number of service units per truck load N times the number of loads K. Inserting these values into Eq. 15.4 and rearranging the variables results in the number of loads that a given vehicle can serve per day

$$K = \frac{Y - (A + E + F + G - C_2)}{(C_1 + C_2 + D + TN)} \qquad (15.5)$$

When considering the entire collection network, the total number of vehicles V required for the task can be determined from

$$V = \frac{M H}{S W} \qquad (15.6)$$

in which M = total number of service units; H = weekly collection frequency; W = number of work days per week; and S = average number of units serviced per vehicle per day. Once S has been determined, waste generation districts can be set by dividing areas into equal workload sections according to the day of the week. An additional step could include dividing each daily workload section into specific vehicle routes on the basis of the route balancing procedure previously described.

Microrouting   The next step in short-range solid waste collection planning is microrouting. This is the determination of the best path to be followed by each collection vehicle and crew on the basis of the existing street pattern of the waste generation area. So that the most efficient collection path can be determined, it is necessary to minimize nonproductive time spent on repeated travel routes, travel through streets with no service requirements, and delays resulting from U-turns, left turns, and congested streets. An intuitive technique for the development of reasonably efficient routings is to allow the drivers to select their own routes with no guidance from management. This method works well when drivers know their areas and are interested in maximizing collection efficiency (for example, because they can go home when the route is done). A more complex method is to describe the collection system mathematically by determining quantitative relationships between its various components. Although various mathematical programming techniques have been utilized in this manner to obtain theoretically optimal routing, they are highly complex and have a low probability of being accepted by local planners except in the most sophisticated operations.

Other approaches to microrouting have been developed which are neither theoretical nor intuitive, but instead heuristic (19). A heuristic approach is one that applies human intelligence, experience, common sense, and certain rules of thumb to develop an acceptable but not necessarily optimal solution to a problem. Heuristic approaches to problem solving are useful in situations where rigorous mathematical solutions have been found to be impossible, infeasible, or impractical. The EPA heuristic routing method (35) involves a simple manual solution to the path selection process on the basis of the following rules of thumb:

1. Routes should not be fragmented or overlapping. Each route should be compact, consisting of street segments clustered in the same geographical area (see Fig. 15-11).

2. Total collection plus haul times should be reasonably constant for each route in the community (equalized workloads).

3. The collection route should be started as close to the garage or motor pool as possible, taking into account heavily traveled and one-way streets (see rules 4 and 5).

4. Collection should not be attempted in heavily traveled streets during rush hours.

5. On one-way streets, it is best to start collection near the upper end of the street (see Fig. 15-12).

6. Services on cul-de-sacs can be considered as services on the street segment that they intersect, since collections can start only from the intersecting street segment. To keep left turns at a minimum, collect from cul-de-sacs when they are to the right of the vehicle. They must be collected by walking down the cul-de-sac, backing the vehicle down it, or making a U-turn at the far end. Do not drive into the cul-de-sac and then back out into the traffic flow.

7. When practical, collection on steep inclines should be done on both sides of the street while vehicle is moving downhill. This practice is recommended for safety, ease, speed of collection, and reduction of wear on vehicle, and to conserve gas and oil.

8. Collection should begin at higher elevations and proceed to lower areas.

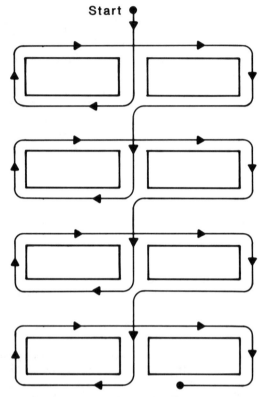

Fig. 15-11. Specific routing pattern for one-way street, one-side-of-street collection (35)

9. For collection from one side of the street at a time, it is generally best to route with many right turns (clockwise) around blocks (see Fig. 15-13).

10. For collection from both sides of the street at the same time, it is generally best to route with long, straight paths across the grid before looping clockwise (see Fig. 15-14). (Note that rules 9 and 10 emphasize the development of a series of clockwise loops in order to minimize left turns, which generally are more difficult and time consuming than right turns. In addition, right turns are safer, and especially so in the case of right-hand drive vehicles.)

11. For certain block configurations within the route, specific routing patterns should be applied (see Fig. 15-15).

To use the heuristic approach just outlined, the planner needs maps of the waste generation area under study and information on the number and type of service units on each side of each street segment. He or she also must know which streets are one-way or dead end, the level

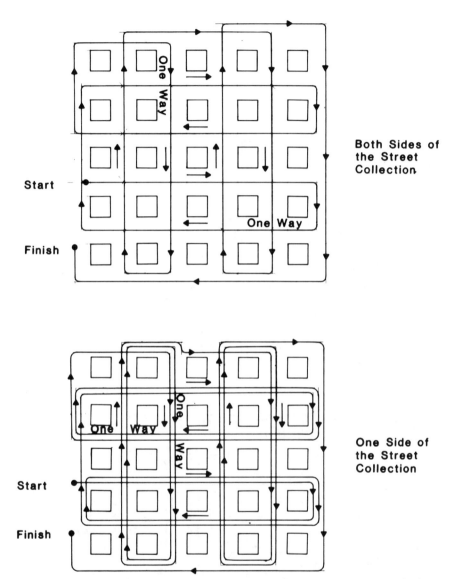

Fig. 15-12. Specific routing patterns for multiple one-way streets (35)

of congestion in these streets, and the locations to which users are required to deliver their wastes. The application of the rules of thumb listed will result in characteristic paths in given urban development patterns. Typical solutions for specific block and street configurations are shown in Figs. 15-11 through 15-15. Of course, other street config-

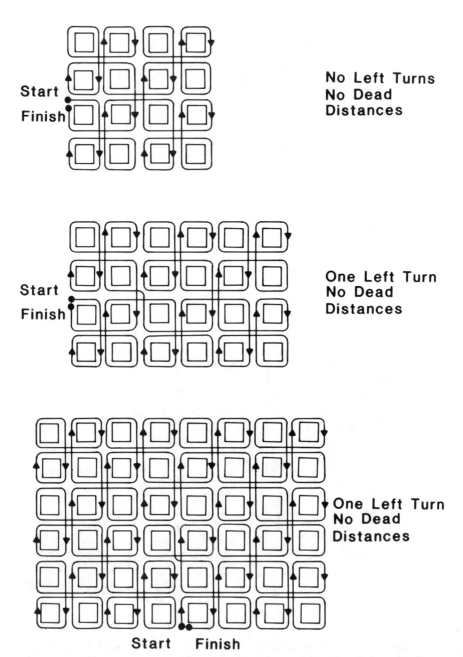

Fig. 15-13. Combinations of four-block pattern, one-side-of-street collection (35)

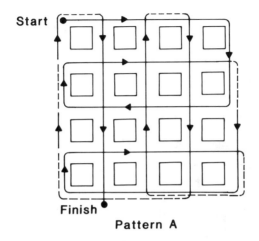

Pattern A

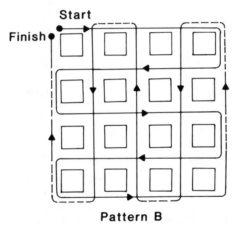

Pattern B

Fig. 15-14. Specific routing patterns for both-sides-of-street collection (35)

urations will result in different patterns as a result of the application of the heuristic rules.

Where the street patterns are not simply sets of rectangular blocks, and where two-sided collection is common, the method described can be improved by other heuristics, which will minimize deadheading (empty or wasted travel). The planner should try to find the minimum-distance continuous tour through a network which covers all streets. This problem was considered as early as 1736 by Euler in the famous problem of the seven bridges of Koenigsberg.

Microrouting must deal satisfactorily with the odd node—an intersection with an odd number of arcs incident upon it. Odd nodes cause the vehicle to repeat a street segment. Consider, for example, a Y-shaped

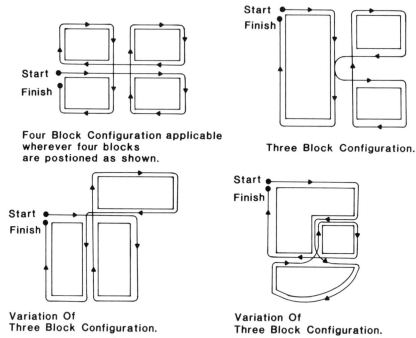

Four Block Configuration applicable wherever four blocks are postioned as shown.

Three Block Configuration.

Variation Of Three Block Configuration.

Variation Of Three Block Configuration.

Fig. 15-15. Specific routing patterns for three- and four-block configurations (35)

intersection, an odd node with three incident arcs. The first time the vehicle passes through this intersection it collects from two of the arcs. On the second pass, it collects from the third, reaches the center of the Y, and must travel one of the three arcs a second time. The same is true of intersections with five, seven, or any other odd number of branches. A dead end is the trivial case of a one-branch node. The planner needs to determine which street segments must be covered twice. These are paths between odd nodes. Essentially, the planner should pair the odd nodes to minimize the total distance traveled twice (once for collection and once for deadheading). The procedure is as follows:

1. Identify and mark the odd nodes for easy bookkeeping.
2. Choose a set of feasible pairing of odd nodes.
3. Inspect these pairings, looking for negative cycles.
4. If a negative cycle is found, reverse the pairing on it. Go back to 3 and continue the inspection.
5. Distance is minimized when no more negative cycles can be found.

A negative cycle is a loop in the network where more than half is covered by deadheading. If this is true on any loop, time can be saved by revising the pairing, as shown in Fig. 15-16.

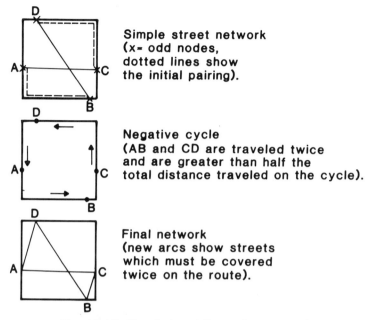

Simple street network
(x= odd nodes,
dotted lines show
the initial pairing).

Negative cycle
(AB and CD are traveled twice
and are greater than half the
total distance traveled on the cycle).

Final network
(new arcs show streets
which must be covered
twice on the route).

Fig. 15-16. Simple heuristic routing example

The street network of one district is shown in Fig. 15-17. Figure 15-17(a) shows the street network with X marking odd nodes. Initial pairing of odd nodes is shown in Fig. 15-17(b), and pairing revised to optimal in Fig. 15-17(c). Three minimum distance routes are generated attempting to minimize the number of U-turns [Fig. 15-17(d)]. The best of these, the last, should probably be the truck route.

The routing process itself can be done very quickly and easily, given the correct boundaries. Ten minutes per route would be a reasonable time requirement, so that a full plan for a 40-route system could be generated in a worker-day, or an hour for each driver. Copies of the maps or lists of the streets traveled would be the output. Perhaps the most important characteristic of this method is that other approaches, such as the heuristics described earlier, can be applied to the results, with knowledge that deadheading has already been minimized.

15.6 REFERENCES

1. American Public Works Association, *Solid Waste Collection Practice*, American Public Works Association, Chicago, 1975.
2. Bacow, L.S., and Sanderson, D.R., *Facility Siting and Compensation: A Handbook for Communities and Developers*, MIT Energy Laboratory, Cambridge, Mass., 1980.

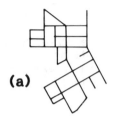

(a)

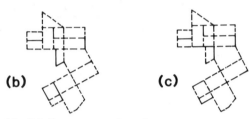

(b) **(c)**

(Solid lines are street segments to be covered twice).

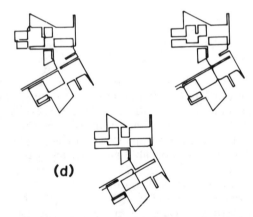

(d)

Fig. 15-17. Heuristic routing example: (a) Street network (x ≡ odd node); (b) initial pairing of odd nodes; (c) final pairing; (d) three possible Euler tours

3. Bender, D.F., Peterson, M.L., and Stierli, H., eds., *Physical, Chemical, and Microbiological Methods of Solid Waste Testing*, (PB-220 479), U.S.E.P.A. National Environmental Research Center, Cincinnati, Ohio, 1972.
4. Blair, L.H., and Schwartz, A.I., *How Clean Is Our City?* The Urban Institute, Washington, D.C., 1972.
5. Cardile, R.P., and Verhoff, F.H. "Economical Refuse Truck Size Determination," *Journal of the Environmental Engineering Division*, ASCE, Vol. 100, No. EE3, June 1974, pp. 679–697.
6. Clark, R.M., and Helms, B.P., "Fleet Selection for Solid Waste Collection

Systems," *Journal of the Sanitary Engineering Division,* ASCE, Vol. 97, No. SA1, February 1972, pp. 71–178.

7. Colonna, R.A., and McLaren, C., *Decision-Makers Guide in Solid Waste Management,* 500, U.S. Environmental Protection Agency, Washington, D.C., 1977.

8. Dajani, J.S., Vesilind, P.A., and Hartman, G., *Measuring the Effectiveness of Solid Waste Collection,* Duke University, Department of Civil Engineering and the Institute of Policy Sciences and Public Affairs, Durham, N.C., 1975.

9. De Neufille, R., and Stafford, J. H., *Systems Analysis for Engineers and Managers,* McGraw-Hill Book Co. Inc., New York, 1971.

10. Deese, P.L., Miyares, J.R., and Fogel, S., *Institutional Constraints and Public Participation Barriers to Utilization of Municipal Wastewater and Sludge for Land Reclamation and Biomass Production,* prepared for the President's Council on Environmental Quality, Washington, D.C., September 1980.

11. DeGeare, T.V., and Ongerth, J.E., "Empirical Analysis of Commercial Solid Waste Generation," *Journal of the Sanitary Engineering Division,* Vol. 97, No. SA6, December 1971, pp. 843–850.

12. Ecke, D.E., and Linsdale, D.D., "Fly and Economic Evaluation of Urban Refuse Systems—Part I: Control of Green Blow Flies (Phawnicia) by Improved Methods of Residential Refuse Storage and Collection," *California Vector Views,* Vol. 14, No. 4, April 1967, pp. 19–27.

13. Ecke, D.E., Linsdale, D.D., and White, K.E., "Migration of Green Blow Fly Larvae from Six Refuse Container Systems," *California Vector Views,* Vol. 12, No. 6, August 1965, pp. 35–42.

14. "Financing," in *Resource Recovery Plant Implementation: Guides for Municipal Officials,* SW-157.4, U.S. Environmental Protection Agency, Office of Solid Waste Management Programs, Washington, D.C., 1975.

15. Fuertes, L.A., Hudson, J.F., and Marks, D.H., "Solid Waste Management: Equity Trade-off Models," *Journal of Urban Planning and Development,* ASCE, Vol. 100, No. UP2, Proc. Paper 10913, November 1974, pp. 155–171.

16. Gilbert, G., and Dajani, J.S., *Measuring the Performance of Transit Service,* Duke University Institute of Policy Sciences and Public Affairs, Durham, N.C. 1975.

17. Golueke, C.G., and McGauhey, P.H., *Comprehensive Studies of Solid Waste Management,* U.S. Department of Health, Education, and Welfare, Public Health Service, Washington, D.C., 1970.

18. Helms, B.P., and Clark, R.M., "Locational Models of Solid Waste Management," *Journal of Urban Planning and Development,* ASCE, Vol. 97, No. UP1, April 1971.

19. Hudson, J.F., and Marks, D.H., "Routing and Siting," *Handbook of Solid Waste Management,* D.G. Wilson, ed., Van Nostrand-Reinhold, New York, 1977.

20. Hudson, J.F., and Marks, D.H., "Solid Waste Generation and Service Quality," *Journal of the Environmental Engineering Division,* ASCE, Vol. 103, No. EE2, Proc. Paper 12871, April 1977, pp. 245–258.

21. Hudson, J.F., Grossman, D.S., and Marks, D.H., *Analysis Models for Solid Waste Collection,* MIT Department of Civil Engineering Cambridge, Mass., 1973.

22. Klee, A.J., "Let DARE Make Your Solid-Waste Decisions," *The American City,* Vol. 86, No. 2, February 1970, pp. 100–103.

23. Liebman, J.C., "Model in Solid Waste Management," in *A Guide to Models in Governmental Planning and Operations,* U.S. Environmental Protection Agency, Washington, D.C., 1974.

24. Marks, D.H., "Modeling in Solid Waste Management: A State-of-the-Art Review," *Proceedings of the EPA Conference on Environmental Modeling and Simulation*, W. Ott, ed., U.S. Environmental Protection Agency, Washington, D.C., 1976.

25. Marks, D.H., and Liebman, J.C., "Locational Models: Solid Waste Collection Example," *Journal of Urban Planning and Development*, ASCE, Vol. 97, No. UP1, April 1971.

26. Marks, D.H., and Liebman, J., *Mathematical Analysis of Solid Waste Collection*, U.S. Department of Health, Education, and Welfare, Public Health Service, Washington, D.C. 1970.

27. Marks, D.H., "Routing for Public Service Vehicles," *Journal of Urban Planning and Development*, ASCE, Vol. 97, No. UP2, December 1971.

28. McMahon, R., Ernst, C., Miyares, R., and Haymore, C., *Using Compensation and Incentives When Siting Hazardous Waste Management Facilities*, SW-942, EPA Office of Solid Waste, July 1982.

29. National Commission on Productivity, *Report of the Solid Waste Management Advisory Group on Opportunities for Improving Productivity of Solid Waste Collection*, National Council on Productivity, Washington, D.C., 1973.

30. Niessen, W.R., "Estimation of Solid-Waste-Production Rates," *Handbook of Solid Waste Management*, D. G. Wilson, ed., Van Nostrand-Reinhold, New York, 1977.

31. Niessen, W.R., "Properties of Waste Materials," *Handbook of Solid Waste Management*, D.G. Wilson, ed., Van Nostrand-Reinhold, New York, 1977.

32. O'Hare, M., "Not on My Block You Don't—Facility Siting and the Strategic Importance of Compensation," *Public Policy*, Vol. 25, No. 4, 1979.

33. Roberts, T.H., "The Planning Process", in *Planning for Solid Waste Management*, U.S. Environmental Protection Agency, Washington, D.C., 1971.

34. Savas, E.S., et. al., *The Organization and Efficiency of Solid Waste Collection*, (see especially Chap. 7 by B.J. Stevens), Lexington Books, Lexington, Mass., 1977.

35. Schur, D.A., and Shuster, K.A., *Heuristic Routing for Solid Waste Collection Vehicles*, SW-113, U.S. Environmental Protection Agency, Washington, D.C., 1974.

36. Shuster, K.A., *A Five-Stage Improvement Process for Solid Waste Collection Systems*, SW-131, U.S. Environmental Protection Agency, Washington, D.C., 1974.

37. "The Solid Waste Disposal Act," Title II of Public Law 89-272, October 20, 1965, as amended by Public Law 91-512, October 26, 1970, as amended by Public Law 93-14, April 9, 1973, and as amended by Public Law 93-611, January 2, 1975.

38. "Solid Waste Recovery and Management," *Environmental Quality Bond Act*, Title 5, Chapter 659, New York State Laws of 1972.

39. Steiker, G., *Solid Waste Generation Coefficients: Manufacturing Sectors*, RSRI Discussion Paper 70, Regional Science Research Institute, Philadelphia, Pa., 1973.

40. Stern, H.I., "Regional Interindustry Solid Waste Forecasting Model," *Journal of the Environmental Engineering Division*, ASCE, Vol. 99, No. EE6, December 1973, pp. 851–872.

41. Systems Control, Inc., *Solid Waste Management Planning: Snohomish County, Washington*, Palo Alto, Calif., 1971.

42. Toftner, R.O., *Developing a Local and Regional Solid Waste Management Plan*, SW-101ts.1, U.S. Environmental Protection Agency, Washington, D.C., 1973.

43. Truitt, M.M., Liebman, J.C., and Kruse, C.W., *Mathematical Modeling of Solid Waste Collection Policies,* Public Health Service Publication No. 2030, U.S. Department of Health, Education, and Welfare, Washington, D.C., 1970.
44. U.S. Environmental Protection Agency, *Reports to Congress: Resource Recovery and Source Reduction,* Office of Solid Waste Management Programs, Washington, D.C.
45. U.S. Environmental Protection Agency, *WRAP: A Model for Regional Solid Waste Management Planning,* draft of User's Manual, Washington, D.C., 1976.
46. Ulmer, N.S., *Physical, Chemical, and Microbiological Methods of Solid Waste Testing: Four Additional Procedures,* U.S.E.P.A., Cincinnati, Ohio, 1974.
47. Warner, D., and Dajani, J.S., *The Impact of Water and Sewer Development in Rural America,* D. C. Heath and Co., Lexington, Mass., 1975.
48. "Waste Disposal Bonds," *Referendum Bill 26,* Chapter 127, Washington State Laws of 1972.
49. Wilson, D.G., ed., *Handbook of Solid Waste Management,* Van Nostrand-Reinhold, New York, 1977.
50. Winkler, P.F., and Wilson, D.G., "Size Characteristics of Municipal Solid Waste," *Compost Science,* Vol. 14, No. 5, September-October 1973.
51. Zausner, E.R., *Financing Solid Waste Management in Small Communities,* SW-57ts, U.S. Environmental Protection Agency, Washington, D.C., 1971.

CHAPTER 16

ENERGY[a]

16.1 INTRODUCTION

16.1.1 Framework and Objectives

Despite the glut of information available regarding energy, we do not know enough about how to become an energy efficient nation. The best we can do is to draw on the results of completed and ongoing research about the relationship of energy to various facets of planning in the United States. This chapter has been written primarily for the urban and regional planner who is interested in approaching and understanding serious problems facing humankind involving the importance of energy supply, demand, and costs. Its objective is to provide an introduction to issues and techniques of energy planning, energy conservation, and energy as it relates to the quality of life, for use by the planning practitioner.

16.1.2 Energy and Society

"Everything is based on energy. Energy is the source and control of all things, all value, and all the actions of human beings and nature" (20). However, the United States can conceivably be at the beginning of an energy crisis, because certain fuels on which we place great reliance, such as petroleum, are nonrenewable and are being depleted at a rate that makes replacement hard. To add to our difficulties, energy supplies are inadequate, unpredictable, and vulnerable to being cut off, because a large proportion comes from politically volatile sources. For a nation that has become accustomed to cheap energy, this is a disconcerting realization. There is immediate need to conserve energy, develop alternative energy technologies, increase the efficiencies of various components of our infrastructure, particularly transportation and housing, develop policies to conserve energy in every sphere, and educate society regarding energy issues.

Energy is a social as well as a technological issue. Yet in many discussions of the factual basis of energy, the cultural and social contexts tend to be left implicit. This problem arises chiefly from our growing dependence on large institutions and decreased self-reliance of both individuals and groups. Such dependence has led to increased govern-

---

[a]Prepared by C. Jotin Khisty, M.ASCE, Associate Professor, Dept. of Civil and Environmental Engineering, Washington State University, Pullman, WA.

ment planning and reliance on expertise. Major choices in energy planning are often made in the context of conflicting perceptions and beliefs
(19).

16.1.3 Energy Crisis

A crisis is defined as a turning point. The oil crisis of 1973–74
constituted a turning point in postwar history, delivering a powerful
economic and political shock to the entire world. Miller (17) states, "The
term energy crisis refers either to a shortage, or a catastrophic price rise
for one or more forms of useful energy, or to a situation in which energy
use is so great that the resulting pollution and environmental disruption
threaten human health and welfare."

The key issues and related problems in dealing with the energy
crisis are dependency on foreign oil sources, heavy outflow of U.S.
dollars, political instability and attitudes of many foreign governments
supplying oil, the competing demand of other countries for petroleum,
and the relatively high price of oil.

16.1.4 Energy Systems

Energy systems may be divided into nonrenewable, renewable,
and derived, as shown in Table 16-1. Nonrenewable systems are characterized by finite supplies which can be exhausted in the course of time.
Renewable systems (at least theoretically) are characterized by infinite
supply, although the cost and the rate at which the resource is used may
be a crucial factor. Each of the derived fuels listed in Table 16-1 is also
based on a raw material that is either nonrenewable or renewable. The
single most complex, difficult, and urgent problem facing the world is a
smooth transition to the use of a mix of environmentally acceptable
energy resources (17). The impediments to this transition are large
investments in existing facilities, the cost of derived fuels, the real or
perceived reliability of some renewable fuels, and the reluctance of
society to shift to new energy sources and adapt to new life-styles.

A survey of the energy sources potentially or actually available to
the United States is shown in Table 16-2. Note that the estimates
indicated in Table 16-2 have been derived from several sources. Energy
estimates are constantly changing and are generally noticed to be increasing, based on an ongoing search for new sources. However, some
reserves included in such estimates may not actually exist, or may be
economically unrecoverable. All estimates of energy reserves should
therefore be generally considered approximations.

16.1.5 Energy Units and Measurements

A bewildering array of units and conversion factors is used to
express energy values. In the International System of Units (SI), which
is used all over the world, the common units are the kilogram (mass), the

TABLE 16-1 Classification of Energy Resources (17)

Nonrenewable (1)	Renewable (2)	Derived fuels (3)

Fossil fuels
  petroleum
  natural gas
  coal
  oil shale (rock containing solid hydrocarbons that can be distilled out to yield an oil-like material called shale oil)
  tar sands (sand intimately mixed with an oil-like material)
 	
Nuclear energy
  conventional nuclear fission (uranium and thorium)
  breeder nuclear fission (uranium and thorium)
  nuclear fusion (deuterium and lithium)[a]
 	
Geothermal energy (trapped pockets of heat in the earth's interior)[b]
	Energy conservation[c]
	
	Water power (hydro-electricity)
	
	Tidal energy
	
	Ocean thermal gradients (heat stored in ocean water)
	
	Solar energy
	
	Wind energy
	
	Geothermal energy (continuous heat flow from earth's interior)[b]
	
	Biomass energy (burning of wood, crops, food and animal wastes)
		Synthetic natural gas (SNG) (produced from coal)
		
		Synthetic oil and alcohols (produced from coal or organic wastes)
		
		Biofuels (alcohols and natural gas produced from plants and organic wastes)
		
		Hydrogen gas (produced from coal or by electrical or thermal decomposition of water)
		
		Urban wastes (for incineration)

[a]The supply of deuterium (a form of hydrogen) produced from seawater would be so large if nuclear fusion becomes feasible that this resource could be reclassified as a renewable resource.

[b]The high-temperature geothermal energy trapped in underground pockets is a nonrenewable resource, but the slow to moderate flow of heat from the interior of the earth is a renewable resource.

[c]Technically, conservation is not a source of energy. Instead of providing energy itself, it reduces the use and waste of energy resources.

Source: *Energy and Environment, The Four Energy Crises*, Second Edition, by G. T. Miller, Jr., © 1980 by Wadsworth, Inc. Reprinted by permission of Wadsworth Printing Company, Belmont, Calif. 94002.

meter (length), the second (time), the newton (force), the watt (power), and the joule (energy). To understand what these units signify, some commonly known approximate equivalents are given as follows (23):

TABLE 16-2 Estimates of Sources of Energy in the United States [a] (24)

Depletable Sources [b]		
Resource	Known and economically recoverable reserves	Potential reserves under certain economic and technological conditions
Petroleum	11.2	21 to 37 [c]
Natural gas	10.9	20 to 36 [c]
Coal	169	~440 [c]
Oil shale	16.9	82
Nuclear fission		
conventional reactors	25.3	
breeder technology		~1800
Nuclear fusion		
deuterium-deuterium		~10^9 [d]
deuterium-tritium		~275 [e]
Geothermal heat		
steam, hot water, and		
geopressured fluids	0.2 [d]	~11 [f]
hot rock		>100 [f]

Renewable Resources [d]	
Resource	Amount of energy continuously supplied per year
Solar radiation	650
Wind power	4
Ocean thermal gradients	>5
Hydropower	0.12
Photosynthesis	0.20
Organic wastes	0.1
Tidal energy	0.1

[a]Numbers are in units of total U.S. energy consumption in 1975, or 1.79×10^{19} calories. They are equivalent to the number of years the resource would last if all energy came from that source alone.

[b]Except as noted, data are from *A National Plan for Energy Research, Development and Demonstration: Creating Energy Choices for the Future,* Vol. I, Chap. II, ERDA, U.S. Government Printing Office, Washington, D.C., 1975.

[c]"Energy Facts II," Subcommittee on Energy Research, Development, and Demonstration, U.S. House of Representatives, 94th Congress, Library of Congress, Serial H, August 1975, p. 44.

[d]Adapted from A. Hammond, *Science,* Vol. 177, 1972, p. 875, using 1975 energy consumption value.

[e]Assumes tritium is obtained from lithium-6, the U.S. supply of which is ~74×10^9g; from A. Hammond, *Science,* Vol. 191, 1976, p. 1037.

[f]D. E. White and D. L. Williams, eds., "Assessment of Geothermal Resources of the U.S.—1975," *Circular 726,* Geological Survey, Washington, D.C., 1975.

Source of this table: Environmental Science in Perspective, by T. Spiro and W. Stigliani, © 1980 by State University of New York Press, Albany, NY. Reprinted by permission of the State University of New York Press.

- 1 kilogram (kg) = about 2 lb (mass)
- 1 meter (m) = about 3 ft or 1 yd
- 1 newton (N) = about 1/4 lb (force)
- 1 watt (W) = the power required to operate an electric clock
- 1 joule (J) = the energy used by an electric clock while operating for 1 sec, or the energy required to lift a 1/4-lb weight 3 ft (1 N-m)

In SI practice, the approved units of energy and power are the joule and the watt, respectively:

- 1 joule (J) = (1 meter) × (1 newton)
- 1 watt (W) = 1 joule per second

A summary of the most common units, dimensions, and conversions for energy is given in Table 16-3. Table 16-4 lists heat content for various fuels.

16.2 ENERGY ISSUES IN URBAN AND REGIONAL PLANNING

16.2.1 Spatial Form and Structure

Urban spatial structure refers to the order and relationship among physical elements and land uses in urban and regional areas as they evolve from interactions among the key systems—individuals and households, firms, and institutions—and pass through transformations in time and space. Land-use planning generally utilizes the normative approach in deciding what the future ought to be (4). A land-use arrangement which is most efficient and least costly to the city and its citizens is a basic concern. Elements such as health and safety, convenience, environmental quality, social equity and social choice have been and are being taken into account.

In recent years, studies relating to energy-efficient patterns of land development have assumed importance. Energy efficiency is a special case of cost efficiency, and in view of the nature of the energy problem and the long-range implications of the built environment, spatial form and structure have emerged as interests to many disciplines. Also, because the transportation sector is such a heavy consumer of fuel, it can be concluded that land-use alternatives which involve the least amount of aggregate travel are generally considered as the most energy-efficient solutions. Another consideration is the development intensity with which the land is put to use. For example, a city which suffers from urban sprawl and ribbon development would have more miles of streets, water pipes, and sewer lines than a more compact city. Not only would the initial cost of developing and constructing the infrastructure be high, but the cost of maintaining it would also be high as compared to that for a compact city with the same population. In reality, the crucial issue is the costs the citizens are willing to pay in order to satisfy their wants.

TABLE 16-3 Energy Conversions

Unit converted from (1)	Foot-pound (2)	Kilogram-meter (3)	Horsepower-hour (4)	Metric horsepower-hour (5)	British thermal units (6)	Kilowatt-hour (7)	Joule (8)
ft-lb	1	0.1383	5.0505×10^{-7}	5.12×10^{-7}	1.285×10^{-3}	3.766×10^{-7}	1.356
kg-m	7.233	1	3.655×10^{-6}	3.704×10^{-6}	9.295×10^{-3}	2.724×10^{-6}	9.80655
hp-hr	1.98×10^{6}	2.7375×10^{5}	1	1.0139	2544	0.7457	2.6845×10^{6}
metric hp-hr	1.953×10^{5}	270,000	0.9865	1	2510	0.7555	2.648×10^{5}
BTU	778.2	107.6	3.93×10^{-4}	3.985×10^{-4}	1	2.931×10^{-4}	1055
kWhr	2.655×10^{5}	3.671×10^{5}	1.341	1.3596	3412	1	3.6×10^{6}
joule	0.7376	0.10197	0.3725×10^{-6}	0.3777×10^{-6}	0.9478×10^{-3}	0.2778×10^{-6}	1

1 quad BTU = 0.4724 million barrels crude per day = 0.1724 billion barrels crude per year.

TABLE 16-4 Heat Content for Various Fuels

Type of fuel (1)	Heat content (2)	Unit (3)
Fuel oils		
crude	138,100	BTU per gal
residual	149,700	BTU per gal
distillate	138,700	BTU per gal
Automotive gasoline	125,000	BTU per gal
AVGAS	124,000	BTU per gal
Jet fuel (kerosene)	135,000	BTU per gal
Jet fuel (naphta)	127,500	BTU per gal
Diesel oil (#2)	138,700	BTU per gal
Coal products		
crude light oil	130,000	BTU per gal
crude coal tar	150,000	BTU per gal
Crude petroleum	138,100	BTU per gal
Ethane	73,390	BTU per gal
Still gas	142,286	BTU per gal
Natural gas		
liquid	95,800	BTU per gal
wet	1,095	BTU per ft^3
dry	1,021	BTU per ft^3
Coal		
anthracite	25.4×10^6	BTU per short ton
bituminous	26.2×10^6	BTU per short ton
lignite	13.4×10^6	BTU per short ton
Electrical generation and distribution efficiency:		30%
Lubricants	144,405	BTU per gal
Waxes	155,643	BTU per gal
Petroleum coke	143,423	BTU per gal
Asphalt and road oil	158,000	BTU per gal
Natural gasoline and cycle products	110,000	BTU per gal

Note: 1 BTU per gal = 278.7 J per l = 2.787×10^5 J per m^3
1 BTU per short ton = 942.0 J per metric ton

This willingness to pay is a function of a society's values, attitudes, and preferences.

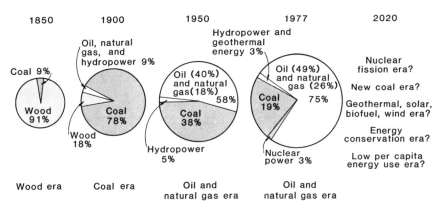

Fig. 16-1. Changing patterns in the use of energy (From *Energy and Environment, The Four Energy Crises,* by G. Tyler Miller, Jr., 2nd ed., © 1980 by Wadsworth, Inc., Reprinted by permission of Wadsworth Printing Company, Belmont, Calif. 94002.)

16.2.2 Energy Demand

The shift in the use of energy sources in the United States is shown in Fig. 16-1 (circle size represents relative amount of total energy used). About 43% of all oil used in the U.S. each year is refined into gasoline to power automobiles.

In general, Americans use energy in four basic sectors: transportation, residential, commercial, and industrial. The breakdown of energy uses in each sector is shown in Fig. 16-2. In 1976, transportation accounted for about 40% of the energy used, with about 23% (direct energy) used to move people and goods, as indicated in Fig. 16-2, and another 17% (indirect energy) used to build and maintain vehicles, highways, and other vehicle support services (17). The indirect energy is accounted for in the industrial and commercial sectors. If the energy used in the residential and commercial sectors is combined, then over half of the 24% (12.78%) of the total energy is utilized for space heating. Industry uses more energy than any other sector of the American economy. The biggest single purpose is to produce process steam. This is a comparatively wasteful use, since the product (steam) cannot be stored and is frequently underutilized (17).

A comparison of energy and productivity of the United States with some of the other eight industrialized countries of the world is given in Table 16-5. Public policy in the United States has been to control the price of energy; consequently, community development and industrial processes in the past were built around the assumption that energy was cheap and abundant. In Europe and Japan, on the other hand, public policy has been one of resource conservation. This conservation is fostered in part by taxing energy, and machines using energy, at a

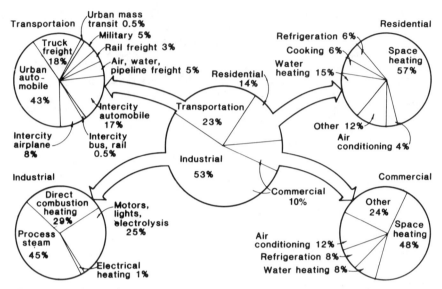

Fig. 16-2. Uses of energy in the United States in 1976 (from *Energy and Environment, The Four Energy Crises,* by G. Tyler Miller, Jr., 2nd ed., © 1980 by Wadsworth, Inc. Reprinted by permission of Wadsworth Printing Company, Belmont, Calif. 94002.

higher level as compared to the United States. Table 16-5 shows the consequences of these public policies, and it is evident that the U.S. energy consumption per unit of gross domestic product ranges from 35% to 85% higher than that of other industrial countries. It may be possible for the United States to reduce energy consumption without fundamental changes in life-style.

Another look at energy consumption with respect to gross national product (GNP) is given in Fig. 16-3. Here, it will be noted that the per capita energy consumption, for example, in Sweden is less than half that of the United States, although the average standard of living in Sweden is apparently in no way inferior to the U.S.

A sketch of energy flows through the U.S. economy is shown in Fig. 16-4. On the left side are the inputs from coal, petroleum, natural gas, water, and nuclear power in units of 10^{17} calories. Note the extent of energy wasted. More energy is ultimately wasted than used productively. The picture has not changed significantly today.

16.2.3 Energy Supply and Alternative Images

It is customary to think in terms of three time frames when we evaluate energy alternatives: the short term, up to 10 years; the intermediate, 10 to 25 years; and the long term, 25 to 50 years. For each alternative we need to know the following: the estimated supply avail-

TABLE 16-5 Energy Consumption and Gross Domestic Product (GDP) Compared, for Developed Countries (2)

Country (1)	GPD per capita, in dollars (2)	Energy per capita, in millions of BTU (3)	Energy-GPD ratio, in thousands of BTU per dollar (4)	GDP index[a] per capita (5)	Energy index[a] per capita (6)	Energy index-GPD index ratio (7)
United States	5643	335.5	59.5	100	100	100
Canada	4728	336.6	71.1	84	100	120
France	4168	133.1	31.9	74	40	54
West Germany	3991	165.6	41.5	71	49	70
Italy	2612	95.7	36.6	46	29	62
Netherlands	3678	188.1	51.1	65	56	86
United Kingdom	3401	152.9	45.0	60	46	76
Sweden	5000	213.4	42.7	89	64	72
Japan	3423	116.6	34.1	61	35	57

[a]For index numbers, U.S. = 100.

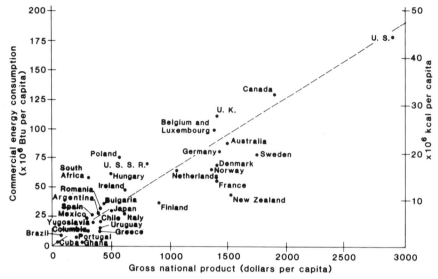

Fig. 16-3. Energy consumption and gross national product (from *Environmental Science in Perspective*, by T. Spiro and W. Stigliani, © 1980 by State University of New York Press, Albany, NY. Reprinted by permission of the State University of New York Press.)

able in each time frame; the estimated net useful energy yield; projected costs for development; and the potential environmental impact. Based on extensive research, Miller (17) draws three important conclusions:

1. The best short-, intermediate-, and long-term alternative for the United States (and other industrialized nations) is energy conservation. It buys time to develop other energy alternatives, saves money, and reduces environmental impact by decreasing energy use and waste. Indeed, it is estimated that the United States could meet all of its energy needs up to the year 2005 by implementing a strong and comprehensive energy program.

2. Total systems for future energy alternatives in the world including the United States will probably have low to moderate net useful energy yields and high to very high development costs. Since there may not be enough capital available to develop all alternative energy systems, they must be carefully chosen now so that capital will not be depleted on systems that will yield too little net useful energy or prove to be environmentally unacceptable.

3. In the future, energy should be provided by a diverse mix of alternative sources based on local availability and conditions rather than relying primarily on one resource (such as our present primary dependence on oil).

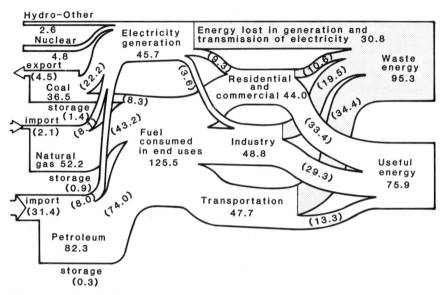

Fig. 16-4. Production and consumption of energy in the United States, 1975 (From *Environmental Science in Perspective,* by T. Spiro and W. Stigliani, © 1980 by State University of New York Press, Albany, NY. Reprinted by permission of the State University of New York Press.)

The world supply of energy has been measured and estimated by scores of scientists. There is an ongoing debate between the pessimists and the optimists, with the former concluding that fossil fuels are nearly exhausted, and the latter arguing that there are undiscovered resources many times greater than the amounts used to date. The one point about which there is agreement is that fossil fuel resources are finite and will be exhausted to the point where further use as fuels is uneconomic some time in the next century (23). One view provided by Dantzig and Saaty (7) is illustrative (see Table 16-6). However, it should be noted that the forecasts summarized in Table 16-6 are made on the assumption that consumption rates are ten times current per capita rates.

16.2.4 Scenarios of Future Spatial Form

A fundamental factor in metropolitan expansion, particularly in the United States during the years 1945 to 1970, was the availability of cheap energy. Other elements which contributed to this expansion were the rapid increase in real per capita income, rapid diffusion of the automobile, development of beltways and freeways at the expense of public transportation, and planning policies that encouraged low-density residential development. Since 1973, five major factors have changed patterns of metropolitan development: (1) Recessions; (2) high inflation and interest rates; (3) continuing decline in the size of households; (4) new

TABLE 16-6 World Supply of Energy, Assuming Consumption Rates Worldwide Ten Times Current Per Capita Rates (7)

Energy source (1)	Reserve status (2)	Years before exhaustion (3)
Coal, oil, gas	known reserves	13
	potential reserves	270
Uranium (U_3O_8)	accessible known reserves	6
	accessible potential reserves	6
	less accessible reserves	10^4
Fusion power	deuterium from the ocean	3×10^9
Solar radiation	life of the sun	10×10^9

Source: Compact City: A Place for a Livable Urban Environment, by G. D. Dantzig and T. L. Saaty, 1973. Reprinted by permission of George D. Dantzig.

environmental and land use controls; and (5) rising energy cost and uncertain energy futures (30).

Van Til (29) has provided five scenarios of alternative images of energy supply:

1. Pre-1973 trends projected, with a continued growth in energy use of 3.5% per yr.

2. Modest growth, with 1.9% growth per yr (this is a conservation strategy).

3. Steady state of energy availability after 1990 (a conservation strategy, with coal replacing oil).

4. Steady state of 1977 level of usage through the year 2000 and beyond (a conservation strategy accompanied by dramatic decline in per capita energy).

5. Decline to 75% of 1977 level of usage by the year 2000 (a pessimistic view, in which frequent crises develop).

Table 16-7 presents the likely amount of energy available for transportation, residential, and industrial-commercial use under each of the five energy scenarios. Table 16-8 gives the transportation energy scenarios through the year 2000. There is a wide variation in future energy use projections. Even the modest growth scenario calls for a 31% increase over 25 years.

William (30) examines four energy futures in the context of a basic set of assumptions consisting of a moderate rate of economic growth, a 1% to 2% increase in personal disposable income, unemployment exceeding 5%, and a continuation of present low levels of fertility. Only three of the four futures are described here:

1. Business as usual: moderate growth of energy supply accompanied by a 3% per yr rise in real energy prices.

2. Conservation incentives and mandates: little or no growth of energy supply, accompanied by a sharp rise in energy prices.

3. Acute shortage: short-term, acute shortage of energy, accompanied by a sharp rise in energy prices.

Figures 16-5, 16-6, and 16-7 show the magnitude of adverse effects for metropolitan trends (in housing, land use, employment, and transportation) for social groupings by income, location, race, age, and family size, for the three scenarios.

Policy implications that emerge from scenario building literature (30) are:

1. Reduce waste and inefficient use of energy through conservation.

2. Decrease energy requirements in transportation through more efficient vehicles, by using vehicles more efficiently, and through land-use patterns that are conducive to energy conservation.

3. Rehabilitate housing stock with emphasis on energy-efficient retrofitting.

4. Change the structure of energy pricing.

5. Establish construction and appliance standards for energy use.

The choice between a "hard" and a "soft" energy future is probably the major social and moral decision facing our generation (10, 15). There is an ongoing debate about whether intermediate (10 to 25 yr) and long-term (25 to 50 yr) energy strategies for the United States should follow a "hard" path or a "soft" path. Miller (17) compares the two paths thus:

> The hard path symbolizes the conventional strategy where the emphasis is placed on building a number of huge, centralized coal-burning or nuclear fission power stations until the year 2000. In sharp contrast the soft path emphasizes energy conservation, cogeneration (using industrial waste heat to generate electricity) and a crash program to greatly increase the use of renewable and more environmentally benign energy flows—sunlight, wind, and vegetation. Effective conservation efforts could cut energy waste in half, reduce the need to build additional coal-burning and nuclear power plants, decrease the environmental impact of energy use, and buy precious time to phase in a diverse and flexible array of decentralized soft energy technologies.

There are four elements of purpose that must be specified, according to Daly (6), when we plan for the future: (1) Size of population or rate of growth to be maintained; (2) level of per capita energy use, and how it is distributed; (3) time period (indefinitely or for 20 yr); and (4) technology to be used, with reference to relative investment and volume

TABLE 16-7 Energy Available in Year 2000 for Major Purposes, Under Five Scenarios (29)

Purpose (1)	Pre-1973 projected (2)	Modest growth (3)	Energy available, in quadrillion BTU			
			Steady state after 1990 (4)	ZEG from 1973 (5)	Decline to 75% 1973 levels (6)	Comparison 1973 pattern (7)
Transportation	38.4	24.7	17.2	13.5	9.0	18.8
Residential use	30.1	19.3	17.0	15.0	14.0	16.3
Industrial-commercial	118.2	80.0	65.8	46.5	33.25	39.9
Total	186.7	124.0	100.0	75.0	56.25	75.0

Source: "Spatial Form and Structure in a Possible Future," by J. VanTil, 1979. Reprinted by permission of the *Journal of the American Planning Association.*

TABLE 16-8 Transportation Energy for Scenarios 1 through 5 (Year 2000) (29)

Use	1: Pre-1973 projected	2: Modest growth	3: Steady state after 1990	4: 1973 ZEG	5: 75% decline	Actual 1975 levels
Automobile	_15.2_[a]	_6.8_	_3.8_	_2.0_	_1.0_	_10.0_
Bus	_0.2_	_0.2_	_1.0_	_2.0_	_1.75_	_0.2_
Air	_11.6_ (6.2)	_8.2_ (4.3)	_4.1_ (3.0)	_1.9_[b]	_0.5_[b]	_1.9_ (1.34)
Truck	6.5	4.4	3.7	3.5	2.0	4.2
Rail	_1.7_ (0.09)	_1.9_ (0.11)	_1.7_ (0.16)	_2.0_ (0.3)	_2.0_ (0.3)	_0.7_ (0.04)
Farm machinery	1.5	1.5	1.5	1.1	1.0	1.1
Others (ships)	1.7	1.7	1.4	1.0	0.75	1.0
Subtotals						
Energy for transit	21.69	11.41	7.96	6.2	3.55	11.58
Energy for freight	16.71	13.29	9.24	7.3	5.45	7.52

[a]Energy available for passenger transport is italicized; other energy is for transport of freight, all in quadrillion BTU.
[b]No air freight.
Source: "Spatial Form and Structure in a Possible Future," by J. VanTil, 1979. Reprinted by permission of the _Journal of the American Planning Association._

Metropolitian trends	Social groupings										
	Income			Location		Race		Age		Family size	
	High	Medium	Low	City	Suburb	Black	White	Old	Young	1–2	3 +
Housing Availability											
Mix of energy conserving units											
Land use Density and intensity of use											
Property values											
Employment Job location											
Transportation Distance to work											
Shift to public transit											

■ High   ☐ Medium   ☐ Low

Fig. 16-5. Business as usual scenario (30)

Metropolitian trends	Social groupings										
	Income			Location		Race		Age		Family size	
	High	Medium	Low	City	Suburb	Black	White	Old	Young	1–2	3 +
Housing Availability											
Mix of energy conserving units											
Land use Density and intensity of use											
Property values											
Employment Job location											
Transportation Distance to work											
Shift to public transit											

■ High   ☐ Medium   ☐ Low

Fig. 16-6. Conservation incentives and mandates scenario (30)

of output of different kinds. Miller (17) has summarized hard and soft energy strategies applicable in the United States in the form of a comparison given in Table 16-9. It must be emphasized that the hard and soft energy paths are by no means mutually exclusive, and the possibility of

Metropolitian trends	Social groupings										
	Income			Location		Race		Age		Family size	
	High	Medium	Low	City	Suburb	Black	White	Old	Young	1–2	3 +
Housing Availability											
Mix of energy conserving units											
Land use Density and intensity of use											
Property values											
Employment Job location											
Transportation Distance to work											
Shift to public transit											

■ High ▫ Medium ▫ Low

Fig. 16-7. Acute shortage scenario (30)

blending the two paths based on realistic criteria would probably best serve the country.

16.3 ENERGY CONSERVATION

There are at least three basic strategies for meeting energy needs: (1) Develop new sources of energy; (2) reduce energy waste; and (3) adopt new life-styles which use less energy. Although some combination of all three strategies is called for, the one that holds out the most promise, keeping in mind actual and potential environmental impacts, is energy conservation. Energy conservation is indeed energy efficiency. If the United States were to make a collective effort to conserve energy, it could save between 30% and 40% of the 1980 consumption level, and still enjoy the same or even a higher standard of living (25).

Conservation can take on several forms: out-and-out curtailment is one way if we are faced with emergencies. A second category is overhauling, in which cities reduce suburbanization, or adopt certain minimum and maximum standards of urban density in order to encourage a substantial amount of mass transit. A third category is a form of adjustment so that energy efficiency is greatly improved.

16.3.1 Transportation

Conservation of energy used for transportation is of vital concern to the nation. A major area for potential energy savings lies in the

TABLE 16-9 Comparison of Hard and Soft Energy Strategies for the United States (17)

Hard energy plan (1)	Soft energy plan (2)
Increase the supply of energy to meet greatly increased total and per capita energy demand.	Emphasize energy conservation to reduce waste and to provide ample energy without large increases in total and per capita energy use.
Greatly increase the use of electricity to provide energy for both high-quality and low-quality energy needs.	To conserve energy quality, use electricity only for appropriate high-quality energy needs.
Depend primarily on nonrenewable energy resources (energy capital)—oil, natural gas, coal, and uranium.	Greatly increase the use of renewable energy flows (energy income)—sunlight, wind, and vegetation (biomass).
Continue to increase the use of oil and natural gas.	Increase the use of oil and natural gas only slightly to prevent rapid depletion of domestic supplies and more dependence on imports.
Greatly increase the use of large, complex, centralized coal-burning and nuclear fission power plants, followed by a shift to centralized breeder fission power plants, and then a shift to centralized nuclear fusion power plants (if they become feasible).	Greatly increase the use of a diverse array of intermediate, relatively simple, small-scale, dispersed energy production facilities using sunlight, wind, and vegetation, depending on local availability. Slightly increase the use of coal by burning it in intermediate-sized fluidized gas turbine power plants coupled with home heat pumps. Phase out the use of conventional nuclear fission power by 2005, and do not develop breeder fission and nuclear fusion energy.
Minimize pollution by building complex safety and pollution control devices into energy production facilities and assume that global climate changes from increased production of carbon dioxide and heat either won't be serious or can be dealt with by some technological breakthrough.	Minimize pollution by using energy sources that have relatively low environmental impacts and that decrease the possibility of changing global climate.

Source: Energy and Environment, The Four Energy Crises, by G. T. Miller, Jr., 2nd ed., © 1980 by Wadsworth, Inc. Reprinted by permission of Wadsworth Printing Company, Belmont, Calif. 94002.

transportation sector, which accounts for one-quarter of the total energy and about one-half of the petroleum used in the U.S. This is called the total direct transportation energy consumption. If indirect energy consumption is included, however, then transportation accounts for more than 40% of total energy consumption. Indirect energy consumption attributed to transportation is in the refining and distribution losses of transportation fuels, manufacture and maintenance of vehicles and equipment, and construction, operation, and maintenance of fixed transportation-related facilities, such as highways, airports, truck-terminals, railroad tracks, and ports. Accordingly, a large share of the savings required in the total national conservation effort must come from the transportation sector, directly and indirectly, especially from the automobile, which represents the largest fuel consumer.

The alternatives for reducing transportation energy consumption can be listed as follows (26):

1. Shift traffic to more efficient modes, by lowering the BTU per seat mile.

2. Increase load factor, by raising the passenger mile per seat mile.

3. Reduce demand, by reducing passenger miles.

4. Increase energy conversion efficiency, by lowering the BTU per seat mile.

5. Improve use pattern, by lowering seat miles.

Figure 16-8 shows the alternatives under each category. Increasing the energy conversion efficiency of highway vehicles is the most important option in the short term, for the following reasons:

1. The savings potential of improving vehicle efficiency is much larger than that of any of the other approaches since motor vehicles now consume the major share of transportation energy.

2. Gains in vehicle efficiency will have little adverse impact on service quality.

3. Implementing improvements in vehicle efficiency will reduce total cost of transportation. Load factor (occupancy) improvements are also important. Although inconveniences might make them unattractive for some users, such improvements could be implemented quickly with little or no capital cost and could add significantly to energy efficiency. Operational improvements in use patterns and declines in growth rates will reduce energy consumption. Modal shifts offer theoretical savings although they are not likely to be induced by fuel price increases of the magnitude experienced since 1973 (26).

Transportation energy solutions are quite varied. Long-term solutions include increased supplies through synthetic fuels and land-use development patterns that reduce the need to travel. In the short term, outside of converting stationary liquid fuel users to natural gas or coal, the solutions are focused in the conservation arena. Rationing, taxes,

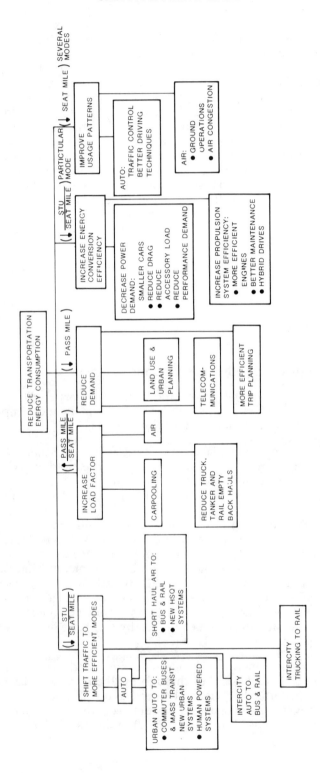

Fig. 16-8. Alternatives for reducing transportation energy consumption (From *NCHRP Synthesis of Highway Practice* #43, Transportation Research Board, National Research Council, Washington, D.C., 1977.)

decontrol of prices, and vehicle fuel efficiency improvements all have the highest potential fuel saving but require government regulations or politically sensitive actions. Improved driving habits, vehicle maintenance, and ride-sharing all have potential but require changes in social behavior. A summary of highway energy conservation strategies is presented in Table 16-10, indicating estimated savings ranging from 0 to 50%.

Energy-efficient cost effectiveness of urban transportation actions is a good indicator for making decisions regarding strategies likely to be adopted by a planner. For instance, signal optimization is estimated to cost a transportation agency only $0.03 to $0.04 per gallon of gas saved. In other words, each dollar invested in this type of project would result in about 25 gal (95 l) of fuel saved. Table 16-11 shows the cost effectiveness of some selected actions applicable in an urban area. In general, the strategies are listed in order of increasing cost and difficulty.

The cost effectiveness of different actions is highly variable. Planners should therefore carefully assess each action at the planning stage to assure that the greatest impacts are achieved from expenditures on urban transportation energy efficiency programs.

Energy conservation strategies concerned with substituting communication for transportation is a viable area for investigation which may lead to a replacement of up to 50% of current face-to-face business meetings in the future (14). Other strategies, such as those connected with "congestion pricing" and parking, are also promising (12, 13). Good parking management, for instance, can lead to the following results: (1) Increase in automobile occupancy levels; (2) decrease in vehicle trips; (3) faster travel times and decrease in travel delays; (4)increase in transit usage; (5) reduction of air pollutants; (6) lower ambient noise level; and (7) decrease in congestion. The first four results directly reduce energy consumption.

16.3.2 Land Use

A long-term perspective is essential if the urban transportation planning process is to deal with problems of providing transportation in an environment characterized by fuel shortages. Land-use plans provide a pattern or arrangement of land uses adopted by a city to achieve the city's goals and objectives. The cost of public services, such as transportation, water supply, sewers, telephones, gas and electricity, is almost directly dependent upon land form. Urban sprawl tends to increase public service cost as well as energy consumption, whereas multicenter plans have generally lower infrastructure costs and lower energy consumption.

In recent studies (8, 9), it has been shown that structural changes

TABLE 16-10 Summary of Highway Energy Conservation Strategies (2)

Program area (1)	Elements included (2)	Estimated saving[a] (3)

1. Vehicle technology improvements	downsizing model lines
	design improvements
	  reduce weight
	  reduce drag
	  improve transmissions and drive
	    trains
		10 to 20%

2. Ride-sharing	ride-sharing matching program ride-sharing marketing employer programs high occupancy vehicle (HOV) incentives	2 to 5%
3. Traffic flow improvements	traffic signal improvements one-way streets reversible lanes intersection widening ramp metering freeway surveillance and control	1 to 4%
4. Other transportation system management strategies	fringe parking alternative work schedule priority lanes for HOVs pedestrian and bicycle improvements pricing parking and highway facilities	1 to 4%
5. Goods movement efficiency improvements	improved routing and scheduling of urban goods delivery truck size and weight changes truck deregulation trailer on flat-car	1 to 4%

6. Transit improvements	modal shifts to transit through:
	  park and ride
	  improved service
	  marketing
	  preferential highway lanes
	  fare reduction
	improved routing and scheduling
	improved maintenance
	vehicle rehabilitation
		1 to 3%

7. Construction and maintenance	improved highway maintenance
	resurfacing, rehabilitation and
	  reconstruction
	substitute sulfur-based materials for
	  asphalt
	pavement recycling
		1 to 3%

8. 55 miles per hr speed limit	better enforcement and compliance to achieve fuel saving and reduced fatalities	0 to 2%
9. Improved driving habits and vehicle maintenance	radial tires higher tire inflation improved maintenance travel planning trip linking	5 to 20%
10. Rationing	private autos taxis and trucks	15 to 30
11. Pricing, decontrol	gas tax parking fees and policies road pricing vehicle registration	5 to 25%

[a]Total direct energy consumption

TABLE 16-11 Cost Effectiveness of Urban Transportation Energy Efficiency Actions (11)

Energy efficiency action (1)	Estimated project expenditures per gallon saved, in dollars (2)	Estimated gallons saved per project dollar expended (3)
Ride-sharing (car pooling and van pooling)	0.06 to 0.26	4 to 17
Compressed work weeks	0.043	23
Flexible work hours	0.28	4
HOV priority treatments	1.20 to 5.40	0.2 to 0.8
Signal optimization	0.035 to 0.047	21 to 29
Signal interconnection and coordination	0.042 to 0.15	7 to 24
Advanced computer control of signals	0.19	5
Signal removal and flashing	negative cost	
Freeway traffic management	1.29 to 1.58	0.6 to 0.7
Areawide express bus services	4.57	0.2
Broad transit expansion programs	7.62	0.1

Note: Where single values appear in the table they should be interpreted as midpoints of ranges. All estimates are approximate orders of magnitude based on generalized cost analyses.

Source: "Energy Impacts of Transportation Improvements." Reprinted by permission of the Institute of Transportation Engineers, Washington, D.C.

in transportation and land-use patterns can produce significant reductions in energy consumption for urban passenger travel (Fig. 16-9). Four dimensions of urban form were examined: (1) Shape of city: concentric ring or grid, pure linear, polynucleated, and pure cruciform; (2) the extent to which the city is compact or sprawling (its geographic extent); (3) population concentration; and (4) employment concentration. Some important conclusions drawn from this study are:

1. From the average work trip length one can determine the total amount of energy required for transport in that city.
2. Energy consumption in concentric ring cities rises fairly rapidly with increasing average work trip length, whereas the rate of increase is much lower in polynucleated cities.
3. A city with most employment concentrated in the downtown

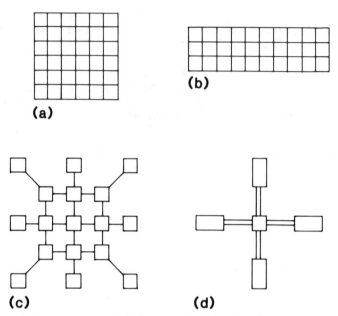

Fig. 16-9. Urban shapes: (a) Concentric (grid); (b) pure linear; (c) polynucleated; (d) pure cruciform

area will consume energy quite differently from one in which most
business and industry is located along a beltway.

4. Transportation level of service is an important factor because
traffic congestion, with its inefficient fuel use, can swallow up any
advantage to an urban area's shape.

The research suggests the desirability of controlling the spread of cities
and of channeling development into higher density, nucleated forms. Its
findings may also serve in the short term as a policy on rezoning
requests and building permits, and as a criterion for incremental improvement to the urban infrastructure. There is need to improve traffic
operations to reduce congestion without building new freeway type
facilities. Such facilities can be self-defeating, because they encourage
horizontal spread of cities, unless strict land use controls are applied.
Moving more people by transit is a promising energy-minimizing strategy. Because transit solutions reduce accessibility, better ways of providing service must be found if people are to use transit by choice (9).

Schofer and Peskin (9, 21) have expanded and refined Edwards's
work (8) and come to the conclusion that polynucleated urban structures
hold more promise for energy conservation than do other spatial arrangements. A USDOT study recently conducted suggests that it would
be advisable to encourage: (1) Filling of city space, thus utilizing existing
infrastructure; and (2) contiguous development, thereby avoiding scattered site development remote to the urban area.

In general, there is a growing concern over some of the effects of the interaction between land use and transportation. Not only have transportation systems covered large areas of land (in many cases very expensive land), but the increased accessibility created by trucks and autos has encouraged activities to disperse, and has contributed to the decline of population densities and the economy of some central areas. Transportation and general development policy adopted by a city can be designed to reduce land-use consumption, improve accessibility and reduce environmental damage in inner cities. Where new development is being undertaken, it may be designed to reduce dependency on cars. Economic techniques, such as value capture and joint development, may be used to transfer to public transportation authorities some of the profits accruing to property owners from improvements in accessibility. The principles of value capture, joint development, and mixed use can be used to intensify these benefits, including energy conservation (27).

The Costs of Sprawl (22), published in 1974, has become one of the most widely cited sources in planning literature. The objective of the study was to examine the effects of suburban development at the urban fringe. It reports significant savings from high-density planned development for economic costs, land-use requirements, environmental impacts, energy and water use, and certain personal effects, such as travel time, traffic accidents, crime, and psychic costs. These savings are reported at two different scales of development: neighborhood prototype costs, and community prototype costs.

The alternative neighborhood housing types compared are: (1) Single-family conventional; (2) single-family clustered; (3) townhouse clustered; (4) walk-up or garden apartment; and (5) high-rise apartment. Each neighborhood considered had 1000 units. The second level of analysis compares five alternative communities with mixed housing types constructed in communities of 10,000 units on fixed sites of 6000 acres (2430 ha):

1. Low-density sprawl: 75% single-family conventional, 25% single-family clustered.

2. Low-density planned: 75% single-family clustered, 25% single-family conventional.

3. High-density planned: 10% single-family clustered, 20% townhouses, 30% walk-up apartments, and 40% high-rise apartments.

4. Planned mix: 20% each of the 5 housing types, characterized by coordinated development.

5. Sprawl mix: 20% each of the 5 housing types, characterized by leapfrog development.

Neighborhood prototype costs and community prototype costs are shown in Tables 16-12 and 16-13, and are broken down into several categories, including energy use. These tables are taken from a cogent critique of *The Costs of Sprawl* (31). The principal environmental impacts indicate that there is a nonautomobile energy saving of about 56% and

TABLE 16-12 Neighborhood Prototype Costs (31)

Category (1)	Neighborhood Prototypes (1000 units)									
	Single-family conventional (2)		Single-family clustered (3)		Townhouse clustered (4)		Walk-up apartment (5)		High-rise apartment (6)	
	Capital costs per unit									
Recreation	$ 220	—%	$ 274	1%	$ 274	1%	$ 252	1%	$ 203	1%
Schools	5354	11	5354	12	4538	17	4538	21	1646	8
Roads and streets	3080	6	2661	6	2111	8	1464	7	801	4
Utilities	5483	11	3649	8	2369	9	1579	7	958	5
Infrastructure[a]	14,137	29	11,938	26	9292	34	7833	37	3628	18
Residential	32,146	66	31,724	69	16,263	60	11,766	55	15,188	73
Land	2628	5	2596	6	1704	6	1683	8	1900	9
Total capital costs	$48,911	100%	$46,258	100%	$27,259	100%	$21,282	100%	$20,696	100%
Public proportion	15%		15%		20%		25%		13%	
Public costs	$ 7337		$ 6939		$ 5452		$ 5321		$ 2690	
	Annual nonresidential operating and maintenance costs per unit									
Operating costs	$ 1721		$ 1720		$ 1388		$ 1319		$ 548	
Public proportion	67%		67%		72%		74%		57%	

Public costs	$ 1153	$ 1152	$ 999	$ 976	$ 312
	Land required for 1000 units				
Total acreage	500	400	300	200	100
	Principal environmental impacts for 10,000 units				
Nonautomobile air pollutants[b]	1420	1420	951	738	644
Sewage effluent[c]	4.5	4.5	4.5	4.5	4.5
Water use[d]	1205	1059	913	730	639
Nonautomobile energy use[e]	2398	2398	1595	1232	1056

Source: RERC, Vol. 1, *Executive Summary. Source of this table:* A critique of "The Costs of Sprawl," by D. Windsor, 1979. Reprinted by permission of the *Journal of the American Planning Association.*

Notes: All dollar figures are per dwelling unit in 1973 dollars. Total prototype costs are obtained when multiplied by 1000.
[a]Infrastructure is the subtotal of recreation and open space, schools, transportation, and utilities.
[b]Pounds per day. 1 lb = 0.37 kg.
[c]Billion liters per year. 1 l = 0.26 gal.
[d]Million gallons per year. 1 gal = 4.5 l.
[e]Billion BTUs per year.

TABLE 16-13 Community Prototype Costs (31)

Category (1)	Community Prototypes (10,000 units)									
	Low-density sprawl (2)		Low-density planned (3)		Sprawl mix (4)		Planned mix (5)		High-density planned (6)	
Capital costs per unit										
Recreation	$ 268	1%	$ 297	1%	$ 268	1%	$ 297	1%	$ 297	1%
Schools	4538	9	4538	9	4538	12	4538	13	4538	16
Public facilities	1662	3	1626	3	1645	4	1622	5	1630	6
Roads and streets	3797	7	3377	7	3235	9	2708	8	2286	8
Utilities	6197	12	4744	10	3868	10	3323	9	2243	8
Infrastructure[a]	16,462	32	14,582	30	13,556	36	12,487	35	10,995	38
Residential	32,040	62	31,629	65	21,417	57	21,417	60	16,030	56
Land[b]	2954	6	2569	5	2311	6	1849	5	1681	6
Total capital costs	$51,456	100%	$48,981	100%	$37,283	100%	$35,753	100%	$28,706	100%
Public proportion	19%		12%		24%		16%		18%	
Public costs	$ 9777		$ 5878		$ 8948		$ 5720		$ 5167	
Annual nonresidential operating and maintenance costs per unit in year 10										
Operating costs	$ 2111		$ 2067		$ 1965		$ 1937		$ 1873	
Public proportion	57%		51%		61%		55%		55%	
Public costs	$ 1203		$ 1054		$ 1199		$ 1065		$ 1030	

Land required for 10,000 units

Developed acres	4590	4113	2780	3040	2173
Vacant, improved acres	459	206	278	152	109
Vacant, semi-improved acres	951	617	1390	456	326
Vacant, unimproved acres	—	1064	1552	2352	3392
Total vacant acres	1410	1887	3220	2960	3827

Principal environmental impacts for 10,000 units

Nonautomobile air pollutants[c]	1420	1420	1034	1034	809
Sewage effluent[d]	4.5	4.5	4.5	4.5	4.5
Water use[e]	1170	1100	910	910	760
Nonautomobile energy use[f]	2355	2355	1750	1750	1400

Source: RERC, Vol. 1, *Executive Summary. Source of this table:* A critique of "The Costs of Sprawl," by D. Windsor, 1979. Reprinted by permission of the *Journal of the American Planning Association.*

Notes: All dollar figures are per dwelling unit in 1973 dollars. Total prototype costs are obtained when multiplied by 10,000.
[a]Infrastructure is the subtotal of recreation and open space, schools, public facilities, transportation, and utilities.
[b]Land dedication by developers varies across prototypes and rises with density.
[c]Pounds per day. 1 lb = 0.37 kg.
[d]Billion liters per year. 1 l = 0.26 gal.
[e]Million gallons per year. 1 gal = 4.5 l.
[f]Billion BTUs per year.

40%, respectively, if high-rise apartments and high-density planning are adopted rather than single-family conventional. Significant savings are also found in automobile energy, to the tune of about 50% (31).

16.3.3 Residential and Building

The residential sector uses about 14% of all energy consumed in the United States. The breakdown of this use is given in Table 16-14 (also see Fig. 16-2). Increased efficiency in existing and new buildings and residences can be achieved from incentives, regulations, research and development, changing techniques and methods of operation, and most importantly, changing human attitudes. Recent studies made in this direction (17, 23) indicate that the following actions would result in substantial savings in energy:

1. Insulating roofs, walls, floors, and windows.
2. Enforcing insulation standards.
3. Using solar heat for space heating and hot water.
4. Reducing heating requirements by planting trees.
5. Changing personal life-style by wearing heavier clothing during winters and setting lower temperatures.
6. Requiring utility companies to provide long-term loans for reducing energy waste.
7. Making use of the topography, if possible, to construct earth-covered buildings.
8. Developing comprehensive heating systems that use local conditions (solar, wind, geothermal, industrial waste).
9. Retrofitting older buildings and residences (since housing stock turns over comparatively slowly).

TABLE 16-14 Energy Used in Residences

Energy use (1)	Range, as percentage (2)	Mean, as percentage (3)
Space heating	50 to 60	55
Water heating	14 to 16	15
Air conditioning	3 to 7	4
Refrigeration	3 to 5	4
Lighting	2 to 4	3
Cooking	3 to 5	4
Other	8 to 20	15

16.3.4 Commercial and Industrial

Industry uses more energy than any other sector of the American economy—53% of the total (see Fig. 16-2). About 99% of that energy is used for three purposes: (1) Producing steam, 45%; (2) providing heat for manufacturing processes and buildings, 29%; and (3) running motors, lights, and electrolytic processes, 25%. From these data it is apparent that process heat and steam are important considerations in industrial energy management. Most of the steam used is produced by the plants themselves, whereas most electricity is purchased from utilities. Over 52% of the energy consumed by industry is concentrated in three sectors: primary metals (especially iron, steel, and aluminum), chemicals (including synthetic fibers and plastics), and petroleum refining (17). The field of process energy is so broad that caution must be exercised in applying any general conservation strategy. Process energy tends to be site- and process-specific.

16.4 PLANNING FOR ENERGY MANAGEMENT

16.4.1 Planning the Program

Urban and regional planners take energy considerations into account in a wide variety of their work. Most planners are concerned with economic development and energy costs. Planners are also called upon to formulate energy conservation strategies for general application or for a sector of activity, such as for a public building system or a transportation related project. Siting energy facilities, such as generating power plants, power lines or pipelines, is becoming increasingly important in planning, and so are locational characteristics and site requirements for life support systems. Occasionally, planners are called upon to plan district heating systems, determine options for cogeneration, and deal with the planning and disposal of solid waste. Although energy management programs and energy plans are often prepared by energy experts, the coordination of these plans with comprehensive plans at the city, county, or regional level often falls on the shoulders of planners.

Energy management programs begin with a commitment from the city, community or organization. The first step is to formulate an energy management committee with a coordinator to look after the day-to-day affairs of the committee and act as its secretary. The committee as a whole must be convinced of the need and the potential economic returns that will result from investing time and money in the program. Table 16-15 outlines the basic steps in three phases: (1) Initiation; (2) audit and analysis; and (3) implementation. It is necessary toward the early part of the program to establish suitable economic criteria for evaluating potential projects. The ultimate success of a program depends on training, personnel awareness, public participation, and human motivation, apart from the introduction of new technology or methodology (23).

TABLE 16-15 Planning an Energy Management Program (23)

Phase (1)	Activity (2)
Initiation	commitment by management to an energy management program assignment of an energy management coordinator creation of an energy management committee of major plant and department representatives
Audit and analysis	review of historical patterns of fuel and energy use facility walk-through survey preliminary analyses, review of drawings, data sheets, equipment specifications development of energy audit plans conduct facility energy audit, covering (a) processes and (b) facilities and equipment calculation of annual energy use based on audit results comparison with historical records analysis and simulation step (engineering calculations, heat and mass balances, theoretical efficiency calculations, computer analysis and simulation) to evaluate energy management options economic analysis of selected energy management options (life-cycle costs, rate of return, benefit-cost ratio)
Implementation	establish energy effectiveness goals for the organization and individual plants determine capital investment requirements and priorities establish measurement and reporting procedures; install monitoring and recording instruments as required institute routine reporting procedures ("energy tracking" charts) for managers and publicize results promote continuing awareness and involvement of personnel provide for periodic review and evaluation of over-all energy management program

Source: *Energy Management Principles*, by C. B. Smith, copyright 1981 by Pergamon Press, Inc. Reprinted by permission of Pergamon Press, Inc., Elmsford, NY.

16.4.2 Energy Audits of Existing Buildings and Sites

Energy audits, consisting of building and site surveys, are useful tools for the energy planner. First, audits can provide important guidelines to the energy planner and insights into major areas of energy use. Second, they can also lead to immediate savings by making people

TABLE 16-16 Principles of Site and Building Surveys (23)

Category (1)	Activity (2)
Important activities	coordinate with operating management (solicit assistance of people working at facility) obtain and review historical data prior to survey conduct preliminary walk through of facility plan energy audit survey (who does what, where does survey team go, when does team meet, etc.) conduct energy audit survey, following plan as a guide and using proper facility energy audit forms after survey, review forms to assure completeness, readability, and reasonableness of values recheck suspicious entries before leaving site
Important survey items	lighting: check for unnecessary lighting in halls, stairwells, unused areas, storage areas and parking lots, excessive levels HVAC: check thermostat settings (too high or too low), filter maintenance and other system maintenance performed at proper intervals, controls, system capacity, over-all operation process areas: check total capacity measured against needed capacity, heat losses and vapor losses, equipment use schedules furnace and ovens: check total capacity measured against needed capacity, idling temperatures, need for constant operation plant air systems: check for leaks and maintenance procedures boilers and steam lines: check for efficiency of burner settings, steam leaks, and lack of insulation, opportunities for heat recovery numerical controlled machines: check need for full operating pressures to maintain hydraulic fluid flows and temperatures electrical and other special building equipment: check need for continuous operation, demand control, power factor, etc. water: check pumping capacity requirements, pump efficiency, head losses material transport: check for more direct routes, less energy intensive modes, and operating requirements general: verify need for all energy-using equipment

Source: *Energy Management Principles*, by C. B. Smith, copyright 1981 by Pergamon Press, Inc. Reprinted by permission of Pergamon Press, Inc., Elmsford, NY.

aware of how energy is being used or wasted. Third, they assist in setting priorities and provide mechanisms for evaluating the effectiveness of an energy management program (23). The general principles of a site and building survey are outlined in Table 16-16.

16.4.3 Energy Planning for Proposed Building Systems

Generally, the energy used in buildings accounts for about one-third of the total energy used. Of the energy used in buildings, over one-half is used for heating, over 10% is used for lighting, and about one-fourth is used for other purposes such as hot-water heating. The energy used in buildings is a function of a number of parameters: micro- and macroclimate, site location, building orientation, building design, building functions, occupancy and use, and building configuration (23).

The choice of site determines the climatic conditions to which a building will be exposed. The building envelope (or building shell) determines how site conditions influence the occupants of the building. The building system, consisting of the various subsystems—building envelope, HVAC, lighting, etc.—supplements the natural available light, heat, and cooling power of the environment. Energy use in building systems can be minimized if the envelope and site characteristics are carefully chosen and integrated (23). General guidelines for energy management in building systems are given in Table 16-17 under three headings: (1) Site; (2) building envelope; and (3) building system.

16.4.4 Energy Planning for Cities

A planner can significantly affect energy demand in a city in several ways. Identifying the potential impacts of energy use on every element of comprehensive planning is an important task. Energy conservation and effciency should be practiced aggressively. Energy planning policies for both current operations and short-term and long-term planning should be coordinated by:

- Designs and renovations that attain satisfactory living conditions at reduced levels of energy consumption
- Priority for energy supply systems that offer opportunities to improve and sustain the quality of life in cities and regions
- Recognition that the appropriate solutions will vary according to individual situations.

The acceptance of an energy planning program can be strengthened through a public participation plan. The program can be set up with the objectives of building: (1) Local awareness regarding energy conservation; (2) local resources and capability to handle energy management activities; and (3) local capability to handle emergency measures in a crisis situation (23). The basic elements of a municipal energy management plan are shown in Table 16-18.

TABLE 16-17 Energy Management Principles for Integrated Building Systems (23)

Item (1)	Action for energy management (2)
Site	take advantage of microclimate conditions orient building for most favorable wind and sun conditions take advantage of shading provided by plants or topographical features use plants or topography for wind breaks use vegetation to influence microclimate (reduce heat absorption, provide evaporative cooling) use bodies of water (natural or artificial) to influence microclimate select a site which minimizes transportation energy
Building envelope	provide shading to reduce solar heat gain and protect against wind losses optimize building volume, area, and layout for energy efficiency maximize use of daylighting tighten building envelope—minimize infiltration and exfiltration insulate building envelope heavily. minimize conduction losses improve glazing, reduce window losses provide thermal energy storage capability, either passive or active incorporate solar heating collectors as structural elements in building envelope proper design of entrances (vestibules)
Systems	design lighting and heating systems to make use of daylight and solar heat gain optimize lighting and HVAC systems to deliver lighting and comfort conditions only to occupied areas; use unoccupied areas as buffers against unwanted heat gains and losses provide automatic controls for lighting and HVAC with local override capability, including the use of computers optimize use of summer or winter outside air employ heat recovery from lights, equipment and environment group systems so heat producing and using activities are adjacent to facilitate heat recovery cogeneration of heat and power

Source: Energy Management Principles, by C. B. Smith, copyright 1981 by Pergamon Press, Inc. Reprinted by permission of Pergamon Press, Inc., Elmsford, NY.

TABLE 16-18 Basic Elements of Municipal Energy Management Plan (23)

Phase 1: The City Sets the Example

1. Energy Management Goals Element
   Set citywide energy use goals
   Establish methodology for tracking energy use and comparing actual performance with goals
2. Public Buildings Element
   Energy audits of selected public buildings
   Engineering and economic analyses
   Certain buildings chosen for demonstration projects
3. City Personnel Training Element
   Trained for more effective facility maintenance and operation
   Trained to train other personnel
4. Design Standards for More Efficient New Public Buildings
5. Vehicle Fuel Conservation Element
   Training of police, fire, and other vehicle drivers
   Selective replacement of fleet vehicles with more efficient types
   Development of ride-sharing, public transportation, and other programs for city employees
6. Municipal Utilities Element
   Exercise leadership in city facilities
   Train their customers
7. Traffic Controls and Street Lighting Element
8. Schools Element
   In-house programs
   Importance of training future energy users
9. Energy Usage Data Reporting Element
   Citywide data reporting and comparison with energy management plan goals
   Department-by-department reporting to department heads

Phase 2: Broadening the Impact

1. Public Information Meetings, Seminars, School Programs
   Report on energy and money savings due to city program
   Provide technical information to citizens
   Training of key personnel in selected community organizations (an "energy extension service")
2. Energy Audits and Retrofit of Private Facilities
   Provide city tax incentives
   Encourage through codes, standards, building permits
   Publicize successful private demonstration projects with awards and publicity
3. Residential Electricity and Gas Element
   Provide checklists of EMOs
   Show typical economic savings
   Make monthly public awards to homeowners and apartment dwellers who institute innovative programs in their homes

TABLE 16-18 continued

Phase 2: continued

4. Energy Management Incentives for Commerce, Agriculture, and Industry
   Personal and political appeals
   Financial incentives (taxes, rebates, business license credits, etc.)
5. Building Codes and Regulations for Private Facilities
   An energy efficient building code for new construction
   Standards for energy efficient retrofit and remodelling
6. Community Transportation Plan
   Car pooling efforts
   Improved public transportation
   Promotion of bicycles and energy efficient vehicles
7. Emergency Energy Curtailment Plan
   Establish priorities for curtailment of different classes of service
   Publicize the curtailment plan
8. Solar and Alternative Energy Technologies
   Guidelines and costs
   Tax and other incentives

Source: *Energy Management Principles*, by C. B. Smith, copyright 1981 by Pergamon Press, Inc. Reprinted by permission of Pergamon Press, Inc., Elmsford, NY.

16.4.5 Infrastructure Energy Demand Estimating

A typical framework for estimating community or regional energy, or both, is (3):

1. Collect population and basic employment projections, information on transportation and service infrastructure, data on the physical characteristics and limitations of the region, and local growth preferences, for use in determining the probable future development pattern of a region.

2. Apply to regional or city planning agencies, which can usually provide most of the information described in item 1. Planning agencies with strong transportation planning functions are particularly useful sources of the specific kinds of information mentioned. The transportation and land-use plans currently in force in a region will provide information on such items as population density, housing distribution, housing types, trip length, trip length duration, and modal splits. They will also be useful for determining growth factors and preferred locations for activities.

3. Calculate the energy intensity, or energy required per unit for

different land uses, using projected quantities and patterns of growth under each scenario. Energy use factors are developed for different types of residential housing units and also for commercial characteristics. If possible it is advisable not to use the Standard Industrial Classification, because this classification has not yet been done on energy intensiveness.

4. Develop transportation energy intensity factors for automobiles, trucks and buses based on a broad view of existing data.

5. Combine residential, commercial, and industrial energy intensity factors with land-use growth projections to produce energy demands by sector for a region. Some of these demands can be fuel specific.

6. Combine transportation energy intensity factors with projections of the future numbers of vehicle-miles traveled to obtain an estimate of transportation energy demand for the region. National or regional data on the number of daily trips per household for different purposes by different income groups, on mode choice, and on vehicle occupancy rates, are combined with local estimates of average trip lengths to determine the future vehicle-miles traveled.

7. Once sector energy demands and the fuel specific or nonfuel specific nature of these demands are determined for each scenario, develop a fuel allocation matrix for use in allocating different fuels to the various sectors, with the objective of satisfying demand, given any constraints on supply.

8. Compare the energy demands of the various scenarios. Alternatives can then be ranked according to their energy demands. This comparison permits decision-makers to identify the energy consequences of each alternative and make appropriate trade-offs.

16.5 ENERGY CONTINGENCY STRATEGIES

Among the greatest vulnerabilities of the U.S. energy system is its heavy reliance on oil imported from a region with a history of instability, halfway around the world. Central to the supply-demand balance underlying this universal vulnerability is our voracious appetite for oil.

The principles of resilient design—dispersion, diversity, redundancy, interconnection—are widely applied in industry, such as in aircraft and power plants. They are now being applied to our energy system. It is only by spreading awarenes of the threat, knowledge of local energy potential, and readiness to act, that we can prepare ourselves for an energy crisis (16).

In recent years several national actions have been taken to reduce the shock of another oil embargo. They include the gradual decontrol of fuel prices to stimulate greater domestic production, acceleration of synfuels development, and establishment of the strategic petroleum reserve. In the short run, local and regional approaches can contribute to energy security much more quickly than the actions the federal government is likely to take (5).

Conservation planning is generally thought of as a continuing, long-range strategy to encourage reduction in energy consumption. Contingency planning is considered to be those actions implemented quickly in response to an unexpected, but possible, emergency situation. In our energy situation, conservation and contingency planning are so interwoven that the two must occur as part of the same process. Thus, it is true that the best contingency plan is to have in place an aggressive conservation strategy, and an efficient conservation plan must include an effective contingency strategy.

The objective of contingency planning is twofold: first, to ease short-term crises and help people cope with the problems generated by such situations; and second, to do so in a manner which helps to solve the long-term problem of reducing fuel demand. Actions that satisfy both objectives are the most desirable contingency actions (28).

16.5.1 Energy Contingency Strategy for Transportation

To be adequately prepared for the energy climate of the future, all levels of government need to prepare a variety of conservation and contingency strategies that can be employed as necessary in response to a wide variety of energy supply scenarios. Inconsistent actions by different levels of government will increase confusion and anxiety when a major reason for the plans is to reduce anticipated confusion and anxiety.

The contingency planning process should yield three principal products: first, the process itself. The interaction among many levels of government and private institutions can generate conflicts over roles, responsibilities, and finance. To avoid confusion this conflict should be resolved before energy shortages occur. Second, the process should lead to ongoing working relationships among various levels of government, private businesses, and institutions for implementation of strategies. Third, the process should produce contingency plans and implementation strategies designed to cover several different types of shortages, for example:

- Expected shortages over a long period of time
- A local, 3 week long, 8% to 12% shortfall resulting from a local misallocation of fuel
- A national, 6 month long, 8% to 12% shortfall that results from an international event
- A more severe 12% to 20% shortfall
- A shortfall of over 20% accompanied by rationing.

All relevant actors need to know what actions they must take under these contingencies, what actions they can rely upon others to take, how their actions will be financed, where their trained personnel will come from, and what the limits of their effectiveness will be. This information should be specific enough to serve as a basis for estimating real potential of transit, paratransit, and ride-sharing as well as the cost of providing this potential. In short, the plans should clearly delineate implementation responsibilities, expected results, and appropriate timetables (28).

Almost all metropolitan planning organizations (MPO) have prepared transportation energy contingency plans in response to federal directives. Recommendations of one MPO, based on an exhaustive study (1), are as follows:

1. Modify state and federal fuel contingency regulations to provide priority fuel allocations to public transportation providers.

2. Maintain the present metropolitan carpool programs.

3. Expand or develop fuel storage reserves.

4. Designate a local energy coordinator (LEC) in counties and major cities.

5. Encourage flexible work hour programs.

6. Increase transit system bus availability.

7. Modify state laws to permit the use of school buses for the general public under emergency conditions.

8. Investigate the impact of an energy shortage on taxicabs and their possible role in local mobility during an emergency.

9. Develop regional park-and-ride programs and an exclusive lane bus plan.

10. Draft contingency agreements to be used between local governments, transit operators, and taxicab operators for mutual assistance.

11. Begin intergovernmental dialogue regarding possible energy contingencies and local solutions.

Naturally, each MPO will evolve its own priorities and mechanisms for implementing contingency plans, depending on such factors as population, economics, city configuration, level of service of transit and its extent, and employment characteristics (1, 28).

16.6 ENERGY AND QUALITY OF LIFE

16.6.1 Life-style and Quality of Life

"Life-style is a term that has been used by social scientists to refer to value preferences" (18). North American life-style varies across the continent and is continually changing. Ever since the oil embargo in 1973 there has been considerable concern that a constraint on the use of energy will result in a decline in the quality of life. Nader and Beckerman (18) have examined this concern and come to the conclusion that there is no evidence that an increase in energy use will improve the quality of American life. Both global and restricted perspective show unambiguously that energy consumption and quality of life vary with substantial independence, particularly in the so-called industrial world. Indeed, the current challenge facing Americans is this: are there changes in technology and life-style that can enhance the quality of life while lowering the level of energy consumption?

Little institutional attention has been given to exploring impacts of high energy costs on urban form and on such matters as life-styles, human values, and social organizations. A diversified set of controls may have to be devised to take into account the unpredictable nature of regional and urban activities. In fact, it is possible that current paradigms of the over-all planning process and its results will have to be reexamined. This would necessarily include the economic, social, and spatial aspects. Along with this, there is need for a revised system of human values, related to the growth of productive forces, changing socioeconomic relations, and use of natural resources.

Taken collectively, most futurists consider that energy policy is a key area of social decision-making for this generation because energy policy permeates the whole pattern of culture. As has been stated by the National Academy of Sciences:

> It is critically important, therefore, that major policy decisions are not made solely on the basis of political expediency, bureaucratic self-interest, narrow and specialized perspectives, or short-term profit considerations at the expense of future generations. (19)

16.6.2 Conclusions

If the definition of "quality of life" in a region were to be appraised as a weighted sum of all opportunities that are important for the population, such as recreation, housing, environment, education, medical care, job opportunities, etc., then the conclusion could be made that increased transportation costs would influence the value of all such opportunities and accessibilities. The effect would probably be mixed. There may be an adverse effect on the quality of life as a result of lower accessibility, but conversely there may be a favorable effect due to a decrease in traffic volume. Less traffic could result in fewer accidents, less air pollution, lower noise levels, and less land area needed for the transportation system. Lower accessibility could, however, result in less recreation, less education, and fewer job opportunities. Whether benefits would outweigh disbenefits is difficult to judge. Decisions cannot be made solely on the basis of objective standards or data. Each specific case may have to be assessed for benefits and disbenefits on an aggregated and disaggregated basis in order to come to any decision.

Among the several concerns raised by Nader and Beckerman (18) for improving the quality of life in relation to energy policy, the following appear to be most significant:

1. Abrupt rises or declines in energy use should be avoided.

2. Production should be matched to consumption in scale; that is, neither process should be overwhelmingly larger than the other.

3. Production should respond to consumption, and consumers, in administrative decisions. There should be channels for the influence of consumer needs on producer policy.

4. Consumption should respond not only to production but to future possibilities of production. There should be channels for the influence of information about possibilities of production on consumer decisions.

5. Technologies that are vulnerable in terms of civil rights and liberties, and in terms of health and safety, require a focus on the supply form, and emphasis upon the necessity for consumers rather than producers of energy to answer the question of needs.

6. Decisions about quality of life issues that are arrived at oligarchically are decisions imposed rather than agreed upon and thus run contrary to American tradition.

16.7 REFERENCES

1. Barker, W.G., and Cooper, L.C., *An Approach to Local Transportation Planning for National Energy Contingencies,* North Central Texas Council of Governments, Arlington, Tex., January 1978.
2. Cannon, B., "Federal Highway Administration Program on Energy Conservation," presented at the ASCE Annual Meeting held at Spokane, Wash., October 3, 1980.
3. Carrol, T.O., "Calculating Community Energy Demands," *Energy and the Community,* R.J. Burby and A.F. Bell, eds., Ballinger, Cambridge, Mass., 1978.
4. Chapin, F.S., and Kaiser, E.J., *Urban Land-Use Planning,* 3rd ed., University of Illinois Press, Urbana, Ill., 1979.
5. Clark, W., "National Security and Community Energy Systems," *The Energy Consumer,* Dec.–January 1981, p. 8.
6. Daly, H.E., "On Thinking About Future Energy," *Sociopolitical Effects of Energy Use and Policy,* C.T. Unseld et al., eds., Supporting Paper 5, National Academy of Sciences, Washington, D.C., 1979, pp. 229–242.
7. Dantzig, G.D., and Saaty, T.L., *Compact City: A Place for a Livable Urban Environment,* W.H. Freeman, San Francisco, Calif., 1973, p. 130.
8. Edwards, J., "The Effect of Land Use on Transportation Energy Consumption," *Energy and the Community,* R.J. Burby and A.F. Bell, eds., Ballinger, Cambridge, Mass., 1978.
9. Edwards, J., and Schofer, J., "Relationships Between Transportation Energy Consumption and Urban Structure," *Transportation Research Record,* No. 599, Transportation Research Board, 1976.
10. Ford Foundation, *A Time To Choose: America's Energy Future,* Energy Policy Project of the Ford Foundation, Ballinger, Cambridge, Mass., 1974.
11. Institute of Transportation Engineers, *Energy Impacts of Transportation Improvements,* ITE, Washington, D.C., 1980, p. 19.

12. Khisty, C.J., "Energy Conservation Through Parking Policy and Management," Compendium of Technical Papers, Institute of Transportation Engineers, Washington, D.C., 1979.
13. Khisty, C.J., "Some Views on Traffic Management Strategies," *Traffic Quarterly*, Vol. 34, No. 10, October 1980, pp. 511–522.
14. Khisty, C.J., "Select Strategies for Energy Conservation," presented at the ASCE Specialty Conference on Energy in the Man-Built Environment, held at Vail, Colo., August 1981.
15. Lowins, A.B., *Soft Energy Paths: Toward A Durable Peace*, Ballinger, Cambridge, Mass., 1977.
16. Lowins, A., and Lowins, H., "Getting Ready for a Surprise-Full Future," *The Energy Consumer*, Dec.–January 1981, p. 6.
17. Miller, G.T., *Energy and Environment*, 2nd ed., Wadsworth Publishing House, Belmont, Calif., 1980.
18. Nader, L., and Beckerman, S., "Energy as it Relates to the Quality and Style of Life," *Annual Review of Energy*, March 1978, pp. 1–28.
19. National Academy of Sciences, *Energy Choices in a Democratic Society*, Supporting Paper 7, Washington, D.C., 1980.
20. Odum, H.T., and Odum, E. C., *Energy Basis for Man and Nature*, McGraw-Hill Book Co., New York, 1976.
21. Pesking, R.L., and Schofer, J.L., "The Impacts of Urban Transportation and Land-Use Policies on Transportation Energy Consumption," NTIS, Springfield, Va., April 1977.
22. Real Estate Research Corp., *The Costs of Sprawl: Environmental and Economic Costs of Alternative Residential Development Patterns at the Urban Fringe*, Vols. 1, 2, 3, Washington, D.C., 1974.
23. Smith, C.B., *Energy Management Principles*, Pergamon Press, New York, 1981.
24. Spiro, T.G., and Stigliani, W.M., *Environmental Science in Perspective*, State University of New York Press, Albany, N.Y., 1980, p. 12.
25. Stobaugh, R., and Yergin, D., *Energy Futures*, Report of the Energy Project at the Harvard Business School, Random House, New York, 1979.
26. Transportation Research Board, "Energy Effects, Efficiencies, and Prospects for Various Modes of Transportation," *Synthesis of Highway Practice #43*, NCHRP, Washington, D.C., 1977.
27. U.S. Department of Transportation, *Innovations in Urban Transportation in Europe and Their Transferability to the United States*, Washington, D.C., February 1980.
28. U.S. Department of Transportation, *Transportation Energy Contingency Strategies*, Washington, D.C., March 1980.
29. Van Til, J., "Spatial Form and Structure in a Possible Future," *Journal of the American Planning Association*, Vol. 45, No. 3, July 1979, pp. 318–329.
30. William, J.S., et al., "Metropolitan Impacts of Alternative Energy Futures," *Sociopolitical Effects of Energy Use and Policy*, C. T. Unseld et al., eds., Supporting Paper 5, National Academy of Sciences, Washington, D. C., 1979, pp. 37–77.
31. Windsor, D., "A Critique of The Costs of Sprawl," *Journal of the American Planning Association*, Vol. 45, No. 3, July 1979, pp. 279–292.

CHAPTER 17

ENVIRONMENTAL ASSESSMENT[a]

17.1 INTRODUCTION

The purpose of this chapter is to present a process for conducting environmental assessments (EA). The process outlined is generic, i.e., it can be applied to any type of planning project—transportation project, wastewater facility, water resources project, solid waste management facility, etc. For the sake of consistency, however, examples used in this chapter are drawn from the water quality area.

A few words of caution are in order. This chapter does not outline specific impact assessment techniques for specific impact issues, such as air quality or employment. There are scores of potential physical and socioeconomic impact issues for any project, and describing assessment techniques for each impact is beyond the scope of this chapter. The reader is directed to the bibliography (Sec. 17.6) for useful publications that cover specific impact assessment techniques.

Most environmental assessments are conducted in an institutional and regulatory context that influences the EA process. The scope, the type of issues to address, the EA area—all may be governed by specific rules and procedures. The reader should keep this context in mind when applying the generic EA process outlined in this chapter.

17.1.1 Statutory and Regulatory Basis for Environmental Assessment

Federal The enactment of the National Environmental Policy Act (NEPA) in 1969 provided a new dimension to planning and decision-making in all levels of government. Prior to the environmental movement that swept NEPA into being, planning decisions generally centered on traditional cost and technical considerations. When Congress passed the comprehensive NEPA legislation in 1969, it symbolized the recognition of environmental values as important ingredients in federal planning and decision-making. The key dimension added by NEPA is the notion that our natural environment is a scarce resource which fulfills a variety of societal needs—social, psychological, and physical. NEPA institutionalized environmental considerations by mandating federal agencies to carefully assess their decisions which had the potential to alter the environment.

The Council on Environmental Quality (CEQ) is the federal agency

---

[a]Prepared by Robert F. McMahon, Providence Parks Department, Providence, RI.

that oversees and monitors the implementation of NEPA. CEQ has issued clarifying regulations (see current Code of Federal Regulations) over the years to provide guidance for those involved in preparing environmental impact statements and environmental assessments.

In addition, federal agencies have also developed more specific guidance on NEPA that should be consulted. By leaving detailed requirements to specific federal agencies, CEQ indirectly stimulated substantial litigation on NEPA. Court decisions will continue to shape and redefine the requirements of the EA process. Finally, revised federal agency regulations, guidebooks, and technical manuals are important sources of assistance in preparing EAs and environmental impact statements (EIS) involving federally assisted projects.

State   Since the federal involvement in the EA process began, many states have introduced EA requirements of their own.

There is considerable variation among the states on requirements and in effectiveness. Some states, like Nevada, only require environmental assessment for specific types of activities, such as power plant siting. Many states have initiated comprehensive land use legislation that has used the environmental assessment tool in "critical areas" and "developments of regional impact." Hawaii, Florida, Oregon, and Vermont are states that have been particularly active in using environmental assessments in land use decision-making. In some states, such as Massachusetts, the environmental assessment requirements cover only state-initiated actions and do not cover private actions that require state permits or licenses. This distinction is important because it determines whether a state agency or private developer is required to actually prepare the assessment.

Much like the federal NEPA experience, the state mini-NEPAs have had mixed success. Depending on one's point of view, the state environmental assessment processes are seen as a technique for protecting environmental values, a tool for developing a rational growth policy, or another layer of government that causes costly delays in development. To determine EA requirements in a particular state, check with that state's Office of State Planning.

Local   Many federal programs involve the distribution of funds for the development of local plans and the construction of local projects. Two primary examples are the EPA wastewater treatment plant construction grants program and the HUD Community Development Block Grants (CDBG) program. Several thousand grants from these two programs are given each year to communities. In each case, EPA and HUD have delegated some responsibility to the grantee, or the local community, and communities generally rely upon a consultant to assist them through the EA process. In the case of EPA grants, 40 CFR 8 is the governing regulation; for CDBG projects, 24 CFR 58 applies.

In many communities, environmental questions are being considered in land use and growth management issues. In particular, communities have developed environmental performance standards as a way of assessing proposed new developments. Environmental performance standards rarely replace traditional land use specifications found in a zoning ordinance; rather they supplement them by providing environmental considerations to the local land use regulatory process. Performance controls have to be supplemented by a natural resources data base and inventory in order to be effective. Placing the burden on developers to provide this information on a site-by-site basis is not as effective as a community's developing and updating a community-wide natural resources inventory. The cost of developing these inventories and the difficulty in developing performance standards have been two practical constraints in using environmental performance controls in local environmental assessments.

17.1.2 Overview of the Environmental Assessment Process

Before proceeding to the details of the process, it is useful to examine first a few key questions.

What is an environmental assessment?   The EA process is an attempt to identify, measure, and evaluate the consequences or impacts of a particular course of action. Any action, whether it be a development, a program, or a strategy, will change an existing system. In short, impacts occur when the characteristics of a particular course of action interact with a particular setting. In the EA process, proposed courses of action are evaluated in terms of their effects on environmental resources.

What is an environmental resource?   Environmental assessments should not be confined to so-called "hard science" issues. In fact, there are several resources that can be examined for impacts, as shown in Fig. 17-1.

What are the principal EA activities?   Four distinct activities should take place within an EA process:

- Impact identification
- Impact measurement
- Impact evaluation
- Impact mitigation.

Each of these is defined in the following paragraphs and described in more detail in Secs. 17.2 through 17.5

Impact Identification.   In this activity, the planner is concerned with: (1) Determining potential direct and indirect impact issues; (2) identifying potential geographic areas affected; and (3) identifying potential group interests affected. The ability to identify impacts will be dependent on the level of detail of the plan, program, or strategy.

Impact Measurement.   In this activity, the planner is concerned with

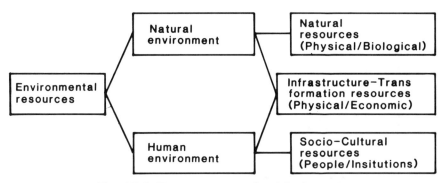

Fig. 17-1. Resources examined for impacts

measuring or quantifying impacts. Impact magnitude and direction (adverse or beneficial) are determined and related to group and area incidence. The specific steps within this activity include selection of appropriate indexes, selection of assessment methodologies, estimate of impact magnitude and direction, and determination of significance. The selection of assessment methodologies to determine impact magnitude should be influenced by the level of detail required to make a decision and by the skills and data available for assessment.

Impact Evaluation. Associated with each impact issue for a particular strategy or plan may be a corresponding objective, that of either maximizing or minimizing some specific attribute. The evaluation task, then, involves a ranking process which attempts to order plan alternatives so that beneficial impacts are maximized and adverse impacts are minimized. Since it is doubtful that any one alternative will be clearly better in all respects, the ranking process will involve making trade-offs among the impact categories.

Impact Mitigation. A particular plan or strategy may be basically attractive for a number of reasons, but may have one or more adverse impacts associated with it. In such cases, it may be appropriate to consider mitigation measures to modify those adverse impacts. The measures may include two types: impact prevention or impact management measures. Prevention measures involve changes or alternatives in the strategy itself, whereas management measures represent additional or after-the-fact activities to deal with expected impacts.

How does the EA process relate to the planning process? A fundamental principle of this chapter is that the EA process must be integrated into the over-all planning process. Environmental assessment is often perceived as an "end-of-the-line" step that is accomplished only after the technical planning is completed. This notion is fraught with problems.

Environmental assessment must go hand in hand with the technical planning process to assure that there is adequate evaluation of the alternatives. As shown in Fig. 17-2, EA should be integrated into the planning process in several key areas. If EA issues are considered during

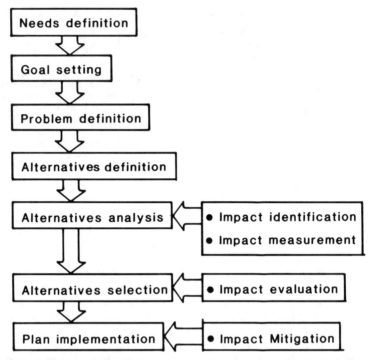

Fig. 17-2. Relationship between planning process and environmental assessment activities

the planning process, project delays can be avoided. In addition, adequate resources can be targeted to EA activities to avoid project cost overruns.

17.1.3 Organization of this Chapter

Each of the next four sections deals with a major EA activity—impact identification, impact measurement, impact evaluation, and impact mitigation. A brief bibliography is presented in Sec. 17.6.

17.2 IMPACT IDENTIFICATION

Impact Identification is one of the most important steps in environmental assessment. The success of tasks that follow—impact measurement, impact evaluation, and impact mitigation—is dependent on the adequacy of the impact identification step. It should serve the following purposes:

- Identify potential direct and indirect impact issues
- Identify potential geographic areas affected

● Identify potential group interests affected.

The identification of potential impact issues should be systematically done by the planning agency for each alternative strategy under consideration. In most planning, impact identification is typically an improvised process. A few general impact categories are selected for use in the assessment, and varying degrees of description are used in each of the categories to assess the impact of alternative strategies. This approach runs the risk of missing relevant impact issues altogether. The process should be systematic and consider a variety of impact issues.

The spatial distribution of impacts is an important aspect of their identification. Spatial incidence may include a variety of geographic areas, such as: (1) Neighborhoods within immediate sensory contact of a facility; (2) a waterfront area of a lake that is affected by development restrictions; (3) a watershed affected by water quality regulations; (4) an entire community affected by a new transit system; or (5) an entire region that is directly affected by a proposed energy facility.

It is important to note that areas affected by strategies or plans may include not only the areas for which a strategy is intended. There may be important indirect or secondary effects on neighboring areas resulting from the application of a specific strategy. For example, the imposition of growth management controls in one community, may, under given circumstances, be instrumental in channeling new development to another community.

The incidence of impacts on particular groups is clearly an important dimension in environmental assessment. Identification of impacted groups will enable the planning agency to incorporate affected interests in the planning process. By including potentially affected interests throughout the planning process, there will be less likelihood of groups emerging at the end of the process and derailing implementation strategies.

17.2.1 How Impacts Occur

Two primary ingredients are necessary for impacts to occur: (1) A change or stimulus represented by a plan, program, or strategy; and (2) a context or set of conditions within which the change occurs. Thus, the characteristics of a proposal and the specific setting will determine whether an impact occurs and how it occurs.

Direct impacts   Direct impacts may result from a variety of features or characteristics of a plan or project. In general, it is important to examine three aspects of a proposed plan or project:

1. Physical characteristics that modify or alter physical resources.
2. Implementation measures, i.e., incentives or inducements that spur an action. These may include regulations, economic incentives, enforcement measures, and the like.
3. Institutional arrangements, or the nature of the institutions

and financing used to manage a proposed action. Particularly important is the distribution of responsibilities among private and public entities. These characteristics will affect the type of direct impacts likely to occur in any given area as well as the incidence of the impact. Again, it is important to emphasize that location or site-specific conditions will shape the types of impacts and their incidence.

Indirect impacts   If the impact identification process stopped with the identification of direct impacts, i.e., those attributable directly to the proposed strategy, it would fail to capture many of the most significant impact issues. Indirect impacts represent those impacts that are stimulated by the direct impacts themselves. Frequently, indirect impacts are referred to as "secondary impacts."

Figure 17-3 and Table 17-1 illustrate direct and indirect socioeconomic impacts of a proposed sewage treatment plan. Smithville is a small bedroom community of 5,000 population located along Interstate 24 about 20 miles (32 km) south of Center City. Because of poor soils that limit development with on-site wastewater systems, the town is considering its first sewage treatment facility. About 2,000 of the town's residents will be served by the first phase of the project. Local capital costs for the project will be financed by long-term general obligation bonds which will be paid off by property taxes, benefit assessments, and user charges. Local capital costs will total $3,000,000. The only two industries in town, two leather tanning firms, presently discharge to the North River. The proposed plan calls for them to discontinue their present direct discharges of tanning wastes, and to pretreat their wastes and tie into the new advanced sewage treatment plant. Because of a shortage of sites along the North River, the plant will be built in an area characterized by large-lot single-family homes.

The likelihood of indirect impacts is dependent on these conditions: (1) The likelihood of the preceding impact; (2) the magnitude of the preceding impact; (3) the strength of relationship between impacts; and (4) the context of the impact area. One implication of this dependency is that higher order impacts tend to be less certain because the number of variables affecting them increases with each link on the chain. Thus, attribution of higher order impacts requires great care and judgment.

The strength of the relationship between impacts is perhaps one of the most important concepts in indirect impacts. Certain impacts will potentially always trigger other specific impacts. For example, there is a natural and strong correlation between impacts in the chain running from population through housing and land use to public services. Clearly, the ability to quantify indirect impacts is directly related to the relative quantification of preceding impacts. For example, if 1,500 housing units are expected to be developed in the western part of town, then the quantification of population effects is fairly straightforward. If, on the other hand, new housing starts in that area are expected to be "substantial," then it becomes more difficult to attach a quantified population estimate to the housing impact.

17.2.2 Impact Identification Procedures

The six steps to take in identifying impacts are as follows:

1. Describe the alternative. The key to identification of impacts is a systematic description of the project under consideration and each of the alternatives being considered. In particular, each of the components—physical characteristics, implementation measures, and institutional arrangements—should be summarized.

2. Describe the existing or projected conditions. In this step, the conditions or contexts for the action are examined to determine if they are ripe for impacts to occur. This step works well if a checklist of potential impact issues is developed. For example, if a water-intensive energy facility is being proposed for development, the water supply situation will be one area to examine carefully. Similarly, if a highway is proposed in an undeveloped area, conditions to check should probably include the existence of archeological sites, existing land use and the potential for development, and critical natural environmental areas.

3. Determine direct impacts. There are two types of general and reasonably quick approaches. The simplest is to use a checklist of potential impact issues under each resource type, i.e., air, water, economic, amenities, ecological, etc. Detailed impact issues concerning each of these natural and human environmental resources can be found in the environmental assessment manuals cited in Sec. 17.6. In the checklist approach, the planner is simply concerned with yes or no answers to each potential impact issue. A slightly more complicated approach would be to use a matrix in which potential impact issues are arranged in the rows of the matrix and the characteristics or features of the plan or project are arranged in the columns. A simple check in the intersecting boxes would be shown in this approach. Its advantage over the checklist approach is that the causes of the direct impacts can be shown. This is important later, when impact mitigation strategies are being considered.

4. Determine direct impact incidence. This step requires that potential groups and areas be identified for each direct impact issue identified in step 3. The detail of the proposed alternative or action will affect the ability to identify incidence. The suggested approach for identifying both groups and areas is to use a checklist. The major categories of potentially affected groups include users, beneficiaries, those adversely affected, those who pay, and those who manage or administer the proposed actions. Not all of these groups may be applicable for a particular strategy. Planning agencies may wish to develop a checklist with specific groups relevant to their study area. The checklist for potentially affected areas should be developed according to local conditions using general categories, e.g., service areas; political jurisdictions; special geographic areas, such as watersheds, lakeshore areas, neighborhoods, geographic sections of a community, regions, economic and housing market areas; and areas defined by natural or environmentally sensitive conditions.

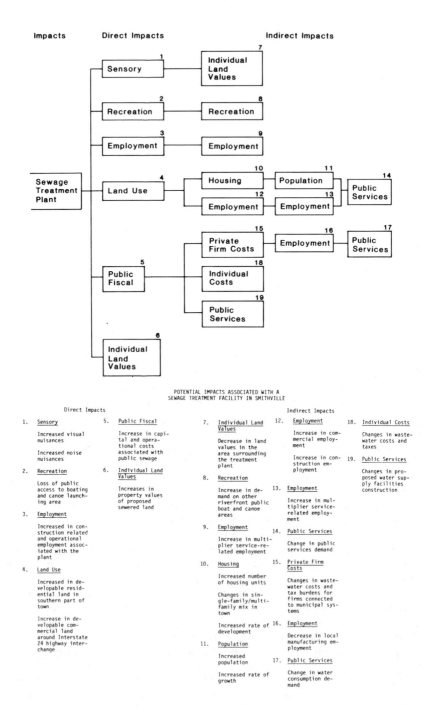

Fig. 17-3. Potential direct and indirect impacts for Smithville sewage treatment plant

TABLE 17-1 Potential Impacts Associated with Sewage Treatment Facility in Smithville

Direct impacts (1)	Indirect impacts (2)
1. Sensory Increased visual nuisances Increased noise nuisances 2. Recreation Loss of public access to boating and canoe launching area 3. Employment Increase in construction-related and operational employment associated with the plant 4. Land use Increase in developable residential land in southern part of town Increase in developable commercial land around Interstate 24 highway interchange 5. Public fiscal Increase in capital and operational costs associated with public sewerage 6. Individual land values Increase in property values of proposed sewered land	7. Individual land values Decrease in land values in the area surrounding the treatment plant 8. Recreation Increase in demand on other riverfront public boat and canoe areas 9. Employment Increase in multiplier service-related employment 10. Housing Increased number of housing units Changes in single-family/multifamily mix in town Increased rate of development 11. Population Increased population Increased rate of growth 12. Employment Increase in commercial employment Increase in construction employment 13. Employment Increase in multiplier service-related employment 14. Public services Changes in public services demand 15. Private firm costs Changes in wastewater costs and tax burdens for firms connected to municipal systems 16. Employment Decreases in local manufacturing employment 17. Public services Change in water consumption demand 18. Individual costs Changes in wastewater costs and taxes 19. Public services Changes in proposed water supply facilities construction

5. Determine indirect impacts. For each individual direct impact, a checklist may be used to identify potential indirect impacts. These higher order impacts should be identified only to the extent that the planner feels is reasonable given the existing conditions and characteristics of the plan or project. A chart similar to Fig. 17-3 is a useful way to show the relationship of the indirect to the direct impact issues.

6. Aggregate and display information. This is simply a mechanical step in which information is summarized as shown in Table 17-2.

TABLE 17-2 Potential Impact Incidence for Smithville Sewage Treatment Facility

Direct impact issues (1)	Groups affected (2)	Areas affected (3)

1. Sensory
  Increased visual
  nuisances
  Increased noise
  nuisances
	property owners	Pleasant Valley neighborhood adjacent to plant

2. Recreation
  Loss of public access
  to boating and canoe
  launching area
	boat and canoe owners	Smithville

3. Employment
  Increase in
  construction-related
  employment associated with the plant
	construction industry	Center City metropolitan area

Increase in operational employment with the plant	none	none
4. Land Use Increase in developable residential land	property owners	proposed sewer service area, particularly vacant areas
Increase in developable commercial land	property owners	proposed sewer service area, particularly Interstate II interchange area

5. Public Fiscal
  Increases in capital
  and operational costs
  associated with public sewerage
	sewer users	Smithville

6. Individual Land Value Increase in property value	property owners	proposed sewer service area

17.3 IMPACT MEASUREMENT

Impact measurement represents the core activity of the environmental assessment process. Its purpose is to determine the change or effect of a proposed action. Before describing the steps involved in impact measurement, it is useful to first consider what change should be measured.

The correct conceptual approach should be to define an impact in two stages. First, a "future baseline" should be established, indicating conditions which would be likely to arise if present conditions continue and none of the proposed alternatives are implemented. In this step, current conditions for each impact issue under consideration are extrapolated to an appropriate point in the future. This future baseline projection is sometimes referred to as the "future without project." Second, "future with project" projections should also be made for each proposed alternative.

Using this conceptual approach, the conditions arising from implementation of one of the proposed alternatives should be compared to the future baseline conditions rather than the current conditions, as the future baseline conditions could be expected to arise even if none of the alternatives were actually implemented. Thus, the "future with" conditions must be compared with the "future without" conditions, rather than "future with" versus "current without." The impacts of the proposed alternatives may then be expressed as deviations from the future baseline, as shown in Fig. 17-4: the actual impact of action A is the difference between curves 2 and 3.

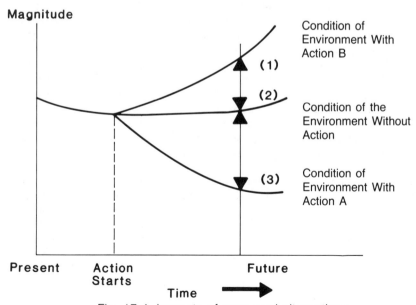

Fig. 17-4. Impacts of proposed alternatives

17.3.1 Types of Measurement

Impacts may be measured at different levels, and may be described in several ways—with monetary, other quantitative, or qualitative measures. Depending on the type of measurement, various mathematical comparisons may or may not be valid in the impact evaluation activity. Four types of measurement are described next.

Categorical scales   These scales place impacts into discrete categories, but one generally cannot say whether one category is "better" than another. In this classification type of measurement it is possible, however, to design categories such that the information can be used to screen out alternatives in the later evaluation steps. For example, one can categorize an impact as short term or long term.

Ordinal scales   These scales imply a ranking measurement. For example, ordinal measurements for one impact may be expressed in the following five categories: extremely beneficial, moderately beneficial, neutral, moderately adverse, extremely adverse. Arbitrary numerical measures may also be employed correspondingly, such as $+2$, $+1$, 0, -1, and -2. One cannot assume that the difference in magnitude involved in moving from a measurement of 0 to a measurement of $+1$ is equal to the difference between impact levels $+1$ and $+2$.

Interval scales   These scales provide equal intervals between impact levels and indicate the differences or distances of impact levels from some arbitrary origin. Interval scales provide a means of measuring more precisely than ordinal scales the dimensions of an impact. Since a continuous scale is used, relative differences between impact levels may be compared. For example, if alternatives for a particular impact category are measured on an arbitrary 10–100 scale with 10 representing the lowest impact level and 100 indicating the highest, then one can actually say how much better a particular alternative is compared to another. If four alternatives, A, B, C, and D, measure 100, 80, 60, and 50 respectively, then the difference between A and B is the same as the difference between B and C. The mathematical operations of addition and subtraction are valid with interval scales along with multiplication or division by a non-negative constant.

Ratio scales   These scales, like interval scales, provide equal intervals between impact levels; but unlike interval scales, ratio scales use a nonarbitrary zero point. Using a ratio scale, impacts can be expressed in dollar terms or in natural physical units, such as length, weight, time, changes in air pollution levels, or changes in employment. Multiplication and division by interval or higher order variables are valid, as are the operations of addition and subtraction. Thus, if a household cost for sewage treatment is \$150 per yr, it is twice as expensive as household costs totaling \$75 per yr.

In general, it is desirable to measure impacts on the highest order scale possible. Measurement, no matter what scale is used, inherently involves some degree of abstraction. Ratio scales obviously involve less abstraction than ordinal scales. It will be impossible, however, to use ratio scales for all socioeconomic impacts. Many impact categories, such as visual quality, can only be qualitatively defined. In these cases the planner simply has to resort to lower order measurement scales to describe impact levels adequately.

For some impact categories normally described in qualitative terms, it may be possible to employ surrogates that permit use of higher order measurement scales. For example, it may be possible to use measures of crowdedness and accessibility as surrogate measures for the quality of recreational experience.

Table 17-3 lists different types of measures for selected impacts associated with a sewage treatment plant. The impacts are drawn from those in Table 17-1.

17.3.2 Impact Measurement Dimensions

So far this review of impact measurement has focused primarily, though not explicitly, on the magnitude aspect of impacts. Clearly, impact magnitude is a major dimension of impact measurement. There are, however, other aspects that may be considered. The following paragraphs summarize the most important dimensions.

TABLE 17-3 Different Measures to Describe Impacts of Smithville Sewage Treatment Facility

Impact indicator (1)	Measurement (2)	Type of measure (3)
X_1 visual nuisances	acceptable	categorical
X_2 noise nuisances	exceeds 45 dB more than 8 hr per 24 hr	interval
X_3 loss of public boat launching areas	2 sites pre-empted	ratio
X_4 construction-related employment	+300 new temporary jobs	ratio
X_5 developable residential land	1500 acres (600 ha) opened up for development	ratio
X_6 public fiscal cost	$169,000 annual debt service costs	ratio
X_7 residential land values for southwest sewer service area	moderate increases	ordinal

Magnitude   This aspect is concerned with the amount or size of the impact.

Direction   Direction deals with the adverse or beneficial nature of an impact. Thus, if the impact indicator is change in employment levels, direction might be indicated as -300 jobs, for example, or $+700$ jobs. It is also possible to indicate direction within an impact indicator. For instance, in the above example, the impact indicator could have been expressed as "loss of employment" or "increase in employment."

Timing   Timing refers to the occurrence of the impact, and may refer to different periods or times in the future. For example, it may be important to note that a given impact will not take place until five years from now. This is particularly important in projects, such as sewage treatment plants, that may take 5 to 10 years or more to plan, design, and build. In this particular case, it is very possible that conditions will alter the magnitude of the impact before the impact is scheduled to occur. See Fig. 17-5 for an illustration of how certain impacts vary over time.

Duration   Complementing the concept of timing is the issue of impact duration. A traditional classification of this aspect is "short term" and "long term." It is particularly important where the impact magnitude is large; for example, the construction of a sewage treatment plant may

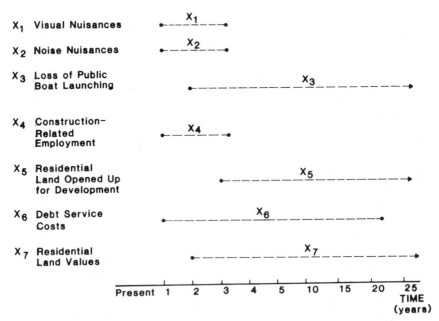

Fig. 17-5. Temporal dimensions of socioeconomic impacts for Smithville sewage treatment facility

stimulate 300 new construction jobs, but the impact may be for only a short period. Similarly, on the negative side, a sewage treatment plant may result in visual and noise nuisances due to construction-related traffic, but the impacts will be of a limited duration.

Incidence As was noted earlier in this section, an important dimension of impact assessment is group and geographic incidence. Measurement cannot really occur in a vacuum. The magnitude and direction of an impact will vary by geographic area and by group. Using the construction employment example described previously, the 300 new jobs have little meaning unless the impact area is defined. The new jobs may represent a major impact in a rural community, but may have virtually no significance if the impact area under consideration is a large region.

One of the implications of varying time streams for socioeconomic impacts is that the selection of a time-frame for the impact assessment will have a significant influence on the types and magnitude of impacts captured in the impact analysis. A relatively short time-frame of, say, 10 years, may not capture all of the impacts from a project.

17.3.3 Impact Measurement Procedures

The following steps are recommended as general procedures for the impact measurement activity:

1. Perform scoping analysis.
2. Determine measurement approach.
3. Determine baseline conditions.
4. Perform impact measurement.
5. Present and display impacts.

Step 1—Perform scoping analysis The essential issue addressed in this step is: does the impact issue appear to be an impact and thus warrant further consideration?

Answering this question involves verification of the potential impacts identified in the impact identification module. Up to this point, identified impacts are only potential impacts—based primarily on the attributes or characteristics of the proposed alternatives. In this step the context or the setting for the proposed action is considered. The analysis should attempt to determine whether conditions are ripe for the potential impact to occur.

It should also be emphasized that direct impacts are screened first. If a direct impact issue is eliminated using the key conditions test, then there is no need to screen for the indirect issues related to it.

Step 2—Determine measurement approach Several issues are addressed in this step: What level of analysis should be applied to the impact? What technique should be used to measure the impact? What impact indicator should be used? What time-frame is most appropriate?

In considering the desirable level of analysis, the planner should determine what impact issues are most important or significant. Significant impact issues may be defined in several ways, so the planning agency should consider incorporating public participation in this decision. For example, the selection of significant impact issues may be judged by the following criteria:

- Impact issue is perceived by the public at large as important
- Considerable controversy has surrounded the issue on previous occasions
- A particular group or area that will be potentially affected requires special attention
- The magnitude of the impact is expected to be severe
- The proposed action or project is large in scope
- The proposed action or project is precedent setting in nature.

Ideally, those impacts that are considered the most important would be given the most attention in terms of measurement approaches. More resources would be devoted to those issues that are of the most concern. The allocation, however, will in fact be dependent on the impact measurement methodologies available for that issue. Impact measurement approaches vary from intuitive judgments and desk-top analysis to data intensive models requiring computer analysis. For some important impact issues, the more sophisticated measurement approaches may be simply beyond the means of available resources. The methodology may require a vast amount of data, or it may involve a model that is not completely understood by the planning agency. In general, the following factors should be considered in choosing a methodology for measuring impacts: (1) Level of measurement requirements; (2) confidence in measurement approach; (3) comprehensibility to user and public; and (4) resource requirements (time, cost, staff).

Closely tied to the selection of measurement techniques and the level of analysis is the selection of impact indicators. Impact indicators are measures used to describe the impact. When approaching the selection of impact indicators, the following considerations are appropriate:

1. Impact indicators should relate to readily identifiable or familiar concerns as much as possible. For example, aggregate costs of a project are more difficult to relate to than per household costs or changes in the property tax rate. This factor essentially calls for a focus on end impacts, where possible, rather than on intermediate ones. This factor also recognizes the desirability of indicators that are traditionally used, such as the unemployment rate, dwelling units per acre, and average daily traffic.

2. Legal or mandatory requirements should be met. Federal, state, or local requirements may spell out certain concerns to be evaluated for certain projects. For example, EPA regulations for wastewater treatment plants call for per household costs for wastewater projects to be indicated.

3. Indicators should be understandable. Impact indicators represent the attributes of a proposed action in the evaluation of alternatives. If they are complex and not easily understood by the public, then the evaluation task may be rather difficult. Abstract indexes or indicators involving technical jargon should be avoided whenever possible.

4. Where necessary, use surrogate or proxy indicators. For many impact issues of a qualitative nature, it will not be possible to estimate the impact directly. In these cases, surrogate indicators may be appropriate if they are not too abstruse and are used with care and explained in footnotes. An example of a traditional indicator used for school crowdedness is the teacher-pupil ratio.

Finally, the measurement determination step should delineate the time-frame for analysis. It is generally easy to estimate most impacts during the short term, but the estimate becomes much more speculative as the time period extends beyond 10 years. Generally, the period used in water quality impact assessment is 20 years, apparently for reasons of convenience—many local and state socioeconomic projections use a 20-yr time period. While the 20-yr time period is a reasonable compromise to use, it should be emphasized that impacts of short and longer duration may occur.

Step 3—Determine baseline conditions   This step is concerned with developing a profile of existing conditions for each of the impact issues being considered for impact measurement.

In establishing the baseline conditions, the planner is primarily interested in the existing conditions for those impact indicators that describe the impact issue. Establishing the baseline will be more straightforward for some impact indicators than others. For example, if the impact indicator is the increase in construction jobs associated with a new sewage treatment plant, then a profile of baseline construction employment would include the number and distribution of construction jobs in the impact area.

Step 4—Perform impact measurement   In this step, impacts are measured in as many of the dimensions indicated as possible, namely magnitude, direction, timing, duration, and incidence. The most intensive aspect of this step will be measurement of the magnitude of the impact.

Section 17.6 lists several manuals which present techniques for actually measuring different types of impacts. While the appropriate measurement technique will have been selected prior to this step, the actual measurement process may reveal the need to select an alternative approach. If, for example, a broad-brush measurement technique reveals an impact in an important impact area of greater than expected magnitude, the planner may wish to use a more sophisticated technique.

Step 5—Present and display impacts   The portrayal of impact information is a key aspect of impact assessment. Information has to be presented in a clear and understandable format. When impact assessment is concerned with the comparison of alternatives, impact information should be presented in a framework that will enable the selection of alternatives to take place. Various mapping and graphic techniques are useful in presenting individual impact information for one or more alternatives. Some are presented in Figs. 17-6, 17-7, and 17-8.

The presentation of impact information in environmental assessment is complicated when there are several impact measures to be considered and more than one decision-maker. The problem results

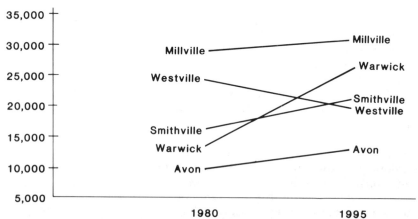

Fig. 17-6. Impact presentation: population changes due to regional wastewater treatment plant

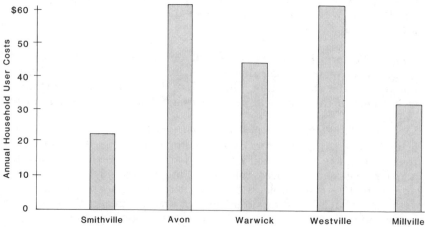

Fig. 17-7. Impact presentation: annual household user cost impacts of regional wastewater treatment plant

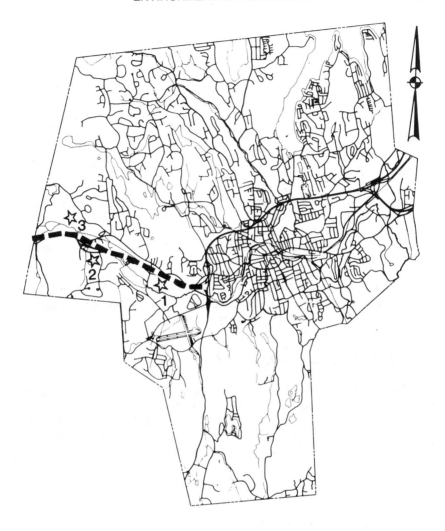

☆1 — **Valley View Farmstead National Register Site**

☆2 — **Town Square Historical District**

☆3 — **Chepachet Indian Burial Area**

Fig. 17-8. Impact presentation: historic locations affected by Interceptor Route A

from the number of dimensions associated with impact measurement, i.e., magnitude, direction, timing, duration and incidence. When all of these dimensions have to be considered for several alternatives involving several impact indicators, then the presentation of impact data is particularly difficult in a two-dimensional matrix. It is impractical to attempt to create a single matrix with all of the desired information.

Different types of matrices, shown in Tables 17-4 and 17-5, are suggested as appropriate for displaying these dimensions given more than one alternative. Table 17-4 is an impact-type matrix in which, for a specific impact indicator, impact magnitude is displayed for various alternatives in various affected areas. (In the table, A, B, C, D, and E are various sewage interceptor routes for a proposed regional sewerage facility.) This type of matrix is most relevant when an impact issue, say household user costs, is perceived as particularly important in the evaluation of alternatives. The alternative-type matrix shown in Table 17-5 evaluates impact indicators for one alternative, interceptor Route A. This kind of matrix highlights the differences among areas in several impact categories for one particular alternative.

The choice of matrix type will depend on the type of evaluation that will take place in the assessment process, importance of individual impact issues, the number of geographic areas of interest, and the number of alternatives. The alternative-type is the most commonly used impact display matrix. It is particularly useful when there are substantial differences among alternatives in several areas.

17.4 IMPACT EVALUATION

The next major task in the EA process involves the evaluation of the predicted consequences associated with each alternative. The proposed alternatives may be described by a variety of impact measures, expressed in various terms, some monetary, some quantitative, and others qualitative. The essence of the evaluation process is the comparison of the

TABLE 17-4 Impact-Type Matrix

| Area | Annual Household User Costs, in dollars per household | | | | |
	Alternative A	Alternative B	Alternative C	Alternative D	Alternative E
Smithville	26	50	55	89	31
Westville	67	61	48	29	64
Millville	31	58	51	79	28
Warwick	41	70	62	48	27
Avon	67	58	57	36	78

TABLE 17-5 Alternative-Type Matrix

Impact indicators (1)	Area				
	Smithville (2)	Westville (3)	Millville (4)	Warwick (5)	Avon (6)
Visual conflicts	slight	extensive	slight	moderate	slight
Annual household user costs, in dollars	26	67	31	41	67
Annual household nonuser costs, in dollars	15	16	20	11	28
Population increases 1980–1995, number of persons	1200	400	2000	800	350
Land preempted, in acres	75	220	100	50	300
New manufacturing jobs	0	600	700	100	1500
Historic locations adversely affected	0	1	4	0	12

Note: 1 acre = 0.405 hectare.

impacts associated with each alternative, in order to illustrate the significant similarities and differences among them and to select the preferred alternative.

The selection of a preferred or best alternative, however, is a difficult decision problem. Each of the alternatives, described by various impact measures, represents an imperfect achievement of goals and objectives. Since it is very unlikely that there will be an alternative that is clearly superior to another alternative in all impact categories, the ranking process will involve trade-offs among the impact categories. The process is made more complicated by the fact that some individuals in the community may view a particular impact as beneficial, while others might perceive it as adverse. In addition, various individuals may also assign different relative levels of importance to each of the impact categories. In the following subsections three approaches to the impact evaluation problem are described. First, some basic screening techniques are briefly reviewed.

17.4.1 Screening Techniques

Screening provides a process of sequentially comparing alternatives on the basis of impact values, so that they may be either eliminated or retained for further consideration. Alternatives are generally classified into one of two categories, acceptable or unacceptable. Without further information no choice may be made among the acceptable alternatives. Therefore, a ranking approach must then be applied to this possible smaller set of options, involving less effort than if it were applied to the entire set of alternatives.

As a first step, screening may eliminate from further consideration alternatives unlikely to be contenders for the best choice. The unacceptable alternatives may then be assigned a rank or score at some arbitrary level less desirable than the least desirable of the acceptable alternatives. Several screening techniques are listed in the following paragraphs.

Conjunctive screening Conjunctive screening implies that all constraints must be satisfied for an alternative to be considered acceptable. All factors are used simultaneously and an alternative must be acceptable with regard to each coequal factor. The procedure cannot differentiate among acceptable alternatives, since no preference information is employed. The methodology is simple and assures that all relevant constraints are satisfied. The approach may be used to eliminate alternatives which do not reach minimum acceptable levels (lower bounds) or which exceed maximum acceptable levels (upper bounds) of various impact measures. For an alternative to be acceptable, all such constraints must be satisfied. Figure 17-9 illustrates the concept. In Fig. 17-9, A, B, C, D, E, and F = various public sewerage interceptor location alternatives; x_1 = number of vacant acres opened up for development, and x_2 = number of existing industries capable of connecting to the sewerage system—these are socioeconomic impact indicators. Constraints l_1, l_2 = minimum acceptable levels for x_1, x_2 , respectively, and all constraints must be met.

Disjunctive screening This approach represents a variation of the conjunctive screening technique, in which an alternative need only pass some specified fraction of the conditions to be acceptable rather than being required to satisfy all criteria. No one condition may be considered exclusionary by itself.

In Fig. 17-10, symbols used are the same as in Fig. 17-9, and the two environmental impact indicators x_1 and x_2 are shown. In this particular case, alternatives pass the screening test if any two of the constraints are met. Thus, alternatives A, B, C, D, and E are all acceptable.

Lexicographic screening Unlike the disjunctive screening process, lexicographic screening assures that the most important criteria are always considered. In disjunctive screening, the most important criterion might be violated, but an alternative could still be acceptable if the other, less

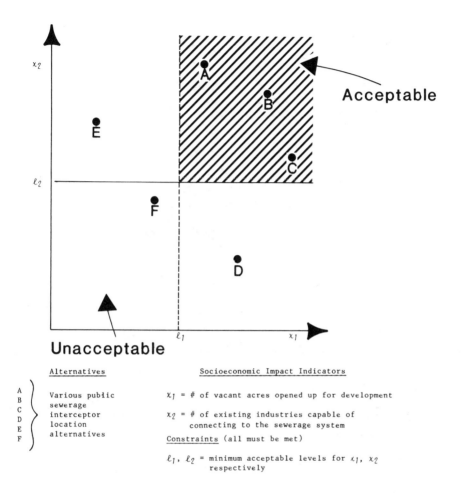

Unacceptable

Alternatives	Socioeconomic Impact Indicators

A
B
C
D
E
F

Various public sewerage interceptor location alternatives

x_1 = # of vacant acres opened up for development

x_2 = # of existing industries capable of connecting to the sewerage system

<u>Constraints</u> (all must be met)

l_1, l_2 = minimum acceptable levels for x_1, x_2 respectively

Fig. 17-9. Conjunctive screening

important, conditions are satisfied. In the lexicographic screening approach, however, the lower ranked factors need not necessarily be considered. If all factors are considered, then the lexicographic approach is identical to the conjunctive screening approach. The alternatives are first screened with respect to the most important criterion. Those that survive are then screened according to the next highest ranked criterion, and so on. The process stops when a single alternative remains, all of the factors have been considered, or the set of alternatives has been sufficiently reduced in size to permit more detailed evaluation. Figure 17-11 illustrates the technique. Symbols used are the same as in Fig. 17-9, and constraint l_1 must be met.

Conjunctive ranking   This approach combines a screening technique

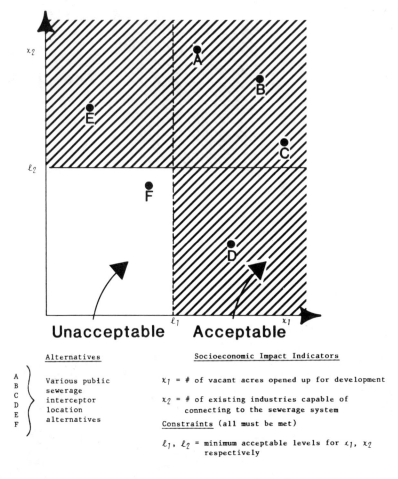

Fig. 17-10. Disjunctive screening

and a ranking process. It assumes that the value of an alternative may be expressed in terms of a single impact measure or attribute.

Referring to Fig. 17-12, symbols used are the same as in Fig. 17-9, and additionally x_3 = number of acres of community parks disturbed by construction, and x_4 = municipal bonded debt. Constraints l_1, l_2, = minimum acceptable goals and l_3, l_4 = maximum acceptable levels; all constraints must be met. Assume that x_1 serves as the exclusionary or most important factor. The unacceptable alternatives D, E, and F would be eliminated during the conjunctive screening process. Ranking the surviving alternatives with respect to x_1, then, it appears that alternative C provides the greatest amount of x_1. If two alternatives are desired for final ranking, B and C would pass this screening test.

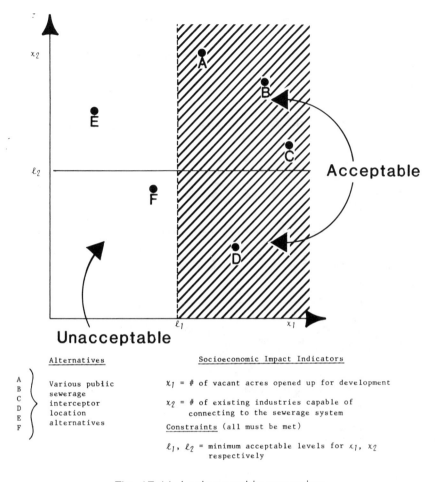

Fig. 17-11. Lexicographic screening

17.4.2 Comprehensive Evaluation Techniques

There are several techniques for comparing alternatives. Two of the most common are presented here.

Balance sheet method   The balance sheet method is one of the techniques most widely used in evaluating alternatives. In this approach, the information from the impact measurement step is presented without alteration to the decision-maker. Impact information is not reduced to commensurable units or compared to standards or objectives. Each decision-maker simply implicitly superimposes a set of values and weights on the information to reach an over-all judgment regarding the "best" alternative.

A variation on the simple balance sheet method is the ranked

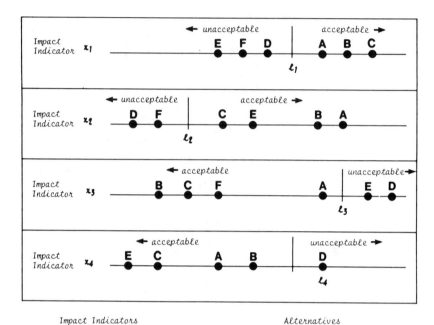

Impact Indicators

x_1 = # of vacant areas opened up for development

x_2 = # of existing industries capable of connecting to the sewerage system

x_3 = #of acres of community parks disturbed by construction

x_4 = municipal bonded debt

Alternatives

A, B, C, D, E, F are various sewerage interceptor location alternatives.

Constraints (all must be met)

l_1, l_2 = minimum acceptable goals

l_3, l_4 = maximum acceptable levels

Acceptable Alternatives

A, B, C

Unacceptable Alternatives

D, E, F

Fig. 17-12. Conjunctive screening

balance sheet approach. The same implicit approach is applied by the decision-maker. Instead of singling out a best alternative, alternatives are ranked. The ranking is typically done on an ordinal basis (A, B, C, D, E), or on whatever basis is derived. It is possible to say, for example, that alternative A is preferred to B, or B is preferred to C, but one cannot say how much more preferred. Figure 17-13 illustrates the ranked balance sheet approach.

Decision Criteria

1. The preferred alternative is that alternative whose impacts are considered to maximize the decision-maker(s) goals.

Impact Information

1. Aggregate impacts of interceptor alternatives A,B,C,D,E on South River Basin (Smithville, Westville, Millville, Warwick, Avon).

Impact indicators	Alternatives				
	A	B	C	D	E
Visual conflicts	slight	slight	moderate	moderate	extensive
Annual household user costs, in dollars	39	61	57	65	30
Annual household nonuser costs, in dollars	17	22	20	24	15
Population increases 1980–1995 (persons)	4750	6500	3200	9000	8500
Land pre-empted, in acres	745	600	650	300	550
New manufacturing jobs	2900	3800	3000	3200	4000
Historic locations affected	17	5	13	2	31

Evaluation Results

The South River Basin Citizens Advisory Committee ranked the alternatives as follows: A > E > C > D > B.

Fig. 17-13. Ranked balance sheet method

Balance sheet methods avoid many of the technical problems associated with scoring impact results or weighting impact attributes. A nonscored plan is attractive largely because it ignores the practical and political difficulties associated with scoring and weighting. While the balance sheet approach can be considered an optimization technique, it fails to consider explicitly how the best alternative or ranking is determined. This makes it impossible to consider trade-offs among alternatives or to suggest impacts that should be modified by mitigation measures.

The balance sheet approach is often a good technique to use initially in an evaluation process. It commits decision-makers to a choice. These choices, in turn, then can be considered by the decision-makers in explicitly defining weights and values. Without giving some explicit consideration to these issues, the balance sheet method resembles a black box approach to evaluation.

Linear additive utility function The utility function evaluation method is a means of generating a single over-all index of preference for an alternative that can be compared with other alternative preference indexes. This preference, expressed on an interval scale, is referred to as a linear additive utility function. It represents the aggregated weighted scores of each impact or attribute. The linear additive utility function can be mathematically expressed as

$$u\ (x_{1m},\ x_{2m},\ \ldots\ x_{mm})\ =\ W_1 v_1(x_m)\ =\ w_2 v_2(x_{2m})\ +\ \ldots\ w_m v_m(x_{mm})\ (17.1)$$

in which w_m = a weight associated with impact categories, and v_m (x_{mm}) = scoring (expressed on an interval scale) placed on the impact consequence. The scorings indicate the relative size or desirability of various levels of the corresponding impacts. Weights, on the other hand, represent the relative importance of a change in one impact compared to a change in another. The ratio of two weights, say w_{x1}/w_{x2}, represents the trade-off that the decision-maker is willing to make in terms of how much impact x_1 can be given up to gain an additional unit of impact x_2.

The end product of a linear additive utility function approach is shown in Fig. 17-14. It requires several steps:

1. Determine the score or value of each impact consequence and express on an interval scale.
2. Determine the weighting factors for each impact attribute.
3. Determine the weighted values of each impact attribute.
4. Aggregate the weighted values for each alternative.
5. Compare aggregated preferences across alternatives.
6. Select the optimal alternative, i.e., the alternative with the highest score.

In Fig. 17-14, impacts have been scored on the basis of 0.00: least preferred, 1.00: most preferred. In the table, score is in upper left of each divided box, and weighted score in lower right.

The linear additive utility function involves relatively easy computations and is desirable in terms of generating rankings that reflect variations in preference. In addition, like any of the approaches that involve impact weighting, it allows decision-makers to perceive and make trade-offs among alternatives.

On the negative side, many decision-makers will be reluctant to use an approach that involves reducing all of the impact attributes to a single index. The use of a single number to express an alternative may simply be too abstract and artificial for some. This approach also requires the most involvement by decision-makers of any approach presented in this chapter. Not only must weights be determined for the impacts, but much more specific and explicit scores must also be developed for the impact consequences. Using this approach will therefore require a great deal of time and interaction between decision-makers and a technical planning staff.

Decision Criteria

1. The preferred alternative is that alternative which yields the highest aggregated preference score.

Impact Information

1. Aggregate impacts of interceptor alternatives A,B,C,D,E on South River Basin (Smithville, Westville, Millville, Warwick, Avon).

Impact indicators	Alternatives				
	A	B	C	D	E
Visual conflicts	slight	slight	moderate	moderate	extensive
Annual household user costs, in dollars	39	61	57	65	30
Annual household nonuser costs, in dollars	17	22	20	24	15
Population increases 1980–1995 (persons)	4750	6500	3200	9,000	8500
Land pre-empted, in acres	745	600	650	300	550
New manufacturing jobs	2900	3800	3000	3200	4000
Historic locations affected	17	5	13	2	31

(Continued)

Weighting factor	Impact indicators	Alternatives				
		A	B	C	D	E
4.0	Visual conflicts	0.80 / 3.20	0.80 / 3.20	0.40 / 1.60	0.40 / 1.60	0.00 / 0.00
15.0	Annual house-hold user costs	0.80 / 12.00	0.10 / 1.50	0.20 / 3.00	0.00 / 0.00	1.00 / 15.00
12.0	Annual house-hold nonuser costs	0.70 / 8.40	0.20 / 2.40	0.40 / 4.30	0.00 / 0.00	1.00 / 12.00
10.0	Population increases, 1980–1995	0.70 / 7.00	0.50 / 5.00	1.00 / 10.00	0.00 / 0.00	0.10 / 1.00
1.0	Land pre-empted	0.30 / 0.30	0.50 / 0.50	0.50 / 0.50	0.00 / 0.00	1.00 / 1.00
12.0	New manufacturing jobs	0.00 / 0.00	0.80 / 9.40	0.10 / 1.20	0.20 / 2.40	1.00 / 12.00
6.0	Historic locations affected	0.40 / 2.40	0.30 / 5.40	0.60 / 3.60	1.00 / 6.00	0.00 / 0.00
		33.30	27.60	24.70	10.00	41.00

Evaluation Results

Alternative E is the preferred alternative; the ranking of alternatives is as follows: E > A > B > C > D.

Fig. 17-14. Linear additive utility function approach

17.5 IMPACT MITIGATION

The purpose of mitigation is to alleviate adverse impacts resulting from proposed plans and strategies. Mitigation is often given minimal attention in the assessment of plans and alternatives. By failing to include mitigation considerations in the assessment process, however, the planner will undermine the legitimacy of the planning process. It is often possible to rectify adverse impacts with mitigation measures and thus save an otherwise unacceptable alternative.

17.5.1 Types of Mitigation Measures

There are basically two types of mitigation measures: those that attempt to alter or prevent the impact, and those that accept the impact and attempt to address it by lessening its adversity. For the sake of classification, these two types will be referred to as impact prevention measures and impact management measures.

Impact prevention measures Impact prevention measures primarily involve changes in the plans and strategies themselves. The focus of impact prevention measures is on the characteristics of the strategy that are responsible for the impact. Generic examples include reduction in the scope of the project, changes in its location, alterations in the regulatory requirements, changes in the financing mechanisms, and shifts in responsibility in the institutional arrangements of a strategy. Typical impact prevention measures are shown in Fig. 17-15.

Impact management measures Impact management measures represent additional measures or activities to deal with expected impacts. The use of impact management measures is particularly suitable in those situations where the use of impact prevention measures is not feasible or would create additional impacts. For example, consider a proposed stormwater detention pond for an existing residential neighborhood. There are objections to the pond for several reasons, particularly for visual and public safety impacts. A first approach to mitigation would be to consider changes in the location or the size of the facility. Evaluation of these options might indicate, however, that the cost would be prohibitive or the effectiveness of the stormwater strategy would be greatly diminished, or both. Thus, impact management measures might be more appropriate. For this particular example, safety fencing and shrub or tree plantings would be proposed and incorporated in the strategy. Other examples of impact management measures are shown in Fig. 17-15.

17.6 BIBLIOGRAPHY

1. Abt Associates Inc., *Man and Water: A Social Report*, prepared for the Bureau of Reclamation, U.S. Department of the Interior, under Contract No. 14-06-D-7342, Washington, D.C., 1973.
2. Abt Associates, Inc., *Social Assessment Manual: A Guide to Preparation of the Social Well-being Account*, prepared for the Bureau of Reclamation, U.S. Department of the Interior, under Contract No. 14-06-D-7342(5), Washington, D.C., 1975.

IMPACT ISSUE: Growth impacts of wastewater treatment facilities
Impact Prevention Measures: • Reduce the capacity of the wastewater treatment facility • Reduce the capacity of the sewer interceptors • Reduce service area coverage • Stage the construction of interceptors
Impact Management Measures: • Use zoning density controls to limit the amount of potential growth in service areas • Use sewer tap-in fees to regulate the amount of connections • Use growth management controls, such as building permit quotas and capital improvement requirements, to stage growth • Use public acquisition techniques to regulate amount of land available for growth
IMPACT ISSUE: Increased cost to users of a proposed wastewater treatment facility
Impact Prevention Measures: • Reduce scope of project • Use a mix of alternative and conventional systems • Alter financing mechanisms to distribute some costs to nonusers • Regionalize with neighboring community to get economies of scale
Impact Management Measures: - • Provide cost sharing via users' loan program • Seek additional cost sharing from outside community to lessen user burden

Fig. 17-15. Mitigation: impact prevention and impact measurement measures

3. Bureau of Reclamation, U.S. Department of the Interior, *Environmental Quality Assessment in Multiobjective Planning*, Denver, Colo., 1977.
4. California Office of State Planning, *Economic Practices Manual: A Handbook for Preparing an Economic Impact Assessment*, Sacramento, Calif., 1978.
5. Harbridge House, Inc., *Socioeconomic Impact Assessment of Proposed Air Quality Attainment and Maintenance Strategies*, EPA (Region 1), Boston, Mass., June 1976.
6. Heer, J.E., Jr., and Hagerty, D.J., *Environmental Assessment and Statements*, Van Nostrand Reinhold Co., New York, 1977.

7. Leistritz, F.L., and Murdock, S.H., *Economic, Demographic, and Social Factors Affecting Energy-Impacted Communities: An Assessment Model and Implications for Nuclear Energy Centers,* North Dakota State University, Williston, N.D., April 1977.
8. Muller, T., *Economic Impacts of Land Development: Employment, Housing and Property Values,* Urban Land Institute, Washington, D.C., 1976.
9. Skidmore, Owings and Merrill, *Notebook 3: Economic Impacts,* part of the Environmental Notebook Series prepared for the U.S. Department of Transportation, U.S. Government Printing Office, Washington, D.C., 1975.
10. Skidmore, Owings and Merrill, *Notebook 4: Physical Impacts,* part of the Environmental Notebook Series prepared for the U.S. Department of Transportation, U.S. Government Printing Office, Washington, D.C., 1975.
11. Stenejhem, E.J., Regional Studies Program, *Forecasting the Local Economic Impacts of Energy Resource Development: A Methodological Approach,* Argonne National Lab., Argonne, Ill., December 1975.
12. U.S. Department of the Interior, *Preparation of Environmental Statements: Guidelines for Discussion of Cultural (Historic, Archaeological, Architectural) Resources,* Washington, D.C., 1974.
13. Urban Systems Research and Engineering, Inc., *Air Quality Reviews for Wastewater Treatment Facilities: A Guidebook on Procedures and Methods (Draft),* prepared for U.S. Environmental Protection Agency (Contract No. 68-01-7490), Washington, D.C., September 1981.
14. Urban Systems Research and Engineering, Inc., *Secondary Impact Assessment Manual,* prepared for U.S. Environmental Protection Agency, Washington, D.C., January 1981.
15. Urban Systems Research and Engineering, Inc., *Socioeconomic Impacts of Water Quality Strategies,* prepared for U.S. Environmental Protection Agency, Washington, D.C., September 1981.

CHAPTER 18

CAPITAL IMPROVEMENT PROGRAMS[a]

18.1 INTRODUCTION

Government bodies at all levels are finding more and more difficulty in meeting the service demands and needs of their constituents. Governmental resources, both human and financial, are increasingly stretched to meet the raised expectations from residents and businesses within their jurisdictions. Both the elected officials, who are responsible for final decision-making, and their staffs, who must provide daily responses to citizens, however, are better educated and trained than their predecessors and are exercising their skills to try to use limited resources in the most efficient manner. More sophisticated problem solving techniques and technological improvements help them to clearer analysis of budgets and costs. In addition, widespread awareness and understanding of governmental responsibilities and problems have encouraged the participation of citizens in governmental processes. The capital improvement programs of government, therefore, have become an increasingly necessary and acceptable part of the governmental budget process.

The definition of capital, as it is used in this chapter, is the amount of property, such as real estate, buildings, and equipment above a specified value (usually $100) and of long life (more than one year). The purpose of a capital improvement program (CIP) is to maintain and increase the value of the capital of the government or private company using the program. Capital improvement programs are used by both private companies and government agencies, but since the emphasis in this book is on planning, and most planners work for the government, either directly or indirectly through their private clientele, the capital improvement process described herein will deal more often with its use by governmental bodies.

It can be said, in the broader view, that government capital includes both public and private holdings. In the literal sense, governmental budgeting can only directly concern itself with its own property, such as municipal buildings, infrastructure systems, parks, schools, airports, etc., but the manner in which governmental capital investments are made affects the value of private capital investments as well. Since a great share of government income derives from the value of private capital, through taxes, if governmental capital investments in-

---

[a]Prepared by Gloria S. McGregor, M.ASCE, Director, Integrated Environmental Planning, Southern California Association of Governments, Los Angeles, CA.

crease the value of private capital, then government income is also increased. Thus, it could be said that one of the goals of the governmental capital improvement program could be considered to be to assist in the appreciation of its capital, both public and private (16). In both the public and private sectors, sound investment, adequate research as to the effects of the investment, and long-range planning will maximize the goal of capital appreciation.

When marketing governmental long-term debt instruments to investors, as is necessary in the sales of general obligation and revenue bonds, or buyers in lease-back arrangements, it is essential to demonstrate that the agency has a well organized and effective budgetary process. The CIP is a valuable asset in this regard.

The CIP is a rational, informed and organized way to plan for long-term expenditures in either the public or private sector. The national concerns for infrastructure improvements across the United States and how to provide national funding assistance have even led to considerable support for the development of a national capital improvement program. This chapter will outline the evolution of the CIP; its purpose and elements (Section 18.2); the CIP process (Section 18.3); and the conclusions and evaluation (Section 18.4). A glossary of terms follows (Section 18.5).

18.2 PURPOSE AND ELEMENTS

18.2.1 Comprehensive Plans

Comprehensive planning, as it is practiced today, deals not only with land use, but with social, environmental and economic elements of the area covered by the plan. Early planning efforts produced some noteworthy results, such as the Chicago Plan by Daniel Burnham (1), but the implementation of those plans was difficult to effect on a continuous basis. There was changing emphasis and priorities with different administrations and generally little involvement of the planner in the budgetary process. Governmental budgets were often short-term and simple revenue-expenditure comparisons, on an annual basis. Land was cheap, service expectations by constituents were low, population pressures were not as great as they are today, and people generally were less mobile. Public improvements expensive to build and maintain, such as secondary sewage treatment plants, sanitary landfills, and treated water systems, were rare.

In the past, planners were trained to organize the use of land, to segregate uses which were not compatible, and to provide projections of the future for the area in which they worked. They were seldom asked the cost of implementation, so plans were often partially implemented, because they were too costly. Of course there were also many other reasons for poor implementation, such as no support by citizens or political bodies.

Concerned planners, elected officials, and citizens debated how to make planning more effective. A common statement by citizens was that if the government were just run "like private industry" these problems wouldn't occur. This is not to say that private industry wasn't inefficient, but rather that, in profit-oriented companies, there was apt to be a better organized money management system. In identifying which aspects of private company financial management were transferable to public agencies, it became apparent that staff trained in budgeting and money management was an important item. With professional budgeting officials, governing bodies would receive adequate information, on a regular basis, about their revenues and expenditures. Standards of education and training required of government staff were tied to performance expectations for particular agency employees, as was common in private industry. Patronage systems became less common.

Planners were not exempt from these performance requirements. Training and education standards began to require knowledge of economics, and competition for government resources became more intense. Professional planners became involved in assisting in long-range financial planning for the agency or private company for which they worked. The value of involvement of planners in governmental and private sector budgeting was then established.

18.2.2 Budgets

Both public and private financial planning and management must follow a rational process if funds are to be spent efficiently. A budget, or plan for money management, in either public or private institutions, is based on a financial statement of estimated income and expenses over a stated period of time, usually on an annual basis. A budget can take many forms.

General　The budget can simply be an allocation of a percentage of the revenue to each specific department, to be spent as designated by the executive of that department.

Line item budget　It can be a line item budget (12), in which the department reports its expenditures of the previous year for various items, and requests that these expenditures be allowed to continue, be increased, decreased or expanded. Line item budgets, for either government or private industry, are the easiest to prepare and maintain. They have all expenditures explained in terms of a particular type of equipment, supply or personnel, such as postage, telephone, vehicle, stationery, desks, accountants, engineers, etc. These items are not tied to the particular functions of the department.

If set by the governing board, the line item budget is difficult to adjust, except by percentage increases or decreases. It is not easy to determine, for example, how many new trucks are required to increase garbage pickups from once to twice a week, when the costs of garbage service are only a part of the public works department budget. Based on his or her knowledge of the operations, the public works director probably has a good feeling about whether increasing staff or acquiring bigger trucks or different garbage containers is the answer. All costs of running the garbage service are line items—items such as laborers, gasoline, mechanics, bookkeepers, repairs and telephone service. The line item budget, however, makes assembling information to support the director's recommendations for program changes in the CIP complicated and time consuming.

Program budget The program budget provides excellent backup information for the capital improvement program. It is designed to identify, as part of the budget process, the costs of particular programs or services provided by the public or private sector agency or company. In these budgets, costs of supplying services, both capital and maintenance, are under separate program listings.

In outlining the costs of building and maintaining roads, the program budget would include capital equipment, such as road graders, paving machines and rollers, as well as maintenance materials, such as asphalt, gravel and sweeper brushes, and personnel. Capital equipment costs could be divided between several programs with a percentage applied to each. In developing a CIP such cost information will help to identify needs for funding and allocation of costs, as well as assist the long-range planning required to develop a successful CIP.

18.2.3 Capital Improvement Programs

The appreciation of capital assets, including land, roads, buildings, parks, factories and equipment, proceeds on a planned course when the CIP is used to assure funding of necessary maintenance and expansion replacements (9). As planners are expected to have a central role in planning for the future, they become key actors in the development of any capital improvement program, public or private. Their estimates of the sequence of development, the parts of the jurisdiction which need improvement, and the over-all value of improvements to the economic health of the area for which they are planning, provide important background information in establishing priorities for capital expenditures.

Planners continually receive input from other jurisdictions or private sources which allows them to better understand the costs and benefits of projects that they must review. A planner who becomes an essential part of long-range budgeting becomes a more effective player on the financial planning team, whose recommendations are based on solid economic facts.

The nonrecurring nature of large capital improvements is an integral part of the long-range planning process: both are mutually supportive (7). In many long-range plans developed today, an implementation section will contain a capital improvement plan related to the comprehensive plan. It will suggest funding mechanisms and timing, thus demonstrating the practicality and financial validity of the plan.

In private development plans, a CIP which includes costs and schedules helps determine profit margins. Planning and budgeting by a public agency, although not organized for profit, must assure that funds will be available for both the necessary capital expenditures and maintenance and operations. Information defining all the financial requirements of the public or private plan should be made available early in the planning process, so that a determination can be made of the feasibility of each part of the plan. Priorities can then be set to mesh with timing of available funding.

The comprehensive plan and the capital improvement program operate in tandem, with the underlying goal of appreciation and maintenance of the economic base of the area to which they apply. In developing the CIP and assuring its effectiveness, all the service beneficiaries should be participants in the process. As in any complicated undertaking, the broader the participation, the wider the support. If the CIP is developed by staff only, without ongoing discussion with the governing board or company management, its acceptance may be uneven.

For a public sector agency, a representative group of constituents, in the form of one or more citizens' advisory committees, should be appointed by the governing board. If more than one group is appointed, each can review needs for a particular form of service, e.g., parks, roads, public health services. Each group can also recommend priorities, and should support the adoption and implementation of their recommendations for CIP. In the case of private development, the benefits of using similar groups include support for and understanding of the projects.

Public works departments in public agencies have traditionally been responsible for the CIPs. However, all departments should be used in the development of the comprehensive plan and the CIP. This can be effective in creating a budget which is broad in its coverage, is integrated, and receives support from all departments. (An integrated budget is one in which purchases and programs are complementary between departments. An example would be the selection of computer equipment which adapts to needs of several departments.) For instance, police and fire departments generally have an intimate knowledge of the condition of roads and which ones are vital to their ability to respond effectively to emergencies in all parts of the jurisdiction. They can provide valuable input when the governing board is trying to establish priorities between more snow removal equipment, a new bridge, or an arterial street improvement.

The most difficult part of establishing a CIP which will receive support by the majority of participants is in setting priorities and timing for expenditures. Often there is not enough money for all items determined desirable in a particular year. The public agency goals, objectives, and policies contained in the comprehensive plan can be useful in this exercise, particularly if they have been established with in-depth participation by various departments, the governing board and citizen groups. In a private development process, it will be equally helpful to involve the in-house engineers and planners, as well as bankers, future users, local officials, realtors, and others who can provide useful information to the company management and decision-makers.

18.2.4 Goals, Objectives, and Policies

Any successful organization, public or private, should have its own goals, objectives, and policies. By definition, a goal is a statement of the long-range, desirable, complete result of a series of actions. An objective is a short-range definable step in reaching a goal. A policy is a statement describing a selective factor to be used in making a decision on a course of action. The more clearly these goals, objectives, and policies are stated and understood, the more helpful they are in setting priorities in the CIP. The over-all goal for the CIP might be to identify and plan for the investments necessary to the community, in an efficient, cost-effective manner, within limits of community ability to pay. A typical goal for a public agency might be:

> Provide adequate transportation systems for all segments of the population.

A support objective for this goal might be:

> Provide a public bus system by 1990.

A policy to assist in decision-making regarding this objective might be:

> Public bus systems must have provisions for the handicapped.

When the public agency begins to develop costs for input into its capital improvement program, the agency will know that they should plan to have the system ready for operation by the year 1990, if it is to meet the objective established in the comprehensive plan. It should also plan that at least some percentage of the buses will provide service for the handicapped. Timing for the CIP will then have been established, and some measure of quality for the equipment to be purchased will have been determined.

The comprehensive plan can be a useful tool in setting needs and priorities for the CIP, although there may still be conflicting objectives. If the comprehensive plan has recommended current funding sources for particular aspects of its captial requirements, these too will be a good source of information in the development of the CIP.

Similarly, in the case of private development, the company may have as its stated goal:

Develop an integrated new community of sufficient size to be economically independent.

A supporting objective could be:

Develop an office/industrial park of 400 acres by 1990.

A policy for use in decision-making could be:

Limit industrial park occupants to those classified as light industry.

The CIP developed by this company should include improvements needed to support an office-industrial park of the defined size, knowing that roads, water and sewer systems, landscaping, and building designs will be of a particular type required by light industry and office development.

18.2.5 Benefits

The development of a comprehensive plan requires many forms of capital improvements, usually to public standards set for the particular density of development and use. In the case of the large-scale planned development—a freeway, school system or other large project—these improvements are usually too costly to be accomplished in one year. The ordinary annual budget cannot respond to the financial needs of these projects.

There is, of course, the option of building each year what the revenues will allow. The government agency or private company reviews the annual expected income for the following year and decides how much of it will be spent on capital improvements. There may be some understanding, written or unwritten, of priorities over several years, but decisions are generally made only on an annual basis, with little long-range planning. Funding for capital improvements would use available funds within the agency or the company, because those involved in budgeting may not be sure what projects will be funded in subsequent years.

With the use of a capital improvement program, which implies planning for capital projects at least five years ahead, long-range funding options can be explored more fully, with knowledge of the amounts and types of funding required. Funding programs available from public and private sources can be reviewed, analyses of their continued viability established, and capital improvements can be matched with anticipated funding.

Most state and federal programs, such as those providing gas tax money, hospital funding, and revenue sharing, usually have a known life, stated in the enabling legislation. Legislation will be altered over time, depending upon political goals. However, these programs help in identifying funding sources. Similarly, the bond market can provide funding for general obligation, tax-increment or revenue bonds. The marketability and interest rates of these bonds will depend on the national and local economy and the economic health of the agency which guarantees their repayment.

Some of the benefits of an effective CIP can be:

1. Services and facilities included in the comprehensive plan can be provided for in an orderly and integrated manner (15).

2. Projects can be developed in the sequences which fit stated goals, objectives, and policies in the comprehensive plan.

3. Each department in the government agency or private company will have its own segment of the capital improvement program outlined and approved in relationship with those of other departments. Each can understand more clearly the needs, pressures, and functions of other departments, when they are all team participants in the development of the CIP.

4. The public, or the clients of the private company, when they are participants in the priority and ratification process of the CIP, will more readily support capital expenditures as planned, as well as financing methodology. This will lessen pressure on staff, management, and the governing board to change priorities.

5. The comprehensive plan will become more effective in achieving its goals and objectives. Its policies will also provide more effective assistance in capital expenditure decisions, and the plan can be monitored by evaluating achievement of objectives (7).

6. Projects requiring large capital expenditures are more likely to be completed on schedule and in orderly progression, since the sources of funding have been identified and allocated over a long period.

7. Inevitable changes in political direction or company management will be less likely to alter an orderly and effective long-range expenditure plan designed to meet goals and objectives which were established with broad participation by service recipients and providers.

8. Public or private agencies or companies will be better able to understand the value of federal or state funding or tax programs if they can review them in the context of assuring implementation of the established CIP. They will be less likely to accept funding or assistance for a capital improvement which is not a currently planned addition to the capital asset system (4).

9. Multiyear projects can be scheduled and funded, and provision for long-range management, maintenance, and operations can be carefully planned and given financial support.

10. All participants in the CIP can achieve better understanding of various services provided which require capital improvements, and may be better able to provide mutual support in establishing investment priorities.

11. Tax stabilization can more easily be achieved on a long-term basis, because community (or company) financial standing and knowledge of funding and revenue sources should be enhanced.

12. Large capital purchases, e.g., land, buildings, etc., can be made when opportunities are available for acquisitions at an advantageous cost (5).

13. Bond purchasers and other investors in the area will be more likely to support capital improvements financially if they can see that they are part of a carefully planned, long-term improvement plan. More favorable bond ratings may result.

14. Projects can be accomplished in a more cost-effective time sequence. For example, a new road improvement will not be scheduled before the underlying sewer system repairs have been made.

15. The capital improvement program and the comprehensive plan will operate in partnership, and each will be more effective in enabling the achievement of community investment objectives in a timely and effective manner.

18.2.6 CIP Policies

As has been previously stated, comprehensive plan policies are helpful in guiding expenditure decisions. There is also a need for policy development in connection with the CIP process itself. These policies can set the direction for CIP allocations and, as with the comprehensive plan policies, work best when developed with the participation of those involved in the process. In the public agency, the chief executive, the governing board, and departmental staff leaders can all provide useful input, with the governing board making the final selections. If informed citizen input can be obtained, such as from banks, financial planners, and business leaders, the product will receive even wider support and benefit. In the private company, although the board of directors and chief executive officer are final decision-makers, the comptroller, department heads, and selected client representatives can also be of considerable assistance in developing policies which will guide the final selection of CIP components.

The issues which capital improvement policy guidelines could address include:

1. The percentage of the budget to be devoted to capital improvements (7). There should be careful attention to outside funding sources.

2. The willingness of the governing board and staff management to accept outside governmental assistance. This is important, because to some, accepting such assistance means giving up some options in making budget decisions. It can also mean having to make decisions based on priorities established by external funding agencies.

3. The types of bonding and other financial mechanisms which are acceptable to the government jurisdiction or to the company. For example, in periods of economic difficulty, will general obligation bonds be supported? Will developers be expected to pay their way entirely, partially, or not at all?

4. How should the end-of-the-year surplus, if any, be used?

Should it be allocated to reserves, next year's CIP, reduction of taxes, or be undesignated?

5. How should the process itself be directed? In some agencies, budget directives include such statements as: "Next year's budget can exceed the current year's by 10%," or " . . . must be reduced by 10%." This approach does not allow for changes in selected service levels, for new projects or new emphasis. It assumes that all functions are equal, and, in general, is difficult to implement. It is better to state the expected revenues, that expenditures must balance them (if that is the goal), and that all involved participants will have to agree to discuss how these goals will be reached.

6. What part of the revenue should be committed to debt service and operating expenses (4)? This information is often difficult to clarify, and yet it is important in the CIP process.

7. Which officials should have final determinations of changes, allocations, and priorities in the CIP?

Ideally, all departments, the executive officer, the citizens, and the governing board should have been involved in the development of adopted policies. Technical questions should be answered by those trained to do so. Planners should contribute advice on such issues as how to maintain economic viability and quality of life within the jurisdiction or project boundary. Planners are often good sources of comparative statistics and are aware of what is happening in similar localities elsewhere.

The finance officer, or comptroller, responds to funding needs and seeks innovative ways to provide revenue necessary to implement the CIP, utilizing information available from peers, as well as information from other participants in the CIP process. The finance officer is also responsible for packaging all the accumulated information in an understandable manner.

Forecasts of land use needs, population growth expectations, economic development goals, social issues, development costs and government funding programs can be generated from the planning and public works departments. Locally derived population statistics are particularly important with respect to sewage treatment, water supply, and educational facilities.

18.2.7 Financing

Of major importance in the locational investment decision of industrial, residential, or commercial developers are the current levels of municipal services and the ability of the municipality to accommodate additional capital improvements for serving new development. If present conditions indicate deficiencies in the sewage treatment plant, or inadequate school facilities or other services which would hinder proper operation or investment returns of development, economic upgrading of the community may not occur. Progress toward the goal of capital appreciation may be slow.

Conversely, if the governmental agency or the company can demonstrate that there is a workable CIP which will correct any deficiencies by a certain time, then the investor should have a positive attitude toward development in that location. Private investment capital may be attracted to financing various capital improvements in an area which has an effective CIP.

Large portions of major local capital projects have traditionally been financed by long-term "loans," either through general obligation (GO), tax-increment, or revenue bonds. GO bonds pledge the full faith and credit of the jurisdiction of issuance. Tax-increment or revenue bonds are honored through the success of a particular project which generates revenue or additional tax income, e.g., a sports stadium or redevelopment project.

General obligation bonds must be used within the constraints of the legal debt limit of the jurisdiction (for more details, see Sec. 18.3), while revenue bonds may be sold without debt limitation constraints of the jurisdiction although respecting market limitations. The attractiveness of revenue bonds to investors depends on the perceived viability of the project. GO bond use is declining as compared to the use of revenue bonds (70/30 in 1960 to 30/70 in 1981), because of the need for voter approval in most jurisdictions (13). Every capital improvement program, therefore, must have its funding mechanisms tied to its capital projects. These linkages should be easily understood and practical.

There are many sources of state or federal government assistance, which vary from year to year in their utility. It is important to keep abreast of changes in these programs. Since they are changing, specific programs will not be reviewed herein.

Private funding mechanisms are also under constant change. Income tax provisions, interest rates, pension investment regulations and banking practices all affect private investments. There are, however, opportunities to develop public-private financing partnerships (such as sale-leasebacks), where new or existing facilities are sold to private investors. These investors, in effect, issue a mortgage to the government agency, payable over a specified number of years, at the end of which the agency will own the facility free and clear. The attractiveness of the sale-leaseback arrangement is that it may not be required to be subject to voter approval and still can be tax exempt.

Specific taxes such as sales taxes can be directly designated as revenue to pay back long-term debt obligations, or their revenue can be directed to the general fund. Special assessment districts can be formed for the purpose of financing localized capital improvements such as fire stations, street lighting, recreational facilities, and water and sewer systems. Such districts can be either single purpose, to finance and maintain a particular facility, or general purpose. General purpose districts, often called "community service districts," have the authority to build any facilities approved by their members. Some special districts, such as U.S. Resource Conservation Districts, can cover very large areas and finance very large projects, such as dams.

18.2.8 Citizen Involvement

Citizen involvement in the CIP process will vary with the locality. Its value in establishing improvement priorities and funding support cannot be underestimated. The planner can be helpful in maximizing the usefulness of citizen input by helping to organize the process and information flow. The citizen group or individuals interested in participating must have access to all background data, objectives, costs, and funding options available. Staff support should also be provided in the form of scheduled meetings, reports, and full disclosure of pertinent information.

Citizen participation in the budget decisions, particularly capital improvement programs, can create better understanding among differing groups in the area and cause the budget process to be a strong element in community politics. Capital investments made by a governing body for a community or area without strong citizen support can result in dissensions within the community which could have been avoided. Input from citizen groups may be required as a part of the approval process for receipt of federal or state funding. Examples are revenue sharing, block grants, and mass transit programs. The planner can help assure that input in these situations is meaningful for everyone involved by organizing the effort and providing information to aid in achieving viable decisions. Citizens can be helpful in researching the needs for projects and private funding opportunities.

If the media have a good working relationship with the agency, and are supplied with pertinent information, broad coverage can be given about the program. This coverage can alert interested persons and notify them of opportunities for participation. Various views about the benefits or disadvantages of particular choices can also be published. Areawide surveys soliciting ideas about improvement needs and priorities can be distributed with the help of the local newspaper, radio, or TV station, or enclosed with utility bills. When these surveys provide support for particular capital improvements, the decision-makers' choices become easier. Passage of related bond issues will probably be expedited.

Citizen groups and individuals, as part of the comprehensive plan process, help in establishing expected growth rates in the community. They can also provide assistance in agreeing on the rate of public investment in capital improvements for the area (15). Technical expertise can be obtained at little or no cost to the jurisdiction by soliciting knowledgeable individuals to be a part of the process. Bankers, engineers, realtors, financial planners and analysts, developers and contractors are some of the groups who can provide technical evaluation of projects and financing arrangements for the CIP program.

Citizen committees can also function as channels to monitor and disseminate information about the value of capital improvements. As an example of this type of action, fire insurance rates are determined in part by the level of firefighting capability in the area, including such elements as water pressure, fire engines, and distance and response time necessary to fight fires in each district. If the firefighting capability is raised to a more acceptable level by the installation of new water storage tanks, and insurance rates are thereby lowered, there can be enough savings in insurance payments across the area to encourage citizens to support a tax increase to pay for the new tanks.

Further, if capital improvements made in the areawide road system substantially lower the accident rate in the same area, automobile insurance rates may decline. Unless the citizens are aware of these implications, however, achieving support for the expenditures and necessary financing may be much more difficult than it need be.

Planners should investigate these less well understood benefits of capital improvements so that they can be ready to provide appropriate data to the citizen groups and individuals. They are in a position, through implementation of the comprehensive plan, to affect levels of all public services and to communicate with all service providers. They can ask appropriate questions to clarify the implications of various capital improvements on the ability to provide services.

Citizen groups, in turn, can inform the planners and governing boards about the effects various capital improvements may have on their quality of life, economic viability, and neighborhood functioning. They may be able to suggest refinements on the proposed projects which will make them more effective or less expensive.

18.2.9 Monitoring

A capital improvement program provides a vital link between the comprehensive plan and the implementing of improvements. It should be used to analyze the effects of the plan and the improvements on the desired growth of the area. The value of monitoring the CIP in terms of its expressed objectives should be recognized. If the comprehensive plan, for example, has included the goal of providing and enhancing economic stability in the area which it covers, then the CIP should be developed to reach that goal by working towards defined objectives in the plan. The returns from particular investments in the CIP, in terms of economic improvements in the area, should be measured to determine whether, in fact, the investment has enhanced economic development.

A typical example of a capital improvement financed by a public agency is an interchange built on the expectation that it will generate additional commercial or industrial development for the community, by providing access to undeveloped land. The development thus encouraged will be expected to provide additional tax returns to the community in sufficient amounts to repay the debt service on the interchange costs. The costs and benefits of the improvement appear clear and developer promises have been received. However, before the interchange is completed, the economics of developing in the area may change.

A major industry, to be served by smaller industries which were to develop in the new tract, may close. Developer priorities may change, or there may be an areawide or national economic reversal. Factors such as these can cause change in the best planning. They can also cause shortfalls in expected revenues to repay the obligations incurred in building the interchange. If the effects of building the interchange are monitored, and the proposed development does not occur, the governing board may be precluded from making a similar decision in the future. Another agency reviewing the benefits a new interchange might bring could also be affected by the results of the monitoring. Public agencies providing similar services should accumulate information about reaching set objectives connected with capital improvements, and should communicate with one another, so that monitoring will have more than local value.

Another common example of a publicly financed CIP project is the provision of curb and gutter improvements in a defined area. They are expected to raise property values because of storm drainage control and general enhanced attractiveness in the neighborhood. An assessment distict may have been formed, and may have received support from residents because they believed the cost of debt repayment would be reimbursed by appreciated capital gains when property was sold. Monitoring property sales before and after the improvements are installed, over a period of years, will provide solid information for residents in other areas who may be considering similar projects.

Changes in intersection designs may be implemented by capital improvements expected to reduce the level of accidents and related property and personal damage costs. The design may be one which the jurisdiction is testing before adopting it as a standard throughout the area. If the accident rate is monitored over time before similar intersection improvements are installed in other locations, the community may discover that the design did not achieve its stated objective of reducing accidents. They could be saved additional investments in a system improvement which was not effective.

The effects of capital improvements can be monitored through record-keeping and systematic observation—by clearly stating the objective of the capital improvement in the CIP, and recommending the desired monitoring system and its estimated costs. When the approving body requires this monitoring and establishes regular reporting periods, it will be continually increasing its understanding of the long-term value of the improvements to the area.

18.3 PROCESS

18.3.1 Inventory

The first step in establishing a capital improvement program is to make a complete inventory of the capital assets of the area or the private development. Facts about public facilities or private capital projects should be collected by the group responsible for the need and upkeep of the facilities or equipment and sent to the financial officer or controller for verification. Information to be obtained and recorded includes the date of purchase or construction completion, expected life, condition, use, additions, repairs or improvements, and replacement value.

When this basic list is completed and reviewed by all departments or divisions involved with purchase, maintenance and development of capital equipment or projects, it will constitute the foundation of the program. The inventory should be updated annually, and records should be kept on a regular basis concerning maintenance and operation costs. These costs become a significant part of the ongoing CIP.

18.3.2 Capital Project Justification

After completion of the inventory, and publication in an orderly format, capital project justification sheets should be prepared. These should be developed by the departments or divisions which will be responsible for purchase, construction, operation or maintenance of the particular capital project (Fig. 18-1). In order to analyze the project effectively, various kinds of information and comments should appear on the project data sheet, including such background data as the area density and numbers of persons or buildings which will be served by the project, as well as conformance to the comprehensive plan in terms of its stated goals and objectives and demonstrated needs. It is important to state whether the project is required to maintain or enhance existing service delivery or to provide a new service.

The project should be identified as an independent item, e.g., a lighting system along an existing road which merely extends the existing lighting network, or an integral part of a group of projects which must be accomplished together. Another question to be answered is whether approval of this project will automatically generate the need for supportive investments. For example, if a street is extended into an undeveloped area, will the need be generated for sewer, water, and other necessary urban services, and what will be their costs and schedule of installation?

Funding sources must be identified. Other data necessary are whether matching funds are needed, how long the funding will be available, where the project is located, and project justification. From records on related projects, either within the agency or private company or obtained from sources elsewhere, expected maintenance and operation (M&O) costs should be stated. An analysis of the total effect on the agency or company budget should be included, so that both the short-term and long-term effects on the budget will be known. This analysis should state the purchase or development costs, the M&O costs, debt service costs, and the length of time before the project must be replaced. When data on debt service and M&O costs are not well defined, the budget can accumulate unexpected debits which can affect planned balance between debits and credits.

18.3.3 Scheduling

Management of the CIP process should early be delegated to one person, department, or division. From that responsibility should come

Project _____ Responsible Dept. _____ Project No. _____

_____ _____ Date _____

Funding Source: Local _____ Priority Rating:*

(Agency-Dollars)

Other _____ Committed _____ Urgent _____

Sure _____ Uncertain _____ Alternatives _____ Necessary_____ Desirable _____

Description _____

_____

Estimated Project Costs: Design: _____ Equipment: _____

Total: _____ Land: _____ Annual M&O: _____

Construction: _____ Other: _____

Project Cost Spread

Year 1 _____ 5 _____ Beyond _____ Project Status: % Complete

2 _____ 6 _____ Pre Design _____

3 _____ 7 _____ Final Plans _____

4 _____ 8 _____ Land Acquired _____

Contracts Let _____

Justification: _____ Construction _____

_____ Potential Generation Other

Relationship to Comprehensive Plan Capital Investment

_____ Public: _____

Location and Relationship to Neighborhood Private: _____

_____

_____ Annual Estimated Budget Effect

Gains

Relationship to Other Jurisdiction(s) Property Sale _____

_____ Property Income _____

_____ General Rev. _____

Cost/Benefit Ratio _____ Sub Total _____

Recommendations Department _____ Losses

Advisory Committee _____ M&O _____

Finance Officer _____ Debt Service _____

Executive Officer _____ Sub Total _____

Chairman Governing Board _____ Net Effect _____

*Rating systems using numbers have also been used.

Fig. 18-1. Capital project justification

organization and direction, so that the process will be well understood by all participants. The responsible party should send out explanations, directives, and schedules well in advance of any actions. All service participants should be involved and have opportunities to discuss the projects.

The coordinator should first set a mutually agreeable calendar of events which will allow the completion of the process in time to proceed with projects or purchases at the most advantageous period or to meet budget deadlines. The process can be lengthy, and this must be recognized well in advance. For an example of the public process, see Fig. 18-2.

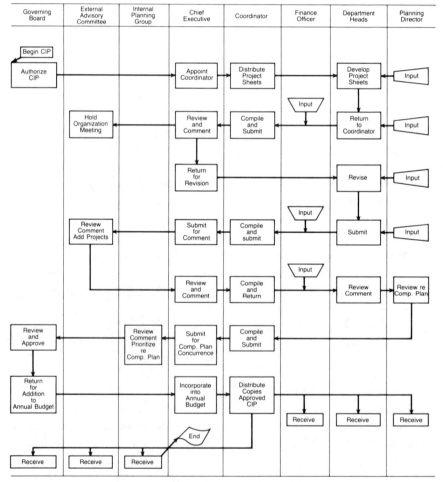

Fig. 18-2. Flowchart—public process Capital Improvement Program

The decision-making body should set a date by which it will give final approval for the project. The calendar (Table 18-1) can be established by working backward from that date so that an adequate amount of time is provided for each step. Final approval dates must mesh with the required final approval date for the over-all budget for the jurisdiction or company. In the case of government agencies, the approval date for the complete budget is often set by law, or because it must fit into budget sequences at a higher level.

Time should be allowed for citizen input, technical advice, price estimates by manufacturers and other providers, and for information gathering. The planner should provide whatever information is available concerning area statistics, related data from other similar agencies or companies, and local and national economic trends, in addition to appropriate information from outside sources. The process can easily consume six months, so that for a July deadline, January would be an appropriate starting date. The schedule should be widely distributed, not only internally, but also to the public, any outside sources of cost estimates, and others who may provide useful input.

There are several easily identified milestones in the process which should be stated. Some of these milestones are:

1. Appointment of a coordinator (7). In a public agency, this could be the finance, public works or planning director, or the assistant executive director. In a private company, it could be the controller, a vice-president, or the construction manager or some similar responsible person. The coordinator selected must have adequate staff, complete

Table 18-1 Sample Capital Improvement Program Schedule

Task	Date Due[a]
Appoint advisory committee	September 15
Develop CIP policies	September 30–December 15
Inventory	Ongoing
Department head meeting	January 15
Planning commission/citizen input	February 15
Project request forms submitted to coordinator	February 28
Compilation and financial projections	March 15
Department head review/recommendations	April 1
City manager review/recommendations	April 15
Planning commission review/public hearing	May 15
Governing board review/public hearing	June 15
Governing board recommendations	July 1
Over-all budget adoption	August 1

[a]Approximate schedule according to regular meeting dates for various groups.

understanding of the process, and enough delegated authority to keep the process moving.

2. A meeting should be called and arranged by the coordinator as soon as possible after the start date. It should include the internal department or division heads. Its purpose is to explain the process, agree on the schedule and deliver any appropriate forms for use in the process (12). Inventory forms should be available to identify any additions or deletions which have occurred since the last annual inventory. Capital justification forms and any established costing or accounting procedures should be presented. Following this meeting, published copies of the schedule should be provided to outside parties who will be participating in the process. In the case of public agencies, a media notice and accompanying article will assist the public in following the process and participating, if they so desire.

3. Appointment of a public advisory group by the governing board if the CIP is for a public agency. If it is for a private company, appointment of an advisory committee can be helpful also. (The private company committee could include potential clients, bankers, and builders, who are able to provide technical and consumer inputs to aid in selection of projects.) The appointment of these groups can occur at any time before the beginning of the process. They can be ongoing, that is, continue the same from year to year, or can be a new group appointed each year. Some continuity of membership is helpful, however. Staggered terms are advised.

4. Due dates for department or division requests for inclusion of capital purchases or projects in the CIP. These requests should be sent to the coordinator, then on to the chief executive, with comments by the coordinator. Requests should include anticipated operation and maintenance costs, potential funding sources, and justification.

5. A meeting date should be set between the chief executive and the originators of capital requests to receive the executive's comments and recommendations. These should include review of revenue sources and comments on perceived priorities. There should be general agreement as to which projects should be dropped and which presented for further review to the citizens' advisory committee or the company appointed review committee.

6. Specific meetings of the review committees should be held.

7. A review should be made of the preliminary CIP by the planning commission or other public advisory group in a public setting, or by the private company planning group in a public or private location as appropriate. These groups should review for conformance to the comprehensive plan and for priorities related to implementation of the plan.

8. A review should be made of the CIP as recommended by the planning advisory group to the governing body of the jurisdiction or company. If the planning advisory group has recommended changes in the preliminary CIP, these should be highlighted and explained. In the case of a public agency, there should be a public review of the decision-making process.

9. The approved capital improvement program should be incorporated into the over-all annual budget of the public agency or private company.

18.3.4 Financing and Revenue Sources

The financial capacity of the community or company must be carefully evaluated so that the CIP will be realistic in its expectations of funding. Sources of revenue differ for the public and private sectors, related to size of jurisdiction, geographic location, and availability. Common public sources include property and sales taxes, user fees, permits, licenses, and government loans and grants. Private companies can also receive money from government grants, user fees, and sales of products. Local, state or federal agencies may receive revenue from income taxes.

Other revenue sources include: special assessment district taxes, donation by private citizens, rents or leasing revenue from public or private property, sales of assets or recovered personal property for which the owner cannot be found, severance taxes, and shared taxes with other jurisdictions. These must be identified and carefully quantified as to amount, timing, and reliability, within the bounds of available knowledge. Annual income will, of course, vary from year to year, and estimates should be averaged over several years.

Property tax revenues, since they are based on nonmoving assets, are reasonably easy to estimate. It is important to keep assessments current, so that revenue is not incorrectly estimated because of lack of current (within two years) knowledge of property values. Sales taxes, on the other hand, vary with the economy, with new or failing commercial and industrial development, and population shifts in both numbers and age. For estimating purposes, several years should be averaged. The planner can supply useful information concerning what is happening with commercial and industrial development as well as forecasts about growth in the area.

Government grants can be one-time-only grants, can be funded to continue on the same level for several years, or can be fluctuating. The planner should keep a high level of awareness about existing programs, what new ones are being developed, funding levels and timing, and should be ready to notify the agency or the company about the potential sources of funding which will be available from government sources. These sources can change or be eliminated entirely. When capital projects are approved based on funding from programs such as these, it should be understood that the project will change in priority if the funding source fails, unless there is substitute funding from another source.

If carefully administered and controlled, the use of state and federal grant funds can be beneficial. It is not uncommon for such money to be authorized by the legislature as seed money, with the intention of helping a new service to get started or upgrade an existing one. The prospective user should carefully evaluate the ability of the jurisdiction or company to carry on with the maintenance and operation of such a service. An evaluation should be made of any additional required capital investment as well as the desirability of the program itself, in terms of already established service objectives. There are instances, for example, where there is grant money to build buildings, but no local money to operate and maintain the function within the building.

User fees are a good source of funding revenue for many capital improvement projects. These are fees charged to the users of the improvement. Sometimes users can be clearly identified, as in the case of a bridge, where toll fees can be charged, or a sewer service district, where monthly service fees are levied. Police and fire services are usually difficult to quantify clearly enough in terms of costs and benefits to establish user fees. Philosophically, many public jurisdictions feel police and fire services should be funded out of general revenues so that all residents will receive service, no matter what their ability to pay. Special assessment districts have, however, been formed to provide firefighting protection.

Libraries, too, are reluctant to charge user fees which are self-supporting, but more revenue may have to be raised in this manner in the future. User fees can be used to support provision of services by either public agencies or private companies. The only difference is that private companies often plan to make some profit from the operation, and are so authorized. User fees in public agencies, on the other hand, are carefully monitored to be sure they are solely related to the costs of the service being provided and no more.

In order to establish user fees, the service provider must utilize the same information as that on the capital project data sheet. The capital costs, debt service costs, M&O, capital replacement and improvement costs must be identified. Total annual costs, together with the costs of collecting user fees, are compared to the number of users. Appropriate monthly, quarterly, semiannual or annual fees are established. If these fees are not paid when billed, they can become liens on private property (providing such a program is authorized by a public agency), or the service can be terminated. Some private companies, such as those supplying gas and electric services, are monitored by public agencies to assure reasonable user fees.

For a public agency, income from most licenses, permits and fees for various transactions tend to be similar from year to year. A large source of revenue for community development agencies in growing areas is building permit fees. They will vary depending on the growth rate of the area.

Private funding of public improvements is also a good revenue source. Developers are able to include the costs of improvements in the costs of development, to be ultimately paid by consumers. Some jurisdictions expect funding on a broad basis, asking for assistance with offsite interchanges, schools, recreation facilities, police and fire stations, and community centers. The extent of the use of such funding often is dependent upon: (1) The ability of the jurisdiction to pay for such improvements out of its own revenues; (2) the rate of growth—if it is growing fast, the community may not be able to provide funds quickly enough; and (3) the perception by existing residents of need for new services which are generated by new growth. The developer may volunteer to provide funding if it will enhance the success of the development.

Revenue from long-term financing is generally utilized for very large projects, although capital is sometimes accumulated over several years for such purposes. Some of the common mechanisms for long-term financing are described in the following paragraphs.

General obligation (GO) bonds These bonds, usually in minimum purchase designations of multiples of $1,000 to $5,000, are sold by bond sales firms and are guaranteed by the good faith and assets of the jurisdiction (2). They are often designated to be spent on a particular capital project, since the voters must approve the authorization to issue.

A prospectus, much like one developed for the issuance of corporate stock, is the common vehicle used to establish this good faith and credit. The prospectus can contain such data as the size and location of the jurisdiction, its current regular revenue and obligations, its rate of growth, fire insurance ratings, and school and recreation systems. GO bonds can be compared to the stock sold by private companies for financing expansion, except that there is no expectation that stock will ever be paid off and can appreciate in value.

GO bonds have been widely used and, if the prospectus demonstrates ready ability to repay the obligation, rather easy to sell. Interest rates on the bonds depend on current market interest rates for other types of loans and the credit rating of the jurisdiction (AA, A, B, etc.). In times of shifting interest rates, they are more difficult to market, since investors are not attracted to fixed interest returns when continuing trends seem to be for interest rates to rise. GO bond repayments are generally income tax free to investors, so they are attractive for that reason.

Revenue bonds Revenue bonds, like GO bonds, are fixed interest rate bonds, long term, marketed through bond sales firms, and offered with a prospectus. Their payback is tied to revenue which is expected from the capital project that they are to fund. Their attractiveness to investors is related to investor perception of how accurate income projections are and whether the project will function as planned (11). Revenue bonds usually do not have to receive voter approval, as do GO bonds, for they are not backed by the good faith and credit of the jurisdiction. Governing boards, however, frequently request advisory voter approval through the referendum process. Referendum returns are not binding on the governing board, but the board may decide not to proceed if they perceive broad voter disapproval.

Tax-increment bonds   Tax-increment bonds are similar to revenue bonds because the guarantee of repayment of debt comes from the rise in tax revenue from the improved property (2). They are a common source of funding for redevelopment projects. The governing body of the jurisdiction, as well as any other agencies receiving taxes collected on a general tax roll, can designate any new tax income generated by improved property, over a specified period of years, to pay off the bonds. School districts can be greatly affected by the loss of designated revenue for tax-increment financing, since they receive a large share of the property taxes in most jurisdictions. After the tax-increment bonds are redeemed, the additional property taxes generated by increased property values become a part of the general revenue funds of the jurisdiction as well as any special districts which are receiving property tax revenue.

Lease purchase   This form of long-term financing comes from private sources. In lease-purchase financing, the capital improvement is financed from private capital sources which either build the new facility or buy an existing one and lease it back to the jurisdiction. This kind of financing can also be used by private companies. For example, company pension funds might be used to build an office building for a private company and then it could be "leased" back to the company, while including in the lease enough capital repayment to retire the debt obligation. It has been used where the jurisdiction or company for some reason cannot obtain any other type of long-term financing.

    Lease-purchase financing does not require voter approval, since the repayments come from the general fund, although sometimes advisory approval votes are requested. Lease-purchase interest costs are generally higher than GO or revenue bonds, since the obligation to repay is not as fully guaranteed. Investor interest payments may or may not be tax free. It is possible to "sell" an existing building to investors on a lease-purchase arrangement as a means to raise operating general fund revenue. Use of this financing rose in the United States from $250,000,000 in 1977 to over $1 billion in 1981.

Special taxing districts   When a capital improvement benefits a defined area, and the property owners in the area agree to accept the obligation, a district can be formed to finance and manage one or more services or improvements. Community service districts, used as a governmental form prior to establishing a formal incorporated city, can supply all the services a city or county is authorized to supply. They can levy taxes, sell bonds, obtain private financing, and operate in many ways as though they were a general-purpose local government agency. Special districts can even be formed within the confines of an incorporated city or town, where there is an improvement related to a particular area. Such improvements, for example, can be sewers, street lighting, or curbs and gutters. Special assessment districts can also be formed citywide for single-purpose improvements such as street lighting or sewers. Special assessment districts complicate local government as they can put deci-sion-making about revenues and expenditures on a less carefully regu-lated basis. Their actions are often not publicized as well as those of general-purpose government. They are, however, a useful mechanism for provision of financing for localized capital improvements.

General fund financing   This is often referred to as "pay-as-you-go" financing. Many capital improvements, particularly those of a shorter life, such as equipment, or those of smaller cost, such as street improve-ments, are paid for out of current annual revenues. A larger capital improvement to be built in phases may also be funded out of annual revenues. Within the annual revenue funds, separate "savings account' funds can be established. These would set aside given amounts annually until enough money has been accumulated to pay for the improvement. In private companies, the same technique can be used with annual revenues.

Long-term financing methods compared   There are other iterations of financing, sometimes combining several of the sources listed. In general, the two most desirable forms of financing are general obligation and revenue bonds, since they have the lowest interest rates and therefore are the least costly to the jurisdiction. Tax-increment financing, in a sense, diverts property tax revenues from its usual assignments, using future revenues to pay for current improvements. Only the increase in tax revenues is diverted until the improvement cost is repaid. Then the tax diversion ceases and taxing bodies receive their normal tax flow. The tax increment provision is sometimes the only viable source of funding. Neither tax-increment financing nor lease-purchase financing require voter approval; therefore voters lose some control over debt obligations they will be repaying through their taxes. Lease-purchase financing is also more costly than GO or revenue financing, because the interest rates are those of the general market. Variable rate securities or addition of "windows" can add to attractiveness (see Sec. 18.5 for explanation of terms).

18.3.5 Limits of Debt

In public agencies or private companies, there are either legal, practical, or implied limits of debt (13). For example, financing advisors working with a private company might recommend that the ratio of debts to assets should be no more than 1:2. Investors may use their own rule of thumb about what they will accept in terms of municipal debt ratios, which they may establish by debt to asset ratios or debt to revenue ratios. In some states, the legislature sets legal limits on the amount of debt a local government may assume. These limits are generally related to the property tax base, and can range from 2% to 20% of the referenced property tax base. If these limits are operable in the area where the capital improvement is planned, it is important to be current on assessments. Local government methods of property assessment vary. Some jurisdictions tax on only a percentage of the market value; others tax on full market value.

Local jurisdictions themselves may, as a matter of policy by the governing board, or through voter referenda, establish some limitation on allowable long-term debt in the jurisdiction as a part of management policies. Private company governing boards generally have some type of internally established limitation. The marketplace itself, through investor interest in general obligation bonds, will place externally imposed limitations. A bond prospectus must state the rating that is given to the jurisdiction by stock and bond market analysts such as Moody's or Standard and Poor.

There are many ways to measure debt other than by comparing it to annual revenues or property tax base. Debt per capita is one measurement. Some analysts suggest that $500 per capita is appropriate. This measurement has nothing to do with current revenue or assets, growth rates or decline, outside financing or other variables. It is a static measurement. Debt compared to income per capita in the area is another method of appraising local economic ability to pay, implying that the wealthier the local residents, the higher the property and sales tax revenues are likely to be. A late 1970s debt limit compared to per capita income, used in the United States nationally, was 7% (7).

Debt service as a percentage of the total budget can also be used to measure ability to pay. (Debt service in this instance means interest and capital repayment.) For areas using this measurement, 10% has been considered acceptable and 25% the upper limit (7). Ratio of debt to market value of capital assets in the jurisdiction has been used also, with an acceptable figure of 10% debt to market value of capital assets. Banks and insurance companies often use this concept in establishing their internal loan limits.

In summary, debt limits are set and measurements of debt made in different ways, from agency to agency and company to company. In an efficiently managed organization, it is desirable to understand the concept of debt limits, which ones are most useful in a particular situation, and which measurements of debt are of the most value in the area developing the capital improvement program. The ratio of debt service to annual revenue is one of the most useful, since it is easily measured and understood.

18.3.6 Maintenance and Operation Costs

An often overlooked or poorly defined part of the capital improvement program is the estimated maintenance and operation costs which will be incurred when the facility is completed. The departments or divisions to be responsible for these functions will be able to furnish estimates. As in private capital replacement projects, a frequent question is whether it is more cost beneficial to continue upgrading the existing facility and accept often higher repair and maintenance costs over a longer period, or to build a new facility and hope that the added capital costs will be compensated for by lowered repair and maintenance costs. These tradeoffs should be evaluated to the best extent possible and the comparisons made a part of the information given to the advisory and governing bodies when they are to decide on a new capital expenditure. The high cost of heating and air-conditioning in recent years has become an important factor in life-cycle building costs, and sometimes causes significant design changes.

18.3.7 Debt Service Costs

Interest rates in localized borrowing situations are heavily affected by external factors. The prime rate, established by the U.S. Federal Reserve Bank Board for the best credit risks, is the basis for all interest rates. To this extent, the local area or company can have no effect on interest rates and related debt service costs. They can, however, affect the attractiveness of the bonds which are offered. They can also affect the lease-purchase costs by the amount of debt already obligated, the stability of debt repayment, and the general management of the agency or company.

When an agency or company contemplates financing long-term debts by the sale of bonds, it should retain bond marketing consultants and attorneys. The bond marketing consultant will be able to inform the agency about expected interest rates, availability of interested investors, and other agencies which may be competing for funds. Just as in stocks issued by a private company, achieving attractive interest rate sales when bonds are issued by a public agency is a factor of the time of year or the particular economic cycle currently affecting investments. Since the obligation will be assumed for many years, it may be advisable to delay the capital improvement until the market is more favorable.

18.3.8 Net Worth

The principle of defining net worth in private company accounting also can be a useful technique in government accounting. Net worth is the difference between credits and debits, or between assets and liabilities. For the purpose of deciding whether or not new capital expenditures and related obligations should be approved, a net worth statement will establish the relationship between assets and liabilities. A standard relationship between assets and liabilities should be adopted as a guideline for the private company or public agency which is acceptable to the management, stockholders, or voters.

When assets are defined, in either public or private organizations, existing capital assets must be evaluated as to their current worth. This should be done annually. If the capital asset has declined in value because of inadequate maintenance or destructive acts, then the net worth will decline. Consequently, the ability to take on new liabilities will also decline.

Evaluation through usual accounting practices of fixed assets (e.g., buildings, bridges, etc., absent any maintenance to restore those assets to like-new condition), will establish a fixed depreciation of an equal percentage each year over the life of the project. If a bridge, for example, has a life of 50 yr, its value as an asset will decline 2% per year. In periods of inflation, when the value of the asset will be determined in inflated dollars, the worth must also be reevaluated annually in terms of appreciated dollars. For example, if in year 1 the bridge is worth $100,000, and there is an inflation factor of 10%, then the value in year 2 will be $100,000 plus 10% or $110,000, minus the 2% depreciation, which will yield a depreciated value of $107,800.

In determining net worth of a governmental jurisdiction or a private company, the current value of assets should always be used. Once net worth is established, and it is determined that the ratio of liabilities to assets is not greater than 1:2 (if that is the adopted standard), current cash flow must also be determined in order to establish the ability to meet debt service demands for new financing. Gross cash flow is simply revenue minus expenses. Net cash flow is debt service cost plus recurring capital expenditures subtracted from gross cash flow. Net cash flow minus operating and maintenance costs, and net capital expenditure reserves, will define the amount still available to meet new debt service demands for the long-term financing needs of new capital projects (9).

18.3.9 CIP Policies

After all information is assembled for use by decision-makers and their advisors, conflicts can arise in setting priorities or determining which projects most nearly meet community or company needs. It is helpful to establish some policies before the process begins which will help in reaching final decisions. The comprehensive plan's goals, objectives, and policies can provide a good start, but additional policies adopted by the governing body, directly related to capital improvements, can also aid in making choices between projects.

A first draft of these policies can be developed by the planner. They can then be reviewed, amended and approved by the advisory committee before being sent to the governing board for adoption. Policies affecting CIP decision-making will be less controversial, and discussions will be more productive, if the policies are developed between the final budget adoption of one project and beginning the process for the next. It is important to have policies adopted without considering them in the context of particular projects.

When the advisory committees and the governing board are considering which projects to recommend, they can evaluate them in terms of such policies previously adopted. Policies will not be the only approval criteria, but they will provide substantial assistance in making choices. Some typical policies which might be considered include:

1. Service completed to already developed areas of the jurisdiction before it is extended to new areas.

2. Services delivered to all parts of the area on an equitable basis, according to standards set for acceptable levels of service.

3. No approval of levels of debt service which are more than $x\%$ of the annual revenue of the jurisdiction, in which x = debt limit percentage established by the governing body.

4. Use of life-cycle costing to determine capital costs, with an attempt to select equipment or facilities with the lowest life-cycle costs.

5. Identification of operation and maintenance costs for new capital projects and the assurance of adequate funding in the annual budget before approval of project.

6. Protection of public health and safety when possible.

18.3.10 Comprehensive Plan Implementation Costs

The cost of implementing the comprehensive plan is often not evaluated, nor are different alternatives compared in terms of costs. The capital costs for implementation should be identified and a phasing plan developed according to the expected growth rate. Although land uses are not identified in the compehensive plan as precisely as they might be on a zoning map, densities, types of uses, and public facilities (such as school, administration and recreation facilities) are usually shown on the comprehensive plan. The costs of servicing these developments with major sewer and water lines, fire and police stations, roads, etc., can be estimated. These costs can be compared to expected revenues and estimates developed for slowing the mix of land uses to assure adequate revenues to fund required improvements.

Some cities have gone to extremes in this regard. The City of Industry in California nearly exclusively has industrial development. It, therefore, has a high rate of tax return because services related to residential development are not necessary. This type of plan may be criticized as ignoring housing and other quality of life needs for its workers, and may be an extreme situation. In general, a more equitable distribution of land uses is to provide worker housing in close association with employment opportunities. Planning should be done to more nearly provide revenues which meet improvement funding needs.

If it appears that a comprehensive plan cannot practically be implemented because of CIP costs, then it may be possible to supply services in some other manner. Services can be provided with private sector franchises, whereby the city or county designates one or more private companies to provide services according to mutually acceptable standards or costs. Garbage collection is commonly accomplished in this manner.

Another alternative may be to consider a system of regional, fiscal interrelationships and tax revenue sharing. An example is the system used in the Minneapolis-St. Paul seven-county region, where tax income from commercial and industrial development is shared: through this concept communities with high percentages of housing can share the tax revenue coming to areas with high percentages of industrial and commercial development. This plan was adopted in the mid 1970s.

In the seven-county region, agreement was reached, through the Minneapolis-St. Paul Council of Governments, to require that a jurisdiction where commercial and industrial development was located would receive only about 50% of the tax income. The other 50% would be shared among jurisdictions within the seven counties which had a disproportionate share of housing (10). Agreement was possible because it was realized that people commuted to work from many locations throughout the region where there were high concentrations of residential units and little commerce and industry. The arrangements took many years to finalize, because of the sensitive nature of sharing locally generated revenues. Sharing income between communities for mutual benefit may be difficult to arrange, but it is a viable option to consider. In the Minneapolis-St. Paul case, the high percentage commercial-industrial communities realized that it was desirable not to have the service costs and problems of increased residential development. They preferred to help support such development elsewhere.

Another aspect of the comprehensive plan implementation costs is that some capital improvement costs may be considered to be seed money. This money can be spent by the local jurisdiction to attract income-generating developments, such as a large stadium, shopping center, or manufacturing plant. Evaluating the cost-benefit ratios of such investments is important, so that revenue expectations will be realistic. It may be possible to reach agreement with neighboring jurisdictions on sharing predevelopment public infrastructure costs in return for a fixed percentage share of the additional tax revenue generated by the new development.

The comprehensive plan should be flexible. It can be amended if it becomes apparent that the arrangement of development planned is more expensive in terms of its required capital investment (for provision of service) than expected revenues will support. In the case of the landmark Palo Alto, California plan (8), the community, through careful study, determined that it would be cheaper for the town to buy a large amount of foothill area within the town boundaries and leave it as open space than to allow it to develop in urban uses and pay for related service costs. Bonds were approved for purchase, and the comprehensive plan was amended to reflect that decision.

18.3.11 Cost-Benefit Analysis

Individual capital improvement projects should be evaluated in terms of costs and benefits to the area or the company, where this is feasible. In building a new freeway, for example, savings to users can be estimated in terms of time and lower motor vehicle operating costs. On the other hand, the added design and construction costs in raising the esthetic appeal of the freeway are not easy to define in terms of benefits returned for the expenditure. For example, the possiblity of reduction of stress, resulting from a beautiful view, which thereby lowers the accident rate in the area, might be considered as cost benefit. Higher accident rates resulting from the distraction to drivers caused by the enhanced view might be termed an unacceptable cost. Wherever possible, benefits should be explained in terms of quantified value received.

The expenditure of capital by a public agency to provide a service, and the benefits received by the users, can be evaluated in terms of the costs of the same service provided by private companies. In some cases, public agencies have decided privately provided services have smaller over-all costs to the consumers than those publicly provided. They have decided that large capital expenditures can be diverted to the private sector, which may have more financing options. Maintenance and operation expenses as well as over-all management expenses may be lowered, perhaps because of lower salaries and benefits to private company employees, or lowered liability and related insurance costs. There may also be lower capital purchase costs because of dispensing with the bidding requirements and other government regulations. These comparisons are not clear cut and public agencies may change back and forth as governing bodies have changing views on the issue.

A less direct cost involved with capital improvements is the potential effect of government borrowing on the rates for private borrowing (14). The term M_1 represents currency held by the nonbank public, plus commercial bank demand-deposits held by the nonbank public (excluding those held by foreign banks and official institutions), and other checkable deposits of all depository institutions, including traveller's checks. Because it represents money readily available for spending, it is considered by many analysts to be an important determinant of economic activity and inflation. The greater the demands on M_1, the higher may be the interest rates for private borrowers. Heavy government borrowing may have the effect of slowing industrial or commercial expansions in the jurisdiction, and thus limiting the tax flow which was expected to help pay for the public improvement. A reasonable approximation of this cost of capital can be a weighted average of the municipal bond rates and the rates of interest for other capital investments in the area, such as mortgages and business development loans.

Cost-benefit ratios can be affected if inflation has had an impact on cost of borrowing or the cost of capital investment between the time the project was evaluated and the time it is actually purchased or constructed. Market interest rates should be continuously monitored so that funds or products can be obtained at the most favorable time. Delays in project completion can be favorable or adverse in the over-all costs to the agency, depending on whether the national or local economy is in a recessionary or an inflationary cycle. Even seasons of the year can affect costs. Projects bid in the summertime, when construction companies are busy, may be bid at a higher price than in an off-season, simply because the contractors are not so eager for additional work when they have several jobs.

18.3.12 Intergovernmental Coordination

Capital improvement projects may be part of an areawide system and can have impacts on neighboring jurisdictions. The extension of an important traffic artery, terminating at the boundary of a neighboring jurisdiction, can affect the traffic in that jurisdiction either positively or negatively. If affected positively, the neighboring municipality may consider sharing some of the costs. For example, building an extensive well system to supply one community with water can affect the water supply of an adjacent area, especially if the first municipality is upstream of the second over the aquifer which is the water supply source. The construction of a convention center in one location can provide customers for hotels, restaurants, and shopping centers over a large area. Neighboring communities may be willing to share in the financing according to the benefits they can envision in terms of tax revenue.

A financial concern which can affect the region is the marketing of bonds or other debt instruments by several municipalities in an area at the same time. This may have an effect on the capital available for investment in the area and cause interest rates to rise because of competing demands. If the municipalities, on the other hand, agree to alternate their marketing over several years, the effect on the capital supply may lessen. Marketing at the same time may also tend to play one public agency against another and cause higher marketing costs in the form of a more elaborate prospectus or other sales tools.

Another potential problem that can be caused by lack of coordination between public agencies is the burden which investments by one can place on another. Since federal, state, and local agencies are not bound by the comprehensive plans of others in the same manner as private developers, these agencies can originate development in areas of a municipality which may not be according to the municipality's comprehensive plan and its scheduled infrastructure improvements. The construction of a regional post office, for example, may occur in a location that has less expensive land, and good access for the users as well as for the large semitrailers which transport the mail. It may, however, employ large numbers of people and attract new housing or commercial construction to nearby areas, in conflict with the comprehensive plan covering the adjacent jurisdictions.

The use of an environmental assessment or other information document—required if federal funding is involved—may be helpful in selecting alternatives which are a more positive addition to the area. Regional agencies which have been created in most areas can be used as a means of coordinating capital improvement and comprehensive planning efforts of local jurisdictions. They can be helpful in disseminating information and accumulating areawide information for use in planning and funding decisions by all public agencies and private developers in the area.

State and federal funding cycles may be out of sequence with local government budgeting cycles, in terms of both funding priorities and sequential programs. Local governments and private companies should be aware of the need for coordination with these funding programs so that they can be in the best position to take advantage of state and federal funding when it is available.

As was stated previously, cooperative capital investment programming can be helpful (5). If an interchange is planned that will benefit each of two municipalities, for example, CIPs in both jurisdictions must be planned so that the capital required will be available from both agencies at times which allow the interchange to be built. The jurisdictions can be overlapping public agencies, such as a city or county, or public and private groups, such as a county, state, and private developer. Objectives which are mutually supported, have acceptable funding percentages, and whose timing is appropriate to the needs of all parties, must be carefully negotiated. This kind of shared capital investment can be an effective way of funding a capital project which no one of the parties could accomplish individually. In this process, each party may be responsible for its own financing mechanisms, although if bonds are to be used as a financing mechanism, some attempt should be made to stagger bond sales, so that both jurisdictions will not be competing for funds at the same time.

18.4 CONCLUSIONS AND EVALUATION

The capital improvement program should include the capital improvement budget over a selected span of years (often five), an annual operating budget, a long-range public services plan, and a revenue program. The capital improvement schedule should include a list of major capital improvement projects, estimates of the cost of each, suggested sources of financing, and recommended timing. These should be summarized in a standard format (see Figs. 18-3 and 18-4).

The CIP budget should include a statement of goals, objectives and policies, all related to both the comprehensive plan and the CIP process itself (3). It should include a breakdown of capital improvements by program area or department. Capital items included in the budget can be projects such as acquisition of land; construction or reconstruction of or additions to buildings; development of infrastructure facilities, parks, etc.; or equipment with a life of more than one year. The value of capital projects varies, depending upon standards set by municipality or private company, from the purchase of typewriters to the building of a sewer plant. The costs of planning and design, if these are required, are usually included as a part of the package of construction or purchase costs.

Funding mechanisms are often general obligation or some form of revenue bonds. Funding can be shared between public agencies and private companies, depending on need and agreement. Costs of financing vary according to the types of instruments used, the general eco-

REVENUES

Fund Number	Description	Amount
(1)	Special grants	$ 144,500
(2)	Equipment replacement	12,000
(3)	Topics	120,000
(4)	State transportation funds	216,000
(5)	Gas taxes	159,000
(6)	Revenue sharing	360,000
(7)	Clean water grant	350,000
(8)	Federal aid urban	42,000
(9)	Residential construction tax	20,000
(10)	General obligation bonds	275,000
(11)	Community development block grant	159,000
(12)	General fund	452,000
	Total C.I. revenue	$2,309,500

EXPENDITURES

Fund Number	Description	Amount
(3)	Traffic signal installation	$ 120,000
(5)	Alley paving, E-F Sts.	100,000
(4)	Bike lane additions	200,000
(5, 4)	3rd and 4th R.R. protection	75,000
(7)	El Hunda sewer interceptor	350,000
(6)	Civic Center site acquisition	250,000
(6)	Minipark land acquisition #10	50,000
(9, 12)	Westwood Park development	472,000
(10, 11)	Senior citizens center	434,000
(8)	Wheelchair ramps	42,000
(1)	Corporation yard addition	144,500
(6)	Water well #21	60,000
(2)	Police vehicle	12,000
	Total C.I. expenditures	$2,309,500

Fig. 18-3 Capital Improvement Program annual budget—Year 1

Item	Year				
	1	2	3	4	5
Traffic signal installation		$120,000			
Alley paving, E-F Sts.	$100,000				
Bike lane additions		200,000			
3rd and 4th R.R. protection		75,000			
El Hunda sewer	350,000				
Civic Center site acquisition			$250,000		
Minipark land acquisition			50,000		
Westwood Park development				$472,000	
Senior citizens center					$434,000
Wheelchair ramps					42,000
Corporation yard addition			144,500		
Water well #21		60,000			
Police vehicle			12,000		
Total	$450,000	$455,000	$456,500	$472,000	$476,000
Total expenditure $2,309,500					

Fig. 18-4. Five-year planned expenditures

nomic health of the area, and the over-all economic cycles of the nation and the world.

Capital improvement programs receive benefit from the involvement of technical and citizen advisory committees and general public knowledge. Prudent financial management by the agency or company, and scheduling the process to allow time for rational decision-making, are effective in securing public support for capital expenditures. The use of bond marketing consultants and attorneys is necessary for most jurisdictions.

18.4.1 Evaluation

It is useful to compare tax rates and bonded indebtedness with other communities which may be similar in population, income per capita, commercial and industrial development, or locational resources. This comparison should be used to obtain feedback on community investments and funding mechanisms. Information obtained may help to decide whether capital investments and related debt burdens are acceptable and what returns can be expected from them. It is also helpful for a jurisdiction to compare past to present budgets and municipal statistics. It must be recognized that new financing mechanisms and service expectations continue to develop, for which there may be no comparisons. Local economic health can be compared from past to present, using such per capita factors as expenditures, property and sales tax revenue, income, property and sales tax base, and rate of revenue growth. These comparisons may be useful in evaluating the change in economic health of the area.

In evaluating these statistics, identification of changed management or investment processes over time should be included to determine their effectiveness. Rate of outside income from state or federal sources, or use of private capital, should be compared with other areas. If data show a significant difference, investigation of methods used by other agencies should follow. Such information can be obtained by planners from the other agencies themselves; municipal leagues; various publications (such as those of the Municipal Finance Officers Association); from stock and bond firms, and other similar sources.

There are also revenue sources which may not be used in the community because of habit or lack of understanding about use of the technique. Development fees of various sorts, related to the cost of providing services (for provision of sewer services, for example), called hookup fees, are often used. These are usually charged directly to the developer and then passed to the eventual owner of the developed property in the form of increased purchase costs. Local sales and income taxes are revenue sources in some areas. They meet with varying success, because sometimes they will cause residents to buy or live elsewhere. Variable interest rate bonds and securities may be useful (see Sec. 18.5).

As a part of the evaluation of impacts of a development, the developer may be asked to underwrite planning costs. A typical case is when owners of undeveloped lands pay for the development of a specific or comprehensive plan covering their lands, usually by assessment of a few dollars per acre. Developers may be asked to help pay for general public services, such as child care, recreational facilities, social service agency operations, schools, and fire and police service buildings. The planner is the central focus in negotiating these shared costs. The CIP and the comprehensive plan provide a rational basis on which to found planning requests (6).

Ineffective capital improvement programs can be caused by such factors as:

1. Failure to allow for increased construction costs from changes in labor and materials prices.

2. Failure to include funds for maintenance and operation costs and escalating materials prices, as well as future escalations of land acquisition costs.

3. Failure to have alternative financing options for projects which apparently will be provided with federal, state, or private funding.

4. Overlooking the need for other capital projects which may be generated by the proposed project.

5. Lack of goals, policies, and objectives to guide the development of the CIP.

There are, of course, many other factors which can affect the success or failure of the CIP. Planners should be aware of these and advise their constituencies appropriately.

18.4.2 Conclusion

A capital improvement program requires investment of time and money to develop, but it is of significant advantage to the planner, the agency, the community, and the private company. Some of the advantages include:

1. Gaining public support through a high level of public information and involvement.

2. Capital project investments which are scheduled and chosen to implement the comprehensive plan.

3. Effective use of municipal or company capital to raise the economic health of the community and lower the costs of obtaining capital.

4. Increased opportunities for local intergovernmental, regional, and private company cooperation in funding projects.

5. Better use of outside funding programs, such as federal and state grants and loans.

6. Effective and planned use of funds, leading to a more stable financial state for the public agency or private company.

7. Provision of a vital link between the comprehensive plan and the actual construction of public improvements.

In summary, capital improvement programming is one of the most important tools available for guiding urban development and implementing a comprehensive plan. When governing boards can refer to the CIP where improvements are scheduled in an orderly, logical, financially prudent manner, they can do so knowing that the studied negotiations and public involvement in the programming process were justified.

18.5 GLOSSARY OF TERMS

Ad Valorem Tax.   A tax based on the value or assessed value of real and personal property.

Amortization.   The systematic reduction of debt through use of serial bonds with sinking funds on an actuarial basis. The gradual and periodic reduction of premium and discounts on bonds purchased or sold, so as to reflect the true rate of interest and to show the amount of assets or liabilities represented by premiums or discounts.

Assessed Valuation.   The valuation placed on real estate or other property by a government for the purpose of levying taxes.

Special Taxing Districts.   Districts formed to construct and operate one or more public improvements, usually financed through revenue bonds.

Bond. A written promise to pay a specified sum of money, called the face value or principal amount, at a specified date or dates in the future, called the maturity date(s), together with periodic interest at a specified rate. The difference between a note and a bond is that the latter runs for a longer period of time and requires many more legal actions before the money is available.

Bonded Debt or Indebtedness. That portion of indebtedness represented by outstanding bonds.

Budget. A plan of financial operation embodying an estimate of proposed expenditures for a given period and the proposed means of financing them. The term usually indicates a financial plan for a single year, but can be modified to extend further. The budget can be preliminary, which means it has not been officially adopted by the implementing body, or final, which means that it has been adopted and will be used during the ensuing budget period.

Capital Budget. A plan of proposed capital outlays and the means of financing them for the current fiscal period. It is usually a part of the current budget.

Capital Program. A plan for capital improvements to be incurred each year over a fixed period of years to meet capital needs arising from the long-term work program or otherwise. It sets forth each project or other contemplated expenditure in which the government is to have a part, and specifies the full resources estimated to be available to finance the projected expenditures.

Capital Projects Fund. A fund created to account for all resources used for the acquisition of designated fixed assets by a governmental unit except those financed by special assessment and enterprise funds.

Debt Limit. The maximum amount of debt which a governmental unit may incur under constitutional, statutory, or charter requirements. The limitation is usually a percentage of assessed valuation and may be fixed upon either gross or net debt.

Debt Ratio. The ratio of the issuer's debt to a measure of value such as assessed valuation or real value.

Debt Service Requirement. The amount of money required to pay the interest on outstanding debt, serial maturities of principal of serial bonds, and required contributions to a debt service fund for term bonds.

Delinquent Taxes. Taxes remaining unpaid on and after the date on which a penalty for nonpayment is attached. Even though the penalty may be subsequently waived and a portion of the taxes may be abated or cancelled, the unpaid balances continue to be delinquent taxes until abated, cancelled, paid, or converted into tax liens.

Default. Failure to pay bond or loan principal or interest, or both, promptly when due.

Determination of Worth. When the present value of estimated flow of benefits, discounted at community's cost of capital, exceeds or equals its cost. When the project is recommended, the stream of net future benefits exceeds the capital outlay.

Fiscal Year. The 12-month period at the end of which a governmental unit or private company defines its financial condition and the results of its operations, and closes its books.

General Obligation Bond.   A bond for which the full faith and credit of the issuer has been pledged for repayment guarantee. More commonly, but not necessarily, general obligation bonds are payable from ad valorem taxes and other general revenues.

Issuer.   A governmental agency or private company which borrows money through sale of bonds.

Marketability.   The measure of ease with which a bond can be sold in the bond market.

Municipal.   Municipal refers to local jurisdictions such as cities, counties, townships, villages, etc., and also includes state governments. "Municipals" (i.e., municipal bonds), as used in the bond trade, include not only the bonds of all local subdivisions such as cities, towns, villages, counties, and school, park, sanitary and other taxing districts, but also bonds of states and agencies of the state.

Net Revenue Available for Debt Service.   Gross operating revenues of an enterprise less operating and maintenance expenses, but exclusive of depreciation and bond interest. Net revenue, as thus defined, is used to compute coverage on revenue bond issues.

Pay-as-You-Go Financing.   The basis upon which a governmental unit operates when it meets its capital expenditure obligations and current operation from current revenues, without borrowing.

Public Service Program.   A long-range plan for all public services. The program determines the level of services to be provided and the maintenance and operation costs of those services.

Ratings.   The financial viability of the jurisdiction as established by a reputable rating firm such as Standard and Poor. A study by the Municipal Finance Officers Association showed a marketing cost differential in 1979, between Aa and Baa rating, of $102,400 on a bond of $10,000,000.

Revenue Bond.   Bonds whose principal and interest are payable exclusively from earnings of a public enterprise. In addition to a pledge of revenues, such bonds sometimes contain a mortgage on the enterprise property and then are known as Mortgage Revenue Bonds. Marketing costs for revenue bonds can be considerbly higher than GO Bonds— interest rates on revenue bonds in 1979 were about 51% higher than those on GO Bonds.

Special Assessment.   A compulsory levy made by a local government against certain properties to defray part or all of the cost of a specific improvement or service which is presumed to be of general benefit to the public and of special benefit to such properties. The assessment is usually not levied without a majority vote of those affected.

Tax Base.   The total resources available for taxation.

Tax Exempt Bond.   Bonds exempt from federal, state income, or state or local personal property taxes. Municipals are exempt from federal income taxation and may or may not be exempt from state taxation, income or property, in the state where originated or held. Some states do not tax municipals issued by their own subdivisions, but subject municipals issued in another state but held therein to either income or personal property taxes or both.

Tax Increment Financing. A form of financing used for large-scale development and redevelopment projects. A special district is formed, the existing tax base for the underlying district is certified, and bonds are sold. The tax base is frozen in time, but tax revenues increase because the property has a higher value after improvements are completed. All future tax receipts collected above the frozen tax base are guaranteed to be used to repay the bonds. When the bonds are repaid, the tax revenues are distributed normally.

Taxes. Compulsory charges levied by a governmental unit for the purpose of financing services performed for the common benefit. The term does not include user charges for services rendered only to those paying such charges as, for example, sewer service charges.

Tax Limit. The maximum rate or amount of tax which a local government may levy.

Tax Rate. The amount of tax stated in terms of a unit of the tax base: for example, 25 mils per dollar of assessed valuation of taxable property.

Variable Rate Securities. Bonds marketed with varying interest rates, indexed to follow trends of competing investments. An example would be a bond interest index of "50% of the prime rate." Floating or variable rate securities primarily appeal to investors who expect that interest rates are on an upward trend. To these investors variable rate bonds may sell at lower rates than fixed rate bonds.

Window Options. Such options allow investors, at a fixed time, such as three to five years, to cash in their bonds plus accrued interest. Thus there is a measure of protection from changing interest rates to the investor. An issuance of $150,000,000 by the Louisiana Housing Finance Agency in 1981, for example, traded at 11% with a 5-year window option and at 15% without the window option.

18.6 REFERENCES

1. American Planning Association, *Practice of Local Government Planning*, ICMA Municipal Management Services, Washington, D.C., 1979.
2. California State Office of Planning and Research, *Economic Practices Manual*, Sacramento, Calif., 1978.
3. City of Davis, *Final Budget*, Davis, Calif., 1976–77.
4. Collins, K.R., *Capital Improvement Programming, A Guidebook to South Dakota Municipalities*, South Dakota Planning Bureau, Pierre, S.D., 1980.
5. Korbitz, W.E., *Urban Public Works Administration*, International City Managers' Association, Washington, D.C., 1976.
6. Lennox, M.L., *Administration of Local Government Debt*, Municipal Finance Officers Association, Washington, D.C., 1970.
7. Lennox, M.L., and Hillhouse, A.M., *Concepts in Local Government Finance*, Municipal Finance Officers Association, Washington, D.C., 1974.

8. Livingston and Blayney, *Open Space vs. Development*, City of Palo Alto, Calif., 1971.
9. Meyer, N.L., *Programming Capital Improvements*, Western Rural Development Center, Corvallis, Ore., 1980.
10. Minneapolis-St. Paul Metropolitan Council, *The Impact of Fiscal Disparity on Metropolitan Municipalities and School Districts*, St. Paul, Minn., 1971.
11. Mountain West Research, *A Guide for Methods for Impact Assessment of Western Coal/Energy Development*, Missouri River Basin Commission, Omaha, Nebr., 1979.
12. Municipal Finance Officers Association, *Management Practices in Local Governments*, ICMA Municipal Management Series, Washington, D.C., 1975.
13. Peterson, J.E., and Hough, W.C., *Creative Capital Financing for State and Local Governments*, Municipal Finance Officers Association, Washington, D.C., 1983.
14. Shaul, M., *Capital Shortages in the Next Decade*, Academy for Contemporary Problems, Columbus, Ohio, 1977.
15. U.S. Department of Housing and Urban Development, *Local Capital Improvements and Development Manual*, Office of Policy and Research, HUD, Washington, D.C., 1980.
16. Van Caspel, V., *The New Money Game*, Reston Publishing Co., Reston, Va., 1978.

INDEX